£19.95

PASCAL
FROM
BEGIN
TO END

PASCAL
FROM
BEGIN
TO END

Thomas C. Wilson
University of Guelph

Joseph Shortt
Sheridan College

Addison-Wesley Publishing Company

Reading, Massachusetts ▪ Menlo Park, California
Don Mills, Ontario ▪ Wokingham, England ▪ Amsterdam
Sydney ▪ Singapore ▪ Tokyo ▪ Madrid
Bogotá ▪ Santiago ▪ San Juan

Sponsoring Editor	James T. DeWolf
Production Supervisor	Mary Coffey
Copy Editor	Jerrold Moore
Editorial, Design, and Production Services	Quadrata, Inc.
Illustrator	Intergraphics
Manufacturing Supervisor	Hugh Crawford
Cover Design	Marshall Henrichs

The programs and applications presented in this book have been included for their instructional value. They have been tested with care but are not guaranteed for any particular purpose. The publisher does not offer any warranties or representations, nor does it accept any liabilities with respect to the programs or applications.

Library of Congress Cataloging-in-Publication Data

Wilson, Thomas C.
  Pascal from begin to end.

  Includes index.
  1. PASCAL (Computer program language)   I. Shortt,
Joseph.   II. Title.
QA76.73.P2W554   1987   005.13′3   86-26597
ISBN 0-201-08344-2

Reprinted with corrections May, 1987

5 6 7 8 9 10 MU 9594939291

To the memory of Thomas and Elaine Wilson

T.C.W.

To the memory of Joseph Shortt, Teresa Shortt, and
William Bell

J.S.

Preface

*I*t was a dark and stormy night when we met to choose an introductory text for our first-year computer science course. Sure, there were plenty of books around, but we wanted one that explained problem solving as it should be practiced and Pascal as it should be applied. We had hoped for a book that gave an integrated view of the entire programming process and maintained a modern perspective throughout. Finding one that was also interesting to read further compounded the problem. Alas, we were on the brink of compromising our expectations and settling for last year's text. Then the solution came: To get what we wanted, we would write it ourselves. At that moment the storm abated, the skies cleared, and we set to work. That night has now become a legend and the book a reality.

Audience and Orientation

Depending on the goals of the course, the material in this book could cover the first quarter, the first semester, or the first two quarters of a computer science course. Although the book is intended for computer science majors, it is also suitable for anyone with a serious interest in programming, including students with no background in computing. Our basic goal was to explain the entire process of programming in language that students could readily understand. The explanations are thorough and technically rigorous. However, we have kept the examples realistic and the style personable, so that the text is accessible to beginners while managing to engage readers with some programming experience.

We present programming as part of the larger process of problem solving. We give ongoing attention to modular design, maintainable code, user interaction, error prevention, and program testing. Language features appear in examples that show when they are appropriate, where they are dangerous, or how they interact in typical programming situations.

Pedagogical Aids and Exercises

Nearly 170 exercises are included in this text, the majority of which require programming. Some reinforce points in the text, whereas others explore new applications or data organizations. Many exercises entail several parts, usually either successive extensions to a particular approach or alternative approaches to the same problem. Taken together, the exercises specify about 200 programming assignments. Other pedagogical aids include margin notes for each chapter as well as a review of rules at the end of each chapter. Appendixes provide reserved words, standard identifiers, and a summary of predeclared subprograms.

Problem Solving and Programming

Problem solving and programming are developed side by side throughout the book, with each topic receiving comparable attention. We teach both skills primarily in the context of tangible, motivating examples in which their practical application and interdependence are evident. Example problems lead to discussion of alternative approaches, identification of subproblems, and description of a solution in pseudocode. This problem-solving process culminates in a program, usually after considering alternative implementations and the consequences of each. We also explain how to use the entire ISO Standard Pascal language.

Software Engineering Themes

We stress modern software engineering practices right from the beginning, including top-down design and stepwise refinement of solution approaches. Our orientation is heavily interactive, and we consider user efficiency far more important than machine efficiency. We advocate and practice modular design, testing of both algorithms and code, clarity of coding, descriptive documentation, adherence to standards, and anything else that would promote program correctness and portability. Throughout, we emphasize appropriate use of each language construct and steer users away from potential pitfalls.

Chapter Organization and Overview

The first two chapters set the tone and establish the major themes of the book. Chapter 1 introduces problem solving, modular design concepts, and the programming process, and provides enough Pascal to get started. Chapter 2 acquaints readers with important software engineering issues, including user interaction, maintainable code, and thorough testing.

Chapters 3–10 comprise the bulk of the material in a typical course. In terms of the Pascal content, Chapters 3–5 cover control structures, while Chapters 6–10 feature data types and data structures. The final two chapters present specialized or advanced material more suitable for an accelerated class or a course lasting two quarters.

We introduce procedures early but not before covering enough material to motivate their use in nontrivial situations and permit thorough discussion of their operation. If procedures were to appear earlier, they would seem conspicuously artificial, and their coverage could not be so complete.

Chapters 7–10, which present structured data, include a large number of applications. We stress top-down design of data structures, which often results in a hierarchy of procedures to manipulate corresponding levels in the hierarchy of data objects.

Topic Flexibility

Although most of the material in the first seven chapters is essential for any introductory course, the instructor should be able to pick and choose topics (especially those in the later chapters) to adapt to the needs of a specific course. The diagram on the following page indicates which sections of the book are prerequisites for others. The topics are arranged in tiers, with those near the bottom being what we consider least essential for an introductory course. Instructor preference, of course, should dictate the actual choice and ordering. For example, an instructor who wants to introduce recursion earlier than our placement suggests could include most of this topic right after Chapter 4 or cover all of it by the end of Section 7.2.

Applications

Certain application themes continue throughout the later chapters and the exercises. These applications serve primarily to demonstrate algorithm development or to highlight particular language features. They include text processing, user interfaces, various searching and sorting techniques, nonstochastic simulation, and such data management issues as updates, merging, and data entry.

Numeric applications include check sums, successive approximation, finding roots of equations, random number generation, matrix manipulation, Gaussian elimination, and numeric integration. However, the more mathematical of these appear only in the exercises.

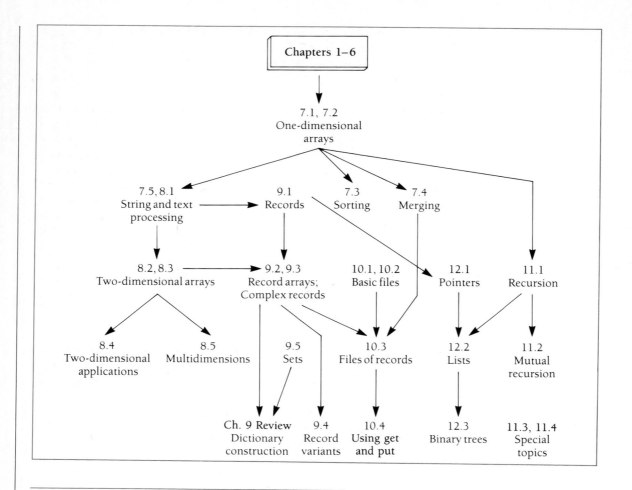

Style

So far as possible we have tried to maintain a style that is comfortable to read without sacrificing technical accuracy. Down to earth, realistic, and thorough, the explanations are designed to appeal to both the beginner and the more experienced programmer alike. The use of English received as much attention from the authors, reviewers, and editors as did the use of Pascal. We hope the resulting text provides an inviting as well as challenging introduction to the world of programming.

Acknowledgments

During the preparation of this book, we have depended heavily on the patience and support of many people. Our wives and children deserve our greatest thanks, for they have endured and given the most. Many friends and colleagues have also continued to provide encouragement as they awaited our return from this enterprise to normal life.

Producing the manuscript required heroic typing efforts by Susan Sutter and Moira Shortt, whose work we especially appreciate. We also thank Martha Smart and Bonnie Miller for their assistance. We credit (with slightly mixed emotions) Antonio Salvadori and Bill Gruener for inspiring this project in the first place and Charles Silio for suggesting the title.

Many people at Addison-Wesley have helped in innumerable ways while we tested their patience to new limits. Our thanks go to editors James DeWolf and Mark Dalton, to the design and production teams, including Mary Coffey and Katherine Harutunian, and to many others who have contributed in ways we may not even realize. Special thanks go to Robert Fiske, our developmental editor who helped us organize and streamline the text, and to Geri Davis at Quadrata, Inc., who is largely responsible for the visual appearance of the book.

Various versions of the manuscript were reviewed by many people, including Stephen J. Allan, *Utah State University;* Peter F. Ash, *St. Joseph's University;* George Beekman, *Oregon State University;* Les Hays, *Pima College;* Robert M. Holloway, *University of Wisconsin—Madison;* Jerry Waxman, *Queens College—CUNY;* and Lawrence Wright, *Williams College.* We especially appreciate the many detailed suggestions provided by reviewers John A. Lutts, *University of Massachusetts—Boston* (who also prepared the Instructor's Manual); William M. McCormick, *Amdahl Corporation;* Terry M. Smith, *Northeastern University;* and J. P. Weston, *University of Lowell.* Of course, any errors that remain after so much attention by so many people are solely the responsibility of the other author.

Guelph, Ontario   T.C.W.
                                                                                          J.S.

Contents

4.   Modular Programming   159

5.   More about Input and Output   209

8.   Packed and Multidimensional Arrays   333

9. Records and Sets   371

10. File Processing Fundamentals   429

Appendixes

Index   555

PASCAL
FROM
BEGIN
TO END

1

Getting Started

You are about to start programming a computer. You have heard that computers can be a lot of fun, that they are extremely important to modern society, and that every educated person should know something about them. Now you are itching to get your hands on a terminal and put a computer through its paces.

Good! Computers *are* fun, influential, and important to know about. This book will explain what you need to know in order to get started. You may not be able to implement your own video game or chess-playing program by the end of the course, but you will have acquired fundamental programming skills and familiarity with a major programming language called Pascal.

However, before you reach for that computer terminal, we have some news that might surprise you: The most interesting and creative aspects of programming do not directly involve computers. Programming is not a matter of pushing keys until a computer responds. The real action requires only pencil and paper and takes place in the privacy of your room or office.

program

A **program** is a carefully reasoned set of instructions for the computer. You can conjure up only the most trivial programs while sitting at a terminal. You must first sketch some ideas, outline an approach, and develop the outline by trimming, modifying, or expanding parts of it. This process produces a succession of progressively refined outlines. The final version will be a detailed specification of the steps that the computer should take in order to solve the original problem.

This part of programming, like creative writing, requires insight, involves originality, and takes time. Moreover, it employs only the English language and exists only on paper. However, programming does not allow the freewheeling organization, construction, and style often used in popular writing. A program must be understood by an unfeeling, unquestioning, totally literal machine and so must be correct and unambiguous to the last detail.

Achieving this level of accuracy requires an unusual amount of care and discipline. The first and most important requirement for programming, then, is acquiring the necessary discipline. This can be learned with practice, and we will make several suggestions in this chapter to help you achieve it.

programming language

In addition, the final version of a program must be written in a special, unambiguous notation called a **programming language.** Programming languages can be deciphered by computers. Only after you have developed a program on paper and expressed it in a programming language can you involve the computer. The primary purpose of this book is to help you acquire a facility with one of the many programming languages: Pascal.

1.1 An Overview of Computing

The computer forms the context for programming. Thus you should begin with some notion of what a computer does and how it works. Getting results from a computer is not unlike getting a meal from the kitchen of a restaurant. This analogy is illustrated in Fig. 1.1. Ingredients enter the kitchen, where they are combined and transformed, and emerge as dinner. The ingredients

input data

used by a computer are called **input data** and are often entered through a terminal. The computer transforms these data to produce results, called

output

output.

There are even parallels between the interior of a kitchen and the interior of a computer system. The kitchen counter is where most of the work takes

main memory

place. The **main memory** of a computer is where data and programs of current interest are stored. The pantry and cupboards provide extra storage

secondary storage

in the kitchen. Disks, tapes, and other devices, collectively called **secondary storage,** provide comparable large-volume storage in a computer system.

When beginning to prepare a meal, the chef places the ingredients in various containers on the counter. The counterparts in main memory are the

memory locations

memory locations, which contain pertinent data to be used. In order to produce the final meal, the chef measures, pours, mixes, chops, or otherwise prepares the ingredients. They are moved from place to place, with transformations occurring in a blender, oven or other appliances along the way. Extra vessels may be required to hold intermediate concoctions. In a computer the circuits that can modify or combine data are known collectively as the

arithmetic–logic unit

arithmetic–logic unit. Data are transformed by being moved through these circuits. Many intermediate results may be generated, requiring additional memory locations.

Of course, a chef directs the entire process by mixing the ingredients, activating the transforming appliances, and controlling the time and temper-

control unit

ature of cooking. The corresponding **control unit** in a computer system

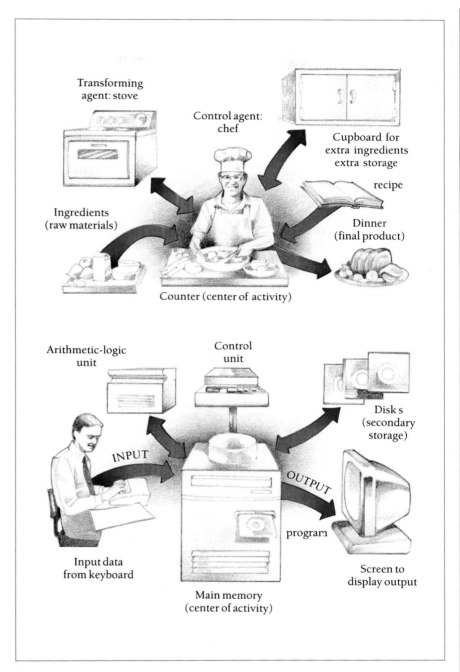

■ Figure 1.1
Analogy between cooking and computing.

coordinates the movement and transformation of data. Like a chef, the control unit follows a recipe. This recipe, or program, prescribes exactly what to do to convert the input data into the desired results.

Role of the program   Just as a recipe prescribes a chef's activities in a kitchen, a program determines the behavior of a computer system. Even with the same chef, kitchen, and ingredients, a different recipe will yield a different result. Similarly, a different program will yield a different result from the same computer system.

The analogy weakens at this point because a chef—unlike a computer—can interpret the recipe and improvise if necessary. However, the program dictates every detail of the computer's activity. The program must be right if the results are to come out right.

Incidentally, just as a chef can reuse a recipe to prepare any number of meals, so we can use a program over and over with different data. This underlines the distinction between devising the program and actually running it on a computer, which is called program execution.

Programming begins by devising a solution approach to a problem. For now, we will leave the discussion of computers and concentrate on problem solving in general.

1.2 Problem Solving

The essence of good problem-solving ability is a careful, systematic approach rather than a carefree, impetuous attack. The ability to approach problems calmly and rationally need not be a hereditary accident; it is a skill that can be learned and practiced with the aid of a few simple guidelines. One especially useful and succinct statement of problem-solving guidelines was given by Rene Descartes, a mathematician and philosopher, in his *Discourse on Method*:

1. Never accept anything as true unless it is certainly and evidently such: carefully avoid all precipitation and prejudgement.
2. Divide each of the difficulties into as many parts as possible.
3. Think in an orderly fashion, beginning with the things which are the simplest and easiest to understand, and gradually reach toward the more complex.
4. Make enumerations so complete and reviews so general that it is certain nothing is omitted.

Although Descartes developed them more than 300 years before the first electronic computer was built, these guidelines are still valid, and we will adopt them as rules. In general, Descartes pleaded for a more systematic and less impulsive approach to problem solving. We echo this plea. A careful, thorough approach to identifying and stating a problem is essential to a successful outcome, especially when dealing with computers.

The individual rules, which focus on different aspects of problem solving, are so simple that you may be tempted to dismiss them. Even though they are ignored far too often, their mastery is by far the major requirement for using computers. In the remainder of this section, we recast these rules in more modern terms.

Understanding a Problem

Problems often seem more complex than they really are because we do not clearly understand them. A hazily grasped problem leads to a fuzzy solution, which is often no solution at all to the real problem. One interpretation of Descartes' first rule is to be sure of what you want. Do not make rash assumptions and jump to conclusions. Instead, try

RULE I
Analyze the problem carefully, attempting to understand its specific aspects and the requirements of an acceptable solution.

Understanding what constitutes an acceptable solution may tell you two things: whether there is any feasible solution and, if so, how far to proceed with it. You should assess the level of result you want at an early stage. This is a frequently neglected consideration, but unless your goals are feasible and within your means, they are not worth pursuing. This discussion could well be summarized by the old adage: Understanding a problem is half the solution. The more complete and precise the understanding, the more apparent may be the course of action.

Decomposing a Problem

As your understanding of a problem increases, your statement of the problem becomes correspondingly more detailed. Of course, as the problem becomes more detailed and constrained, it also becomes more difficult to deal with *all at one time*. This is where Descartes' second rule comes into play, which we rephrase as

RULE II
Attempt to break the problem into simpler, relatively independent parts and then focus on the separate parts.

Various approaches to problem decomposition can be used. The most useful is probably

RULE II(a)
Attempt to break the problem into a *sequence* of smaller problems, so that the solution of one subproblem followed by the solution of the next, and so on, will provide a solution to the original problem.

The purpose of decomposing problems is to spare you from the details of *how* other solution steps perform their functions when you are developing one step. However, you must never lose sight of *what* the other parts of the solution are supposed to do because they are seldom completely independent. Usually, certain steps must precede others because the later steps rely on earlier results.

The solution of many problems involves dealing repetitively with similar situations and conditions (customers, financial transactions, experimental data items). When facing such a problem, you should first concentrate on how to handle an individual case. If your solution for one case is sufficiently general, you can easily repeat that solution procedure for all cases.

RULE II(b)
If the problem involves performing some *repeated* process, attempt to isolate the action that is required in one instance from the repetitive aspect of the process.

If you cannot decide where to begin, perhaps it is because special cases make the problem appear too confusing. It might help to *temporarily* ignore special and unusual cases. This would allow you to concentrate on the standard or routine cases. Later, you could handle most of the exceptional cases by making minor modifications to your standard solution.

RULE II(c)
First attempt to solve the problem for the *simplest* case or the most likely set of circumstances. When you reach a satisfactory solution for this, then extend the solution to cover special cases or less likely contingencies.

In an initial design you should provide for the eventual inclusion of special cases but not become entangled in their details. After all, if your solution will not work for the standard situation, it does not matter how well it handles exceptional cases.

The Problem-Solving Process

The rules for refining the approach to a problem can be applied in a variety of ways. To be effective, they should be applied slowly and carefully. The overall decomposition of a problem should follow

RULE III
When breaking a problem into simpler parts, perform the decomposition gradually in several stages. Use general criteria in the early stages and more specific criteria later.

The early stages involve more global, general considerations, whereas later stages focus more and more on details. Moving from the general to the specific

stepwise refinement

gives this style of problem solving the name top-down design with **stepwise refinement.**

We suggest that each step in the decomposition of a problem produce no more than five simpler problems. As for how many steps are needed, the only rule of thumb is to keep analyzing and refining until you have isolated subproblems that are simple enough to solve easily. The ability to do this is a skill requiring intuition and experience, but it is a skill well worth developing.

Nevertheless, no matter how thoroughly you analyze, you will almost invariably overlook some feature or special circumstance when designing the first (second, third, and fourth) version of a solution procedure. Never try to save time by ignoring

RULE IV

At every stage in its development, review and reconsider your proposed solution to ensure that it is complete and correct.

Unfortunately, one review is seldom sufficient. Rule IV should be applied at every step in the solution. As you solve one subproblem, reconsider your proposal to make sure that it does precisely what is required by that subproblem. Whenever you combine separate subsolutions, make sure that they are compatible. Check to see that you have covered all the special cases. Never hesitate to review a proposed solution procedure; you will almost always find something to add, modify, or delete.

1.3 Algorithms and Pseudocode

When you decide to have a house built, you may have only a general idea of what you want. The architect talks with you and tries to pinpoint your desires and preferences. You then expect the architect to provide you with a satisfactory solution.

This is not quite the case if you turn to a computer for assistance with a problem. Your relationship with the computer is more like the architect's relationship with a construction crew. The workers do not help decide how the house should be built; they follow the specifications on the blueprints. Similarly, a computer does not directly assist you in organizing your thoughts or inventing a solution procedure. You must have your procedure in hand; the computer merely manipulates symbols according to your prescription. If your solution procedure is wrong, the computer's output will be wrong. This is why you must master the art of problem solving if you hope to use a computer effectively.

The analogy between the architect and the computer programmer is not complete. The architect can revise parts of the plan to allow for changing, or unanticipated, circumstances after construction has begun. The construction crew can report omissions or ask for clarification of ambiguous instructions.

However, the procedure that you would have a computer follow must specify precisely what to do in all cases. There is no room for sloppiness because the computer is a machine—devoid of compassion and insight—that does exactly what it is instructed to do. Your proposed solution must be expressed at a level of detail and precision far in excess of that required for normal human communication; it must be in a form known as an algorithm.

algorithm   An **algorithm** is a complete, unambiguous procedure for solving a specific problem, expressed as a finite number of rules, and guaranteed to terminate in a finite number of applications of these rules. The notation used to describe algorithms ranges from a natural language (such as English) to a programming language (such as Pascal), depending on the level of development of the algorithm. Only when the algorithm is ready for presentation to a computer

code   is it written in **code,** that is, expressed in a programming language. During the development process, the algorithmic notation often progresses gradually from English toward the programming language notation. Any notation, short

pseudocode   of the actual programming language itself, is often referred to as **pseudocode.**

Before looking at some examples of algorithms, it will be instructive to look at a nonalgorithmic procedure that is typical of most human communication. We take for granted how much meaning we convey with gestures, facial expressions, inflections, and the context of our words. A procedure may be correct in the sense that it could be performed successfully by a person of reasonable intelligence, but it may be far from an algorithm.

For example, consider the following procedure for frying eggs.

> A little melted butter or oil lining a moderately hot pan will eliminate sticking. Break eggs in directly from shell, or pour from cup. Pan should be hot enough so white sets speedily but not so hot that white burns or sticks. Choose a flexible spatula for turning; tip the pan slightly forward toward the spatula so that the egg almost slides onto it.

This sort of solution, known as a recipe, is correct in the human sense. A chef could follow its instructions and fry eggs perfectly every time because a chef understands the terminology of a recipe, can follow its instructions, and has enough background to make correct assumptions whenever something is left unspecified in the recipe.

Most of us, however, are not chefs. We might have no idea about what type of pan to use, what temperature to set the stove (what stove?), or when to turn the eggs. The recipe says nothing about the type of pan and is imprecise regarding temperature: "Pan should be hot enough . . . but not so hot. . . ." Not only does the recipe fail to say when to turn the eggs, it never explicitly says to turn them; it only hints at turning by recommending a flexible spatula for that purpose. Someone who takes things too literally might even go on frying the eggs forever because the recipe says nothing about when to stop! At a lower level of understanding, this recipe fails to communicate how to fry eggs. It is imprecise, incomplete, and ambiguous.

In contrast, consider an algorithm that describes exactly how to compute the product of two positive integers, using only the process of addition. If we

■ Figure 1.2
Algorithm to find the
product of two
positive integers
using only addition.

1. Determine values for J and K (both positive).
2. Set the value of P to zero.
3. If the value of K is zero, then the product is the value of P. If not, then proceed to step 4.
4. Add the value of J to the value of P.
5. Deduct 1 from the value of K.
6. Proceed to step 3.

denote the two integers (the multiplicand and the multiplier) by the symbols J and K and represent the product by P, the algorithm would read as shown in Fig. 1.2. For algebraic reasons, the value of K will eventually become zero. Consequently, this procedure is guaranteed to halt ultimately at step 3.

This algorithm is based on the fact that multiplication of two positive integers is derived from repeated addition. That is, $3 \times 4 = 3 + 3 + 3 + 3$, and $6 \times 2 = 6 + 6$. Although we hardly expect many people to do multiplication in this way, our purpose is to show a finished algorithm, so completely prescribed that anyone who can add and subtract could carry out multiplication *without* knowing anything about the multiplication process. This mimics the operation of a computer, which must act on your instructions (program) as presented—without any understanding whatsoever of your goals or how your algorithm achieves these goals.

Note that the steps in the algorithm are listed sequentially so that when one has been carried out, the next consecutive step is to be followed immediately. This progression through consecutive steps is always assumed in every algorithm unless there are explicit instructions to the contrary, as in steps 3 and 6 of Fig. 1.2.

Besides announcing the result at the end, the role of step 3 is to determine whether an additional application of steps 4 and 5 is necessary. This role becomes clearer when the algorithm is expressed in the form shown in Fig. 1.3. Here, the progression from step 3.2 to step 4 is not automatic; completion of step 3.2 does not imply that all of step 3 has been completed. Only when step 3 determines that enough applications of steps 3.1 and 3.2 have occurred will step 4 be applied. We also removed some of the wordiness from the algorithm. Steps 3.1 and 3.2 correspond directly to steps 4 and 5 of the

■ Figure 1.3
The multiplication
algorithm restated.

1.   get values for J and K (both positive);
2.   set P to zero;
3.   while $K \neq 0$ do steps 3.1 and 3.2;
3.1   let $P = P + J$;
3.2   let $K = K - 1$;
4.   the product is the value of P;
5.   stop.

original version. Finally, an explicit instruction to stop appears in Fig. 1.3 to indicate the end of the algorithm. Although stated more succinctly, this version of the algorithm carries out exactly the same operations as the version shown in Fig. 1.2.

Pay particular attention to the use of symbols such as J, K, and P to refer to actual but unspecified positive integers. These symbols simply denote algebraic variables, the values of which may differ from one application of the algorithm to the next and may change during the course of carrying out the algorithm. Algorithms suitable for computer implementation make heavy use of variable names to denote whatever data are to be processed. In fact, these algorithms usually revolve around a few variables, whose values they keep changing and examining. For example, most steps in the multiplication algorithm either alter or compare the values of P and K. Thus variables are the common thread connecting one step of an algorithm with the other. Identifying which values to denote by variables is a crucial decision. If you decide which values are to be processed before you design your solution procedure, the steps of your eventual algorithm will be more compatible, since they will be dealing with the same data.

Because of this unifying role of the data, we propose the following special rule for problem solving.

RULE V
Identify at the beginning the data that are necessary for the solution and develop every stage of the solution procedure with them in mind.

This rule is often the key to organizing a proposed solution into an algorithm suitable for a computer. At every step of any proposed algorithm you should answer the following questions in a way appropriate to the current level of refinement.

1. What (input) data must be supplied to enable the current step to make its decision or carry out its action?
2. What (output) data should be produced by this step, so that its results may be conveyed to other steps?
3. What other (temporary) quantities should be generated for the private internal use of this step in order to simplify or facilitate its operation?

Looking back at Fig. 1.3, we see that step 1 requires two integers (J and K) that are used throughout step 3 in conjunction with another integer (P) that is introduced at step 2. All three integers participate in the manipulations of step 3, even though only K and P are modified. The variable P is needed to display the ultimate result in step 4.

Such analysis is helpful in showing how the separate steps pass data from one to the other and in revealing how the steps interact. Understanding this interaction and the flow of data is crucial to the development of more complex algorithms.

Algorithm Development

Now that you know what an algorithm is, we will use the techniques of problem solving to actually derive an algorithm.

Suppose that you are asked to automate the vote counting in an election between two candidates for one office. Each ballot contains two boxes, and each voter is supposed to mark an X in the box for one of the candidates. Your first task is to develop an algorithm, and you should begin by applying the general rules of problem solving.

Rule I says that you should understand the problem and the required result before doing anything else. In this case, the desired result is a pair of numbers: the total vote for each of the candidates. A good way to begin is to consider how you would achieve the desired result manually.

One approach might be to start with a blank sheet of paper and divide it into two sections where the vote count for each candidate would be recorded. Then you would inspect each ballot in turn, updating the count for whichever candidate received that vote. At any point in the counting the latest numbers on the sheet represent the current vote count for each candidate. This is the approach that we will pursue in developing an algorithm for the solution of this problem.

Rule V tells you to identify the data that are required for the solution. In this case you need two variables to maintain two running totals, which we will call "total1" and "total2." The variables are to be *incremented* (increased by 1) until all the votes have been recorded. Variables used in this way are called **counters.** A counter variable must have an initial value to which the first increment can be added. In most cases this initial value is zero. Whatever it may be, every counter variable must be set explicitly to some initial value.

counters

With this in mind, we follow Rule II(a) and decompose the solution into a sequence of basic steps:

1.   set both counters to 0;
2.   tally the votes;
3.   display the results (the two counters);
4.   stop.

Step 2 obviously needs refinement, so we apply Rule II in an attempt to elaborate on it. Tallying votes involves repeatedly inspecting very similar ballots, and Rule II(b) suggests isolating the action taken on each ballot from the repetitive aspect of the counting process. Hence step 2 becomes

2.   while any unprocessed ballots remain do:
2.1   process the next ballot;

Note that step 2 specifies that step 2.1 should be repeated until all the ballots have been counted.

We again apply Rule II(a), this time to the processing of one ballot (step 2.1). This involves two actions: inspecting the ballot and adding 1 to the appropriate counter. Now we have

2.   while any unprocessed ballots remain do:
2.1   inspect the next ballot;
2.2   increment the appropriate counter;

At this point we may realize that some of the ballots will be invalid and that we need a method of handling this situation in step 2.2. However, Rule II(c) suggests bypassing this complication for the moment and dealing with the standard (valid ballot) case first. In addition, as we encounter each ballot, we must also note the contents of both boxes. We will let "box1" and "box2" refer to the contents of the boxes on the ballot currently being examined. Hence step 2.2 becomes

2.2.1   if box1 is X then increment total1;
2.2.2   if box2 is X then increment total2;

Now we can extend these steps to handle invalid ballots. Suppose you recognize two types of invalid ballot: (1) a ballot on which no marks appear; and (2) a ballot on which both boxes are marked with an X. The first case will cause no difficulty because our solution alters a total only when it encounters an X. However, the second would cause *both* totals to be incremented. Therefore we must refine the solution so that totals are changed only when *one* box contains an X.

2.2.1   if box1 is X and box2 is not X then increment total1;
2.2.2   if box2 is X and box1 is not X then increment total2;

Rule IV tells us to review each stage of the solution. A review at this stage may call to our attention a third type of invalid ballot: a ballot on which one box contains an X and the other box contains a mark other than an X. A ballot with an X in one box and a check mark in the other would be incorrectly presumed valid. Therefore a box that does not contain an X must be specifically blank, and so we now have

2.2.1   if box1 is X and box2 is blank then increment total1;
2.2.2   if box2 is X and box1 is blank then increment total2;

Satisfied that every possibility has been covered, we now collect all these components of the solution into one algorithm:

1.   set total1 and total2 to 0;
2.   while any unprocessed ballots remain do (level 2):
2.1   inspect the next ballot;
2.2.1   if box1 is X and box2 is blank then increment total1;
2.2.2   if box2 is X and box1 is blank then increment total2;
3.   display results (total1 and total2);
4.   stop.

One more review (Rule IV) does not reveal any other omissions, and so we are ready to try our algorithm.

1.4 Programming Languages

When given a programming problem, you first have to devise a solution procedure and refine this procedure into an algorithm. When you are satisfied with the algorithm, you must rewrite it in a programming language that the computer is able to interpret. English is too imprecise; meanings of words depend too much on nuance, context, and human experience. A programming language, on the other hand, has only a limited vocabulary and extremely precise grammatical rules for building unambiguous instructions from its basic vocabulary.

Programming languages

Several programming languages are in common use. You may have heard of the BASIC, FORTRAN, COBOL, Ada, C, PL/I, and Pascal languages. You may be less familiar with others, including MODULA-2, LISP, SNOBOL, LOGO, ALGOL, and Smalltalk. Various languages may reflect the preferences that prevailed at the time they were introduced, or they may have been designed to facilitate some particular programming technique. Yet, despite superficial differences, most computer languages (with a few notable exceptions) are basically similar. Like the variety of human languages, certain programming languages may express certain things especially well, but most are capable of somehow expressing what needs to be said. After all, they are merely different notations for specifying algorithms.

Pascal is a particularly straightforward member of the mainstream group of programming languages. It was designed during the early 1970s and encompasses most of the important features found in earlier languages such as FORTRAN, COBOL, PL/I, BASIC, and ALGOL. It is especially popular as an introductory language because, unlike some of the others, it handles key features in a clear, consistent manner. In fact, learning to program in Pascal will help you to use other languages later. The hard part is learning to develop algorithms and to specify typical computer processes. This can be done well using Pascal. Learning the peculiarities of another programming language is comparatively easy after you have mastered Pascal. From here on we will discuss only the Pascal language, but many of the issues and themes presented apply to programming in general, regardless of the language used.

Returning to the analogy of preparing a meal in a kitchen, you could write the same recipe for a meal in a number of human languages. You would probably write the recipe in English. Now suppose the chef at your restaurant understands only Hungarian. The chef could execute your recipe only if it is first translated from English into Hungarian.

The same applies to programming languages. The computer itself does not directly respond to any of the more human-oriented programming languages, such as Pascal. Its own language, called **machine language,** is at a much more primitive level. Before a program can execute, or start to run, it must be translated into an equivalent program in machine language. This is done by a **compiler.**

machine language

compiler

Each language has its own compiler. For example, a FORTRAN program would be translated by the FORTRAN compiler. Of course, when you write a program in Pascal, you must compile it on a computer system that has a Pascal compiler. This step is trivial for the user; it usually requires only one command to the computer system.

The compiler inspects an entire program before it can be executed by the computer and can catch certain types of errors you may have made. If the compiler finds problems, it reports the error and prevents the program from reaching execution. Although it can detect misuse of the Pascal language, the compiler cannot detect errors in your logic or thought process. If your algorithm is wrong, the corresponding program will produce wrong answers, even though your use of Pascal may be flawless. Although the compiler can filter out many problems, it does not eliminate the need for careful algorithm development and careful testing of the final program.

The overall programming process, including compiling and executing programs, will be described later. Meanwhile, let's see what a Pascal program looks like.

Consider the simple problem of finding the area of a rectangle that has a length of 114 and a width of 62. A possible algorithm is shown in Fig. 1.4(a). The corresponding Pascal program is shown in Fig. 1.4(b). The portion of the program between BEGIN and END is the rewritten version of the algorithm. The correspondence between the algorithm and program should be obvious.

■ Figure 1.4
A first program.

1. let the length be 114;
2. let the width be 62;
3. the area is length times width;
4. display the area;
5. stop.

(a) Algorithm for the area of a specific rectangle.

```
PROGRAM First (input,output);
VAR
  Length,
  Width,
  Area: integer;
BEGIN
  Length := 114;
  Width := 62;
  Area := Length * Width;
  writeln (Area)
END.
```

(b) Corresponding Pascal program.

After the program has been entered into the machine, compiled, and executed, the ultimate result, a single integer, appears on the screen or printer:

7068

This is, of course, the area of the rectangle under consideration.

Note that in Fig. 1.4 the words PROGRAM, VAR, BEGIN, and END are

reserved words

entirely in upper case. These are special symbols, called **reserved words,** that have special roles in Pascal. The convention that we use throughout this book is to show all reserved words entirely in upper case. In the following sections we explain the details of each statement in the program shown in Fig. 1.4.

1.5 Overall Pascal Program Structure

A Pascal program consists of a heading and a block. The heading names the program and indicates how the program communicates with the outside world, while the block contains the details of the data manipulation that the program is to carry out.

program heading

The **program heading** is usually just the first line and always begins with the word PROGRAM. The most common form of a program heading is

PROGRAM ⟨program identifier⟩ (input,output);

The identifier is simply some name by which the program can be recognized. The special notation ⟨. . .⟩ designates one specific selection from the class of objects described inside the angle brackets. Here the class is all legitimate program identifiers. In Fig. 1.4, "First" was chosen as the identifier. A program identifier can be almost any reasonable name you care to use. (Precise rules governing identifiers are given in Section 1.6.) Another example of this notation is ⟨digit⟩, which refers to any one of the ten symbols 0, 1, . . . , 9.

The "(input,output)" part of the program heading refers to the way in which the program will communicate with the user. For now, you can take these names as standard, required parts of the program heading. If you use a terminal, *input* refers to the keyboard and *output* to the screen or printing device. Unlike the symbols ⟨ and ⟩, the parentheses themselves appear in the actual heading.

block

Following the heading, the remainder of the program is called the **block.** Just as a recipe identifies required materials before describing how to use them, a program block contains some definitions before describing what to do.

statement part

The algorithm that the program represents is encoded between BEGIN and END. This section of the program is called the **statement part** and prescribes the actions for the computer to take. However, this specification

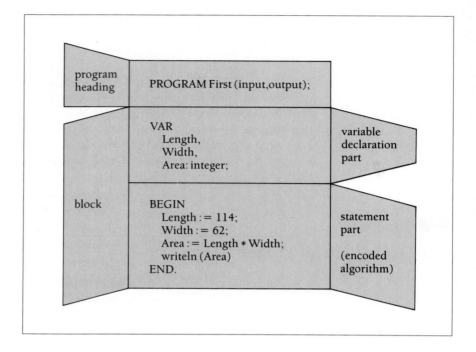

makes use of symbolic names, which must be defined prior to the statement
part itself. In Fig. 1.4 the lines introduced by VAR explain how certain
symbols—Length, Width, and Area—are to be used later on. These lines
constitute the **variable declaration part,** which is just one of several possible
preliminaries to the statement part. Figure 1.5 shows these basic parts of a
Pascal program.

variable declaration
part

   Note that statements in Pascal are separated from each other by semicolons
(;). The final END is followed by a period (.). Capitalization is used only to
help the reader identify the symbols that have special meanings in Pascal and
to identify the structural form of a program.

1.6 Variables and the Variable Declaration Part

You are already familiar with the use of variables in algebraic formulas, such
as

$$A = l \times w,$$

which relates the area A of a rectangle to its length l and width w. When l
and w represent specific values, say 4 and 3, the formula shows how to find

the area of the corresponding rectangle. By letting *l* and *w* represent other values, we can use the same formula to find the area of other rectangles. Of course, a formula containing values rather than variables for length or width, such as $A = 4 \times 3$, may also show how to compute an area—but only for one specific rectangle. You should remember three key points: (1) the use of symbolic names (variables) rather than specific values makes a formula more widely applicable; but (2) before the formula can be used to make an actual calculation, the variables have to be given specific values; and (3) the particular choice of symbolic names is really not important. The formula

$$s = a \times b$$

expresses exactly the same relationship between area *s* and the lengths of the sides *a* and *b*. The *structure* of the formula is what matters, not the letters employed.

Similar observations apply to programs. We usually write programs to solve a class of problems rather than one specific instance. Thus we use symbolic names, or variables, to designate whatever values may be involved in a particular execution. Variables lie at the very heart of programming.

variable identifiers In Pascal, the symbolic names are known as **variable identifiers.** We have great freedom in choosing symbolic names, so we must announce the variable identifiers that we are using in a program. We list them in the variable declaration part, introduced by VAR. For example, in the program shown in Fig. 1.4, we declared Length, Width and Area to be the variable identifiers.

Just as variables in a formula are associated with actual values before computing a specific result, the variables in a program will also be associated with values during program execution. However, since a program is carried out by a computer, there is an underlying physical reality to giving a value to a program variable. A computer memory contains a vast number of "places," called *memory locations,* that can each store one item of data or one value. A distinct memory location is set aside for each variable identifier declared in a program, and every occurrence of that variable identifier throughout the program refers to the same memory location (at least in simple programs). Of course, the computer will manipulate only the *contents* of memory locations; the identifiers themselves merely designate which locations to use.

The variable declaration part of Fig. 1.4 will enable the statement part to utilize three memory locations:

Length   [ ]

Width   [ ]

Area   [ ]

Note that none of these locations contain any values before program execution begins. In Section 1.7, we describe how to give values to these locations and how to change their contents during execution. Meanwhile, however, let's consider some more details of writing variable declarations in Pascal.

Identifiers

identifier

You are free to select almost any "reasonable" name for your program and the variables you use. However, the rules governing names in programs are precise and must be strictly observed.

A program or variable name in Pascal is known as an **identifier.** The general rules for constructing valid identifiers are very simple:

1. Each identifier must begin with a letter of the alphabet.
2. Subsequent characters may be any letter of the alphabet or any of the 10 digits (0 through 9).
3. Reserved words may not be used as identifiers.

Note that there is no general limit on the length of an identifier. But different implementations (that is, different versions of Pascal such as Turbo, VAX-11, UCSD, and Waterloo) may impose a maximum number of characters for an identifier. Although some implementations make allowance for other characters in an identifier, it is advisable to use only letters and digits because they are universally acceptable.

Most versions of Pascal permit long identifiers, so you should use names that are meaningful. In Fig. 1.4 we used Length, Width, and Area as identifiers to make their roles clear. Without affecting the outcome of the program, we could have selected $i, j,$ and k instead, but these names give no clue about what they represent. Unfortunately, many programmers use short, uninformative names. The extra time spent on selecting descriptive identifiers is insignificant compared to the time that can be wasted later in trying to decipher an unreadable program.

As a convention in this book, we will use capital letters for the first letter of an identifier. If the identifier is a composite of several words, each word will be capitalized. Thus you will see identifiers such as

```
CurrentBalance
TimeOfDay
SpeedLimit
```

Note that spaces are not permitted within an identifier; all its constituent characters must be consecutive.

Recall that the (capitalized) reserved words, such as PROGRAM, BEGIN, VAR and END, are symbols that have special meanings. They may not be used as identifiers. A complete list of reserved words is given in Appendix A. Another set of symbols, although not strictly reserved and not strictly off limits, should never be declared as your own identifiers. They are called *required* or *predeclared* symbols, or **standard identifiers,** and also have special meanings in the Pascal language. Four of these (input, output, integer, and writeln) appear in Fig. 1.4. A complete list of these identifiers is given in Appendix B.

standard identifiers

The Notion of Data Types

The computer can store information of different types. For example, it can store either characters or numbers, and the numbers can be either whole numbers (integers) or numbers with a decimal point and a decimal fraction (real numbers). There are other data types as well.

Each variable can hold only one type of data. Even though the value stored there may change from time to time, each successive value of the same variable must have the same type (for example, all must be integers). Data type can be compared to geometric shape, where all integers are round, all real numbers are square, and all characters are triangular. Just as you cannot put a square peg in a round hole, neither can you store real numbers in integer variables.

data type

Therefore you must announce the type of each variable as well as its name. The **data type** is a particular property permanently associated with that variable. In Fig. 1.4 all three variables are declared with the integer type. This allows them to hold integers and only integers. Because every computer has a finite capacity for storing data, you cannot store any integer whatsoever in an integer variable. For instance, most computers currently available could not fit the integer 28000000000 into an integer variable.

maxint

Pascal utilizes a standard identifier, called **maxint,** which always contains the value of the largest permissable integer in a computer system. To discover the largest allowed integer in your computer system, all you need do is display the value of maxint, as in

```
PROGRAM Biggest (input,output);
BEGIN
  writeln (maxint)
END.
```

According to standard Pascal, the allowed values for integers lie in the range − maxint to maxint, inclusive.

1.7 The Assignment Statement

To see how variables may be given values and used in a program, let's focus on the statement part of the program shown in Fig. 1.4. The first two statements

```
Length := 114;
Width := 62;
```

produce the following results during execution:

Length | 114 |

Width | 62 |

Area | ▨ |

Each of the statements is an **assignment statement** because it includes the **assignment operator** (:=). This symbol, formed by a colon followed immediately by an equals sign, specifies that the value on its right is to be placed in the variable identified on its left. Thus 114 is stored in Length, and 62 is stored in Width.

The value to be stored may be a **constant,** that is, an explicitly written value such as 114. Another possibility is to use the value of some other variable. If the third assignment statement had been

```
Area := Width;
```

the net effect would have been to place a copy of the current value of Width into the variable Area:

Length | 114 |

Width | 62 |

Area | 62 |

Note that the value of Width is not affected by its assignment into Area. The assignment operator can alter only the variable on its left.

Furthermore, a variable (such as Width) can have its value inspected or used any number of times without changing the value that is stored in that memory location. Storing a value in a memory location is analogous to recording a song on tape: You can listen to the tape over and over and hear the same song each time.

However, whenever a recording is made on tape, its previous contents are completely lost by recording over them. A similar thing happens to a value stored in a memory location. If a new value is placed there, the previous value is lost from that location. A variable may contain only one value at a time—the one given to it most recently. If a subsequent assignment statement had been

```
Area := -37;
```

the previous value of Area would then be replaced by the new one:

Length | 114 |

Width | 62 |

Area | −37 |

The Assignment Statement

⟨variable identifier⟩ := ⟨expression⟩;

The expression on the right-hand side of the assignment operator (:=) is evaluated and stored in the variable identified on the left-hand side of the assignment operator (sometimes referred to as the target variable). The expression must yield a value of the same type as the target variable.

Returning to the program shown in Fig. 1.4, we can see that the third assignment is actually

```
Area := Length * Width;
```

Here the value to be placed in Area is neither a constant nor the value of another variable. It is computed by multiplying the current values of Length and Width; that is,

Length | 114 |

Width | 62 |

Area | 7068 |

The asterisk (*) is used in Pascal as the symbol for multiplication. There are many such operators and possible ways of deriving a new value from combinations of existing values. The right-hand side of the assignment operator may even contain an enormously complex expression. We explain some of these possibilities in the following section and others throughout the rest of the book.

For now, we simply note the overall operation of the assignment statement:

1. The expression on the right-hand side of := is evaluated.
2. This value is then placed in the memory location identified by the variable on the left-hand side of :=, replacing whatever was there before.

Since it is the major means of changing the values of variables, assignment is by far the most widely used statement in Pascal.

1.8 Arithmetic Expressions

arithmetic expression

An **arithmetic expression** indicates how to calculate a single numeric value. The right-hand sides of all the assignment statements used so far are examples of arithmetic expressions. The right-hand side of an assignment statement is probably the place where arithmetic expressions most commonly occur, but it certainly is not the only place.

The simplest arithmetic expressions are either numeric constants (such as -18) or numeric variables (such as Width), which supply the value of the expression directly. Other arithmetic expressions produce their results by combining or transforming these basic ingredients—constants and variables—

arithmetic operators   by means of various **arithmetic operators** and functions. In fact, most arithmetic expressions closely resemble algebraic expressions and are evaluated according to rules that resemble the normal rules of algebra.

For example, addition and subtraction in Pascal are denoted by the conventional plus $(+)$ and minus $(-)$ signs. Assuming that the variables all contain appropriate values, we could express the total number of widows and orphans as

Widows + Orphans

and the amount by which a group's average age exceeds 40 as

AverageAge − 40

(This number may turn out to be negative.)

We have already observed that multiplication in Pascal is denoted by an asterisk $(*)$, rather than by a dot, a cross, or by juxtaposition, as in ordinary algebra. When multiplication is required, you must write the asterisk explicitly. Thus the algebraic expression $4N$ must appear as 4 ∗ N (or 4∗N) in Pascal.

The other basic arithmetic operator is division. In Pascal, conventional division is denoted by a slash $(/)$; 11 divided by 4 is written 11/4. Even though both constituent values are integers, the result (2.75) is *not* an integer; it is a real number. Such a value could not be stored in a variable of integer type.

In order to remain within the world of integers, another division operator, written DIV, is used in Pascal. To see how it works, consider the arithmetic expression

11 DIV 4

which has a value of 2. The DIV operator divides the first integer by the second but uses only the integer portion of the result as its value. Note that it does not round 2.75 to the nearest integer; it simply ignores the fractional part. This discarding of any fractional part of a number, even though it be as

truncation   much as .999, is known as **truncation.** As with conventional division, the divisor (second number) must not be 0, and if the two original values have different signs, the result is negative.

Pascal provides another fundamental operator that is related to division and remains within the world of integers. Given two positive integers, this operator, written MOD, performs a division, ignores the integer quotient, and yields the remainder as an integer for its value. Thus

11 MOD 4

has the value 3—the amount left over after dividing 4 into 11. The second value must be greater than 0. In rare situations, the first integer may be negative, but a somewhat different result may be produced in this case, depending on the version of Pascal being used; in some cases, for example, −11 MOD 4 yields the value −3 (the true remainder after division), whereas other versions may yield the value 1 (adhering strictly to the rules of modulus arithmetic).

You can form more elaborate arithmetic expressions by using combinations of the basic operators. Again, the values are obtained following rules resembling those in conventional algebra. For example, the expression

    5 + 3 * 2

contains two different operators. It yields the value 11 because the multiplication (*) is performed before the addition (+). Hence 5 is added to the result of evaluating 3 * 2.

You may use parentheses to alter (or clarify) the order in which operators are evaluated. Hence

    (5 + 3) * 2

causes the expression in parentheses to be evaluated first. The result then is 16. Again, note that the multiplication operator must be explicitly written.

In the absence of parentheses, which may be used to override these conventions, certain kinds of operators are always applied before others. Those performed first are said to have higher **operator precedence.** Among the arithmetic operators, the *multiplicative operators* (*, /, DIV, MOD) have higher precedence. The *additive operators* (+, −) have lower precedence. All operators from the same group (say, multiplicative) share the same precedence.

operator precedence

If an expression contains two or more consecutive operators having the same precedence, they are evaluated from left to right in order of appearance. For example, the expression

    6 − 3 − 2

is equivalent to (6 − 3) − 2, whose value is 1. The left to right order of evaluation is significant because the other order, specified by 6 − (3 − 2), yields a value of 5. Similarly, the expression 17 DIV 4 MOD 3 has a value of 1, whereas 17 DIV (4 MOD 3) has value 17.

In any event, the rules of Pascal conform closely to the rules of ordinary algebra. Thus you should find writing and understanding arithmetic expressions in Pascal to be straightforward.

1.9 The writeln Statement

It would be a shame if, after toiling for hours to develop a program that produces long-awaited results, you never get to see those results. That is exactly what will happen if you do not explicitly request your program to

The writeln Statement

writeln (⟨list of values⟩)

The value of every item in the list is displayed on the output device in the same order as it appears in the list. The list may contain constants, variables, and/or expressions. After all the values have been displayed, the cursor advances to the start of the next line.

display some values. All you need to do is include the statement

writeln (⟨list of values⟩)

and the values indicated in the list will be printed on the terminal screen or printer. You will frequently encounter the notation ⟨list of "things"⟩. In this context, a list is a collection of individual items, separated by commas when more than one item appears in the list.

writeln
statement

For example, the **writeln** (pronounced *write line*) **statement** in Fig. 1.4 will cause the computer to display the current value of the variable Area. If we had wanted to display the values of all variables in this program, that statement might have read

```
writeln (Length, Width, Area)
```

These values are displayed in the same order in which the variables are listed in the *writeln* statement. The result would look something like this:

114   62   7068

The values displayed can also be specified by constants or more involved arithmetic expressions. For example, the statement

writeln ($-6, 3 * 5$)

would generate the following line of output:

-6 15

1.10 Flow of Control

Recall that the statements in algorithms do not need to say "proceed to the next statement." When executing an algorithm, you would move through the list of instructions in order, one at a time, unless explicitly directed to skip or repeat some.

Similarly, when the program shown in Fig. 1.4 is being executed, each statement is executed in the order in which the computer encounters it. The

flow of control

concept of a computer completely executing one statement of a program before executing some other statement is extremely important. The sequence in which the statements are executed is called the **flow of control.**

If we ignore, for the moment, the initial parts of the program shown in Fig. 1.4, which supply special getting-started information, the computer starts execution with BEGIN and continues sequentially through the statement part until it encounters the END of the program. This program's flow is extremely simple, since it proceeds sequentially from the top of the block to the bottom. However, most programs do not have such a simple flow of control. Most programs, like most algorithms, contain statements that may be repeated or bypassed in some situations. Nevertheless, every execution of a program has some particular flow of control, since statements must be executed in some order.

Clearly, the order in which the program statements are placed is vital to the correct execution of the program. For example, if we had mistakenly interchanged the statements

```
Area := Length * Width;
```

and

```
writeln (Area)
```

the program would not execute properly; the computer would have encountered the writeln statement before any value had been stored in the variable Area. We would then be asking the computer to display a nonexistent or incorrect value (Area).

1.11 Executing a Program on a Computer

Suppose that you have developed an algorithm, have refined it to the point that you feel confident of its correctness, and have coded it as a Pascal program. The creative process now gives way to the purely mechanical one of getting the program to run on a computer. Unfortunately, at this point the peculiarities of your machine and computer system become so important that little can be said here except to explain the procedure in a very general way. You must obtain the details about using your system from your own instructor or local computer center. However, three basic steps are always required:

1. The program, now existing on paper, must be entered into the machine (usually through the keyboard).
2. The Pascal version of the program must be internally transformed (compiled), so that it can be executed.
3. The machine must execute the program so that you can see the result.

file

In step 1 the program statements are entered directly through the terminal keyboard. The machine-readable copy of your program is stored electronically inside the computer system in what is called a **file.** Like a file in an office, your newly created program file need not be used (executed) immediately. It also remains in the system from one use to the next, so that you need not retype the code. (We assume that you have terminal access to your computer; if not, the procedures would be slightly different.)

text editor

As you enter your program in a file, a **text editor** assists you with text-entry problems. By typing certain commands to the text editor, you can cause selected lines in your program file to be inserted, deleted, or modified. You can easily correct spelling and other mistakes.

Compilation

After your program has been stored in a file, it is almost—but not quite—ready for execution. The Pascal compiler still has to translate the program into machine language form so that it can be executed by the computer. The compiled version then has to be combined with some other things in a process called **linking** before it is fully ready to execute. Only then can you request execution. On some systems you can request compilation and linking with a single command. On other systems, you may have to request these steps separately. In any case, when a program resides in a file, simple commands to the system activate the following steps:

linking

1. Compile.
2. Link.
3. Execute (or run).

As we mentioned earlier, the compiler may not permit the process to continue if it finds errors in your use of the Pascal language. When informed of an error by the compiler, you must return to the text editor, repair the program file, and compile again. If the errors are especially severe, subtle, or persistent, you may have to leave the terminal and give the problem more attention.

Execution

Only when the program has been compiled and linked without error can it begin to execute, displaying its results on the screen or printer. You may think the task of programming ends here. Unfortunately, it does not. There is still the possibility of error. The compiler cannot detect all errors, especially errors in logic. Sometimes the results either fail to appear or are conspicuously wrong. Sometimes they look plausible but, in fact, are incorrect. You must always review the results of execution.

If the results are not acceptable, some part of the problem-solving process contains an error that needs to be corrected. This may entail returning to any of the earlier steps in program development. Sometimes the error is trivial and can be repaired with the text editor. Other errors are problems with logic and may require repairs to the algorithm and recoding of significant parts of the program. Sometimes the problem is so severe that a whole new approach is called for, requiring a return to square one. This is not meant to be discouraging, just realistic. The requirement for program accuracy is so stringent that programs rarely work correctly the first (or second) time.

The process of correcting errors is easily the most tedious and frustrating of all the steps involved in programming. Unfortunately, far too many programmers spend a large portion of their time on program repairs. If more

■ Figure 1.6
The problem-solving
process.

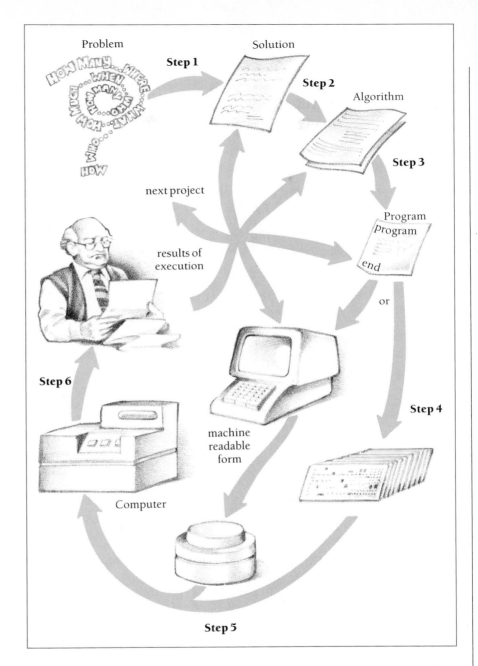

Problem

Step 1

Solution

Step 2

Algorithm

Step 3

next project

Program

Program

end

results of
execution

or

Step 6

Step 4

machine
readable
form

Computer

Step 5

time and attention were devoted to initial program preparation—and to
problem solving in particular—there would be fewer errors to eliminate
(ideally none).

The entire programming process is summarized in Fig. 1.6, as well as in
the following review of rules. Again, we emphasize that this is only an outline
of typical interactive processing. Details about the operation of your local
installation must be taken into consideration.

1.12 Review of Rules

A. A systematic approach to general problem solving involves adherence to the following rules.

 1. Analyze the problem carefully, attempting to understand its specific aspects and the requirements of an acceptable solution.
 2. Attempt to break the problem into simpler, relatively independent parts and then focus on the separate parts.
    (a) Attempt to break the problem into a *sequence* of smaller problems, so that the solution of one subproblem followed by the solution of the next, and so on, will provide a solution to the original problem.
    (b) If the problem involves performing some *repeated* process, attempt to isolate the action that is required in one instance from the repetitive aspect of the process.
    (c) Attempt to solve the problem for the *simplest* case or the most likely set of circumstances. This may suggest a structure for a more general solution.
 3. When breaking a problem into simpler parts, perform the decomposition gradually in several stages. Use general criteria in the early stages and more specific criteria later.
 4. At every stage in its development, review and reconsider your proposed solution to ensure that it is complete and correct.
 5. Identify at the beginning the data that are necessary for the solution and develop every stage of the solution procedure with them in mind.

B. The process of solving problems with a computer involves the following steps.

 1. Program preparation.
    (a) Devise a solution procedure for the problem (applying the general problem-solving rules).
    (b) Refine this procedure into an algorithm by specifying in detail how to perform the sequence of actions.
    (c) Express this algorithm in a programming language.
    (d) Enter the resulting program in a file through a computer terminal.
 2. Program execution.
    (e) Try your program on the computer:
       (i) Compile.
       (ii) Link.
       (iii) Execute (or run).
 3. Review of results.
    (f) Inspect the results of program execution. If they are not satisfactory, you must (depending on the severity of the difficulty)

revise your approach (return to step a); modify your algorithm (return to step b); correct language errors (return to step c); correct transcription mistakes (return to step d); and then try again.

C.   The standard structure of a simple Pascal program is

PROGRAM   ⟨program identifier⟩ (input,output);
VAR
.
.
· declaration of variables
.
.

BEGIN
.
.
· encoding of algorithm
.
.

END.

Semicolons are used to terminate each variable declaration and to separate the statements comprising the algorithm.

D.   An identifier must

1.   begin with a letter of the alphabet;
2.   be made up only of letters of the alphabet or the digits 0 through 9, and
3.   not be a reserved word (see Appendix A).

These rules apply to any sort of identifier (such as a program name or variable name). It is advisable not to use the standard identifiers listed in Appendix B. Theoretically, there is no limit to the number of characters that you can use in an identifier. In practice, most implementations do impose a limit.

E.   The assignment statement is the primary means of placing new values in variables. Its format is

⟨variable⟩ : = ⟨expression⟩

For now, the variables hold integers, and the expression is some arithmetic expression involving integers and/or integer variables. Eventually, other data types will be introduced. The target variable and the value resulting from the expression must be of the same type.

F.   The integer arithmetic operators are $+$, $-$, $*$, DIV, MOD. Unless overridden by parentheses, any $*$, /, DIV, and MOD operations are performed before $+$ and $-$, and operators of equal precedence are evaluated from left to right. The operator / performs conventional division, but produces a real (not an integer) result.

G. One of the output statements in Pascal is writeln, which may take various forms, including

>   writeln (⟨value⟩)

or

>   writeln (⟨list of values⟩)

where constants and expressions may be included with variable names to comprise a list; items in such a list are separated by commas. After printing the indicated values from left to right across the same line, writeln positions the output device so that subsequent output will be displayed at the beginning of a new line.

KEY TERMS

algorithm	main memory
arithmetic expression	maxint
arithmetic operators	memory locations
arithmetic–logic unit	operator precedence
assignment operator	output
assignment statement	program
block	program heading
code	programming language
compiler	pseudocode
constant	reserved words
control unit	secondary storage
counters	standard identifiers
data type	statement part
file	stepwise refinement
flow of control	text editor
identifier	truncation
input data	variable declaration part
linking	variable identifiers
machine language	writeln statement

EXERCISES

1.1   Circle the terms that are valid Pascal identifiers for your computer system.

(a) FirstOne   (b) Second One
(c) Third_One   (d) Fourth-One
(e) AnEspeciallyLongOne   (f) 2ndTime
(g) WhyNot?   (h) Rate@2%
(i) R2D2   (j) Begin
(k) Finish   (l) AuRevoir

1.2   Which of the following assignment statements are valid for your computer system? Assume that all the variables have been declared as type integer.

(a) A := B + C DIV D;   (b) Cost + Tax := Price;
(c) Tax = Gross * Rate;   (d) X := A + B * C MOD D ** E;
(e) 7 := 3 + 4;   (f) Triple := 3Single;

1.3   Assume that all the following variables are of type integer. What values will be displayed by each fragment of code?

(a) N := 1;   (b) K := 13;
    N := 2;   L := 4;
    N := N + 1;   M := K DIV L DIV 3;
    writeln (N);   N := K DIV (L DIV 3);
                                             writeln (M,N);

(c) K := 5;   (d) K := 276;
    L := K;   L := 394;
    M := K DIV 2 * 2;   K := L;
    writeln (M);   L := K;
                                             writeln (K,L);

1.4   The following program is supposed to compute and display the squares of the first three natural numbers. Why does it fail to do so? Repair it so that it will work correctly.

```
PROGRAM Squares (input,output);

VAR Num,NumSquared: integer;

BEGIN
  Num := 1;
  NumSquared := Num * Num;
  Num := Num + 1;
  NumSquared := Num * Num;
  Num := Num + 1;
  NumSquared := Num * Num;
  writeln (NumSquared)
END.
```

1.5   What values will be displayed by the following program?

```
PROGRAM What (input,output);

VAR Old,Next,D1,D2: integer;

BEGIN
  Old := 47;
  D2 := Old MOD 10;
  D1 := Old DIV 10;
  Next := D2 * 10 + D1;
  writeln (Old,Next)
END.
```

1.6   Design an algorithm to separate a positive three-digit integer into its component digits and compute their sum. For example, if the number is 394, the sum of the digits is $3 + 9 + 4 = 16$. Implement your algorithm as a Pascal program. *Hint:* See Exercise 1.5.

1.7   Although standard Pascal defines the range of integer values to be from $-$ maxint to maxint, inclusive, some implementations allow an additional negative integer. Run the following program to determine whether your version of Pascal permits integers in the range `[-maxint-1,maxint]`.

```
PROGRAM InterRange (input,output);
BEGIN
  writeln (-maxint-1,maxint)
END.
```

1.8   In this exercise you will write some algorithms in pseudocode to search for a "Target" value from among a list of values, such as a list of numbers written in a column down the side of a sheet of paper. "Current" represents the particular item from the list that is currently under consideration. The algorithms must be expressed in terms of the following primitive operations. (Do not write out the detailed steps of those primitives.)

- *Basic Actions*
  - initialize (Current)   . . . start at 1st item
  - advance (Current)   . . . to next item
  - obtain (Target)   . . . get target value from user
  - obtain (List)   . . . get list of values
  - stop
  - announce result
- *Selecting and Controlling Actions*
  - *if* ⟨condition⟩ then ⟨action⟩
  - *repeat* the following while ⟨condition⟩
    - ⟨list of actions⟩
  - where ⟨condition⟩ is one of
    - Current < Target
    - Current = Target
    - Current > Target
    - not-at-end-of-list

(a) Devise an algorithm to discover whether Targer occurs anywhere in the list; stop the search as soon as Target is encountered. Remember to allow for the possibility that Target is not in the list.

(b) Suppose you want to know the POSITION in the list where Target appears. What additional mechanism (and primitives) would be required?

(c) Devise an algorithm to locate *all* occurrences of the Target value in the list. Display the positions where these instances occur.

(d) Suppose that the list is in ascending order, with the smallest value appearing first and the largest value appearing last. Find the first value in the list, if any, that is larger than Target.

(e) Devise an algorithm to find ALL values in the list, if any, that are smaller than Target.

(f) Using the following additional primitives

> copy(Current)   . . . from this list to another
> delete(Current)   . . . from this list

adapt the algorithm from part (e) to divide the original list into two lists, with one new list containing all values smaller than Target and the other list containing all values larger than Target.

1.9 (a) Consider how you would scan a list of several numbers to find the smallest number. Try to do it, and observe carefully how you proceed, what you must remember as you go, and what decisions you make along the way. Write this process as an algorithm.

(b) Finding the smallest element in a list is the basic step in another ordering strategy, known as the *selection sort*. The idea is to repeatedly locate, display, and then remove the smallest remaining element. Each application of this procedure deals with an ever-shrinking list of values that are larger than any that were previously selected and displayed. Write this procedure as an algorithm, in which finding the smallest value may be considered a primitive operation.

1.10 Suppose you have an ordered list of several numbers, say: 3, 6, 10, 12, 17, 20, 24, 29, 30, 32, 37, 40. Now suppose that you want to search the list for three specific values, say: 32, 10, and 24.

(a) By counting the number of times pairs of values must be compared, evaluate each of the following ways of handling these searches.

(i) Conduct three independent searches, one for each desired value.

(ii) Consider the three desired values in numeric order (10, 24, 32), and search for all three during a single sweep through the list.

(b) Assuming that the desired values will be found and ignoring the problem of getting them in order, write an algorithm for the general approach suggested in part (a, ii).

1.11 The number n, raised to the kth power, is just n multiplied by itself $k - 1$ times. Write an algorithm in pseudocode that calculates n to the kth power by successive multiplication. The algorithm must be able to handle any n and positive integer k. You may assume that appropriate values will be supplied.

1.12 A prime number is an integer greater than 1 that is exactly divisible only by 1 and by itself: 2, 3, 5, 7, and 11 are examples. Write an algorithm to test whether an arbitrary positive integer ≥ 2 is prime. You may assume that it is possible to test whether one number exactly divides another. You do not need to use all integers between 1 and the candidate value as test cases. State any special arithmetic assumptions you use (if any) to simplify the testing.

1.13 (a) The product of all positive integers from 1 through k is defined as k factorial and is written $k!$. Thus 4! is the product $1 \times 2 \times 3 \times 4 = 24$. Write an algorithm to compute $k!$.

(b) The number of ways in which to select k objects at a time from a collection of n candidate objects is called "n-choose-k" and is given by the formula

$$\frac{n!}{(k!)(n - k)!}$$

Write an algorithm to evaluate n-choose-k, assuming that computing a factorial is a primitive operation for this purpose.

(c) Even though *n*-choose-*k* may be small enough to represent, the actual value of *n*! may be so large that a computer cannot hold it in a single memory location. Devise another way to compute *n*-choose-*k* that avoids calculating such large values as *n*! itself.

1.14 For several years a merchant has been selling *n* units of his product at a base price of *b* dollars per unit. The market seems stable, and market research has shown that for every *r* dollars he is willing to lower the price, *m* additional units can be sold. The problem is to determine the selling price that will maximize total profit. Although this problem has an algebraic solution, a systematic enumeration of prices and total profits might be both easier and more informative. Write an algorithm to find the best price in this way.

1.15 One method for finding a path through a maze is to walk through it, always keeping your right hand on a wall. Stated another way, this becomes the rule: Go forward along corridors; at corners, intersections, and dead ends, turn right when you can do so without your right hand losing contact with a wall, and turn left only when you must. Now consider a robot that has the following limitations:

- It can move forward (only) one pace at a time.
- It can turn right (90°).
- It can turn left (90°).
- It can determine whether there is a wall immediately ahead of it.
- It can determine when it has left the maze.
- It can perform only *one* of these functions at a time.

If the robot is placed facing into a maze, describe an algorithm that will help it to enter the maze and then find its way to an exit. Assume that the maze has no circular pathways, that is, no path leads back to itself.

2

A Closer Look at Programming

The program in Fig. 1.4 represents the bare minimum of complexity and utility. The computation was trivial and used specific, known values. When the result was displayed on the screen, the user was expected to know what the value meant and the data it was derived from. It is hardly worth the effort to solve such a simple problem by computer.

Most useful programs are more general, complex, and helpful to the user. Instead of always computing the same result from the same starting values, a more versatile program may rely on the user to supply particular values to be used as the program is being executed. Instead of just displaying the unadorned result, a good program should generate additional information to help the user understand the results. In fact, a program and a user may carry on a dialogue in which each responds to the data supplied by the other. This mode of operation is called **interactive computing.**

interactive
computing

input process

output process

The responsiveness of such programs depends on executing statements that copy values between program variables and a terminal in an appropriate sequence. In Section 2.1, we introduce the **input process,** or the process by which a program obtains values *from* a user. In Section 2.2, we consider the **output process,** or how to display data and provide guidance *to* a user in an intelligible way.

This exchange of information is not restricted to integers. For one thing, computers can manipulate *real numbers,* that is, numbers with decimal points and, possibly, fractional parts. They can also manipulate alphabetic and other kinds of *characters,* that is, symbols like those you see on a terminal screen or printed page. We introduce the realms of real numbers and character data in Sections 2.3 and 2.4, respectively.

Besides exchanging data with a program while it is executing, humans must also be able to read and understand its code in order to modify or correct it during its development and useful life. Several stylistic guidelines are available to promote program readability. We introduce the topic of programming style in Section 2.5 and continue the discussion in later chapters.

In Section 2.6, we present another subject that you will continue to encounter: how to make programs work correctly. In that section, our concern is with program testing, diagnosis, and repair.

2.1 Input: The read Statement

A practical program usually applies to a whole class of problems. Rather than always finding the product of the same two specific integers, why not have the program find the product of *any* two integers? Instead of computing the duration and total amount involved in a particular loan repayment plan, it might be preferable to analyze a variety of possible repayment plans, with different down payments, monthly payments, interest rates, and so on. In other words, we often write programs to be versatile: to solve any problem from a class of related problems rather than just one specific instance. Not until that program is executed can it possibly "know" the features (or parameters) of the particular problem it is dealing with right then.

input data

Such a program must rely on a user to supply specific values, called **input data,** whenever the program is executed. Each time it is executed, the user can supply a different set of data. This is like using a general formula, such as

distance = speed × time,

which requires a user to supply numbers for speed and time whenever distance is to be calculated. Unlike a formula, however, a program that requires input data must include statements to copy user-supplied data into program variables.

Consider the program in Fig. 2.1(a) for finding the sum of *any* two integers. Instead of having fixed, predetermined values assigned to the variables First and Second inside the program, it requires two user-supplied integers as input data. The program obtains the data by executing two read statements. Each of these read statements transfers one integer from an input device to the variable named within the parentheses.

read statement

As you will soon see, the **read statement** can transfer other types of data from the outside into program variables. The read statements in Fig. 2.1(a) seek integer data because the indicated variables are both of type integer. *Only integer values may be placed in integer variables,* regardless of whether the values arise from an assignment statement or from a read statement.

To complete execution of this program, the user must supply two integer values. However, the user does not enter them until after the program has begun to execute. Only when the flow of control reaches a read statement, will the computer look to the terminal for data to be typed in.

```
PROGRAM AddTwo (input,output);

VAR First, Second, Total: integer;

BEGIN
    read (First);
    read (Second);
    Total := First + Second;
    writeln (First,Second,Total)
END.
```

(a) Program to find the sum of any two integers.

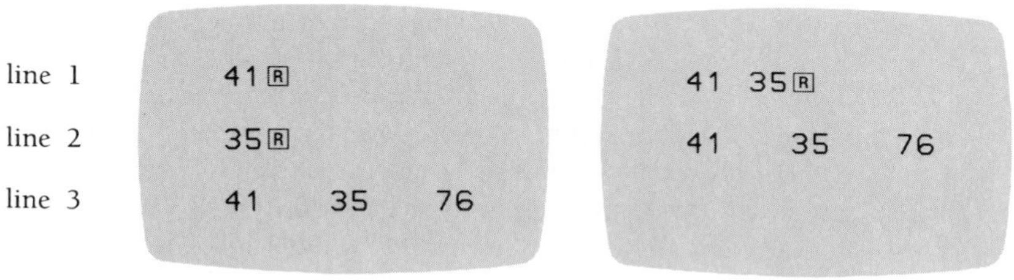

line 1	41 Ⓡ
line 2	35 Ⓡ
line 3	41 35 76

(second screen)
```
41   35Ⓡ

41      35      76
```

(b) Two methods of supplying integers as input data.

■ Figure 2.1

An input line is any sequence of characters terminated by hitting the return key, which we denote by Ⓡ.† The user may type the data either on separate lines or on the same line, so long as two integers are supplied. If both are typed on the same line, they must be separated by one or more blanks; that is how numeric values on a single line can be distinguished from each other. The two methods of supplying input data shown in the terminal screens in Fig. 2.1(b) yield equivalent results for the program in Fig. 2.1(a). In both cases the bottom line on the screen is generated by the writeln statement in the program; the preceding lines are typed by the user.

All the input supplied during program execution appears to the system as a single, continuous stream of arriving data. This **input stream** includes *everything* the user types in, including punctuation, blanks, and Ⓡ characters. It doesn't matter whether successive integers appear on separate lines because the read statement ignores blanks and RETURNs when looking for a numeric value. It will scan past any number of intervening blank characters or blank lines to find the next numeric value.

However, when a numeric value is encountered in the input, either a blank or an Ⓡ will signal that the number has come to an end. Therefore

input stream

---

† Note: On many keyboards the return key shows an arrow (↵) or simply says RETURN.

the user must enter the sign and individual digits comprising a number with consecutive key strokes. No commas are allowed inside numbers, and an attempt to carry an integer over to the next line will cause the separated parts to be misinterpreted as distinct values. (Incidentally, the contents of a line of input cannot be read until the return key has been pressed, so do not forget to press it.)

The user must supply enough values of the appropriate type (such as integer) to satisfy all the executed read statements. The read statements copy values in the order that they arrive from the terminal. Each read statement always takes the *next* value in the input stream that has not already been read. If there is no next value when flow of control reaches a read statement, the program will simply wait for the user to provide one. Sometimes a program that seems to be doing nothing is merely stalled at a read statement waiting for the user to enter some input values. If you supply more values than the program requires, it just never encounters unneeded values.

The program in Fig. 2.2 for multiplying three arbitrary integers together illustrates how successive read statements copy successive data items into variables. The statements in the program are interspersed with "snapshots" of the variables to show how each statement affects the flow of data. Note how the final read statement replaces the old contents of Factor with a new value. The read statement affects its target variable in exactly the same way as the assignment operator changes the variable on its left. The difference between read and assignment is in the way the new value is obtained.

As read statements execute, they progress steadily through the input
sequential processing stream. This is called **sequential processing.** A program cannot go back to an earlier value or a previous line that has already been "consumed" by read statements. Similarly, if the user enters a value having a data type that does not match the current read statement's expectations, the system will not skip ahead in the hope of finding a value of the correct type. Thus the sequence of executed read statements and the input data typed by the user must agree in two ways:

1. Enough distinct data values must be supplied to satisfy the data requirements of all the executed read statements.
2. The data types of the input data must occur in the same order as expected by the executed read statements.

Just as a single writeln statement can display more than one value, so a single read statement can also read more than one value. The read statement can take either of the forms:

   read (⟨variable⟩)

or

   read (⟨list of variables⟩)

In the latter form, values from the input stream are stored in the variables in their order of occurrence in the list. That is, the first value goes into the first

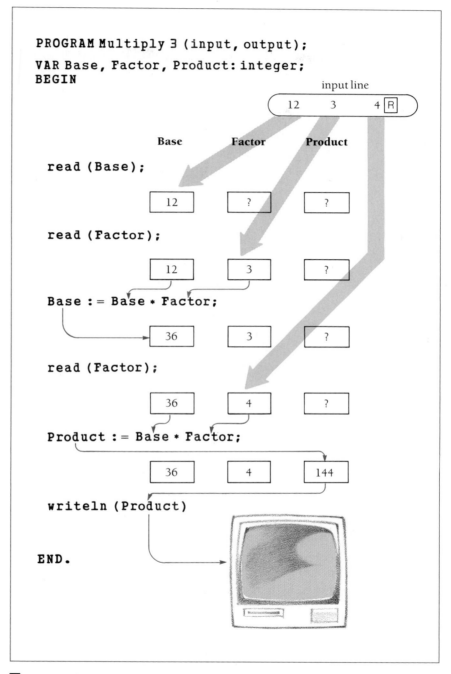

```
PROGRAM Multiply 3 (input, output);
VAR Base, Factor, Product: integer;
BEGIN
```

input line

| 12 | 3 | 4 R |

Base   **Factor**   **Product**

`read (Base);`

| 12 | ? | ? |

`read (Factor);`

| 12 | 3 | ? |

`Base := Base * Factor;`

| 36 | 3 | ? |

`read (Factor);`

| 36 | 4 | ? |

`Product := Base * Factor;`

| 36 | 4 | 144 |

`writeln (Product)`

`END.`

■ Figure 2.2
Program control of data flow.

```
PROGRAM Volume1 (input,output);

VAR Length,Width,Height,Volume: integer;

BEGIN
    read (Length,Width,Height);
    Volume := Length * Width * Height;
    writeln;
    writeln ('dimensions:',Length,Height,
             Width);
    writeln ('volume is:',Volume)
END.
```

```
                                    Input
12    3R
4R

dimensions: 12 3 4
volume is: 144
```

■ Figure 2.3
Labeling output of a program.

variable, the second value into the second variable, and so on. The following sets of code are equivalent.

```
read (V1);      read (V1,V2,V3,V4);      read(V1,V2);
read (V2);                               read(V3,V4);
read (V3);
read (V4);
```

Figure 2.3 shows another program for multiplying three integers together. Its behavior is similar to the program in Fig. 2.2. However, this version uses only one read statement. Again, it does not matter whether the data are entered on one, two, or three separate lines. A read statement progresses sequentially through the input stream until values have been copied into *all* the variables in its input list (assuming that no error occurs).

The read Statement

read (⟨list of variables⟩)

The input stream contains data values separated by spaces or R. As many values are read from the input stream as there are variables in the list and the data values must be entered in the same order as the variables appear in the list. These values are stored in the corresponding variables and must be of suitable type. Extra data values are ignored by read and may be picked up by subsequent read statements.

2.2 Making Programs Communicate with People: Output

The ultimate purpose of a great many programs is to convey information to people. However, displaying raw results, called output, on a screen or a printer is often not enough. When the results are complicated or voluminous, the user often cannot grasp their meaning without considerable thought and time or even knowledge of how the program was written. Much of the mystery can be removed if the program generates its output with human readers in mind. The results do not change; only their method of presentation does.

People-Oriented Output

The program in Fig. 2.3 contains three writeln statements, each of which contributes in a special way, as the output on the screen shows. Note that the first writeln statement is not followed by words in parentheses. The purpose of a plain writeln is to skip to the next line, leaving a blank line on the screen. Although blank lines convey no information themselves, they are useful for separating different kinds of information on the screen. In this case the input is isolated from the results, making them easier to locate and absorb.

Another technique is illustrated by the third writeln statement. The three integers represent the dimensions of a rectangular solid, such as a brick or a room. The result is the volume of the solid and is clearly labeled as the volume by

```
writeln ('volume is:', Volume);
```

character string

Execution of this statement displays two items, side by side, on the output line. The first is called a **character string.** It consists of the character v, followed by the characters o, l, u, m, and e, a blank, the characters i, s, and ":". In other words, the character string is exactly what appears inside the apostrophes (not including the apostrophes themselves). The second item displayed is the current value, 144, of the variable Volume. Assuming the same input values as before, the net result is the output line

```
volume is: 144
```

If the identifier Volume had been enclosed in apostrophes, it too would have been interpreted as a character string, displaying the characters V, o, l, u, m, and e, rather than the current value of the variable with that name.

echoing

The second writeln statement in Fig. 2.3 displays the three input data values that were just read. This technique, known as **echoing,** assures the user that the program correctly accepted the values that were entered. The label "dimensions," provides additional background to help the user understand the meaning of the result.

The writeln Statement without Parameters

writeln

When the writeln statement appears without a list of values its effect is to terminate the current line on the output device and move the cursor to the start of the next line.

Note that each writeln statement generates a separate line on the screen. Furthermore, the number of items generated on a line is limited by the capacity of the line and not by any property of the writeln statement. It may include any number of items in its output list.

Programs often generate messages on the screen that tell the user what to do or what to expect. This is especially important if the user is not familiar with the program or if the input must be supplied in a particular form. The program shown in Fig. 2.4 begins by identifying itself and explicitly instructs

prompts

the user to supply three integers as input. Such instructions, called **prompts,** are very helpful in obtaining the right amount of input data and preventing input of the wrong type.

If the input varies even slightly or is complex, the user should receive some guidance as the data are being entered, not just at the beginning. Every input item or every few items are solicited by a prompt that provides needed instructions or reminders. These prompts for input give users the impression that they are involved in a dialogue with the computer.

Although hardly necessary for such simple input, the program in Fig. 2.4 includes three writeln statements to provide ongoing assistance. A typical screen is also shown, where prompt messages generated by the program are interspersed with lines typed by the user. Each output line generated by the program is numbered to indicate which writeln statement produced it.

Pascal Output Statements

writeln statement

The **writeln statement** does two things: first it displays the values of all the items in its output list; and it then causes the display device to terminate the current output line and move to the beginning of the next output line.

Of course, executing writeln without parameters causes only the second of these actions. Pascal provides another statement that causes only the first:

write statement

the **write statement.** The write statement has the form

write (⟨list of output items⟩);

output item

An **output item** is any value to be displayed, and the "list" may contain only

```
PROGRAM Volume2 (input,output);
                                                            writeln
VAR Length,Width,Height: integer;                           Statements

BEGIN
    writeln ('To find volume of a rectangular solid,');        1
    writeln ('enter integer dimensions as requested...');      2
    writeln ('Enter the length:');                             3
    read (Length);
    writeln ('Enter the width:');                              4
    read (Width);
    writeln ('Enter the height:');                             5
    read (Height);
    Volume := Length * Width * Height;
    writeln;                                                   6
    writeln ('Volume of object is:',Volume)                   7
END.
```

Corresponding
Output Lines

```
              To find volume of a rectangular solid,         1
              enter integer dimensions as requested...       2
              Enter the length:                              3
Only      →12ℝ
lines
typed         Enter the width:                               4
by        →3ℝ
user
              Enter the height:                              5
          →4ℝ
                                                             6
              Volume of object is:      144                  7
```

■ Figure 2.4
Interactive prompts for input.

a single item. Items are displayed on the current output line, exactly as they would be by writeln. However, unlike writeln, the *write statement does not move on to the next output line after its execution. The output device remains on the same line, causing subsequent output to continue farther to the right along the same line.*

formatted output   The programmer can use **formatted output** to control the general appearance or format of the line. Every output item appears in an imaginary

field   space called a **field.** Think of a field as a rectangle one character high and w field width   characters wide; w is called either the **field width,** or format specifier. Consecutive items on the same output line appear in adjacent fields across the line, and the choice of field widths controls the horizontal spacing between these items. The programmer can specify the field width for each item in an output list by placing a colon (:) and the field width immediately after the item, that is, a colon followed by a number designating the maximum number of characters the field is to contain, as in

> writeln (ItemA:w1, ItemB:w2, ItemC:w3);

or

> write (ItemA:w1, ItemB:w2, ItemC:w3);

These field widths may be any reasonable, positive, and integer-valued expression. By reasonable, we mean that the width should be sufficient to accommodate the item being displayed while leaving enough space around it to make it readable. In most applications the field widths are given as constants.

Suppose that an output item is 5 characters long. When it is displayed in a field of width 8, it will appear in the *rightmost* 5 positions of the field, preceded by 3 (or $8 - 5$) blanks. More generally, if an output item of s characters is displayed in a field of width w, it will appear in the rightmost s positions preceded by $w - s$ blanks. In most cases the field width should be larger than the number of characters in the value to be displayed, so that the value will be separated from whatever appears in the field to its left on the same line. Figure 2.5 shows how different format specifiers produce different looking output lines, even when the same output items are used.

Since the size of the output value may be difficult to predict, generous field widths should normally be used. If they are not wide enough, the output may look cramped, may run together into an unintelligible mass, or may be partially missing. If the size, s, exceeds the field width, w, and the value being displayed is numeric, the field is stretched to size s, so that the entire number gets printed, but with no preceding blanks. If s exceeds w and the value is a character string, only the first w characters are shown, and the final $s - w$ characters fail to appear.

When no field width is specified, a default field width is assumed by the system. For numeric items, this width is always quite large, just to be on the safe side. This is why consecutive numbers on the same line have been so widely separated until now. Character strings normally appear in fields that exactly match their lengths.

Figure 2.6(a) on p. 46 shows a program for displaying the square and cube of any integer between 1 and 99. This time the prompt for input is generated by write instead of writeln. As a result, the value typed by the user appears on the same line as the prompt. In addition, the final line appearing on the screen is generated by three separate output statements, each of which contributes one additional value to the line. Whenever an output line is

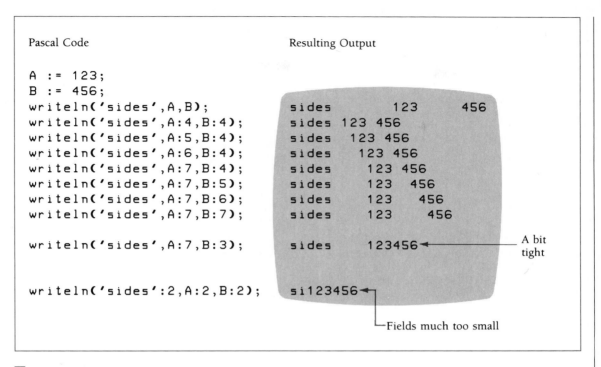

Pascal Code

Resulting Output

```
A := 123;
B := 456;
writeln('sides',A,B);              sides          123        456
writeln('sides',A:4,B:4);          sides 123 456
writeln('sides',A:5,B:4);          sides  123 456
writeln('sides',A:6,B:4);          sides   123 456
writeln('sides',A:7,B:4);          sides    123 456
writeln('sides',A:7,B:5);          sides    123  456
writeln('sides',A:7,B:6);          sides    123   456
writeln('sides',A:7,B:7);          sides    123    456

writeln('sides',A:7,B:3);          sides    123456   ←———  A bit
                                                            tight

writeln('sides':2,A:2,B:2);        si123456 ←—┐
                                              └— Fields much too small
```

■ **Figure 2.5**
The effect of format specifiers.

produced piece by piece, the line must be terminated by writeln, and each preceding part must be produced by write.

This example also illustrates the care that you should give to the presentation of output. Each output value is displayed *under* a heading that explains its significance. These headings and the values themselves are spaced across their respective output lines, so that they will appear aligned in columns.

Rather than guess at the required spacing, we prepared a detailed sketch of a typical display, as shown in Fig. 2.6(b). After placing the labels at uniform distances across their output line, we filled in the numeric values on the line below. Each X represents a digit position, and we assumed the maximum possible number of digits in each case. (The user is asked by the program to keep the input value under 100, so that its square will not exceed 4 digits and its cube 6 digits.)

After arranging the sample output on a grid, we easily determined the required field widths. Figure 2.6(c) shows how the program's output would actually look to the user. Note the use of plain writeln statements to produce blank lines between parts of the display.

```
PROGRAM Display (input,output);

VAR                                                   Corresponding
  N,Power: integer;                                   Display Line

BEGIN
    writeln ('To find square and cube');                   1
    writeln ('of a number between 1 and 99...');           2
    writeln;                                               3

    write ('Enter number: ');
    read (N);                                              4
    writeln;                                               5

    writeln ('value','square':10,'cube':8);               6

    write (N:4);
    Power := N * N;
    write (Power:10);                                      7
    Power := Power * N;
    writeln (Power:10)
END.
```

(a) Program to compute square and cube of an integer.

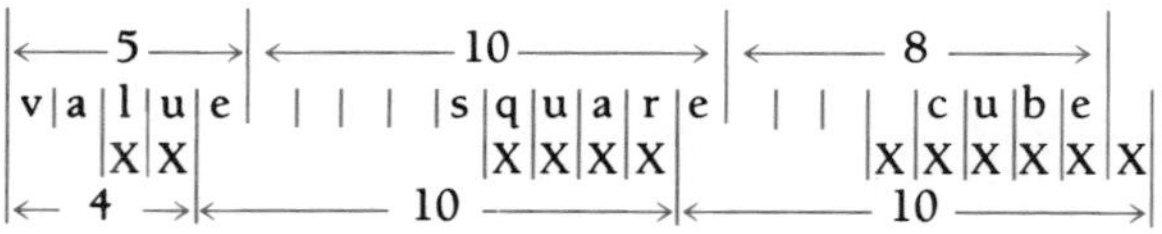

(b) Planning the output.

```
1    To find square and cube
2    of a number between 1 and 99...
3
4    Enter number: 23
5
6    value       square       cube
7      23          529        12167
```

(c) What the user sees.

■ Figure 2.6
Formatting output.

The write and writeln Statements and Formatted Output

```
write (V1:w1,V2:w2, . . . ,Vn:wn)
```
or
```
writeln (V1:w1,V2:w2, . . . ,Vn:wn)
```

Each of the values in the output list (V1, V2, . . . , Vn) is displayed in a field whose width is specified by the corresponding field specifier (w1, w2, . . . , wn). Values are right-justified in the field and padded with preceding blanks, if necessary, to fill up the field. Numeric values that require more characters than given in the field width cause the field width to be expanded to a size sufficient to accommodate the value exactly. Character values that are too long to fit in the specified width are truncated on the right to fit the field.

2.3 Numeric Data Types

Pascal makes a distinction between integers and numbers with decimal points. In this section we will discuss the combination of various numeric values to form new ones, and elaborate on numbers with decimal points (real numbers).

More about Arithmetic Expressions

We introduced the arithmetic operators (+ , − , *, /, DIV, MOD) in Section 1.8. The values that they combine or manipulate to produce results are known as their **operands.** When an operator requires two operands to produce its result, it is called a **binary operator;** if only one operand is needed, it is called a **unary operator.** The difference is depicted in the following data flow diagrams.

operands
binary operator
unary operator

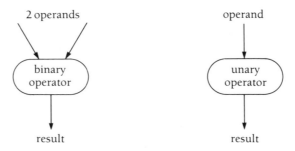

Our previous discussion covered binary operators only, but Pascal also has two unary arithmetic operators: identity (+) and negation (−). A plus sign in front of a numeric quantity yields the original numeric value; a minus sign in front of it generates a value with a sign opposite to the original. Thus the code

```
A := - 3;
writeln(A, +A, -A);
```

displays the line of output:

```
-3        -3        3
```

The first and second values are simply those placed in A by the assignment statement, namely, the negative of 3. The final value displayed is an unsigned 3, which is the value of A (− 3) with its sign reversed. Note that unary (−) does not force the resulting value to become specifically negative, but instead reverses whatever sign that operand already has. Also, placing the minus sign in front of A does not alter the value still stored in A; rather it reverses the sign of the value retrieved from A for use in another context. As in ordinary algebra, the context determines whether the unary or binary version of the (+) or (−) operator is being used.

Returning to the binary operators, we need to take a closer look at the evaluation of arithmetic expressions. Recall that, in an arithmetic expression, operands may be constants, variables, or the values of simpler arithmetic expressions enclosed by parentheses. These basic operands are then combined by the arithmetic operators to yield an overall value for the expression. When two or more arithmetic operators are used, the result of one may serve as an operand to the other.

Evaluating expressions

The following rules for evaluating expressions merely reflect the different priorities given to operators and our ability to override these priorities with parentheses.

1. First, evaluate all subexpressions enclosed in parentheses, beginning with the innermost ones.
2. Perform all multiplications and/or divisions and/or MOD operations (from left to right).
3. Finally, perform all additions and/or subtractions (from left to right).

Ignoring rule 1 for the moment, rules 2 and 3 reaffirm that, in the absence of parentheses, multiplicative operators have higher precedence than additive ones, and the order of evaluation is always from left to right among operators of equal precedence. For example, consider the expression

A + B DIV C * D − E

and its evaluation, which is illustrated by the data flow diagram in Fig. 2.7(a). Both the order of evaluation and the interaction among the operators are shown clearly by this diagram. We gave A, B, C, D, and E specific values, so that you can follow the intermediate values as they lead to the final result.

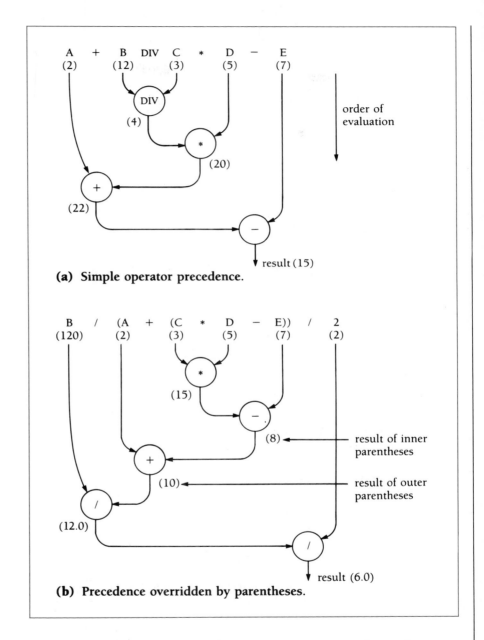

■ Figure 2.7
**Data flow diagrams
for arithmetic
expressions.**

(a) **Simple operator precedence.**

(b) **Precedence overridden by parentheses.**

Parentheses are used to identify an interior expression, whose value serves as one operand within a higher level expression. Rule 1 insists that such parenthesized expressions be evaluated first. Of course, an expression in parentheses may be *any* arithmetic expression, including one containing further sets of parentheses. No level can be evaluated until after its own "parenthesized" expressions have been evaluated. This is why evaluation starts with the innermost set of parentheses and proceeds to successively higher levels.

Consider an expression that contains *nested* parentheses:

B / (A + (C * D − E)) / 2

The innermost expression, C * D − E, is evaluated first. Then its value can be added to A, so that the outer level has the form B / (value) / 2, which can then be evaluated from left to right. The data flow diagram for this case is shown in Fig. 2.7(b).

Certain parentheses may be essential to the correct evaluation of an expression. On the other hand, additional parentheses that do not change the order of evaluation may enhance our understanding of what the expression does. Whenever you are in doubt about the order of evaluation, use parentheses to enforce the order you desire. A lack of parentheses in complicated expressions only makes them harder to understand.

Incidentally, some versions of Pascal provide a basic operator for exponentiation. Sometimes two consecutive asterisks are used, so that A ** N is interpreted as A raised to the power of N. However, an exponentiation operator is *not* standard Pascal, and its use is generally discouraged because it may prevent programs from being transported from one machine to another.

Introducing the Real Numbers

We pointed out in Chapter 1 that integer values are confined to a specific range. For example, on the VAX series of computers, an integer may lie only in the range from −2,147,483,648 to 2,147,483,647, inclusive; using Turbo Pascal on the IBM PC, the range is from −32,768 to 32,767, inclusive. In some applications this is a serious limitation. An equally serious limitation is the inability of integers to express decimal values (that is, numbers with fractional parts or very small magnitudes). Decimal values are essential for expressing monetary values (10.98), the number of kilometers in a mile (1.62), the rate of interest on a loan (0.15), the result of dividing 5 by 4 (1.25), and numerous other quantities.

real number

Therefore, in order to manipulate values outside the range of integers or to use numbers having fractional parts, another kind of number—known as a **real number**—must be used. Even real numbers must lie within a certain range, but this range embraces values of very great and very small magnitudes. (There is nothing in the realm of reals that corresponds to maxint for integers.) For example, in the VAX implementation of Pascal, real numbers have seven significant digits and fall roughly into the range from $\pm 10^{-38}$ to $\pm 10^{38}$.

decimal notation

Real numbers may be written in two different ways. In the first form, called **decimal notation**, a number *may* have a sign, *must* have a decimal point, and *must* have at least one digit before *and* one digit after the decimal point. No commas or spaces are permitted, regardless of the number of digits written. The following are examples of valid real numbers in decimal notation.

$$-1.2$$
$$139.8257$$
$$-0.125$$
$$38.0$$
$$0.0$$

The following are invalid for the reasons noted.

.25	No digit before decimal point
18.	No digit after decimal point
−1980	No decimal point
462,340.0	Contains a comma

Decimal notation is often inconvenient for very large or very small numbers. For example, the approximate mean distance of the planet Pluto from the sun is 3670000000 miles. We can write this more conveniently in scientific notation as 3.670×10^9 miles without loss of precision or meaning. The second way of expressing real numbers is called **exponential notation,** in which we replace the "$\times 10^n$" in scientific notation with the notation "En". Thus 3.670E9 means "3.670 times 10 to the power of 9," or exactly the same as 3.670×10^9 or 3670000000. The following are examples of valid real numbers in exponential form.

exponential notation

Number	Meaning
3670E6	3670×10^6
1.67339E−24	1.67339×10^{-24}
−3.141593e0	-3.141593
0.57721e+3	0.57721×10^3 or 577.21

Note that the decimal point is optional, but at least one digit must appear to its left and one to its right if a decimal point is present; note also that you can write either E or e. You may use either the decimal or exponential notation in specifying the values of real numbers; the choice is strictly a matter of personal taste.

Manipulating Real Variables

Just as integers can be stored only in integer variables, real numbers can be stored only in real variables. Such variables are identified in the VAR section as

```
VAR X: real;
```

If a variable is so defined, values can be stored in and copied from the real variable by the usual assignment, input, or output statements. For example, to assign the value of zero to X, you could use either of the following statements.

X := 0.0;

or

X := 0e0;

Not only can you move real numbers in and out of real variables, you can also combine and manipulate them by using arithmetic expressions. The unary operators (+) and (−) apply to reals as they do to integers. The (binary) arithmetic operators that produce a real-valued result from real-valued operands are

    +   addition
    −   subtraction
    *   multiplication
    /   division

The addition, subtraction, and multiplication operators are the same for both real and integer values, but only the division operator shown here (/) is applicable to the reals. The DIV and MOD operators are *never* used for real numbers. The (/) operator produces a real-valued result that is more conventional because the fractional part is retained.

The operators retain the same precedence as before: Multiplication and division are performed before addition and subtraction, unless the order is overridden by parentheses. Thus the expression (6.1 + 2.5)/2.0 computes the value 4.3. If Celsius is a real variable containing a number interpreted as a metric temperature, then the statement

Fahrenheit := 1.8 * Celsius + 32.0;

stores the Fahrenheit equivalent in a real variable having a suitable name.

Real numbers can be copied from an input device to a real variable by executing a read statement as before. If X is a real variable, the statement

read (X);

will accept a data value in either of the real number notations. For example, the user could enter any of the following input data, all of which are equivalent.

    −82.6   −8.2600E+01
    −8.26E1   −8260e−2
    −0.826e+02   −8260.0E−02

Whatever notation you choose, you must separate the real numbers that appear on the same input line by one or more blanks and in general follow the input conventions described for integers.

When real numbers are written out, a particular exponential notation is used by default. For example, the code

```
VAR X: real;
BEGIN
  X := 976.1;
  writeln (X);
    .
    .
    .
```

will produce the output

9.761000000E + 02

on a VAX computer. Note that one digit appears to the left of the decimal point, and (for this particular implementation) 10 digits are printed before the E. The default notation varies from computer to computer, but the exponential form is always used.

In many applications the use of exponential rather than decimal notation and the display of so many digits (even though we may desire only three or four) is downright annoying. Fortunately, we can request a different form for the output by adding another component to the field format specifier. By executing the statement

writeln (X:10:2);

the value 976.10 is displayed. In general, use of

⟨RealItem⟩:w:d

in an output statement prints the real value in *decimal* form and shows d digits to the *right* of the decimal point. The value of w specifies the total field width, which must now include at least enough space for any sign, the integer portion of the number, the decimal point, and d fractional digits. If the number to be displayed has fewer than d digits to the right of the decimal, zeros are appended to make up d. If the number has more than d digits to the right of the decimal, only the most significant d decimal digits are displayed. In some versions of Pascal, rounding occurs in this case. Figure 2.8 on p. 54 provides several examples of these concepts.

Some Implications of Data Type

Real numbers are more than a notation. They belong to a particular class of objects that can be manipulated by a computer in a special way. Real numbers are fundamentally different from any other kind of data that a computer can handle—even different from integers. Though numerically equal, the integer 5 and the real number 5.0 are represented in quite different ways inside the computer and exhibit different properties in operation. A class of objects, such as the integers, belongs to a specific **data type** in Pascal. The real

data type

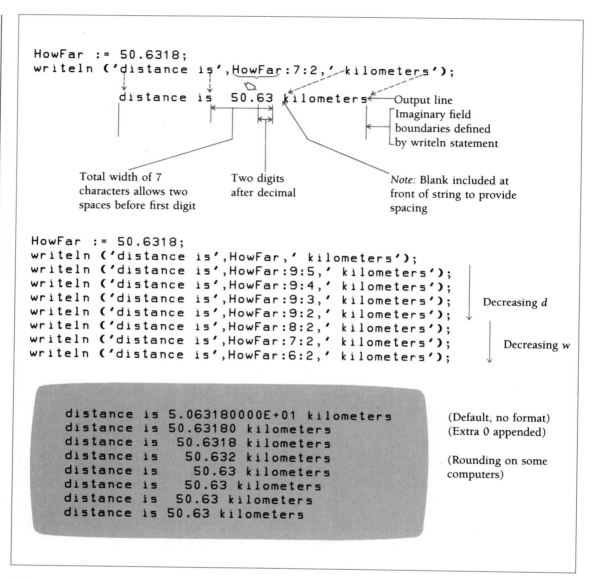

■ Figure 2.8
Effect of field width on output.

numbers belong to a separate, very distinct data type. Yet another data type is composed of characters. Each data type is a world of its own, in which only certain operations can occur and in which objects belonging to other data types generally have no place.

A data type in Pascal consists of a number of basic objects or component data items, such as integers, together with appropriate operators, such as $+$,

−, ∗, MOD, DIV. The values from a particular data type may be stored only in variables that have been declared with that type. For example, declaring

```
VAR U,V: integer;
```

makes variables U and V capable of holding integers and *only* integer values. After this declaration, it would be an error to write

```
U := 0.03;
```

in an attempt to store a real value in an integer variable. Even a real value like 12.00, which is numerically equal to the integer 12, cannot be stored in an integer variable! Most attempts to cross boundaries between types by using values, variables, or operators of the wrong type will be considered an error and will be prevented by the compiler. Another common error is attempting to read a real value into an integer variable. It can't be done.

In most practical cases, different data types pertain to objects so completely different (such as characters and reals) that there is little temptation to confuse or intermix them. However, both integers and reals involve numeric values and both types often occur within the same arithmetic expression. Therefore we need some rules to determine the type of result produced when a mixture of integers and reals is involved. The +, −, and ∗ operators will produce a real-valued result if either or both operands are real. If both operands are integers, the result will be an integer. The (/) operator may also be used with integer operands, but the result is *always* real valued. These observations are summarized in Fig. 2.9.

For example, 6 ∗ 2.0 yields the real number 12.0 (not the integer 12) and may not be stored in an integer variable. The value of 36/3 is also the real number 12.0, even though both operands, 36 and 3, are integers.

Although the separation between the data types is usually strictly enforced, Pascal does make one concession in the case of real and integer values. Because all integer values happen to be special cases of real numbers, *integer values can be stored in real variables,* by either the assignment statement or the read statement. The integer is automatically converted into the equivalent real value before being stored. The technical term for this is **assignment compatibility;** integers are assignment compatible with reals because they can be placed in real variables. Note that when an integer value has been stored in a real variable, the integer value cannot be recovered directly from that variable: The value stored in real form continues to remain real.

assignment
compatibility

■ Figure 2.9
Type of result
produced by
arithmetic operators.

Operand		Operator		
First	Second	+, −, ∗	/	DIV, MOD
integer	integer	integer	real	integer
integer	real	real	real	invalid
real	integer	real	real	invalid
real	real	real	real	invalid

The converse is not true. *A real number, even if it is algebraically equal to an integer, can never be stored in an integer variable*

Predeclared Arithmetic Functions

In comparison to the number of special function keys on a typical calculator, the number of basic operators in Pascal does not seem large. It would be useful to have other operators, such as square root, to derive other kinds of values. Unfortunately, such symbols are rarely found on input–output devices. However, you can request many such operations in Pascal by using a function, which is merely a special operator notation. For example, to find the square root of X, you would write sqrt(X) rather than $\sqrt{X}$. To store the square root of 3 in variable Y, simply write

```
Y := sqrt(3.0)
```

predeclared
functions

The functions described here are called **predeclared functions** because they are always available as part of the Pascal language. The mathematical functions provided in Pascal all require one operand and therefore act like unary operators. In the language of functions, this operand is called an

argument

argument. The parentheses following the function name enclose its argument. The argument may be any suitable arithmetic expression, and the result of the function may be used like any other value within an arithmetic expression. *The argument(s) of a function must always be evaluated before the function itself can be evaluated.*

For example, the Pascal equivalent of $\sqrt{x - y}/\sqrt{x + y}$ is

sqrt(x − y) / sqrt(x + y)

Its data flow diagram is

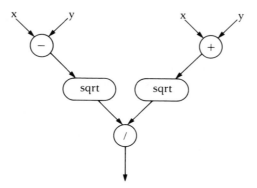

Pascal provides several other basic mathematical functions that are similar to the ones found on a standard electronic calculator. Those functions (shown in Fig. 2.10) take either real or integer arguments and always give real results.

■ Figure 2.10
Predeclared real-
valued mathematical
functions.

Name	Explanation	Example
exp	Exponential of argument, e^x	exp(x)
ln	Natural logarithm of argument, $\log_e x$, where $x > 0$	ln(x + 2.0)
sqrt	Positive square root of argument, $\sqrt{x}$, where $x \geq 0.0$	sqrt(7.46)
sin, cos	Trigonometric functions sine and cosine, where the argument is expressed in radians	sin(x), cos(2*f*t)
arctan	The angle, in radians, the tangent of which is the argument value	arctan(x)

You can use any of these functions in an expression wherever you would use a variable or a constant. For example,

```
Tangent := sin(X) / cos(X) ;
writeln (X,sqrt(X))
```

Although the functions in Fig. 2.10 *always* produce real values, they will accept integer-valued arguments such as

sqrt(16)	yields	4.0
ln(1)	yields	0.0
exp(0)	yields	1.0

Pascal provides two other mathematical functions that produce a result of the same type as the argument: (1) abs, the absolute value function; and (2) sqr, which returns the square of the argument. In symbolic terms, abs(x) yields $|x|$, and sqr(x) yields x^2. The matching of argument and result type is illustrated by the following:

abs(-4)	yields	4
abs(-4.0)	yields	4.0
sqr(4)	yields	16
sqr(4.0)	yields	16.0

Bridging Arithmetic Types: Transfer Functions

Sometimes it is necessary to convert an integer to the real representation of the same value. Because of assignment compatibility, integer values may be placed in real variables, causing an automatic conversion to real form before the assignment can occur. Thus, to convert *from* integer *into* real, you simply assign the value to a real variable.

transfer functions

The reverse is not quite so straightforward. It is *always* an error to assign a real value to an integer variable. Instead, Pascal provides two **transfer functions,** which will convert *from* a real value *into* a nearby integer value.

trunc

round

These two functions, **trunc** and **round,** differ in the way they select the "equivalent" integer value. Trunc (for truncate) gives the integer part of the real-valued argument by simply lopping off any decimal digits, no matter what they are. Thus

trunc(6.75)	yields	6
trunc(5.2)	yields	5
trunc(−4.8)	yields	−4

Round yields the *nearest* integer to the real-valued argument; for instance,

round(6.75)	yields	7
round(5.2)	yields	5
round(−6.75)	yields	−7
round(−5.2)	yields	−5

The round function uses the conventional rule for rounding. Specifically, round(X) yields trunc(X + 0.5) if X is positive and trunc(X − 0.5) if X is negative.

These functions are often used to prepare the value of an entire real-valued arithmetic expression for storage in an integer variable or to display it as an integer. For example, if A and B are integers, trunc(A/B) is equivalent to A DIV B.

2.4 Character Data

Computers are as adept at handling text and other forms of character data as they are at dealing with numeric data. We are so familiar with reading, writing, looking up words in dictionaries, and other forms of text processing that we tend to take the underlying operations for granted. Perhaps we even assume that, if computers can do such things, they do them "instinctively," as we seem to do.

Computers can manipulate the symbols we use in written communication, but certainly not by instinct. As in the case of numerical manipulation, nonnumeric data are processed by applying appropriate operations to these symbols as prescribed by a program. These symbols, the fundamental units of text, are individual characters and comprise another data type in Pascal:

char data type

the **char** (for character) **data type.**

A character is basically any individual letter, digit, punctuation mark, or delimiter, such as a left parenthesis. A character may also be invisible to the eye, as in the case of a blank. When you hit one key of a terminal, usually one character is generated. Characters are the objects displayed on screens and printed out on paper.

You can represent a single character constant within a program by enclosing it within apostrophes (often called single quotation marks). Recall that the statement

```
writeln ('a');
```

will cause the character a to be displayed on the output device. With a program, you must use apostrophes to denote character constants; without them the letter would be mistaken for an identifier.

Characters, like other types of data, may be stored in variables that are defined as type char. For example,

```
VAR One, Other: char;
```

declares two variables, each of which may contain a *single* character. These variables may be given values by either the assignment or read statements. If the input data is about to supply the letter i, the sequence

```
One := 'H';
read (Other);
writeln (One,Other);
```

would display the output Hi; that is, the character 'H' that was assigned to variable One, followed immediately by the character 'i' that was read into variable Other. The default field width for characters is 1, so that each character appears alongside characters occupying adjacent fields.

Note that character variables may hold only single characters. It would be illegal to attempt the assignment

```
One := 'Hi';
```

Of course, you may write out the character string 'Hi', but this object is a composite of two characters and is not an instance of the type char; it will not fit in a character variable.

The following fragments of code will both produce exactly the same output, assuming that the variables are of type char.

```
write('j');          First := 'j' ;
write ('o');         Last := 'e' ;
writeln('e');        writeln(First,'o',Last)
```

On input, execution of a statement like

```
read (NextChar);
```

copies precisely *one* character—the next unread character—into the character variable indicated. Except for certain control keys, anything you type can be read as a character, including blanks, apostrophes, digits, punctuation marks, and so forth. It makes no sense to separate character data by blanks, because blanks are themselves characters. They can only separate a numeric value from what precedes it.

In order to read an entire word, say of five letters, it is necessary to read each of the five letters into separate character variables. Assuming that all five variables have type char, the read statement

```
read (Char1,Char2,Char3,Char4,Char5);
```

would be capable of reading any one of the following five-character sequences in their entirety.

```
Hello       I am.        -3.75
```

Note how blanks and punctuation count the same as alphabetic characters. Incidentally, in Pascal the uppercase (capital) letters are considered to be different from their lowercase (small letter) counterparts.

In the third situation above (-3.75), '$-$' would go into Char1, '3' into Char2, '.' into Char3, and so on. What was typed to look like a single number—and *could have been read as one numeric value into a single real variable*—would instead be input as five totally independent characters with no numeric significance. The fact that these five characters occupied consecutive positions in the input stream would be purely coincidental to the program. The fact that they *look* numeric is also of no significance in the world of characters.

As you may already realize, the apostrophes surrounding characters in write statements do not appear when the characters are displayed on the output device. Similarly, apostrophes should *not* be used to delimit input data that are to read as characters. Plain characters typed at the terminal may be read as char data without confusion. In fact the apostrophe itself, if typed, would be read as just another ordinary character.

Blank   Two characters deserve special mention. The first of these is the blank, denoted in Pascal by ' '. The blank is a bona fide character, of equal stature with all other characters, even though it cannot be seen. Although the space between the apostrophes indicates a blank, you must realize that blanks—not just emptiness—separate other characters on input and output media.

Apostrophe   The other special character is the apostrophe. Because of its unique role in specifying other character constants, it requires a different representation itself within a program. To depict an apostrophe inside a program, write *two* consecutive apostrophes (''). This requires two separate strokes of the apostrophe key. Two apostrophes are not the same as one double quotation mark (''), which is a completely different character.

If an apostrophe is called for within a character string, two consecutive apostrophes are all that is required. However, if an apostrophe appears as an isolated character constant, the pair of apostrophes must be enclosed by another set of apostrophes, making a total of four apostrophes in a row. Consider how the following write statement produces its line of output.

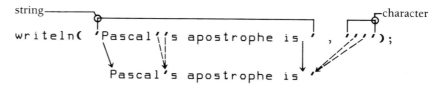

```
PROGRAM Reverse3 (input,output);

VAR First, Middle, Last: char;

BEGIN
    writeln ('Please enter a 3-character string:');
    read (First,Middle,Last);
    writeln ('Reverse order:    ',Last,Middle,First)
END.
```

■ Figure 2.11
Program to reverse three-character input.

One other "character," namely ⓡ, is sometimes read into a character variable, often by mistake. In standard Pascal, if *return* is read as a character, it is converted into a blank before being stored. It is then indistinguishable from any other blank and therefore loses its identity as the end-of-line indicator.†

Consider the problem of reversing the letters of any three-letter word that you have typed in; that is, you want a program that can convert don into nod, nip into pin, and so on. Obviously, the strategy is to read in the characters and then write them out in the opposite order. Since the characters must be read from left to right and written from left to right, the first character written will be the last one read. Therefore all input precedes any output (excluding prompts), and enough variables must be defined to store all three characters read. These observations lead to the program shown in Fig. 2.11. Although the program is very simple, its results can be instructive, as illustrated by:

Input	Output	Remarks
Tom	moT	Upper case differs from lower.
$ Q	Q $	Note the blank character.
357	753	Each digit is a character.
.",	,".	So are quotes and other punctuation.
.30	03.	Special numeric symbols . . .
−65	56−	get no special treatment.

Character data and other data types do not mix in Pascal. Although the integer 5 and the character '5' may look similar, they are totally different things inside the machine. If variable CharVar is declared with type char, it

---

† Turbo Pascal treats the return differently if it is read into a character variable. The ⓡ is actually treated as its two component parts: a carriage return and a line feed.

makes no sense to write

```
CharVar := 5;          {error}
```

because an integer cannot be stored in a character variable and vice versa. It is equally meaningless to write either

```
'3' + 5     or     '3' + '5'
```

because you cannot involve characters in arithmetic operations. If this were possible, you would expect expressions like 4.28 * '#' to mean something.

In fact, you cannot do much with individual characters except to move them from place to place and inspect them. Their main use is in combination with other characters to make up words, sentences, paragraphs, essays, programs—in a word, text.

2.5 Making Programs Easier to Understand and Modify: Part 1

Programs must be intelligible to people as well as executable by machines. In practice a program is often handed on to others for further use and even further development. This is standard practice with commercially important programs. Other people besides the original author must be able to comprehend how it works.

An indecipherable program is difficult (if not impossible) to diagnose, repair, or extend. Regardless of how well a program may be understood today, by tomorrow some of its conventions and assumptions will likely be forgotten, even by its originator. Consequently, you will save yourself and others hours of frustration if you clearly reveal your program's secrets. It is well worth the effort to arrange the statements in ways that reflect their logical relationships and to supplement them with ample, descriptive text, which is called

documentation   **documentation.**

We customarily use special conventions to enhance the clarity of ordinary English text. These include spacing, margins, indentation, underlining, page numbers, and overall neatness. Corresponding layout and documentation

programming style   conventions exist to enhance the clarity of programs. **Programming style** refers to those aspects of program writing that make the code easier for people to comprehend. Although programming style has no impact on execution, it can greatly influence the successful development and future use of programs. Programs should be written "with style" right from the beginning to improve their chances of ever working correctly.

Even though our program examples up to this point have been quite simple, we have already used several clarifying techniques. We will continue to use the conventions listed in the box on the next page (and add some others later); you should also use them in programs that you write.

You may be tempted to ignore the suggestion about meaningful identifier names in favor of cryptic names requiring less typing. When observed,

Program Style and Documentation

1. Write each program statement and each identifier in the variable declaration part on separate lines.
2. Indent the executable statements (between BEGIN and END) and the identifiers in the variable declaration part one tab position to indicate the section of the program to which they belong.
3. Enter the reserved words (PROGRAM, VAR, BEGIN, END) in upper case to draw attention to the structural units they introduce or terminate.
4. Use self-explanatory identifier names for the program name and all variable names.
5. Use blank lines between major sections of the program (such as between the variable declarations and BEGIN) or between logically distinct subsections. Blank lines cost nothing and assist the reader in locating distinct program units.

however, this suggestion can be most helpful, especially in larger programs where dozens or even hundreds of identifiers may be involved. We further suggest the use of multiword identifiers, in which each component word begins with an uppercase letter (such as AmountOwed, CurrentBalance, TimeToGo).

Comments

A program may contain descriptive text that is intended solely for the reader and has absolutely no influence on program execution. Such text is known
comment as a **comment** and consists of almost any string of characters enclosed between the special symbols { and }. These characters, called braces (or curly brackets) are the common delimiters in standard Pascal. It is also acceptable to use (* in place of { and *) in place of }. Because of their special role, the symbols } and *) cannot appear inside a comment. We will use the brace notation, as in

{ This is my program }

With more complicated programs, you cannot always tell from the code exactly what the program is supposed to do. Comments supplement the limited powers of expression of computer languages and explain the underlying algorithm, assumptions, limitations, and motivations of a program. Comments comprise part of the program documentation. For large and complex programs, comments are indispensable in revealing what a program is supposed to do. They are surprisingly helpful even with simple programs.

```
PROGRAM Circle (input,output);

   {Given the radius of a circle,
    compute its area and circumference}
VAR
   Radius,           {input data}
   Area,             {of circle}
   Circumference:    {of circle}
                     real;

BEGIN {Circle}
   writeln ('Please enter radius:'); {prompt}
   read (Radius);
   writeln; {provide spacing on screen}

   Area := 3.1416 * Radius * Radius;
   writeln ('area of circle:',Area:10:3);

   Circumference := 2 * 3.1416 * Radius;
   writeln ('circumference:',Circumference:10:3)
END. {Circle}
```

■ Figure 2.12
Program to find area and circumference of a circle.

Figure 2.12 shows comments incorporated into a program for finding the area and circumference of a circle, given its radius. The program implements the standard formulas $A = \pi r^2$ and $C = 2\pi r$. Even though we do not go through the development of the program, its operation should be perfectly clear. That is precisely the point: A well-written program should be easy to understand.

In this program we used comments in four different ways. First, we stated the purpose of the program, as well as any general limitations or assumptions, at the beginning. This overview should be included in every program.

variable dictionary

Then we explained every identifier in the variable declaration part with a separate comment. This set of comments is often referred to as the **variable dictionary.** The simplicity of this program does not allow us to illustrate the full value of the variable dictionary. However, one of the major causes of errors in and frustration with larger programs is the failure to give each variable a clear, consistent role. Creating a variable dictionary forces you to decide the exact purpose of every variable and serves as a record of your decision, so that each variable will be used consistently throughout program development.

Next, we used comments to explain the purpose of two of the writeln statements, in case that purpose would not be clear to the reader. And, finally, we wrote matching comments for BEGIN and END. We did this in anticipation of programs having several BEGINs and ENDs, where comments can assist in making the correct associations.

Note how blank lines are used in the program shown in Fig. 2.12. They separate major sections of the program, and, within the statement part, they separate the input process, the area calculation, and the circumference calculation.

CONSTant Definition

symbolic constants

The program in Fig. 2.13 is the program for finding the area and circumference of a circle but rewritten with one new feature: the use of **symbolic constants.** When a constant value, such as 3.1416, has some special role, it is good

```
PROGRAM Circle (input,output);

    {Given the radius of a circle,
     compute its area and circumference}

CONST
    Pi = 3.1416;
    Prompt = 'Please enter radius';

VAR
    Radius,         {input data}
    Area,           {of circle}
    Circumference: {of circle}
                    real;

BEGIN {Circle}
    writeln (Prompt);
    read (Radius);
    writeln; {provide spacing on screen}

    Area := Pi * Radius * Radius;
    writeln ('area of circle:',Area:10:3);

    Circumference := 2 * Pi * Radius;
    writeln ('circumference:',Circumference:10:3)
END. {Circle}
```

■ Figure 2.13
Program containing definitions of symbolic constants.

practice to identify it by some name that reflects that role. This usually makes expressions containing that constant more readable. In fact, it is common practice in algebra to use the symbol π, to represent the actual value for which 3.1416 is only an approximation. Greek letters are not generally available keyboard symbols, so we chose the identifier Pi and used it in Fig. 2.13 wherever 3.1416 was used in Fig. 2.12. Wherever Pi appears, it is as though the actual value 3.1416 had been written there. However, we first had to make the association between the identifier Pi and its intended value in the **constant definition part** of the program. This part, introduced by CONST, precedes the variable declaration part.

constant definition
part

Identifiers defined there must not be confused with variable identifiers. When a symbolic constant has been defined, it cannot be modified by any subsequent statement. The constant Pi can no more be assigned a new value than can the constant 3.1416. The use of an equals sign (=) in the definition of Pi emphasizes the permanence of its association with 3.1416. Similarly, when Pi has been defined as a particular constant, the symbol cannot be redefined as anything else, such as a variable (at least within the same program module).

Besides improving the readability of the program text, the definition of symbolic constants offers another advantage. Though the value of Pi remains fixed throughout execution of the program, it may require redefinition at some later point in the lifetime of the program. If you decide that 3.1416 is not a sufficiently precise value for π, you can employ a value with more decimal digits (say, 3.141593). Instead of having to replace every instance of the former value by the new one, you need only to redefine the value of Pi and recompile the program to know that the revised value is effective in every expression containing Pi.

Figure 2.13 contains another symbolic constant, the identifier Prompt, which represents the entire character string used to prompt an interactive user of the program. Representing long character strings by short names can remove clutter from the executable statements and saves tedious typing if the string appears in more than one location.

2.6 Making Programs Work Correctly

Getting a program into operation involves three major stages. The longest is stage one: *the design and coding stage,* where an approach to the problem is gradually refined into an algorithm and eventually encoded as a program. We have urged you to do this carefully. If your program is well-designed and written, you can avoid many later problems and make necessary changes more easily.

The first real test of your program occurs at stage two: *when it is submitted to the compiler.* We mentioned this phase in Chapter 1 and expand on it here. Before transforming a program into executable form, the compiler must make sure that the program is at least reasonable, that is, syntactically correct. Misuse of the Pascal language, whether caused by haste, ignorance, or typing errors, is identified and reported to the user. Problems identified by the compiler are called either **syntax errors** or **compile-time errors.** You must repair such errors before the compiler will produce an executable version of the program. This entails making changes, additions, or deletions so that your program conforms to the rules of Pascal. After making the necessary changes, which often are of a minor nature, you submit the program to the compiler again. If more syntax errors are found, you must repeat the process until you either (1) decide on a major overhaul and return to the first stage; or (2) achieve a successful compilation and move on to the third stage.

syntax (compile-time) errors

Far more subtle than syntax errors are **logic errors.** Just as a sentence may be grammatically correct but meaningless, you can write a syntactically correct program that does the wrong thing. The compiler can only verify that the combination of Pascal constructs you wrote is superficially acceptable. It cannot verify that the program will execute correctly or that it represents a solution to your original problem. There is no way for the computer to know what problem you intend to solve with the program. Likewise, a program that runs and produces results does not necessarily produce correct results.

logic errors

The only way to find out whether it works is to try the program and compare its results with what you expect. This is stage three: *run-time program testing.* You must execute a program over and over with different data to ensure that it conforms to the underlying algorithm and that the algorithm actually solves the original problem. Such testing often reveals problems that must be fixed.

You may discover that certain input values cause unexpected results, or you may see no results at all. From such symptoms of trouble (called **run-time errors**) you must diagnose the cause of the problem. It may be a minor flaw or omission that can be easily repaired, or it may be a major logic error requiring massive revision or even a fresh start. Finding subtle logic errors often requires great care and patience. The easiest way to avoid them is by applying care during the design stage. Whatever the problem, considerable testing and possibly some fixing is required before you can be fairly confident the program does what it is supposed to do. Since run-time errors are sometimes called **program bugs,** the testing and repair process is known as **program debugging.**

run-time errors

program bugs
program debugging

In the remainder of this section, we present some practical suggestions for detecting and fixing errors. The topic of program testing reappears throughout the book, as new opportunities for errors and new ways to detect them are introduced.

Fixing Compile-Time Errors

When you use a programming language, the opportunities for errors are numerous. They range from typing mistakes to wholesale abuse of the language syntax. These errors—and combinations of them—are so many and varied that all we can do here is present a few typical examples and suggestions for avoiding trouble.

Figure 2.14 shows the code and the error messages generated by VAX-11 Pascal after an unsuccessful attempt to compile a program for finding the area and circumference of a circle. (The correct version was shown in Fig. 2.13.) At first glance, the program in Fig. 2.14(a) may look correct, but an attempt to compile it produces a dismaying list of errors, as shown in Fig. 2.14(b). Although these error messages are from the VAX-11 Pascal compiler, another Pascal compiler would produce a similar list. The error messages follow the program statements that the compiler believes to be in error.

We numbered the error messages for reference. Error message #1 is straightforward. An assignment operator was mistakenly used where an equals sign belongs in the constant definition part.

```
PROGRAM Circle (input,output);

   {Given the radius of a circle,
    compute its area and circumference}

CONST
   Pi := 3.1416;
   Prompt = 'Please enter radius';

VAR
   Radius,          {input data}
   Area,            of circle}
   Circumference: {of circle}
                  real;

BEGIN {Circle}
   writeln (Prompt);
   read (Radius)
   writeln; {provide spacing on screen}

   Area := Pi * Radius * Radius;
   writeln ('area of circle:",Area:10:3);

   Circumference := Pi * Radius;
   writeln ('circumference:',Circumferance:10:3)
END. {Circle}
```

(a) Program containing syntax errors.

■ Figure 2.14

```
1     PROGRAM Circle (input,output);
2        {Given the radius of a circle,
3         compute its area and circumference}
4
5     CONST
6        Pi := 3.1416;
            1
%PASCAL-E-SYNEQL, (1) Syntax: "=" expected                    #1
7        Prompt = 'Please enter radius';
8
9     VAR
10       Radius,     {input data}
11       Area,       of circle}
              1           2
%PASCAL-E-SYNRESWRD, (1) Syntax: reserved word  ⎫
                          cannot be redefined   ⎬    #2
%PASCAL-E-SYNASCII, (2) Illegal ASCII character  ⎭
12       Circumference: {of circle}
            1
%PASCAL-E-SYNCOMCOL, (1) Syntax: "," or ":" expected         #3
13               real;
14
15    BEGIN {Circle}
16       writeln (Prompt);
17       read (Radius)
18       writeln; {provide spacing on screen}
            1
%PASCAL-E-SYNSEMI, (1) Syntax: ";" expected                  #4
19
20       Area := Pi * Radius * Radius;
21       writeln ('area of circle:'',Area:10:3);

%PASCAL-E-QUOBEFEOL, (1) Quoted string not terminated        #5
                         before end of line
22
23       Circumference := Pi * Radius;
            1
%%PASCAL-E-SYNPARMLST, (1) Syntax: actual parameter list     #6
24       writeln ('circumference:',Circumferance:10:3)
                                1
%PASCAL-E-UNDECLID, (1) Undeclared identifier CIRCUMFERANCE  #7
25   END. {Circle}
```

(b) Errors raised by compiling program in (a) under VAX-11 Pascal.

■ Figure 2.14 (*continued*)

Message #2 identifies two errors in line 11. Just because the compiler indicates two errors does not necessarily mean that you have to make two corrections. None of the characters on line 11 is inherently illegal. If you reread line 11 carefully, you should note that there is only one brace; the left one is missing. Without the opening {, the comment is not understood as a comment, the word "of" (a reserved word) is taken as another identifier following Area, and the closing } makes no sense to the compiler. Adding the balancing bracket will correct the error.

Message #3 is a bit of a mystery. Although it indicates a problem with line 12, nothing appears to be wrong with the actual line. In fact, there is nothing wrong with line 12. The compiler at this point was misled by the error on line 11, and is not expecting what appears on line 12. After line 11 has been repaired, message #3 will also disappear.

Use the messages to locate the approximate point of the error, but do not always take the error message literally. The actual error may be something different from what the compiler suggests, and it may have occurred earlier in the program; only its effects are still causing confusion.

Message #4, for example, identifies line 18 as the source of the problem, but the real difficulty is the missing semicolon on the line above. Because of this omission, the compiler identifies line 18 as a continuation of a read statement, which permits nothing but a ";" to appear after the right parenthesis.

Message #5 is straightforward and on target. The string on line 21 was terminated with a double quotation mark where an apostrophe is required.

Message #6 is another red herring, left over from the previous error. Line 23 is syntactically correct, but the compiler is still looking for the missing apostrophe to close the string on line 21.

Message #7 depicts a common problem: a misspelling (or typing error), which causes an identifier in an executable statement to differ from the identifier defined in the CONST or VAR parts, and therefore to appear undeclared. If the misspelling had occurred in the variable declaration itself, every occurrence of the (correct) identifier would have had an "undeclared identifier" message—except, of course, the misspelled version. If you see such messages associated with multiple copies of an identifier, be sure to check its initial declaration, even though the declaration did not contain an error message.

Since such obviously small things can cause compile-time errors, it should be clear why your knowledge of the language must be good and your coding accurate.

Run-Time Errors: Program Testing

After you have fixed the compile-time errors from Fig. 2.14, the resulting program, shown in Fig. 2.15 can be compiled, linked, and executed. It still contains an error, but you must test it with actual data to discover this fact. If the program seems to work the first time, you may just have been lucky.

```
PROGRAM Circle (input,output);

   {Given the radius of a circle,
    compute its area and circumference}

CONST
   Pi = 3.1416;
   Prompt = 'Please enter radius';

VAR
   Radius,        {input data}
   Area,          {of circle}
   Circumference: {of circle}
                  real;

BEGIN {Circle}
   writeln (Prompt);
   read (Radius);
   writeln; {provide spacing on screen}

   Area := Pi * Radius * Radius;
   writeln ('area of circle:',Area:10:3);

   Circumference := Pi * Radius;
   writeln ('circumference:',Circumference:10:3)
END. {Circle}
```

■ Figure 2.15
A syntactically
correct program
containing a run-time
error (based on the
program in Figure
2.13).

It must be tried more than once to demonstrate acceptable performance over the range of expected input values. However, all possible input values cannot be tested. Therefore you should select a few, well-chosen test cases to represent extreme situations (that is, the smallest and largest values anticipated), special cases (such as 0 and 1), and a few typical values for which you know the correct result.

Each problem and each program has its own characteristic behavior and typical input–output values, so we cannot give precise guidelines. The most important thing is that you know in advance what should be produced by a correct program. You must be able to distinguish right answers from wrong answers at the testing stage.

Suppose you were to run the program in Fig. 2.15 using the value of 16.37 for the radius. The result would not be immediately recognizable as correct. Thus you should use very simple test data.

The first test uses a radius of zero. Although this represents a degenerate circle, the formulas will still apply, and the program should give correct results for this extreme (smallest) case. The program does produce answers and they are correct—in this particular case. But we cannot stop testing here. Next, we try a radius of 1 with the formulas

$$A = \pi r^2 \quad \text{and} \quad C = 2\pi r.$$

When $r = 1$, A should be equal to π and C equal to 2π (that is, the value of C should be twice that of A). However, when 1 was supplied as input, the program produced *equal* values for A and C, namely, 3.142. Therefore we know that the program contains an error. The fact that the value of A is correct but that of C is not suggests (but does not prove) that the problem is confined to the calculation of the circumference.

Another convenient value is a radius of 2, because when $r = 2$, $A = 4\pi$, and $C = 4\pi$; in this case, A and C should have equal values. Testing the program with this value produces a correct area (12.566) but an unequal and incorrect circumference (6.283). The evidence suggests that the computed circumference is one-half its correct value.

One look at the program statement that performs this calculation confirms that we used the wrong formula; the factor of 2 is missing. When we correct this omission, the correct program (Fig. 2.13) results. Of course, we must test it further in order to convince ourselves of its correctness. The test values we used were 0, 1, 2, 100, 1000000 (all of which produce results that are simple to verify), as well as 6.2 to demonstrate that the program could handle real-valued input, and -1 just to see what would happen with negative input. The results were satisfactory, so we can consider this program to be correct for nonnegative input.

In this example, the error was easy to find and easy to repair. However, the problems uncovered during testing are often subtle and their solutions often elusive. Discovering the true difficulty can involve considerable investigative and diagnostic skill. Again we urge care during program development, so that logic errors will be minor or avoided altogether. Above all, you should never make random changes in the hope that they will correct some problem that you do not understand. Guessing has no place in program development, repair, or maintenance.

Another outcome of testing is to fine tune and humanize the output, so that results are clearly identified, output is correctly aligned, and prompts are intelligible and appropriate. However, such cosmetic repairs are not as important as finding and fixing true errors and should therefore be postponed until the basic results are acceptable.

2.7 Pascal Grammar and Syntax Diagrams

syntax diagrams

At the very least, a program must conform to the rules of the programming language in which it is written. Knowing the rules is essential for preventing compile-time errors and for fixing those that do occur. **Syntax diagrams** provide a notation for clearly and pictorially describing the rules of Pascal and are a handy reference when you are coding or fixing a Pascal program. However, we first need to say something about programming languages in general.

For a sentence in English to be meaningful, it must at least contain appropriate vocabulary and conform to the rules of English grammar. These rules specify the acceptable ways of combining words into phrases, clauses, and ultimately into sentences. Although they are rarely invoked explicitly outside English class, these rules lie in the background of all that we hear and say. They provide the criteria for deciding whether a sentence is constructed correctly.

Programming languages can also be characterized by a particular vocabulary and grammar. Compared to the richness of human languages, their grammars are sparse and simple. Nevertheless, they serve a function similar to the rules of human language. When we want to know whether a program statement, or for that matter an entire program, is correctly constructed, we merely consult the grammar for the corresponding programming language.

Pascal grammar can be described by syntax diagrams. In the remainder of this section we introduce these diagrams and show how to interpret them.

The basic symbols, in a sense the vocabulary, used in Pascal include the digits 0 through 9, the alphabetic characters, and certain punctuation marks. We show such basic symbols inside circles in syntax diagrams. For example, a digit is described as

digit
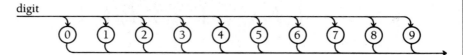

Such a diagram resembles a map in which some path is sought from the entrance at the upper left to the exit somewhere on the right. Any path is acceptable provided it follows the arrows. Any symbols encountered along the way are collected. When the exit is reached, this collection of symbols constitutes one instance of the class of object named at the entrance.

For example, there is a path from the entrance through the 8, which terminates at the exit. Thus 8 is an instance of one particular digit. Because of the simplicity of the digit diagram, there are only ten different paths, and ten different instances of this class.

For a slightly more interesting example, consider the syntax diagram that defines an unsigned integer:

unsigned
integer

First note the box labeled "digit." Such a box indicates some other construction in the language defined by another syntax diagram. To determine whether 8

is an unsigned integer, we start at the entrance to this diagram and encounter the digit box. At this point, if any doubt existed, we could look at the digit syntax diagram and discover that 8 is indeed a valid digit. Then we would return to the unsigned integer diagram, find a path directly to the exit, and conclude that 8 is therefore also an unsigned integer. Defining one construction or concept in terms of another occurs with human languages as well; for example, we say that the predicate of a sentence must contain a verb.

The other point of interest is that the path leading out of the digit box branches to either the exit or back to the digit box. Thus we could return to the digit box any number of times, choosing any one of the ten possible digits on each visit before finally branching to the exit. This means that 0, 93764, and 888 are also unsigned integers, whereas +6 is not because no path exists that leads to the symbols (+) and 6 in that order.

We can depict an identifier consisting of a letter followed by any combination of letters and digits (including none) as follows:

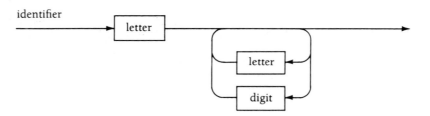

Consider, finally, a portion of the syntax diagram for a block, that is, the main body of a Pascal program:

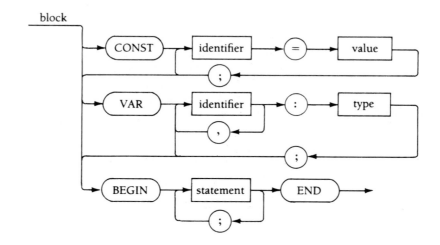

This diagram indicates that the CONSTant definition part (if any) must precede the VARiable declaration part (which, in rare cases, may be omitted)

and that both of these parts must precede the BEGINning of the statement part. It also shows that identifiers X and Y may be declared as real by either

```
VAR X: real;    or    VAR X,Y: real
    Y: real;
```

On the other hand, the use of VAR more than one time is *not* allowed; the code

```
VAR X: real;
VAR Y: real;
```

is an error.

Just as the rules of English grammar say nothing about penmanship and layout, so the rules of Pascal syntax say nothing about spaces, margins, identations, use of separate lines for separate statements, and so on. These matters of style pertain only to making a program readable for people. Although important, they are not prescribed by Pascal. However, other constraints may apply. For example, there may be practical limits on the length of an identifier (such as 31 characters in VAX Pascal) or the size of an unsigned integer (recall maxint). Such limitations may vary from one computer system to another. However, you should not feel too constrained by such limitations at this stage.

Just because a sentence in English conforms to the rules of English grammar, it does not necessarily become true or even convey any meaning. Similarly, a program written in Pascal that obeys the rules of Pascal will not necessarily do what you want it to do and may not do anything at all. Conformity to the rules of Pascal does not guarantee success for a program. A programming language is a tool for communicating algorithms to a computer. If your algorithm is flawed, your program will also be defective. On the other hand, strict conformity to the grammar of a programming language is absolutely essential. Without it, success is impossible. Programming languages allow no poetic license, no deviation from the rules. Thus, besides designing algorithms carefully, you must know the programming rules precisely.

2.8 Review of Rules

A. Input data may be transferred from an input device to a program variable by executing a statement of the form

> read (⟨variable⟩);

or from consecutive positions in the input stream into several variables by the statement

> read(Variable1,Variable2, . . . ,VariableN);

Reading is sequential; that is, each read begins at whatever point in the input stream a previous read left off. The data type of the variable determines the data type that is expected as input. If the type is numeric, the input value must be separated by one or more blanks from any preceding numeric value on the same line. If the type is char, precisely one character—the next character—is read, be it alphabetic, blank, quote, digit, apostrophe, or whatever.

B. Executing the writeln statement can display several values across the same line on the output device. Its syntax diagram is

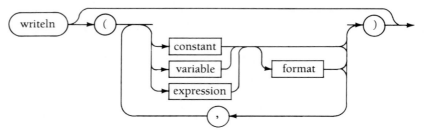

The constants may be character strings—sequences of characters enclosed by apostrophes—in order to display literal messages. These may be interspersed with values from variables and expressions during output and are used to label or highlight these other values. Writeln always leaves the output device positioned at the start of a new line. When used without output values, writeln produces an empty output line.

C. Consecutive output values are displayed in consecutive fields, the widths of which may be indicated by a format specifier. An integer value or a character string constant may be displayed in the right-hand portion of a field of width w as follows:

⟨value⟩:w

Real numbers may be written in decimal notation, using the form

⟨real-number-value⟩:w:d

This displays the number at the right of a field of width w, which must include the sign, decimal point, and d digits to the right of the decimal point.

D. The write statement has syntax and behavior similar to writeln, except that it does not advance to a new line following output. It must be supplied with a value to be displayed.

E. A data type consists of a set of characteristic values that belong only to this type and no other, along with operations appropriate to data of this particular type. The data types encountered so far are integer, real, and char (character).

F.   The character (char) data type includes only individual characters as members (not character strings). A character constant must be enclosed in apostrophes within a program although these delimiters are not needed on input and are not shown on output. The apostrophe character itself is depicted by two consecutive apostrophes, enclosed by two additional apostrophes when used as an isolated character constant.

G.   The real data type includes numbers with decimal points and fractional parts. It also allows numbers of much smaller and larger magnitudes than are possible with integers. There are two notations for real numbers: decimal (such as -60.3) and exponential (such as $62.407E-12$ and $-0.214E3$). Their syntax diagrams are

decimal
notation

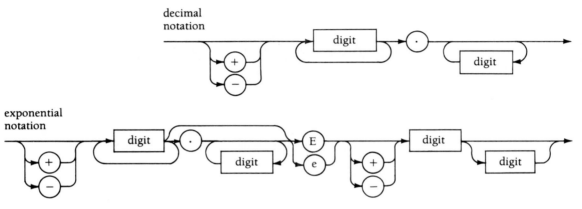

exponential
notation

H.   Members of the real and integer data types may be combined using the operators $+$, $-$, $*$, and $/$. Division $(/)$ always produces a real result; the other three operators produce a real result if one or both of the operands are real. The operators DIV and MOD are restricted to integers.

I.   In a special case, known as assignment compatibility, integers may be read into or assigned to real variables (after automatic conversion to real form). However, the converse is never possible. Other data types (such as char and numeric types) remain separate and do not mix.

J.   Pascal also provides several unary numeric operators and functions:

   1.   The unary operators are identity $(+)$ and negation $(-)$.
   2.   The arithmetic functions abs and sqr yield the same type of result as their (numeric) arguments.
   3.   The arithmetic functions sqrt (argument ≥ 0), ln (argument >0), exp, sin, cos, and arctan, produce real values but accept integer or real arguments.
   4.   The transfer functions trunc and round convert real values to integers; the reverse is accomplished by assigning an integer value to a real variable.

K. Symbolic constants may be defined in the constant definition part, which precedes the variable declaration part. Its syntax diagram is

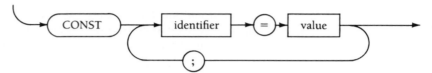

L. A comment may be inserted into a program at any point where a free blank is permitted. Comments are any message enclosed in braces (except that } and *) may not be part of a comment). Comments do not affect the program's behavior in any way and are intended only to inform anyone who reads the code.

KEY TERMS

argument
assignment compatibility
binary operator
char data type
character string
comment
compile-time errors
constant definition part
data type
decimal notation
documentation
echoing
exponential notation
field
field width

formatted output
input data
input process
input stream
interactive computing
logic errors
operands
output item
output process
predeclared functions
program bugs
program debugging
programming style
prompts

read statement
real number
round
run-time errors
sequential processing
symbolic constants
syntax diagrams
syntax errors
transfer functions
trunc
unary operator
variable dictionary
write statement
writeln statement

REVIEW PROBLEM

Consider the plight of a parent whose child plays ball almost every night at the same ballpark (8 miles from home). The child bicycles to the park at a speed depending on energy level, interest in the game, and time of departure. However, once a speed has been established, the child maintains that speed all the way to the park, since the road is level and free of traffic.

Unfortunately, the child almost always forgets to take some piece of equipment or the sandwich required to get through the game. When realization of the missing item dawns, the child stops briefly at one of the many phone booths along the way and calls home. The parent is asked to deliver the missing item(s) by car and that the delivery be made before the child reaches the ballpark.

The problem is for the parent to decide whether sufficient time remains to catch up with the child before the child reaches the ballpark and without violating the speed limit.

To be precise, the parent must calculate the speed required to arrive at the park just as the child arrives. A greater speed will result in them meeting earlier along the route; driving at a slower speed will cause a late arrival, so that the parent might just as well stay home. The rate required for simultaneous arrival at the park is the slowest feasible speed. If it happens to exceed the speed limit, the parent will decide not to go.

Fortunately, the family owns a personal computer, on which this daily calculation can be performed, but they need help in writing the program. We begin by considering the desired result. The result is a rate, expressed in miles per hour, which can be compared mentally with the speed limit. Since distance, speed, and travel time are related by the standard formula:

distance = speed × time

the desired result is therefore the total distance (to the ballpark) divided by the available time. Only one value is known in advance: the distance from the home to the ballpark (8 miles). Assuming that the remaining available time (following the phone call) can be determined, the first level of the algorithm is already apparent:

1. calculate the available time;
2. required speed is total distance/available time;
3. display the required speed in mph;
4. stop.

Step 1 requires further refinement. It might help to consider the available input. When the phone call occurs, two things can be determined: (1) the distance of the child from home; and (2) the time elapsed between departure and the phone call. This time is most conveniently expressed in minutes.

When calculating times, we can safely ignore the time spent placing the call and the parent's reaction time, because they should be very small in comparison to travel times. The time available to the parent (step 1) is the difference between the child's total travel time and the time elapsed so far, that is, before the phone call. The elapsed time can be obtained as input, but the child's expected total travel time must be calculated. Thus the next level of refinement is to calculate time available (step 1):

1.1   determine time elapsed so far (from the child);
1.2   calculate child's expected total travel time;
1.3   time remaining is the difference: child's total − time elapsed;

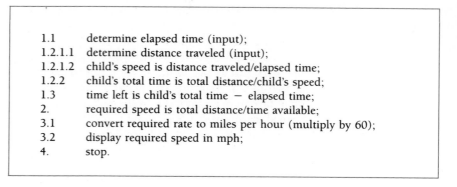

■ Figure 2.16
Algorithm for
interception-of-child
problem.

1.1   determine elapsed time (input);
1.2.1.1   determine distance traveled (input);
1.2.1.2   child's speed is distance traveled/elapsed time;
1.2.2   child's total time is total distance/child's speed;
1.3   time left is child's total time − elapsed time;
2.   required speed is total distance/time available;
3.1   convert required rate to miles per hour (multiply by 60);
3.2   display required speed in mph;
4.   stop.

The child's expected total travel time (step 1.2) is simply the (known) total distance divided by the child's rate of travel. The problem assumes that the child keeps to a steady speed, and so the speed calculated to the point of making the call will be maintained over the remaining distance to the ballpark. Calculating the rate of travel is elementary; we can learn both the elapsed time and the distance covered at the time of the call directly from the child.

Now that all the parts seem to be in place, they can be collected into the complete algorithm, shown in Fig. 2.16. Note that step 3 was subdivided into two parts. If all times are measured in minutes, the required speed computed in step 2 will be in miles per minute. This rate must be converted to miles per hour prior to output. Let us now consider the corresponding code (Fig. 2.17).

The total distance to the ballpark is known to be 8 miles. However a symbolic constant represents this distance. This makes the later arithmetic expressions more descriptive and will simplify a subsequent change should the child start playing at a ballpark a different distance from home.

Real variables are used throughout the program. Although the various times may be expressed in integral minutes, the distances and speeds will probably contain fractional parts. In any case, the frequent use of the division operator (/) will generate real values that can be stored only in real variables. Also, it causes no problem if an integer value happens to be read into or assigned to a real variable.

The variables required are all evident from the algorithm. They have descriptive identifiers and a variable dictionary, giving details of their meanings and units of measurement.

Since the program is designed for interactive use, prompt messages are issued before reading each input value. Note that the prompts include the expected units of measure (minutes and miles) to avoid problems with input expressed in the wrong units.

Although not mentioned in the algorithm, an extra output statement is included to tell the parent how much time remains. This information might also prove to be useful during testing. All real numbers are displayed in decimal notation to improve readability, and appropriate units are also shown.

The conversion of the required speed to mph (multiplication by 60) is incorporated inside the final writeln statement. Of course, this conversion could have been done before the writeln statement.

■ Figure 2.17
Calculating time and speed.

The program in Fig. 2.17 contains no syntax errors and will compile correctly—unless some typing mistakes are made while entering it. Once any such errors have been repaired, testing of the program can begin.

```pascal
PROGRAM BallPark (input,output);

    { Calculate time to overtake child
      en route to ball park }

CONST ParkDist = 8.0; {distance to park in miles}

VAR
    ChildSpeed, {miles per min.}
    ElapsedTime, {in minutes}
    TotalTime, {for child to reach park}
    TimeAvailable, {to overtake child}
    CarSpeed, {to overtake child (miles/min)}
    DistanceGone: {by child since leaving home}
                                    real;

BEGIN {BallPark}
    writeln ('Enter elapsed time in minutes');
    read (ElapsedTime);
    writeln ('Enter distance travelled in miles');
    read (DistanceGone);

    {compute child's speed}
    ChildSpeed := DistanceGone / ElapsedTime;
    {compute total time for child to reach park}
    TotalTime := ParkDist / ChildSpeed;
    {compute time available to overtake child}
    TimeAvailable := TotalTime - ElapsedTime;

    writeln (TimeAvailable:5:1,' minutes to catch up');
    {compute required speed to catch up}
    CarSpeed := ParkDist / TimeAvailable;
    writeln ('Drive at',CarSpeed*60:5:1,' mph')
END. {BallPark}
```

Thanks to thorough, systematic algorithm development and careful coding, the program contains no logic errors. The results will be correct if the input values are reasonable. Test data might include a few (two or three) different distances traveled, and for each of these, a few (two or three) different elapsed times.

For any particular distance, increasing the elapsed time implies a slower speed for the child and allows a slower speed for the parent to catch up. Such trends are useful to know when you are attempting to judge whether the test results are reasonable. Note too that a convenient test value for the distance traveled is one-half the total distance (4 miles); the parent's remaining time will then be equal to whatever elapsed time has been used.

If you test this program—as you should—with extreme values for input data, you might receive a surprise. If you supply an elapsed time of 0, the program will abruptly terminate, and a run-time error message will be issued. The problem occurs in the very first assignment statement, where the elapsed time is the denominator in a division operation. Any attempt to divide by 0 will bring any program to a halt. The error occurs at run time, because the actual value of the denominator cannot be known until the program is executed.

Certain other numeric input values will cause premature program termination and some input values will produce ridiculous results. A negative value for either time or distance makes no sense; neither does a distance traveled that is greater than the distance to the ballpark.

When such impossible or anomalous situations are recognized, a warning can be incorporated into the program. One way is to note the limitations in the documentation, that is, in comments. Another is to indicate the reasonable range for input values in the prompt messages. For example, when asking for elapsed time and distance traveled, the respective prompt messages could be generated by

```
writeln ('Enter elapsed time in minutes (time > 0)');
                          .
                          .
                          .
writeln ('Enter distance traveled in miles (0 < distance < ',
         ParkDist:3:1,')');
```

In this last statement, note the use of the symbolic constant between two character string constants. Unless the symbolic constant is redefined, the message that appears will include

```
    . . . (0 < distance < 8.0).
```

EXERCISES

2.1 Identify and explain the errors (if any) in the following statements.

(a) `read (x+y);`   (b) `writeln (x+y);`
(c) `read (X,Y,Z);`   (d) `read (A,B,A);`
(e) `read (X,'Y');`   (f) `writeln (X,'Y',2);`
(g) `Sum := Sum + '1';`   (h) `CONST E := 2.71828;`

2.2 Assuming that J and K are integer variables and P and Q are real variables, what values will be displayed by each of the following sections of code? Be sure to give the exact format.

```
(a) K := 15;
    J := K DIV 2;
    P := K / 2;
    writeln (J:4,P:7:2);
(b) P := 15;
    Q := P / 2 * 2;
    J := round (P / 2) * 2;
    writeln (Q:7:2,J:4);
(c) K := 23;
    Q := 17;
    writeln (sqr(K),sqr(Q));
(d) K := 36;
    Q := 36;
    writeln (sqrt(K),sqrt(Q));
```

2.3 Suppose that the following program reads the values 2, 3, and 4 from the terminal. What values will be displayed?

```
PROGRAM Q3 (input,output);

VAR A,B: real;

BEGIN
  writeln ('enter three values');
  read (A,B,A);
  writeln (A,B,A)
END.
```

2.4 Write a program to read a temperature in degrees *Fahrenheit* and convert it to its equivalent in degrees *Celsius*.

2.5 Write a program to read a temperature in degrees Celsius and convert it to its equivalent in degrees Fahrenheit.

2.6 Write a program to read a measurement in miles and convert it to kilometers. *Note:* 1 km is approximately 0.6214 mi.

2.7 Write a program to read a measurement in meters and convert it to yards. *Note:* 1 yd is approximately 0.9144 m.

2.8 Write a program to:
   (a) Read a value representing the distance in miles traveled by a rocket.
   (b) Read a value representing the number of days taken to travel that distance.
   (c) Compute the speed of the rocket in kilometers per hour (km/h).

2.9   Write a program to read the price of an item (Price) and display the cost to the customer (Cost) as Price plus tax at the rate of 6%. The Cost should be given to 2 decimal places, since it represents dollars and cents.

2.10 Write a program to read the total sales for each of five days and compute and display the average daily sales total.

2.11 Any quadratic equation can be written in the standard form $ax^2 + bx + c = 0$. Assuming that the equation has real solutions, these solutions are given by the formula

$$x = \frac{-b \pm \sqrt{b^2 - 4ac}}{2a} .$$

(a) Write programs to compute the roots of the following equations.
   (i) $x^2 - 9x + 36 = 0$
   (ii) $x^2 - x + 1 = 0$
   (iii) $ax^2 + bx + c = 0$,   where a, b, and c are supplied by the user, so that a real solution exists.

(b) State exactly what conditions must be met by a, b, and c, to guarantee a valid solution in part (a, iii). What conditions make the two roots equal? If a, b, and c are entered on separate lines and are obtained by separate read statements, suggest a prompt message preceding each read statement that would encourage the user to enter values producing a real solution.

2.12 A straight line has the equation $y = ax + b$. Two straight lines intersect at a point if they are not parallel. Consider how to find the $x-y$ coordinates of this intersection point for the two lines given by

$$y = ax + b \quad \text{and} \quad y = cx + d.$$

(a) Write a program to accept values for a, b, c, and d from the user and to calculate the coordinates of the intersection point, assuming that one exists.

(b) Include prompt messages to ensure that the lines will not be parallel. Assume that each equation is specified by a single line of input (containing two values).

2.13 (a) Write a program to accept a value between 0 and 359, interpreted as degrees of arc. Display the equivalent value in radians, as well as the sine, cosine, and tangent of the angle.

(b) Allow the program to accept any nonnegative value as the original angle.

2.14 Write a program to accept any number as input and display its value as the nearest real number with exactly two digits following the decimal point. In addition, display the nearest integer value without any decimal point.

2.15 A common way to specify a date is to supply three separate numbers in the order month, day, year, with a blank as separator (such as 12 25 85).

(a) Suppose the user will always supply two digits for each component of the date, even for a month, day, or year less than 10. Write a program to generate the equivalent metric date, expressed as six consecutive digits, yymmdd (such as 851225).

(b) Comment on the problem of displaying leading 0's when the day or month is less than 10. Write an algorithm (not a program) to handle this problem when the input does not always supply two digits per component, such as 8 2 57.

3

Repetitive and Alternative Execution

Although it would hardly be worth the effort to write a payroll program for one employee, you might consider writing one for 50 or 500 employees. More than the problems we presented earlier, this problem lies in the realm of the computer; one of the computer's great strengths is its ability to repeat some task over and over.

Recall how the algorithms in Chapter 1 involved repeating some basic process, such as adding a number to a total or inspecting a ballot. Many programs perform relatively simple calculations but repeat them again and again. We say that the basic process is subject to **repetitive execution.** In this chapter we introduce some of the features in Pascal that will enable you to program repetitive algorithms.

repetitive execution

Most realistic programs also handle different situations in different ways. They must recognize when specific situations apply and be able to select the code to carry out the appropriate action. The code chosen to calculate the next loan payment depends on whether it is the first, the final, or some other payment. The way a ballot is marked determines which candidate (if any) gets credit for the vote. Selecting one action from a set of alternatives is called **alternative,** or conditional, **execution.** We also discuss the techniques for coding alternative actions in this chapter.

alternative execution

The need to know when to stop the repetitions requires the ability to ask whether all the ballots have been counted or the bank debt has been paid in full. Other questions are posed to decide how to handle each individual payment or ballot. Such questions are expressed in a program as assertions, whose truth or falsehood determines the course of events. These assertions, called **conditions,** govern both repetitive and alternative execution. Therefore the first topic we consider in this chapter is the expression of conditions in Pascal.

conditions

With more powerful programming tools at our disposal, we will be able to solve far more interesting and useful problems. But as problem complexity increases, so do the number of possible solution approaches and the number of opportunities for error. The need for careful program development and thorough testing becomes much more important in this context. We will deal with these issues in the final portion of this chapter.

3.1 Boolean Expressions

relational operator

One way to express a condition in Pascal involves comparing two values. For example, you could ask whether your current debt is greater than zero. The phrase *is greater than* is an example of a **relational operator** and describes the way in which the two numbers current debt and 0 are being compared.

Relational Operators and Simple Boolean Expressions

There are several other relational operators. For example, you could ask whether your current debt *is equal to* 0, or whether it *is less than or equal to* 500 dollars. Pascal uses special symbols to represent its relational operators, as shown in Fig. 3.1. If the amount of debt is recorded in a variable named Debt, the expression Debt > 0 in the proper context indicates whether your debt is greater than zero or not.

Note the similarity between the symbols used in Pascal and those used in mathematics. The least familiar symbol may be < >, which means *is not equal to*. This operator is made up of the < and > characters without any intervening blank. (The operators <= and >= are also comprised of two adjacent characters.)

boolean expression

Comparison of two values, such as Debt > 0 is called a simple **boolean expression** (in honor of George Boole, the father of logical calculus). Like anything described as *boolean,* this expression has only one of two possible values: true or false. At any one time, either your current debt is greater than

■ Figure 3.1
Basic relational
operators in Pascal.

Pascal Symbol	Mathematical Symbol	Meaning
=	=	Is equal to
< >	≠	Is not equal to
<	<	Is less than
>	>	Is greater than
< =	≤	Is less than or equal to
> =	≥	Is greater than or equal to

■ Figure 3.2
Values for some
boolean expressions.

Variable	Value
I	3
J	4
K	5
Boolean Expression	Value
I <> J	true
I <= K	true
J > 6	false
K >= 5	true
9 < J	false
I = J − 2	false
(2 * J) = (I + K)	true

0 or it isn't. No third alternative, no "maybe true," exists. The proposition that 35 is less than 27, written $35 < 27$, is either true or false. (This boolean expression happens to be permanently false.)

The relational operators are all binary and have the form

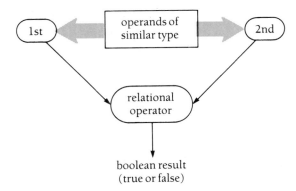

boolean result
(true or false)

The true or false value of the boolean expression itself may be quite different from the two other values being compared. You should verify that the boolean expressions shown in Fig. 3.2 do indeed have the values shown (at least while the variables involved have the values shown for them).

What makes boolean expressions useful in Pascal is their ability to compare the *current* values of variables or expressions during execution. Their outcomes can be used to control the action within a program. As long as your debt really is greater than 0, you must keep making payments. Once the debt becomes less than or equal to 0, you may cease paying. In

other words, payments should continue as long as the boolean expression
Debt > 0 remains true. Once it becomes false, the payments should stop.

Although we have used integers in our examples so far, any two simple
values can be compared, provided they have the same data type. Again, a
concession allows relational operators to compare real and integer values.
The following four boolean expressions all have the value "true."

$$6.7315 < 6.7342 \qquad -124.2 < 0.003 \qquad 7 = 7.0 \qquad 14.95 < 15$$

Note that any negative value is less than any positive value. Also, the fact
that $7 = 7.0$ is true implies only that their signs are the same and that their
magnitudes are numerically equal; they still belong to different data types
and are still represented differently inside the machine.

Comparing characters

The relational operators can also be used to compare two items of
character-type data. Hence, when the character variable Letter contains a
question mark, the boolean expression Letter = '?' will be true; otherwise it
will be false.

Another boolean expression that is always true whenever both uppercase
and lowercase letters are available is 'A' <> 'a'. When used as data within a
program, the uppercase and lowercase versions of the same letter are two
distinct characters and are therefore never equal.

Even when two characters are not the same, they may still have a particular
relationship similar to alphabetic ordering. It is true that 'A' < 'B' because 'A'
occurs prior to 'B' in every Pascal internal ordering. You can test whether a
lowercase letter lies beyond 'm' in the alphabet by asking whether

SmallLetter > 'm'

or, equivalently,

SmallLetter >= 'n'

When both characters being compared are digits ('0' through '9'), the
relational operators indicate the normal numeric ordering. Thus '4' <= '6' is
true.

collating sequence

Any two characters—even punctuation marks and nonprintable characters—may be compared using relational operators. All characters belong
somewhere in an ordering called the **collating sequence,** and the relational
operators test the relative positions of the characters in this sequence.

Unfortunately, the collating sequence may be different on different
machines. It is always true that all uppercase letters are ordered alphabetically,
all lowercase letters are ordered alphabetically, and all numeric characters are
ordered numerically. Therefore the expected ordering exists *inside* these three
groups, i.e.,

'A' < 'B' < · · · < 'Z'
'a' < 'b' < · · · < 'z'
'0' < '1' < · · · < '9'

However, the relative ordering among these three groups depends entirely on the machine. On some machines it is true that 'A' < 'a'; on others this is false. You have to be careful when comparing a character from one of these groups with a character from another group.

ASCII code

We ran the programs in this book on machines using the **ASCII code** (American Standard Code for Information Interchange). In this code numeric characters are less than—that is, come before—uppercase letters, which in turn are less than lowercase letters. Punctuation and other characters are interspersed here and there. We provide complete collating sequences for the most common series of computers in Appendix C. To determine the proper order for your computer, ask your instructor or consult your user's manual.

Recall that character data and other data types do not mix in Pascal. It makes no sense—in fact, it is an error—to try to make a comparison like

> '5' = 5   {an error}

Numeric values can be compared only with other numeric values, and characters must be compared with other characters. It is also an error to compare a character with a (longer) character string. For example, it would be wrong to ask whether

> '2' < '385'   {an error}

(As you will see later, two character strings can be compared but only if they have *exactly the same length*.)

Incidentally, the relational operators can also compare two boolean values. For example, we could ask whether two numbers have the same signs by writing

> (X >= 0) = (Y >= 0)

When both numbers are positive (both assertions true) or when both numbers are negative (both assertions false), the overall result is true because the two assertions are the same.

Boolean Operators and Compound Boolean Expressions

boolean operators

Often we need to express a condition involving more than two quantities or involving a relationship more complex than simple equality or ordering. For these occasions Pascal provides three **boolean operators** (AND, OR, and NOT) to generate more complex boolean expressions. Although their use in Pascal parallels their use in ordinary English, all three operators require true/false operands and produce true/false results. Their operands are often simple boolean expressions. The boolean operators combine these simple expressions into a compound boolean expression.

For example, we could ask whether X and Y are both positive by writing

> (X >= 0) AND (Y >= 0)

AND operator

*The **AND operator** has a value of true only when both of its operands are true.* If either X or Y or both were negative, at least one of the simple comparisons would be false, making the entire expression false.

The AND operator is often used to combine two (or more) conditions that must *all* be true in order for a particular action to occur. For example, some event may occur only when X is within a particular range of values. Being in a range requires that X be simultaneously above one limit and below another. We can test by asking whether

$$(X >= \text{LowerLimit}) \text{ AND } (X <= \text{UpperLimit})$$

This test will fail if X is either too small or too large. If X must also differ from 0 as well as fall within the prescribed range, we could write

$$(X >= \text{LowerLimit}) \text{ AND } (X <= \text{UpperLimit}) \text{ AND } (X <> 0)$$

On the other hand, it may be when X is *outside* the range that special action is required. We can test this with

$$(X < \text{LowerLimit}) \text{ OR } (X > \text{UpperLimit})$$

OR operator

*The **OR operator** has a true value if either (or both) of its operands are true.* If X is either too small or too large, this expression becomes true because either the condition (X < LowerLimit) or the condition (X > UpperLimit) becomes true. The AND operator would be completely inappropriate in this situation, since these two conditions will never both be true, assuming that UpperLimit is at least as large as LowerLimit.

The OR operator is often used to combine conditions when any *one* of them is sufficient to cause a particular action. For instance, a bank could require that payments be made until the borrower became too old or too poor, or the debt was paid. We can express this situation by

$$(\text{Age} > 100) \text{ OR } (\text{Assets} < 200) \text{ OR } (\text{Debt} <= 0)$$

NOT operator

*The **NOT operator** is unary and has the effect of reversing the true/false value of its operand.* If (Temp > 20) happens to be false, the expression

$$\text{NOT } (\text{Temp} > 20)$$

will have the opposite value, namely, true. In the domain of boolean expressions, NOT is similar to negation (unary minus) in arithmetic expressions. The NOT operator is written to the left of its operand. It does not force an expression to become false; instead it yields the true/false value opposite to that possessed by its operand, just as the arithmetic negation operator reverses the sign.

We can ask whether X and Y differ in either of these two equivalent ways:

$$X <> Y \qquad \text{or else} \qquad \text{NOT } (X = Y)$$

Sometimes it is helpful to read NOT as *It is not the case that.* . . .

Operands			Operands			Operand	NOT
1st	2nd	AND	1st	2nd	OR		
F	F	F	F	F	F	F	T
F	T	F	F	T	T	T	F
T	F	F	T	F	T		
T	T	T	T	T	T		

■ Figure 3.3
The boolean operators.

truth table

The action of the three boolean operators is shown in the truth tables in Fig. 3.3. A **truth table** indicates how a boolean operator responds to every combination of operand values. Since each operand can have only two values (true or false), the number of different combinations is small enough to be listed completely.

Boolean, relational, and arithmetic operators can all appear in the same expression. For example, it is perfectly valid to ask whether it is true that

$$((X * 2 > Y - 3) \text{ OR } (X > Y - 1)) \text{ AND } (Y > 5)$$

Thanks to a generous use of parentheses, we can be fairly sure of what is being tested. Figure 3.4 shows the data flow within this complex condition. Without any parentheses, this expression would (1) confuse the reader; (2) associate the components in a different way; and (3) fail to compile for attempting to combine or compare items of different types.

Parentheses are always recommended and often required in boolean expressions, both for readability and because, in their absence, Pascal tends to group things differently from what we might expect. Parentheses are usually needed to guarantee a correct interpretation.

When parentheses are missing, the precedence rules determine the order of evaluation. The operators that we have used so far have the following precedence.

```
NOT                              (highest)
AND * / DIV MOD                     .
OR + -                              .
 =  <>  <  >  <=  >=           (lowest)
```

Note that AND is considered multiplicative, and OR is considered additive; NOT is in a class by itself and is applied before any other operator. As usual, operators of equal precedence are evaluated from left to right as they appear in an expression, and parentheses may override any of these rules.

■ Figure 3.4
Analysis of a complex
boolean expression.

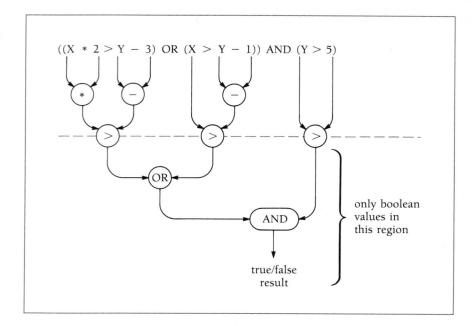

3.2 Repetitive Execution with the WHILE Statement

Repeating a group of instructions is a common feature of algorithms and programs. Thus one of the most important statements in Pascal is WHILE, which governs such repetitive actions. This is the only statement encountered so far that can divert the flow of control at execution time from its conventional sequential course to some other group of instructions.

Introducing the WHILE Statement

WHILE statement

The **WHILE statement** causes the computer to repeatedly execute a subsequent statement as long as some condition remains true. The general form of WHILE is written:

        WHILE ⟨condition⟩ DO
            ⟨statement⟩

For example, the construction

        WHILE 7 < 10 DO
            writeln ('Hello');

in which the condition $7 < 10$ is permanently true, would continue writing Hello on separate lines until forcibly stopped by the user or the system.

Such *runaway* programs are clearly undesirable. In order to make such repetitions stop, two things are required. First, the condition must be capable of becoming false; it usually contains some variables whose values may change. Second, the ⟨statement⟩ must be able to change these values, causing the condition to actually become false. An example of code having these two properties is

```
X : = 0 ;
WHILE  X < 3  DO
    X : = X + 1 ;
```

When control first reaches the WHILE statement, the condition $X < 3$ will be true. Therefore WHILE will start repeated execution of the following assignment statement. After each execution, the value of X will be 1 greater than before, and the condition will be reevaluated to determine whether it remains true. After the third execution, the value of X will be 3, the condition $X < 3$ will then be false, and the repetition will stop. Unfortunately, this code accomplishes little and wastes time.

In practice, we usually want to repeat more than one statement at a time (that is, a group of statements). If it were possible to repeatedly *both* write Hello *and* increment X until X reached 3, then we would have a program to write Hello three times.

You identify such a group of statements by enclosing them between the reserved words BEGIN and END, which act rather like giant parentheses. This construction is a **compound statement,** and we normally write it as

compound statement

```
BEGIN
    ⟨statement⟩;
    ⟨statement⟩;
        .
        .
        .
    ⟨statement⟩;
    ⟨statement⟩
END
```

The interior statements execute in the order in which they appear. Semicolons are used to separate the constituent statements from each other. (No semicolon is needed between the last statement and END.)

At the outer level a compound statement acts like a single, ordinary statement, even though its execution may involve executing a whole sequence of interior statements. You can use a compound statement anywhere an individual statement can occur.

When the compound statement is combined with WHILE, we get the following construction:

WHILE ⟨condition⟩ DO

   BEGIN
     ·
     ·   (sequence of statements to
     ·   be repeated while the
     ·   condition remains true)
     ·
   END

In Fig. 3.5(a), we used this pattern to write Hello three times, as suggested earlier. We unravelled the flow of control through this code and depicted it in Fig. 3.5(b).

Execution of the WHILE statement proceeds as follows: When flow of control arrives, the condition is first evaluated; if its value is true, the entire (compound) statement following DO is executed; then control transfers back to the WHILE statement. The entire process, including testing of the condition and execution of the (compound) statement, is then repeated and will continue to be repeated as long as the condition is found to be true at each testing. Presumably, some execution of the (compound) statement will make the

▶

The WHILE Statement

WHILE ⟨condition⟩ DO
  ⟨statement⟩

The rules associated with the WHILE statement are

1. There is only one way in and one way out of the loop. In fact the WHILE statement itself serves as both entry point and exit point.
2. The condition is tested before and after every execution of the loop (including the first and last).
3. If the condition is false when WHILE is first encountered, the statement following DO is never executed.
4. If control does flow into the loop, it will remain in this loop as long as the condition remains true.
5. Something within the loop must therefore modify the value of the condition in order to stop the repetitions.
6. If the condition should become false while control is within the loop, this situation is not recognized by the WHILE statement until control has returned to it in the normal way.

```
HowOften := 0;
WHILE HowOften < 3 DO
  BEGIN
    HowOften := HowOften + 1;
    writeln ('Hello')
  END;
writeln ('Goodbye');
```

Output from
Program

Hello
Hello
Hello
Goodbye

(a) **Program fragment to illustrate WHILE statement.**

Operation	Value of HowOften	Value of Condition	
initial assignment	0	true	
test condition	0	true	
increment HowOften	1	true	
writeln ('Hello')	1	true	
test condition	1	true	When
increment HowOften	2	true	condition
writeln ('Hello')	2	true	is tested
test condition	2	true	
increment HowOften	3	false	
writeln ('Hello')	3	false	
test condition	3	false	
writeln ('Goodbye')			

(b) **Execution of program fragment.**

■ Figure 3.5
An example of WHILE with a compound statement.

condition false. On the next execution of the WHILE statement, the false condition value will be detected, and the entire WHILE construct finishes its execution. This causes the (compound) statement to be bypassed and the subsequent statement to begin its execution.

flowchart

This process is shown in Fig. 3.6. Such a diagram is called a **flowchart** because it depicts the flow of control among statements or components of a program. The WHILE statement causes the flow of control to cycle through

loop

a loop. The term **loop** is frequently used with any construct that causes the computer to execute instructions repetitively. The execution of the loop interior does not stop the instant the condition becomes false. Control must reach the end of the (compound) statement and go back to the WHILE before the change in condition can be recognized.

■ Figure 3.6
Flowchart of the
WHILE statement.

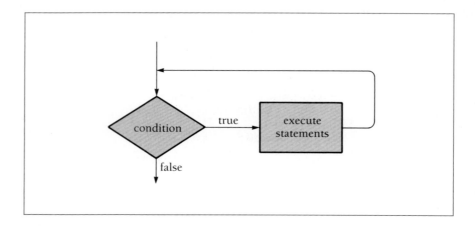

An Example Using WHILE with a Counter

Counters   Suppose that you make 50 stock transactions every day. The net dollar profit and loss on each transaction is recorded by a signed integer (a positive integer for profit, negative for loss). Thus you want a program that will compute the net profit for one day, by adding together the 50 signed integers. You might first try the algorithm:

1. obtain 50 values;
2. add these 50 values together;
3. display the result;
4. stop.

Although technically correct, this algorithm requires all 50 values to be available between steps 1 and 2. The corresponding program would therefore require at least 50 different variables and contain either very long or very many statements.

A much neater approach is to recognize that the same simple process is being repeated 50 times. A single application of this process involves (1) obtaining a value for a transaction; and (2) adding this value to a total. The resulting algorithm is

1.   initialize the total to 0;
2.   do (the remainder of level 2) 50 times;
2.1   obtain a value for one transaction;
2.2   add this value to the total;
3.   display the total;
4.   stop.

Note that you must give the total its proper starting value explicitly in step 1, so that it will have a value of zero when the first legitimate data value is to be added to it.

This second algorithm still requires some refinement to keep track of the repetitions. One method is to maintain a count of how many values have been processed so far. This count would be initialized to 0 to reflect the fact that no values have been obtained before the processing begins. After processing each value, the count is increased by one. The processing would then continue as long as the count remained less than 50 and stop after a count of 50 is attained. This strategy yields the algorithm shown in Fig. 3.7(a) and the program in Fig. 3.7(b).

Remember to use the BEGIN . . . END construction to identify which statements are to be repeated. Without a compound statement, the code may appear syntactically correct and thus be compiled without an error. However, in the absence of BEGIN . . . END only the one statement immediately after DO would be repeated at execution time. And that statement would be repeated (almost) forever because the only statement capable of changing the WHILE condition would not be encountered.

Even with a compound statement, if you forget to increment the count, the program might continue in the loop forever. Here, however, it would pause after the fifty-first printing of the prompt because the user would have run out of data. When a repetitive program appears to do nothing, it may be repeating endlessly. The first things to check are missing BEGIN and END statements and a missing increment statement.

Initializing counters   All counters in a program must be set to some initial value, usually 0 or 1. The decision to initialize the counter to 0 or to 1 often depends on the answer to the question: Do you want to count the things you have done successfully or the things you are going to do? *If you want to count completions, you must initialize the counter to 0,* since in the beginning you have done nothing (as in Fig. 3.7).

On the other hand, *if you prefer to let the count indicate which transaction is about to be processed, you should initialize the count to 1,* since you presumably start with transaction number 1. You still want to include the fiftieth value, so you do not want to stop the repetitions when the count reaches 50. Rather, you want to continue repetitions for every value of the count less than *or equal to* 50 (or if you prefer, less than 51). Thus, when you use a counter to control a WHILE loop, you must consider at least three factors: (1) the initial value; (2) the final value; and (3) the relational operator used to test for termination.

We could have included additional criteria for halting the tally of gains and losses in the original problem. Suppose that you cannot face knowing about net losses in excess of $5000. Regardless of the number of transactions processed, you decide to stop whenever the net amount drops below -5000.

When using WHILE, you must indicate the conditions for continuity— not those for stopping. In this case, processing should continue as long as two conditions are both met:

1.   the number of stocks processed is still less than 50 *and*
2.   the Total so far is still at or above -5000.

1.1 initialize total to 0;
1.2 initialize count to 0;
2.   while count < 50 do (remainder of level 2);
2.1   obtain a value for one transaction;
2.2   add this value to total;
2.3   increase count by 1;
3.   display total;
4.   stop.

(a) Algorithm to add 50 values.

```
PROGRAM Add50 (input,output);

   {program to add 50 integer values}

VAR
   Total,     {running total of 50 values}
   HowMany,   {no. of values processed so far}
   OneValue: {current value to be processed}
            integer;

BEGIN {Add50}
   Total := 0;
   HowMany := 0;

   WHILE HowMany < 50 DO
      BEGIN
         writeln ('Enter profit or loss value:');
         read (OneValue);
         Total := Total + OneValue;
         HowMany := HowMany + 1
      END;

   writeln ('Net profit : ',Total)
END. {Add50}
```

(b) Program to implement the algorithm.

■ Figure 3.7
An example of the use of WHILE.

English, like Pascal, uses AND to connect conditions that must hold together. The conditions for continuing can be expressed with either of the following equivalent forms, assuming both variables start out at 0.

```
WHILE (HowMany < 50) AND (Total >= -5000) DO
  . . .

WHILE (HowMany < 50) AND NOT (Total < -5000) DO
  . . .
```

A Biological Modeling Example

To illustrate another sort of repetitive process, we will look at a simple model of the growth of some primitive, fictional creatures called "munchies." Munchies live a simple life: They feed until they are full and then they split in two, doubling the population. The munchies' sole diet is a crop called "varmint grass," whose growth rate is negligible compared to the appetite and reproduction rate of the munchies. Each colony of munchies invades a stand of varmint grass and remains there, feeding and reproducing, until the food supply has been exhausted; then they move on to greener pastures.

We will develop a computer model to investigate the number of generations of munchies that will be produced for any given quantity of varmint grass. The model will enable students of "munchie dynamics" to investigate growth patterns under various combinations of food supply, appetite, and starting population. The main output from the model will be the number of generations that can be sustained under the particular starting conditions.

An important thing to notice is that each generation does the same thing; munchie life is a repetitive process—at least while food supplies last. Also since the number of generations is the desired result, we must initialize, maintain, and finally display the value of a generation counter. Without our worrying yet about the dreary details of munchie life, these observations give rise to the following overall algorithm:

1. obtain starting values for food supply, population, and appetite;
2. initialize generation counter to 1;
3. while food supply lasts do the following:
3.1   simulate one generation of munchie life;
3.2   add 1 to the generation count;
4. display the result—generation count;
5. stop.

Here the repetitions are controlled by the remaining food supply rather than by a counter. The number of repetitions is not known in advance; the role of the counter is to record rather than to control the number of generations. A generation counter must still be initialized before the loop and be incremented inside the loop, but it will not be involved in the (WHILE) condition controlling the loop. Furthermore, this counter begins with a value of 1, since there will always be at least one generation, even if it turns out to be the last.

Step 3.1 still requires refinement. A generation of munchie life is a two-phase affair. The munchies first consume varmint grass. The net effect of this phase is to reduce the remaining food supply by the number of munchies times the appetite of each. Next, they split in two, doubling the number of munchies for the next generation. Knowing the current food supply, population, and appetite at the start of a generation enables us to calculate the food supply and population at the end; the individual appetite remains the same.

Now consider the condition for controlling repetitions. An apparent choice would be to continue the life cycle while the food supply remains greater than 0 (Food > 0). However, this supply, though positive, could be too small to feed even a single munchie. In this case, the generation count would be incremented even though no reproduction could occur in a "realistic" situation.

Another choice would be to demand sufficient food to satisfy all the munchies (Food >= Munchies * Appetite). Even if all the munchies were 99% full, no reproduction would occur in a democratic munchie society. On the other hand, this condition seems a bit severe and the democratic assumption unrealistic.

More likely some "munching order" exists in which the "fittest" munchies will eat to capacity and reproduce, even if not all the others are able to do so. As long as some members are produced for the next generation, it seems fair to increase the generation count. If the munching order is rigorous, then all we need is sufficient food to feed just one munchie (Food >= Appetite).

We use this third alternative in the following algorithm:

1. obtain starting values for Food, Appetite, Munchies;
2. Generations := 1;
3. while Food >= Appetite do:
3.1   Food := Food − Munchies * Appetite; {feed}
3.2   Munchies := Munchies * 2; {reproduce}
3.3   Generations := Generations + 1;
4. display Generations;
5. stop.

Of course, there are valid arguments for, and objections to, each of these alternatives. There are also many other alternative stopping conditions not discussed here. The important thing is to know precisely what assumptions are being made so you can properly assess the program's results and the correspondence between your model and reality.

Notice that even though the generation count may be correct, the final values for the food supply and number of munchies may not be. A more refined model that avoids these problems will be developed later. Of course, these (possibly) erroneous numbers are of no interest for the time being. Our objective was to determine the generation count, and that we have done.

We can now translate our algorithm into Pascal once we have decided on the data types for our variables. The number of munchies and generations are clearly of type integer. We can also use integers for both the food supply and the appetite of one munchie simply by assuming small enough units. These decisions allow us to write the program in Fig. 3.8.

```pascal
PROGRAM Munchie1 (input,output);

    {Simulating munchie growth under
     varying conditions}

VAR
    Generations,
    Munchies,              {number of munchies}
    Food,                  {units of food available}
    Appetite: integer; {units of food consumed by
                            one munchie at a feeding}

BEGIN {Munchie1}
    write ('Enter initial amount of varmint grass:');
    read (Food);
    write ('How much grass eaten by one munchie?');
    read (Appetite);
    write ('Enter initial number of munchies:');
    read (Munchies);
    Generations := 1;

    WHILE Food >=Appetite DO
        BEGIN {generation cycle}
            Food := Food - Munchies * Appetite; {eat}
            Munchies := Munchies * 2; {reproduce}
            Generations := Generations + 1
        END; {cycle}

    writeln (Generations,' generations sustained')
END. {Munchie1}
```

■ Figure 3.8
An elementary biological model.

3.3 Using Sentinels to Control Input

The program in Fig. 3.7(b) reads and processes 50 stock transactions using an application of the following general algorithm:

initialize count to 0;
while count < number of data values do:
    read next value;
    process that value
    increment count;

The major shortcoming of this algorithm is its need to know the number of input values in advance. We can make such algorithms more general by allowing them to process values as long as there are still values to be processed. In other words, the number of repetitions should not be governed by a counter that approaches a preset limit but, instead, should continue as long as data remain to be processed.

One approach is to have the program recognize the *last* value in the input stream and stop subsequent looping when the last value shows up. Unfortunately, the final data value may be unrecognizable; frequently, there is nothing unique about it.

However, we can often include a special, recognizable *extra* value at the end of all the legitimate values. An extra value used in this way is called a

sentinel   **sentinel.** Its role is analogous to that of the period at the end of a sentence, which conveys no information other than to announce the end of the sentence. The program keeps testing to determine whether the sentinel value has been encountered and, until it is discovered, keeps on reading and processing. When the sentinel does show up, it merely signals the end of the data; it is *not* processed as data.

Use of a sentinel requires that we restructure our basic algorithm. At first sight the following general form looks plausible.

{WARNING: this structure does not work correctly}

while current "value" is not the sentinel do:
    read a "value";
    process the "value";

However, there are two drawbacks to this approach. When control first reaches the WHILE statement, no *value* is available for comparison with the sentinel because no value has been read. It is not clear whether the loop can even be entered or whether the program will continue to execute. When the last legitimate data value has been read and processed, the loop is executed again because no sentinel value has been read. During this (full) execution, the sentinel value is first read and then processed as if it were ordinary data—

which it definitely is not. A sentinel *must not be processed,* lest it corrupt the values computed from legitimate data.

The Basic Sentinel Structure

The solution to these problems lies in the special input structure:

read first value;
while value <> sentinel do:
    process previously obtained value;
    read a new value;

To see how this structure works, let's apply it to an input stream containing two regular data values A and B, followed by a sentinel value denoted by S. The complete input stream is therefore:

ABS

The resulting sequence of actions is

Action	Value read	Value processed	Condition: value <> sentinel
Read	A		
Test condition			true
Process		A	
Read	B		
Test condition			true
Process		B	
Read	S		
Test condition			false
Continue beyond			

Note that the sentinel is not processed, because it is read at the end of the loop, immediately before testing the condition that terminates the loop. Although the first value is read before entering the loop, it is processed immediately upon entering with no intervening input. Values other than the first or the sentinel are read at the end of one loop execution and processed at the beginning of the next. The sequence of reading and processing will therefore be correct.

This standard structure should be used whenever a sentinel signals the end of the input data. This structure will process an arbitrary number of data values, including the case where there are no values and only the sentinel appears.

The only problem remaining is to choose an actual value for the sentinel. In rare situations the programmer knows nothing about the permissible data values. In these cases a different termination technique is advisable, since any choice of value for the sentinel could occur within the data and prematurely terminate processing.

Choosing a sentinel value

     Fortunately, the programmer is usually aware of the range of possible values the program is required to manipulate. For example, if the program reads and processes integers representing student identification numbers, you know that all such numbers are greater than zero. Any negative value or zero itself would make a suitable sentinel. If the program is processing the ages of people, you can reasonably assume that all values will fall in the range of 0 to 120. Choosing any negative number or a large positive number would be safe. There are three requirements for the sentinel value:

1. The sentinel value must be unique; that is, it must be easily distinguishable from other data.
2. The sentinel must be of the same type as the true data values, so that either can be read by the same input statement.
3. The value actually used to terminate the input data must be the same value expected by the program.

Interactive programs expecting a sentinel should include a prompt to make sure that the user eventually supplies a sentinel value and that this value is the one expected.

     The clearest way of specifying a sentinel value within a program is to define it as a symbolic constant. After all, its value must not change during the program, and by calling it something sensible, like Sentinel, we make the basic input loop more readable.

A Character Counting Example

     When processing text you rarely know how much data will be encountered. A string of text may be a character, a word, a sentence—even a book.

     Let's confine this example to reading a single sentence and counting the number of characters. For now we will define a sentence as any character string that ends with a period. That is, we specifically exclude sentences ending with a question mark or exclamation point. We also consider everything preceding the period to be a character, regardless of whether it is a letter, digit, punctuation mark, or blank. The period is not to be included in the count of characters and thus serves as a sentinel. We can write the solution directly in the general form:

1.   count := 0;
2.   read first character;
3.   while character <> period do:
3.1   count := count + 1;
3.2   read next character;
4.   display count;
5.   stop.

     Note the initialization, repetitive updating, and final display of the count. In fact, processing the next character consists only of updating a counter to

record that another character was encountered. The program will need only
two variables: (1) an integer variable to maintain a count of the characters
read; and (2) another of type char to receive each character as we read it.
These considerations, when combined with the algorithm, lead to the program
shown in Fig. 3.9. Note that the prompt to the user specifies that the sentence
must end with a period. Also note that defining the sentinel as a symbolic
constant clearly reveals how the loop is controlled.

One problem in practice is that the period may not be sufficiently unique
for use as a sentinel. The first occurrence of any period would halt the loop.
This means that no periods would be allowed in the interior of a sentence,
precluding abbreviations, real numbers, and similar uses of the period.

Incidentally, if sentences were allowed to end with a period, question
mark, or exclamation point, the loop control condition in Fig. 3.9 would
have been

```
WHILE (Symbol <> '.') AND (Symbol <> '?')
    AND (Symbol <> '!') DO . . .
```

```
PROGRAM Sentence1 (input,output);

    { Counting the number of characters in
      a sentence which ends with a period.}

CONST Period = '.';

VAR
    CharCount: integer; {characters in the sentence}
    Symbol: char;        {current character in sentence}

BEGIN {Sentence1}
    CharCount := 0;
    writeln ('Enter sentence ending with a period.');
    read (Symbol);

    WHILE Symbol <> Period DO
        BEGIN
            CharCount := CharCount + 1;
            read (Symbol)
        END;

    writeln (CharCount,' characters read')
END. {Sentence1}
```

■ Figure 3.9
Counting characters.

Whenever Symbol becomes equal to one of the three termination characters, precisely *one* of the inequalities becomes false. The AND operator thus makes the entire expression false, and the repetition will cease. You must resist the temptation to use the OR operator because at least two of the simple inequalities will always be true.

Calculating Averages

Consider the problem of finding the average of an arbitrary number of values. The words *arbitrary number* immediately suggest the standard sentinel structure for the input process.

We obtain the average by summing the input values and dividing by the number of values read. This implies the need to maintain both a running total and an item count, both of which must be set to 0 before encountering the data. For each input value we need to add the value into a running total *and* update the count of values processed so far. When these two actions are inserted into the standard structure, we have the algorithm:

1. set total and count to 0;
2. read first value;
3. while value <> sentinel do:
3.1   total := total + value;
3.2   count := count + 1;
3.3   read next value;
4. average := total / count;
5. display average;
6. stop.

A Nested Loop to Process Two-Level Input

We now combine the concepts from the two preceding sections in order to find the average length of an arbitrary number of sentences, each of which ends with a period. We will also display the length of each individual sentence.

To begin, consider only the input process in isolation from the required calculations. Scanning an arbitrary number of sentences suggests a sentinel structure, as usual. However, reading an entire sentence is not a primitive operation. Since only one character can be read at a time, the sentinel can be a single character. (We chose the symbol # because it seems sufficiently unusual.) Only one character beyond the end of a sentence needs to be read to determine whether another sentence has begun or the input has terminated. This leads to the overall sentence-level process, shown in Fig. 3.10(a).

One step in this algorithm is to read a sentence. We have already discussed input of a single sentence using the sentinel structure shown in Fig. 3.10(b). This entire structure *almost* matches the box labeled "read and process one

■ Figure 3.10
Pseudocode to
process several
sentences.

read 1st character of 1st sentence
WHILE current character <> Sentinel (#) DO
  BEGIN

        read and
        process one sentence

    read 1st character of next sentence
  END

(a) Structure for processing a sequence of sentences.

read 1st character of sentence
WHILE current character <> period (.) DO
  BEGIN

        process one character

    read next character
  END

**(b) Structure for processing one sentence as a sequence
      of characters.**

read 1st character of 1st sentence
WHILE current character <> sentinel (#) DO
  BEGIN

        .
        .
        .

    WHILE current character <> period DO
      BEGIN

            process one character

        read next character
      END;
        .
        .
        .

    read 1st character of next sentence
  END;

(c) Combined structure for processing several sentences.

sentence" in the overall procedure. The only part of Fig. 3.10(b) that would not transfer is the very first line:

read 1st character of sentence

because the first character is already provided by the outer control structure due to its need to detect the sentinel. When we place the details from Fig. 3.10(b)—without this first line—in the box of Fig. 3.10(a), we get the combined structure shown in Fig. 3.10(c). Here the boxes represent "processing one sentence" and "processing one character." The dots in the figure indicate that processing a sentence may include other actions to prepare for, and analyze the results of, scanning a sentence.

Although the input is physically just one stream of characters, our need to identify sentences within it led to a two-level view: (1) at the higher level we see only a sequence of sentences ending with #, and (2) at the lower level we seen an individual sentence comprised of characters ending with a period. The resulting structure of Fig. 3.10(c) reflects this two-level view of input.

nested loops   Such structures are called **nested loops** because the *outer loop* that governs the overall process contains a step that is implemented by a loop of its own, called the *inner loop*. The code in the inner loop would usually be executed several times for *each* execution of the outer loop. The general structure of nested loops is shown in Fig. 3.11.

Whenever a problem imposes a multilevel view of input, a nested loop structure often emerges in both the algorithm and the processing program. If

■ Figure 3.11
General nested loop
structure.

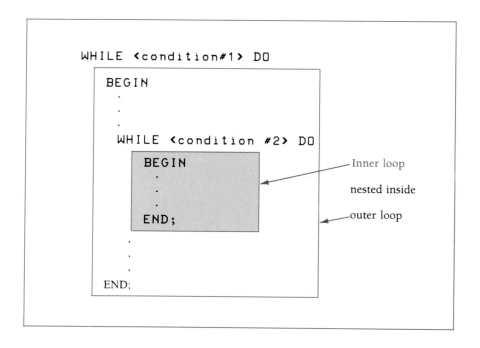

■ Figure 3.12
Top-down
development of
algorithm to compute
average length of
several sentences.

1. set total length and sentence count to 0:
2. while sentences remain do:

2.1   process next sentence

2.2   add its length to total length;
2.3   increment sentence count;
3.   average := total length / sentence count;
4.   display average;
5.   stop.

(a) Finding the average length of several sentences.

{assume first character already read}
1.   set current length to 0;
2.   while interior characters remain do:
2.1   increment current length;
2.2   read next character;
3.   display current length;

(b) Finding the length of a single sentence.

set total length and sentence count to 0;
read first character;
while sentences remain do:
    set current length to 0;
    while interior characters remain do:
        increment current length;
        read next character;
    display current length;
    add its length to total length;
    increment sentence count;
average := total length / sentence count;
display average;
stop.

(c)   Details of finding average length of several sentences.

you develop the algorithm carefully in a top-down fashion, the levels of looping will appear quite naturally.

Now let's put aside the input structure and focus on the other part of the problem: finding the average sentence length. As you saw in the preceding section, finding an average requires updating an item count and a running total for each value included in the average. The major difference here is that the values are not read directly from a terminal; they result from processing entire sentences. The general process is shown in Fig. 3.12(a).

```
PROGRAM Sentences (input,output);

   { Computing the average length of several
     sentences. }
CONST
   Sentinel = '#';  {terminator of all sentences}
   Period = '.';    {terminator of a single sentence}
VAR
   NextChar: char; {current character in input}
   GrandTotal,     {of characters in all sentences}
   CurrentLength,  {characters in current sentence}
   SentenceCount: integer; {number of sentences}
   Average: real;

BEGIN {Sentences}
   GrandTotal := 0;
   SentenceCount := 0;
   writeln ('Enter any number of sentences.');
   writeln ('End each with a period. Put a #');
   writeln ('IMMEDIATELY after the final period.');
   read (NextChar); {first character}

   WHILE NextChar <> Sentinel DO
      BEGIN {sentences}
         CurrentLength := 0;

         WHILE NextChar <> Period DO
            BEGIN {characters}
               CurrentLength := CurrentLength + 1;
               read (NextChar)
            END; {characters}

         writeln ('Current length = ',CurrentLength:4);

         GrandTotal := GrandTotal + CurrentLength;
         SentenceCount := SentenceCount + 1;

         read (NextChar) {sentinel or 1st char
                               of next sentence}
      END; {sentences}

   Average := GrandTotal / SentenceCount;
   writeln;
   writeln ('Average length = ',Average:6:1)
END. {Sentences}
```

■ Figure 3.13
Computing average sentence length.

Processing one sentence (that is, filling in the box) entails counting its interior characters and displaying its length, as we did before. The general approach (ignoring input and sentinels) is shown in Fig. 3.12(b).

When we place these details from Fig. 3.12(b) in the box in Fig. 3.12(a), we get the combined algorithm shown in Fig. 3.12(c). Here, too, a nested loop appears because we are again dealing with two levels of processing: (1) an outer level with basic units that are entire sentences; and (2) an inner level that deals with the characters comprising a single sentence.

Now that we have an input structure and a processing structure, we must synthesize the two into one program. Blending the nested loops from Figs. 3.10(c) and 3.12(c) yields the complete program shown in Fig. 3.13.

3.4 Two More Repetitive Control Structures

The WHILE statement in Pascal is the primary means of controlling the number of repetitions in a program loop, and every conceivable loop could be governed by this statement. However, Pascal provides other loop control mechanisms for special situations. Two of these are the FOR statement and the REPEAT statement.

The FOR Statement

FOR statement

When using a counter to govern the repetitions, you must explicitly (1) initialize a counter outside the loop; (2) increment it by 1 each time through the loop; and (3) test whether its value has exceeded some predetermined maximum before each potential execution of the loop. The **FOR statement** may prove to be more convenient when a loop is to be executed a predictable number of times (that is, under control of a counter). Contrast the approach using WHILE in Fig. 3.14(a) with the equivalent code using the FOR statement in Fig. 3.14(b).

These two fragments of code behave in exactly the same way, but the FOR statement consolidates initializing, incrementing, and testing the variable in one place. This code starts off by setting Count to 1. By convention, the value of the variable is always incremented by 1 at the completion of each execution of the loop. When you use FOR, the increment is implied and must not be explicitly included as a separate assignment statement. The basic action of the loop is repeated for each successive value of Count from 1 through MaxCount, inclusive. The FOR statement has the form:

FOR ⟨variable⟩ := ⟨initial value⟩ TO ⟨final value⟩ DO ⟨statement⟩

As usual, BEGIN and END are needed only if the ⟨statement⟩ associated with FOR is a compound statement.

```
Count := 1;
WHILE Count <= MaxCount DO        FOR Count := 1 TO MaxCount DO
  BEGIN                             BEGIN
  ┌─────────────────────────┐       ┌─────────────────────────┐
  │ .                       │       │ .                       │
  │ .                       │       │ .                       │
  │ .                       │       │ .                       │
  │ perform basic action    │       │ perform basic action    │
  │ .                       │       │ .                       │
  │ .                       │       │ .                       │
  │ .                       │       │ .                       │
  └─────────────────────────┘       └─────────────────────────┘
    Count := Count + 1             END;
  END;
```

(a) Using the WHILE statement.   **(b)** Using the FOR statement.

■ Figure 3.14
Executing a loop a known number of times.

control variable

The initial and final values need not be constants; they may be supplied by variables or by more general expressions. However, these values must not change during the execution of the loop. The ⟨variable⟩ in the FOR statement is known as the **control variable,** and the code in the loop should not tamper with it. Of course, the current value of the control variable may be inspected and used at any point inside the loop. As long as the final value is greater than or equal to the initial value, the ⟨statement⟩ will be executed precisely

⟨final value⟩ − ⟨initial value⟩ + 1

times. If the final value is less than the initial value, the ⟨statement⟩ is not executed at all! This is not considered an error; in fact, this feature is often useful.

Figure 3.15 contains a program for generating the squares of all the integers from 1 through whatever positive value the user specifies. Although the number of squares to be generated is not known before the program starts execution, the user specifies it by the time control reaches the loop. The predetermined limits and the need to generate every consecutive integer make the FOR statement suitable for this problem. Although the starting value here is fixed at 1, it too could have been read from the terminal or calculated.

DOWNTO

Another form of the FOR statement allows you to move *backwards* through a range of values. In this form the reserved word TO is replaced by **DOWNTO:**

FOR ⟨variable⟩ := ⟨large initial⟩ DOWNTO ⟨small final ⟩ DO ⟨statement⟩

Execution will continue as long as the value of the control variable is greater than or equal to the final value, and after each execution of the ⟨statement⟩, the loop variable is decremented (reduced) by 1. The following sets of code produce equivalent output: a list of consecutive integers from 10 down to 1.

```
K := 10;
WHILE K >= 1 DO                    FOR K := 10 DOWNTO 1 DO
  BEGIN                              writeln (K);
    writeln (K);
    K := K - 1
  END;
```

Standard Pascal *always* leaves the value of the control variable undefined when the FOR loop terminates normally. After finishing the loop, K should not be accessed until it has been reinitialized.

Instead of just their squares, suppose that you want to generate the cubes, as well as the fourth, fifth, and sixth powers of the integers. These powers can be displayed in tabular form, in which any particular row contains various powers for the same integer. Since the range of successive integers is determined as it was in the program in Fig. 3.15, the overall structure of the program for this problem will be exactly the same. However, instead of merely writing its square when the next integer is generated, we must now generate an entire output line containing several powers of the integer.

A systematic way to generate several consecutive powers of N is to compute each power as *N times the previous power* and to display the result

```
PROGRAM Squares (input,output);

VAR
    Limit,      { the largest integer }
    N:          { current integer }
       integer;

BEGIN

    write('enter integer from 1 through 99: ');
    read(Limit);

    FOR N := 1 TO Limit DO
      writeln(N,sqr(N))

END.
```

■ Figure 3.15
Generating squares with a FOR statement.

as soon as it is computed. The following code does this, using a FOR statement.

```
{generate the first six powers of N}
Power := 1;
FOR Exponent := 1 TO 6 DO
  BEGIN
    Power := Power * N;
    write(Power)
  END;
writeln; {to terminate current output line}
```

When we place this code inside the structure from Fig. 3.15 to generate successive values for N, the result is the program in Fig. 3.16. Comparing it with Fig. 3.15, we see that the new code replaces the single writeln statement as the interior of the outer FOR loop. The new code contains several statements, so we must enclose it with BEGIN and END. Since this code contains its own FOR loop, we have another nested loop structure.

The FOR Statement

FOR ⟨variable⟩ := ⟨initial value⟩ TO ⟨final value⟩ DO ⟨statement⟩

or

FOR ⟨variable⟩ := ⟨initial value⟩ DOWNTO ⟨final value⟩ DO ⟨statement⟩

The rules associated with the FOR statement are

1. The control variable, initial value, and final value must all be the same type, but *the real type is not permitted.* The initial and final values may be generated by expressions.
2. Before the first execution of the loop, the control variable is assigned the initial value.
3. The last execution of the loop normally occurs with the control variable equal to the final value. In other words, the control variable takes on each successive value from initial to final, inclusive. However, if the initial and final values are ordered so that the control variable can never reach the final value, the interior of the loop is not executed.
4. When the reserved word TO is used, the control variable is incremented to the successor (next higher) value after each iteration through the loop.
5. When DOWNTO is used, the control variable is decremented to the predecessor (next lower) value after each iteration through the loop.
6. It is illegal to attempt to modify the control variable within the loop.
7. The value of the control variable is undefined on normal termination of the loop.

```
PROGRAM PowerTable (input,output);
VAR
   Limit,     {the largest integer = number of rows}
   N,         {current integer = current row number}
   Exponent,  {identifies power of N being computed}
   Power:     {value of "Exponent"th power of N}
        integer;
BEGIN
   write('Enter integer from 1 through 30: ');
   read(Limit);
   {generate table headings...}
   writeln;
   writeln('Powers of N':36);
   writeln('N':10,'Square':10,'Cube':10,'Fourth':10,
        'Fifth':10,'Sixth':10);
   writeln;
   {now generate successive values of N = row of table}
   FOR N := 1 TO Limit DO
      BEGIN {another row}
         {N contains the current integer value...}
         {generate the first six powers of N}
         Power := 1;
         FOR Exponent := 1 TO 6 DO
            BEGIN
               Power := Power * N;
               write(Power:10)

            END; {another entry}
         writeln {to terminate current row}
      END {another row}
END.
```

```
Enter integer from 1 through 30: 4

                 Powers of N
   N    Square   Cube  Fourth   Fifth   Sixth

   1       1      1       1       1       1
   2       4      8      16      32      64
   3       9     27      81     243     729
   4      16     64     256    1024    4096
```

■ Figure 3.16
Nested FOR loops to generate table of powers.

The REPEAT Statement

REPEAT statement

There are some repetitive situations in which at least one repetition is *always required.* The WHILE statement can be cumbersome as a control structure for such applications. To complement it, Pascal also provides the **REPEAT statement,** which resembles WHILE in spirit but differs from it in two important ways.

First, the REPEAT statement tests the condition for continuation at the *end* rather than at the beginning of the loop. This means that the loop is *always* executed *at least one time* regardless of the condition. You can consider using REPEAT only if you are certain that at least one loop execution is always needed; otherwise, use WHILE. The form in which the statement is written emphasizes that the test occurs at the end of the loop:

> REPEAT
>
> ·   (statements to be repeated until
> ·   condition becomes true)
> ·
> ·
>
> UNTIL   ⟨condition⟩

UNTIL

The use of **UNTIL** before the condition suggests the second major difference between REPEAT and WHILE. The loop governed by REPEAT continues until the condition becomes *true,* that is, as long as the condition remains false. This is the opposite of WHILE, which requires a true condition for another repetition. The difference between using a true or false condition to terminate repetitions is a matter of phrasing the condition. However, the execution of the interior before testing the condition can make REPEAT more convenient when (1) it is always safe to execute the interior at least once; and (2) some artificial contrivance would be needed to force a WHILE condition into a true state to cause the first execution. You can avoid the extra mechanism for entering a WHILE loop the first time by using REPEAT. The flow of control associated with each statement is illustrated in Fig. 3.17.

Another difference between the syntax of the two structures is the omission of BEGIN and END in the REPEAT version. The words REPEAT and UNTIL identify the extent of the loop, implying that everything between them is subject to repetition. The compound statement delimiters would be redundant in this context.

Consider the two fragments of code in Fig. 3.18, both of which control the input of a negative number. If the value read is greater than or equal to zero, both fragments try again and again until the user supplies the kind of value requested. The shorter and clearer option obviously is REPEAT. Note that the conditions in the two loops are boolean opposites: For any number, whenever one is true, the other is false.

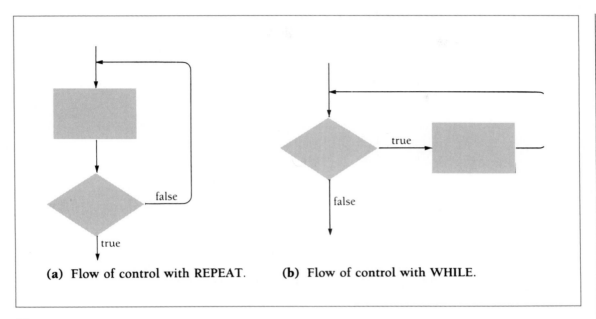

(a) Flow of control with REPEAT.   (b) Flow of control with WHILE.

■ Figure 3.17
Comparison of flowcharts for REPEAT and WHILE.

```
write ('Negative number?');
read  (Number);
WHILE Number >= 0 DO
    BEGIN
        write ('Negative number?');)
        read (Number)
    END;
```

(a) Control with WHILE.

```
REPEAT
    write ('Negative number?');
    read (Number)
UNTIL Number < 0;
```

(b) Control with REPEAT.

■ Figure 3.18
Comparison of code for WHILE and REPEAT.

The REPEAT Statement

REPEAT
  ⟨statement1⟩;
  ⟨statement2⟩;
     ·
     ·
     ·
  ⟨statementN⟩
UNTIL ⟨condition⟩

The rules associated with the REPEAT statement are

1. The statements governed by REPEAT are always executed at least once.
2. The condition is tested after every execution of the loop.
3. Control remains within the loop as long as the condition is false.

3.5 Alternative Execution with IF

Let's return to the analysis of 50 stock transactions. We now want more information than the net profit. We also want to know the total amount earned by profitable stocks and the total amount lost by unprofitable ones. We will call these quantities "total gain" and "total loss," respectively. Total gain is the sum of all positive values in the input, and total loss is the sum of all negative ones. Consequently, the algorithm for maintaining these two running totals will repeatedly obtain an individual amount, determine whether it is positive or negative, and add this value to the appropriate total. Since net profit is merely the sum of these two totals (net loss being negative), it may therefore be computed at the end when these first two totals have been established. The resulting algorithm is shown in Fig. 3.19.

The most striking difference between this algorithm and the algorithm used to find only net profit (Fig. 3.7a) is the choice between two alternative actions in steps 2.2 and 2.3. There each transaction amount is added to one total or the other but never to both. The decision about which total to update depends on whether the amount under consideration is positive, that is, on the boolean expression Amount $>= 0$. If the value of this boolean expression is true, the first alternative (updating total gain) should be used. Otherwise, the expression is false and the second alternative should be used.

```
1.1  initialize total gain and total loss to 0;
1.2  initialize count to 0;
2.   while count < 50 do;
2.1      obtain amount for one transaction;
2.2      if amount is positive then
              add amount to total gain;
2.3      otherwise
              add amount to total loss;
2.4      increment count by 1;
3.   net profit is total gain + total loss;
4.   display total gain, total loss, and net profit;
5.   stop.
```

IF-THEN-ELSE

IF statement
A construction called an **IF statement** provides the ability to make just such decisions by executing one of two alternative statements, based on the truth or falsehood of a boolean expression. We can express steps 2.2 and 2.3 of our algorithm in Pascal code as follows:

```
IF Amount > = 0 THEN
   Gain := Gain + Amount
ELSE
   Loss := Loss + Amount;
```

Note how closely this code resembles the original steps in the algorithm. In Pascal, ELSE corresponds to the English word *otherwise*. The general form of the IF statement is

```
IF ⟨boolean expression⟩ THEN
   ⟨statement #1⟩
ELSE
   ⟨statement #2⟩;
```

Regardless of which alternative statement in the IF construct is executed, the statement *following* this entire construct will be executed next.

In Fig. 3.20 (the program corresponding to Fig. 3.19) the count is incremented regardless of which total was adjusted by the preceding IF statement. Figure 3.20 includes an additional IF statement to choose between two alternative output messages, depending on whether NetProfit was truly profit (nonnegative) or actually a loss (negative). In case NetProfit is negative, the negative of *this* value will be displayed so that no sign will appear. The minus sign on Loss is similarly reversed and removed from the output.

Because semicolons are used to separate statements in a program, programmers sometimes unconsciously insert a semicolon after ⟨statement #1⟩ and before the ELSE. However, this is an error, since it separates the ELSE from the rest of the IF statement. Be on guard: You *cannot* put a semicolon before an ELSE. The entire IF-THEN-ELSE construction is just a single Pascal statement. As such it contains no interior semicolons to separate its key words from its statements.

```
PROGRAM Stocks (input,output);

   { Computing total profit, loss and net profit
     from 50 stock transactions }

VAR
   Gain,           {running total of profitable sales}
   Loss,           {running total of losing sales}
   NetProfit,      { Gain + Loss }
   Amount,         {amount of current sale}
   HowMany: integer;

BEGIN {Stocks}
   Gain := 0;
   Loss := 0;

   FOR HowMany := 1 TO 50 DO
      BEGIN
         write ('Enter one transaction amount: ');
         read (Amount);
         IF Amount >= 0 THEN
            Gain := Gain + Amount
         ELSE
            Loss := Loss + Amount
      END;

   NetProfit := Gain + Loss;
   writeln;
   writeln ('Total gain =: ',Gain);
   writeln ('Total loss =: ',-Loss);
   IF NetProfit >= 0 THEN
      writeln ('Net profit =: ',NetProfit)
   ELSE
      writeln ('Net loss =: ',-NetProfit)
END. {Stocks}
```

■ Figure 3.20
Computing total gain, total loss, and net profit from stock transactions.

The IF Statement

IF ⟨boolean expression⟩ THEN
   ⟨statement 1⟩
ELSE
   ⟨statement 2⟩

The rules associated with the IF-THEN-ELSE statement are

1. When control reaches IF, the boolean expression is evaluated. If the expression is true, then ⟨statement 1⟩ is executed; otherwise ⟨statement 2⟩ is executed.
2. Precisely one of ⟨statement 1⟩ or ⟨statement 2⟩ will be executed, and, regardless of which of these alternatives is selected, the next statement to be executed will be the one following ⟨statement 2⟩.
3. Note that no semicolons appear between THEN and ⟨statement 1⟩, between ⟨statement 1⟩ and ELSE, or between ELSE and ⟨statement 2⟩.

Using IF without ELSE

Sometimes one of the alternatives in a decision is to take no action. In other words, you may want to perform a certain action when some condition is true and simply bypass that action otherwise. In such cases the ELSE is superfluous. The resulting form of the IF statement is:

IF ⟨boolean expression⟩ THEN
   ⟨statement⟩;

To illustrate its use we will modify the character counting program shown in Fig. 3.9. The original program counted all characters in a sentence up to the first period. The program might be more useful if it counted only nonblank characters. To achieve this we increment the counter *only* if the character happens not to be a blank. In other words, the increment statement becomes the object of an IF statement and is executed subject to the condition Symbol <> Blank. The modified program is shown in Fig. 3.21 on p. 122. Note the use of the symbolic constant Blank.

Finding Largest and Smallest Values

Consider the problem of finding the largest value in a set of similar items. Without knowing any special properties of the set, we would have to inspect every value in the set before we could identify the target value. In a computer environment, the difficulty is that we must inspect the values one at a time, and we do not wish to (or cannot) look back over all previously encountered values.

The strategy is to keep track of the largest value encountered *so far,* as we progress through the set. Each new value encountered is compared with the largest value previously observed. If the current value is greater than the already recorded largest value, we have a new candidate for the largest value; we can forget the old one and need to remember only the new one for future comparisons. On the other hand, if the current value is not greater, the already recorded value still stands as the best candidate, and nothing more need be done.

We can write the basic step, to be repeated for every item in the set in

```
PROGRAM Sentence2 (input,output);

   { Counting the nonblank characters in
     a sentence ending in a period. }
CONST
   Period = '.';
   Blank = ' ';

VAR
   CharCount: integer; {no. of nonblank characters}
   Symbol: char; {current character in sentence}

BEGIN {Sentence2}
   CharCount := 0;
   writeln ('Enter a sentence ending in a period.');
   read (Symbol);
   WHILE Symbol <> Period DO
      BEGIN
         IF Symbol <> Blank THEN {count it}
            CharCount := CharCount + 1;
         read (Symbol)
      END;

   writeln ('Number of nonblank characters was: ',
            CharCount)
END. {Sentence2}
```

■ Figure 3.21
Counting nonblank characters.

■   Figure 3.22
Finding the largest
input value (using a
sentinel for
termination).

```
        .
        .
        .
    read (ThisItem); {first value encountered}
    CurrentMaximum := ThisItem;

    WHILE ThisItem <> Sentinel DO
      BEGIN
        IF ThisItem > CurrentMaximum THEN
          CurrentMaximum := ThisItem;
        read (ThisItem)
      END;
    {CurrentMaximum now contains true maximum}
        .
        .
        .
```

Pascal as

> IF ThisItem > CurrentMaximum THEN
>   CurrentMaximum := ThisItem;

This statement updates CurrentMaximum whenever a more promising candidate is found, and does nothing otherwise. By the time this comparison has been made for the *final* value, the "largest value encountered so far" will be the largest value in the entire set.

We must have an initial candidate for CurrentMaximum with which to make the first comparison. A suitable choice for an initial value would be the first member of the set to be inspected. This, after all, is the largest value encountered after looking at only one value.

When finding the largest value from an input stream terminated by a sentinel, we can use the basic pattern of Fig. 3.22. When control first enters the loop, CurrentMaximum is compared to the first input value, which it already equals. However, after this first (fruitless) comparison, all subsequent repetitions involve new values from ThisItem.

Situations may exist in which the first value is not easily obtainable prior to entering the loop (such as when input is controlled by a counter). In these cases, another suitable starting value for CurrentMaximum would be some extremely small value, that is, smaller than any legitimate data value expected in the set. This artificial value is not in the set and remains a candidate for CurrentMaximum only until the first true set member is encountered. The first true value, being larger than the artificial starting value, is guaranteed to become the candidate for CurrentMaximum as a result of the first comparison.

We can find the smallest value in a set in a similar manner: We continually seek a value *smaller* than "the smallest value encountered so far."

Using IF with Compound Statements

We have already noted that a compound (BEGIN . . . END) statement may be used anywhere in place of a single statement. Used in conjunction with an IF statement, the compound statement enables the IF to select (or bypass) many statements arbitrarily. Any number of statements may constitute the alternatives.

Recall the problem of simulating munchie existence discussed earlier. In its original version, we were concerned only with the number of generations that could survive on the food supply. The program (Fig. 3.7) did not bother to compute the correct value for the final number of munchies; it merely doubled the number from the previous generation, even if not all these had eaten and reproduced.

Now suppose we do want to know how many munchies are left at the end. Eventually the problem must be faced. When the last generation does not find sufficient food for everyone, only a certain number of munchies can eat. Those who are fortunate enough to eat do so and reproduce, leaving the rest of the population to some unspecified fate. The number of munchies participating in the final feast is the quotient of varmint grass left divided by appetite. Having eaten, these munchies split in two to yield the final population. (Even if the surviving munchies do not quite finish the food supply, the next munchie in the "munching order" does by consuming part of its capacity.)

To summarize, when there is insufficient food for the whole population, the actions taken are these:

1. Reduce the munchie population to match food supply (thereby eliminating munchies who will not eat).
2. Double this remaining population.
3. Reduce food supply to 0.

Of course, all this is just one possible course of action. The alternative, which is taken whenever food supply is adequate, is the normal food consumption and reproduction cycle, as implemented before. The heart of the (revised) algorithm becomes:

```
3.    while Food > = Appetite do:
3.1       if Food sufficient for whole population then
3.1.1         feed population;
3.1.2         double population;
3.2       otherwise
3.2.1         reduce population to match food supply;
3.2.2         double this remaining population;
3.2.3         reduce food supply to zero;
3.3       increment generation count;
```

This form of solution requires that we perform both steps 3.1.1 and 3.1.2 if the food supply is sufficient; similarly, we do 3.2.1, 3.2.2, and 3.2.3 only if it is not. When finally translated into Pascal, this will require compound statements to group these sets of actions into single (composite) actions. Of course, the generation count is increased in either case. The corresponding program is shown in Fig. 3.23.

```
PROGRAM Munchie2 (input,output);

   {Simulating munchie growth under
    varying conditions}

VAR
   Generations,
   Munchies,              {number of munchies}
   Food,                  {units of food available}
   Appetite: integer; {units of food consumed by
                       one munchie at a feeding}

BEGIN {Munchie2}
   write ('Enter initial amount of varmint grass:');
   read (Food);
   write ('How much grass eaten by one munchie?');
   read (Appetite);
   write ('Enter initial number of munchies:');
   read (Munchies);
   Generations := 1;

   WHILE Food >= Appetite DO
      BEGIN {generation cycle}
         IF Food >= Munchies * Appetite THEN
            BEGIN {normal feeding}
               Food := Food - Munchies * Appetite; {eat}
               Munchies := Munchies * 2 {reproduce}
            END {normal}
         ELSE
            BEGIN {final feast of the munchies}
               Munchies := Food DIV Appetite; {survivors}
               Munchies := Munchies * 2; {reproduce}
               Food := 0
            END; {final feast}
         Generations := Generations + 1
      END; {cycle}

   writeln (Generations,' generations sustained');
   writeln (Munchies,' munchies survived')
END. {Munchie2}
```

■ Figure 3.23
Improved biological model.

```
WHILE Food >= Appetite DO
    BEGIN
        IF Food >= Munchies * Appetite THEN {adequate}
            Food := Food - Munchies * Appetite
        ELSE {not enough food for all}
            BEGIN {final cycle}
                Munchies := Food DIV Appetite;
                Food := 0
            END; {final cycle}
        Munchies := Munchies * 2; {reproduce}
        Generations := Generations + 1
    END;
```

■ Figure 3.24
IF statement with one compound alternative.

Notice that step 3.2.1, which determined how many munchies can be fed by the remaining food supply, is interested in fully fed munchies only. This translates into Pascal as:

```
Munchies := Food DIV Appetite;
```

since any remainder would be meaningless.

You may have noticed that either alternative set of activities includes doubling the (surviving) munchie population. A different approach to formulating the algorithm might have included just one, common doubling operation, at the conclusion of each cycle following both basic alternatives. In this case the code might have been written as shown in Fig. 3.24.

In this version, only the second (ELSE) alternative needs a compound statement, because only this alternative involves more than one statement. Note that the munchies reproduce and another generation is counted, regardless of which alternative is executed.

3.6 Sequences of Decisions Using Nested IFs

You have seen how repetitive processes can be nested within larger repetitive processes and that such nesting occurs naturally in the solution of various types of problems. An analogous nesting may occur with decision-making statements, particularly with IF statements. If the outcome of one decision leads to another, the second decision will be one of the alternatives chosen by the first.

Some Basic Concepts and Cautions

Suppose that you want to compare the scores of two teams, A and B, and print a message that announces the winning team or proclaims a tie. A correct but lengthy solution is to test separately for every possible situation:

if A's score > B's score then
  announce A the winner;
if B's score > A's score then
  announce B the winner;
if A's score = B's score then
  proclaim a tie;

Regardless of the scores, all three comparisons would be made, with only one being true and initiating its corresponding action. If A's score really is larger than B's, the second and third IF statements will accomplish nothing; their conditions, predictably, will be false. Perhaps those two IF statements should be executed only in the event the first condition is false, that is, when A's score is not greater than B's, or

1. if A's score > B's score then
  announce A the winner
2. else {since A did not win}
  decide whether B won or a tie occurred.

Of course, deciding whether B won or there was a tie (step 2) now requires only a *single* decision, since the possibility that A won was eliminated in step 1. Thus the outcome can be chosen from the two remaining possibilities:

2.1 if A's score < B's score then
  announce B the winner
2.2 else
  proclaim a tie

The combined algorithm is shown in Fig. 3.25(a). Because the second decision is a direct consequence of the first, we say (in terms of control structure) that it is *nested* inside the first. The corresponding code shown in Fig. 3.25(c) has exactly the same structure.

decision tree

Note the **decision tree** in Fig. 3.25(b). Such a structure is called a *tree* because its *branches* continue to diverge as they progress from the *root* at the top toward the leaves at the bottom (actually an upside down tree). Decision trees are useful for organizing sequences of decisions. The first decision is made at the root and its branches clearly show which decisions should follow which others. A decision tree can serve as a helpful alternative, or complementary, technique for use with an algorithm when you are writing the parts of a program that involve complex logic.

One special advantage of the decision tree is its clear depiction of the alternative paths for eventual flow of control. Whenever the code in Fig.

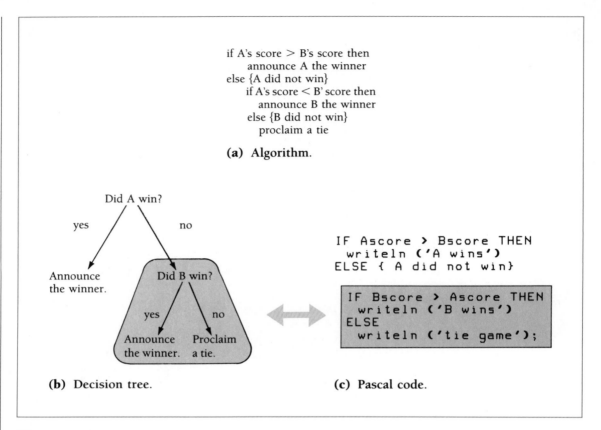

■ Figure 3.25
Deciding the winner (if any) of a game.

3.25(c) is executed, only one of the three messages will be displayed. The sequence of executed tests will correspond to one of the paths from the top of the decision tree to the appropriate action at the bottom. A decision tree is therefore a specialized kind of flow chart.

This problem of determining the winner or loser (if any) is actually a problem of *classifying* an enormous number of possible scores into three distinct categories: win, lose, or tie. An individual IF statement is capable of subdividing the set of all possible scores into only two categories. Any resulting category that is not sufficiently refined requires a subsequent decision to further subdivide that category into two distinct parts. Of course, this process of successive subdivision may continue to whatever level of nesting is required to achieve the desired refinement of classification. The way in which the classification begins makes little logical difference. An alternative approach (and different sequences of decisions) is illustrated in Fig. 3.26. Obviously, there are several correct ways to make such complex decisions.

■ Figure 3.26
Classification starting
with test for a tie.

```
IF Ascore = Bscore THEN
   writeln ('tie game')
ELSE {clear winner}
   IF Ascore > Bscore THEN
      writeln ('A wins')
   ELSE
      writeln ('B wins');
```

There are also several incorrect ways to proceed. One of these is shown
in Fig. 3.27. The difference between this code and that of Fig. 3.26 is the
absence of the first ELSE. This seemingly small omission makes a world of
difference to the results. The second IF statement in Fig. 3.27 is *always*
executed, regardless of the outcome of the first. Thus, if A's score is higher
than B's, *two* messages result: the first giving the win to A and the second
proclaiming a tie. According to the second IF, there is a tie if B does not win.
Of course, this is true after the case where A won is eliminated, but only in
that case and not in general.

Clearly, this (incorrect) program *is not* an example to be followed. It *is*
an example of what can happen if you are careless or too hasty. The compiler
does not notice such problems; this code follows the rules of Pascal and looks
perfectly correct. The problem reflects an error in either the logic or encoding
of the algorithm into Pascal. Although this logic is not particularly complex,
even here great care is required to produce correct code.

One lesson from Fig. 3.27 is that, in case of doubt, an ELSE matches the
nearest preceding IF within the same block (compound statement) whose
associated ELSE has not already been encountered. Your indentation scheme
should clearly show which ELSE goes with which IF, but the indentation
scheme does not *cause* the desired association to occur.

■ Figure 3.27
A completely wrong
implementation.

```
{ WARNING -- THIS DOES NOT WORK}

IF Ascore > Bscore THEN
   writeln ('A wins');
IF Bscore > Ascore THEN
   writeln ('B wins')
ELSE
   writeln ('tie game');
```

Another common error is to include a semicolon somewhere in the midst of all these IFs and ELSEs. But remember: No matter how deep the nesting, the entire structure is just one Pascal statement and should contain no semicolons. The only semicolons that may appear are those used to separate statements within some interior compound statement.

A Small-Business Decision Problem

Imagine that a small company is managed by three people who always confer when making a business decision. Despite their tradition of group decisions, not every opinion is of equal importance. One of the three is the founder, who is now chairman of the board. The second is his favorite son, who is president, even though he is only 22 years old. The third is a key employee with 15 years' service, who, unfortunately, is not a member of the founder's family. We will call these three people "chairman," "son," and "employee," respectively.

Whenever the three decide on a proposal, each one eventually votes *yes* or *no*. As a result of the vote, a corporate decision is announced. This decision may be one of three distinct alternatives: reject, reconsider, or accept the proposal. The decision resulting from every possible outcome of the voting is shown in Fig. 3.28. Note the departure from strict democratic majority voting.

We now consider the implementation of this decision-making process by computer. There are various approaches to the solution of this classification problem; although all produce correct programs, some obviously will be more satisfactory than others.

Solution 1: The first, and in some ways the safest approach is to build a complete decision tree to consider each person's vote in turn until a final decision is reached. Although we could consider the individual votes in any

■ Figure 3.28
The small-business decision.

	The Vote		
Chairman	**Son**	**Employee**	**The Result**
no	no	no	reject
no	no	yes	reject
no	yes	no	reject
no	yes	yes	reconsider
yes	no	no	reconsider
yes	no	yes	accept
yes	yes	no	accept
yes	yes	yes	accept

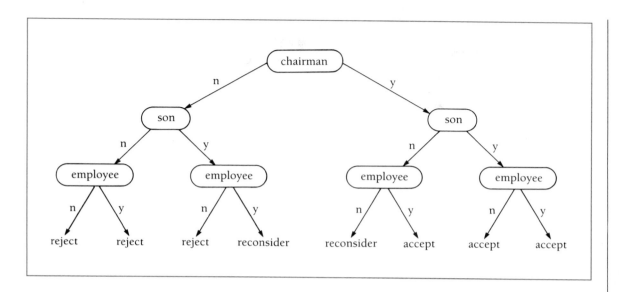

■ Figure 3.29
The small-business
decision tree.

order, we have chosen to consider them in the order: chairman, son, and employee. The decision tree is shown in Fig. 3.29. We could encode this tree directly using an IF statement for each decision. Even though it would be correct, the code would require seven IF statements and three levels of nesting.

Solution 2: The first thing to notice about solution 1 is its length and complexity. An obvious simplification is to remove useless tests. For example, if the chairman and son vote the same way, the vote of the employee is irrelevant. Once the outcome is clear, further tests (that is, nesting other IF statements) serve only to complicate the algorithm. We can avoid useless IF statements altogether by noticing when *all* decision paths from some point on the decision tree lead to the *same* outcome. Thus

should become simply *accept,* and

should become simply *reject.*

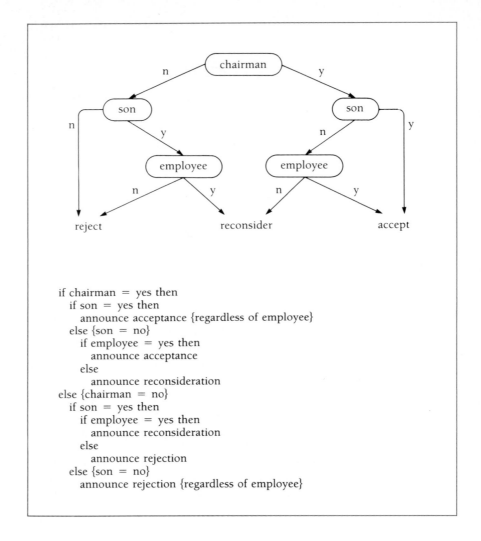

```
if chairman = yes then
  if son = yes then
    announce acceptance {regardless of employee}
  else {son = no}
    if employee = yes then
      announce acceptance
    else
      announce reconsideration
else {chairman = no}
  if son = yes then
    if employee = yes then
      announce reconsideration
    else
      announce rejection
  else {son = no}
    announce rejection {regardless of employee}
```

The resulting reduced, or merged, decision tree and its corresponding algorithm are shown in Fig. 3.30. As a general rule, useless decisions are more evident when the decision tree begins with the most influential test.

Solution 3: Perhaps by considering the problem from a different perspective, we can generate an even simpler solution. One possibility is to consider the classification of all possible voting situations into three distinct sets, that is, those that will produce decisions to reject, reconsider, or accept a proposal. In order to do this, we need some simple way to characterize these sets.

The general pattern we might adopt would be to test first for acceptance and, failing that, to then choose between rejection and reconsideration, as follows:

```
if vote indicates acceptance then
    announce acceptance
else {either reject or reconsider}
    if vote indicates rejection then
        announce rejection
    else {no clear decision}
        announce reconsideration
```

Note that this structure is analogous to the win, lose, or tie decision in the preceding section. However, the tests here are much more involved than merely comparing two scores.

The brute force approach would be to completely specify every voting situation leading to a particular outcome, but this would involve some very cumbersome boolean conditions. On the other hand, a review of Fig. 3.30 reveals that the chairman *must* vote *yes* and that either the son or the employee (or both) must also vote *yes* for acceptance of a proposal. This observation greatly simplifies the characterization of acceptance; that is

```
if (chairman = yes) and ((son = yes) or (employee = yes)) then
    announce acceptance
else . . .
```

The conditions for rejection are similar, leading to the complete classification shown in Fig. 3.31.

Solution 4: The conditions for acceptance and rejection are so similar that we should be struck by their symmetry. They can be summarized as follows: If either the son or the employee agrees with the chairman, the chairman will prevail. The alternative (to reconsider) occurs only when the other two agree in opposition to the chairman. This translates into the general structure:

```
if (chairman = son) or (chairman = other) then
    {do whatever the chairman wishes}
else {reconsider}
```

■ Figure 3.31
Solution 3: Using boolean conditions to characterize acceptance and rejection situations.

```
if (chairman = yes) and ((son = yes) or (employee = yes)) then
        announce acceptance
else
        if (chairman = no) and ((son = no) or (employee = no)) then
            announce rejection
        else
            announce reconsideration
```

■ Figure 3.32
Solution 4: Further
consideration yields a
simpler classification
scheme.

```
if (chairman = son) or (chairman = employee) then
    if chairman = yes then
        announce acceptance
    else {chairman voted no}
        announce rejection
else {no clear decision}
    announce reconsideration
```

Choosing between acceptance and rejection involves only one more IF statement to test how the chairman voted. Thus we have the solution shown in Fig. 3.32, the clarity and simplicity of which should be immediately appealing.

3.7 The CASE Statement

**Selecting one of
several actions**

In the preceding section we explored the problem of analyzing votes in order to announce the result of a business decision. The algorithms that we developed suggested announcing the decision as soon as it could be determined within a sequence of decisions. However, we do not need to do this when encoding the algorithm into Pascal. Determining the result and displaying it are two separate activities, which can be handled by two different sections of code. This may be especially desirable if either process is elaborate; for instance, if the announcement must be conveyed through a formal decree requiring several lines of code to generate. Of course, the vote analysis would have to come first, and its outcome would have to be represented in some manner, so that the output section would know what action to take. The simplest way to convey the result of one step to the next is by encoding the possible outcomes and storing the appropriate encodings in a variable.

One way of implementing an encoding scheme for this problem is to represent the possible outcomes by symbolic constants and to declare a variable for storing the actual outcome:

```
CONST
    Accept = 1;
    Reject = 2;
    Reconsider = 3;
VAR
    Result: integer;
```

Then the Pascal code to determine and display the result could resemble that in Fig. 3.33.

```
IF (Chairman = Son) OR (Chairman = Employee) THEN
    IF Chairman = yes THEN
        Result = Accept
    ELSE
        Result = Reject
ELSE
    Result = Reconsider;
    {Here Result contains the outcome of the vote}
    .
    .
    .
    {Now take appropriate action}
IF Result = Accept THEN
    writeln ('accept')
ELSE
    IF Result = Reject THEN
        writeln ('reject')
    ELSE
        writeln ('reconsider');
```

■ Figure 3.33
Separation of analysis and output functions in small-business decision problem.

Our focus here is not on the vote analysis but rather on the use of an encoded value to select one of several alternative actions. Because this sort of selection is so common, Pascal provides a special construct for this purpose: the **CASE statement.** The general form of the CASE statement is

CASE statement

CASE ⟨expression⟩ OF
⟨constant1⟩: ⟨statement1⟩;
⟨constant2⟩: ⟨statement2⟩;
    .
    .
    .
⟨constantN⟩: ⟨statementN⟩
END

Figure 3.34 contains two examples of code that are equivalent in their actions, both to each other and to the second part of the code in Fig. 3.33. In particular, each will display one message as output. The only difference between the two versions is in the use or absence of symbolic constants to denote the integer constants 1, 2, and 3.

When control reaches the CASE statement, the value in Result will be one of the three values 1, 2, or 3 (for Accept, Reject, or Reconsider). We list these possibilities, called **case constants,** between CASE . . . OF and END.

case constants

case index

The case constants are merely labels to distinguish the various alternative actions. The value of Result, called the **case index,** must be one of the case constants. Depending on the current value of Result, the action following the matching case constant is taken. For example, if Result contains the value 1, only the message 'reject' will be displayed. Consequently, one and only one action is taken each time the CASE statement is executed. A case constant

case list element

together with its associated statement is known as a **case list element.** END is used to terminate CASE, just as it terminates BEGIN; thus it indicates how far the case list elements extend. The whole purpose of the CASE statement therefore is to select one action from among many, determined by the current value of the case index.

Comparison of Figs. 3.33 and 3.34 should indicate the benefit of using the CASE construct. It makes the list of alternative actions and the value of Result, which activates each alternative, immediately apparent. This clarity is an even greater advantage when you are dealing with a large number of alternative actions.

Figures 3.33 and 3.34 also indicate what the CASE statement does *not* do well: It does not "make" complex decisions involving the complex logic of the IF statements. However, it can handle multiway branching that is based on only a single value. This value does not always need to reside in a variable; it can be generated from an expression having a result among the case constants.

Suppose that the small business in our previous example has expanded and has new directors, whose decisions can be one of five alternatives: definitely, probably, reconsider, unlikely, and no. Whenever the decision is positive, whether definite or probable, they issue the same, somewhat qualified

■ Figure 3.34
Use of CASE
statement to select
one of three actions.

```
{Here Result contains outcome of vote}

CASE Result OF
   Accept:     writeln ('accept');
   Reject:     writeln ('reject');
   Reconsider: writeln ('reconsider')
END; {case}
```

or, alternatively, the code fragment

```
CASE Result OF
   1: writeln ('accept');
   2: writeln ('reject');
   3: writeln ('reconsider')
END; {case}
```

```
CONST
   Definitely = 1;
   Probably = 2;
   Reconsider = 3;
   Unlikely = 4;
   No = 5;

VAR Decision: integer;
   .
   .
   .
   {Assuming Decision contains one of the vote values}
```

CASE Decision OF   CASE Decision OF
   Definitely,   No,
   Probably: BEGIN   Unlikely: BEGIN

   ┌─────────────┐   ┌─────────────┐
   │ produce   │   │ produce   │
   │ positive   │   │ negative   │
   │ report   │   │ report   │
   └─────────────┘   └─────────────┘

                  END;   END;
   Reconsider:;   Probably,
   Unlikely,   Definitely: BEGIN
   No: BEGIN

   ┌─────────────┐   ┌─────────────┐
   │ produce   │   │ produce   │
   │ negative   │   │ positive   │
   │ report   │   │ report   │
   └─────────────┘   └─────────────┘

                  END   END;
END; {case}   Reconsider: {no action}
                                     END; {case}

(a) First ordering.   **(b) Alternative ordering.**

■ Figure 3.35
Equivalent ways to select appropriate report.

positive announcement to shareholders. Similarly, either negative decision results in the same negative announcement to shareholders. When they decide to reconsider, no announcement is made. Two equivalent case constructs for issuing these reports are shown in Fig. 3.35.

We used compound statements with the alternative actions because printing a shareholder report involves more than one statement. Of course, compound statements may appear wherever a simple statement is permitted, and this often occurs within CASE statements.

The CASE Statement

```
CASE ⟨expression⟩ OF
    ⟨constant-list1⟩: ⟨statement1⟩;
    ⟨constant-list2⟩: ⟨statement2⟩;
            .
            .
            .
    ⟨constant-listN⟩: ⟨statementN⟩
END
```

The rules associated with the CASE statement are

1. The CASE statement begins with CASE and terminates with END. Its basic elements—statements with their identifying case constants—are separated by semicolons. The final element is not separated from END by a semicolon.
2. The case index and the case constants must all belong to the same data type, and the value of the case index must be one of the case constants. If a case index has a value that is not listed among the case constants, a run-time error will occur.
3. The real data type may not be used for either the index or the case constants.
4. The case constants must be true, explicit constants. Variables and expressions are illegal. However, their order of appearance is not significant; they merely identify the alternative statements.
5. The case constants must all be different; that is, the same constant may not appear more than once. However, as indicated by the notation ⟨constant-list⟩, the same statement may have more than one identifying case constant, separated by commas; for example,

    ⟨constant5⟩, ⟨constant6⟩: ⟨statement⟩;

    or

    ⟨constant5⟩,
    ⟨constant6⟩: ⟨statement⟩;

    A colon separates the case constant (list) from its associated statement.
6. After execution of one of the statements, control transfers to the first statement after the END of the CASE construct.

In both parts of Fig. 3.35, we used more than one case constant to identify the same action, which is the proper thing to do if the same action is required in more than one case. Since both approaches produce exactly the same effect, it should also be apparent that the order in which the case list elements appear is irrelevant—so long as the correct constant is associated with its corresponding statement.

A new feature in Fig. 3.35 is a *no action* alternative in case the directors decide to reconsider. When there is nothing to do, the natural thing to write is nothing. Consequently, in Fig. 3.35(a) "nothing" appears between the colon and the semicolon for the case of 'Reconsider'. This "nothing," which is not even so much as a blank, is technically known as an **empty statement.** The empty statement is a valid Pascal statement with no effect. It usually appears in places like this, where the case of 'reconsider' must appear, but no action is required. The semicolon has nothing special to do with the empty statement but is needed to separate the second case list element from the third.

empty statement

In Fig. 3.35(b) the empty statement appears as the final alternative (non)action, and so it is not even followed by a semicolon. However, we explicitly indicate "no action" by a comment, which we believe should always be done to assure the reader that no action really is intended.

Next, let's suppose that the generation of shareholder reports is either so complex or so delayed that it is handled by an entirely separate program. This program accepts the voter outcome as user input before generating the report.

Since the user input to the second program is coming through the keyboard, we will use single characters to represent the votes. For simplicity, we will consider only the three original possible decisions: accept, reject, and reconsider, coded as 'y', 'n', and 'r', respectively. In order to allow the user to type the vote outcome in either uppercase or lowercase, we allow for six legitimate input values:

Vote Outcome	Encoding
Accept	Y or y
Reject	N or n
Reconsider	R or r

Consequently, each alternative action is selected by two case constants.

The basic structure for generating the correct alternative report is shown in Fig. 3.36. Because we used character constants as the case constants, we had to include the single quotes. Since the value for the case index is arriving from the terminal, there is no guarantee that one of the six allowable characters will be supplied. A moment of distraction or a slip of the finger could cause the user to type a character that is not among the case constants. Such an error would abruptly terminate the program.

Whenever there is any possibility of an illegal case index value, the program should first test it for membership among the case constants before allowing the CASE statement to execute. Although we did not do it in Fig.

```
VAR Result: char;
   .
   .
   .
BEGIN
   write ('Enter vote outcome: Y, N or R');
   read (Result);

   {Assume the input is one of the requested letters}
   {either upper or lower case is acceptable}

   CASE Result OF
      'Y',
      'y': BEGIN

                  ┌─────────────────────────┐
                  │    generate positive     │
                  │          report          │
                  └─────────────────────────┘

                  END;
      'N',
      'n': BEGIN

                  ┌─────────────────────────┐
                  │    generate negative     │
                  │          report          │
                  └─────────────────────────┘

                  END;
      'R',
      'r': writeln ('no decision yet')
   END {case}
   .
   .
   .
END.
```

■ Figure 3.36
The CASE statement with character case constants.

3.36, some preliminary testing should be considered the normal prelude to every CASE statement, unless the program logic guarantees one of the case constants as a value for the case index (which was the situation in Figs. 3.34 and 3.35).†

---

† Not all implementations of Pascal behave according to the standard when executing the CASE construct. Notable exceptions are VAX-11 and Turbo Pascal, which allow catch-all statements within the case list elements. These statements (prefixed by "otherwise" in VAX-11 and "else" in turbo), allow the user to specify a statement to be executed if the case index value does not match one of the case constants.

3.8 Making Programs Easier to Understand and Modify: Part 2

English text that is not broken down into chapters, sections, and paragraphs is difficult to read. Therefore rules for structuring prose were developed to make relationships between ideas more apparent to the reader and to highlight certain aspects of the writer's thoughts.

There is a similar need for programming style to display the logical structure of your programs to readers (including yourself). We made some suggestions in Chapter 2, such as indenting the lines of detail within each major program section and separating distinct sections of code with blank lines and explanatory comments. Now that we have programs with nontrivial flow of control, it is even more important to show the reader how the program is structured, precisely which sections of code may be executed repeatedly, and which sections may be selected or bypassed through the action of an IF statement.

As with English text, no single, universally accepted "correct" programming style exists. The particulars may involve personal preference, or they may be dictated as company policy. Whatever the situation, the need for some stylistic conventions is universally acknowledged.

The following are some additional style rules that extend those presented in Chapter 2, in order to accommodate the new control structures and more complex programs introduced in this chapter. We use these conventions in the programs throughout the rest of this book. Your instructor may prescribe some additional rules or may wish to modify ours somewhat. Nevertheless, these style rules represent a good starting point; you should use this set or a similar set of conventions in every program you write.

An important feature of style is indentation. Various levels of indentation show fine structure within broad structure within even broader structure, and so on. Each level should correspond to one stroke of the tab key on a terminal.

We also recommend matching each BEGIN and END with similar comments to identify them as a matching pair. We hasten to add that these comments do not necessarily make the pair match, but they do serve as a reminder that the programmer intended them to match. If an error occurs in compilation, the comments will be a useful aid to finding the error, and after the error has been corrected, they will properly identify a matching pair.

3.9 Making Programs Work Correctly

As the logic of a program becomes more complex, associated errors can become harder to diagnose and correct. Because a major source of error is an incorrect algorithm, you should check it by hand with several examples even

**Program Style
and Documentation**

1. Major program sections and major groups of lines or statements within
    each section should be separated by blank lines and (often) introduced
    by comments.
2. Compound statements are coded as follows:
    (a) Each simple statement is indented one level from its BEGIN.
    (b) END appears at the same level of indentation as the corresponding
        BEGIN.

    ```
    {Example}
      BEGIN
        Count := Count + 1;
        read (Symbol)
      END;
    ```

3. IF statements are coded as follows:
    (a) THEN appears on the same line as IF.
    (b) The statement associated with THEN is indented one level.
    (c) ELSE appears at the same level of indentation as the corresponding
        IF and on a line by itself.
    (d) The statement associated with ELSE is indented one level.

    ```
    {Example}
      IF A > B THEN
        writeln (A)
      ELSE
        writeln (B);
    ```

4. Rules 2 and 3 are combined to cover the case of compound statements
    used with IF, as in

    ```
    IF A > B THEN
      BEGIN
        writeln (A);
        read (A)
      END
    ELSE
      BEGIN
        writeln (B);
        read (B)
      END;
    ```

5. The object of a WHILE statement is indented one level from the controlling
    statement.

    ```
    {Example}
      Fact := 1;
      K := 1;
    ```

```
WHILE K < 16 DO
  BEGIN
    Fact := Fact * K;
    writeln (K,Fact);
    K := K + 1
  END;
```

6. The object of a REPEAT statement is indented one level from REPEAT, and UNTIL appears at the same level of indentation as the corresponding REPEAT.

```
{Example}
  Fact := 1;
  K := 1;
  REPEAT
    Fact := Fact * K;
    writeln (K,Fact);
    K := K + 1
  UNTIL K = 16;
```

7. The object of a FOR statement is indented one level from the controlling statement.

```
{simple FOR}
  FOR Symbol := 'a' TO 'z' DO
    writeln (Symbol);
{compound FOR}
  Psn := 26;
  FOR Symbol := 'Z' DOWNTO 'A' DO
    BEGIN
      writeln (Psn,Symbol);
      Psn := Psn - 1
    END
```

8. Case constants are indented one level from the governing CASE statement. Multiple constants associated with the same statements are listed on separate lines. A statement appears on the same line as the corresponding (last) constant. The END appears at the same level of indentation as the CASE.

```
{Example}
  CASE Status OF
    Class1: FirstClass := FirstClass + 1;
    Class2,
    Class3: Regular := Regular + 1;
    Class4: BEGIN
              SlowPay := SlowPay + 1;
              writeln ('Adjust credit rating.')
            END
  END; {case}
```

desk checks   before you begin coding. Even if your **desk checks** of the algorithm and the
code seem to work, and even after you compile the code and perhaps run it
(correctly) a few times, some error may eventually show up. You should
never rule out the algorithm as a possible cause. When designing the solution
approach, you may have overlooked some particular circumstances that never
happened to occur until a late stage in testing. As long as errors persist, you
should subject the algorithm to review and possible revision.

Assuming that the algorithm is correct, there is often a lack of correspondence between the algorithm and the code. Even if the program compiles
and sometimes runs, it still may not be doing what it should do in every case.
Even when a program is correct, a mistake made while improving it may
introduce new errors or undermine a section that worked previously.

So, how do you find out whether your program is working correctly?
We have already stressed the importance of testing programs with a variety
of both typical and rather extreme or unusual input combinations. This is
even more important when the logic is complex. The number of different
cases and alternative paths through the program may be very large, and you
should try as many as possible with judicious test cases. The most important
thing to remember is to keep the test cases simple, so that you know whether
the program's response is correct. Simple tests of specific situations may help
to zero in on the code that is in error, greatly simplifying the diagnosis and
repair. Problems do arise; that much is certain. What you should look for
depends on the symptoms you observe during testing.

BEGIN–END Problems

One source of trouble is the misuse of BEGIN . . . END constructs. If some
ENDs are missing, the compiler will usually indicate that another END was
expected. However, the compiler often recognizes this only at the bottom of
the program, where it issues the message. But this is not necessarily the place
where the missing END belongs. Make sure that your repair matches the
specifications of your algorithm, and consider the compiler's message as
simply an indication of trouble *somewhere*.

Since every BEGIN and every CASE must have a matching END, you
can inspect an existing program, associating each END with its parent BEGIN
or CASE and perhaps see where your nesting went wrong and where you
should place a missing END. The technique is simple: For each END
encountered while reading the program from top to bottom,

1. scan backwards to the first preceding BEGIN or CASE that does not
    already have an associated END; and
2. make the association by drawing a line (or box) between the END and
    its matching BEGIN or CASE.

When you have finished this procedure, your lines (or boxes) will reflect the nesting structure as understood by the compiler. If it does not agree with your algorithm, then you must make changes.

These BEGIN–END, CASE–END constructs form the basic structural components of the program. You must properly nest them, which means that none of your lines may cross. This is illustrated in Fig. 3.37.

A much more subtle error is the *failure* to use a BEGIN–END block when more than one action must be selected (by IF or CASE) or repeated (by WHILE or FOR). Such omissions are often not noticed by the compiler and result in run-time errors. For example, if you forget the compound statement after WHILE, only the first statement after the WHILE gets repeated, instead of the sequence intended to constitute the loop. If this first statement does not change the loop condition, it gets repeated potentially forever—a common cause of *infinite loops*.

■ Figure 3.37
Discovering the major sections of a program by identifying loops and compound statements.

```
BEGIN
    S1;
    IF  C0 THEN
        WHILE ...  DO
          ┌─BEGIN
          │     S2;
          │     IF  C1  THEN
          │         IF  C2 THEN
          │             S3
          │         ELSE
          │           ┌─BEGIN
          │           │     S4;
          │           │     S5
          │           └─END
          │     ELSE
          │       ┌─BEGIN
          │       │     S6;
          │       │     IF  C3  THEN
          │       │         S7;
          │       │     S8
          │       └─END;
          │     S9
          └─ END
    ELSE
        S10
END.
```

Semicolon Problems

In Pascal semicolons are used to separate the statements or to separate the case list elements of the CASE construct. Sometimes complex statements (especially nested IF statements) become so long that some people have a tendency to insert an extra semicolon here and there—simply because semicolons are used so often at the end of other statements. However, this indiscriminate use of semicolons can be fatal. If not caught by the compiler, the statements may be broken apart, destroying dependencies implied by the algorithm and intended by the programmer.

Two examples of semicolon problems are shown in Fig. 3.38. The semicolon in Fig. 3.38(a) isolates the FOR statement from its intended object. The syntax is valid, but at run time the empty statement between the DO and semicolon is executed ten times and the compound statement once. In Fig. 3.38(b) the *second* semicolon would cause a syntax error by ending the second IF statement just before an ELSE, leaving the ELSE unattached to any IF. A semicolon preceding an ELSE is *always* an error. After removing the second semicolon, the code would execute, but probably not as intended. The first semicolon terminates the first IF causing the second IF to choose its actions independently, regardless of whether X < 6 is true.

In an existing program an easy way to highlight what the semicolons tell the compiler is simply to scan the executable part of the program for semicolons. Whenever you find one, circle it and draw a line separating the preceding line from the following line. If this does not separate the statements

■ Figure 3.38
Some problems
caused by extraneous
semicolons.

```
FOR J := 1 TO 10 DO;
    BEGIN

        ┌─────────────────┐
        │ code that is    │
        │ to be repeated  │
        └─────────────────┘

    END
```

(a)

```
IF X < 6 THEN;
    IF Y <> 6 THEN
        Y := Y * Z;
    ELSE
        Y := (Y-1) * Z;
```

(b)

Figure 3.39
Isolating separate
statements in each
block by locating
semicolons.

```
┌BEGIN
│   S1;
──────────────────
      IF C0 THEN
            WHILE ... DO
               ┌BEGIN
               │   S2;
            ──────────────────
                  IF C1 THEN
                        IF C2 THEN
                           S3
                        ELSE
                           ┌BEGIN
                           │   S4;
                        ──────S5
                           └END
                  ELSE
                     ┌BEGIN
                     │   S6;
                  ──────IF C3 THEN
                  ──────────S7;
                           S8
                     └END;
               ──────────────────
                     S9
               └END
         ELSE
               S10
└END.
```

at the intended boundaries, changes are needed. Be especially wary around nested IFs; determine whether they really are nested. However, it is important that the separating line be entirely within the BEGIN–END or CASE–END construct; the latter are the major components, and semicolons are only separators within them. See Fig. 3.39 for an example of this construction.

Nested IF Problems

When sequences of decisions are required in which earlier decisions determine the course through later ones, nested IF statements are usually involved. Sometimes the logic is so complex that the nesting becomes too deep to be understood clearly. We have already mentioned the problems of leaving out BEGIN–END groupings or using semicolons except to separate statements within a BEGIN–END block. Another source of error is to accidentally leave out an ELSE or to include an extra one. These errors cause ELSE clauses to be associated with the wrong IF statement.

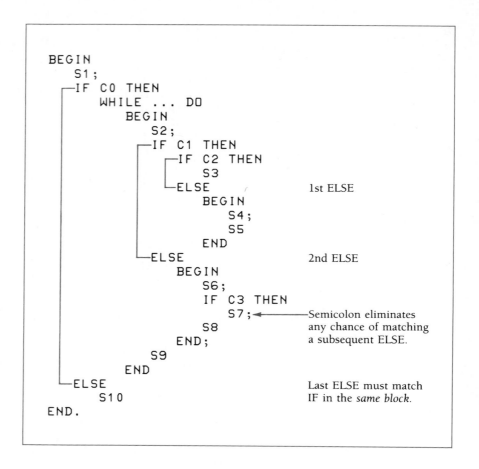

To check an existing program for the correct association, scan a program (or a single BEGIN–END construct) to match ELSEs with the same IF as the compiler. For each ELSE encountered while reading the program (or block) from top to bottom,

1. scan backwards to the preceding IF (in the same block) that does not already have a matching ELSE; and
2. make the association by drawing a line between the ELSE and the matching IF.

Once again, no lines should cross. In fact, such associations must lie within the same compound structure, which means that the lines cannot cross BEGIN–END (and similar) boundaries. Figure 3.40 completes the analysis of this program by matching corresponding IF-THEN-ELSE constructs.

Such a pictorial analysis of a program greatly facilitates comparison of the program with the decision tree and/or algorithm that served as its

inspiration. Comparisons like this often reveal a discrepancy that can be cured
by including an ELSE clause or rearranging parts of the nested IF structure.
You also might find it helpful to draw the decision tree implied by the
program to see whether it resembles the original.

For example, Fig. 3.41(a) shows a decision tree and Fig. 3.41(b), a faulty
attempt to encode it. In Fig. 3.41(c), the matching process reveals an erroneous
association. Note that the indentation (alignment) has no effect on the logic;

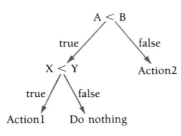

(a) Decision tree.

```
IF A < B THEN
  IF X < Y THEN
    Action1
ELSE
  Action2
```

(b) Incorrect implementation.

```
IF A < B THEN
 ┌IF X < Y THEN
 │   Action1
 └ELSE
     Action2
```

(c) Problem revealed by pictorial association.

```
┌IF A < B THEN
│ ┌IF X < Y THEN
│ │   Action 1
│ └ELSE {no action}
└ELSE
    Action2
```

(d) Inclusion of another ELSE with empty statement produces correct association.

```
┌IF A < B THEN
│ ┌BEGIN
│ │   IF X < Y THEN
│ │     Action1
│ └END
└ELSE
    Action2
```

(e) Enclosing the inner IF yields another correct solution.

■ Figure 3.41
Making correct IF-THEN-ELSE associations.

its only role is to improve readability. We cured the problem by using the code shown in Fig. 3.41(d). In this last (correct) version, the first ELSE leads to an empty statement, causing no effect, but its inclusion is essential. We also solved the problem in a different way, as shown in Fig. 3.41(e). By enclosing the second IF statement in a BEGIN–END block, we eliminated any possible association with an element outside the block. (Make sure you understand why a semicolon would not solve this problem.)

Problems with Conditions

Sometimes a trade-off is necessary between the depth of nested IFs and the complexity of the boolean expressions used to express the conditions. When rearranging THEN and ELSE clauses to make nested IFs correct or when reducing their depth by revising the test conditions, great care must be taken to ensure that the original logic is preserved.

Our attempt in Fig. 3.42(a) to encode the decision tree of Fig. 3.41(a) may look straightforward, but this is not a correct implementation. It performs Action1 when it should, but it performs Action2 in all other cases, even in the case where it should perform no action. Figure 3.42(b) shows another attempt that reverses the first condition and order of actions and that does correspond to the logic of Fig. 3.41(a). The point is that altering conditions is tricky. You should test every possible case by hand to make sure that the new version takes the correct action in all cases.

When reversing a compound condition, say

$$(Q > R) \text{ OR } (S < T)$$

be very careful. Its exact opposite can be expressed by either

$$(Q <= R) \text{ AND } (S >= T)$$

or

$$\text{NOT } ((Q > R) \text{ OR } (S < T))$$

```
IF (A < B) AND (X < Y) THEN        IF A >= B THEN { A<B false }
   Action1                            Action2
ELSE                                ELSE { A < B true }
   Action2                            IF X < Y THEN
                                         Action1
```

(a) An incorrect implementation.   **(b)** A correct implementation.

■ Figure 3.42
Attempts at rearranging the conditions of Fig. 3.41(a).

On the other hand, the expression

$$(Q <= R) \text{ OR } (S >= T)$$

is neither the same nor opposite. Do not leave any case unchecked when testing the equivalence (or difference) between two logical expressions.

The Loop Index Problem

loop index

Loops often are controlled by some variable, which is first given a starting value, then changes by a constant amount each time through the loop, and eventually causes termination of the loop by reaching or exceeding some final value. Such a variable is called a **loop index.** We used several counters in this chapter as loop indices. However, an index does not have to be a counter. It need not start with 0 or 1, and it need not be modified by 1 inside the loop.

Sometimes the starting value or final value for the loop index is not immediately apparent from the problem statement, and the programmer must deduce it. This is not as easy as it sounds. Choosing the correct limits for a loop index is a very common problem that is too often solved incorrectly. In practice it is likely that the loop will execute one time more or one time less than it should. Good programmers are always wary of this possibility and tend to double-check loop indices during both the development and testing stages.

For example, consider the problem of adding n consecutive integers starting with a. In other words, a and n are parameters specifying the range of integers to be added. For $a = 0$ and $n = 4$ we want $0 + 1 + 2 + 3 = 6$. For $a = 6$ and $n = 2$, we want $6 + 7 = 13$. For $a = -1$ and $n = 3$, we want $-1 + 0 + 1 = 0$.

The solution obviously involves a repetitive process governed by a loop index that equals the integer being added to the sum. The starting value of the index is given directly (a), and the index will be incremented by 1 each time. However the final value—the largest integer in the sum—is not usually the same as n. Take another look at the examples in the preceding paragraph for evidence.

We want to determine the final value for the index and might be tempted to try $a + n$. After all, the nth integer beyond a is $a + n$. But this is wrong. We do not want the nth integer beyond a; we also need to include a itself in the range. The correct choice for the final value is one less, namely, $a + n - 1$. You can confirm this by again looking back at the sample sums.

The important point is that we do have two or three simple examples on which to try our choice of a final value. Trying them on paper at this stage can prevent much grief later, when the program starts generating wrong answers for no apparent reason. You should, of course, use some other simple examples at the testing stage, so that you know whether the program is generating correct answers.

The loop index problem is often more subtle than the one shown here. Among the issues to be resolved are which loop control statement to use and if WHILE or REPEAT is chosen, how to select the relational operator used in the loop condition. But even for seemingly simple loop index problems, we recommend pretrial using examples in which only one or two—or possibly no—repetitions of the loop are expected. If your loop does not work on the trivial cases, it certainly will not work in general.

It is good defensive programming to use inequalities rather than = or <> in loop conditions. This helps to guard against problems with precision that would prevent the index variable from exactly reaching some specific value. It is generally safer to allow the index to migrate toward some boundary and then stop the loop whenever that boundary is met *or* passed. Hence,

```
WHILE N > 5 DO
```

is preferable to

```
WHILE N <> 5 DO
```

because the latter has only one opportunity to cause loop termination. If N is never exactly 5, the latter loop will never stop.

3.10 Review of Rules

A. A condition (or simple boolean expression) has the form

⟨expression⟩ ⟨relational operator⟩ ⟨expression⟩

and has a value of either true or false. The expressions must both be of comparable type. If they are characters, the condition refers to their relative ordering in the machine's collating sequence.

Simple boolean expressions may be operands for the boolean operators (AND, OR, NOT) that produce compound boolean expressions. AND has a true value when both of its operands are true. OR has a true value whenever either or both of its operands are true. NOT is a unary operator, and reverses the boolean value of its operand.

B. The syntax diagram for the WHILE statement is

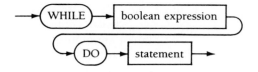

WHILE causes repeated execution of its constituent statement so long as the condition is true. If the condition is false when WHILE is first encountered, the statement is not executed.

C. The syntax diagram for a compound statement is

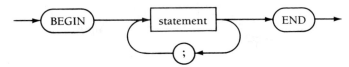

The compound statement groups other statements so that the entire collection can be treated as a single statement at a higher level.

D. The FOR statement is used to control the number of iterations through a loop. The more common of its two general forms is

FOR ⟨variable⟩ : = ⟨expression1⟩ TO ⟨expression2⟩ DO
    ⟨statement⟩;

The ⟨variable⟩ must not be of real type, and both expressions must be compatible with its type. On successive executions of the ⟨statement⟩ the ⟨variable⟩ will take on successive ordinal values from ⟨expression1⟩ to ⟨expression2⟩, inclusive. If ⟨expression2⟩ is less than ⟨expression1⟩, the ⟨statement⟩ will not be executed. To force execution in this case, the second form of FOR must be used, as in

FOR ⟨variable⟩ : = ⟨expression1⟩ DOWNTO ⟨expression2⟩ DO
    ⟨statement⟩;

In this form the values of the ⟨variable⟩ progress backward. In either form the value of the ⟨variable⟩ is undefined on completion of the FOR statement. The syntax diagram is

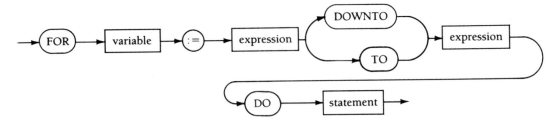

E. REPEAT is used to control the execution of a loop until some condition becomes true. It has the general form:

REPEAT
    ⟨statement1⟩;
    ⟨statement2⟩;

        .
        .
        .

    ⟨statementN⟩
UNTIL ⟨condition⟩.

The statement(s) between REPEAT and UNTIL will always be executed

at least once because the condition is tested only at the end of the loop. The syntax diagram is

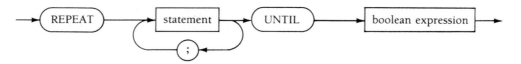

F.   The syntax diagram for an IF statement is

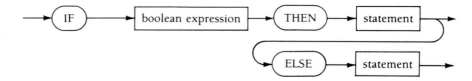

The IF statement is used to direct flow of control through one of two alternative statements. If the second alternative is "nothing," the ELSE may be omitted.

G.   The CASE statement permits the selection of a single statement for execution based on the value of some nonreal expression; this expression is often referred to as the CASE index. The general form of CASE is

```
CASE ⟨CASE index⟩ OF
    ⟨constant-list1⟩: ⟨statement1⟩;
    ⟨constant-list2⟩: ⟨statement2⟩;
        .
        .
        .
    ⟨constant-listN⟩: ⟨statementN⟩
END
```

The ⟨case index⟩ is evaluated and then the statement prefixed by the constant corresponding to that value is executed; the execution continues with the first logical statement after the END of the CASE construct. If the ⟨case index⟩ evaluates to an unlisted constant, the result is an error. The syntax diagram for CASE is

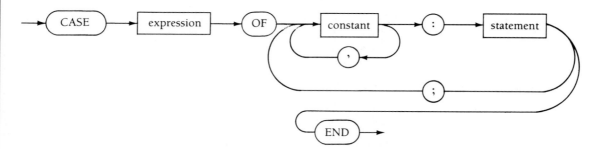

KEY TERMS

alternative execution	empty statement
AND operator	flowchart
ASCII code	FOR statement
boolean expression	IF statement
boolean operators	loop
case constants	loop index
case index	nested loops
case list element	NOT operator
CASE statement	OR operator
collating sequence	REPEAT statement
compound statement	repetitive execution
conditions	relational operator
control variable	sentinel
decision tree	truth table
desk checks	UNTIL
DOWNTO	WHILE statement

EXERCISES

3.1   Identify and explain the errors (if any) in the following statements.

```
(a) IF A = B = C THEN
      writeln ('all equal');
(b) IF A = B THEN
      writeln ( 'A equals B');
    ELSE
      writeln ('A different from B');
(c) IF A = B THEN
    ELSE
      Sum := Sum + 1;
(d) CASE Change OF
      0.05: write ('nickel');
      0.10: write ('dime');
      0.25: write ('quarter');
      0.50: write ('half')
    END;
(e) read (Next);
    WHILE Next <> Sentinel DO
      Total := Total + Next; {add to total}
      Count := Count + 1; {no. of values read}
      read (Next);
```

3.2   How many times will each of the following loop interiors be executed?

```
(a) K := 10;
    WHILE K > 1 DO
      BEGIN
        writeln (K);
        K := K - 2
      END;
```

```
(b) FOR K := 10 DOWNTO 1 DO
      writeln (K);
(c) K := 0;
    WHILE K <= 10 DO
      BEGIN
        writeln (K);
        K := K + 1
      END;
(d) L := 2;
    REPEAT
      writeln (L);
      L := L + 2
    UNTIL L = 10;
(e) K := 0;
    WHILE K = 0 DO
      K := K + 1;
(f) K := 1;
    WHILE (K > 0) OR (K < 10) DO
      K := K +1;
```

3.3 Which of the following correctly tests whether the character just read into the variable Ans is NOT the letter q (uppercase or lowercase)?

```
(a) IF (Ans <> 'q') OR (Ans <> 'Q') THEN ...
(b) IF (Ans <> 'q') AND (Ans <> 'Q') THEN ...
(c) IF NOT ((Ans = 'q') OR (Ans = 'Q')) THEN ...
(d) IF NOT ((Ans = 'q') AND (Ans = 'Q')) THEN ...
(e) none of the above
```

3.4 The program to calculate averages in Fig. 3.13 will fail with a run-time error if no data values are given, that is, if it is supplied with only the sentinel value. Modify the program so that it issues the message "No data values read" if this condition is detected.

3.5 The grades for a class of unknown size fall in the range 0 to 100, inclusive. Write a program to read the grades, calculate the average, and count how many grades fall into each of the following categories.

Category	Grade range
A	$79 < \text{grade} \leq 100$
B	$69 < \text{grade} < 80$
C	$59 < \text{grade} < 70$
D	$49 < \text{grade} < 60$
F	$\text{grade} \leq 49$

3.6 A perfect square is an integer whose square root is also an integer. Write a program to discover the perfect squares between any two input integers. The program should reject negative input and may not assume that the first number is necessarily smaller than the second.

3.7 Write a program to read a sentence terminated by a period and tabulate the frequency of each of the vowels (whether upper or lower case) in the sentence.

3.8 Write a program to read an arbitrary number of temperatures in either Fahrenheit or Celsius and convert the temperatures to the other scale. The input data will consist of a real number, a single space, and either the letter F or the letter C, say, 98.6 F or −5.0 C. The program should produce output of the form:

98.6 degrees Fahrenheit is equivalent to 37.0 degrees Celsius.

3.9 Write a program to raise an arbitrary number n to the kth power, as described in Exercise 1.11.
  (a) Assume that k is a strictly positive integer.
  (b) Allow k to be any integer.
3.10 (a) Write a program to compute $n!$ (n factorial), as described in Exercise 1.13(a).
  (b) Write a program to compute n-choose-k, as described in Exercise 1.13(b).
3.11 Write a program to compute the roots of a quadratic equation, with the standard coefficients entered as input. (See Exercise 2.11.) Make sure that the coefficients entered will produce real roots. In case the values supplied will not yield real roots, your program should give the user the option of either quitting or entering new coefficients until suitable values are obtained.
3.12 Write a program to accept the coefficients for two straight lines, as described in Exercise 2.12. Your program should tell the user whether these lines are parallel, coincide, or intersect at a point. In the last case, it should display the coordinates of the intersecting point.
3.13 Extend any of the preceding exercises (3.9–3.12) by allowing the user to apply the basic operation over and over to new data. For example, if computing factorials, the user should be able to enter a succession of integers and see the factorial of each computed. Processing should terminate when a suitable sentinel value is entered. Your program should inform the run-time user about this sentinel, at least at the beginning of execution.
3.14 Triangles may be grouped into four classes: scalene, isosceles, equilateral, and right-angled. An isosceles triangle is one with any two sides equal; an equilateral triangle is one with all three sides equal; a right-angled triangle is one where the square of the longest side is equal to the sum of the squares of the other two; a scalene triangle is a triangle with none of the above properties. In any triangle, the sum of the lengths of any two sides exceeds the length of the third.

  Design an algorithm to examine an arbitrary number of triplets of integers representing the sides of a triangle. Decide whether they could form a triangle and, if so, to which one of the four classes it belongs. (Some triangles may belong to more than one class.) Implement your algorithm by a Pascal program that produces as output the three sides considered and any of the applicable messages: SCALENE, ISOSCELES, EQUILATERAL, RIGHT-ANGLED, or NOT A TRIANGLE.
3.15 Recall that a prime number is a positive integer greater than 1 that is exactly divisible only by itself and 1. (See Exercise 1.12.)
  (a) Write a program to determine whether a given number is prime.
  (b) Write a program to generate the first 25 prime numbers.
  (c) Write a program to generate all the prime numbers between two given numbers.
3.16 A perfect number is a positive integer, all of whose positive divisors (except itself) sum to the number. Thus 6 is a perfect number because its divisors (3, 2, and 1) add up to 6. On the other hand, 8 is not a perfect number because its divisors are 4, 2, and 1, which sum to 7. Write a program to find all perfect numbers which are less than or equal to some given number.

3.17 Implement the algorithm developed in Exercise 1.14 to find the best selling price for a product. Read values for N, B, R, and M. Display the results as a table, with each line showing a proposed price, the number of units to be sold at this price, and the total income from these sales. The first row should show these values for the starting (base) price.

(a) Stop after ten prices have been tried or when the price would become 0 or negative, whichever happens first.

(b) After you check to determine that the input values are reasonable for this problem, try different prices and generate lines of output until the total income begins to decrease. In a well-formed problem solution, the income should increase to its maximum point and then decrease forever. The first decrease signals that the maximum has been passed.

(c) Bonus: After getting near the price that produces maximum income by trying prices at fixed increments from the base price, see if you can find the very best price (to two decimal places) that produces the absolute maximum income; that is, find the *best* price by doing a more refined search among prices in the vicinity of the *good* price.

3.18 In Exercise 2.15, your program displayed a metric date, given some user-supplied date in another standard format. Character data had to be used in order to provide leading 0's, so that single-digit components of the date would appear as two-digit numbers.

(a) Solve this problem without using the char data type. While allowing the user to supply only as many digits as required, display each component of the date with two digits. Assume that the input utilizes blanks as separators.

(b) Check each date supplied for validity. You should make sure that each value is in its proper range, accounting for the correct number of days in each month. (Do not worry about leap year; assume that February has 28 days.)

(c) Now account for leap year. N represents a leap year if N is exactly divisible by 4, except when N is exactly divisible by 100, it must be divisible by 400 also. Hence, while 2000 will be a leap year, 1900 was not.

3.19 Write a program that will accept a metric date as input and give the correct NEXT N metric dates as output. You should keep track of leap years. See the previous exercise for pertinent information.

3.20 Sometimes part numbers and other identification numbers have an extra digit, called a *check digit,* to help verify that the number is valid and has not been altered. A valid number is one having digits, including this check digit, that satisfy some internal algebraic relation, such as: the sum of the digits of the original part number, when taken mod 10, must be equal to the check digit. For example, if the rightmost digit is the check digit, the number 2653 is valid because the sum of 2, 6, and 5, or 13, taken mod 10, is 3. When people make a typing error or when a number is accidentally changed, the alteration is usually confined to a single digit. If one digit has been changed, the expected relation will not hold, and the number can be recognized as invalid. Write a program to test the validity of a four-digit part number, using the consistency check described, and refuse to accept the part number until it passes the consistency check.

4

Modular Programming

By now you should be accustomed to designing algorithms that display different levels of detail at different stages of development. Once the overall, high-level algorithm has been designed, subalgorithms may be written to show the finer structure of particular steps. Then, certain steps may be further refined by still other levels of algorithm, and so on, until a clear, understandable solution to the problem has been achieved.

Program development itself can proceed in exactly the same way. As soon as a suitable high-level algorithm has been produced, it can immediately be encoded as the main program. Wherever the high-level algorithm contains a step that requires elaboration by a subalgorithm, a reference to some *subprogram* is inserted in the main program. A **subprogram** is a separate auxiliary program that will specify how to implement a particular step. The main program remains at the same high level as the initial algorithm. This version of the main program is the complete and final version. Missing details are simply relegated to subprograms that remain to be written.

A similar approach can be used with the subprograms. When a more detailed subalgorithm has been designed, it can then be encoded to become the required subprogram. If any subalgorithm contains steps that require even more detailed specification, the corresponding subprogram will contain references to even lower-level subprograms, and so on. The resulting subprograms will have a hierarchical relationship similar to that of the various components of the algorithm.

The final program will not contain just a single, massive block of executable code. Instead it will consist of a family of individual, conveniently *modules* small programs known as **modules.** These modules retain their identity as separate programs. Only references to them appear in the higher level code that requires their action.

Because code development can occur in parallel with algorithm development, it can share the advantages of top-down design and stepwise refinement. Since each module focuses on only one aspect of the solution, the modules are easier to write, understand, test, and change. When an error does occur, the problem is often confined to a single module that can be located quickly, and can be repaired without disturbing other parts of the program.

From another viewpoint, subprograms are simpler programs that can be used as building blocks to construct more complex programs. Writing a new module is somewhat like adding a new feature or operation to the language, which can then be used as if it had been provided from the start. Thus previously written modules can often be incorporated into new programs.

With so many advantages, modular programming has become standard practice for all but the simplest problems. In this chapter we introduce the techniques of modular programming as well as *procedures* and *functions,* the two kinds of subprogram modules provided by Pascal.

4.1 Procedures without Parameters

Just as we make the distinction between writing a program and executing it, we must distinguish between the declaration of a procedure and references to it in programs that use it. Declaring a procedure involves writing code to specify how it works, similar to coding any other program.

A program may use a procedure merely by referring to it. If a procedure reference is encountered at run time, control is redirected to the procedure, the procedure is executed, and control then returns to resume execution of the referencing program. The effect is to cause the procedure's action to occur at the point where a reference to the procedure appears.

Using Procedures

procedures
predeclared
procedures

Perhaps without realizing it, you have been using **procedures** right from the start. In particular, read, write, and writeln are **predeclared procedures,** which means that they are already defined and built into Pascal. They are predeclared because they perform fundamental, commonly needed tasks. However, their use is similar to procedures you define for yourself. These particular procedures perform some fairly sophisticated tasks in regulating the flow of data in and out of programs. As with any procedures, you do not need to know the details of their internal operation in order to use them.

When you want to display the value of X, the X is placed within parentheses following the appropriate procedure name—for example, write(X).

parameters

The items that appear in parentheses are **parameters,** which cause the procedure to produce its effect using different selected values. We will deal with parameters shortly, but for now let's consider only procedures that do not use parameters. You have had some experience with this in the form of writeln—which allows you to skip a line without transferring data. Another example of a predeclared procedure that does not require parameters is "page," which causes the printer to begin at the top of a new page.

calling program
procedure call
called procedure

Note that you may have a program invoke either of these procedures simply by mentioning the procedure name at the appropriate place. A program that invokes a procedure is known as a **calling program.** Reference to a procedure, known as a **procedure call,** constitutes a complete statement in the calling program. The procedure being referenced is then the **called procedure** (or called subprogram). If the procedure requires parameters, you must include them in parentheses in the reference; otherwise you only use the procedure name (without parentheses). Thus the four-statement sequence

```
read(X);
page;
writeln;
writeln;
```

contains four procedure references and, if executed, would leave the output device positioned two lines below the top of a new page.

procedure identifier

Exactly the same holds true for procedures you define yourself. Every procedure has its own unique name, called the **procedure identifier.** By simply using this identifier as a separate statement, your program can cause the indicated procedure to produce its effect at that point during program execution.

Suppose that your program is generating reports on paper, and you want a special heading to be printed at the top of each page. Rather than put all the required output statements in the body of the program, you decide to call a procedure to print the headings. Since this is not a predeclared procedure, you must define your own. We will explain how to do this in the next section. However, at this stage we do not care how the procedure will work—only that it can be defined.

Now, assume you will have a procedure named NewPage to generate page headings. All that you have to do in the main program is refer to NewPage whenever a heading is needed, as in

```
BEGIN {Report}
  NewPage; {generate header for first page}
```

```
      recognize that new page
      should be generated
```

```
  NewPage {generate header for next page}
END. {Report}
```

Declaring Your Own Procedures

A procedure is little more than a self-contained program. Therefore you should not worry about any other program that might use it. You can concentrate exclusively on the specific task the procedure is supposed to perform.

A procedure resembles the programs we have developed so far: It is the encoding of an algorithm, along with appropriate definitions. Writing a procedure declaration involves little more than writing the code to perform the desired action. The code to produce a page heading might look like:

```
page; {skip to top of new page}
writeln (' ':30,'My report':20);
writeln; writeln {skip 2 lines}
```

procedure heading

To convert this code into a procedure declaration, merely enclose it by BEGIN and END and introduce it by a line called the **procedure heading.** This heading always begins with the reserved word PROCEDURE, followed by the identifier of your choice. This identifier is the name by which another program can reference and invoke the procedure. (Just make sure it is a unique name.) If there are no parameters, that is all there is to the heading. Simply add a semicolon to separate the heading from the *block* of code that describes its workings, and the procedure declaration is complete. A complete procedure declaration is shown in Fig. 4.1.

Procedure placement

The NewPage procedure is ready to use when we position its declaration correctly within the overall program. Like any other object to be referenced by a Pascal program, we must declare a procedure before the executable statements that use it. All subprogram declarations must appear immediately before the statement part of the program.

Figure 4.2 shows an example of the NewPage procedure embedded within the report-generating program. Notice how the entire declaration of NewPage appears just before the statement part of the main program. Incidentally, this procedure calls two other (predeclared) procedures to complete its work: writeln and page.

■ Figure 4.1
Complete procedure
to generate page
headings.

```
PROCEDURE NewPage;
   BEGIN
      page; {skip to top of new page}
      writeln (' ':30,'My report':20);
      writeln; writeln {skip 2 lines}
   END;
```

```
PROGRAM Report (input,output);
    .
    .
VAR ....;

┌─────────────────────────────────────────────┐
│ PROCEDURE NewPage;                           │
│    BEGIN                                      │
│        page; {skip to top of new page}       │
│        writeln (' ':30,'My report':20);      │
│        writeln; writeln {skip 2 lines}       │
│    END;                                       │
└─────────────────────────────────────────────┘

BEGIN {Report}
    .
    .
    .
    NewPage; {header for first page}
    .
    .

        {recognize that new page          References
         should be generated}              to procedure

    NewPage;
    .
    .
    .

END. {Report}
```

Flow of control   Even though the procedure declaration physically precedes the other executable statements, there is no danger of it being executed first. Execution always begins at the statement part of the PROGRAM block. A subprogram can be executed only when control reaches a *reference* to it. The flow of control during execution of the report-generating program is shown in Fig. 4.3 on p. 164.

Local Identifiers

The first thing an interactive program may do is ask whether the user wants instructions in its use. If the user responds positively, the program then prints some preliminary information. This initial interaction is an optional prompt

■ **Figure 4.3**
Flow of control
through procedures.

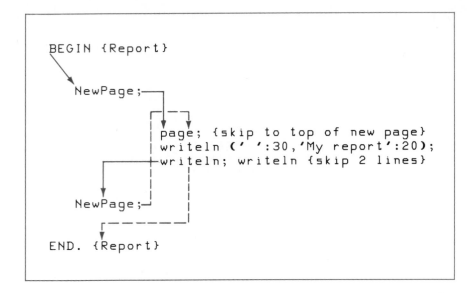

and has nothing to do with the operations performed by the program. Rather than clutter up the main program with it, you can relegate the initial prompt to a procedure.

For now, let's concentrate on such a procedure without concern for the program that it explains. Its algorithm is simple:

1. ask user if explanation is desired;
2. read user's response;
3. if response is positive, then
3.1   display desired information.

We turn this into a procedure directly, as shown in Fig. 4.4. The procedure consists of an encoding of this algorithm, enclosed by BEGIN and END and introduced by a procedure heading.

However, this procedure also contains its own variable declaration section because a variable is needed for storing the user's response. Since a procedure is just another program that is used in a special (auxiliary) way, so it can define whatever identifiers of whatever sort it needs to carry out its task. Thus procedures may declare constants, variables, and all the other elements that a main program can declare.

local identifier   An identifier declared inside a subprogram is called a **local identifier;** if
local variable   the object is a variable, such as Choice, it is called a **local variable.** The qualifier "local" emphasizes that the identifier is the local, private, exclusive property of the subprogram in which it is declared. In other words, although the main program may call on Prompt, it cannot access anything *inside* of Prompt that the procedure declared for its own use. In particular, the main program could not use or change the value of the local variable Choice. An

```
PROCEDURE Prompt;
   VAR
      Choice: char; {for private use of procedure}
   BEGIN
      write('Instructions? Type Y or N: ');
      read(Choice);
      IF (Choice = 'Y') OR (Choice = 'y') THEN
         BEGIN {output of instructions}
         writeln('                              ');
         writeln('                              ');
         writeln('       INSTRUCTIONS           ');
         writeln('                              ');
         writeln('                              ')
         END {output of instructions}
      END; {procedure definition}
```

■ Figure 4.4
Declaration of a procedure containing a local variable.

attempt by the program block to reference Choice (assuming it had not declared a version for its own use) would cause a compile-time error. The variable, Choice, is simply undefined outside the confines of the procedure. This should not be surprising, since the main program is not concerned with how its procedures carry out their activities.

On the other hand, you may suspect that, by declaring the identifier Choice inside the procedure, we have used up this variable name and must not reuse it anywhere else in the program. However, this is *not* the case. Regardless of what may be declared in its subprograms, we are still free to declare any valid identifier in the calling program. In other words, each program and each procedure may be written independently, without regard for the symbolic names declared inside any other module. This is one of the great advantages of modular programming: Each module may be developed on its own without having to worry about the details of how any other module was or will be developed.

Now suppose that we have also declared the identifier Choice as, say, an integer variable in the main program. Is there not a conflict? After all, the same identifier cannot be used in more than one way in a single module. But here we are dealing with two modules, each containing its own declaration of Choice. There is no confusion about which version is intended with each use of the identifier in the code. Whenever we use the variable Choice anywhere inside the procedure, we are referencing the char-type variable declared in the procedure. Whenever we mention the identifier Choice in the

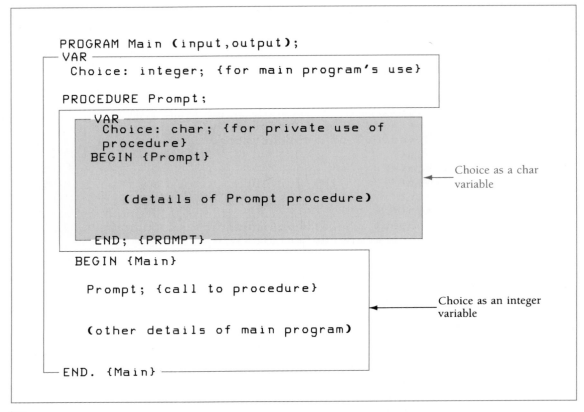

```
PROGRAM Main (input,output);
 VAR
   Choice: integer; {for main program's use}

 PROCEDURE Prompt;

    VAR
       Choice: char; {for private use of
       procedure}
    BEGIN {Prompt}


       (details of Prompt procedure)


    END; {PROMPT}
 BEGIN {Main}

    Prompt; {call to procedure}


    (other details of main program)


 END. {Main}
```

Choice as a char variable

Choice as an integer variable

■ Figure 4.5
Two nonoverlapping definitions (scopes) for the same identifier.

main program, we are referencing its own integer-type variable. If we want to store something in Choice in either module, that value is simply not available to the other module, even if we had declared the identifier with the same data type in both modules. The two variables are as distinct as if they were named Ralph and Alice. See Fig. 4.5 for an illustration of these points.

These observations apply to any kind of identifier and any number of modules. Any two modules may declare whatever objects they require without any interference from use of the same identifier in some other module.

Procedures That Call Other Procedures

Suppose that you are still writing an interactive program that will provide initial instructions to the user. Again, you give this task to a procedure. However, unlike the previous example, you have to break the instructions into two parts. The basic introduction is displayed to all users in all cases.

Only after seeing this information is the user given a choice about seeing additional instructions. The explanation about the system is then dispensed according to the following algorithm.

1. display basic information;
2. ask user if more information is desired;
3. read user's response;
4. if response is positive, then
4.1   display additional information.

The procedure governing this output, shown in Fig. 4.6, is a restatement of this algorithm in Pascal without elaboration. The explanations themselves have not yet been specified. They have been left as details to be completed in two other procedures: ShowBasics and Examples. The procedure of Fig. 4.6 merely delivers the services of one procedure followed by the services of another—after receiving the user's permission. It handles the *logic* of the display, not the *content*.

Each of the other two procedures is merely a sequence of writeln statements to display its portion of the output. By separating the control logic and the two blocks of text into three separate procedures, we ensure that each procedure remains small and clearly focused. The purpose and operation of the control procedure in particular is immediately apparent: It is not cluttered with output statements that might distract a reader.

It makes no difference to the main program whether these introductory messages are the product of one procedure or three. It merely calls on Information and leaves the details to this procedure (and, as it happens, its allies).

The only question that remains is the placement of the three new procedure declarations in the overall program. Of course, all three declarations must appear between the VAR part and the executable code of the program block. Just as the procedure Information must be defined before it is referenced (in the main program), the other two procedures must be declared before

■ Figure 4.6
Procedure to control output.

```
PROCEDURE Information;
   VAR
      Choice: char;
   BEGIN {Information}
      ShowBasics; {display initial information}
      write ('Do you want examples? (Y or N): ');
      read (Choice);
      IF (Choice = 'Y') OR (Choice = 'y') THEN
         Examples {display additional information}
   END; {Information}
```

■ Figure 4.7
Placement of
procedure
declarations.

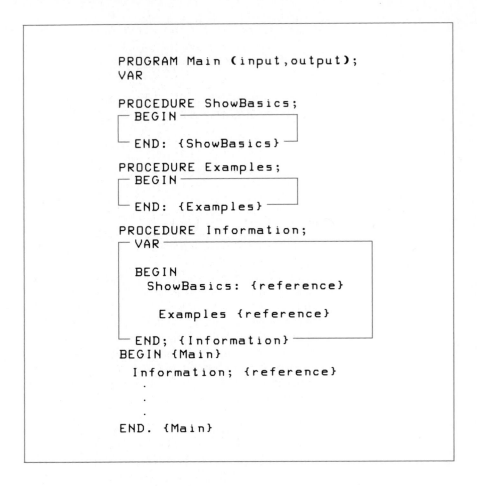

```
PROGRAM Main (input,output);
VAR

PROCEDURE ShowBasics;
┌ BEGIN ──────────────────────────┐
│                                  │
└ END: {ShowBasics} ───────────────┘

PROCEDURE Examples;
┌ BEGIN ──────────────────────────┐
│                                  │
└ END: {Examples} ─────────────────┘

PROCEDURE Information;
┌ VAR ─────────────────────────────────┐
│                                       │
│  BEGIN                                │
│    ShowBasics: {reference}            │
│                                       │
│      Examples {reference}             │
│                                       │
└ END; {Information} ───────────────────┘
BEGIN {Main}

  Information; {reference}
    .
    .
    .

END. {Main}
```

■ Figure 4.8
A tree structure
showing intermodule
references.

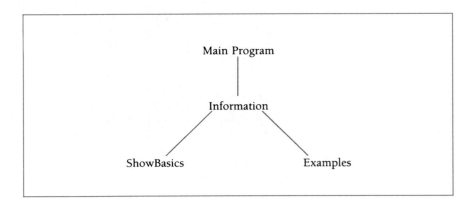

they are referenced (in Information). Hence, both their definitions must precede the definition of Information. One possibility is shown in Fig. 4.7.

The tree diagram in Fig. 4.8 shows which modules contain references to which other modules. Each line represents an intermodule reference, with the calling module at the top and the called module at the bottom. Trees are useful for depicting the hierarchical relationship among modules. *Execution* can proceed only from the top toward the bottom. On the other hand, *placement* of the subprogram declarations inside the main program proceeds from the bottom toward the top.

4.2 Procedures with Value Parameters

The procedures that we have dealt with until now have been entirely self-sufficient. Their only interaction with any other part of the program was to call or be called by some other module. The most familiar was the simple call writeln without parameters.

However, in practice most calls to the writeln procedure include some parameters, for example, writeln (X,Y). As you know, the parameters indicate which particular values *originating within the calling module* are to be displayed as output. Parameters are the means by which we enable one module to share some of its values with another. A **value parameter** allows a value to be transferred *from* the calling module *to* the called module. The value is said to be *passed* from one module to the other. Thus X and Y refer to values in the calling program that are passed to the writeln procedure for further processing. The procedure mechanism becomes much more powerful when we permit modules to communicate by passing values through parameters.

value parameter

A View from Inside a Procedure

Recall the NewPage procedure from Fig. 4.1, which printed a heading at the top of a page of output. Now suppose we extend this heading to include the current page number. The page number is a value that differs from one use of the procedure to the next. Consequently, our new procedure must be told the current page number every time it is called. Hence, it needs a parameter.

The code for the modified procedure NewPage2 is shown in Fig. 4.9. The interior of the procedure is the same as before, except that the output line now includes the value of PageNo, the current page number.

At first PageNo may look like an ordinary variable, but it is not. We neither declared it as a variable nor gave it an initial value inside the procedure. Its role is revealed by the procedure heading, where we listed it within parentheses.

■ Figure 4.9
Declaring a procedure
with a value
parameter.

```
PROCEDURE NewPage2 (PageNo: integer);
   BEGIN
      page;
      writeln (' ':30,'My Report':20,' ':20,
         'page ':6,PageNo:3);
      writeln; writeln
   END;
```

This appearance of PageNo in the heading declares it to be a (value) parameter. This means that whenever NewPage2 is called, a value will be provided by the calling program, and this value will be known as PageNo inside this procedure. Since PageNo will identify a value, we must also specify its data type. The heading indicates that PageNo will always identify integer-type data.

This parameter declaration resembles the declaration of variables in the VAR part. What makes it a parameter instead of an ordinary variable is its appearance in the procedure heading. Of course any name declared as a parameter *must not* be redeclared as a (local) variable.

A parameter is expected to already contain a value from the "outside" when the procedure begins execution. Therefore it does not need to be explicitly given a value before being used. On the other hand, once the procedure has been called, parameters *behave* exactly like variables within the procedure. They can be accessed or given new values in the usual ways (such as by assignment statements). To the procedure then, its parameters are similar to variables, except that they already have values when the procedure starts executing.

A View from Outside a Procedure

To make use of our new procedure, we merely mention its name as before in the calling program, but this time the calling program includes an integer value within parentheses to be used as the parameter value. Thus successive calls to NewPage2 presumably employ successive integer values for the parameter. Two possible patterns are outlined in Fig. 4.10.

Each time NewPage2 is called, a different value is supplied from outside the procedure. As Fig. 4.10 suggests, this value can be a constant, the value of a variable, or even the result of evaluating a more complex integer-valued expression. However it may be produced, it is called the *argument,* or **actual parameter.** This term distinguishes it from the **formal parameter,** which is the permanent symbolic identifier used in a procedure to denote a value.

actual parameter
formal parameter

Figure 4.10
Calling a procedure
with one value
parameter.

```
NewPage2(1);                       N := 1;
     .                             WHILE . . . . DO
     .                                BEGIN
     .                                   NewPage2(N);
NewPage2(2);                                .
     .                                      .
     .                                      .
     .                                   N := N + 1
NewPage2(3);                          END; {loop}
```

(a) Supplying constants as   **(b)** Supplying parameter val-
parameter values.   ues through a variable.

The actual and formal parameters pertain to the two ends of the communication link between modules. Actual parameters are the property of the calling module, whereas formal parameters are the private property of the called procedure, just as are its local variables. Consequently, the calling module cannot access the called procedure's formal parameters. If a procedure alters the value of one of its (value) parameters, the calling program will not be affected. It doesn't matter whether the identifiers used by the caller and the called procedure happen to be the same or different, as shown in Fig. 4.10.

Placement of a procedure definition is unaffected by the presence of parameters. Figure 4.11 on p. 172 shows NewPage2 defined in the context of its calling program.

How Value Parameters Actually Work

In a procedure heading, we may declare any number of formal parameters by listing their identifiers, together with their respective data types. Consider the procedure declared in Fig. 4.12 to display the maximum of any three real numbers. This procedure expects *three* real values from the module that calls it. The procedure itself refers to these numbers by the formal parameters A, B, and C, which we declared in its heading. The formal parameters must be simple identifiers, since their role is to receive starting values from outside the procedure and then act as ordinary variables inside.

Note that we specified the common data type only once for the entire list of identifiers. The syntax is similar to declarations that occur in the VAR part. For example, if a procedure named StirUp expects a character, two real numbers, and an integer as parameters, its heading might be the following:

PROCEDURE StirUp (Letter: char; X,Y: real; M: Integer);

■ Figure 4.11
Modules
communicating
through a value
parameter.

```pascal
PROGRAM Report2 (input,output);

VAR N: integer;

PROCEDURE NewPage2 (PageNo: integer);
    BEGIN
        page;
        writeln (' ':30,'My Report':20,' ':20,
            'page ':6,PageNo:3);
        writeln; writeln
    END;

BEGIN {Report2}
    .
    .
    .
    N := 1; {current page number}
    NewPage2 (N);
    .
    .
    .

    N := N + 1;
    NewPage2 (N);
    .
    .
    .

END. {Report2}
```

```pascal
PROCEDURE Max (A,B,C: real);
    {determine and display the largest of A,B, and C}
    VAR
        Largest: real   {largest seen so far}

    BEGIN {Max}
        Largest := A; {initial estimate}
        IF B > Largest THEN
            Largest := B;
        IF C > Largest THEN
            Largest := C;
        writeln('Maximum value is: ',Largest)
    END; {Max}
```

■ Figure 4.12
Procedure to display the largest of three values.

A procedure that expects three real values as parameters must be given three real values as arguments every time it is called. As you realize, the values can be supplied by arbitrary expressions, and different references may use different expressions to generate these values. For example, we could call Max with either of the following references, assuming that the variables are all real and the references appear in context.

```
Max(X,Y,Z);
```

or

```
Max(2.4,S+T,abs(T));
```

Formal to actual parameter correspondence

How then do we establish the binding, or association, between actual parameters and formal parameters? The answer is simple: by corresponding position. The first value generated is placed in the first formal parameter; the second actual parameter value is placed in the second formal parameter; and so on. This evaluation of actual parameters and assignment of values to formal parameters occurs each time a procedure reference is executed. This is why it makes no difference whether the values are generated in the same way each time.

This parameter mechanism has two important consequences, which are really rules governing the relationship between subprogram declarations and subprogram references.

RULE I:

The *number* of actual parameters supplied in a reference must be equal to the number of formal parameters specified in the declaration.

RULE II:

The *type* of each actual parameter must be assignment compatible with the type of the corresponding formal parameter.

Once again, *assignment compatible* means that the generated value could legally be placed in the formal parameter variable under the type constraints of an ordinary assignment statement. The required correspondence is

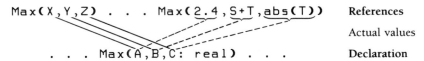

```
Max(X,Y,Z) . . . Max(2.4,S+T,abs(T))        References
                                            Actual values
    . . . Max(A,B,C: real) . . .            Declaration
```

Rule II is especially important when the formal parameters are of different types. The type of each actual parameter supplied must match the type defined in the heading for its corresponding formal parameter.

Now consider a reference to Max:

```
Max(A + B, B/2, abs(B))
```

In this reference we incorporated the variables A and B in expressions that generate actual parameter values. However, these symbols identify variables

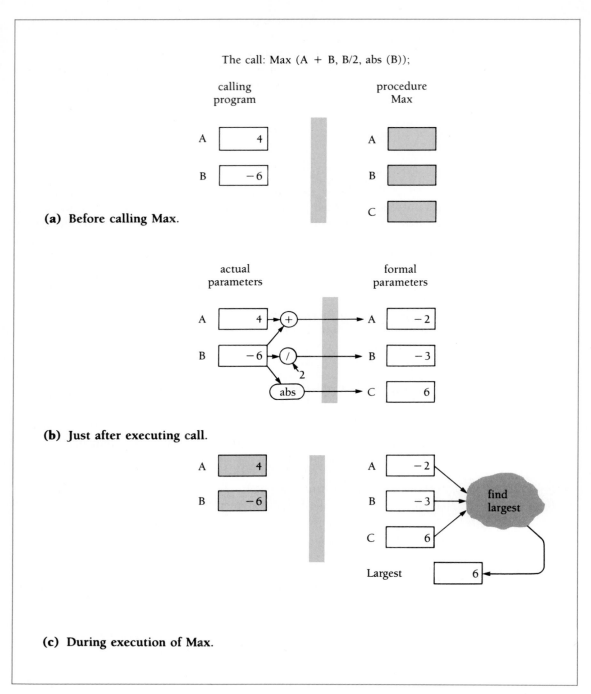

The call: Max (A + B, B/2, abs (B));

(a) Before calling Max.

(b) Just after executing call.

(c) During execution of Max.

■ Figure 4.13
Copying value parameters when a procedure call is executed.

in the referencing program. They are completely separate from the formal parameter identifiers used inside the procedure. The referencing program and Max are really two (almost) independent "programs," each of which is free to choose its own variable names. If these names happen to resemble each other, it really does not matter; they still designate different variables residing in their respective (sub)programs.

Figure 4.13(a) shows the variables containing values in the referencing program before this reference is executed. Figure 4.13(b) shows the result of executing the reference. Note the "barrier" between the main program and the procedure, which is crossed only at the moment of reference execution. Figure 4.13(c) shows how the execution of Max proceeds independently.

Figure 4.13 provides some insight into why a subprogram's local variables and formal parameters cannot be referenced from outside. For example, an attempt by the main program to access "A" results in an access to its own A, not the parameter A in Max. An attempt to access C or Largest from outside is simply not allowed (unless these identifiers have been declared as something else in the outside module).

A Modular Programming Example

In this section we encounter a problem whose solution may not be apparent at the beginning but will emerge quite naturally when we use modular programming techniques. The resulting program will contain several modules that pass information among themselves by means of (value) parameters.

Generating triangles   The problem is to write a program that can generate several isosceles triangles of various sizes until it is instructed to stop. The triangles have the form shown in Fig. 4.14(a). The parameter S determines the size of each triangle; S is equal to the number of stars along either of the sides (excluding the stars at the apex and base).

The overall program should repeatedly determine a value for S and generate the corresponding triangle, until encountering a sentinel value. Thus our algorithm is

1. read a value for S;
2. while S $<>$ sentinel do:
2.1   generate a triangle of size S;
2.2   generate 5 blank lines; {to separate triangles}
2.3   read a value for S;
3. stop

Step 2.1 is clearly the crux of the problem. However, we do not need to deal with it yet. Instead, we can write the main program to carry out the high-level control logic. We leave the actual generation of a triangle to a procedure, OneTriangle. This procedure will need to know the value of S and will therefore have one (integer-type) parameter. This is all we need to know to complete the code for the main program block shown in Fig. 4.15(a).

■ Figure 4.14
Triangle structure

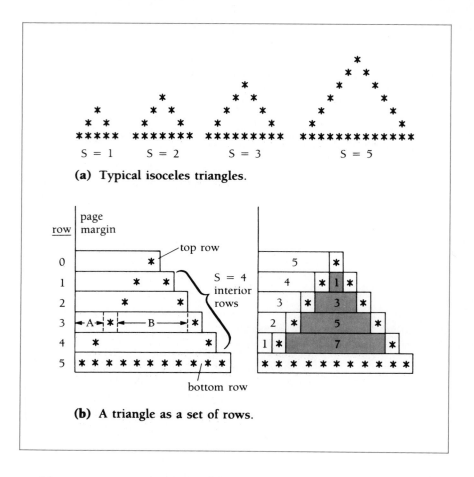

(a) Typical isoceles triangles.

(b) A triangle as a set of rows.

Now we can concentrate on the problem of producing a single triangle (step 2.1). The shape of a triangle comes from the pattern of stars on the output device. Since we can generate the output only one row at a time, we need to refer back to Fig. 4.14(b) to see how to generate a triangle as a series of distinct rows in which

1. the top row contains one star;
2. interior rows each contain two stars; and
3. the bottom row contains several stars.

Since the triangle is so symmetrical, we are fairly safe in lumping all the interior rows into one group; they will probably be handled in similar ways. If S is greater than or equal to zero, the number of interior rows is S. This observation leads to the following algorithm for generating *one* triangle.

1. generate top row;
2. generate S interior rows;
3. generate bottom row;

```
PROGRAM Triangles (input,output);
CONST Sentinel = -1;
VAR S: integer; {interior rows}

    ┌─────────────────────────────┐
    │ procedures defined here     │
    └─────────────────────────────┘
BEGIN
  read (S);
  WHILE S <> Sentinel DO
    BEGIN
      OneTriangle (S);
      writeln; writeln;
      writeln; writeln;
      writeln; {5 lines}
      read (S)
    END {loop}
END. {Triangles}
```

(a) Main program block.

```
PROCEDURE OneTriangle
      (S: integer);
   VAR R: integer; {row}
   BEGIN
     TopRow (S);
     FOR R := 1 TO S DO
       InnerRow (R,S);
     LastRow (S)
   END; {OneTriangle}
```

(b) Procedure OneTriangle.

```
PROCEDURE TopRow (S: integer);
  VAR Blank: integer;
  BEGIN
   FOR Blank := 1 TO S+1 DO
     write (' ');
   writeln ('*')
  END; {TopRow}
```

(d) Procedure TopRow.

```
PROCEDURE LastRow (S: integer);
  VAR Star: integer;
  BEGIN
   FOR Star: = 1 TO 2*S+3 DO
     write ('*');
   writeln
  END; {LastRow}
```

(c) Procedure LastRow.

```
PROCEDURE InnerRow (R,S: integer);
  VAR Item: integer;
  BEGIN
   FOR Item := 1 TO S+1-R DO
     write (' ');
   write ('*');
   FOR Item := 1 TO 2*R-1 DO
     write (' ');
   writeln ('*')
  END; {InnerRow}
```

(e) Procedure InnerRow.

■ Figure 4.15
Procedure interaction when generating triangles.

Rather than deal with the detailed calculations to determine the proper spacing within each kind of row, we now focus only on the overall structure of a triangle, as reflected in the three steps above.

Each step will be carried out by calling the corresponding subprogram. Further study of Fig. 4.14 shows that each of these new procedures will require knowledge of S in order to complete its calculations. In addition, the procedure used in step 2 must know which row it is currently supposed to generate. These observations determine the parameter requirements for all the subprocedures. We can now completely encode the procedure to supervise construction of a single triangle, as shown in Fig. 4.15(b).

We now have three new procedures to develop, but fortunately each has only one specific task to perform. Let's begin with the simplest: LastRow, which generates the bottom row.

By observing that the bottom row contains one star under the topmost star, one star under each of the stars of each of the S interior rows, and two more stars for its own endpoints, we need a total of $(2 \times S) + 3$ stars. We will supply the value of S as a parameter. That is all we need to know. The code for LastRow is shown in Fig. 4.15(c).

The next simplest procedure appears to be TopRow. This procedure must generate a sequence of blanks followed by a single star. (See Fig. 4.14b.) We must allow one blank above the first star in each succeeding row. Since there are S interior rows and one bottom row, S + 1 blanks are required before the star. See Fig. 4.15(d) for the code.

All that remains is to design the InnerRow procedure. Note that an interior row consists of four parts: a sequence of blanks (part A); the first star; another sequence of blanks (part B); and the final star. This suggests a four-step algorithm:

1. generate preceding blanks (A);
2. generate first star;
3. generate intervening blanks (B);
4. generate 2nd star;

The number of *preliminary* blanks (A) depends on both the total number of interior rows S and the current row number R, both of which should be parameters. Each row has one fewer leading blank than the row above it. We just decided that the topmost row of the triangle contains S + 1 blanks. Therefore the first interior row contains $(S + 1) - 1$ leading blanks; the second, $(S + 1) - 2$ blanks; and so on. In general, interior row R contains $(S + 1) - R$ leading blanks.

The space *between* the stars in each interior row (B) contains two more spaces than the row above it, except for the first row. Row 1 contains 1 interior blank, row 2 contains 3 blanks, row 3 contains 5, and so on. In general, row R contains $(2 \times R) - 1$ interior blanks. We are now ready to write the code for InnerRow, as shown in Fig. 4.15(e).

Now that we have written all the procedures, we collect them together to produce the complete program shown in Fig. 4.16(a). Although this final

```
PROGRAM Triangles (input,output);

CONST

VAR

PROCEDURE TopRow (S: integer);
   ┌──VAR─────────────────────────────┐
   │  BEGIN                           │
   │                                  │
   │      See Figure 4.15(d)          │
   │                                  │
   └──END;────────────────────────────┘

PROCEDURE InnerRow (R,S: integer);
   ┌──VAR─────────────────────────────┐
   │  BEGIN                           │
   │                                  │
   │      See Figure 4.15(e)          │
   │                                  │
   └──END;────────────────────────────┘

PROCEDURE LastRow (S: integer);
   ┌──VAR─────────────────────────────┐
   │  BEGIN                           │
   │                                  │
   │      See Figure 4.15(c)          │
   │                                  │
   └────────────END;──────────────────┘

PROCEDURE OneTriangle (S: integer);
   ┌──VAR─────────────────────────────┐
   │  BEGIN                           │
   │                                  │
   │      See Figure 4.15(b)          │
   │                                  │
   └──END;────────────────────────────┘
 ┌─BEGIN {Triangles}──────────────────┐
 │        See Figure 4.15(a)          │
 └─END. {Triangles}───────────────────┘
```

(a) Complete program.

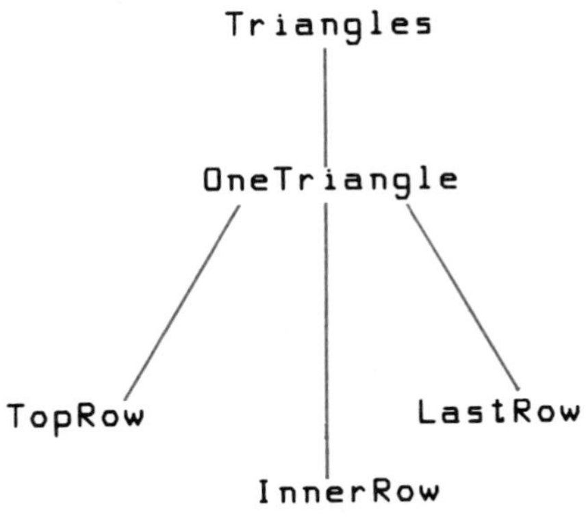

(b) Tree of intermodule references.

■ Figure 4.16
Complete solution for triangle generation problem.

version looks complex, its step-by-step derivation was not. However, this program is sufficiently complex that finding a good solution in one shot and without having to make successive refinements is highly unlikely.

Note the relative placement of procedure declarations. We defined the lower-level procedures first, so that their definitions precede the code containing references to them. Figure 4.16(b) shows the tree diagram of intermodule references; the more detailed modules appear at the bottom of the tree.

Also note that we used the same identifiers, namely, S and R, for all the procedure parameters. This uniformity is intended to assist readers of the program. These identifiers still refer to quite separate things inside each module. It would have made no real difference if each module had used completely different identifiers for its parameters.

Our choice of local variable names also shows some overlap, but not as much. Again, this makes no difference. We coded each module independently, without risk of a conflict with similar names that might appear elsewhere.

4.3 Procedures with Variable Parameters

None of the user-defined procedures that we have described so far has had any real impact on the calling program. These procedures have carried on their own dialogues with the user, displayed their own results, and possibly called upon other procedures. However, the only communication between procedures up to this point has been by means of value parameters *from* the calling module *to* the called module, never the reverse.

Yet, there is obviously a need for communication in this reverse direction. Sometimes we use a procedure to produce results that are of use directly to the calling program. The procedure may perform only one of several steps in processing the data, and its outcome may be of use only to the calling module or another module that its caller will invoke.

We cannot convey results *back* to a calling program with any of the procedure mechanisms that we have encountered so far. We use value parameters and local variables, in particular, to expressly prevent the calling program from inspecting their values after the procedure has finished execution.

A View from the Outside: Using Variable Parameters

Nevertheless, a procedure can use parameters to communicate its resulting values back to its calling module. Consider the familiar read procedure as an example. Read provides values to whatever variables appear as actual parameters in the call. Thus read(B,C) alters the values of both B and C. When read has finished execution, B and C may have different values than they had before. The call read(X,Y) will update the values of X and Y. You can also write your own procedures to update variables in the calling module.

variable parameters   Since these altered parameters cannot be value parameters, they must be some other kind. They are called **variable parameters.** A variable parameter allows a procedure to change its value and the calling module to inspect this updated value when the procedure has finished.

How does the calling module "know" which parameters may be changed by a procedure and which may not, that is, which are variable type and which are value type? Unfortunately, you cannot answer this question just by looking at the call to a procedure. It depends on how you defined each formal parameter inside the procedure itself; your procedure declaration may or may not have given this capability to a parameter. Whether it does depends on how the parameter is supposed to be used. Actually, the question of parameter data type is similar; your procedure declaration determines whether each formal parameter will convey char, real, or other values, depending on the purpose of the parameter.

Of course, the user of a procedure is always expected to know why and how the procedure is being used. The user calls read(X) precisely for the purpose of obtaining a new value for X. When a procedure is supposed to change a value of X, then X must correspond to a variable-type parameter. On the other hand, the user calls write(X) to copy an existing value to the output device. There is no intention to have the write procedure alter the valueof X in the calling module

The same holds true of the procedures you will write. Some parameters are used only to provide starting values to the procedure for its own use; these are the value parameters. Other parameters are expected to change. They are intended to give back results from the procedure. These will be— in fact must be—variable parameters. In the next section we look inside the procedure definition to see what makes a parameter a variable type.

Meanwhile, we need to consider one special restriction concerning the calling module. Any actual parameter that might be altered by a procedure *must be a variable.* It cannot be a constant or a more complex expression for the same reason that only a variable may be the target of an assignment statement. We cannot say read(X + Y); an expression containing operators generates its own value and cannot be assigned another. Similarly, we cannot say read(3). It makes no sense to try to alter the value of 3. Thus we add one more rule to the list governing actual to formal parameter correspondence:

RULE III:
Any actual parameter corresponding to a variable-type formal parameter must be a variable.

In order to see a variable-type parameter in operation, assume that we have a procedure Maxi to find the largest of three real numbers. Unlike the earlier version Max in Fig. 4.12, which immediately displayed its answer, this version will report the result back to the calling module. The calling program can then do whatever it wants with this value.

The following fragment of code calls read to obtain three numbers, Maxi to find the largest of these values, and writeln to display this value.

```
read(A,B,C);
Maxi(A,B,C,Result);
writeln('Largest is:',Result);
```

Note the call to Maxi. We now have four parameters. The first three provide Maxi with the values just read from the terminal. The fourth is used by Maxi to return some value to this calling level. Maxi involves a combination of parameter types: three value type and one variable type. The fourth parameter, Result, has no particular value before Maxi is called but will have the desired value after Maxi has finished executing. Maxi's ability to supply a value for Result should be no more surprising than the ability of the read procedure to supply values for A, B, and C.

Note the flow of data from one procedure to the next. In this fragment of code we use procedures to accomplish all the processing. Its role is simply to call the procedures in the correct sequence and to convey the results from one procedure to the next. Obviously, our choice of variable names at this level is arbitrary—as long as they all have the appropriate data types.

A View from the Inside: Declaring Variable Parameters

Two-way communication path

The purpose of variable parameters is to serve as a *two-way* communication path between two modules. These parameters may be given initial values when a reference is executed, may be modified during the course of subprogram execution, and make their resulting values available to the calling program. We must give this capability to return updated values to a parameter explicitly in the declaration in the subprogram heading.

To see how this is done, consider the declaration of Maxi, the procedure to find the largest of three values. Maxi requires a total of four parameters: three for the values being compared and one for the result, the latter being a variable-type parameter. Figure 4.17 shows this procedure inside a calling program.

In the procedure heading for Maxi, we declare Big as a variable parameter by preceding it with VAR. Since we do not use VAR to introduce X, Y, and Z in the heading, they remain value parameters. The parameter type is completely determined by the presence or absence of VAR in the subprogram heading.

When the call to Maxi in the main program is executed, the current values of A, B, C, and Result becomes known as X, Y, Z, and Big, respectively, within the procedure. The correspondence between actual and formal parameters is still determined by relative position. As before, for every reference to

■ Figure 4.17
A procedure with a
variable parameter.

```
PROGRAM Context (input,output);

VAR A,B,C,Result: real;

PROCEDURE Maxi (X,Y,Z: real; VAR Big: real);
    BEGIN {Maxi}
        Big := X;
        IF Y > Big THEN
            Big := Y;
        IF Z > Big THEN
            Big := Z
    END; {Maxi}

BEGIN {Context}
    read (A,B,C);
    Maxi (A,B,C,Result);
    writeln ('largest is ',          )
END. {Context}
```

a procedure you must use the correct *number* of actual parameters, and these must correspond in *type* to their formal parameter counterparts (Rules I and II in the preceding section).

As Maxi executes, all its parameters, including Big, may be manipulated like ordinary variables. The difference is that any change made by Maxi to Big is reflected as a change to Result in the main program. In particular, the last value assigned to Big within Maxi becomes the value of Result for later use in the main program. Result takes on a new value only because it is the fourth parameter in the reference to Maxi, corresponding to the *variable*-type parameter position in the declaration of Maxi. This is precisely how the procedure can have an effect on the calling program.

A procedure may have more than one variable parameter. Each use of VAR allows two-way communication through all the parameters following it, up to the next colon. Consider the procedure heading:

```
PROCEDURE P1 (A,B: integer; VAR C,D: real;
                  E: char);
```

This heading declares five formal parameters: two integer, two real, and one char. Only the two reals are variable parameters; the others, by default, are value parameters. Now consider

```
PROCEDURE P2 (X: real; VAR Y: real; Z: real;
                  VAR B: char);
```

This heading specifies only one real (Y) parameter and one char (B) parameter as variable type; X and Z are value type.

Incidentally, when Maxi is first referenced in Fig. 4.17, Result has no particular value. This causes no problem because Big is immediately assigned a value by Maxi. If Maxi had first tried to use the value of Big in an expression, an initial value would have been expected (through Result) from the main program. Variable parameters are capable of communicating values in both directions, although only one direction is significant in this example.

Maintaining an Account Balance

We now examine a part of the problem of maintaining bank account balances. Suppose, at some point in its processing, that a program has available the next account number and the previous month's balance for that account. Given this information, a procedure is asked to update that balance and reports on the resulting status of the account. Accounts with a final balance of more than $1000 are designated as GoldStar; others are designated as either Normal or Overdrawn (if negative). These are encoded as 0, 1, and 2, respectively. The procedure will use the account number in prompting an interactive user to enter the net change to the account. A positive change implies an increase; a negative change, a decrease.

In designing the procedure, we must recognize that four items of information are exchanged between the main program and the updating procedure: (1) the account number; (2) the old balance; (3) the new balance; and (4) the status of the account. The first two are supplied by the main program to the procedure, and the last two are the results returned by the procedure to the program.

Since the account number is not changed by the procedure, it should be supplied as a value parameter. Both of the results must be returned through variable parameters (otherwise they could not be returned). Assuming that the main program does not need the old balance after it has been updated, the old balance and the newly updated balance can both be transmitted through the *same* parameter—the old balance upon entrance to the procedure and the new upon exit. Consequently, only three formal parameters are required.

Figure 4.18 shows the complete procedure declaration, surrounded by pertinent parts of the main program. Figure 4.19 on p. 186 depicts the flow of data among the program, procedure, and user.

In this example some of the actual and formal parameter names are the same, whereas others differ—but this does not matter. One set of identifiers belongs to the program and the other set to the procedure; the matchup is strictly by position. Also, note that Bal receives the old balance from the program when the procedure's execution begins and conveys the new balance back to the program when the procedure's execution is completed. This variable parameter really does involve two-way communication.

```
PROGRAM BankAccounts (input,output);

CONST
   GoldStar = 0;
   Normal = 1;
   Overdrawn = 2;
VAR
   Account: integer;
   Balance: real;
   Status: integer;

PROCEDURE UpdateBalance (Acct: integer; VAR Bal: real;
                         VAR Status: integer);
   VAR NetChange: real;
   BEGIN {UpdateBalance}
      writeln ('Enter net change for account# ',Acct);
      read (NetChange);
      Bal := Bal + NetChange;
      IF Bal > 1000.00 THEN
         Status := GoldStar
      ELSE
         IF Bal >= 0.0 THEN
            Status := Normal
         ELSE Status := Overdrawn
   END; {UpdateBalance}

BEGIN {BankAccounts}
   {execution begins here}
   .
   .
   .
   {at this point Balance = old balance}
   UpdateBalance (Account,Balance,Status);
   {at this point Balance = updated new balance}
   CASE Status OF
      GoldStar:  _ _ _ _ _ _ _ _;
      Normal:    _ _ _ _ _ _ _ _;
      Overdrawn: _ _ _ _ _ _ _ _
   END; {case}
```

■ Figure 4.18
Relevant code to update an account balance.

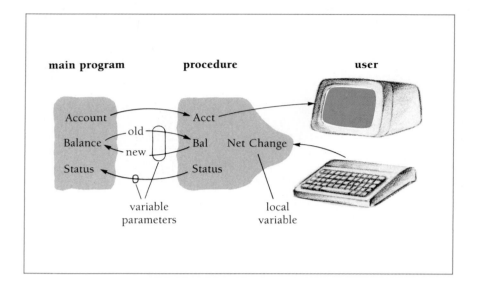

At this point, we can provide a more detailed explanation of the variable parameter mechanism. Consider Fig. 4.20, which shows the step-by-step changes in all the variables from Fig. 4.18 when a net change of -200 is entered from the terminal.

Before executing a reference, value parameters are true variables awaiting initial values. However, variable parameters are simply names waiting to be associated with variables outside the subprogram (Fig. 4.20a). Once a reference occurs, these names inside the subprogram are associated with the outside variables indicated by the corresponding actual parameters (Fig. 4.20b). During execution, any reference to its formal parameters causes the subprogram to reference the actual associated variables outside itself. Consequently, whatever values remain in its formal parameters upon completion are, in fact, stored in the referencing program's own variables. It is almost as if the variables identified by actual parameters are allowed to straddle the boundary between the two programs during the subprogram execution. Of course, when control leaves the subprogram, the association is broken, and a completely different set of associations may be established the next time the subprogram is referenced. You should compare this variable parameter mechanism (Fig. 4.20) with the value parameter mechanism of Fig. 4.13.

Modular Programming Using Variable Parameters

Sorting three values   Instead of simply finding the largest of three values, as we did with Max and Maxi, we now want to know the largest, second largest, and smallest of three values. In particular, we want to rearrange the three numbers so that the largest appears first and the smallest last.

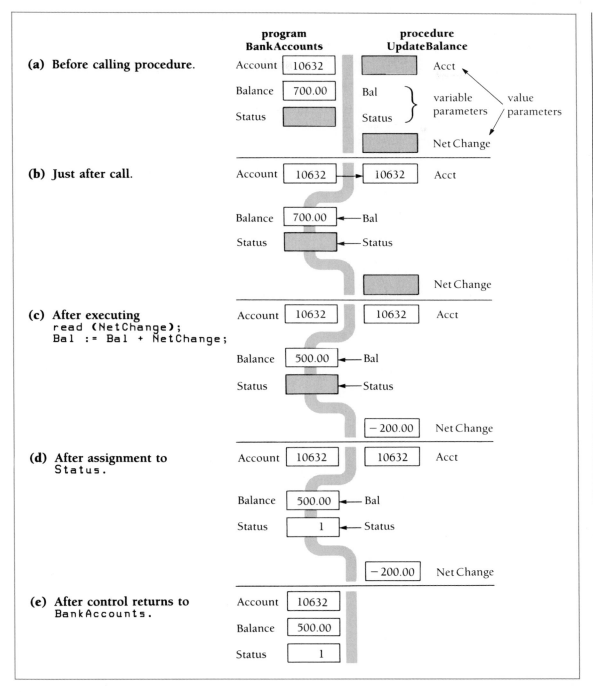

(a) Before calling procedure.

(b) Just after call.

(c) After executing
`read (NetChange);`
`Bal := Bal + NetChange;`

(d) After assignment to
`Status.`

(e) After control returns to
`BankAccounts.`

■ Figure 4.20
Details of variable parameter mechanism.

The actual rearrangement can be carried out by a procedure, so the main program is trivial:

```
read(A,B,C);
Reorder(A,B,C);
writeln(A,B,C)
```

The key action is the call to the procedure Reorder. Immediately before the call, A, B, and C contain three arbitrary numbers in the order supplied as input. Immediately after execution of Reorder, A will contain the largest of the three values, B the next largest, and C the smallest. Although the original values are still represented, any particular variable may contain a different value than it had before the call.

In this example, A, B, and C must all correspond to variable-type

```
PROCEDURE Reorder (VAR First,Second,Third: real);
   BEGIN
      IF First < Second THEN
         Swap(First,Second);
      IF First < Third THEN
         Swap(First,Third);
      IF Second < Third THEN
         Swap(Second,Third)
   END; {Reorder}
```

(a) Code to define Reorder.

Point in Execution	First	Second	Third
When called	3	6	7
compare first and second			
After 1st swap	6	3	7
compare first and third			
After 2nd swap	7	3	6
compare second and third			
After 3rd swap	7	6	3

(b) Detailed execution of Reorder.

■ Figure 4.21
A procedure to reorder three real values.

parameters, as reflected in the heading of the procedure Reorder:

```
PROCEDURE Reorder (VAR First,Second,Third: real);
```

In order to devise an algorithm for rearranging three values, think about how you might solve this problem with three physical objects of different sizes aligned in a row on a table. You might compare the first with the second and interchange them if the first was smaller than the second. Knowing that the first object was now the larger of the first two, you could compare the first with the third and swap them if necessary. The first item in the row would then be the largest overall. One more comparison and possible transposition would correctly order the second and third items, leaving all three in the desired order.

The key process, repeated three times in this approach, is the comparison and possible rearrangement of a *single pair* of items. We can do the rearranging with a procedure, Swap. It will have two parameters that can contain arbitrary real numbers before its call but that will always return the larger value in the first parameter and the smaller value in the second. The declaration of Reorder, employing the Swap procedure, is shown in Fig. 4.21(a). Figure 4.21(b) shows the step-by-step execution of Reorder for the three initial values 3, 6, and 7, in that order.

Exchanging two values

In the declaration of Swap, we must define both of its formal parameters as variable type. The actual exchange of two values between two (formal parameter) variables is more subtle than it might at first appear. Exchanging values is analogous to exchanging the contents of two bottles—red and white wine, for instance. To do so, you must pour the contents of one bottle (say, the white wine) into a third, empty container. Having emptied the white-wine bottle, you can pour the red wine into it. Finally, you can pour the white wine from the spare container into the red-wine bottle. This involves a total of three transfers, corresponding to three assignment statements. The complete declaration of Swap is

```
PROCEDURE Swap (VAR White,Red : real);
  VAR
    Spare : real;
  BEGIN
    Spare := White;
    White := Red;
    Red := Spare
  END; {Swap}
```

The complete program, including both procedure declarations, is shown in Fig. 4.22. Again, we used different identifiers in each module but only to dramatize that each module defines its own names. The major point is that both procedures use their parameters in two-way communication with their calling modules: they receive starting values and return their results through the parameters.

```
PROGRAM Sort3 (input,output);

VAR
    A,B,C : real;

PROCEDURE Swap(VAR White,Red : real);
    VAR
        Spare : real;
    BEGIN
        Spare := White;
        White := Red;
        Red := Spare
    END; {Swap}

PROCEDURE Reorder (VAR First,Second,Third : real);
    BEGIN
        IF First < Second THEN
            Swap(First,Second);
        IF First < Third THEN
            Swap(First, Third);
        IF Second < Third THEN
            Swap(Second,Third)
    END; {Reorder}

BEGIN {Sort3}
    read(A,B,C);
    Reorder(A,B,C);
    writeln(A,B,C)
END. {Sort3}
```

■ Figure 4.22
Sorting three real values.

4.4 Some Implications of Scope Rules

As you have seen, at any point in a program certain variables are accessible while others are not. Also, the same identifier may refer to different things in different modules. **Scope** refers to the extent of a program over which any particular declaration of an identifier applies.

scope

Nested Subprograms

Local subprograms   Just as a subprogram may declare local variables for its own private use so it may declare other objects that serve its purposes. Of special interest here is that a subprogram may declare its own local procedures or functions for its exclusive use.

Figure 4.23 shows another version of the program to rearrange three numbers (originally presented in Fig. 4.22). Here the swap procedure is declared *inside the* Reorder *procedure.* After all, we devised Swap to implement one of the subtasks of Reorder, and it has no role in the main program.

```
PROGRAM Sort3 (input,output);

VAR
    A,B,C : real;

PROCEDURE Reorder (VAR First,Second,Third : real);

    PROCEDURE Swap(VAR White,Red : real);
        VAR
            Spare : real;
        BEGIN {Swap}
            Spare := White;
            White := Red;
            Red := Spare
        END; {Swap}

    BEGIN {Reorder}
        IF First < Second THEN
            Swap(First,Second);
        IF First < Third THEN
            Swap(First, Third);
        IF Second < Third THEN
            Swap(Second,Third)
    END; {Reorder}

BEGIN {Sort3}
    read(A,B,C);
    Reorder(A,B,C);
    writeln(A,B,C)
END. {Sort3}
```

■ Figure 4.23
A nested subprogram.

Consequently, we can declare Swap as a local procedure for the exclusive use of Reorder.

Comparing the two versions of the program (Figs. 4.22 and 4.23), we see absolutely no changes in the executable code of any module. At run time there will be no difference in execution; each module will behave exactly the same. The *only* difference is where the definition of Swap appears.

The major implication of declaring Swap inside (as opposed to beside) Reorder is that we now prevent the main program from calling Swap directly. The main program contains only one procedure of its own (Reorder) and can no more access Reorder's local procedure than it can Reorder's local variables (if it had any). In this case, we say that swap is *nested* inside Reorder.

Of course, in this example there is no reason for the main program to access both procedures. In a sense, it is better if the main program does not "know" anything about an object it does not directly use. Another advantage of the nested approach is that Reorder now "owns" the Swap procedure, and we may customize their mutual interaction (such as in parameter specification) without affecting any other parts of the main program. Nesting a subprogram not only restricts access to it, but also limits the number of clients it may be required to serve. These considerations are more than aesthetic for programs of any complexity.

On the other hand, if some subprogram is sufficiently important to be needed widely, it cannot be hidden from view by being nested inside another. Defining the procedures at the same level (but in the correct order) would be more appropriate in such a case.

Global Variables and Procedure Interactions

global variables

In addition to variable parameters, another mechanism called **global variables,** allows two-way communication between programs. Global variables are common to both programs and are permanently known inside both programs by identical names.

Since global variables are truly shared, the referencing module may leave values in global variables for use by a subprogram, which also may use and alter them; any values remaining in the global variables when the subprogram terminates are, in turn, available to the calling module. Global variables differ from variable parameters in two ways: (1) no special declarations are required in the subprogram (in fact, none are allowed); and (2) the exact same names must be used for such variables in both modules.

Global identifier

As you already know, if you declare any identifier (say, as a parameter or as a local variable) in a subprogram, that identifier—at least with that declared meaning—cannot be referenced by the higher level module in which the subprogram is defined. On the other hand, *any identifier declared in a higher level module and not redeclared in one of its subprograms, is known and available to the subprogram.* The subprogram can use that same identifier and thereby access the object declared at the higher level. This is why the procedure Reorder in Fig. 4.22 can use the procedure Swap, even though Swap is defined within the higher module Sort3.

Thus a global variable is simply a variable identifier declared in some program but *not* redeclared in a subprogram. The subprogram still has access to the original variable by using the original identifier.

The program in Fig. 4.24 implements the same logic as the program fragment in Fig. 4.18, but uses global variables instead of parameters for transferring values between the main program and the procedure. Note also our use of the CONSTants as global identifiers.

At first glance this version looks simpler than the version using parameters. However, to avoid parameters, we had to give up some clarity, flexibility, and independence because global variables, unfortunately, cause hidden and permanent interconnections between modules. Because of this, you should use global variables only in certain circumstances and, even then, with great care.

Clarity is sacrificed because the procedure does not indicate the types of variables with which it deals. Nor does it indicate which variables contain incoming values and which return results. You should provide such information in comments, but, unlike declarations, comments cannot be enforced. Any attempt to declare the variables would render them either parameters (if declared in the heading) or local variables (if declared in the block).

Clarity is also sacrificed at the point of reference. The subprogram is executed simply by naming it (that is, ReviseBalance). This reference contains no hint of which variables transmit values to and from the subprogram. To find out, you must look in three places: the declaration of the variables, the subprogram, and the neighborhood of the reference.

Global variables also cause the programs involved to be less flexible. You can use the subprogram in Fig. 4.24 to manipulate values in the variables Account, Balance, and Status only. The calling program must always use the same identifiers for every reference. You no longer have the freedom to provide values from different variables, let alone from complex expressions.

Global variables also result in interdependence between the two modules. In order for the subprogram to operate, you must declare it within the program that contains its variable declarations; it depends on the surrounding program for the meaning of those variables. If you were to modify the outer program and redeclare a variable, the subprogram might not work. You cannot reuse the subprogram in another context. You must write the two programs specifically to work with each other and to behave more like one module than two.

Similarly, if the subprogram is ever rewritten or modified, the higher level programs could receive some surprises. The subprogram might modify some global variable that the higher level program did not expect would change. Such unanticipated values, passed back "under the table" through global variables, are called **side effects** of the subprogram.

side effects

```
PROGRAM BankAgain (input,output);

CONST
   GoldStar = 0;
   Normal = 1;
   Overdrawn = 2;

VAR
   Account: integer;
   Balance: real;
   Status: integer;

PROCEDURE ReviseBalance;
   VAR
      NetChange : real;
   BEGIN
      writeln ('Enter net change for # ', Account);
      read (NetChange);
      Balance := Balance + NetChange;
      IF Balance > 1000.00 THEN
         Status := GoldStar
      ELSE
         IF Balance >= 0.0 THEN
            Status := Normal
         ELSE
            Status := Overdrawn
   END; {ReviseBalance}

   BEGIN {BankAgain}
   .
   .
   .
   ReviseBalance;
   CASE Status OF
      .
      .
      .
   END. {BankAgain}
```

■ Figure 4.24
Use of global identifiers.

Through side effects, an innocent-looking subprogram can inflict terrible damage on its user. This kind of disaster often arises when the referencing program and the subprogram use the same loop index variables. Programmers frequently get into the habit of using single letter identifiers for such variables in the interest of brevity. Figure 4.25 is an example of the kind of trap into which the unwary might fall. The program is supposed to use the procedure BadFact to compute the factorial of each of 10 input values. However, as soon as it has processed an input value greater than 9, the program comes to a normal halt. Further, until it receives this large a value, the program continues to process input, not necessarily stopping after the first 10 values.

```
PROGRAM SideEffect (input,output);

VAR N,FactN,K: integer;

PROCEDURE BadFact (N: integer; VAR FactN: integer);
   {Fact(n) = 1x2x3x...xn, Fact(0) = 1}
   BEGIN {BadFact}
      IF N < 0 THEN
         BEGIN {factorial not defined}
            writeln ('Factorial undefined for:', N);
            writeln ('Value of zero returned.');
            FactN := 0
         END {warning}
      ELSE
         BEGIN {valid}
            FactN := 1;
            K := 1;
            WHILE K <= N DO
               BEGIN
                  FactN := FactN * K;
                  K := K + 1
               END
         END {valid}
   END; {BadFact}

BEGIN {SideEffect}
   K := 1;
   WHILE K <= 10
      BEGIN
         read (N);
         BadFact(N,FactN);
         writeln (N,FactN);
         K := K + 1
      END
END. {SideEffect}
```

■ Figure 4.25
An example of side effects from the careless use of global variables.

The problem lies in the line

```
WHILE K <= N DO
```

inside the procedure. The identifier K is not declared within BadFact and thus refers to the same K declared in the surrounding program. There, K is used to control an input loop and is incremented by 1 after each return from BadFact. Thus, while K is supposed to progress steadily from 1 to 11 in the outer program, it also varies from 1 to one more than the most recent input value N inside the procedure. In fact, neither section of code has complete control over the value of K.

Obviously, in this example K was intended for use only in BadFact and we should have made it a local variable. Failure to do so caused the hidden interaction and led to all the trouble. Such interactions are rarely intended. They almost always result from carelessness, that is, failure to declare local variables intended for local use.

In general, you should not use global variables because they are inherently more dangerous and less flexible than parameters. However, they are useful in the right circumstances—for example, when you are defining an entire set of subprograms to operate on one common (usually large and complex) data object. If every procedure manipulates the same object, it might as well be global.

The Notion of Scope

Although the complete rules of scope are somewhat involved, the basic idea is simple. A subprogram may declare its own identifiers to denote whatever objects it requires: its own variables, constants, (nested) subprograms, etc. Whenever a subprogram uses one of these identifiers, reference is always to the object it defined, regardless of other declarations of the same identifier in some other module. Thus there is no conflict with competing declarations elsewhere in the program. Identifiers declared in any module are for that module's own use. No outside module can access its local variables or call its locally defined subprograms.

On the other hand, a module may use some identifier *not* defined in it. It cannot access identifiers defined inside its nested subprograms (their identifiers are local to them and inaccessible). Instead it looks "outside" to the immediately surrounding module. If the identifier is not declared there, then a definition is sought in the module containing that one, and so on. In terms of a tree of nested subprograms, a module in the interior can never use objects defined in its descendants (closer to the leaves); it may look up the tree (toward the root) for objects defined in its ancestors. This explains the phenomenon of global variables, which are simply objects declared in some containing module but not redeclared in the current module. Thus local identifiers and global identifiers are really two sides of the same coin.

In summary, the meaning that applies at any point to any identifier is the one derived from the *nearest* declaration, starting in the current module and working outward through the nesting structure. Of course, if no declaration is found by the time the main program is reached, the identifier is undefined at that point and cannot be used.

4.5 Function Subprograms

functions **Functions** comprise another kind of subprogram, sharing many properties with procedures but also differing from procedures in some important ways. One major difference is the way they are used.

A View from the Outside: Function Use

function call   You have already had the experience of calling predeclared functions such as abs, round, trunc, and sqrt. A **function call,** or reference, entails mentioning the function name, usually followed by one or more actual parameters enclosed in parentheses. For example, the square root of 4 is found by writing sqrt(4).

However, unlike a procedure call, a function call never constitutes a complete statement all by itself. *A function reference always occurs within an expression.* This is because every function always produces a single special

function value   result, called the **function value.** Thus the value of sqrt(4) is 2.0. To say that the value of sqrt(4) is 2.0 means that sqrt(4) behaves exactly as though 2.0 had been written in its place. Just as the constant 2.0 cannot appear in isolation, neither can a function reference. It must occur within some expression or context that uses its value. Hence we see constructs such as

```
X := sqrt(Y) / S;
IF trunc(X) <= 5 THEN . . .
WHILE abs(A - B) < 0.001 DO . . .
```

Although most of the functions you have encountered base their values on only a single argument, this need not be the case. A function, in general, can depend on any number of arguments. However, it should produce only one effect: the function value. This is a special characteristic of functions, which is not shared by procedures. Functions and procedures are compared pictorially in Fig. 4.26.

As you have seen, a function value and its parameters do not need to be all the same type. Recall that sqrt always yields a real value, even with an integer argument, whereas trunc will return an integer value from a real argument.

We can illustrate the use of functions with an example involving the weather bureau. A regional office receives snowfall reports from two stations, each representing three cities. Each day both stations send in data containing

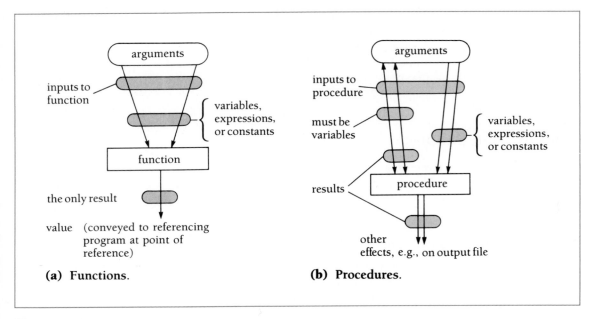

(a) **Functions.**

(b) **Procedures.**

■ Figure 4.26
Functions versus procedures.

three snowfall amounts, and we have to compute the heaviest snowfall in each region. Our algorithm is

1. read the data for region 1;
2. compute the largest of these 3 values;
3. display the result;
4. read the data for region 2;
5. compute the largest of these 3 values;
6. display the result;
7. stop.

Note that finding the largest of three values is a task requiring more than one step. Furthermore, this task is performed at two different points in the algorithm. Either of these facts makes it a possible candidate for a subprogram. Since the maximum of three numbers is always a single value, we can use a function rather than a procedure.

Assuming such a function (Maxy) is available, the overall program is shown in Fig. 4.27. Note the two references to Maxy. Each will provide three values to the function through its parameter list and then get back a result to be stored in the variable Largest.

Note that the variable Largest belongs to the calling program and that the calling program does the updating of its value. All the function does is supply a value for the right-hand side of an assignment statement.

A View from the Inside: Declaring Functions

As Fig. 4.27 indicates, we also place function declarations immediately before the statement part of the defining module. In this respect they are exactly like procedures. All subprograms follow the same rules for the location of their declarations. We may intermix or nest function and procedure declarations, as long as we declare every module before it is to be used and make its identifier known to all referencing modules, according to the rules of scope.

Like that of a main program or a procedure, the body of a function is the encoding of an algorithm, along with appropriate definitions. Writing a function declaration is mostly a matter of writing the code to perform the desired action.

We showed one way of finding the largest of three values in Fig. 4.16. Another approach is

```
Maxy := A;
IF B > A THEN
  Maxy := B;
IF (C > A) AND (C > B) THEN
  Maxy := C
```

```
PROGRAM Snowjob (input,output);

VAR
    Fall1,Fall2,Fall3: real; {amounts from one region}
    Largest: real; {largest of Fall1, Fall2, Fall3}


          +------------------------------+
          | declaration of Maxy          |
          | appears here                 |
          +------------------------------+


BEGIN {Snowjob}
    read (Fall1,Fall2,Fall3);
    Largest := Maxy(Fall1,Fall2,Fall3);
    writeln ('Maximum for region 1 is ':25,Largest:8:4);
    read (Fall1,Fall2,Fall3);
    Largest := Maxy(Fall1,Fall2,Fall3);
    writeln ('Maximum for region 2 is ':25,Largest:8:4)
END. {Snowjob}
```

■ Figure 4.27
Program to compute maximum snowfall in two regions.

function heading

In order to convert this code into a function, we enclose it by BEGIN and END and introduce it with a line called a **function heading.**

The complete declaration for Maxy is shown in Fig. 4.28. It reveals two major differences between function and procedure declarations. The first difference is seen in the function heading

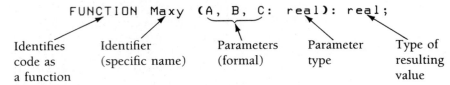

```
FUNCTION  Maxy  (A, B, C:  real): real;
```

| Identifies code as a function | Identifier (specific name) | Parameters (formal) | Parameter type | Type of resulting value |

The new features occur at opposite ends of the heading. First, the reserved word FUNCTION identifies what follows as a function-type subprogram. The identifier and parameter list are written exactly like those in the heading of a procedure. Then we come to another data type (here, real), which is separated from the parameter list by a colon. This final item indicates the data type of the *function value* that is to be returned. Since the function identifier (here, Maxy) conveys this result, the final type declaration is actually declaring the data type for Maxy. Maxy must be used in contexts that are appropriate for this type.

The second major difference in the function declaration occurs inside the statement part. The appearance of Maxy within the code as the target of some assignment statements is not accidental. The value to be returned to the user is always assigned to the function identifier. In Maxy such an assignment occurs in three separate places. The *last* value assigned during any particular execution will be the one returned to the user. It is essential that we assign some value to the function identifier for every possible path of execution within the function.

Whenever we assign Maxy a value, the value it receives must meet the usual requirement of assignment compatibility. Recall that the data type of Maxy is the type defined in the heading for the returned function value.

■ Figure 4.28
Declaration of
function Maxy.

```
FUNCTION Maxy (A,B,C: real): real;
   BEGIN
      Maxy := A;
      IF B > A THEN
         Maxy := B;
      IF (C > A) AND (C > B) THEN
         Maxy := C
   END;
```

On the other hand, Maxy is *not* an ordinary program variable. Within the code specifying a function's operation, the identifier normally appears only on the left-hand side of an asssignment operator. Any other use of the function identifier is considered to be a reference that invokes the function anew and requires all parameters to be specified. (We discuss such techniques in Chapter 11.) Thus, in Fig. 4.28, the IF statement comparisons involve only A, B, and C—never Maxy. For now, assume that the function name must not appear inside the function code, except as the target of an assignment statement.

Like procedures, functions are separate programs that can define any objects they may need for their implementation. In particular they may declare local variables, constants, subprograms, and so on.

According to the rules, a function may also have variable parameters. However, the "spirit" of functions is that they return only a single result through their identifier. This implies that a function should never need a variable-type parameter. If you are tempted to return additional results through variable parameters, you should consider using a procedure instead of a function.

4.6 Making Programs Work Correctly

Many programmers would rather sit down at a computer and start writing code than deal with all the dreary details of problem solving and refinement, but that approach is counterproductive. The less time spent in the early design stages, the longer it usually takes to get a program running correctly. The time you invest in problem solving will be repaid many times over when you finally run the program. One of the benefits of modular programming is that you can decompose your problem solution and get right to the "fun part"—the coding—at the same time.

The Elements of Stub Programming

As before, the module-by-module growth of the program will parallel the step-by-step refinement of the solution. Recall the basic idea: Creating a subprogram is somewhat like adding a new, possibly powerful, operation to the language. Knowing that we have this ability allows us to write higher level programs in terms of operations that are not yet implemented as subprograms, assuming that they ultimately will be. In other words, we can encode each high-level step as a subprogram reference, leaving the details to be filled in at a later time when we write the subprogram declaration.

We can do better than this: We can actually test the flow of logic through the high-level code without having to supply all the details of the subprograms.

Some definition of the subprograms must be present before the compiler will accept your code, but there is no reason for it to be the final definition. One way to test a module that contains calls to other, nonexistent modules is to write trivial or highly simplified versions of the missing modules. The idea is to provide enough values to allow the module being tested to proceed, even if the values are not accurate or even meaningful.

The main consideration is that the temporary version of the subprogram has the same calling conventions as its final version. Thus the calling module can try out the parameters and returned value(s), and should not have to change when we finally implement the real subprogram. This technique of providing dummy subprograms until we write the real ones is called **stub programming.** The dummy subprograms are the *stubs.*

stub programming

We might at some stage in a program have to call a procedure to produce a fairly complex report. We cannot test the driving program until we include the code for either the final report or some interim version of it. Since the calling program will probably not care what the report looks like, we could provide a stub subprogram such as

```
PROCEDURE Report;
  BEGIN
    writeln ('Report will be generated here')
  END;
```

Such code incorporated into the high-level code will permit execution of calls to Report. It will not, of course, produce the desired ultimate report; nevertheless, it serves the immediate objective of testing the code that references it. It even provides the user with visible evidence that control actually did flow through the report subprogram. When you are satisfied that the main code works correctly, you can turn to completing the procedure that writes the report. There will be no need to modify working code, and any subsequent errors will most likely be confined to the newly coded subprogram.

4.7 Review of Rules

A. There are two kinds of subprograms: functions and procedures. Both can be defined within other (sub)programs and thereafter used by those (sub)programs. The execution of functions and procedures is similar to the extent that a reference to such objects causes control to transfer from the point of reference to the subprogram and then back to the referencing program on completion of the subprogram. They differ in that a function reference must occur within an expression, since functions return a single value. A procedure reference itself constitutes a statement, and procedures may return any number of results, usually in the form of altered parameters.

B. The syntax diagrams of a program, procedure, and function are

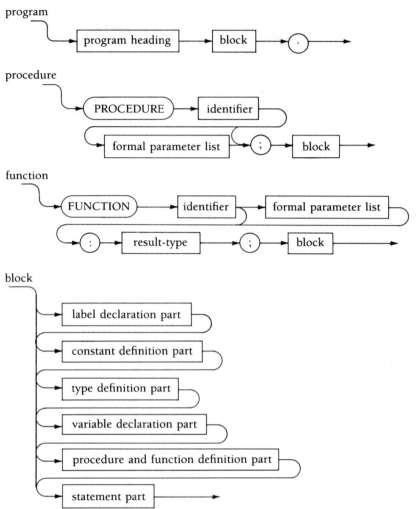

program

procedure

function

block

C. *Formal* parameters are identifiers in the subprogram definition. *Actual* parameters are the values or variables supplied by the referencing module during a particular execution of a subprogram reference. The syntax diagram for a formal parameter list is

formal parameter list

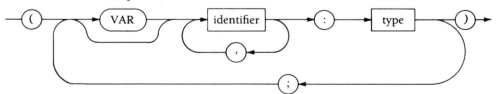

D. There are two kinds of formal parameters:

1. *Value*-type parameters are initialized during execution of a reference but cannot convey results back to the calling program.
2. *Variable*-type parameters are denoted by VAR in the formal parameter list; they can transfer values to the subprogram at the time of reference, and any changes to these parameters are conveyed back to the corresponding actual parameter.

E. Actual and formal parameters must obey these following rules.

1. There must be the same *number* of each; each actual parameter corresponds to the formal parameter in the same relative position in the parameter list.
2. Corresponding actual and formal parameters must be of the same *type* or at least assignment compatible (in both directions if the formal parameter is of variable type).
3. If the formal parameter is of variable type, the actual parameter must be a *variable* (not a constant or more general expression).

F. The scope of an identifier refers to the region over which the identifier has a consistent meaning (that is, refers to the same object or value). In general, the scope is the block in which the identifier is declared together with all other blocks contained in it, excluding those blocks in which the identifier is redefined.

G. A subprogram identifier is technically declared in the immediately containing block, so that the subprogram name is known to its parent. All other declarations in the subprogram are *local* to it and cannot be accessed by the parent. These include its formal parameters, (local) variables, its own subprograms, constants, types, and labels. Any entity declared in a containing block and not redeclared in the subprogram remains accessible to it, using the same identifier; such objects are said to be (relatively) *global*.

KEY TERMS

actual parameter	parameters
called procedure	predeclared procedures
calling program	procedure
formal parameter	procedure call
function call	procedure heading
function heading	procedure identifier
function value	scope
functions	side effects
global variable	stub programming
local identifier	subprogram
local variable	variable parameters
modules	value parameter

EXERCISES

4.1 What values will be displayed by the following program?

```
PROGRAM Proc (input,output);

VAR J,K,L: integer;

PROCEDURE Junk (VAR J,K,L: integer);
  BEGIN
   J := K;
   K := L;
   L := J
  END;

BEGIN
  J := 25;
  K := 36;
  L := 47;
  Junk (K,L,J);
  writeln (J,K,L)
END.
```

4.2 What does the following procedure do?

```
PROCEDURE What (VAR X,Y: real);
  BEGIN
   X := X + Y;
   Y := X - Y;
   X := X - Y
  END;
```

4.3 The Euclidian algorithm to find the greatest common divisor of two positive integers J and K is

```
while J ≠ K do:
   if J < K then interchange their values;
   Temp := J - K;
   J := K;
   K : = Temp;
GCD is J;
stop.
```

Write a function GCD to compute the greatest common divisor of two positive integers, according to this algorithm. The function should verify that its parameters are indeed positive values and return zero if either or both are ≤ 0.

4.4 Rewrite the following function as a procedure.

```
FUNCTION F (A,B,C: real): real;
  BEGIN
   F := 4*A*A + 3*B + 2*C
  END;
```

4.5   Rewrite the following procedure as a function.

```
PROCEDURE P (X,Y: real; VAR Z: real);
  BEGIN
    Z := sqrt(sqr(X-2) + sqr(Y-1))
  END;
```

4.6   A standard terminal screen has 24 lines with 80 columns per line. A chessboard can be displayed in the center of the screen by making each square 3 rows long by 3 columns wide and filling black squares with one character and white squares with another. Using this approach, the first two rows of the board might resemble

```
***...***...***...***...
***...***...***...***...
***...***...***...***...
...***...***...***...***
...***...***...***...***
...***...***...***...***
```

Write a procedure Board to draw a chessboard in the middle of the screen. The procedure should have two parameters, Black and White, each of type char. It should allow the calling program to specify the character to be used for each type of square.

4.7   In banking, the number of days between two dates is crucial for calculating interest. When counting the number of days between any two dates, you do not count the final day. That is, there are 2 days between February 1 and February 3, 30 days between August 1 and August 31, and 5 days between November 28 and December 3. Write a function procedure with the heading

FUNCTION DaysBetween (M1,D1,M2,D2: integer): integer;

which counts the number of days between day D1 of month M1 and day D2 of month M2. If the second date is less than the first, assume that the second date refers to the next year and omit any consideration of leap year.

4.8   Each term in a geometric sequence is the product of the previous term and some common ratio $r (r \neq 0)$. That is, any term $a_n = a_{n-1}r$. For example, 0.25, 0.5, 1, 2, 4 is a geometric sequence with $a_1 = 0.25$ and $r = 2$, while 4, 2, 1, 0.5, 0.25 has $a_1 = 4$ and $r = 0.5$. In general,

$$a_n = a_1 r^{n-1}.$$

Now, suppose that you have been offered a job with the choice of two pay formulas. The first gives you a starting salary of $24,000 and automatic raises of 6% per year. The second gives you a starting salary of $22,600 and automatic increases of 0.5% per month. Write a program to help you decide which option you should choose if (a) you plan to stay on the job for 5 years only, and (b) you plan to stay for 40 years.

4.9   Write a function subprogram to compute $n!$, as described in Exercise 1.13(a) or as encoded in Exercise 3.10. Then write a function that utilizes this factorial function in order to calculate n-choose-k, as described in Exercise 1.13(b).

(a)   Write a main program to test these functions by repeatedly obtaining values from the user for n and k.

(b) When you are satisfied that the functions are working correctly, use them in a program that generates a table of values for *n*-choose-*k*. Let the four columns of the table represent values of *k* from 1 through 4, and the 10 rows of the table represent the values of *n* from 1 through 10. No entry should appear for any $k > n$.

4.10 Implement the metric date problem from Exercise 3.18(b) by using subprograms in the following way. Write a function that accepts the (numeric) month and yields the number of days in that month (ignore leap year); write a boolean valued function to determine whether one given number lies between 1 and some other given number (the maximum allowed), inclusive. Use the latter function to test the validity of both the month number and the day number.

4.11 (a) In this exercise, one user will play a guessing game with another user at the terminal. Two procedures will be required. The first procedure communicates with the first player. It obtains the range of possible values, the particular integer to be guessed by the other, and the number of guesses allowed. In addition to reading these numbers, this procedure should provide some instructions for the first player and output enough blank lines to scroll the numbers off the screen. The second procedure communicates with the second player. Without telling the secret number, it tells the player the possible range and solicits a guess. It then tells the player whether the guess is high, low, or correct. The main program merely coordinates the action and keeps track of the number of guesses made.

(b) To make the play more interesting and allow a single user game, the first procedure can generate a secret number based on input supplied from the terminal without explaining how that number is derived. For example, the player could supply some arbitrary amount of text, and an auxiliary procedure could scan this text and calculate the percentage of words that have more consonants than vowels. The secret number could be the integer having a position in the range proportional to this calculated percentage.

4.12 (a) Implement the program of Exercise 3.17(b) using a procedure to calculate a good selling price for some object. In particular let a procedure handle the details of calculating the number of units sold and the expected income for any particular price. This procedure should also generate a line of output in the table. Another procedure should generate the table heading and column headings before the calculations begin. The main program controls only the overall process and decides when to quit (when a good price has been found).

(b) Once a good price has been found, let another procedure conduct a refined search in the vicinity of this price for the best price, as described in Exercise 3.17(c).

(c) Use an estimate for the number of units sold based on a quadratic relation rather than a linear one: for example, if N is the number of units sold at base price B, and each reduction in price is R dollars in size, the additional number of units sold is expected to be $-N[X - (B + 3R)]^2$, where X is the number of reductions. Incorporating this change in the program should affect only one procedure.

5

More about Input and Output

To this point our programs have dealt with relatively simple input structures. The data have been either all numeric or all character. Variable amounts of data have been terminated by sentinels, and whether data appeared on one or several lines has made little or no difference. The realities of data processing are not so simple. Data often appear on a single line because they pertain to the same customer, experiment, or inventory item, making the distinction between input lines significant. The data on a single line often consist of a mixture of types, and though the number of data values may be unpredictable, they are not always terminated by a sentinel. We now turn to consideration of more complex and realistic input situations and methods of handling them. In this chapter we also stress methods of presenting intelligible output and coordinating the input–output dialogue with an interactive user.

5.1 Reading a Single Line of Text

file

In Pascal each distinct source of input data and each possible destination for output data is known as a **file.** Whenever a program interacts with the outside world, it transfers data between its own storage area and some file. Two of the most important files are the standard text files *input* and *output,* which are associated with the keyboard and the screen of the terminal, respectively.

Even if a user–program dialogue occurs at the terminal, with alternating input and output, the input comes from one file while the output goes to another; these two files are treated independently by the computer system. Regardless of intervening output, everything the user types is seen collectively input stream   as one unbroken sequence of input characters called the **input stream.**

The data entered from a keyboard are always in the form of characters. Even if numeric values are entered, their fundamental constituents (sign, digits, decimal point) are still just characters; the read procedure interprets such characters and generates the corresponding numeric values for use inside the program. The stream of characters arriving at the computer from a terminal is broken only by the occasional **end-of-line component,** an element of the input stream produced by the user hitting the return key. Every input line, *including the last,* is terminated by an end-of-line component.

end-of-line
component

Files containing only characters and end-of-line components are called **text files.** It is possible to have other kinds of input from other kinds of devices, but for now we assume that all input originates from character-oriented devices and comprises text files.

text files

A Closer Look at the read Statement

As input statements are executed by the program, the input stream is transversed, with its contents being copied item by item into program variables. Successively executed read statements consume successive portions of the input stream, each beginning where the previous one left off. There is no way to go back and reread some previously processed data value (at least for input arriving from the terminal). This type of steady, irreversible progression is known as **sequential processing.**

sequential processing

In each read statement we specify one or more variables into which successive items from the input stream are to be placed. These variables determine how the read statement will interpret the input characters. If the next variable to be given a value is of type char, then only the next individual character will be read and placed in that variable. If an end-of-line component is read into a character variable, it is first converted to a blank. Thus, if a character variable contains a blank after input, we have no way of telling whether it was originally typed as a blank or resulted from reading an end-of-line component.

Character input

Numeric input

On the other hand, if the next variable to receive a value is of type real or type integer, the read statement does something much more sophisticated. It scans forward through the input stream looking for the first character that is not a blank or the end of a line. If that character could be the start of a numeric quantity, then as many consecutive characters as could constitute a numeric value are read. This might include a sign, several digits, a decimal point, and even a second sign and letter 'e' if exponential notation is used. The implied numeric value is calculated and this single value is placed in the variable, if possible. The read may produce an error for a variety of reasons: the number may be beyond the range of the corresponding variable; a real value may be read for an integer variable; or the first character encountered may be one that could not be part of a numeric quantity. Thus reading a number is considerably more involved than reading a character. With numeric input, the end-of-line component is treated like a blank; it is usually ignored, unless it indicates where the last number on an input line ends.

Program's input process and input stream must match

All of this emphasizes the importance of coordinating the execution of input statements with the supply of input data, especially when the data contain a mixture of data types. The sequence of variables to be given data values dictates, by the data types of the variables, how the input stream is to be broken up and interpreted. *The data must agree in type with the variables into which they are placed.*

Let's look at what happens when numeric and character data are interspersed in the input. Consider the input data:

First ┐
col. │
      ▼
```
111ƀAⓇ
222ƀBⓇ
333ƀCⓇ
```

Each line contains an integer, a blank (explicitly indicated by ƀ), and some other significant character. With the proper variable declarations, a fragment of code capable of reading the input is

```
FOR Times := 1 TO 3 DO
  BEGIN
    read (Number,Blank,Other);

    ┌──────────────────────────────────────┐
    │ use Number and Other somehow         │
    └──────────────────────────────────────┘

  END;
```

We can stretch out the input and show the corresponding sequence of executed read statements to illustrate how the code progresses through the input data and confirm that this code works correctly.

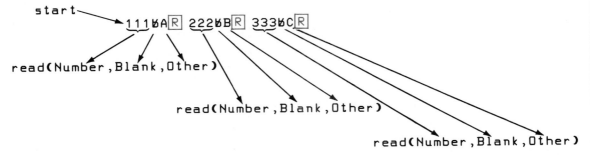

Note how the reading of a numeric value (into Number) bypasses the end of a line in its quest for a numeric character.

Problems with mixed numeric and char input

The blank between the integer and the other character on each line cannot be ignored. If the input statement had been

```
read (Number,Other);
```

its first execution would have placed a blank into Other and reading would have stopped just before A in the input stream. The second execution would have failed by trying to place a nonnumeric object (A) into an integer variable (Number).

If we reverse the order of the data on each input line and modify the read statement accordingly, we have a different problem. The code fragment

```
FOR Times := 1 TO 3 DO
  BEGIN
    read (Other,Number);
      .
      .
      .
  END;
```

cannot successfully process the input

```
A 111 R
B 222 R
C 333 R
```

The difficulty this time is not the blank; it will be bypassed in the search for an integer to place in Number. However, the first execution of this read statement leaves off just *before* the end-of-line component. The second execution then places the end-of-line component (converted to a blank) into Other and fails by trying to place the character B into Number. A primitive solution is to deliberately read the end-of-line into a throw-away character variable. However, there is a much better solution.

The readln Statement

readln statement

To deal explicitly with line boundaries, Pascal provides another input statement: the **readln** (pronounced *read line*) **statement.** Its purpose, besides reading, is to get beyond the next end-of-line component in the input stream. This guarantees that a subsequent input statement will begin at the true beginning of the next line of input. The correct code for the last input stream is

```
FOR Times := 1 TO 3 DO
  BEGIN
    readln (Other,Number);
      .
      .
      .
  END;
```

Specifically, the action of readln is to obtain values from the input data for the variables in its parameter list, exactly as the read statement does. Then, *after* the input of values, readln moves through the input stream to the position immediately following the next end-of-line component. Any inter-

Difference between read and readln

vening values (including blanks) between the last value placed in a variable and the end of the line are simply bypassed—and will never be read again. Thus the primary difference between read and readln is the position in the input stream where they leave off after obtaining their values. Readln is useful when line boundaries are significant to an application. Its use ensures that the next input statement will begin at the start of a new line.

Readln without parameters

Another useful feature of readln is that it may be used without parameters to simply find and bypass an end-of-line component. For example,

```
readln (X,Y,Z);
```

is equivalent to

```
read (X);
read (Y);
read (Z);
readln;
```

To read a line such as

```
3616 209.82 d
```

representing an account number, an amount, and a transaction type, (each separated by a single blank) we could use the following statement.

```
readln (Account,Amount,Blank,Kind);
```

The data types of the variables here are integer, real, char, and char, respectively. Of course, the values need not all be read at once. They may be read in various combinations, involving as many as five input statements:

```
read (Account);
read (Amount);
read (Blank); {and ignore}
read (Kind);
readln;
```

Finally, readln is applicable only to reading text files because only they are divided into lines. See the box on p. 214 for a summary of readln rules.

Detecting the End of an Input Line: The eoln Function

Reading an entire line . . .

Whenever we must treat the data on a single line of input as a related group, we have to know where one line ends and the next begins. Furthermore, it is often necessary to actually read past the end-of-line component as part of reading an *entire* line. We assume this requirement throughout the remainder of this section.

when format is predictable

When we can predict the exact format of a line—the data types and the number of objects it contains—we can use a single readln statement to read the entire line. Such lines are known as **fixed format lines.**

fixed format lines

The readln STATEMENT

readln (⟨list of variables⟩)

or

readln

The rules associated with readln are

1. When readln is used without a parameter list its function is to scan beyond the end of the current line in the input stream, leaving the program ready to read the first character on the next line.
2. When readln is used with a parameter list to read data from a single line of input, as in

    readln (⟨list of variables⟩);

   its action is equivalent to

    read (⟨list of variables⟩);
    readln;

However, some input lines are not so predictable. When we do not know the exact format of a line in advance, the line must be read and analyzed piece by piece. This is done in order to obtain a correct interpretation of what is being encountered and to ensure that no more and no less than one full line is read. However, the sequence of data *types* on the line must be predictable, at least to some extent. After all, we must use the correct type of target variables to receive the data. The most common unknown is therefore the *number* of items on a line. Consider reading a line of text that may contain any number of characters. In order not to miss any, the characters will be read one at a time until the end of the line is reached. The problem, then, is one of end-of-line recognition.

As we already know, it is not possible to identify an end-of-line component simply by reading it because it resembles a blank. Pascal provides the solution with a predeclared **eoln** (end-of-line) **function** to test for the arrival at an end-of-line component in the input stream. Like a boolean expression, eoln will always be either true or false. The value of eoln is true when the current position in the input stream is *immediately before* an end-of-line component. Thus when eoln is true, the entire data portion of the current line will have been read, but not the end-of-line component itself. Because eoln is boolean valued, it can be used in conjunction with IF, WHILE, and REPEAT statements.

The eoln function allows data to be read on the condition that some data still remain on the line (that is, the end has *not* been reached). We code it as

When types are known but number of items is unknown

eoln function

■ Figure 5.1
Reading one line
containing an
arbitrary number of
identical items.

```
WHILE NOT eoln DO
  BEGIN
    read (NextItem);
    ┌─────────────────────┐
    │ process NextItem    │
    └─────────────────────┘
  END;
  readln; { to get beyond end-of-line}
```

follows:

```
IF NOT eolnTHEN
  read (NextItem)
```

If eoln becomes true, the read is not performed. Since the end-of-line component would then be the next item in the input stream, we should skip it by using readln (without parameters), thus completing the entire line and restoring eoln to false (assuming that there are data on the next line).

One common form of a line of input has three properties:

1. Each item on the input line has the same data type.
2. Each item is independently subjected to the same sort of processing.
3. The number of data items on each line is unknown.

Use of eoln to control input loop

These conditions may allow each item to be read into the *same* variable and the input of values to occur within a loop, as in Fig. 5.1. Here, as with the simple IF statement, reading and processing each item is conditional upon the availability of another data value for reading. When the loop terminates, readln is then executed to correctly finish input of the line. This general structure is extremely useful, and you should consider using it whenever the three conditions above are met. It works even when there are no data on the line but just the end-of-line component.

Suppose that each line of input contains an arbitrary amount of text. If the program needs to know the length of each line, counting the number of characters in a *single* line can be implemented as shown in Fig. 5.2.

■ Figure 5.2
Determining the
number of characters
in a line.

```
Length := 0;
WHILE NOT eoln DO
  BEGIN
    read (NextChar);
    Length := Length + 1
  END;
readln;
```

Reading Lines That Have Common Initial Parts

Lines with fixed initial part

We have already considered fixed format lines and lines consisting of many identical data items, but there are other possibilities. A common situation is for an input line to have a standard initial part, followed by an arbitrary number of identical items. Consider a financial transaction system in which the input lines consist of the transaction type (d stands for deposit), the account number, and an arbitrary number of transaction amounts (here deposits), such as

d   24229   2.15   123.67   8.02

The initial part of each line—the character and the following integer—are guaranteed to appear on every input line. Consequently, they can be read without testing for end-of-line. After they have been read, an unknown number of transaction amounts remain. They can be read by using the loop structure shown in Fig. 5.1. The fixed, initial portion of the line must be read *before* the loop that reads the transactions is entered, as shown in Fig. 5.3.

Mixed line formats indicated by initial part

Despite a desire to make all input lines look alike, you will come across many problems that do not permit this. The next best thing for you to do is to identify a few standard line formats and use some feature of the line itself to recognize which format is being read.

Let's expand the financial transaction system example to deal with the transaction system example to deal with the following operations.

d—post deposits for account
w—post withdrawals for account
b—determine balance in account
s—display complete status of account
n—open new account
r—generate report on all accounts

■ **Figure 5.3**
Processing lines with a fixed initial part.

```
read (Kind, Account);

  standard initial processing for line

WHILE NOT eoln DO
  BEGIN
    read (NextAmount);

      process NextAmount

  END;
readln;

  processing following input of line
```

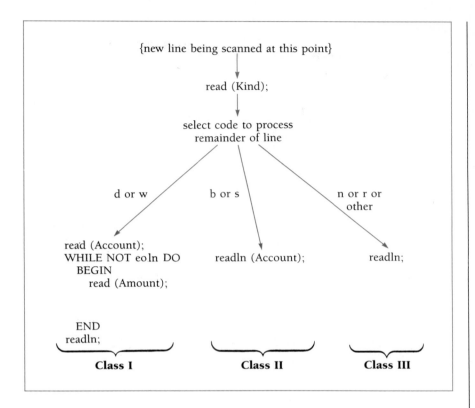

■ Figure 5.4
Reading lines having
formats that belong
to different classes.

The associated line formats are

```
d  acct#  amt1  amt2  .  .  .  amtN
w  acct#  amt1  amt2  .  .  .  amtM
b  acct#
s  acct#
n         {system will generate new account number}
r         {applies to all numbers}
```

The formats fall into three broad classes having one common characteristic:
a single character at the start of each line. This first character immediately
classifies the remainder of the line, enabling the proper code to be chosen
for subsequent processing. Figure 5.4 shows the format classes and the basic
flow of control through the various input structures. Note that every line is
completed by executing readln. Again, we emphasize that this mechanism
reads only a single line of data.

The single characters at the start of each line do more than identify the
line format. They also prescribe the required processing and can be construed
as commands to the financial system. An overall program that cycles through
such a system and responds to the commands is called a *command interpreter,*
which we discuss in Section 5.3.

5.2 Reading Many Lines of Text

Problems with sentinels

We now turn to the problem of reading *several* lines of text. We noted earlier that using sentinels to signal the end of input has its drawbacks. One problem is choosing which value to use. The sentinel must be read as though it were valid data but must not be mistaken for valid data. Thus it is difficult (sometimes even impossible) to choose a sentinel value of the required type and which is known to be outside the range of feasible data.

If several values are read by one input statement, the sentinel must have several components so it can be read in the same way. An interactive system can issue prompts to the user to enter the sentinel, but they may be cumbersome and may have to be repeated often, lest the user forget. Finally, in practice the data may come from various sources, some being remote We should not expect all these data sources to know and include the exact sentinel value for the local application. In summary, sentinels are neither sufficiently general nor foolproof.

The eof Function in General

end-of-file

The alternative to sentinels is to establish a more general condition called **end-of-file.** End-of-file is the way an operating system terminates *all* its files. Whether the file comes from a remotely generated tape, the local card reader, or a disk file produced using an editor, when the last component of the file has been read (or bypassed by readln), the program encounters the end of the file. One exception is data entered directly from a terminal. Since the system cannot guess when the user has finished typing, the user must generate an explicit end-of-file by pressing the appropriate key(s) (such as "control/z" in VAX-11 and Turbo Pascal). In the sense that the user must type something special after the data, end-of-file resembles a sentinel. However, end-of-file is nothing like legitimate data and cannot be confused or mistaken for anything else. Furthermore, it is not specific to any application; it is a standard, systemwide end-of-data indicator.

eof function

Since end-of-file is not a character (or any other data type), it cannot be read or manipulated within a program. The only way it can be sensed or recognized is by invoking the predeclared end-of-file function, or **eof function.** This function returns a boolean result: true if end-of-file has been reached (or if the file contains no data) and false if not.

        IF eof THEN
            writeln ('data exhausted')
        ELSE {data remain}

Eof will not become true until all the data in the input file have been read, including end-of-line components. When eof becomes true no more data can be read from that source. One cannot read "past" the end of a file to get at some additional data. In fact, it is a fatal error to try. Consequently, since the program is usually not sure there will be more data to process, all reading should be conditional upon eof still being false. The general idea for repetitive input is

```
WHILE NOT eof DO
  BEGIN
    .
    .       ┌─────────────────────────┐
    .       │ read more data          │
    .       │ process that data       │
    .       └─────────────────────────┘
  END;
```

To guard against an attempt to read an empty file, WHILE is used in preference to REPEAT.

Detecting the End of Text Files

eof with text files requires end of line to be bypassed

In the case of nonempty text files, another important consideration is that the end of a file can be encountered only after the end of the last line in that file. If there are any data at all, an end-of-line component will immediately precede the end of the file. This implies that when "more data" are read in the interior of the loop (in the preceding code fragment) that data should comprise precisely one line, including the end-of-line component. Reading any more or less than one entire line inside the loop may prevent you from ever discovering the end of the file (except by accident). Therefore, you should conclude the reading of the line with a readln statement to make sure that the input stream will be positioned just beyond an end-of-line component. We summarize this requirement in Fig. 5.5. You could use any appropriate input pattern for reading an entire line inside the loop.

```
WHILE NOT eof DO {test file}
  BEGIN

    ┌──────────────────────────────────────────────────────┐
    │ read and process precisely one entire line including  │
    │ the end-of-line component (implying one occurrence of │
    │ readln)                                               │
    └──────────────────────────────────────────────────────┘

  END;
```

■ Figure 5.5
General repetitive input from a text file using eof.

■ Figure 5.6
Reading an arbitrary
number of lines
containing an
arbitrary number of
identical items.

```
WHILE NOT eof DO
  BEGIN

    Actions before reading next line

    WHILE NOT eoln DO
      BEGIN
        read (NextItem);

          process that item

      END
    readln; {skip past end of line}

    Actions after reading one line

  END;
```

Reading an arbitrary number of variable length lines

When the input lines consist of an arbitrary number of similar items on each line, the input structure shown in Fig. 5.1 should be used to read one such line. This yields the overall structure for reading an arbitrary number of these lines shown in Fig. 5.6. This turns out to be a very useful input process; it is capable of dealing with empty lines and can even handle the case of no lines at all.

For example, consider the problem of finding the longest line from an arbitrary number of input lines. We showed the code for reading and determining the length of one line in Fig. 5.2. We can also use it to implement step 2.1 of the overall process:

1. MaxLength := 0;
2. while lines remain to be read do:
2.1   read next line and determine its Length;
2.2   if Length > MaxLength then
            MaxLength := Length;
3. report MaxLength;
4. stop.

Assuming that we use eof to detect the end of the final line of input, the code fragment in Fig. 5.7 would determine the longest line.

Placement of prompts

Finally, if the text file comes from a terminal, and if an interactive prompt is to precede each line of input, the prompts must be generated at the *two*

```
MaxLength := 0;

WHILE NOT eof DO
  BEGIN {all lines}
    Length := 0;

    WHILE NOT eoln DO
      BEGIN {one line}
        read (NextChar);
        Length := Length + 1
      END; {one line}

    readln;

    IF Length > MaxLength THEN
      MaxLength := Length
  END; {all lines}

writeln ('Longest was:', MaxLength:3,' characters');
```

■ Figure 5.7
Finding the longest line from among several lines.

places shown in Fig. 5.8. The eof function cannot determine whether the input stream is at the end of the file until the user types something. If no prompt is issued, the user may not know what to type. Thus a deadlock can occur, in which the user waits for instructions while the program waits for input. The writeln statement before the loop eliminates this potential stalemate.

```
writeln ('Enter next line or end-of-file to quit');
WHILE NOT eof DO
  BEGIN

    ┌─────────────────────────────────────────────────┐
    │ read and process one entire line of input,      │
    │ including end-of-line component                 │
    └─────────────────────────────────────────────────┘

    writeln ('Enter next line or end-of-file to quit')
  END;
```

■ Figure 5.8
Repetitive input of lines from a terminal, showing interactive prompts.

When this prompt has been issued, the user should not see another one until the program is ready for the next set of data, that is, *after* the current line has been entered. This explains why we placed the second writeln—the one responsible for all subsequent prompts—at the end of the loop.

5.3 Command Interpreters

When you interact with the operating system of a computer, a dialogue is established in which you repeatedly give commands (often with an operand or two, such as a file name), and the system responds by carrying out that command. Each command elicits a response, such as compiling a program, executing a program, or removing a file. Another familiar example is the text editor, which reacts to your commands to store, display, or modify text. The software that reads your commands and directs control to the correct processing module is known as the **command interpreter.**

command interpreter

The command interpreter's job is to select one of a variety of alternative actions, depending on the command just read. If these commands are values of a simple data type, you could implement the selection process with a CASE statement.

Implementation

Basic Structure of Command Interpreters

For commands that are integers or (individual) characters, the general structure of a command interpreter is as shown in Fig. 5.9. Some particular command usually terminates the action; in Fig. 5.9 it is identified as Terminator and acts as a sentinel. The command interpreter must receive at least one command from the user, even if that command is to quit, so the REPEAT structure is the preferred construct.

An Example: Simulating a Calculator

Let's design a program that behaves much like a simple hand calculator. Instead of pushing buttons for each operation, the user will type, at the beginning of each line, one character indicating the operation, followed by a number, if that operation requires one. The operations we will use are

+	add	Requires numeric operand
−	subtract	Requires numeric operand
q	quit	

Our calculator will have only one memory location, which we will call the "accumulator." It starts with the value of zero, and all operations are applied to its current value. Whenever an operation takes place, the resulting value

■ Figure 5.9
Structure of a simple
command interpreter

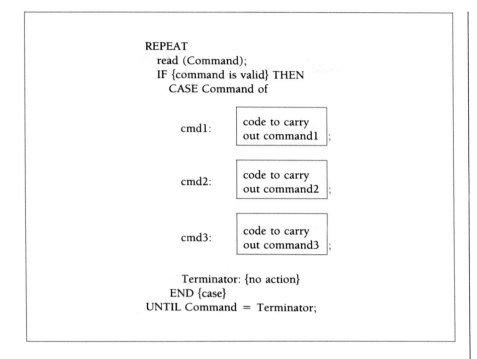

```
REPEAT
    read (Command);
    IF {command is valid} THEN
        CASE Command of


        cmd1:    | code to carry  |
                 | out command1   | ;


        cmd2:    | code to carry  |
                 | out command2   | ;


        cmd3:    | code to carry  |
                 | out command3   | ;


        Terminator: {no action}
        END {case}
    UNTIL Command = Terminator;
```

of the accumulator is displayed. The internal calculations and the output employ real numbers. Thus the following input produces the output shown (and may appear intermixed with the input on an actual terminal screen).

Input	Output	
	0.00	(initial)
$+7$	7.00	
$+28$	35.00	
-12	23.00	
-23	0.00	
$+8$	8.00	
q		

The overall algorithm is

1. start accumulator at 0;
2. repeat until termination command ('q') occurs:
2.1   read and process next command line;
3. stop.

Step 2 is nothing more than a high-level statement of the process shown in Fig. 5.9. Since each of the arithmetic commands requires the additional input of a number from the current input line, step 2 becomes

2.   repeat until command = 'q':
2.1   read command;
2.2   if command is arithmetic then
          read numeric operand from same line;
2.3   select action indicated by command;

Since the individual actions are trivial, we can proceed directly to the program shown in Fig. 5.10.

Observe how the readln statement completes every line of input, regardless of the command it contained. It is important to make sure that the next

```
PROGRAM Calculator (input,output);

    {Simulating an elementary calculator}

VAR
    Command: char;
    Operand, Accumulator: real;

BEGIN {Calculator}
    Accumulator := 0;
    REPEAT
        {Accumulator diplayed for all commands except 'q'}
        writeln (Accumulator:10:2);

        read (Command);
        IF (Command = '+') OR (Command = '-') THEN
            read (Operand); {arithmetic}
        readln; {clear input line in every case}

        IF (Command = '+') OR (Command = '-')
            OR (Command = 'q') THEN
            CASE Command OF
                '+': Accumulator := Accumulator + Operand;
                '-': Accumulator := Accumulator - Operand;
                'q': {no specific action}
            END {case}
        ELSE
            writeln ('invalid command')

    UNTIL Command = 'q'
END. {Calculator}
```

■ Figure 5.10
Program to simulate a simple calculator.

command will be read from the beginning of the next line. Note too that we placed the common action of displaying the contents of the accumulator as the first action inside REPEAT. This calculator will then display a zero as soon as it is activated and will show the result of each command (except q) after it has been executed.

Guarding CASE   Once again we emphasize the importance of having the IF statement guard the CASE statement. We cannot always depend on the user to enter one of the acceptable commands, which can be processed by the CASE statement. Because it is an error when the case selector value does not appear in the case statement list, the IF screens out unacceptable commands entered by the user.

5.4 Special Output Considerations

When designing and doing early testing of a program, you should usually not be concerned with fully formatted, aesthetically pleasing output. In a sense, the presentation of results is just the frosting on the cake. If the results are wrong, it does not matter how beautifully you present them. Thus you should focus initially on program completeness and accuracy.

Planning the Presentation of Results

The display of results, however, should not be just an afterthought or the result of some hastily inserted write statements. Too little planning can cause **Need for output** hours of effort later as you try to align data into columns for output or achieve **planning** uniform spacing in a report. Furthermore, the way you present data to the user greatly influences the ultimate effect and usefulness of the program. In fact, this aspect of the user–program interface deserves more attention than it tends to receive.

All that is usually required is some planning. Before encoding the final, formatted output statements, you should carefully write out one or two typical examples of the desired report. This model should be sufficiently detailed to allow counting of spaces, calculation of field widths, and the like. This may seem tedious, but it allows you, for example, to center headings and align columns correctly on your first attempt. The alternative—tinkering with existing write statements—is far more time-consuming.

More about Field Width Specifiers

We covered most of the material on field width specifiers in output statements in Chapter 2, but two rather technical considerations remain. The first of **Exponential notation** these concerns the display of real values in exponential (rather than decimal) form. This form is important in many scientific applications, which deal with numeric values beyond the range that can be conveniently written using decimal notation. When a real value is followed by a two-component field width specifier,

⟨real expression⟩:w:d

it is displayed in decimal notation. However, if only *one* component is supplied, as in

⟨real expression⟩:w

the resulting number is shown in exponential form in a field of total width w. This field must accommodate all the items displayed, including

$$\left.\begin{array}{l}\text{the sign of the number } (- \text{ or blank})\\ \text{the first digit of the number}\\ \text{the decimal point}\end{array}\right\} \text{ 3 characters}$$

other decimal digits of the number

$$\left.\begin{array}{l}\text{the letter e (or E)}\\ \text{the sign of the exponent}\\ \text{the digits of the exponent (often 2)}\end{array}\right\} \text{ 4 characters}$$

As you can see, the value of w should be at least 7. It is usually much larger to allow several digits of the number to appear, as in

Code	Output
X := − 123.45608;	
writeln (X:8);	− 1.2e + 02
writeln (abs(X):13);	⟶b1.234561e + 02

Blank occupies first of 13 positions.

On the other hand, if w is too large, many nonsignificant digits may be printed. Unlike the case with other data types, this form of real notation consumes all w positions of the field. When the number is positive (or zero), a single initial blank is often used in place of a plus (+) sign; when the value is negative, there are no preceding blanks.

Variable field widths   The other consideration is that the field width does not always need to be specified by a constant. We may use variables or more complex expressions. The writeln statement at the end of the sequence

```
Y  := 789;
N  := 4;
writeln ( Y:N, Y:(N+1) );
```

produces exactly the same effect as

```
writeln ( Y:4, Y:5 );
```

A variable field width allows the programmer greater flexibility in displaying values, regardless of their size.

The function FieldWidth in Fig. 5.11 calculates the field width required to display its real-valued parameter in decimal form, providing one leading blank, at least one digit before the decimal, and two decimal places in every case. For example, it returns 6 when given 24.68 and returns 8 when given −456.78. The minimum field width that meets these constraints is 5 (ƀn.nn). The width must be one greater for each order of magnitude (power of 10) in the number and must include an additional space if a minus sign is involved. We used a value-type parameter so as not to disturb the original values.

We can use the function value directly within the write(ln) statement in place of a constant field width. The code:

```
Number := 2.3;
writeln ('Try',Number:FieldWidth(Number):2, 'for now.');
Number := −725.648;
writeln ('Try',Number: FieldWidth(Number):2, 'for now.');
```

produces the output:

```
Try 2.30 for now.        (field width is 5)
Try −725.65 for now.     (field width is 8)
```

```
FUNCTION FieldWidth (X:real): integer;
   {Assuming one leading blank and two trailing
    decimal places, calculate the field width
    needed to display value of X in decimal form}

   VAR Width: integer;

   BEGIN {FieldWidth}
      Width := 5; {minimum field ƀn.nn}
      IF X < 0 THEN {need extra space for sign}
         Width := Width + 1;

      WHILE abs(X) >= 10 DO
         BEGIN
            X := X / 10; {for each power of 10}
            Width := Width + 1 {one more position}
         END;

      FieldWidth := Width
   END; {FieldWidth}
```

■ Figure 5.11
Calculation of proper field width.

5.5 Making Programs Work Correctly

Anticipating input problems

Despite all the careful design and coding that you put into a program, it is likely at times to fail to perform as expected. In fact, few error-free programs exist—there are only programs in which errors have not yet been detected. The programmer is responsible for ensuring that the program functions correctly in all reasonable environments. Thus the programmer must clearly state the objective of the program, give clear instructions for the program's use (by way of prompts), and test the program under a variety of conditions. Although no one can anticipate *every* possible mistake a user might make, the programmer is obligated to ensure that the program does not give incorrect answers when appearing to run normally.

Identifying and Preventing Input Anomalies

In this section we will reexamine some earlier programs and discover some surprises revealed during testing. These surprises are typical of the anomalies that you need to understand and correct in order to make programs acceptable.

When sentinel is first data item

Refer back to the algorithm to calculate an average on page 106. If we turn it directly into a Pascal program, a serious problem arises if the first value supplied to the program is the sentinel value. This can happen in three cases: (1) the sentinel value may equal the first legitimate data value; (2) the user may decide to exit from the program at once; and (3) there may be no data for this particular execution (a situation that should always be tested).

Prevent division by zero

Regardless of the reason, if the first value entered is the sentinel value, Count will remain zero, and an attempt will be made to compute Average using a Count of 0 in the denominator. Since the rules of arithmetic forbid such an operation, the program will fail with an error message. The algorithm should be modified, so that the process will halt gracefully and a suitable message will be provided if, indeed, the program does not encounter any values. We do this by replacing steps 4 and 5 with the logic:

4.   if Count > 0 then
4.1   compute Average;
4.2   display Average;
5.   otherwise
5.1   display a message saying no values were read;

In general, the programmer is responsible for ensuring that the divisor in a division operation is not equal to zero.

When we design programs, we tend to assume that users will always supply reasonable input data, but users do not always do so. Users may not consciously enter wrong data, but a slip of the fingers or an error in the transmission of the data can cause the program to receive something never

defensive
programming

**Obtaining reasonable
input values**

intended. The programmer is responsible for taking all *reasonable precautions* to trap bad input; this attitude is called **defensive programming.**

We might expect that in our first munchie model (Fig. 3.8) the user will always give positive values to start the model off. After all, we cannot conceive of a negative or zero value for any of the variables requested by the program. Nevertheless, the program in Fig. 3.8 will accept either zero or negative integers as data. If we run it with any positive value for the initial food supply and zero for either (or both) of the other variables, the program will run, and run, and run. No output will appear on the screen; the user will be left looking at a blinking cursor with no indication of why the program is not responding. The reason is that the program does not produce any output until the food supply has been reduced below the appetite of one munchie, a situation that cannot occur if no munchies exist or if those that do have no appetites. A more robust program can be made by requiring all initial values to be greater than zero. This means that on reading each of the initial values, we should proceed only if the one just read is greater than zero.

One approach might be to amend the program, such as:

```
read (Munchies);
IF Munchies <= 0 THEN
   BEGIN {2nd chance}
      writeln ('Population must be > 0. Please re-enter');
      read (Munchies)
   END; {2nd chance}
```

However, should a second unacceptable value be entered, we are back at the same problem. Better still is to keep insisting on an acceptable value until the user finally supplies one. This can be easily implemented by using REPEAT.

```
REPEAT
   writeln ('Enter initial munchie population (> 0)');
   read (Munchies)
UNTIL Munchies > 0;
```

Similar code could be devised for the other input values. Although you may feel that this is a lot of extra code to cover a situation that ought not to happen, such an attitude will only hasten the application of Murphy's Law: "Anything that can go wrong will go wrong."

Of course, users also have a responsibility to follow instructions. If a program expects to receive an integer from the user and it encounters anything other than the decimal digits, the program will be aborted. As a beginning programmer you can do little about this kind of error yet, and whether you ever should depends on the application.

Diagnosis through Tracing

Some errors seem to defy all attempts at understanding; despite reexamination of the algorithm and analysis of the program structure, you can find no explanation. Even when you carefully execute the program by hand, using the same data, you fail to reproduce the error.

This does not mean that the computer made a mistake; it means that you have been misled by the evidence or have made some unjustified assumptions. For example, from having designed the logic, you may *know* that a certain section of code is responsible for the problem or that some other section is never reached and need not be inspected. What you may not know is that you phrased some condition incorrectly, causing control to flow into unexpected territory where the damage occurred.

One way to track down such problems is to "watch" the program in operation and see where control actually flows and what values are actually placed in critical variables. Of course you cannot actually see the flow of control in action, but you can take occasional *snapshots* of the program during its execution and deduce its behavior from this new evidence. Some computer systems supply special programs, called run-time debuggers, to aid you in this activity, but we will describe aids that you can program yourself.

Diagnostic snapshots of execution

These snapshots are simply the output from specially placed writeln statements. They are used only for diagnostic purposes and play no part in the algorithm. When control reaches one of these writeln statements and activates it, the current location in the program and the values of selected variables are displayed. The sequence of these output lines allows you to trace the flow of control and the history of key variables, hence the term **tracing.**

tracing

These traces often provide some surprises and, it is hoped, the insight needed to correct the error. On the other hand, they may not fully expose the problem. This means that more thought, more hand checking, and perhaps even more detailed tracing will be required.

Revealing flow

To be more specific, one basic kind of information desired is the path taken by the flow of control. This means that each trace statement must identify itself by printing either a unique number, or code, or the actual description of where it is located. You can get a general idea of what is happening from just a few strategically placed writeln statements. For example, a tracing statement within a loop will show how many repetitions (if any) actually occurred. An extra writeln inside each subprogram will show how often (if ever) and in what order the subprograms are executed.

Tracing strategy

If this additional output does not provide enough information, you can add more writeln statements to obtain a more detailed trace. Again, judgment is important. Too many trace statements may yield too much data for you to understand easily. Usually the basic error symptoms or a first attempt at tracing lead you to suspect a particular section of code as the source of the problem. You should analyze this section first with more refined tracing before focusing on other sections of the program.

Values to watch

The other basic kind of information needed concerns the values of *key* variables. The meaning of key variables depends on the symptoms of the problem. These variables also determine where you should place the extra trace statements. Typical values to watch for are

1. *Input values:* What your program actually reads and what it is supposed to read may not be the same. It is often helpful to follow each read statement by displaying the values just read. Occasionally this reveals that a supposedly repeated read statement executed only once, and that the same input data were reused repeatedly.

2. *Loop control variables:* Any variables involved in the expressions governing loops should be displayed if looping problems are suspected. They should be displayed both before entering the loop and within the loop at the very end, just before they are tested. Placing a trace statement inside the loop enables you to accurately count the number of repetitions. A trace statement following the loop will reveal exactly why the loop terminated. If many executions are expected, it might be worthwhile to define, maintain, and display a separate counter variable just for diagnostic purposes.

3. *Variables involved in decision making:* In addition to loop control, displaying the variables used to govern IF statements will reveal what paths were actually taken. Doing this before entering a CASE statement or a nested IF construct is very useful. But placing separate writelns along each alternate path will reveal with certainty the path actually taken.

4. *Variables known to contain incorrect values:* Any variables known to contain wrong values should be monitored. They should be checked at the transition points between major sections of the program. In the section where the incorrect values occur, the variables should be displayed after every assignment that can potentially alter them. Although this trace will reveal the exact point where the variables were assigned faulty values, additional traces of contributing variables may be needed to find the ultimate cause.

5. *Parameter values:* Find out whether subprograms are receiving the correct starting values. Variable parameters should be displayed both before and after calling a procedure. This will reveal what effect (if any) the procedure actually had on the program.

Removing trace statements

Wherever you decide to place these extra trace statements, you must remove them when the program is working correctly. A good way to do this is to attach the same distinctive comment to every trace statement, so that they can be easily located and deleted by the editor. For example, if you use the trace statement:

```
writeln ('end of loop2',var1,var2); {trace}
```

you can find all such statements by scanning for {trace}. If a visual scan is required, use an eye-catching pattern such as {*******}.

Enabling and disabling traces

An additional possibility is to build in the ability to turn traces off and on, so that you can disable them for some test runs and reactivate them if errors persist. To do this, simply make each trace statement the object of an IF, which tests a variable set by the user at the beginning of the program.

Potential new errors

If you insert extra writelns in a program, make sure that their inclusion does not introduce new errors by altering the program's flow structure. A common mistake is adding a trace statement to the single-statement object of FOR, THEN, or ELSE, but forgetting to enclose the new writeln and the action statement within a BEGIN–END block. In some cases this causes no syntax error but completely undermines the intended logic.

Use of output procedures

Procedures offer a powerful tool for tracing. You might be interested in the values associated with the variables Gross, Tax, and Net at different points in the program. A simple way to achieve this is to write a procedure such as

```
PROCEDURE Trace;
  BEGIN
    writeln ('Gross =: ',Gross);
    writeln ('Tax =: ',Tax);
    writeln ('Net =: ',Net)
  END;
```

Then, at those points in the program where all three values are needed, simply insert the statement `Trace;`. Note that we used global variables in this procedure, since the objects of interest are values as they appear in the main program, and tracing by its very nature will not alter any values in its calling program.

5.6 Review of Rules

A. A text file has individual characters as its components and may be subdivided into lines (that is, variable length character sequences terminated by the end-of-line component). End-of-file follows the final end-of-line component. The standard files, known as input and output, are text files.

B. The procedures readln and writeln, together with the eoln function, may be used only with text files. Only text files allow end-of-line components.

C. The procedure readln first obtains values for each of the variables in its parameter list from successive positions in the input stream—exactly like read. However, readln then positions the input stream immediately *after* the next end-of-line component (that is, at the start of the following line), bypassing any intervening characters. Readln may be used without parameters to position the file at the start of the next line.

D. The eof function returns a true value when the last component of the input file has been read (or bypassed by readln) or if the input file is empty; its value is false otherwise. When data are arriving from the terminal, the user must enter an explicit end-of-file sequence after the final line of input. It is an error to call eoln, read, or readln when eof is true.

E. The eoln function returns a true value if the input file is positioned at (immediately before) an end-of-line component; it is false otherwise, provided eof is false. Eoln is undefined when eof becomes true. Pressing the return key on most terminals generates an end-of-line component.

F. The field widths for formatted output may be specified by any integer-valued expression, provided the value is greater than or equal to 1. If a real value is displayed in decimal notation, using ⟨real expression⟩:w:d, d may also be given by an integer-valued expression with value $>= 0$. When a real-valued expression is displayed with the field width specified as

write (⟨real-expression⟩:w);

the value will be displayed in exponential (or floating) form.

KEY TERMS

command interpreter	fixed format lines
defensive programming	input stream
end-of-file	readln statement
end-of-line component	sequential processing
eof function	text files
eoln function	tracing
file	

EXERCISES

5.1 In this exercise, each successive part should include all the features of the preceding parts.

(a) Using a positive integer n as input, generate a table in which the lines pertain to the first n positive integers: 1, 2, . . . , n. Each line should contain the value of the integer, its square root, its cube and its fourth root.

(b) Include a title for the entire table and a heading at the top of each of the four columns.

(c) Generate a blank line after every five lines of data. At the end, generate a line of stars.

(d) Below the table, generate the sum of the numbers displayed in each column. These sums should appear aligned under their respective columns. Another line of stars might help to set off this summary line. Extra blank lines should be added to eliminate crowding.

5.2 (a) In Exercise 2.13, you supplied an integer interpreted as degrees of arc and produced an equivalent value in radians. Here, you are to supply a real value interpreted as radians (either positive or negative) and the program will display the equivalent value in degrees, that is, an integer between 0 and 359. In addition, give the sine, cosine, and tangent of the input angle.

(b) Allow an arbitrary number of (radian) angles to be entered, followed by a suitable sentinel. Make sure that your program tells the user what sentinel value to supply.

(c) Display the results of this program as a table, with column headings, blank lines, and column averages, as described in Exercise 5.1(b–d). (This table will have five values per line: two versions of the angle and three trigonometric functions of the angle.) *Note:* When you develop this program interactively, the input and output will appear intermixed on the screen, so that the tabular form of the output cannot be viewed. However, when you are able to display the correct values properly aligned, you can run the program with its input coming from a predefined data file. (Your instructor will show you how.) Then only the program output will show up on the screen, allowing you to see the table.

5.3   Modern car radios allow the owner to preprogram stations into the radio, which can then be tuned in at the touch of a button. This exercise is concerned with writing a command interpreter to simulate an FM car radio having limited capability. The radio has two memory buttons (marked 1 and 2), a seek button (marked S), a memorize button (marked M), and an off button (marked O). When you turn the radio on, it immediately tunes in to the frequency associated with memory button 1. You use the seek button to advance the tuner to the next frequency from that currently tuned. When you press the memorize button and then press one of the memory buttons, you change the station associated with that memory button to the station currently playing. You merely press one of the memory buttons to tune the radio to the station associated with that button.

Write a Pascal program to simulate the action of this radio. Playing a station can be simulated by displaying its frequency on the screen. The usual range for an FM station is from 88.0 to 108.0 Mhz, and stations are separated by at least 0.1 Mhz. Since your simulated radio cannot remember the stations for each memory button from one execution to the next, you should always start with the same station. Finally, you do not have to provide for error checking in your program.

5.4   At the end of the month, information about each account in a small branch bank is entered into a program, summarized, and displayed on the screen. Each account is handled by the following commands.

Name	Format
new	n account-number starting-balance
deposit	d amt1 amt2 . . . amtN
withdraw	w amt1 amt2 . . . amtM
balance	b

The command new introduces the next account and supplies its five-digit account number and starting balance. The commands deposit and withdraw introduce lines containing one or more positive monetary amounts. The command determines whether the amounts on the same line represent successive deposits or withdrawals. No command may extend beyond one line; however, any number of command lines may be employed to provide data for the same account. The first command for any account must be n; all following commands before the next n pertain to that same account. The b command causes a summary output line to be generated. This output line contains the account number, the number of deposits, the number of withdrawals, and the current balance. The d, w, and b commands may appear in any order. However, the final command for an account should be b, so that a summary appears for all the data. In addition a quit command (q) terminates the entire program.

(a) Implement this system using a command interpreter and procedures to handle each nontrivial command. Note that the same auxiliary procedure may be used to read and summarize the numeric data for both the d and w commands.

(b) Assume that the input data (and commands) will be arriving from a file. (Your instructor will explain how.) This allows you to focus on presenting the output lines in the form of a table. Give the table a title and label each column. At the end of the table, the number of accounts and the total number of individual transactions should be printed.

(c) Dispense with the b command (but not the line-generating procedure) and assume that the data for each account will be displayed upon encountering the next n or the q command.

(d) Introduce another procedure to compute a service charge for each account just before its closing balance is derived, as follows:

Conditions	Service charge
min balance $\geq$ 1000	no charge
$0 \leq$ min balance $<$ 1000	$0.15 per withdrawal
min balance $<$ 0	extra $10 charge

The requirement to maintain the minimum balance imposes some extra responsibility on the main program but should cause no changes in the NewAccount, Deposit, or Withdraw procedures. The line-generating procedure should *flag* (by printing an extra asterisk or other symbol next to) every account number that had a minimum balance less than 0 *at any time* during the month.

5.5 In this exercise, you will implement a simple table formatting system that will enable you to display numeric data in tabular form according to specifications provided at run time. This system will first read a number of parameters that describe aspects of table appearance. The data—simply a stream of numbers—will then be provided for display. Table specifications will be provided in response to prompts. The following features can be specified.

Number of columns (no more than 6).
Column width (this must be checked for consistency).
Spacing between title and first line of table.
Number of consecutive rows appearing without a break (called a *table section*).
Whether to delineate sections with a blank line or with a line of stars.

After supplying these parameters, the user types the title (which the system should center over the table), followed by an arbitrary number of numeric values on an arbitrary number of lines.

(a) Test this system with various table configurations using integer data.

(b) Add the ability to handle either integer or real data values; in particular, specify

whether data items will be real or integer; and

if real, how many digits to provide after the decimal point (if 0 suppress decimal point during output).

Be sure to check these specifications to determine whether they are consistent with your column widths. Perhaps the size of the largest expected value can be requested as a check.

(c) Add the option of drawing a border around the entire table (top, bottom and sides) consisting of stars.

5.6 A text filter is a program that performs some simple transformation of text as it passes through the program. In other words, as the text is being read, its transformed version is being written.

(a) Write a program to transform text with the following options.

- Spacing between consecutive output lines:
    consecutive lines
    1 blank line
    2 blank lines
- Spacing between words (across an output line):
    always 1 blank
    exactly 2 blanks
    no change from original
- Spacing between sentences:
    2 blanks
    begin new line
    no change from original
- Valid sentence terminators:
    period
    period plus ?
    period, ?, and !

Assume that end-of-file will terminate the input. *Note:* Since intermixed input and output will interfere with the reformatted output, the output should be directed to a file for later display at the terminal. (Your instructor will show you how to do this.)

(b) Add the option of how to terminate input.

- Terminating input:
    end-of-file
    sentinel

If the sentinel option is chosen, the user should specify its value as input at this time.

5.7 (a) Take any program containing subprograms that you wrote as an exercise for either Chapter 4 or Chapter 5 and insert trace statements that enable you to track the flow of control through the various modules during execution. The trace should also reveal how many times each loop was executed.

(b) Make the trace a run-time option that is either activated or disabled by the first input value.

5.8   Write a program to read an arbitrarily long stream of integers and display the relative numbers of even and odd integers. The result should be expressed as a bar chart. This bar chart will have only two bars, with lengths proportional to the percentage of numbers that are even and odd, respectively.

  (a) Display a bar chart with horizontal bars. Allow 50 spaces across a line to represent 100%. Thus, if 25 integers are read, with 20 being even, the even bar should be 80% of this length, or 40 characters long; the bar representing the number of odd integers would be only 10 characters long. Use stars to form the bars.

  (b) Add the option of specifying the bar width, that is, the number of lines thick each bar should be. Also include the choice of the number of lines to separate the two bars.

  (c) Label each bar as either *even* or *odd* along the left-hand side. This will move the bars themselves a few spaces to the right. Add labels across the top to identify the percentages being represented by the bars. If the line of labels is followed by a line of the form

            – – – – + – – – – + – – – – + – – – –

    the plus signs serve as markers to associate labels with exact positions.

  (d) Since both bars will often be of nearly the same length, make the scale flexible, so that the longer bar will always occupy exactly 50 positions, and the shorter bar will be scaled accordingly.

5.9   Produce as output a downward stairstep pattern in response to a sequence of inputs specifying movement either to the right or downward. For example, if the inputs are either r (right one space) or d (down one line), the sequence rrrrddrdrrrddrrrr should produce the pattern

            # # # #
                *
                * #
                 * # # #
                      *
                      * # # # #
    where # reflects an r, and * reflects a d.

6

Basic Data Types

Pascal provides four basic data types: integer, real, char, and boolean. So far, we have presented all the basic features of the two numeric types, many features of the char type, and some features of the boolean type. In this chapter, we complete our discussion of the definition and manipulation of the char and boolean types. More importantly, we present some typical applications, using these data types to make programs straightforward and understandable. We also show that other data types can be derived from the four basic types—and how to extend the language by defining data types of your own design.

6.1 Numeric Applications

To guard against typing or clerical errors, it is common for part numbers or product numbers to conform to some internal pattern. Then, if one or two digits are entered incorrectly, the pattern will probably be violated, allowing the error to be detected by a program. Typical patterns involve sums of individual digits, called **check sums.**

check sums

Check Sums: An Example Using Integer Arithmetic

Consider a simple check sum in which the first three digits of a four-digit part number must add up (mod 10) to the value of the fourth digit. The reason for taking the sum mod 10 is to ensure it will be between 0 and 9—the only possible values for the fourth digit. For example, 5274 is valid because $5 + 2 + 7 = 14$, and 14 MOD 10 = 4. However, 5074 is invalid because $(5 + 0 + 7)$ MOD $10 = 2 \neq 4$. We will develop a program to test a four-digit part number for validity using this scheme.

If we identify individual digits, left to right, as Digit1, Digit2, Digit3, and Digit4, the actual test for validity is merely to ask:

IF (Digit1 + Digit2 + Digit3) MOD 10 = Digit4 THEN . . .

The difficult part is obtaining the values for these individual digits. They cannot be read one digit at a time, at least not as *numeric* quantities. Only the entire four-digit part number can be obtained as an integer; the values of the individual digits must be obtained later by arithmetic manipulation.

We could start from either end of the number and alternately (1) identify or isolate the end digit for later use in the check sum calculation; and (2) remove that digit from the number. The second step eliminates the end digit from further consideration and shortens the remaining, unprocessed part of the number, thereby exposing the next digit as the end digit. If we choose to identify the rightmost digit each time, division by 10 would seem a natural approach. To capture *only* the rightmost digit of N: (1) compute N MOD 10, which shows the digit that is left over after we divide by 10; and (2) compute N DIV 10, which yields everything *except* the rightmost digit of N.

One approach then is to alternately (1) compute N MOD 10 to capture the next digit; and (2) replace N by N DIV 10 to remove that digit. We keep doing this until we have isolated all the digits in the number, that is, until N = 0. These digits can be summed as we go along. More formally we can say

1.   read Number;
2.   set Sum to 0;
3.   CheckDigit := Number MOD 10;   {isolate and}
4.   Number := Number DIV 10;   {remove 4th digit}
5.   repeat until Number becomes 0:
5.1   RightDigit := Number MOD 10;   {select right digit}
5.2   Sum := Sum + RightDigit;
5.3   Number := Number DIV 10;   {remove right digit}
6.   determine and report on the validity of the number;
7.   stop.

Expanding this logic to cover many part numbers, we get the program shown in Fig. 6.1. Note that the original value of the number in the program must *not* be destroyed because it will be needed when the final result of the program is reported.

Successive Approximation

Especially in the world of science, we encounter equations or systems of equations of such complexity that we cannot write simple (closed form) general solutions. In these cases, we have to solve each particular instance of the equation separately.

```
PROGRAM CheckSum (input,output);

   { Checking the validity of 4-digit part numbers}

VAR
   PartNumber,
   Remainder,    {leftmost portion of PartNumber
                   after removing low-order digits}
   CheckDigit,   {rightmost digit of PartNumber}
   RightDigit,   {rightmost digit of Remainder}
   Sum:          {running total of RightDigit values}
         integer;

BEGIN {CheckSum}
   write ('Enter 4-digit part number,');
   write (' signal end-of-file when done');

   WHILE NOT eof DO
      BEGIN
         readln (PartNumber);
         {strip check digit from part number}
         CheckDigit := PartNumber MOD 10;
         Remainder := PartNumber DIV 10;

         {sum digits of Remainder}
         Sum := 0;
         REPEAT
            RightDigit := Remainder MOD 10;
            Sum := Sum + RightDigit;
            Remainder := Remainder DIV 10
         UNTIL Remainder = 0;

         IF (Sum MOD 10) = CheckDigit THEN
            writeln (PartNumber:5,' is valid')
         ELSE
            writeln (PartNumber:5,' is NOT valid');

      write ('Enter 4-digit part number,');
      write (' signal end-of-file when done')
   END {while}
END. {CheckSum}
```

■ Figure 6.1
Checking the validity of four-digit part numbers.

successive
approximation

A commonly used approach involves the process of **successive approximation.** First, we make an estimate of the solution, evaluate the equation(s) using the estimated solution, and determine the accuracy of the estimate. Depending on the outcome of the first estimate, we make a second and (we hope) more refined estimate. We repeat the process, producing a succession of estimates until we can make only negligible progress in refining the estimates. We then regard the final estimate as sufficiently close to the "true" solution that we can use it as the solution.

A large proportion of scientific computing is devoted to successive approximation of solutions to complicated (systems of) equations. Mathematicians have developed various approximation algorithms and conditions affecting the suitability and effectiveness of these algorithms on different kinds of equations. This area of study, known as numerical analysis, is of considerable interest to computer scientists but is beyond the scope of this book.

We can illustrate the basic idea with the problem of trying to guess a number between 1 and 99. Each time you guess, the person who offered the challenge will tell you whether your guess is lower or higher than the number that person has in mind. A good strategy is to guess a number near the middle of the range, say 50. If you are told that your guess is below the true value, use this new information to correct your guess upward to 75. After learning that this new guess is high, correct it downward to 62. Eventually you will reach the correct answer. By systematically guessing the *midpoint* of the interval where the answer is known to lie, you can tell when you are getting

binary search

close. This method is called the **binary search** because it subdivides the candidate interval in half with each estimate.

Now suppose that you are asked to discover the value of $\sqrt{2}$, which is an irrational number and therefore cannot be exactly represented. You could still make a guess and be told whether you were high or low. (Simply observe whether the square of your estimate is greater than or less than 2.) You can keep making successive refinements in your guess until you have guessed enough correct digits. You decide to stop guessing when successive estimates produce no more changes in these digits. This idea of zeroing in on a value by successive approximation is illustrated in Fig. 6.2.

Pascal already contains the function sqrt for computing square roots, but let's suppose that it does not exist and you have to develop a program to compute a square root by successive approximation. Although other and sometimes faster strategies exist, you decide to use the binary search method: At each step you choose the midpoint of the interval where the answer is known to lie.

Assuming that Number (whose square root you want to find) is nonnegative, its square root will lie in the interval bounded by 1 and Number. This is true for any nonnegative Number (even for numbers between 0 and 1). Your initial estimate would be the midpoint of the interval. Then at each step, depending on whether the square of this estimate is less than or greater than Number, your adjustment would be respectively added to or subtracted

■ Figure 6.2
The idea of
successive
approximation.

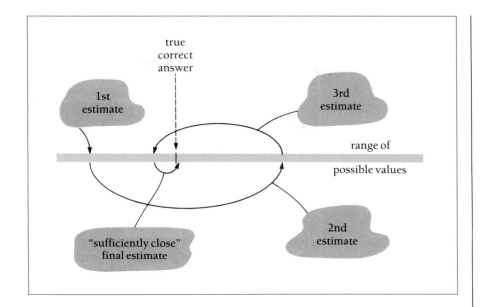

from this estimate to obtain the next estimate, the midpoint of the revised solution interval. This process is depicted in Fig. 6.3 for Number = 2.

Note that the adjustment made at each step is $\frac{1}{4}$ the size of the current interval or, equivalently, $\frac{1}{2}$ the size of the new interval. Thus the adjustment decreases by half at each step. Since this adjustment dictates the difference between any estimate and the next, you can test it directly when deciding whether to terminate the process. We can summarize this process with the following algorithm.

1. obtain the Number whose square root is desired;
2. the initial estimate is the midpoint between 1 and Number;
3. the first adjustment will be $\frac{1}{4}$ the length of the interval between 1 and Number;
4. while adjustment > threshhold value do:
4.1   if estimate * estimate > Number then reduce estimate by adjustment;
4.2   otherwise increase estimate by adjustment;
4.3   halve adjustment (in case more refined estimate is needed);
5. display most recent estimate (interpreted as the square root);
6. stop.

A function procedure to carry out the estimation (steps 2 through 4) is shown in Fig. 6.4. Note that when Number is less than 1, the initial estimate (step 2) is still calculated correctly. However, it is necessary to use care in step 3 to ensure that the length of the interval comes out nonnegative. If it does not, the first adjustment will be negative and the process will terminate immediately. We used the absolute value function abs to overcome this

■ Figure 6.3
Successive estimates
for square root of 2
(1.414 . . .).

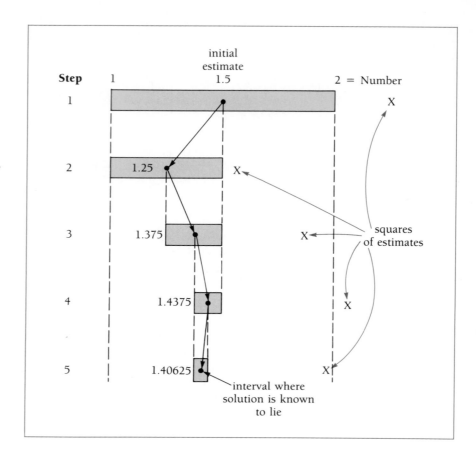

difficulty. Also, by continuing until the adjustment is less than 0.001, the function provides stability in the third decimal position, (that is, three digits of accuracy). A simple modification would permit the calling program to pass the Threshhold value as a parameter and so control function accuracy.

6.2 The Boolean Data Type

boolean data type

Much of the flow of control through programs is based on the truth or falsehood of conditions. Such boolean expressions are but one aspect of another data type in Pascal: the **boolean data type,** which encompasses the world of true/false values.

boolean constants

In fact, the boolean data type contains *only* the two values true and false. These **boolean constants** may seem like unusual values, but true and false are just as much boolean values as 6 is an integer value and 'M' is a character value.

```
FUNCTION SquareRoot (N: real): real;

    { Compute the square root of N
      to 3 decimal places }

  CONST Threshold = 0.001;

  VAR
     Estimate,      {successively refined estimates
                      of square root}
     Adjustment:  {amount by which successive
                      estimates differ}
            real;

  BEGIN {SquareRoot}
     Estimate := 0.5 * (N + 1);
     Adjustment := 0.25 * abs(N - 1);

     WHILE Adjustment >= Threshold DO
        BEGIN {refinement}
          IF sqr(Estimate) > N THEN {too high}
             Estimate := Estimate - Adjustment
          ELSE
             Estimate := Estimate + Adjustment;
          Adjustment := Adjustment / 2
        END; {refinement}

     SquareRoot := Estimate
  END; {SquareRoot}
```

■ Figure 6.4
Computing square roots by successive approximation.

boolean variables   As with other data types, we can declare **boolean variables** and assign
                           values to them, as in

```
VAR
  Done,                {define two boolean}
  IAmHome: boolean;    {variables}
BEGIN
  .

  .

  .

  IamHome := true;     {initialize}
  Done := IAmHome;     {copy value}
```

Boolean values may, of course, be generated by the relational operators and combined with the boolean operators. Their results can be stored in boolean variables; for example,

```
IAmHome := Hour < 9
```

Later the variable can be inspected to recover the value

```
IF IAmHome THEN . . .
```

Note that we do not need to ask whether IAmHome = true because the equality relationship is true or false, depending on whether the variable IAmHome is true or false.

odd function

Pascal also provides three boolean-valued functions. We have already discussed two of these, eof and eoln, which pertain to testing input. The third function, called **odd**, tests whether its integer operand is an odd or even number; its result is true or false, accordingly.

We can ask whether an integer X is odd by writing

```
IF odd(X) THEN . . .
```

Alternatively, we can ask whether X is even by writing

```
IF NOT odd(X) THEN {X is even}
```

The Use of Flags

When we use a WHILE or REPEAT statement to control a loop, the choice between continuing or terminating the loop depends on the value of some boolean expression. If there are several possible reasons for termination, this expression can become quite complex.

Consider the loop in Fig. 6.5, which represents the warranty period for a new car. The owner "drives" the car around the loop while (1) the car has not been in a serious accident; (2) the car has traveled less than MaxMiles; and (3) the car has yet to reach the age of MaxMonths. If any one of these conditions is violated, the warranty becomes void.

flag

Using flags to
terminate loops . . .

Figure 6.5 shows two equivalent ways of implementing this loop. In Fig. 6.5(a), we expressed all the reasons for termination in the loop condition. In Fig. 6.5(b), we reduced the loop condition to a simple boolean variable, called a **flag,** which may be set to false at various points within the loop, whenever a cause for termination is detected. When the flag is tested by the loop control statement, its value is the same as the full set of conditions in the companion structure. For example, if an accident occurs in the final month of coverage, there would be two reasons for termination. In Fig. 6.5(a) two components of the boolean expression would be false, whereas in Fig. 6.5(b) two assignments of false to the flag variable would result in a false value for the loop condition.

The trade-off between the two approaches is a simpler loop expression at the cost of some extra statements inside the loop to conditionally set the

```
VAR                                  VAR
  Accident: boolean;                   InWarranty: boolean;
  Mileage, Age: integer;               Mileage, Age: integer;
  .                                    .
  .                                    .
  .                                    .
Age := 0;                            Age := 0;
Mileage := 0;                        Mileage := 0;
Accident := false; {new}             InWarranty := true; {new}

WHILE NOT Accident                   WHILE Inwarranty DO
  AND (Mileage < MaxMiles)             BEGIN
  AND (Age < MaxMonths) DO
BEGIN                                     .
  .                                       .
  .               ┌─────────┐             .          ┌─────────┐
  .               │ {drive} │             .          │ {drive} │
  .               └─────────┘             .          └─────────┘
                                          .
  IF {serious accident} THEN           IF {serious accident} THEN
    Accident := true;                    InWarranty := false;
  update Mileage;                       update Mileage;
  Age := Age + 1                       IF Mileage >= MaxMiles THEN
END;                                     Inwarranty := false;
                                       Age := Age + 1;
                                       IF Age >= MaxMonths THEN
                                         InWarranty := false
                                     END;
```

(a) Full condition on loop.   **(b)** Use of flag for loop control.

■ Figure 6.5
Two ways of implementing a loop.

bypass parts of a loop . . .

flag to signal the end of the loop. The choice may ultimately depend on which you find easier to understand. Still, there is another reason why the choice of a flag might be preferred. It allows early (and easy) detection of a terminating condition in order to bypass later parts of the loop; this is the logical equivalent of immediate termination at the point where the condition occurs.

This situation is very common in practice. Whenever a special condition is recognized, continuation to the end of the loop (not to mention further iteration) is often useless—or even incorrect. One solution is to check that none of the previously tested special conditions has, in fact, occurred before performing each major step in the interior of the loop. It is usually easier to do this by using a flag (which indicates whether everything so far is normal), than by constructing compound conditions to capture all the possible abnormalities generated within the loop.

Figure 6.6 illustrates this general idea. If step 2 should discover a problem, it would make the flag false, causing step 3 to be bypassed. Similarly, a problem discovered in step 1 would cause both succeeding steps to be bypassed.

For a different application of flags, recall the problem of counting all nonblank characters in a sentence, but this time consider sentences that can end with either a period or a question mark. The program must therefore be on the lookout for either of two sentinel values. Let's also allow sentences containing quotation marks and therefore the possibility of imbedded periods and question marks as part of the quotations, as in

Her question, "Wherefore art thou?" was "rhetorical" at best.

and represent a binary state

The program must recognize that the question mark is within the quotation and is therefore not the sentence terminator. The period is the terminator

■ Figure 6.6
Discontinuing a loop as soon as a problem arises.

```
OK := true;
WHILE OK DO
    BEGIN { all 3 steps }
        .
        step 1
        .
        .
        IF problem1 THEN
            OK := false;

    IF OK THEN {safe to continue}
        BEGIN {step 2}
            .
            step 2
            .
            .
            IF problem2 THEN
                OK := false
        END; {step 2}

    IF OK THEN {safe to continue}
        BEGIN {step 3}
            .
            step 3
            .
            .
            IF problem3 THEN
                OK := false
        END {step 3}

    END; {while}
```

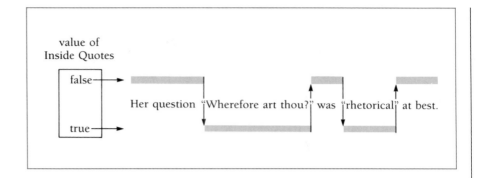

■ Figure 6.7
Alternate excursions
through quoted
material.

because it is *not* inside quotes. Assuming that the boolean variable InsideQuotes
has the value true whenever the program is scanning quoted material, the
loop to control counting and scanning can be governed by

```
WHILE ( (NextChar <> '.') AND (NextChar <> '?'))
       OR InsideQuotes DO
```

This causes scanning to continue inside quoted material regardless of the
value of NextChar. Only when InsideQuotes is false can the other conditions
make the whole expression false and stop the repetition.

For simplicity, we have excluded the possibility of another level of quoted
material within the quotations. Under this assumption every quotation mark
is matched by the one either preceding or following it. The first quotation
mark signals the beginning of quoted material and the second one the end.
With the third quotation mark, we enter the next stretch of quoted material,
to emerge only when the fourth one is encountered. In other words, we
alternately enter and leave quoted material with the occurrence of each
quotation mark. This is depicted in Fig. 6.7.

Reversing current value of flag

Again, if we represent the condition "inside quoted material" by the value
of the boolean variable InsideQuotes, every quotation mark *reverses* its value.
We accomplish this by the statement

```
IF NextChar = Quote THEN
   InsideQuotes := NOT InsideQuotes;
```

Note that the NOT operator inverts the previous value, and the assignment
makes this the new value.

The entire program is shown in Fig. 6.8 and starts with an initial value
of false for InsideQuotes. Note that we also allow sentences to wrap from one
line to the next by skipping over the end-of-line marker. It is also worth
noting that this program still cannot handle such features as numbers with
decimal points or ellipses (. . .).

```
PROGRAM FlagUse (input,output);

   {Counting the number of nonblank characters
    in a sentence which ends in "." or "?". These
    delimiters are allowed inside quoted material.}
CONST
   Blank = ' ';
   Quote = '"';

VAR
   InsideQuotes: boolean; {true scanning inside quotes}
   CharCount: integer; {of nonblank characters}
   NextChar: char; {current character in sentence}

BEGIN {FlagUse}
   InsideQuotes := false;
   CharCount := 0;
   writeln ('Enter any sentence ending in . or ?');
   read (NextChar);

   WHILE ((NextChar <> '.') AND (NextChar <> '?'))
            OR InsideQuotes DO
      BEGIN {scan}
         IF NextChar <> Blank THEN
            CharCount := CharCount + 1;
         IF NextChar = Quote THEN
            {start or end of quotation}
            InsideQuotes := NOT InsideQuotes;
         IF eoln THEN readln;
         read (NextChar)
      END; {scan}

   writeln ('Character count is:',CharCount:3)
END. {FlagUse}
```

■ Figure 6.8
Improved program to count nonblank characters.

Boolean-Valued Functions

A particularly useful application of the boolean data type is in the context of boolean-valued functions: those functions that return boolean results and can be used directly to control loops and make choices. To illustrate, consider again the new-car warranty loop. Figure 6.5(a) shows the criteria for continuing the loop fully specified inside the WHILE statement. We can relegate these detailed conditions to a function, so that the loop control expression can be comprehended more easily. The result is shown in Fig. 6.9, where the function Problem returns a boolean value, indicating whether any problem has arisen to invalidate the warranty. This makes the WHILE statement in the calling program so clear that it reads almost like English. Whenever a long or complicated boolean expression is required, we can often bury it in a boolean-valued function, so that its details will not clutter the higher level code.

```
FUNCTION Problem (Accident: boolean,
                  Mileage, Age: integer): boolean;

   {determine whether warranty should terminate;
    if so return true, indicating a problem}

   CONST
      MaxMiles = 10000;
      MaxMonths = 24;

   BEGIN {Problem}
      Problem := Accident OR (Mileage > MaxMiles)
                 OR (Age > MaxMonths)
   END; {Problem}

BEGIN {program}
   .
   .
   .
   Age := 0;
   Mileage := 0;
   Accident := false;
   .
   .
   .
   WHILE NOT Problem(Accident,Mileage,Age) DO
     BEGIN {another month of ownership}
       .
       . {drive}
       .
       IF {serious accident} THEN
          Accident := true;
       {update Mileage}
       Age := Age + 1
     END; {another month}
```

■ Figure 6.9
Testing conditions with a boolean-valued function.

6.3 Introducing the Ordinal Functions

Collating sequence

Recall that the collating sequence is the ordering of characters according to their internal encodings in the machine. Comparison of characters by relational operators in fact compares their relative positions in the collating sequence. Thus 'a' < 'b' is true because 'a' has an earlier encoding than 'b', and 'a' <> 'A' is true because two different characters cannot have the same encoding.

We mentioned in Chapter 3 that different machines may have different collating sequences and that only three assumptions can be made about them:

1. Numeric characters are in numeric order.
2. Lowercase alphabetic characters are in alphabetical order.
3. Uppercase alphabetic characters are in alphabetical order.

Relating a character to its ordinal position

What we *may not* assume, in general, is the relative ordering among these three sets of characters, the location of the punctuation and special characters in the ordering, and, most importantly, that the alphabetical characters are contiguous, that is, that they occupy adjacent positions in the ordering. Numeric characters, however, are in consecutive positions, so that '9' is located precisely 9 positions beyond '0'.

Pascal provides two functions for conversion between a character and its position in the collating sequence. They are

ord function

ord: Given a character as an argument, ord (⟨ThatChar⟩) indicates that character's integer position in the collating sequence.

chr function

chr: Given an integer argument within the range of the collating sequence, chr (⟨ThatNumber⟩) returns the corresponding character at that position.

Thus chr is the first character-valued function we have encountered. The ASCII character set is one of the most commonly used sets and is the one used on the VAX and IBM PC computers. In Fig. 6.10 we used a fragment of the ASCII code to show how ord and chr link the characters and their positions in the collating sequence. The two functions perform exactly opposite operations; what one does the other undoes. Such functions are called

inverses

inverses.

Special characters

One use of chr is to designate characters that are otherwise unrepresentable. For example, sending a special "invisible" character BEL to a terminal will, in many cases, cause the terminal to beep or ring. This character cannot be typed at a keyboard or included as a character constant in a program. However, it is at position 7 in the ASCII character set, so it can be represented as chr(7). If chr(7) is written to a terminal from an ASCII machine, the terminal may beep. Many other similar special characters are used in communications and for controlling external devices such as terminals.

Numeric character to integer conversion

An interesting use for the ord function is to convert numeric *characters* to actual *integers*. Assume that Digit is a single numeric character ('0' <=

■ Figure 6.10
Numeric characters
in the ASCII collating
sequence.

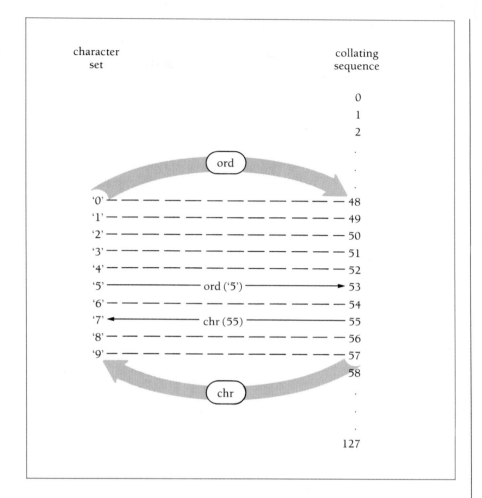

Digit $<=$ '9'). Of course, ord (Digit) is some integer, but *not* the numeric equivalent of Digit. However, since the numeric characters are in consecutive positions of the collating sequence, the difference between ord(Digit) and ord('0') indicates how far Digit is from '0' (that is, the numeric value of Digit). For example, on an ASCII machine, ord('4') − ord('0') = 52 − 48 = 4. Incidentally, ord stands for *ordinal number,* which is just a technical term for position within a sequence.

This provides a whole new approach to the problem of reading and verifying a four-digit part number using a check sum (Section 6.1). Instead of reading the entire number as one integer and breaking its digits apart by algebraic manipulation, we can now think of the number as a sequence of four numeric characters. Each character can be read individually and converted into its equivalent numeric digit. This conversion to integers is necessary to compute the check sum and complete the verification.

**Uppercase versus
lowercase letters**

You can often use either uppercase or lowercase letters when typing commands to the system or submitting a program to the compiler. However, a program does distinguish between uppercase and lowercase letters in its own input. And so it should, since 'a' <> 'A' is always true. If the program is supposed to respond in a special way to 'a', it will not respond in the same way to 'A', unless you have allowed for either character in some way, such as:

IF (NextLetter = 'a') OR (NextLetter = 'A') THEN . . .

If you want your program to accept all uppercase and lowercase letters as equivalent, without distinction, you can convert every uppercase letter to its lowercase counterpart immediately after input. Then all input will appear as lowercase to the rest of your program, regardless of its actual origin.

**Uppercase and
lowercase conversion**

To demonstrate this, we represent the distance through the collating sequence between *any* uppercase alphabetic character (say, Letter) and the letter 'A' by the expression:

```
ord(Letter) - ord ('A')
```

The corresponding lowercase letter will appear at the same relative distance through the collating sequence from the letter 'a'. Thus the actual position of the desired lowercase letter is

```
ord('a') + ord(Letter) - ord('A')
```

and the lowercase letter itself is obtained using the chr function:

```
chr( ord(Letter) + ord('a') - ord('A') )
```

**Machine-dependent
coding**

The ASCII character set (Appendix C) has the convenient property that all uppercase letters span consecutive positions in the collating sequence. The lowercase letters also have consecutive positions but in a higher range of the sequence. The *consecutive position* property of the uppercase letters in the ASCII code also enables us to discover whether Letter actually does contain an uppercase letter by a simple range test:

IF (Letter >= 'A') AND (Letter <= 'Z') THEN {uppercase}

Unfortunately, another major encoding scheme (EBCDIC) used on most IBM equipment (the IBM PC uses ASCII) does not have the uppercase and lowercase letters in consecutive positions. Fortunately, even though gaps exist in the two character sequences, the matching uppercase and lowercase letters are all separated by the same interval, so that the conversion formula still applies. There are even character sets (such as the 64-character CDC) in which no lowercase letters are available, and there is no conversion problem.

**Traversing a
collating sequence**

Two other functions may be used to traverse the character set according to the collating sequence, although the functions make no explicit reference to it. When given a character as an argument, either function returns the *next character* in the sequence. The two functions correspond to the two directions of travel; that is,

succ function
succ returns the successor, that is, the immediately following character; and

pred function
pred returns the predecessor, that is, the immediately preceding character.

Thus succ('b') yields 'c', and pred('b') yields 'a'.

    If you wanted to list the uppercase alphabet backwards, the following code fragment would work (at least in ASCII).

```
This Char := 'Z';
REPEAT
  writeln (ThisChar);
  ThisChar := pred(ThisChar)
UNTIL ThisChar < 'A';
```

The first character, chr(0), has no predecessor, and the last has no successor. Attempting to find a nonexistent predecessor or successor will result in an error.

6.4   Ordinal Data and Type Definition

ordinal data types

The integer, character, and boolean data types all belong to a class known as the **ordinal data types** (sometimes called scalar data types). An ordinal data type has constituent values that can be counted and ordered in some way or, in a word, enumerated.

    As you know, there are only two boolean values: false and true, in that order. Most machines have just over 100 characters, all of which are ordered according to the collating sequence. Although numerous integers exist, they are quite distinct, and consecutive members in their ordering are easily recognizable as such. For any integer (say, 6), you can identify its predecessor (5) and successor (7) without hesitation.

Reals are not ordinal

    Real numbers do not share this property. Although the real numbers are ordered, it is impossible to identify the next largest real number after 6.143 or to say how many real numbers lie between 8.3 and 9.162. The reals are not discrete and, hence, do not constitute an ordinal type.

The Ordinal Functions Revisited

Ord, pred, and succ apply to any ordinal type

The three functions ord, pred, and succ, which were introduced in the context of characters, actually apply within any ordinal type. If Instance represents some variable or constant of a scalar type, then ord(Instance) returns the position of the instance within the ordering pertaining to that type. In any computer using ASCII code, ord('a') has value 97 because 'a' lies at position 97 of the ASCII collating sequence. The value of ord(false) is 0 because false is the first (of two) boolean values, and the sequence numbering always begins with 0. The value of ord(true) is 1.

The integers are given slightly special treatment. Since integers in theory (though not on a computer) extend indefinitely in both the positive and negative directions from 0, the value of ord(AnyInteger) is simply the value of that integer. Hence ord(-7) $=$ -7.

In other words, the ord function provides a mapping from any base ordinal type to the integers. If X and Y are consecutive members of the same ordinal type, with X $<$ Y, then ord(X) $+$ 1 $=$ ord(Y); that is, consecutive members of an ordinal type map to consecutive integers.

The other two functions, pred and succ, move directly from one member of any ordinal data type to its immediate predecessor or its immediate successor in the ordering. Both return a member of the same data type as their argument. If the argument to pred is at the beginning of the ordering and has no predecessor, the value of pred is undefined. Likewise, the final, largest member of the ordering should not be given as an argument to succ. The programmer is responsible for avoiding these situations.

Subrange

Programs often deal with ordinal types for which the range of legitimate values for that application is supposed to be restricted. For example, if your program deals with people's ages, you can use integers to represent these ages. However, a legitimate age would never be negative and would rarely exceed 100. Therefore you could safely assert that any valid age should lie between 0 and 120, inclusive.

Restricting the range of values

Simply knowing that ages should lie within these limits does not prevent an integer variable intended to depict an age from actually taking on some unreasonable value during execution of your program. For example, a computational error could result in -60 being assigned, or a typing mistake at the terminal could cause 500 to be read. Such erroneous values might then be used to generate erroneous results.

However, if you know the range in which acceptable values should lie, Pascal provides a simple mechanism to guarantee that only values within that range will ever be stored in selected variables. Instead of declaring a variable (say, Age) as integer, you define it as a **subrange** of the integers—in this case a variable with values that must lie between 0 and 120, inclusive. The following definition accomplishes this.

subrange

VAR Age: 0 . . 120;

base type

The lower and upper limits of the allowable range of values are separated by two periods. Since the lower and upper limit values are both integers, Age is therefore a subrange of the integers; the integers are said to be the **base type** (or parent type) for this subrange. Any attempt to give Age a value that is not an integer or that is some integer less than 0 or greater than 120 causes an error either at compile time or during execution, depending on when the attempt can be detected.

We can also use most other ordinal types as the basis for subranges. For example, to restrict the character values that can be stored in variables LowerCase and Numeric to what their names imply, we declare

```
VAR
   LowerCase: 'a'..'z';    {at least this}
                           {works in ASCII code}
   Numeric: '0'..'9';
```

Subrange mechanism

Thus the subrange mechanism can automatically restrict the values of a variable to some set of consecutive, ordered values chosen from any one ordinal data type. *Note that it is not possible to define a subrange of the reals because they are not ordinal.*

Advantages . . .

The subrange mechanism has two great advantages. First, it helps a reader to understand the program by explicitly showing the values considered legitimate for many of the variables. In addition, it enforces these limitations so that infractions can be detected before invalid values could otherwise corrupt the results.

and disadvantages

On the other hand, there is a possible disadvantage to using a subrange variable in certain situations. If you are not sure of all the legitimate values for a variable, the subrange could exclude some unanticipated but truly legitimate value.

More serious is the problem of reading an invalid value from an input device—particularly from a keyboard, where one slip of the finger can generate an out-of-range value and prematurely terminate an otherwise correct program. Although this is a risk with the basic data types, it is a greater risk with subrange types. Whether we should allow erroneous input to summarily terminate a program or allow it to be read, checked, and then rejected by an algorithm is arguable. The latter alternative allows a second input attempt by the user in the hope of letting the program continue but at the cost of more complexity. The best approach to dealing with bad input data will depend on the application.

Subranges are new types

When we define a subrange, we are actually defining a new data type. This immediately suggests that a barrier exists between a new subrange type and other data types. In one sense this is true. We can no more give a variable that is a subrange of the integers a real or character value than we can to an ordinary integer variable.

On the other hand, a subrange type is derived from—and has its possible values completely contained within—one of the basic types. To the extent that the subrange and its base type overlap, assignment of values is permitted from a variable of one type to a variable of the other type. For example, if Parent and Child are defined as

```
VAR
   Parent: integer;
   Child: 10..20;
```

the assignment `Parent := Child` is always allowed, since the value in Child is guaranteed to be an integer. However, the validity of `Child := Parent` depends on the current value of Parent. If Parent contains an integer in the range allowed by Child, the assignment will work; otherwise, a run-time error will occur. This is another instance of assignment compatibility between objects of technically different types. (See Section 2.3.)

Incidentally, if X is a value from any subrange of an ordinal type, the value of ord(X) is the position of X in the base type, not necessarily its position within the subrange. Similarly, pred and succ refer to the base type rather than the subrange.

Use of Ordinals with the FOR Statement

FOR progresses through any ordinal type

We have seen the FOR statement cycle through consecutive integers (either forward or backwards). In fact the FOR statement is capable of moving through consecutive members of *any* ordinal data type. Each repetition of a FOR loop actually uses the successor (or predecessor) of the previous loop index value. With an integer index, this is equivalent to incrementing (or decrementing), but it explains why the index value could only be adjusted by 1 for each iteration.

To see how the FOR statement is used with another ordinal type, let's consider two fragments of code, each of which generates the entire lowercase alphabet (in ASCII).

```
ThisChar := 'a';
WHILE ThisChar <= 'z' DO
  BEGIN
    writeln (ThisChar);
    ThisChar := succ(ThisChar)
  END;


FOR ThisChar := 'a' TO 'z' DO
  writeln (ThisChar);
```

Similarly, the following code fragments each generate the uppercase alphabet backwards.

```
Letter := 'Z';
WHILE Letter >= 'A' DO
  BEGIN
    writeln (Letter);
    Letter := pred(Letter)
  END;


FOR Letter := 'Z' DOWNTO 'A' DO
  writeln (Letter);
```

```
{ NEVER TRY THIS }                    {correct version}
VAR Partial: 10..20;                  VAR Partial: 10..20;
      .                                     .
      .                                     .
      .                                     .
Partial := 10;                        FOR Partial := 10 TO 20 DO
WHILE Partial <= 20 DO                    BEGIN
    BEGIN                                     .
        .                                     .
        .                                 END;
        Partial := Partial + 1
    END;
```

(a) Invalid use.   **(b)** Correct use.

■ Figure 6.11
Invalid and valid use of subrange variable in a loop.

You should use the FOR statement to control loops whenever the control variable must take on consecutive values within an ordinal data type or subrange. The reason is that the WHILE or REPEAT statements usually require the control variable to take on a value beyond the final limit in order to recognize the termination condition. However, the FOR statement traverses the sequence of values only between (and including) the indicated limits because these limits may have no successor or predecessor. This explains why the value of the FOR control variable is undefined upon exiting from the loop.

The use of FOR is especially important with a subrange, since the loop control variable may be incapable of holding a value beyond the limiting value of the loop, even if a successor (or predecessor) exists within the base type. Figure 6.11 illustrates the right and wrong approaches. The error in Fig. 6.11(a) occurs when the final assignment statement attempts to increment the value of Partial from 20 to 21, in violation of its subrange type.

The TYPE Definition Part

TYPE definition part
type identifier

As we will show later, Pascal has several mechanisms besides subrange for creating new data types. Rather than specifying the details of new data types inside the variable declaration part, you may first define the new type itself in a separate **TYPE definition part** of the program. This entails defining your own **type identifier,** which you may use like any other type identifier when declaring the particular variables of that type.

For example, each of the following forms of code declares two variables, This and That, as integers in the range 13 to 19, inclusive.

```
                              TYPE
                                Teens = 13..19;
        VAR                   VAR
          This,                 This,
          That: 13..19;         That: Teens;
```

Note the explicit definition and naming of a new data type, Teens, in the second case. This occurs in the type definition part, which must precede the variable declaration part and follow the constant definitions, if any. Here, Teens identifies a type; it is definitely not a variable. It defines a prototype rather than an actual memory location. However, after you have defined it, you can use it exactly like the basic types (such as integer or char) to prescribe the type for specific variables in the variable declaration part.

6.5 A Glimpse of Sets

It is often necessary in a program to ask whether an unknown item is one of several particular values. This sort of test can lead to a very long and awkward boolean expression. For example, to ask whether the character variable NewChar contains a vowel, we might write

```
IF (NewChar = 'a') OR (NewChar = 'e') OR
   (NewChar = 'i')
   OR (NewChar = 'o') OR (NewChar = 'u') THEN
   {vowel} . . .
```

and this covers only lowercase vowels.

IN operator

These tests are so common that Pascal provides a special boolean-valued **IN operator** to ask such questions. We can also write the test for a vowel as

IF NewChar IN ['a', 'e', 'i', 'o', 'u'] THEN {vowel} . . .

The object denoted by square brackets, namely,

['a', 'e', 'i', 'o', 'u']

set constant

is called a SET. A set is a collection of objects of identical ordinal type. Here, the objects happen to be characters, and the collection consists of the lowercase vowels. Since the five characters comprising this set have been explicitly displayed, this is an example of a **set constant.** The square brackets group the values into a single set.

The IN operator is binary. Its left operand denotes a single object of some type (here char), and its right operand denotes a set of objects of that type.

The value of IN is true if the object on its left occurs anywhere in the set; the value is false if the object is not a member of the set. For example,

'e' IN ['a','e','i','o','u']

is true, whereas

7 IN [2,4,6,8,10]

is false, since 7 is not one of the integers shown as members of the set. When used in more complex boolean expressions, IN has the same low precedence as the relational operators.

In Chapter 9 we will work with set variables having members that may vary dynamically and with set operators for manipulating and combining sets. For now, however, set constants are sufficient for our purposes.

There is nothing special about the order in which set members are written; IN tests only *whether* an item belongs to a set, not *where* it appears within the set. The set ['e','u','o','a','i'] specifies the same collection of lowercase vowels as the earlier example.

Subrange notation in sets

If the members of a set happen to be consecutive items of a subrange, we can also specify them by using subrange notation. The set ['3','4','5','6'] is identical to the set ['3' . . '6'], as are [10,11,12,13,14,15,16] and [10 . . 16]. The following two range tests are equivalent.

```
IF (TestChar >= 'A') AND (TestChar <= 'Z') THEN
 . . .

IF TestChar IN ['A'..'Z'] THEN . . .
```

A set can contain several subranges, provided they all come from the same base data type. We can write the set of uppercase and lowercase alphabetic characters—at least in ASCII representation, where they are consecutive—as ['A' . . 'Z','a' . . 'z']. We can write the set of positive two-digit integers beginning with a 2, 5, or 8 as [20 . . 29,50 . . 59,80 . . 89]; this set has thirty members.

Since the gaps in the EBCDIC alphabet occur between the letters I and J and between R and S, on an EBCDIC machine we could ask whether TestChar is uppercase alphabetic as follows:

IF TestChar IN ['A'..'I','J'..'R','S'..'Z'] THEN...

Using sets to guard CASE

The IN operator is commonly used to guard a CASE construct. Before trying to execute a CASE statement you should always make sure that the case index contains one of the values in the case constant list; otherwise an error will occur. The use of SET notation is desirable when the values in the case constant list are widely separated, as in the calculator example in Chapter 5. In that problem, the only valid commands processed by the CASE statement were (+), (−), and (q). We used an IF statement to guard CASE in the code in Fig. 5.10. Rewriting the pertinent parts of the code using SET notation yields

```
IF Command IN ['+','-','q'] THEN
  CASE Command OF
    '+': Accumulator := Accumulator + Operand;
    '-': Accumulator := Accumulator - Operand;
    'q': {no specific action}
  END {case}
ELSE
  writeln ('invalid command')
```

To ask whether the character variable symbol is something other than a lowercase alphabetic, we might write

```
IF NOT (Symbol IN ['a'..'z'] ) THEN
{NOT lowercase}
```

At first glance, NOT used in conjunction with IN often appears stilted. In English we tend to form the complement of a phrase such as "if Kevin is in the house" as "if Kevin is not in the house." However, in Pascal the complement reads more like "if it is not the case that Kevin is in the house."

6.6 User-Defined (Enumerated) Types

Along with the basic predefined types (integer, boolean, char, and real), you may create additional, personalized data types. From time to time it is necessary for a program to represent things like the days of the week or the kinds of transactions being processed. In many programming languages you would be forced to invent a coding scheme using characters or integers to represent such objects. In Pascal, however, you can define a new data type, such as Days to represent directly the days of the week:

```
TYPE Days = (Sun,Mon,Tue,Wed,Thu,Fri,Sat);
```

This statement establishes a new *ordinal* data type having the values shown between the parentheses. These values must be unique, so that they cannot be mistaken for members of any other data type. For example you *cannot* define a data type having any integers or character strings among its values.

Although these values may appear to be character strings (most written symbols look like character strings), they are totally different. Just as the character string 'false' is different from the boolean value false, and the string '24' is different from the integer 24, so the values Sun, Mon, and Tue are not the same as the strings 'Sun', 'Mon', and 'Tue'. Values like Sun and Mon are merely encodings for the separate days of the week; Sun is a single, simple object, whereas 'Sun' is a composite of three separate characters. The single quote marks make all the difference. In other words, you cannot intermix or overlap in any way the data types in Pascal, including the new ones you define.

Variables and assignment

As with other data types, you can declare variables for the types you define and can assign values to these variables. For example, the statement

```
VAR Today, Tomorrow: Days;
```

would generate two variables, each capable of holding one and only one of the seven possible values from the type Days. The statements

```
Today := Wed;
Tomorrow := succ(Today);
```

place the value Wed in one of the variables and its successor Thu in the other (Tomorrow). Again, note the absence of apostrophes, since no character strings or char data are involved.

Use with ordinal functions . . . and FOR

The order in which the values of a user-defined type are specified is crucial; it determines their ordinal numbers. (Recall that, in general, ordinal numbering begins at 0.) The functions pred, succ, and ord may be applied to user-defined types, just as they may be applied to any other ordinal type. Thus pred(Wed) = Tue, succ(Wed) = Thu, and ord(Wed) = 3. In particular, variables of user-defined types can be used as control variables in FOR statements. Thus the following code will display the integers 0 through 6.

```
FOR Today := Sun TO Sat DO
  writeln (ord(Today));
```

When two values from the same type are compared, the outcome is determined by their ordinal numbering. Because of the way we defined Days, the following expressions are all true.

Mon < Thu
Thu <= Fri
Fri > Thu

We can also define subranges:

```
TYPE
  Days = (Sun,Mon,Tue,Wed,Thu,Fri,Sat);
  MidWeek = Tue..Thu;
  GoodTV = Thu..Sat;
```

and sets:

```
IF Today IN [Sun,Tue..Thur,Sat] THEN . . .
```

Note that we had to define the type Days before attempting the definition of MidWeek and GoodTV. Without this prior definition of Days, the subranges for the latter two types would have no reference point, that is, no parent type.

Use with CASE

When used to select the alternative in a CASE statement, user-defined types can greatly improve the clarity of the code. For example, consider the following fragment, assuming that Today has been assigned some value of type Days.

```
{Daily schedule}
CASE Today OF
  Sun: Rest;
  Mon,
  Tue,
  Wed,
  Thu,
  Fri: ToteThatBarge;
  Sat: HaveSomeFun
END; {case}
```

Restriction on use   User-defined types have equal status with the predefined types, except that *in standard Pascal (hence in most versions) it is not possible to read or write a value from a user-defined type.* This restriction tends to confine their use to identifying internal states or special conditions arising during execution. However, in this role they can appreciably improve the clarity and readability of a program. When their values *must* be made visible to the user, you could use a CASE statement with the user-defined type as a case selector to select a corresponding character string.

State Variables

When a loop is controlled by a single condition, the cause of termination is obvious. However, if any of several conditions can cause the repetition to end, some indication of the cause may be required for later use. Although boolean flags can be set when various conditions are detected inside the loop, these simple flags cannot distinguish which condition is forcing termination.

state variable   A common technique is to use a **state variable,** which is an extension of the flag. Instead of a two-valued flag indicating merely whether to stop or not, a state variable may contain several different values. One of these is its *normal* value, which indicates that no special conditions have arisen. All of its other possible values signify particular termination conditions. When a reason for termination is discovered inside a loop, the encoding for that reason is stored in the state variable at that point. This new value may or may not cause later sections of the loop to be bypassed, but it will cause eventual termination and allow some corresponding action to be taken after the loop has finished. A user-defined type is often used for these state variables.

We can extend the warranty example in Section 6.2 (Fig. 6.5) by using a state variable instead of a flag. Its values reflect the three reasons for ending the warranty plus another value to depict the normal warranty period, that is,

    TYPE WarrantyType = (UnderWarranty, TooFar, TooOld, Damaged);
    VAR Status: WarrantyType;

We could rewrite the warranty loop as shown in Fig. 6.12. Note how well the state variable serves as the case index after leaving the loop. By that time it must contain one of the case constants as its value (certainly not the normal value of UnderWarranty).

One of the great causes for error in many systems is erroneous input data. We often want to check to make sure that input values lie within their allowed ranges. Many applications require such **consistency checking.** If the application or the accuracy is sufficiently important, then *all* input data may be subject to a variety of stringent tests before they are allowed to enter the system and affect any other values or results.

consistency checking

Let's consider the problem of adding numbers from an input file into a total. For our problem, we can imagine that the input values represent either positive or negative changes in the flow of fuel into a large industrial furnace over a certain period of time. All changes must be gradual; that is, they must fall within a narrow range near zero. Also, the total flow cannot fall below zero and must remain below the capacity of the furnace. It is possible for a reasonably small negative change to drive a previously low flow below zero, which is unacceptable.

For these reasons we have to check the resulting flow amount as well as the amounts of change. We will keep reading values and incorporating them

■ Figure 6.12
Use of state variable
to terminate loop and
record reason.

```
Status := UnderWarranty; {new car}
WHILE Status = UnderWarranty DO
   BEGIN
      .
      . {drive}
      .
      IF {serious accident} THEN
         Status := Damaged;
      update Mileage;
      IF Mileage >= MaxMiles THEN
         Status := TooFar;
      Age := Age + 1;
      IF Age >= MaxMonths THEN
         Status := TooOld
   END;

CASE Status OF
   Damaged:  _____
   TooFar:   _____
   TooOld:   _____
   END; {case}
```

```
    TYPE Reason = (Normal, EndOfData, DataValue, FlowValue);

VAR
    Status: Reason;
    Flow, Change: real;

          .
          .
          .
BEGIN {fragment to add Change values to Flow}
      .
      .
      .
    Flow := 0;
    Status := Normal;

    WHILE Status = Normal DO
        BEGIN
            IF NOT eof THEN
                readln (Change)
            ELSE
                Status := EndOfData;

            IF Status = Normal THEN
                IF (Change > MaxValue)
                    OR (Change < MinValue) THEN
                        Status := DataValue;

            IF Status = Normal THEN
                IF (Change+Flow > MaxFlow)
                    OR (Change+Flow < MinFlow) THEN
                        Status := FlowValue
                ELSE {everything OK}
                    Flow := Flow + Change

        END; {while loop}

    CASE Status OF
            EndOfData: writeln ('Normal end of data');
            DataValue: writeln ('Change:',Change,
                                 ' outside allowed range');
            FlowValue: writeln ('Change:',Change,
                                 ' will put flow out of range')
    END; {case}
```

■ Figure 6.13
User-defined type to convey reason for termination.

into a net flow until

1. the numbers are deliberately stopped (end-of-file) *or*
2. an input value is outside its allowed range *or*
3. the total falls outside its allowed range.

When one of these events occurs, we will display a message about what happened and then stop. Our general algorithm is

1.   initialize variables;
2.   while no problems encountered do:
2.1   if data remain then
2.1.1   read next value;
2.2   if new value within allowed range
             and new value will not put total outside range then
2.2.1   add new value to total;
3.   print termination message;
4.   stop.

Most of the resulting program is shown in Fig. 6.13. Note how any of the three conditions for termination causes later sections of the loop to be bypassed. The loop of Fig. 6.13 fits the pattern of Fig. 6.6.

6.7 Making Programs Easier to Understand and Modify: Part 3

In Section 6.1, we presented a program that checks the validity of a four-digit part number (Fig. 6.1). The problem is simple and well-defined, thus allowing us to predict reasonable ranges for every variable in the program. The program can be made much more precise by taking advantage of the subrange facility, as shown in Fig. 6.14 on p. 268. Except for their variable declaration parts, the programs in Figs. 6.14 and 6.1 are identical.

Use of Subrange

Documentation and error control

This use of subrange has two advantages. First, it adds a new facet to the documentation. The variable declaration part clearly shows the permissible values as well as the ultimate use of each variable. Second, if the program contains an error or receives erroneous input data, it will tend to terminate much sooner than it would without the use of subranges. In most cases the termination will occur immediately after the error, making the cause of the problem easier to locate and preventing corruption of other data by the erroneous input value.

   If anything other than a four-digit integer is supplied, PartNumber will not accept it. Even if PartNumber were not a subrange type and could contain,

```
PROGRAM CheckSum (input,output);

   { Checking the validity of 4-digit part numbers}

VAR
   PartNumber: 1000..9999;
   Remainder: 0..999;    {leftmost portion of PartNumber
                              after removing low-order digits}
   CheckDigit,           {rightmost digit of PartNumber}
   RightDigit: 0..9;     {rightmost digit of Remainder}
   Sum: 0..27;           {total of RightDigit values}

BEGIN {CheckSum}
   write ('Enter 4-digit part number,');
   write (' signal end-of-file when done');

   WHILE NOT eof DO
      BEGIN
         readln (PartNumber);

         {strip check digit from part number}
         CheckDigit := PartNumber MOD 10;
         Remainder := PartNumber DIV 10;

         {sum digits of Remainder}
         Sum := 0;
         REPEAT
            RightDigit := Remainder MOD 10;
            Sum := Sum + RightDigit;
            Remainder := Remainder DIV 10
         UNTIL Remainder = 0;

         IF (Sum MOD 10) = CheckDigit THEN
            writeln (PartNumber:5,' is valid')
         ELSE
            writeln (PartNumber:5,' is NOT valid');

         write ('Enter 4-digit part number,');
         write (' signal end-of-file when done')
      END {while}
END. {CheckSum}
```

■ Figure 6.14
Another version of Fig. 6.1.

say, a five-digit integer, the Remainder of such invalid input would exceed the permissable range for Remainder. If the user had inadvertently typed 98007 instead of 9807, the error would be caught on the first attempt to store 9800 in Remainder. Such an error might otherwise escape diagnosis, while continuing to cause mysterious results.

Subrange as input variable . . .   As we pointed out previously, the use of subranges can be carried too far in the case of input variables. It might be better to let PartNumber be a general integer variable and test its value each time using an IF statement. Then if an out-of-range value is entered, the user could be notified and given another chance, without the program terminating prematurely.

In other situations though, you should use subranges whenever you know the feasible values for a variable, for both better documentation and better protection. Subrange can also be a useful tool for debugging during program testing.

and as loop control variable   We want to emphasize again the special problem concerning the use of subrange variables in indexing roles. Such a variable must be allowed enough scope to span its full indexing range if it is to be used in WHILE or REPEAT constructs. This usually means allowing it either to start off one unit below its first legitimate value or to finish one unit beyond. Recall that loop indices (other than those used with FOR) usually must exceed some limit to stop the loop. A range defined too narrowly could prevent this.

Promoting Program Portability

program portability   An important goal in the computing industry is **program portability.** Portability refers to the ability (or desire) to run the same program on different machines. When an organization upgrades its system, adds new machines, or replaces old ones, ideally its existing programs should run in the new environment without alteration and produce the same results as before.

Portability problems   Unfortunately, many programs are not portable. They contain features supported by only one particular compiler, operating system, or machine. Code peculiar to the old system may have to be rewritten and retested, involving considerable cost and delay. Even then, the behavior of the revised program on the new machine may not exactly duplicate that of the older version.

Some of these conversion problems may be unavoidable because of different machine architectures. Nevertheless, these problems can and should be minimized by good programming practice right from the start.

Avoid nonstandard Pascal features   One approach is to avoid the use of any nonstandard Pascal features, even if some shortcuts are allowed by your compiler or operating system. A prime example is the exponentiation operator $**$, provided by some but not all Pascal implementations. Instead of using A $**$ N to denote the Nth power of A, we can always use exp (N $*$ ln(A)). It may not be as clear, but it always works if A $>$ 0.

Use standard
identifier names

Another area of possible abuse is the choice of identifier names. Even if your compiler allows some extra symbols in an identifier, stay with alphabetic and numeric characters and be aware that different systems impose various limits on identifier length.

Anticipate problems
with precision . . .

Different machines may allow different numbers of digits to be stored in a variable. This means that on different machines maxint may have different values and that real numbers may contain different numbers of significant digits, which is referred to as the *level of precision*. Whenever your program must make tests near the limits of magnitude or precision, you should use symbolic constants in preference to explicit ones that pertain to particular machines. For example, always use maxint instead of 2147483647 or 32767, because maxint is defined in every version of Pascal but does not have the same explicit value on every machine.

Similarly, if testing whether two real numbers differ by less than 0.000000001, you should define a symbolic constant (say, Threshhold) having this value. On other machines it may be desirable to raise or lower this threshold, which is much easier to do if it is clearly defined in just one place (the CONST section) at the beginning of the program.

and character
encoding

Finally, you should be aware of the possibility of different collating sequences and even different character sets in different machines. Since you may have to modify some character-handling code for other machines, make your definitions clear and your code as straightforward as possible to facilitate any necessary changes.

Confine nonportable
features to
subprogram(s)

When machine-dependent code *must* be used, you should confine it to one (or a few) subprograms. This allows the main program to be transported without alteration and requires only the subprogram(s) to be recoded. For example, the test of whether a character is an uppercase alphabetic differs slightly between machines with ASCII and EBCDIC character encoding. The following two functions carry out the details of this test, one for each possible encoding. The version actually employed depends on the type of machine being used. The functions have the same identifiers and parameters, so that their calls are indistinguishable. This allows the calling program to remain unchanged, regardless of which version of the function is used.

```
FUNCTION UpperCase (Letter:char):boolean;
  {ASCII version of upper case test}
  BEGIN
    UpperCase := (Letter >= 'A') AND
                 (Letter <= 'Z')
  END;

FUNCTION UpperCase (Letter:char):boolean;
  {EBCDIC version of upper case test}
  BEGIN
    UpperCase := Letter IN ['A'..'I','J'..'R',
                            'S'..'Z']
  END;
```

A typical call might look like

```
IF UpperCase(Letter) THEN . . .
```

Thus portability requirements provide another strong argument for modular coding and full documentation.

6.8 Making Programs Work Correctly

As you know, π is an irrational number; this means that it cannot be represented *exactly,* regardless of the number of digits used to specify it. Its value to 10 decimal places is 3.1415926536. Although this is not the true value of π, this number is so close to π that it can be safely used in most applications as though it were the true value. In fact, many applications can make do with a much less precise estimate for π, such as 3.1416 or even 3.14.

Problems with numeric precision
    By using less precise approximations, we introduce more chance for error in the results. After all, the quality of a calculation's outcome depends on the quality of its starting values; if these values are inaccurate, the result of their use will likely be inaccurate. On the other hand, by using fewer digits we reduce the effort required to make the calculations.

The point is that we often do use approximations to actual values, involving fewer digits than the true values would require. We make such approximations in representing distances, lengths, metric conversion factors, populations, altitudes, and a variety of other quantities. Having chosen an approximate value, we then carry on computing as though the data were accurate, and we accept the results as being close enough to be useful. This is not necessarily wrong; after all, we have to be practical.

Computers, too, can store only a certain number of digits in each numeric variable. This number is a physical feature of the particular machine, and it places a limit on the precision with which numeric quantities can be stored and manipulated.

precision
    The capacity of the memory locations restricts the size of the largest integer in a machine to the value maxint. It restricts even further the **precision** of real numbers, that is, the number of meaningful digits a real number can contain. It is not necessary for you to know the technical details, but it is important for you to understand that these limitations exist. Otherwise, your expectations of a computer may be unrealistic, and the results of numeric computations may provide a few surprises.

For example, on a VAX machine, the value of maxint is 2147483647. Yet, two real numbers with even fewer significant digits may not be distinguishable by the machine. For instance the boolean expression

2147483600.00 = 2147483700.0

has the value true in VAX-11 Pascal. Both numbers contain more digits than the machine can store in real number form, and both are approximated by the same number internally.

Continuing with VAX-11 Pascal, the expression

$$2147483600.0 \; = \; 2147483647$$

is also true. When an integer is converted to a real representation before comparison to the real constant, some of its digits may be lost. Here again, the same real number is used to approximate both values.

These anomalies result from trying to use more digits than the computer can represent. Similar phenomena may arise from using irrational numbers that are inherently impossible to represent exactly. To further complicate matters, an innocent-looking decimal number, such as 1.2, turns out to be nonterminating in the binary number system, the system used by the computer. We can perform calculations using 1.2 on paper with perfect accuracy. Yet, since 1.2 has only an approximate representation in a machine, computations involving it may contain small errors.

Error propagation   If such numbers are heavily involved in a computation, or the computation is lengthy and repetitive, the errors may not be so small. A small error in starting values may produce larger errors in the results. When these results are the inputs to subsequent calculations, even larger errors may arise. With more stages of calculation, the errors continue to magnify. To illustrate, consider repeated multiplication of 1.2 by itself. Two powers of 1.2 were computed both by hand and by machine (VAX). The differences in the results are

Value computed	$(1.2)^8$	$(1.2)^{16}$
True value calculated by hand	4.29981696	18.4884258895036416
Approximate value calculated by VAX	$\updownarrow$ 4.29981803 . . .	$\updownarrow$ 18.48843765 . . .
Approximate error	10^{-6}	10^{-5}

For purposes of comparison we carried out the same computations on an IBM-PC using Turbo Pascal. Turbo computed 1.2^8 exactly and gave an error of only 10^{-10} in the value of 1.2^{16}.

Admittedly, such discrepancies are minor and for early applications will probably be tolerable. However, in serious numeric processing, these small inaccuracies accumulate throughout sometimes very lengthy computations. They can accumulate to the point of completely undermining the final results. Consequently, the control and reduction of these effects is the subject of considerable study in the field of numerical analysis.

For now, just be wary when writing conditions that test the (in)equality of two numeric quantities, especially if one or both are real. This is particularly important in loop termination conditions, because the actual values may be different from those expected. For example, the expression $(6/5) * 5 = 6$ is *never* true, even though it should be according to the rules of algebra. Note that 6/5 is our old friend 1.2.

6.9 Review of Rules

A. The value of a boolean expression may be stored in a boolean variable, passed through boolean-valued parameters, or returned as the result of a boolean-valued function. In addition to the relational and boolean operators covered in Chapter 3, another useful operator is IN, written:

⟨item⟩ IN [⟨list of items⟩]

This expression yields a value of true if the item on its left occurs anywhere in the SET of items of similar type on its right; its value is false otherwise. It shares lowest precedence with the relational operators.

B. The programmer may define user-defined data types as

TYPE ⟨type identifier⟩ = (⟨list of values⟩);

These definitions appear in the type definition part, which comes immediately after the constant definition part and immediately before the variable declaration part. Variables can then be declared and assigned any value belonging to this type. These values may not belong to any other type, and their order of specification determines their ordinal numbering (starting from 0). On most systems these values cannot be read from or written to a terminal in standard Pascal.

C. The char, integer, boolean, and user-defined types are all ordinal types, which means that they have discrete, ordered, enumerable values. The reals do not constitute an ordinal type. The following apply to any ordinal type.

1. A restricted, subrange type may be defined to include only those values in the range, including the ends of the range; that is,

TYPE ⟨type identifier⟩ = ⟨lowerlimit⟩ . . ⟨upperlimit⟩;

Both limits must be given as constants belonging to the same ordinal type.

2. The preceding or following member of any ordinal type can be obtained by supplying the current member as the argument to the functions pred or succ, respectively. Pred and succ are undefined (and may raise an error) if their arguments represent the first and last members, respectively, of the ordinal type.

3. The position of a member within an ordinal type can be obtained by supplying the member to the function ord. The position numbers start with 0, except in the case of integers, where

⟨integer value⟩ = ord(⟨integer value⟩).

The ord function, like succ and pred, applies to positions within the base data type and not to subranges.

D. The char data type has an ordering based on the collating sequence of the particular machine. For any position number within this sequence, the function chr determines the corresponding character.

KEY TERMS

base type	ordinal data types
binary search	precision
boolean constants	pred function
boolean data type	program portability
boolean variables	SET
check sums	set constant
chr function	state variable
consistency checking	subrange
flag	succ function
IN operator	successive approximation
inverses	TYPE definition part
odd function	type identifier
ord function	

EXERCISES

6.1   Identify the errors (if any) in the following sets of code.

```
(a) TYPE
      Suits = (Clubs,Diamonds,Hearts,Spades);
    VAR
      BlackCard: Clubs;
(b) TYPE
      Grades := (A,B,C,D,F);
    VAR
      Mark: Grades;
    BEGIN
      MARK := 'A';
(c) TYPE
      Days = (Sun,Mon,Tue,Wed,Thu,Fri,Sat);
    VAR
      Today: Days;
    BEGIN
      Today := Sun;
      WHILE Today <= Sat DO
        BEGIN
          {code to process Today}
          Today := succ(Today)
        END;
(d) TYPE
      Weekdays = Mon..Fri;
      Weekends = (Sat,Sun);
      Days = (Sun,Mon,Tue,Wed,Thu,Fri,Sat);
```

6.2 We have described the control of input when the user terminates input by either signaling end-of-file or entering some sentinel value. Write a loop that will allow the user to enter a stream of integers and stop the input in either of those two ways.

6.3 Rewrite the following code using REPEAT.

```
writeln ('Enter one character per line');
readln (C);
Valid := (C >= 'a') AND (C <= 'm');
WHILE Valid DO
  BEGIN
    {process variable C}
    readln (C);
    Valid := (C >= 'a') AND (C <= 'm')
  END;
writeln('That is enough')
```

6.4 Rewrite the following code using WHILE.

```
read (K);
N := 1;
IF N <= K THEN
  REPEAT
    writeln(N);
    N := N + 1
  UNTIL N > K;
```

6.5 The Fibonacci sequence begins with the integers 0, 1, and each successive term is obtained by adding the two previous terms. The first seven terms in the sequence are 0, 1, 1, 2, 3, 5, 8. You do not have to go too far in the sequence before encountering a term that exceeds maxint in value. Write a program to display the largest Fibonacci number that can be generated in an integer variable on your computer. The program must terminate normally; that is, it must not end on a run-time error. It should also indicate the number's place in the sequence.

6.6 In Canada every worker is assigned a nine-digit Social Insurance Number (SIN). These numbers are valid if they conform to the following pattern.

(a) Double the 2nd, 4th, 6th, and 8th digits.

(b) Add the *digits* of each of the numbers from step (a).

(c) Add the 1st, 3rd, 5th, and 7th digits to the result of step (b).

(d) Subtract the rightmost digit of the result of step (c) from 10; if the rightmost digit of the result of step (c) is zero, the result of this step is 0.

(e) If the ninth digit is the same as the result of step (d) the number is valid.

Consider, for example, the number 714676483.

- Doubling yields 2, 12, 12, 16;
- Summing the digits of these numbers yields $2 + 1 + 2 + 1 + 2 + 1 + 6 = 15$;
- Adding the 1st, 3rd, 5th and 7th digits yields $7 + 4 + 7 + 4 + 15 = 37$;
- $10 - 7 = 3$;
- The ninth digit is 3 and therefore the number is valid.

Write a program to read a nine-digit integer as a sequence of nine separate characters and determine whether it is a valid Canadian Social Insurance Number.

6.7   One of the problems with reading integer data is that if the user accidentally keys anything other than a digit, the program terminates with a run-time error. It is possible to read integers as a sequence of characters and build the corresponding integer as the numerals are read, stopping when a nonnumeric character or end-of-line is encountered.

Write a function subprogram GetInteger which will read digits from the input stream as a sequence of characters, construct the corresponding integer, and return the integer to the calling program.

6.8   Write a function subprogram GetReal to read characters from the input stream, construct the corresponding real number and return it to the calling program. The function should be able to deal with reals in either decimal or exponential form.

6.9   Write a program to analyze a stream of text, terminated by the sentinel '#'. The text consists of words separated by any number of blanks or certain punctuation. By scanning the arriving characters, you are to obtain the following information.

- The number of words.
- The average number of words per sentence.
- The percentage of words containing more than four letters.
- The percentage of words beginning with a vowel.
- The number of occurrences of the word "in";
- The number of occurrences of the words "a" and "at";

   (a)   Assume that all input—even proper names and the first word of each sentence—is in lowercase. The only punctuation allowed is a period at the end of every sentence.
   (b)   Allow either uppercase or lowercase letters, interior commas, and either a period or question mark at the end of every sentence—but nothing else.

6.10 Write a program that will convert a stream of input text to either uppercase or lowercase, as specified by the user.

         desired case of the text on output:
            all uppercase
            all lowercase
            no change

   This feature can be added to the text filter described in Exercise 5.6.

6.11 Another way to convert text is to encode it. An elementary encoding scheme (applicable to lowercase letters of the alphabet only) is to replace each letter with the one to its right in the alphabet. That is every 'a' in the original is replaced with a 'b', every 'b' with a 'c', and so on, until every 'z' is replaced with an 'a'. Other characters in the source data are left untouched.

   (a)   Write a program to read and encode some text using this technique. The program should include a function

```
FUNCTION Change (C: char): char;
```

         which accepts the character to be encoded and returns the replacement character.
   (b)   The basic scheme described uses a one-character shift. A better scheme would allow the user to specify an N-character shift where $1 \leq N \leq 25$.

Modify the function to

FUNCTION Change (C: char; N: integer): char;

where N is the number of characters to be shifted in determining the replacement character.

6.12 In many mathematical problems it is not possible to arrive at an analytic solution and you must resort to approximation. In calculus, one of the formulas used to approximate

$$\int_a^b f(x)\, dx$$

is the trapezoidal rule:

$$f(x)\, dx \approx \frac{h}{2}\left[f(a) + f(b) + \sum_{k=1}^{n-1} 2f(a + kh) \right],$$

where $h = (b - a)/n$ and n is the number of trapezoids.

Write a program to evaluate the integral of $x^2 dx$ from 0 to 2 and show the result using $n = 1, 2, 3, \ldots$ trapezoids, stopping when a value obtained for the integral is within 0.000001 of the previous value. The program will utilize the function subprogram:

FUNCTION Trap (A,B: real; N: integer): real;

where A is the lower value of the range in question, B is the upper value, and N is the number of trapezoids.

7

One-Dimensional Arrays

Looking back over the programs developed in the preceding chapters, we find a common thread: All have required only a few variables. Even when large amounts of data were involved, our usual approach was to read or generate one *unit* of data, process it, and then either display the result or incorporate it into a total or some other summary information. Since each unit of data could be discarded after being processed, the same memory locations were reused to handle a long succession of similar individual items.

Not all applications are of this type. Often the data must either be retained after initial processing or be assembled in memory before processing can begin. In contrast to its *simple data types,* which depict individual values, Pascal also provides several *structured data types,* which allow the programmer to view and manipulate aggregations of data systematically. As the amount and interrelationship of data increase, so does the need to organize the data for effective processing. In fact, the problem of data organization becomes as important as algorithm design because the two are intertwined. In this chapter we begin the ongoing theme of data structuring by introducing one of its most important structures: the one-dimensional array.

7.1 Declaring and Referencing One-Dimensional Arrays

The need for arrays
Suppose that you must find the average of three numbers and then display every number greater than the average. In this case you cannot determine the average until all three numbers have been read. Then you must inspect all the numbers again to find out which ones are greater than the average. It is

279

not feasible to reenter all the numbers, so they must be retained in main memory for later inspection. One algorithm for this problem is

1. read values for A, B and C;
2. compute average of A, B and C;
3. if A > average then display A;
4. if B > average then display B;
5. if C > average then display C;
6. stop.

Although this algorithm may not appear formidable, consider the corresponding solution for 30 or 300 numbers. Trying to invent and declare so many distinct identifiers could easily tax both your imagination and your typing skills. Worse yet, even though many data items are processed similarly, you cannot handle them by identical code because the code must refer to different identifiers in each case.

    With problems like this, where several data items *having identical types* must be available for processing, you should consider using an array. An **array** is simply a collection of memory locations of the same type. It can provide convenient storage for a collection of values and a uniform way of referring to individual values in the collection, allowing the same code to operate on any designated value.

array

Getting Acquainted with One-Dimensional Arrays

one-dimensional array

A **one-dimensional array** is a linear sequence of memory locations of identical type. It bears the same relation to a simple variable as a row of identical townhouses does to a single dwelling unit. (See Fig. 7.1.)

    Suppose that you were making up a party invitation list. You would not explicitly write before each person's name "first invited guest," "second invited guest," and so on. You might instead write "Invited Guests" at the top of a sheet of paper and then assume that each following line would identify a different guest. Similarly, to request a list of 100 memory locations, you do not need to make 100 explicit declarations. Instead, you declare a single array and indicate how many locations are included. For example,

```
VAR List: ARRAY [1..100] OF real;
```

would request an array of 100 variables, known collectively as List, and each capable of holding a single real value.

    Since each name on an invitation list appears on a separate line, you may refer to the fourth name on the list, even though you did not explicitly write "fourth invited guest" before the name. Similarly, the declaration of an array includes enough information to number, or otherwise identify, unique locations in the array. In the preceding declaration, the notation [1 . . 100] specifies that the individual locations within the array are to be numbered

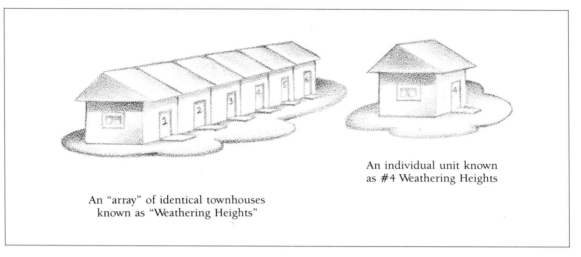

An "array" of identical townhouses
known as "Weathering Heights"

An individual unit known
as #4 Weathering Heights

■ Figure 7.1
The concept of an array.

array bounds
subordinates
array declaration

from 1 *through* 100; these numbers are called the **array bounds.** The location numbers, called **subscripts,** are always consecutive and span a subrange of the ordinal data type specified by the bounds. The **array declaration,** then, has three main parts:

1. the identifier that names the entire array (List in our example);
2. the bounds specify the range and type of the subscripts and, by implication, the number of memory locations (100 locations numbered 1 through 100 with integer subscripts in our example); and
3. the type of values that may be stored in the memory locations (real in our example).

In general, the simplest form of declaration for a one-dimensional array is

VAR ⟨identifier⟩: ARRAY [L . . H] OF ⟨type⟩

where L is the lowest valued subscript, H is the highest valued subscript, and both L and H belong to the same ordinal type. Such an array will have $ord(H) - ord(L) + 1$ storage locations associated with it. These individual locations are called **array components.** When the components are simple variables (as they are throughout this chapter) they are sometimes called subscripted variables, or **indexed variables.** The latter term is used because a subscript is also known as an **index** into an array.

array components

indexed variables
index
**Reference to a
component**

The program can *reference* an individual location in the array by specifying the array identifier, followed by a particular subscript value enclosed in square brackets. For example, to reference the fourth location in the preceding array, simply use List[4], which is just the name of that particular memory location. The other 99 components have similar names: List[1], List[2], . . . , List[100].

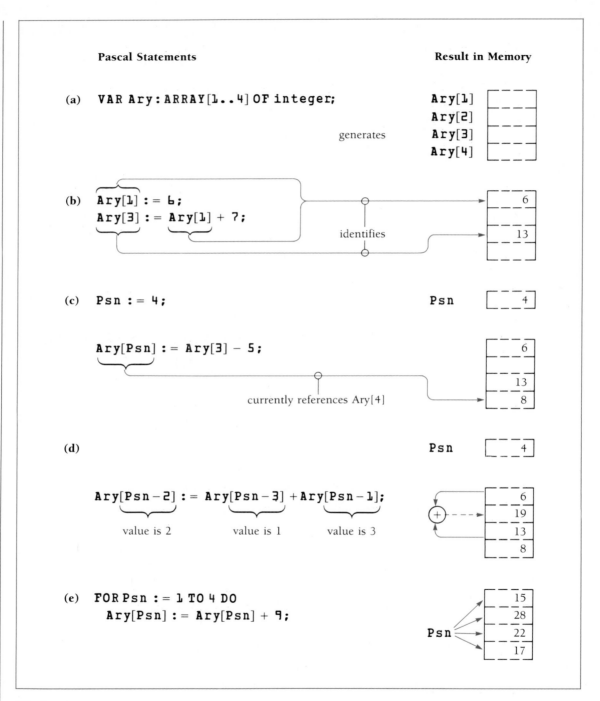

Figure 7.2
Declaring and referencing one-dimensional arrays.

**One-Dimensional
Arrays**

Declaration:

VAR ⟨identifier⟩: ARRAY [L . . H] OF ⟨type⟩

where L and H are both of the same ordinal type and ord(L) <= ord(H).

Effect:
1. The identifier names the entire array.
2. The lowest valued subscript is L and the highest valued subscript is H.
3. There are ord(H) − ord(L) + 1 components associated with the array.
4. Every component can hold a value of the type named in the declaration.
5. An individual location is referenced by a name of the form

    ⟨identifier⟩[⟨expression⟩]

    where the expression has a value of the same type as L and H and lies
    in the range specified by L and H.

A particular reference, such as List[4], identifies an ordinary real variable
that behaves just like any other real variable. Only its name is a bit different
because it is an array component. Such references have to appear in a context
where a variable identifier is appropriate; for instance,

```
writeln (List[4]:10:2);
```

Figure 7.2(a) shows how declaring an array of four integer components
implicitly generates four different variables and variable identifiers. Figure
7.2(b) shows how these identifiers behave like any other variable identifier
in Pascal statements.

Variable subscripts   Figure 7.2(c) illustrates a most important point: The particular array
component being referenced can be denoted by a *variable* subscript. In fact,
the subscript can be generated by an expression, as shown in Fig. 7.2(d).
This allows you to use the same code to refer to different items in the array
merely by executing the code with a different value for the subscript each
time.

Sequential Processing of an Array

Figure 7.2(e) depicts how 9 could be added to every element in the array by
executing the statement

```
Ary[Psn] := Ary[Psn] + 9;
```

■ Figure 7.3
Sequential processing
of an array.

(a) Initial values in array

Ary[1]	6
Ary[2]	19
Ary[3]	13
Ary[4]	8

(b) Code for adding 9 to each component

```
FOR Psn := 1 TO 4 DO
    Ary[Psn] := Ary[Psn] + 9;
```

(c) Step-by-step execution

```
Psn := 1;                          Psn [    1 ]
Since Psn is <= 4, continue loop.
Ary[Psn] := Ary[Psn] + 9;
```

15
19
13
8

```
increment Psn to 2                 Psn [    2 ]
Since Psn is <= 4, continue loop.
Ary[Psn] := Ary[Psn] + 9;
```

15
28
13
8

```
increment Psn to 3                 Psn [    3 ]
Since Psn is <= 4, continue loop.
Ary[Psn] := Ary[Psn] + 9;
```

15
28
22
8

```
increment Psn to 4                 Psn [    4 ]
Since Psn is <= 4, continue loop.
Ary[Psn] := Ary[Psn] + 9;
```

15
28
22
17

```
Since Psn is at upper loop limit, stop loop.
```

■ Figure 7.4
Control structure for
processing an entire
array.

```
FOR Psn := First TO Last DO

    BEGIN
       .
       .        ┌─────────────────────────────────────┐
       .        │ code to process one array component:│
       .        │ that at position Psn                 │
       .        └─────────────────────────────────────┘
       .

    END
```

four separate times with different values for Psn each time. The variable Psn
indicates the location currently being accessed. As its value is systematically
altered, so is the location being referred to in the array.

This example is so important that we display its step-by-step execution
in Fig. 7.3. It typifies the most common way of using arrays, namely, *moving
through* the array, processing each element in a similar way, and processing
only one element at a time. The general control structure for moving through
an array from components First through Last, inclusive, is shown in Fig. 7.4.

This kind of movement through consecutive items is, of course, an
example of sequential processing. The term *processing* includes a great many
possibilities, such as updating values, displaying values, adding values into a
running total, and generating new values. Note how the basic control structure
(from Fig. 7.4) appears in each of the examples in Fig. 7.5.

Use of TYPE and Subrange with Arrays

■ Figure 7.5
Examples of sequential
array processing.

Although an array is a composite of several simpler objects, each array is
itself an object in the language and therefore an instance of some data type.
There is not just one type known as *array*. Arrays are of different types if

(a)	Displaying the values already stored in an array	`FOR Psn := 1 TO 4 DO` `   writeln (Ary[Psn]);`

(b)	Adding the values of array elements into a total	`Total := 0;`
		`FOR K := 1 TO 4 DO`
		`   Total := Total + Ary[K];`

(c)	Storing the first four even integers (2, 4, 6, 8) in an array	`FOR N := 1 TO 4 DO` `   Ary[N] := 2 * N;`

their basic constituents are of different types or if their subscript ranges differ in any way.

Arrays as new types

Thus, when you define a new array structure, you are introducing a new data type into your program. In fact, if two definitions cannot be traced back to the very same type declaration, they are considered distinct types, even if they are structurally identical. For example, the definition

```
VAR
  A,B : ARRAY [1..10] OF char;
  C   : ARRAY [1..10] OF char;
```

creates two different types, with A and B belonging to one type and C belonging to the other, even though all three arrays have similar structures.

To avoid confusion and to avoid a proliferation of types, it is better to describe the new type first in the type definition section and then to create one (or more) instances of the actual array in the variable declaration part, as follows:

```
TYPE
  RealArray = ARRAY [1..100] OF real;
VAR
  Ary : RealArray;
```

Entire arrays may be passed to subprograms as either value-type or variable-type parameters. In either case the actual array parameter and the corresponding formal parameter must be of *exactly* the same type. Thus you must define the array structure as an explicit type, so that you can use the type identifier in the subprogram's formal parameter definition and declare the actual array parameters with that same type.

We might use the upper index limit (100 in our example) not only in the definition of the array type, but also throughout the program to control access to such arrays. We can identify such limits with a more descriptive word than 100 and so permit easy modification of this value in the future by defining this upper limit as a constant, such as

Preferred declaration of arrays

```
CONST
  MaxSize = 100;
TYPE
  RealArray = ARRAY [1..MaxSize] OF real;
VAR
  Ary: RealArray;
  Psn: 1..MaxSize;

BEGIN
  .
  .
  .
  {traverse entire array}
  FOR Psn := 1 TO MaxSize DO
    . . . Ary[Psn] . . .
```

The array subscripts span a subrange, and it is an error to execute an array reference when the subscript is not within this range. To guard against straying outside these limits, you should use a subrange type in the definition either of the array type or the actual array. A common and very readable form is

```
CONST
  MaxSize = 100;
TYPE
  IndexRange = 1..MaxSize;
  RealArray = ARRAY [IndexRange] OF real;
VAR
  Ary: RealArray;
  Psn: IndexRange;
```

Subscript ranges

Now suppose that you use an array to store sales figures for the period from 1956 through 1987, inclusive. Pascal allows you to set up any range of subscripts, provided the lower one is less than (or equal to) the upper one. Although only 32 values will ever be stored there, an array whose subscripts run from 1 to 32 will not be as descriptive as an array whose subscripts run from 1956 to 1987. The array of sales values can be established as

```
CONST
  Start = 1956;
  Finish = 1987;
TYPE
  Period = Start..Finish;
  SalesValues = ARRAY [Period] OF real;
VAR
  Sales: SalesValues;
  Psn: Period;

BEGIN
  .
  .
  .

  FOR Psn := Start TO Finish DO
    . . . Sales [Psn] . . .
```

Noninteger ordinal subscripts

Since subscripts can belong to any ordinal type, we sometimes find it useful to reference array locations by something other than integers. The declaration

```
TYPE
  Rainbow =
    (Violet,Indigo,Blue,Green,Yellow,Orange,Red);
VAR
    Spectrum: ARRAY [Rainbow] OF boolean;
```

generates six boolean variables having the identifiers:

```
Spectrum[Violet]
Spectrum[Indigo]
Spectrum[Blue]
Spectrum[Green]
Spectrum[Yellow]
Spectrum[Orange]
Spectrum[Red]
```

7.2 Some Important Techniques in Array Processing

In this section we explore several examples of array manipulation strategies and programming techniques. These ideas will appear in various combinations in almost all future array-oriented applications.

Reading Values into an Array

Pascal allows you to read values directly into array components; in fact, a common operation is to read a sequence of input values with identical types into successive array components. However, because the supply of data rarely matches the number of array components, input must be done very carefully.

Input need not fill array

Just because you declare an array to consist of a certain number of memory locations, you do not have to use all of them. For example, your party invitation list may be on a sheet of paper with 20 lines, but if you have only seven friends, you will use only seven lines. What is important is that you start with a sheet of paper large enough to accommodate the names of all the friends that you want to invite. Similarly, when dealing with unknown quantities of data to be read into an array, you should declare an array large enough to hold all the data and not worry about whether data will fill it. Unlike the party list, where you can always add another sheet of paper, you cannot change your mind about the size of an array in mid-program.

Test for end of data and end of array

Of course, when filling an array by read statements, you may reach the end of the array before you run out of data. It is an error to attempt an access beyond the end of an array. Your loop governing movement through the array should therefore keep testing the current position to determine whether it is still within the array. The loop should also continue to test for the end of data, since you may exhaust the data before reaching the end of the array. Thus, whatever input structure you use, you must guard against continuing beyond either the end of the data or the end of the array.

The resulting code, shown in Fig. 7.6, is a blend of moving through the array and reading an arbitrary number of values using eof and eoln. Note our

```
CONST
   MaxSize = 10;
TYPE
   IndexRange = 1..MaxSize;
   IntArray = ARRAY [IndexRange] OF integer;
VAR
   Table: IntArray;
   Last: integer;

BEGIN
   Last := 0; {indicates empty array}

   WHILE (Last < MaxSize) AND (NOT eof) DO
      BEGIN {input loop}

         WHILE (Last < MaxSize) AND (NOT eoln) DO
            BEGIN {one line at a time}
               Last := Last + 1; {next component}
               read (Table[Last]) {fill that component}
            END;
         readln

      END; {input loop}
   { Last = number of values read }
```

■ Figure 7.6
Reading values into successive array locations.

use of WHILE rather than FOR; FOR is appropriate only if you know in advance how much data will be read.

Recording amount filled

When the code in Fig. 7.6 finishes executing, the value of Last indicates the final array position that was successfully given a value. It is important to retain this value, since it represents the "frontier" between the occupied and unoccupied portions of the array. Last will indicate the frontier even if no data were available (Last = 0) or if the amount of data reached or exceeded the capacity of the array (Last = MaxSize). If there were more data than required, the excess data will not be read.

Using a Partially Filled Array

As with simple variables, only those array components containing values can be manipulated. Any subsequent processing must be prevented from venturing into unoccupied portions of the array, except to place values there. The *effective size* of the array becomes the number of values actually stored there, rather than the number of defined locations. The effective size (or its equivalent) is often maintained in a simple variable to limit the extent of processing.

For example, if the code in Fig. 7.6 were used to read the data 36 20 47 98 65 2 16, the array would appear as shown in Fig. 7.7. The frontier Last is set by the input process. Conceptually, sequential processing of a partially filled array is the same as processing an entire array; the difference is that the array references must not extend beyond the last occupied position.

Using a partially filled array Figure 7.8 contains some examples of code for processing the array shown in Fig. 7.7. The code in Fig. 7.8(a) determines the average of all the values stored in the array. The code in Fig. 7.8(b) reports all the values larger than the threshold. If the threshold happens to be the average, we have the code required to solve the problem posed at the beginning of this chapter: to find all the values larger than the average.

The code in Fig. 7.8(c) finds the largest value in the array. We now apply the strategy originally proposed for this problem (in section 3.5) to an array rather than to an input stream. The value in the first component becomes the initial candidate for the largest value. The loop begins at the second location, since there is no point in reprocessing the first. If the array contains only one value, the loop is bypassed, but Max still contains the largest value.

■ **Figure 7.7**
Partially filled array.

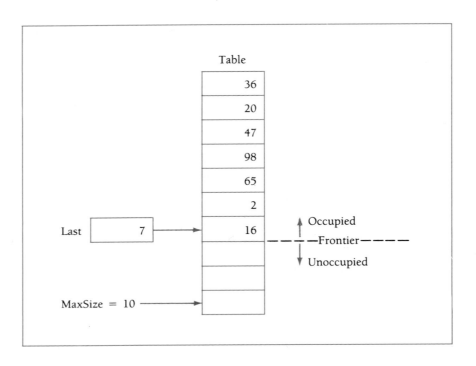

Sequential processing
of partially filled
array.

```
Sum := 0;
FOR K := 1 TO Last DO
   Sum := Sum + Table[K];

IF Last > 0 THEN {array contains data}
   Average := Sum / Last
ELSE {empty array}
   Average := 0; {default}
```

(a) Find average of values in table.

```
FOR Location := 1 TO Last DO
   IF Table[Location] > Threshold THEN
      writeln (Table[Location]:8,
                 'exceeds threshold');
```

(b) Report which values in table exceed threshold.

```
Max := Table[1];
      {1st value is initial candidate}

FOR Entry := 2 TO Last DO
   IF Table[Entry] > Max THEN {new candidate}
      Max := Table[Entry]; {record its value}
{Max now contains the largest value}
```

(c) Find the largest value in table (assume nonempty).

Arrays as Parameters

Passing an entire array

One great advantage of arrays is that they allow a whole collection of values to be passed as a single parameter. As you might expect, the actual parameter in the calling program is the particular array identifier, and in the corresponding formal parameter we declare the object to be an array by including the appropriate type identifier. In order to pass arrays, we must make the actual and formal parameters exactly the same type. Recall that type identity requires more than structural similarity; two arrays have the same type only if their definitions are based on the very same type declaration. Therefore we have to define an explicit type identifier in the TYPE declaration section. This type identifier would then appear in both the actual array declaration and the formal parameter declaration as

PROCEDURE Legal (Ary : ArrayType);

However, the following kind of subprogram heading is illegal.

PROCEDURE Illegal (Ary: ARRAY [1 . . 80] OF char);

When passing an array to a subprogram, we make *all* its components accessible to the subprogram. If the array is passed as a variable-type parameter, any and all of the array components may be altered by the subprogram. On the other hand, when the array is a value-type parameter, *none* of its components may be modified. Thus, whenever an array is being passed to a procedure that alters even a tiny part of it, the formal parameter must be variable-type.

For example, the code from Fig. 7.6 to read integers into an array of type IntArray is shown as a procedure in Fig. 7.9(a). Since the array itself as well

```
CONST
    MaxSize = 10;
TYPE
    IndexRange = 1..MaxSize;
    IntArray = ARRAY[IndexRange] OF integer;
VAR
    Table: IntArray;
    Last: integer;


PROCEDURE ReadArray (VAR A: IntArray; VAR Last: integer);
    BEGIN {ReadArray}
        Last := 0; {indicates empty array}
        WHILE (Last < MaxSize) AND NOT eof DO
            BEGIN {input loop}

                WHILE (Last < MaxSize) AND NOT eoln DO
                    BEGIN
                        Last := Last + 1; {next component}
                        read (A[Last]) {fill component}
                    END;
                readln

            END {input loop}
    END; {ReadArray procedure}
    .
    .
    .

BEGIN {program}
    ReadArray (Table,Last);      {typical call}
```

(a) Procedure to read values into successive array components.

■ Figure 7.9
Initializing and searching an array of integers.

as its effective length will be given values by the procedure, both are variable-type parameters. As with simple variables, the actual and formal parameter identifiers do not need to be identical; Figure 7.9(b) shows their correspondence.

Figure 7.9(c) shows a function to find the largest value in this type of array. As usual, the effective length is also passed as a parameter, so that the function will know how much of the array to inspect. A typical sequence of calls to these subprograms might be

```
ReadArray (Table,Last );
Largest := FindMax (Table,Last );
```

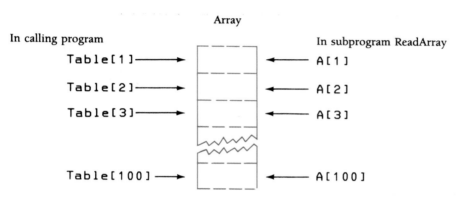

(b) Actual to formal array parameter correspondence after executing ReadArray (Table,Last).

```
FUNCTION FindMax (Table :IntArray; Last integer): integer;

   VAR Max, Entry: integer;

   BEGIN
      Max := Table[1]; {1st value is initial candidate}

      FOR Entry := 2 TO Last DO
         IF Table[Entry] > Max THEN {new candidate}
            Max := Table[Entry]; {record its value}
      {Max now contains the largest value}

      FindMax := Max
   END; {FindMax function}
```

(c) Find the largest value in table (assume nonempty).

■ Figure 7.9
(Continued)

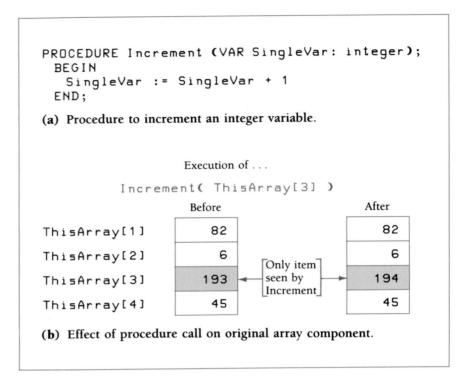

```
PROCEDURE Increment (VAR SingleVar: integer);
  BEGIN
    SingleVar := SingleVar + 1
  END;
```

(a) Procedure to increment an integer variable.

Execution of . . .

Increment(ThisArray[3])

	Before		After
ThisArray[1]	82		82
ThisArray[2]	6		6
ThisArray[3]	193	Only item seen by Increment	194
ThisArray[4]	45		45

(b) Effect of procedure call on original array component.

Passing an array component

An *individual component* of an array may be passed to any subprogram whose formal parameter matches the component type. If the formal parameter is variable type, the subprogram can alter that individual array component, exactly as it would an ordinary variable. For example, Fig. 7.10(a) shows a trivial procedure to increment an integer variable. (You would never actually include such a procedure in a program.) When this procedure is called with an array component as an actual parameter, only that single component is known to the subprogram and, hence, subject to modification, as shown in Fig. 7.10(b).

It is important to distinguish an entire array (such as ThisArray) from an array component (say, ThisArray[3]). The latter is simply the name of an integer variable and can match only a parameter of type integer, whereas the former, being an entire array, can match only a parameter of the same type.

Using an Array of Counters

Suppose that several batches of a particular chemical solution are to be prepared for experimental study. Wide variations in temperature owing to a variety of external factors (light, temperature, pressure, agitation, and the like) can cause the solution to become unstable. The purpose of the experiment is to measure the stability of the solution under various conditions.

As soon as a batch of solution has been prepared, its temperature is recorded at that time and at 10-minute intervals for the next hour (a total of 7 readings). Both the average (Mean) and highest (Max) temperatures for the hour are calculated. The stability of the solution depends on two things: (1) a comparison of its Mean temperature with a threshold temperature beyond which the solution is considered unstable; and (2) the disparity between the Mean and the Max temperatures. These two factors are used to classify the batch into four categories:

1. **Stable**, if Mean $<=$ Threshold and Max $<$ 2*Mean.
2. **Active**, if Mean $<=$ Threshold and Max $>=$ 2*Mean.
3. **Volatile**, if Mean $>$ Threshold and Max $<$ 2*Mean.
4. **Dangerous**, if Mean $>$ Threshold and Max $>=$ 2*Mean.

Our problem is to write a program that performs this classification based on the data from an arbitrary number of batches. The input will consist of one line containing seven real values for each batch under study. End-of-file will indicate when data from all batches have been entered. The output will give the total number of batches and the number in each of the four categories. Figure 7.11 shows the basic algorithm.

Before rushing to code this algorithm, we should consider how to organize the data; in the process we will notice two applications for arrays. First, an array could be used to hold the seven input values for each batch, since they are all real numbers and will be processed in similar ways. An array is not strictly necessary for this purpose because the processing of the data—finding the Mean and Max—can be done as the data are being read. However, by collecting the data first, we can detach the input process from the analysis, and the data become available for other operations (such as output or further analysis) that may be introduced later. Having the data in an array also permits separate calculation of the Mean and Max. This is an important advantage if these subprograms are already available.

Array as input buffer

■ Figure 7.11
Algorithm to process
experimental data.

1. initialize BatchCount and the four "category" counters to 0;
2. while not end-of-file do:
2.1   read temperatures for next batch;
2.2   compute their Mean and Max;
2.3   determine the correct category for this batch;
2.4   increment corresponding category counter;
2.5   increment the (total) BatchCount;
3. display BatchCount and the four "category" counters;
4. stop.

Array of counters

The second application for an array is to hold the four category counters, since all are integers and all are similarly manipulated. When several counters must be maintained, they are frequently collected into an array for uniformity of access. For the array of counters in our solution, we utilize a user-defined type as its subscript, since these subscripts are generated internally and the categories have descriptive names.

Hence we declare our two arrays as

```
CONST
  DataPoints = 7; {values per input line}
TYPE
  TempArray = ARRAY [1..DataPoints] OF real;
  States = (Stable,Active,Volatile, Dangerous);
  CountArray = ARRAY [States] OF integer;
VAR
  Temperature: TempArray; {input buffer}
  Counter: CountArray; {4 category counters}
```

Now consider the program in Fig. 7.12(a). Note how the Counter array is initialized to zeroes at the beginning and displayed at the end. A FOR statement, with its ability to cycle through the values of a user-defined type, is the perfect vehicle for traversing an array with user-defined subscripts.

The first action inside the major loop is to transfer an input line into the Temperature array, which is done by the procedure ReadLine in Fig. 7.12(b). Since we know that there are exactly 7 values per line, the amount of data and the size of the array are perfectly matched, and no extra checking is required. In this case a FOR statement is sufficient to activate the seven read operations. Readln must be included to clear the line, since loop termination is by end of file.

The functions to find Mean and Max borrow their code from Fig. 7.8. Without an array to retain the input values, we would have had to combine both these operations inside the input loop.

A basic decision tree is implemented as the function Classify. Although only one nested IF statement is involved, we made it a subprogram so as not to clutter the main program. Note that this function, Classify, returns a user-defined type. This value, stored in the variable Category, can be used immediately to select the correct counter from the array Counter. Thus incrementing any one of the four categories is accomplished by the statement:

```
Counter[Category] := Counter[Category] + 1;
```

Without arrays, we would have had to use Category as a selector in a CASE statement in order to choose one of four separate assignment statements. The relative simplicity of the array approach should be apparent.

```pascal
PROGRAM Solutions (input,output);
CONST
   Threshold = 27; {celsius; criterion for stability}
   DataPoints = 7; {values per input line}
TYPE
   TempArray = ARRAY [1..DataPoints] OF real;
   States = (Stable,Active,Volatile,Dangerous);
   CountArray = ARRAY [States] OF integer;
VAR
   Temperature: TempArray; {input buffer}
   Counter: CountArray; {4 category counters}
   Category: States; {outcome of classification}
   BatchCount: integer; {no. of experiments = lines}
   Mean, Max: real;

PROCEDURE ReadLine (VAR A: TempArray; Number :integer);

FUNCTION FindMean (Temp :TempArray; Number :integer): real;

FUNCTION FindMax (Temp :TempArray; Number :integer): real;

FUNCTION Classify (Mean,Max: real): States;

BEGIN {Solutions}
   BatchCount := 0;
   FOR Category := Stable TO Dangerous DO
      Counter[Category] := 0;
   WHILE NOT eof DO
      BEGIN {process next experimental batch}
         ReadLine (Temperature,Datapoints);
         Mean:= FindMean(Temperature,Datapoints);
         Max := FindMax (Temperature,Datapoints);
         Category := Classify(Mean,Max);
         Counter[Category]:= Counter[Category] + 1;
         BatchCount := BatchCount + 1
      END; {one experiment}
   writeln ('Batches':10,'Stable':10,'Active':10,
            'Volatile':11,'Dangerous':11);
   writeln; {blank line}
   write (BatchCount:8);
   FOR Category := Stable TO Dangerous DO
      write (Counter[Category]:10);
   writeln;
END. {Solutions}
```

■ Figure 7.12(a)
Evaluation of experimental data.

```
PROCEDURE ReadLine (VAR Temp: TempArray; Number :integer);
   VAR Psn : integer;
   BEGIN {ReadLine}
      FOR Psn := 1 TO Number DO
         read( Temp[Psn] );
      readln
   END; {ReadLine}

FUNCTION FindMean (Temp :TempArray; Number :integer): real;
   VAR Sum : real;
       Current : integer;
   BEGIN
      Sum := 0;
      FOR Current := 1 TO Number DO
         Sum := Sum + Temp[Current];
      FindMean := Sum / Number
   END; {FindMean procedure}

FUNCTION FindMax (Temp :TempArray; Number :integer): real;
   VAR Max, Current : integer;
   BEGIN
      Max := Temp[1];
      FOR Current := 2 TO Number DO
         IF Temp[Current] > Max THEN
            Max := Temp[Current];
      FindMax := Max
   END; {FindMax procedure}

FUNCTION Classify (Mean,Max: real): States;
      {classify experiment}
   BEGIN {Classify}
      IF Mean <= Threshold THEN
         IF Max < 2 * Mean THEN
            Classify := Stable
         ELSE
            Classify := Active
      ELSE {Threshold exceeded}
         IF Max < 2 * Mean THEN
            Classify := Volatile
         ELSE
            Classify := Dangerous
   END; {Classify}
```

■ **Figure 7.12(b)**
Subprograms for Figure 7.12(a)

Sequential Searching

linear search

Inspecting the values in an array to find some particular value or a value with some particular property is a common activity known as *searching* the array. Although many ways of searching exist, the most straightforward is to start at the top of an array and examine its components one by one to see which item (if any) happens to have the sought-after attributes. This is called a **linear,** or sequential, **search.**

Suppose that the object of the search is to locate the value 65 (the current contents of the variable Target). Figure 7.13(a) reproduces the array Table from Fig. 7.7 and shows the route through the array leading to the discovery of the value 65. Figure 7.13(b) shows a full sequential search of Table to discover whether the value of Target occurs anywhere within the array. Note

Full array traversal

that this search proceeds all the way through the occupied portion of Table, regardless of whether 65 occurs. The Target value may have multiple occurrences, but this would not affect the outcome of this search.

Stopping the search

Once an instance of the Target value has been encountered, continued searching of the array in this particular application is unnecessary. By including a boolean flag among the loop conditions, the loop can be terminated as soon as 65 is located. The code shown in Fig. 7.13(c) stops the search as soon as the Target value is found.

At the completion of this search, if the desired value was found (Found = true), the final value of Psn gives the location of the *first* position where that value is located (that is, the Target value resides in Table[Psn]). Although there may be other occurrences of the desired value, this code never discovers them.

We can use an alternative implementation, shown in Fig. 7.13(d), and set a position variable instead of a boolean flag as soon as the Target value is encountered. We initialize this position variable to 0 to indicate that it has not yet been set by the search. The position variable value then becomes part of a condition for continuing the loop and a criterion for testing whether the search was successful.

Figure 7.13(e) shows use of the technique from Fig. 7.13(c) inside a function. However, to its caller this function *behaves* more like the approach used in Fig. 7.13(d): A returned value of 0 indicates failure to find the Target value.

You have to avoid the temptation to place the comparison of array values among the loop conditions; that is, you must not write

WHILE (Table[Psn] <> Target) AND (Psn <= Last) DO {not do}

If the Target value is not in the array, this statement will cause an error when Psn is advanced beyond Last and an attempt is made to access Table[Last + 1]. Rephrasing the condition will not solve the problem. The array references must appear inside the loop to avoid the possibility of an illegal array access.

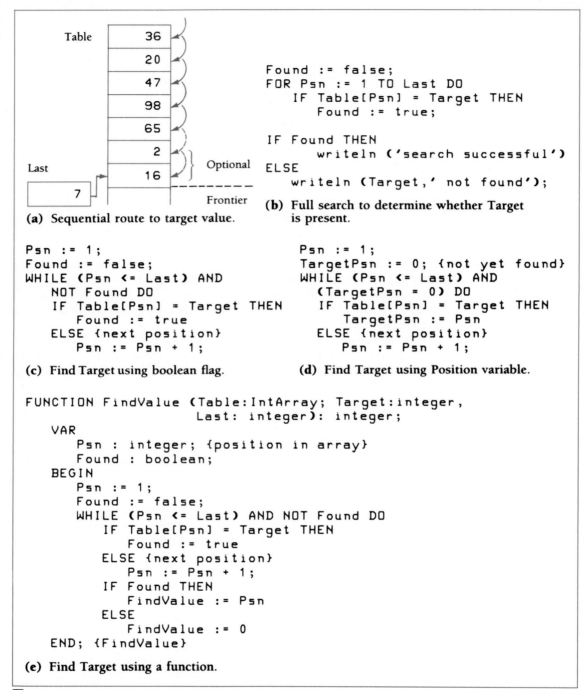

```
Found := false;
FOR Psn := 1 TO Last DO
     IF Table[Psn] = Target THEN
          Found := true;


IF Found THEN
          writeln ('search successful')
ELSE
     writeln (Target,' not found');
```

(a) Sequential route to target value.

(b) Full search to determine whether Target is present.

```
Psn := 1;
Found := false;
WHILE (Psn <= Last) AND
   NOT Found DO
   IF Table[Psn] = Target THEN
      Found := true
   ELSE {next position}
      Psn := Psn + 1;
```

(c) Find Target using boolean flag.

```
Psn := 1;
TargetPsn := 0; {not yet found}
WHILE (Psn <= Last) AND
   (TargetPsn = 0) DO
   IF Table[Psn] = Target THEN
      TargetPsn := Psn
   ELSE {next position}
      Psn := Psn + 1;
```

(d) Find Target using Position variable.

```
FUNCTION FindValue (Table:IntArray; Target:integer,
                    Last: integer): integer;
   VAR
      Psn : integer; {position in array}
      Found : boolean;
   BEGIN
      Psn := 1;
      Found := false;
      WHILE (Psn <= Last) AND NOT Found DO
         IF Table[Psn] = Target THEN
            Found := true
         ELSE {next position}
            Psn := Psn + 1;
         IF Found THEN
            FindValue := Psn
         ELSE
            FindValue := 0
   END; {FindValue}
```

(e) Find Target using a function.

■ Figure 7.13
Examples of linear search.

Updating and Appending to Unordered Arrays

updating   A common reason for searching an array is to select an element for **updating,** that is, modification or replacement. For example, every time you visit the doctor, the receptionist will search the patient files and, if yours is found, increase your bill and add any pertinent medical information to the file.

In order to modify a value when it has been found in an array, its position must be known. In such cases it is not enough to determine simply whether the value occurs. For example, the following code increments the first occurrence of the Target value, provided a call to our search function (Fig. 7.13e) is able to find this value within the array Table.

```
WhereFound := FindValue (Table, Target, Last );
IF WhereFound > 0 THEN {search successful}
  Table[WhereFound] := Table[WhereFound] + 1
ELSE {failure}
  writeln('Target value not found in Table')
```

Effective array size   When a search *fails* to find the desired item, there may be an important consequence: the item is added to the array as a new element. Thus, if you are a new patient, the receptionist will be unable to find your file and will create a new one. Any subsequent search for this same item will successfully discover it. Within the limitation of the number of memory locations declared for an array, its effective size (that is, the number of values actually stored there) may change as the result of searches and updates.

If the values in an array are in no particular order, the easiest place to add a new item is at the end of the occupied portion, that is, in the first
appending   component of the unused part. This operation is called **appending** a value to an array.

Check first to determine whether space is available for the new value. If the entire array is already occupied, no new values can be appended. Assuming that a free location exists, the first free component occurs immediately after the last occupied one. The append operation, then, consists of

1. advancing the frontier to encompass the next array component (by incrementing Last); and
2. storing the new value in this newly identified Last component of the occupied portion of the array.

A procedure to do this is shown in Fig. 7.14.

We have already seen this sort of "growth" within an array; when values were being read into an array, the position indicator was advanced just before installing a new value in this next available location. The differences are that, here, the additions are made one at a time, rather than in a steady sweep through the array, and the new value is no longer arriving directly from the input stream.

Of course, subsequent processing of this array will encounter one more occupied position than before, but this will cause no problem since the

```
PROCEDURE Append (VAR Table: IntArray; VAR Last: integer;
                  NewValue: integer);
   BEGIN {Append}
      IF Last = MaxSize THEN
         writeln ('Cannot add ',NewValue,' array full')
      ELSE {space exists}
         BEGIN
            Last := Last + 1;          {advance frontier}
            Table[Last] := NewValue {install new value}
         END
   END; {Append}
```

■ Figure 7.14
Appending a new value to an array.

effective size of the array is always indicated by the variable Last which has also been updated.

Deleting Elements from an Array

Values may also be deleted from an array, causing the useful portion of the array to shrink instead of grow. Deleting elements from an array is a bit more difficult than appending new values, and we will discuss two approaches to the problem. The choice between the two depends on whether the ordering of elements is important.

Deletion from an unordered array   The first approach to deletion may be used when the order of values in the array does not matter. Here, the value to be deleted is replaced by the last value in that array, and the effective length of the array is reduced by one. The code and the result are shown in Fig. 7.15, where Old identifies the array, Victim indicates the position number of the item to be deleted, and LastValue is the current number of meaningful values in the array. Even when the value to be deleted (Victim) is equal to the last value in the array (LastValue), this approach works. In that case the last value overwrites itself, and, when the frontier recedes, it is effectively forgotten.

Deletion that preserves order   The second approach is more drastic and corresponds to cutting out the deleted item with scissors and pasting together the two remaining parts. However, this technique does preserve ordering and is the recommended method of removing an item from an ordered array. This is achieved by copying each array component below the deleted position into the preceding position. Thus all the following items move up, retaining the original ordering and squeezing out the deleted value. The concept and the code to do the

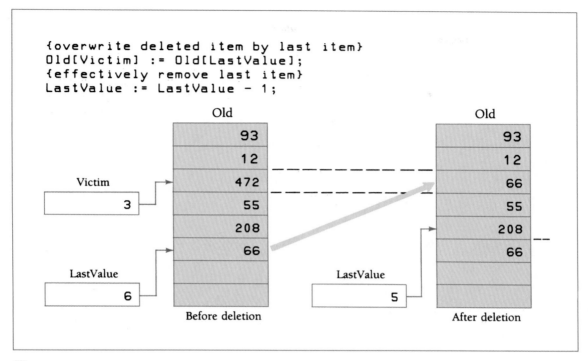

```
{overwrite deleted item by last item}
Old[Victim] := Old[LastValue];
{effectively remove last item}
LastValue := LastValue - 1;
```

■ Figure 7.15
Deletion by replacement with final value.

copying are shown in Fig. 7.16 on p. 304. Because of the considerable amount of processing involved, deletion by physical movement should be used only when the effort is justified by the need to preserve ordering.

Inserting an Item into an Ordered Array

insertion

Backwards movement to make space

When a new value is added to an *unordered* array, the most convenient place to put it is at the end (by appending). However, if the overall ordering must be preserved, the new value must be slipped into the proper position in the array, usually in the interior. This operation is known as **insertion.** The method is the reverse of deletion from an ordered array. All items that will follow the new value must first be moved down one position, so that they retain their original ordering and leave an empty space into which the new value can then be assigned. However, *the last item must be moved first, the second-to-last item next, and so on.* Until the following item is moved, there will be no place for the preceding item to go (without overwriting it). In other words, the loop to move following values out of the way must move *backwards* through the array.

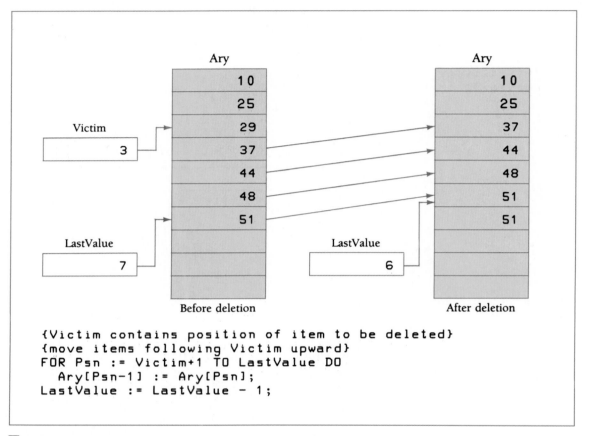

```
{Victim contains position of item to be deleted}
{move items following Victim upward}
FOR Psn := Victim+1 TO LastValue DO
   Ary[Psn-1] := Ary[Psn];
LastValue := LastValue - 1;
```

■ Figure 7.16
Deletion by physical movement of subsequent items in an ordered list.

The code to insert a new item (NewItem) at a specific location (given in the variable Position) is shown in Fig. 7.17. Note the use of DOWNTO in the FOR loop to effect the backwards movement. Also note that the effective length of the array must be incremented after insertion. Even if the new position follows all the other values (making the insertion equivalent to append), this code will work; the FOR statement never activates the code to move larger values out of the way because Position would be greater than Last in that case.

Finding the location to make insertion   In order to determine the position where the new item should be placed, we have to perform a search. But search for what? Assume that the array is in ascending order (the smallest value first and the largest last) and that the search starts at the top. The value of NewItem is presumably not yet in the array, and so we should not expect to find it. However, as soon as we encounter a value that is *larger than* NewItem, we have reached the portion of the array where only larger values reside; in other words, the sequence of larger values that should be moved out of the way. Thus the value of Position should be the *first* location where a value greater than NewItem is discovered.

Figure 7.18 contains the code for this kind of search, followed by the insertion of NewItem. Note how this code behaves in special cases. When the array is empty, Last will be 0, the search loop will be bypassed since Position > Last, and the new item will be placed in the first location. If NewItem is larger than any current values in the array, the search occurs but is unsuccessful. In this case the search will leave the value of Position one greater than Last, which results in appending the new value to the end.

One situation that could cause problems is not covered by this code. If the array is full, there is no way to insert or append any more values. Whenever there is a possibility of array growth, you should first determine whether there is indeed room for growth, as was done in the append code of Fig. 7.14.

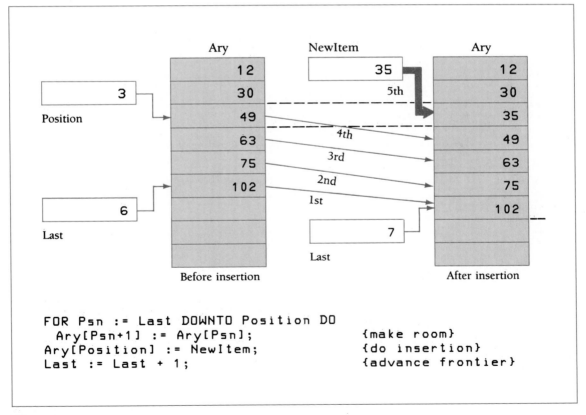

```
FOR Psn := Last DOWNTO Position DO
  Ary[Psn+1] := Ary[Psn];              {make room}
Ary[Position] := NewItem;              {do insertion}
Last := Last + 1;                      {advance frontier}
```

■ Figure 7.17
Inserting an item in an ordered array.

```
{assume NewItem contains value to be inserted
 in ordered array; search for correct Position
 to put it}

StillLooking := true;
Position := 1;
WHILE (Position <= Last) AND StillLooking DO

    IF Ary[Position] < NewItem THEN
        Position := Position + 1 {keep going}
    ELSE
        StillLooking := false;    {far enough}
    {end of search loop}

{now perform insertion at Position}
FOR Psn := Last DOWNTO Position DO
    Ary[Psn+1] := Ary[Psn];       {make room}
Ary[Position] := NewItem;         {do insertion}
Last := Last + 1;                 {advance frontier}
```

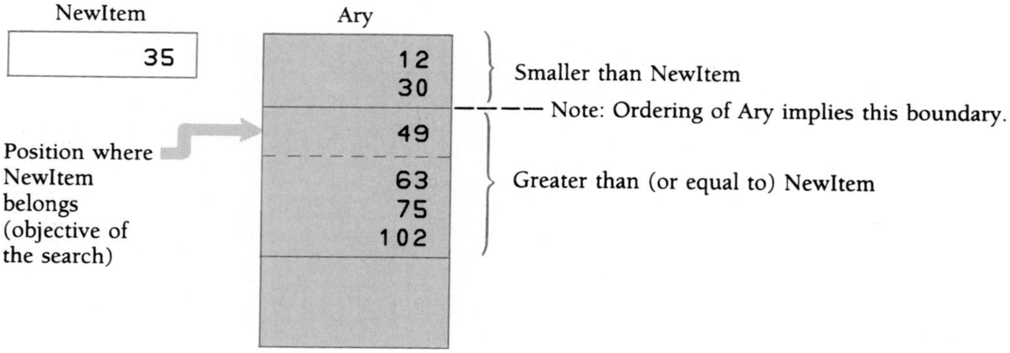

Figure 7.18
Searching for the place to insert item in ordered array.

Referencing an Array by Name Only

The major reason for declaring arrays is to provide a large number of individual locations with similar names that can be manipulated by the same code. Most of the array processing that we encounter deals with one component at a time.

With one exception (see the discussion on PACKED ARRAYs in Chapter 8), only two situations exist in which an entire array can be processed as a single entity:

1. An entire array can be passed as a parameter.
2. One entire array can be assigned all the values from another, using a single assignment statement.

We discussed passing arrays as parameters earlier in this chapter and so will focus only on the second situation here.

Assignment of entire arrays by name only

Provided A and B have identical type, the values of array B can be copied into array A by executing the single assignment statement A := B; . This assignment is equivalent to the following component-by-component assignment, assuming that A and B are of type ARRAY[1 . . MaxSize] OF ⟨some type⟩.

```
{B presumably is filled with values}
FOR K := 1 TO MaxSize DO
    A[K] := B[K];
```

7.3 Sorting

As long as data are stored in an arbitrary order inside an array, linear searching is as good as any other method for finding specific items. However, when large volumes of data are involved, plunging in at the top of the list and inspecting each item in turn can be very time-consuming—for both people and computers.

Need for ordering

What if names appeared in the telephone directory in the order that customers had their phones installed? Under such a system you would have an extremely difficult time finding anyone's number. When you search for a phone number, you rely on the names being in alphabetical order. This permits you to quickly direct your search to the correct page, column, and name.

sorting

Sorting is the process of arranging related data into some ordered sequence, and its motive is to facilitate later searching, whether by computers or people. Computerized search algorithms can take advantage of sorted data to work much more efficiently than linear searching. We describe one such algorithm later in this book.

First, however, let's look at two distinctly different sorting algorithms. One method, the *selection sort* is more natural, whereas the other, the *bubble sort* is usually more efficient. Both methods will reveal even more techniques in array manipulation. That two such entirely different approaches are both able to solve the same problem is not only interesting but also offers insight into problem-solving procedures. In fact, many other algorithms for sorting work as well as and, often, more quickly than either of these.

The Selection Sort

Suppose that someone handed you a list of numbers on a sheet of paper and asked you to sort them into ascending order. You would probably construct a new list by (1) finding the smallest number and writing it at the top of the new list; (2) finding the next smallest number and writing it in the next (second) position of the new list; and (3) continuing this process until every original number had been copied to the new list. To help keep track of which numbers you had already copied, you would probably cross out each number as you copied it and from then on would ignore it. In other words, you would instinctively execute the algorithm:

1.   for as many times as there are numbers, do:
1.1   search original list for smallest remaining value;
1.2   append that number to the end of new list;
1.3   delete that number from the original list;
2.   stop.

Since each application of Step 1 (search–append–delete) moves one more item to the new list, this sequence must be repeated as many times as there are values in the original list. (To sort into descending order, you would search for the largest remaining value each time.)

selection sorting   The general strategy is called **selection sorting,** since the basic step consists of searching remaining elements to *select* the next one for the new list. Obviously, a computer could be programmed to imitate this natural, human method of sorting. If the original values are in an array Old, a second array of the same size, NewAry, will be needed to hold the sorted values. The goal of the selection sort is illustrated in Fig. 7.19.

Sort procedure   A procedure to perform a selection sort is shown in Fig. 7.20, assuming the declaration of AccountNumbers as an array of integers is available. Since NewAry is being loaded with data, it must be variable-type. The other parameters should not change in the calling program; they should be value-type.

■ Figure 7.19
Building a new sorted array from an old unsorted array.

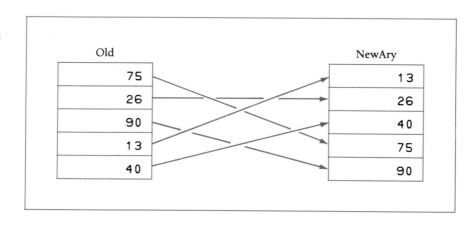

```
PROCEDURE SelectionSort (Old : AccountNumbers;
                         VAR NewAry : AccountNumbers;
                         NumItems: integer);

   { sort the first NumItems values from array Old
     into ascending order in array NewAry }

   VAR
      SizeOfOld: integer; {no. of values to be sorted}
      MinLoc:         {location of smallest value in Old}
      Times: integer; {step count =
                       location being filled in NewAry}


   FUNCTION FindMin (Ary: AccountNumbers;
                     Last: integer):integer;
   VAR
      K, MinPsn: integer;
   BEGIN {FindMin}
      MinPsn := 1;
      FOR K := 2 TO Last DO
         IF Ary[K] < Ary[MinPsn] THEN {new candidate}
            MinPsn := K;
      FindMin := MinPsn
   END; {FindMin}


BEGIN {SelectionSort}
   SizeOfOld := NumItems;
   FOR Times := 1 to NumItems DO
      BEGIN {sort}
         {find smallest remaining element in Old}
         MinLoc := FindMin (Old,SizeOfOld);

         {copy it to location 'times' in NewAry}
         NewAry[Times] := Old[MinLoc];

         {delete it from Old}
         Old[MinLoc] := Old[SizeOfOld];
         SizeOfOld := SizeOfOld - 1
      END {sort}
END; {SelectionSort}
```

■ Figure 7.20
Selection sort procedure.

The sort begins by copying the value of NumItems into the variable SizeOfOld. Because NumItems controls the number of times the find–append–delete operations are performed, its value must not be modified within the loop. Hence a different variable must be used to keep track of the continually shrinking portion of Old that is of interest to the sort.

Since the smallest item will be deleted, the search for it must determine its position in the array. Because knowing the position of an array item allows access to the value itself, we need only keep track of the *position* of the smallest value inspected so far; the function FindMin provides that. Following execution of

```
MinLoc := FindMin (Old,SizeOfOld);
```

Minloc will indicate where the smallest value resides, and Old[MinLoc] will actually reference it.

The append step is quite simple. The overall process uses the loop index variable Times to keep track of how many times the basic search–append–delete step is done. The value of this variable also indicates the next free position in NewAry, whenever it is time to perform an append. That is, the first item copied goes into position 1, the second item into position 2, and so on. The smallest value can be copied from position MinLoc of the Old array by the statement:

```
NewAry[Times] := Old[MinLoc];
```

The selection sort requires that the selected item be deleted from Old so that it will not be rediscovered by a later search. Of the two approaches described previously we use the technique appropriate for an unordered array: overwriting the deleted value by the last value and then contracting the frontier.

The Bubble Sort

Although selection sorting may conform to the natural, human approach to sorting, it is not as efficient as many other methods. One obvious drawback to the selection sort, as we have presented it, is that it requires *two* arrays of the same size. With very large arrays, sufficient space may not be available for both. (It is possible to perform the selection sort on only one array; see the Exercises.) Another problem is that selection sorting takes no advantage of any ordering that may already exist among some of the data; it resolutely performs complete searches of all array locations.

bubble sort

The **bubble sort** is an alternative algorithm that requires only one array and generally achieves its goal more quickly than the selection sort. The bubble sort will quit early if it can speedily sort the data. However, it is not the most efficient sorting method; many more efficient sorting algorithms exist, and whole books have been written on the topic. (There are also many variations of bubble sorting, but the one presented here is probably the most common.)

The bubble sort gets its name from the property of "bubbling" the largest elements in an array to the bottom. This approach involves rearranging consecutive pairs of elements into their desired order; after enough consecutive pairs have been rearranged, the whole array will be ordered. We illustrate the fundamental comparisons made by the bubble sort, with the array shown in Fig. 7.21(a).

Bubble sort strategy

Moving through an array *once* from top to bottom and inspecting every adjacent pair of locations for the possibility of an interchange is called one *pass* through the array. The array in Fig. 7.21 contains 5 numbers and therefore 4 consecutive pairs of locations (1–2, 2–3, 3–4, 4–5). Note that adjacent pairs do overlap. In general, if an array contains N elements, there are N − 1 different adjacent pairs, and therefore N − 1 comparisons and possible interchanges during *one* pass. Because the array is being sorted into ascending order, a pair of values is interchanged only if it violates this order, that is, if the first element is larger than the second. The algorithm for one pass is

1. begin with first pair of elements;
2. for each consecutive pair of elements do:
2.1   if current pair is out of order then
            interchange current pair;
2.2   move to the next pair of elements;

When to stop

Figure 7.21(a) shows that four comparisons are made, resulting in two interchanges. Although one pass through the array yields a more ordered arrangement, it is evidently not enough. How many passes will be needed? The simple answer is to keep making passes until the array is sorted. In our example two passes were needed to sort the array, followed by a third to confirm that the array was, in fact, sorted.

Recognizing order

The array will be in order if, on any pass, no interchanges are performed. This condition is easy to detect by setting a flag to true before each pass and then changing it to false if any interchange is made during the pass. Thus we will have to make another pass whenever the flag is false at the end of the preceding pass, but may quit as soon as one pass leaves the flag as true. Incidentally, in the worst case (where the original array is in reverse order) the bubble sort will require the maximum of N − 1 passes to sort an array of N elements.

Retracting the frontier

A minor modification provides a slightly more efficient implementation of the bubble sort. In Fig. 7.21(a), the largest element is moved to its proper position (the last position) in the array. This element will never move again and may be removed from further consideration on future passes. The same thing happens to the second largest item on pass two (Fig. 7.21b). In general then, we should reduce the effective length of the array by one after each pass, to avoid making comparisons involving elements that cannot possibly change locations. This is like retracting the frontier in the selection sort.

The algorithm, with this refinement, and the resulting procedure are shown in Fig. 7.22. Because the procedure will do the bubble sort in the

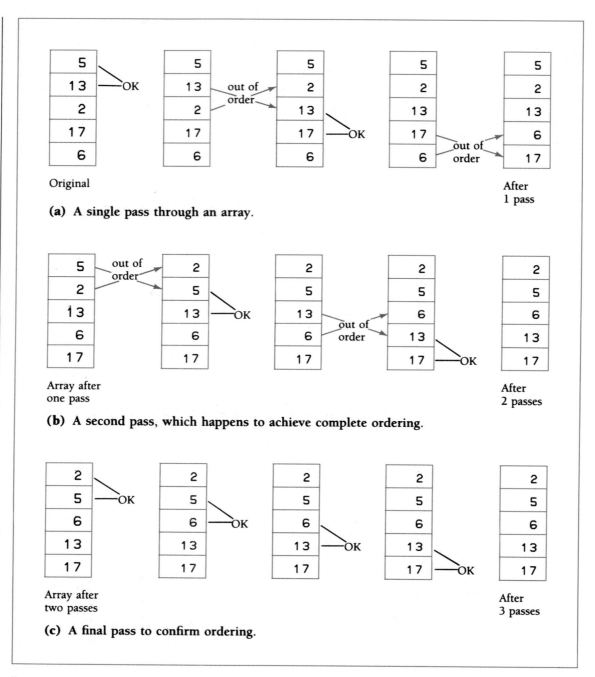

(a) A single pass through an array.

(b) A second pass, which happens to achieve complete ordering.

(c) A final pass to confirm ordering.

■ Figure 7.21
Operation of the bubble sort.

1.   repeat until Sorted:
1.1   Sorted := true; {assume array is sorted}
1.2   begin with first pair of elements;
1.3   do N − 1 times: {once for each consecutive pair}
1.3.1   if current pair is out of order then
1.3.1.1   interchange this pair;
1.3.1.2   Sorted := false; {indicate interchange}
1.3.2   move to next pair;
1.4   N := N − 1; {reduce effective length of array}
2.   stop.

(a) Algorithm.

```
PROCEDURE BubbleSort (VAR Ary: AccountNumbers; N: integer);

    {Sort array Ary into ascending order}

    VAR
        Sorted: boolean; {true when array is sorted}
        K, Temp: integer;
        NumItems: integer;

    BEGIN {BubbleSort}
        NumItems := N;
        REPEAT
            Sorted := true; {assume sorted}
            FOR K := 1 TO NumItems-1 DO
                BEGIN {one pass}
                    IF Ary[K] > Ary[K+1] THEN
                        BEGIN {interchange}
                            Temp := Ary[K];
                            Ary[K] := Ary[K+1];
                            Ary[K+1] := Temp;
                            Sorted := false
                        END {interchange}
                END; {one pass}
            NumItems ;= NumItems - 1
        UNTIL Sorted
    END;{BubbleSort}
```

(b) Procedure.

■ Figure 7.22
Bubble sort of an array with N elements.

same array, the array must be passed as a variable parameter. The three statements required to interchange two values perform exactly the same logic as the Swap operation in Section 4.4. Of course, in the present context the references are array identifiers.

7.4 Merging Two Ordered Arrays

The merge process

In data processing we are frequently faced with the problem of producing one large sorted list by blending two sorted arrays. We might, for example, be given an alphabetical list of women students and a similar list of men students from which we are to construct an alphabetical list of all students. Such a list can be produced by *merging* the two original lists.

Observe how we might merge the following lists to print a report in alphabetical order:

Anne
Moira
Wilma

David
Jack
Mike
Tom

We begin by comparing the first names on each list, Anne with David. Since Anne is smaller (precedes David), we print it.

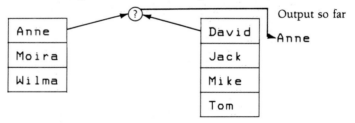

Compare two names and select one

The name printed was a woman's, so we proceed by comparing the next woman's name with the same man's name used in the previous comparison. Thus we compare Moira with David and print David.

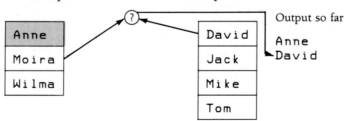

Now compare the next man's name, Jack, with Moira and print Jack.

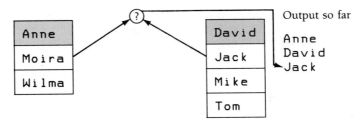

Output so far

Anne
David
Jack

Eventually we will have processed all the names from one of the lists.

Anne		David
Moira		Jack
Wilma		Mike
		Tom

Output so far

Anne
David
Jack
Mike
Moira
Tom

When one list is exhausted, append the other

Since both lists were originally in alphabetical order, we need to print only the names remaining on the unexhausted list, and the result will still be in alphabetical order. The same approach could be used to place the selected names in a third list rather than printing them.

two-way merge

This process is known as a **two-way merge.** The following algorithm produces a sorted array C from two other sorted arrays A (of length N) and B (of length M). Assume that both A and B are in ascending order, so that the resulting array C will be ascending as well.

1. begin at position 1 in both A and B;
2. while elements remain in *both* arrays, A and B, do:
2.1 consider the first "unselected" items from A and B;
2.2 choose the smaller and append it to C;

3. if B is "empty" then
    copy remaining elements from A to C;
4. otherwise {A is "empty"}
    copy remaining elements from B to C;

A more detailed algorithm appears in Fig. 7.23.

Since we copy an element from only one array on any iteration of step 2, we must increase the subscript of that array to avoid reusing the same element. The index for the "other" original array must not be touched because it indicates an element that is still a candidate for selection. Further, since we copy an element to array C on *every* iteration through step 2, we must increase the index for array C by 1 each time.

■ Figure 7.23
Pseudocode for two-
way merge of ordered
arrays.

1. set APsn, BPsn and CSlot to 1;

2. while (APsn $\leq$ N) and (BPsn $\leq$ M) do: {elements in both arrays}

2.1   if A[APsn] $\leq$ B[BPsn] then   {copy item from A}
2.1.1   C[CSlot] := A[APsn];
2.1.2   APsn := APsn + 1;

2.2   else   {copy item from B}
2.2.1   C[CSlot] := B[BPsn];
2.2.2   BPsn := BPsn + 1;

2.3   CSlot := CSlot + 1;   {advance through C}

3. while APsn $\leq$ N do: {copy remaining values from A}
3.1   C[CSlot] := A[APsn];
3.2   APsn := APsn + 1;
3.3   CSlot := CSlot + 1;

4. while BPsn $\leq$ M do: {copy remaining values from B}
4.1   C[CSlot] := B[BPsn];
4.2   BPsn := BPsn + 1;
4.3   CSlot := CSlot + 1;

5. stop.

On exit from step 2, one of the subscripts BPsn or APsn will have exceeded the bounds of its corresponding array. It is impossible for both to have done so because only one of them is incremented at a time. The other subscript will indicate the next element to be copied into the new, merged array. Hence only one of steps 3 and 4 of the algorithm in Fig. 7.23 will ever be executed. Clearly the resulting array C must contain at least N + M components because all the values from A and B are being copied to C.

The two-way merge is central to many problems in data processing and shows up in many forms as the fundamental approach to a solution. Note that it is applicable only to problems dealing with *sorted* arrays.

Variations on basic merge

A minor change to the pseudocode in Fig. 7.23 will enable it to deal with arrays in descending order. In our algorithm if the same value appears in both arrays, it will appear twice in the new, merged array. The decision on how to handle such cases depends on the application in which the problem arises. Other variations on the merge do not copy all N + M original values to the third array. Whenever a pair of duplicates is discovered during the merge, only one of the two is transferred to the new array; the other is simply bypassed and ignored. If the two original arrays are considered sets of values, this operation is equivalent to the "set union" operation.

Another alternative is to bypass any value that does *not* appear in *both* arrays. In other words, only duplicates are of interest, and only one member of each duplicate pair is copied to the new array. The result is the selection of only those values common to both of the original arrays. In terms of sets, this is equivalent to the "set intersection" operation.

7.5 Use of Arrays—Text Processing: Part 1

Getting used to text algorithms

Many of us spend much of our time reading, writing, and manipulating character data. We are so adept at text handling that we take it for granted. When computers are used to manipulate text, however, their operations occur at a much more primitive level and under the direction of a completely specified algorithm. When writing text processing programs, you might find it difficult at first to slow down and adjust to such a primitive level. Yet once you appreciate how machines handle text, the actual text processing algorithms become straightforward.

First of all, the objects of interest are usually *sequences* of characters: words, sentences, paragraphs, reports, and the like. Individual characters have little meaning except in combination with other characters. However, the most appropriate basic data type in Pascal, the char type, is capable of holding and handling only isolated, individual characters. Although we have presented many programs that read and display sequences of characters, none has needed more than a few characters at a time in main memory.

Strings and Substrings as Data

Need to store sequences

Clearly there are occasions for retaining large amounts of character data in memory—not just as an unstructured heap of characters, but as a sequence with a significant relative arrangement. This is required whenever text must be scrutinized, broken apart, reassembled, or otherwise modified in nontrivial ways. Perhaps the most familiar example is the text editor, which, after all, is just a program that can perform all sorts of transformations on sequences of characters, often called character strings.

You are already familiar with character string constants, but, as the name implies, they cannot be modified or manipulated. What we need is a flexible structure for holding arbitrary character sequences and allowing interior inspection, modification, and growth.

Character string "variable"

Standard Pascal does not include a character string variable as such. However, the one-dimensional array is the ideal structure for assembling a large number of individual character variables into a linear sequence. The basic operations of Pascal remain at the level of individual characters, and operations that seem elementary to us, such as finding the next "word" in the sequence, have to be carried out by algorithms. But arrays provide the storage structures on which these algorithms will work.

String length   Character strings have unpredictable and variable lengths. To represent a variable-length string in an array with its fixed number of components, we have to record the number of characters actually stored in the array, that is, the number of array components occupied by the string. The fundamental data structure is therefore an array of char variables for holding the actual string, *together with* an integer variable to indicate its length, as shown in Fig. 7.24(a). It is usually more convenient to depict an array as horizontal when it holds a string of characters; conventionally, the characters begin from the left at location 1.

The length is no more than the frontier that confines processing to the portion of the array containing data of interest. Input of a string consists of the familiar one-at-a-time transfer of characters from the input stream to successive array components. The number of characters read is recorded as the string length. Output may be accomplished by writing characters from successive components until the frontier is reached.

■ Figure 7.24
Representations of strings and substrings.

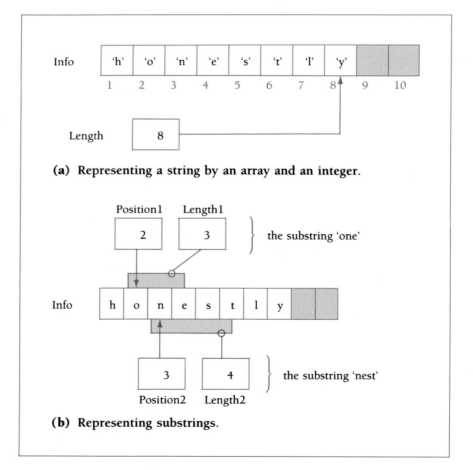

(a) Representing a string by an array and an integer.

(b) Representing substrings.

String operations   Typical operations on character strings are probably familiar to you from using the text editor. These include making a copy, appending more characters to an existing string, and locating some piece of the string to be deleted or replaced by another sequence of characters.

It is often necessary to describe positions within strings and fragments of strings. Any piece of a string consisting of consecutive characters is known

substring   as a **substring.** A substring can be completely specified by

1.   the *string* to which it belongs (the array identifier);
2.   the *position* where its first character occurs; and
3.   its *length* (the number of constituent characters).

Figure 7.24(b) shows how to depict two overlapping substrings of the same parent string. The original string can also be described as a substring starting at position 1 and having the same length as the original.

Manipulating Substrings

Copying   Much string processing involves moving substrings around to construct new strings from the pieces. One of the basic operations is to copy any substring from a *source* string to any position within a *destination* string. The code for a string copy procedure is shown in Fig. 7.25(a), along with a sketch of its operation in Fig. 7.25(b).

As usual, the primitive operations involve individual characters, in this case moving a character from one array to the other. This is repeated for each character that must be copied. As the transfers proceed, each array is traversed in parallel.

The hardest part about writing string processing algorithms is deciding exactly where to start and stop the traversal of the character arrays. In the case of Copy, the number of characters moved from the Source array is given by the parameter SourceLength. The first character is taken from position SourcePsn, and the last from position

SourcePsn + SourceLength − 1

You should *always* verify such formulas by referring to a diagram like the one shown in Fig. 7.25(b). The risks of miscalculating index ranges are too high to take chances.

The starting position for the destination index is given by the parameter DestinPsn. Because the source and destination arrays are traversed in tandem, the final value for the destination index does not need to be computed. The destination index is simply incremented each time through the copy loop, ensuring that both indices progress through their respective arrays at the same rate.

Although the total length of the destination string may change, Copy does not update this length. In addition, the procedure shown in Fig. 7.25 does not check that its parameters are reasonable. However, we assume that

```
PROCEDURE Copy (Source :CharArray; SourcePsn,
               SourceLength :integer;
               VAR Destin :CharArray;
               DestinPsn :integer);

  {copy substring from Source to designated position in
  Destination; length of Destin is NOT adjusted by Copy}

   VAR
      SourceIndex,
      DestinIndex : integer;

   BEGIN {Copy}
      DestinIndex := DestinPsn;
      FOR SourceIndex := SourcePsn TO
         (SourcePsn+SourceLength-1) DO
         BEGIN
            Destin[DestinIndex] := Source[SourceIndex];
            DestinIndex := DestinIndex + 1
         END {copy loop}
   END; {Copy procedure}
```

(a) Procedure.

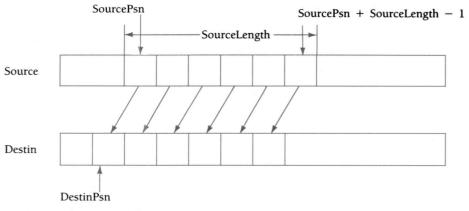

(b) Visual representation.

■ Figure 7.25
The string copy procedure.

Copy will be called only by other procedures where any necessary updating and verification will be done.

Appending   The Append procedure in Fig. 7.26 shows how copy might be used. Its task is to attach a new (Source) substring to the end of an existing (Destin) string. Append merely calls Copy to perform the actual transfer of characters. However, it first makes sure the resulting string length will not exceed the

```
PROCEDURE Append (Source :CharArray;
                  SourceLength :integer;
                  VAR Destin :CharArray;
                  VAR DestinLength :integer );

   {Using the Copy Procedure, attach the string in
    Source onto the END of string Destin;
    DestinLength is updated; checks that resulting length
    will not exceed allowed length of Destin}

   BEGIN
      IF (SourceLength + DestinLength) <= MaxLength THEN
         BEGIN
            Copy (Source,1,SourceLength,Destin,DestinLength+1);
            DestinLength := DestinLength + SourceLength
         END
      ELSE
         writeln('Strings too long; no append occurs')
   END; {Append procedure}
```

(a) Procedure

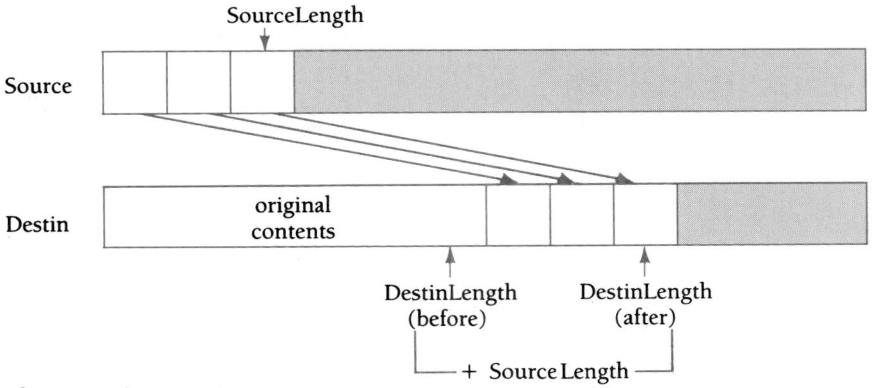

(b) Visual representation.

■ Figure 7.26
The string append procedure.

maximum permitted, and at the end updates the Destin string length to reflect the change.

concatenation

The operation of appending or juxtaposing two strings into one is basic to string processing and is called **concatenation.** You use it to assemble letters into words, which are themselves concatenated to form sentences.

Substring Matching and Replacement

Another important kind of operation is to *find* or *locate* a particular target string within a subject string. The objective is to determine whether the target string occurs within the subject string and, if so, to determine its starting position. This kind of searching might be the prelude to another operation, such as replacement.

Searching for a substring

The basic idea in locating a target string is to compare the target string with various substrings having the same length within the subject string. The target string can be visualized as a template that moves steadily from left to right across the subject string until either a perfect match is found or the template spills over the end of the subject string. This overshoot will occur when the template moves beyond position

SubjectLength − TargetLength + 1

This is illustrated in Fig. 7.27(a) and encoded in Fig. 7.27(b).

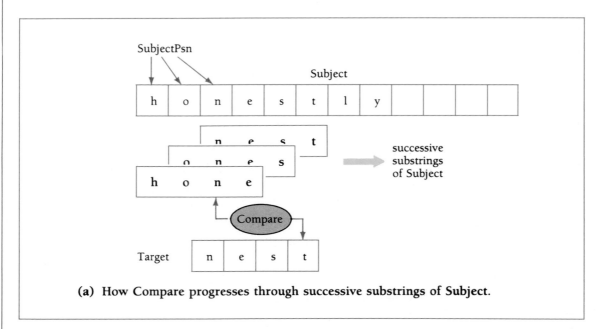

(a) How Compare progresses through successive substrings of Subject.

■ Figure 7.27
Finding a substring within the string subject.

**Comparing
substrings for
identity**
While the motion of this template through the Subject string is like a sequential search, the question asked at each position is much more involved. The task of finding whether a particular substring of Subject matches the Target requires a character-by-character comparison of both. Again, tandem movement through two arrays is involved. This is accomplished by the

```
FUNCTION Compare (Subject :CharArray;
                  SubjectLength :integer;
                  Target :CharArray;
                  TargetLength :integer ):integer;

   {determine the position within Subject string where
    the first instance of Target substring is located;
    if Target not found within Subject,
    return a value of 0}

   VAR
      SubjectPsn :integer;
      Found :boolean;
      ScanLimit :integer;

   BEGIN
      SubjectPsn := 1;
      Found := false;
      ScanLimit := SubjectLength - TargetLength + 1;

      WHILE (NOT Found) AND (SubjectPsn <= ScanLimit) DO
         BEGIN
            Found := Match(Subject,SubjectPsn,Target,
                           TargetLength);
            IF NOT Found THEN {advance through Subject}
               SubjectPsn := SubjectPsn + 1
         END; {search}

      IF Found THEN {announce where substring starts}
         Compare := SubjectPsn
      ELSE
         Compare := 0

   END; {Compare}
```

(b) Finding the position of a substring within a string.

■ Figure 7.27
(Continued)

```
FUNCTION Match (Subject :CharArray;
               SubjectPsn :integer;
               Target :CharArray;
               TargetLength :integer): boolean;

   {perform a detailed, char-by-char comparison to
    determine whether the Target string occurs as a
    substring of Subject, beginning at SubjectPsn}

   VAR
      SubjectIndex,
      TargetIndex :integer;
      Agreement :boolean;

BEGIN
      Agreement := true; {assume match}
      SubjectIndex := SubjectPsn;
      TargetIndex := 1;

      WHILE Agreement AND (TargetIndex <= TargetLength) DO
         IF Subject[SubjectIndex] = Target[TargetIndex] THEN
            BEGIN {advance through both strings}
               TargetIndex := TargetIndex + 1;
               SubjectIndex := SubjectIndex + 1
            END
         ELSE {mismatch}
            Agreement := false;
         {end of match-up loop}

      Match := Agreement
END; {Match}
```

(c) Character-by-character comparison of two strings.

■ Figure 7.27
(Continued)

function Match, shown in Fig. 7.27(c). Match begins by assuming agreement between the two strings and stops as soon as disagreement is found or the ends of both strings are found. (Remember: The two strings inspected by Match have equal length.)

In contrast to locating a specific target string, a more general operation, called pattern matching, attempts to find any substring meeting certain requirements, such as anything beginning with "(" and ending with ")". More general pattern matching employs more sophisticated versions of the Match function.

Substring replacement

Let's consider a more involved example: the problem of replacing one substring by another, as sketched in Fig. 7.28(a). The substring to be removed,

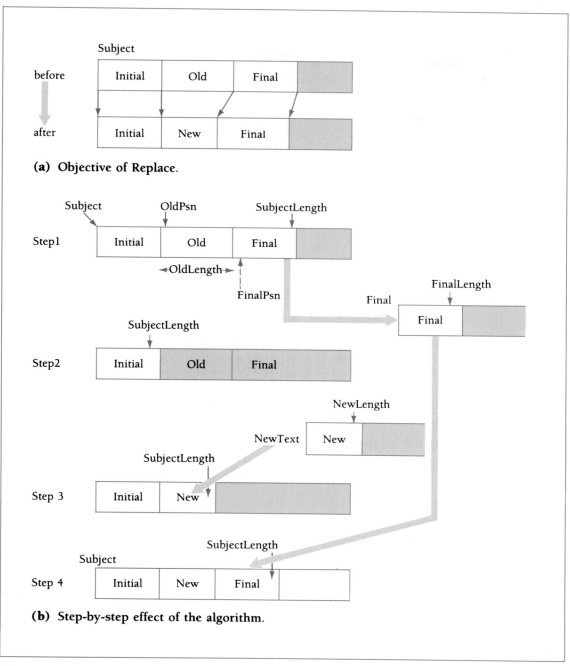

(a) Objective of Replace.

(b) Step-by-step effect of the algorithm.

■ Figure 7.28
Replacing one substring by another.

```
PROCEDURE Replace (VAR Subject :CharArray;
                       VAR SubjectLength : integer;
                       OldPsn, OldLength : integer;
                       NewText : CharArray;
                       NewLength : integer );

   {the Old substring within Subject is removed and
   replaced by the NewText string; update
   SubjectLength if Old and New have different lengths;
   no action if final length exceeds global MaxLength}

   VAR
       Final :CharArray; {hold final section of Subject}
       FinalPsn, FinalLength :integer;

   BEGIN
       IF (SubjectLength - OldLength + NewLength) >
           MaxLength THEN
           writeln('no replacement; strings too long')
       ELSE
           BEGIN
               {save copy of Final section of Subject}
               FinalPsn := OldPsn + OldLength;
               FinalLength := SubjectLength - FinalPsn + 1;
               Copy (Subject,FinalPsn,FinalLength,Final,1);

               {delete all but Initial section of Subject}
               SubjectLength := OldPsn - 1;

               {now append New and Final sections to Subject}
               Append (NewText,NewLength,Subject,SubjectLength);
               Append (Final,FinalLength,Subject,SubjectLength)
           END
   END; {Replace}
```

(c) Corresponding code.

Figure 7.28
(Continued)

Old, was presumably discovered by a search (using a function such as Match) or described directly by the user. We do not need to know what is in the Old substring; its contents are completely specified by its starting position and length. Its replacement has already been stored in another array, NewText. The Subject string conceptually consists of three nonoverlapping parts: (1) an Initial part, which does not change or move; (2) the Old part, which is to be replaced; and (3) a Final part, which may have to be moved to accommodate the new substring. When the replacement has taken place, Subject will then contain Initial, NewText, and Final—in that order.

Devising an algorithm

One way to approach this problem is to imagine the various strings on strips of paper. By cutting and moving the strips, the correct pieces can be assembled into the desired string. One possible algorithm that emerges is

1.   make a *copy* of the Final part to keep for later use;
2.   *delete* all but the Initial part of Subject string;
3.   *append* the substring NewText to the Initial part;
4.   *append* the copy of the Final part after this new part.

You can best see its action in Fig. 7.28(b). The corresponding code is shown in Fig. 7.28(c). Step 1 merely calls the Copy procedure after the starting position and length of the Final portion have been calculated. Having saved a copy of Final elsewhere, we deleted the Old and Final sections of Subject. Note that this is done by merely reducing the length of Subject to encompass only its Initial portion. The original characters are all still physically present in the array but, being beyond the new frontier, have been effectively removed. When the strings NewText and Final are appended, they will be attached at the correct positions, and the length of Subject will grow by the correct amount. In the process of appending, some (or all) of the *original* array Subject is overwritten.

Insertion and deletion

Insertion of additional characters into the interior of a string and deletion of a substring without replacement are simple adaptations of the preceding algorithm and, like replacement, are built on the notion of copying substrings.

7.6 Review of Rules

A.   One-dimensional arrays may be declared as

VAR ⟨identifier⟩ : ARRAY [⟨first⟩ . . ⟨last⟩] OF ⟨type⟩

where ⟨first⟩ and ⟨last⟩ are ordinal *constants* defining the *bounds* of the array, and ⟨last⟩ >= ⟨first⟩. Such an array has ord(⟨last⟩) − ord(⟨first⟩) + 1 storage locations or *components* associated with it. If an array is to be passed as a parameter, its type identifier must be declared, for example;

```
TYPE
   ⟨bound-type⟩ = ⟨first⟩ . . ⟨last⟩;
   ⟨array-type⟩ = ARRAY [⟨bound-type⟩] OF ⟨type⟩;
VAR
   ⟨identifier⟩ : ⟨array-type⟩;
```

B.   To *refer* to an individual array component, use

⟨array name⟩[⟨index⟩]

where ⟨index⟩ is an expression whose value lies within the bounds of the array. Such a reference may be used in any context where an ordinary variable identifier is allowed.

C. Much array processing involves the notion of sequentially moving through the array element by element. This movement may be controlled by structures such as

```
FOR Psn := First TO Last DO
   BEGIN
      .
      .    ┌────────────────────────────────┐
      .    │ process value at position Psn  │
           └────────────────────────────────┘
   END
```

Here, First and Last need not denote the physical bounds of the array but may represent any portion of the array.

D. An array may be a parameter to a subprogram and may be either value-type or variable-type. The most elementary form of array parameter declaration is

⟨identifier⟩ : ⟨array-type identifier⟩

Subprograms employing such parameter declarations may only accept as actual parameters arrays with precisely these bounds. If the parameter is a variable type, then every component of the array may be modified by the subprogram.

KEY TERMS

appending	insertion
array	linear search
array bounds	one-dimensional array
array components	selection sorting
array declaration	sorting
bubble sort	subscripts
concatenation	substring
index	two-way merge
indexed variables	updating

EXERCISES

7.1 Rewrite the following declaration in a form that will allow the array A to be passed as a parameter to a subprogram.

```
VAR
   A: ARRAY ['a'..'z'] OF integer;
```

7.2 Identify the errors, if any, in the following code.
(a) `VAR A: ARRAY [-10..10] OF ['a'..'z'];`

(b) `TYPE Small = 'a'..'n';`
   `VAR A: ARRAY [Small] OF Small;`
(c) `TYPE Ary: ARRAY [1..20] OF real;`
   `VAR A: Ary;`

7.3 A palindrome is any sequence of characters that reads the same from left to right as it does from right to left. When this definition is applied to integers, a palindrome is an integer such as 25652, 686, or 44. To do this exercise, display all the integers between 1 and n that are palindromes and also perfect squares (see Exercise 3.6).

   We suggest that you begin by generating squares and then test them to see if they are also palindromes. Palindrome testing can be done most easily by decomposing the square into its component digits and storing these digits in the elements of a one-dimensional array.

7.4 Devise a program to test whether a character string contained on a single line is a palindrome. To avoid problems with uppercase and lowercase, you may enter all characters in lowercase; for example, "able was i ere i saw elba." Note that blanks count.

7.5 As you saw in Exercise 6.5, the Fibonacci sequence begins with the numbers 0 and 1 and generates each new term by summing the two previous terms. As you proceed in the sequence, you will quickly exceed the value of maxint. This problem can be overcome by decomposing each number into its component digits and storing one digit in each element of a one-dimensional array. These arrays can be added, element by element, ensuring that each element has only one digit in it. Write a Pascal program to generate all the numbers in the Fibonacci sequence until you reach the first number with 100 digits in it.

7.6 Whenever extremely large numbers must be processed, the strategy of storing individual digits as array components can be used (see Exercise 7.5). Of course, this requires your program to carry out the processing digit by digit. Use this approach to compute and display the square of maxint.

7.7 You have already learned how to compute the mean of a set of numeric values. Another common statistical measure is the standard deviation. The sample standard deviation s is defined as

$$s = \sqrt{\frac{1}{n-1}\sum_{i=1}^{n}(x_i - \bar{x})^2}, \quad n > 1$$

where $\bar{x}$ is the mean of the sample. Write two function subprograms to compute the mean and sample standard deviation of an array of integers and return real values as their results.

7.8 Modify the selection sort program in the text so that the sorting is done in place, that is, using only one array. The general idea is that when an item is "removed" from the original array, the logical array contracts by one component, leaving one more component free at the other end of the physical array. Since the new ordered array grows at the same rate, it can be developed in the space at the end of the same physical array.

7.9 Another familiar sorting method, called the insertion sort, is used when placing new folders in an ordered filing cabinet or ordering playing cards in your hand. Two arrays are used, but this time the action centers on the new ordered array instead of the original. Items are removed from the original array in their order of appearance. Each time another item is removed, the second array is searched for the position where this new item should be inserted among the data that have already been ordered. The values beyond this position (that is, larger than the one being inserted) are moved down one position to make room for the new value. Finally the new value is copied into this just-vacated position.

(a) Write a program to sort up to 50 integers using the insertion sort.

(b) Do this sort using only one array, as in Exercise 7.8.

7.10 You now have three sorting methods. One criterion for selecting a method is the "speed" with which it operates. In this exercise, you are to stage a contest to determine which method is fastest, or at least to identify conditions that seem to favor certain methods. Begin by implementing at least two of the three sorting methods—selection, bubble, and insertion sort—applying them to the same (numeric 100-element) array types. Then execute each sort program using the same data in each case. The criterion for speed can be the number of times two items are compared plus the number of executed assignment statements. (Do not count the additional statements required to keep track of these counts.) Besides trying different unordered data, try using data that are already ordered.

7.11 One of the measures used by cryptographers in deciphering coded messages is the frequency with which different characters appear in a string of encoded text. If we assume that the difference between uppercase and lowercase letters is of no interest and that punctuation is to be ignored, an array suitable for use in such counting might be

```
CharCount: ARRAY ['a'..'z'] OF integer;
```

(a) Write a Pascal program to read a string of text and count the frequency of occurrence of each alphabetic character. Then print the characters and their frequency in alphabetic order.

(b) Next print the same information in descending order of frequency.

7.12 This exercise integrates the use of arrays into a command interpreter. The program will offer the user a menu of the following choices.

1. Enter a set of grades.
2. Display the grades one per line.
3. Sort the grades in ascending order.
4. Compute and display the average grade.
5. Compute and display the standard deviation.
6. Exit.

The program will use five subprograms: one to display the menu, one to display the grades, one to sort the array in ascending order, one to compute the average, and one to compute the standard deviation (see Exercise 7.7). Do not attempt to execute choices 2–5 unless the user has entered at least one grade into the array. You may assume that no more than 50 grades will be entered and that they will be in the range 0–100 inclusive. Display the mean and standard deviation to two decimal places.

7.13 When data are stored in order inside an array, you can exploit this ordering to improve the performance of sequential searching. One such strategy is called an estimated entry search. It begins by searching at a spot close to where the desired value is likely to reside. In other words, an educated guess determines the starting position. If the value found there is too small, a sequential search proceeds from that point in the forward direction. If the first value found is too large, the search proceeds in the reverse direction. Let Min and Max represent the smallest and largest values currently stored in the array. If the values are evenly (uniformly) distributed along the array, the relative distance into the occupied portion of the array where Target resides should be approximately (Target − Min)/(Max − Min). Implement the estimated entry search as a function with three parameters: the array to be searched, the number of values it contains, and the desired value. The function returns the position containing the desired value or 0 to signal failure. Test this procedure by entering 30 integers in ascending order into an array and asking for five of their locations.

7.14 Now that you have two search techniques suitable for searching an ordered array, you can stage a contest between them, as we did for sort algorithms in Exercise 7.10. Implement both the sequential and estimated entry searches using the same (numeric 50-element) array type. Use the same data for each program, ask for the locations of at least 10 different values, and keep track of the number of executed comparisons and executed assignment statements in each trial. Try some values near each extreme, as well as some near the middle and at least one that is not present in the array.

7.15 Consider a system to keep track of the vehicles in a fleet of taxicabs. Each cab is known by its ID number. Two properties are of interest: whether the cab is currently in service; and whether the cab currently needs repairs. Two arrays of ID numbers correspond to these two properties. If a cab is on the road, its ID number will appear in one array; if it needs service, it will appear in the other. (It is possible for a cab to appear in both arrays, implying that it needs service but is in operation anyway.) The user will maintain and query these arrays through the following commands and operands, where Array is either 1 (in service) or 2 (needing repair).

a (add)	IDNumber	Array	{specific array}
r (remove)	IDNumber	Array	{specific array}
s (search)	IDNumber	Array	{specific array}
f (find)	IDNumber		{in either array}
d (display)	Array		{entire array}

Write a program to maintain the arrays by implementing each of these commands with a subprogram.

7.16 Modify the program of Exercise 7.15 to maintain both arrays in order at all times. Besides producing a more readable display in response to the d command, this approach also permits the arrays to be merged in various ways. Two new commands use variations of merging to do their work:

b (both)   and   e (either)

These commands cause a display of possibly several ID numbers without showing any number more than once. The b command displays all the cabs that are both on the road and need repairs. The e command displays all the cabs that require monitoring because they are either on the road, need repairs, or both.

7.17 Write a function to accept two character strings that are stored in (unpacked) arrays of equal, known length. Both strings are followed by enough blanks to fill their respective arrays. The function is boolean-valued and returns a true value if the first string precedes (is less than) the second, according to alphabetic ordering. The comparison must be done character by character. Corresponding characters in the two arrays are compared until a mismatch occurs or the strings end. If a mismatch occurs, the first character position that disagrees determines the ordering.

7.18 Once upon a time one of the most popular children's toys was a secret decoding ring. The ring consisted of two concentric circles, each imprinted with the 26 letters (uppercase) of the alphabet. The outer ring was fixed, but the inner ring could be rotated within the outer one. The idea was that we could encode secret messages and send them to a friend; conversely, we could decode secret messages received from the friend. We would first write the message in English. Then we would rotate the inner ring (corresponding to English) to get a transformation for use in encoding the message. For example, if the inner ring were rotated so that its letter 'A' was opposite 'X' on the outer ring, we would encode the message by replacing every A with X, B with Y, C with Z, D with A, and so on. Blanks remain in their original positions. If your friend knew how the rings were aligned, he or she could decode the message by using the same type of secret decoding ring.

(a) Write a program that will generate an array of uppercase alphabetic characters, indexed by uppercase alphabetic characters, equivalent to the decoding ring. The first input to this program should be the letter with which 'A' should be encoded. For example, if 'G' were given as the first input, then 'A' in the original message would become 'G', 'B' would become 'H', and so on. After generating the "encoding" array from this first input, enter an encoded message, and output the secret message.

(b) Extend this program to help the recipient of your secret message with the decoding. In order to recover the original message, the recipient can search the original array for each character in the secret message. However, the decoding process is faster when the recipient can merely index another array by characters from the secret message to find the original equivalent. First, generate this "decoding" array from the data contained in the original "encoding" array. Then enter the secret message in order to recover the original.

(c) The following message was received.

GHCBSG OBR QZOM BCH AIR OBR VOM KWZZ ZOGH
TCF SJSF OBR O ROM

Unfortunately, the secret decoding rings are gone and so is the knowledge of which decoder-ring setting was used to produce this message. Write a program to help you decipher this message.

(d) The encoding/decoding scheme can be more complex than a simple rotation of the alphabet, that is, some fixed displacement through the alphabet. Any permutation of the alphabet could be entered into the original encoding array. Rewrite parts (a) and (b) to allow any arrangement of 26 uppercase letters to be entered from the terminal and stored in the first array. Make sure that every letter is entered and that no letter is entered more than once. Construct the second array from the first and encode and decode some messages.

8

Packed and Multidimensional Arrays

PACKED ARRAY

In Chapter 7 we focused on the algorithms and Pascal language features associated with one-dimensional arrays. Except when an entire array was copied or passed as a parameter, only component-by-component operations were permitted. However, some operations apply more appropriately to an array as a whole. If we declare an array in a special way (as a **PACKED ARRAY**), Pascal permits the entire array to be used in certain ways as if the array were a simple object. This is particularly useful with character strings, where a packed array can represent an entire word or name, allowing the processing program to deal at the level of words rather than characters. The first section of this chapter examines packed arrays, continuing the discussion of character strings begun in Chapter 7.

We devote most of this chapter, however, to arrays having components that are not simple variables but rather are themselves arrays. A quick look back at the definition of an array shows us that this extension is hardly a quantum leap in concept; an array is simply a linear sequence of objects having the same type, with no restriction placed on the type of object. We can therefore have arrays of arrays.

When several linear arrays are arranged in an array, the resulting structure resembles a two-dimensional grid. These so-called two-dimensional arrays can be used to represent tabular, pictorial, and other kinds of two-dimensional data. Although the algorithms for multidimensional arrays are a bit more complex than those encountered earlier, they are fundamentally the same. When dealing with arrays inside arrays, the added level of complexity is similar to that associated with loops inside loops. We are merely adding another level to the hierarchy of data objects.

8.1 Packed Arrays and Character Strings—Text Processing: Part 2

When a structured data type such as an array is defined, its constituent objects are often physically stored so as to facilitate access by the machine to individual components. As a result, the amount of main memory dedicated to the entire structured type may be much more than the sum of the space required by each of its components. In order to store these components in less memory space, we can declare structured data types as PACKED; for example,

VAR Vector : PACKED ARRAY [1 . . 12] OF boolean;

The actual effect on storage depends on the implementation. On some systems the reduction may be from 12 to 2 bytes in this example, whereas on others there may be no net change. One possible penalty for packing may be that more time is required to access individual components. Since this is undesirable in applications dealing primarily with separate components (as many applications do), packing is seldom used to conserve space unless memory space is at a premium.

Need for packed structure

However, many applications tend to access an entire structured type as a single entity and may benefit from the structure being packed or even require this condition. The most important instance of this occurs when we deal with strings of characters (that is, text). Many applications focus on coherent sequences of characters, such as words or sentences. If words are the basic units of information, having access to individual letters may not be too important, but it may be important to have a structure allowing treatment of entire words as entities. Packed arrays of characters provide access to both individual characters and entire strings.

Declaring a structure as packed always turns it into a new data type; a packed array is incompatible with every unpacked array. Even when the number and type of constituent components are the same, if one array is packed and the other is not, neither array can be assigned to the other or be passed as an actual parameter to a formal parameter of the other variety.

Use of Entire Character Strings

Although character strings are not a true primitive type in Pascal, they are informally recognized *as though* they were legitimate data types. You have already encountered character string constants such as 'Hello there' and 'Hi'. Any text enclosed by apostrophes is a character string constant and can be given a symbolic identifier in the CONSTant declaration part or be output as an entity by appearing in a write statement.

string-type variable

As we mentioned in Chapter 7, Pascal does not include a character string variable as such. However, we can declare what amounts to a **string-type variable** as a PACKED ARRAY of type char with subscripts that are integers, beginning with 1 and specifying more than one component. If you declare an array in strict accordance with these requirements, the entire packed array can behave like a simple variable in certain contexts. Consider the string-type variables declared as

```
TYPE
  ShortString = PACKED ARRAY [1..3] OF char;
VAR
  A, B: ShortString;
  X: PACKED ARRAY [1..7] OF char;
```

String assignment and output

We can then make assignments of entire strings and write out the contents of string variables as follows:

```
A := 'Joe';    {give A a value}
B := A;        {make a copy in B}
write(A,B);
```

The result would be to display JoeJoe on the screen. The alternative, using an unpacked array, would have required each array to be initialized or displayed one character at a time.

String comparison

We also can compare entire strings, be they constants or variables. For the preceding values, the following conditions are all true.

```
IF 'Amy' < 'Tom' THEN . . .
IF B <> 'Amy' THEN . . .
IF A = B THEN . . .
```

However, there is one serious limitation: Only strings of exactly the same length can be compared or assigned. We *cannot* legally write

```
X := A;        {invalid-different lengths}
```

because one array (X) has 7 components whereas the other (A) has only 3. Similarly, the statement

```
X := 'Kevin';      {illegal-need 7 characters}
```

is illegal, though it would be possible to assign a string padded with enough blanks to give it the necessary 7 characters, as in

```
X := 'Kevinʬʬ';      {exactly 7 characters}
```

Length determines type

The length of a string constant or the number of components in a string variable determines its type. All strings of the same length belong to the same data type. Thus when manipulating strings (say, words) having a variety of natural lengths, these strings are often filled out with enough blanks to make them equal in length, thereby allowing their assignment or comparison.

Details of comparison

Comparison of two strings—of equal length, of course—proceeds as follows. The leftmost character from one string is compared with the leftmost character from the other. If these characters are the same, then the second characters from the two strings are compared. If required, tandem traversal of the strings continues, comparing pairs of characters from corresponding positions. If every pair of characters is the same, the strings are deemed equal. But if the strings are not identical, the scan stops at the position where the first mismatch occurs. The relative ordering in the collating sequence of the two dissimilar characters determines the relative ordering of the two strings.

Comparing 'fragment' to 'fracture', for example, entails successively comparing the two 'f's, the two 'r's, the two 'a's, and finally the 'c' from fracture with the 'g' from fragment. At this point, the fact that 'c' < 'g' in the collating sequence determines that 'fracture' < 'fragment'. This is illustrated in Fig. 8.1. This process may appear complicated, but it resembles the algorithm we routinely use for ordinary alphabetical ordering.

The blanks usually occur very early in the collating sequence. This makes 'artƀƀƀ' < 'arthur' because the first blank occurs before 'h' in the collating sequence. In order to compare *character strings* of *unequal* length, where both are interpreted as words, enough blanks should be appended to the *right* of the shorter string to make their lengths equal. If the shorter word is identical to the initial portion of the longer, the additional blanks will cause the previously shorter string to evaluate as prior in the ordering.

Padding words on right

Unless you realize how it works, comparing two character strings might provide a few surprises. For example, 'fredƀ' > 'ƀfred' because the first characters in each string differ and 'f' > 'ƀ'. Caution: Be careful where the blanks are added! Moreover, you know that 'ANNE' <> 'anne', but which comes first in the ordering depends on the collating sequence of your particular machine.

Padding "numbers" on left

Fortunately, equal-length strings of numeric characters compare as their integer counterparts would. For example, '247' < '253' because '4' < '5'. In order to compare *numeric sequences* of unequal length, '0's should be inserted to the *left* of the shorter number. For example, to correctly compare '35' with '147', '35' must first be extended to '035'. Trailing blanks do not work (consider '147' < '35ƀ'), and rightmost '0's are equally wrong ('147' < '350'). Furthermore, '4165' < '48.7' because '1' < '8'. (Remember, these are character strings, not numbers.) Although the decimal point did not influence this example, when punctuation and other special characters are involved, the outcome depends on their ordering in your particular machine.

■ Figure 8.1
Comparing two character strings.

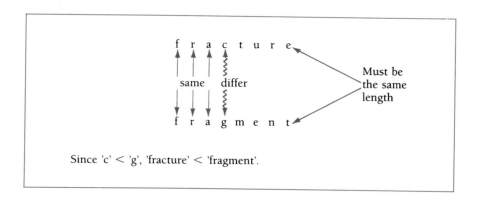

Since 'c' < 'g', 'fracture' < 'fragment'.

Accessing Individual Characters of a String

Component access

Although string variables behave like simple objects at times, they are actually arrays and as such may have their individual components referenced in the usual way. If A is an array with 1 as its first subscript, its second component is denoted by A[2], regardless of whether A is packed or not. Figure 8.2 contains a program that generates an isosceles triangle having an interior that consists entirely of stars (asterisks). The strategy for producing it is to write each row as a character string. Since the entire array is displayed each time, it is initially filled with blanks. This is done one blank at a time. A star placed at the triangle's midpoint is all that appears in the top row. Each succeeding row contains an additional star at each end of the sequence of stars used in the row above. Thus each new row is formed by adding two more stars at selected positions in the existing array. By using a packed array, each row is displayed simply by executing `writeln(Line)`.

Although the components of an array may be packed, each component still retains its original data type. The components of Line in Fig. 8.2 on p. 338 are each of type char and may therefore appear on either side of an assignment or relational operator wherever a character variable is allowed. If Y is declared as

```
VAR Y: {unpacked} ARRAY [0..9] OF char;
```

the statement

```
Line [3] := Y[6]
```

is allowed because Line[3] and Y[6] are of the same type, even though Line and Y themselves are not.

Packed component cannot be VAR parameter

However, there is one situation in which an individual component of a packed array *cannot* be used like an ordinary variable: A component of a packed structure cannot be passed as a *variable*-type parameter to a subprogram. Components of packed structures, however, can be passed to the predeclared procedures read, readln, and new.

Input to String-Type Arrays

String input

Because we can pass a single component of a packed array to the procedures read and readln, we can use the techniques of Chapter 7 to fill packed arrays character by character.† However, before a packed array can be manipulated in its entirety, all its components must have a value. With string-type arrays, this means that trailing positions in the array usually must be filled with blanks.

Two basic alternatives for ensuring that the array is filled are shown in Fig. 8.3(a) and Fig. 8.3(b). These procedures differ in their methods of filling

---

† A few implementations (such as VAX-11 Pascal) allow input of an entire packed array, but these are nonstandard extensions and should not be used unless portability is unimportant.

```
PROGRAM Triangle (input,output);

CONST
   Blank = ' ';
   Star = '*';
   LineWidth = 50; {chars per line}
   MidPoint = 25; {of line}
TYPE
   String = PACKED ARRAY [1..LineWidth] OF char;
VAR
   Line: String;
   Height,      {of triangle; no. of lines generated}
   Extent,      {from midpoint to end of line}
   Psn : integer;

BEGIN {Triangle}
   writeln('Enter desired number of rows:');
   readln(Height);
   FOR Psn := 1 TO LineWidth DO
      Line[Psn] := Blank;

   {first row}
   Line[MidPoint] := Star;
   writeln (Line);

   {succeeding rows}
   FOR Extent := 1 TO Height-1 DO
      BEGIN {current row = Extent + 1}
         Line[MidPoint - Extent] := Star;
         Line[MidPoint + Extent] := Star;
         writeln (Line)
      END

END. {Triangles}

   sample output:

                  *
                 * * *
                * * * * *
               * * * * * * *
              * * * * * * * * *
```

■ Figure 8.2
Accessing individual locations in a packed array.

```
                   {declarations relating to both procedures}
      CONST
         MaxLength = 20;
      TYPE
         String = PACKED ARRAY [1..MaxLength] OF char;
      VAR
         StringArray: String;

      PROCEDURE ReadString1 (VAR Ary: String);
         CONST
            Blank = ' ';
         VAR
            CharCount, Psn: integer;
         BEGIN {ReadString1}
            CharCount := 0;
            WHILE (CharCount < MaxLength) AND NOT eoln DO
               BEGIN
                  CharCount := CharCount + 1;
                  read (Ary[CharCount])
               END;
            {now fill remainder of array with blanks}
            FOR Psn := CharCount+1 TO MaxLength DO
               Ary[Psn] := Blank
         END; {ReadString1}
```

(a) Read data and then supply trailing blanks.

```
      PROCEDURE ReadString2 (VAR Ary: String);
         CONST
            TwentyBlanks = '                    ';
         VAR
            CharCount: integer;
         BEGIN {readString2}
            {first fill array with blanks}
            Ary := TwentyBlanks;
            {now overwrite with valid data}
            CharCount := 0;
            WHILE (CharCount < MaxLength) AND NOT eoln DO
               BEGIN
                  CharCount := CharCount + 1;
                  read (Ary[CharCount])
               END
         END; {ReadString2}
```

(b) Fill with blanks followed by read.

■ Figure 8.3
Reading data into a string-type packed array.

any unused portion of the array with blanks. The first reads each character directly into its proper position in the array and then fills any remaining components with blanks. The second fills the entire array with blanks and then *overwrites* some (or all) of it as each character is read.

Transfer Procedures pack and unpack

Consider the variables:

```
VAR
    PackedCity: PACKED ARRAY [1 . . 6] OF char;
    UnpackedCity: ARRAY [1 . . 6] OF char;
```

We can store the string Boston in PackedCity by executing:

```
PackedCity := 'Boston';
```

Should we need to transfer the characters from PackedCity to UnpackedCity, a simple assignment statement will not suffice because the source and target arrays are not of identical types. One approach is to do the following:

```
FOR K := 1 TO 6 DO (unpack)
   UnpackedCity[K] := PackedCity[K];
```

pack **and** unpack   However, Pascal allows us to obtain directly an ordinary (unpacked) version of a packed array and similarly permits the packing of an unpacked array. Two predeclared procedures, called **pack** and **unpack,** are provided for transferring data in either direction between packed and unpacked arrays. For example, the following call to the unpack procedure is equivalent to the preceding FOR loop.

```
unpack(PackedCity,UnpackedCity,1);
```

The third parameter (1 in this example) indicates the starting subscript in the unpacked array. In practice the data are usually transferred between two entire arrays having the same number of components. However, the unpack procedure allows the data to be moved to selected consecutive locations of an *unpacked* array having more components than the packed array. This is the reason for specifying the starting subscript. Since the *entire* packed array is involved, this subscript must be sufficiently close to the beginning of the unpacked array to allow all the values from the packed array to be transferred. When the arrays are of equal length, the first subscript (usually 1) must be used.

Going the opposite way is similar. To pack the characters from UnpackedCity into the string variable PackedCity, we could execute either

```
FOR K := 1 TO 6 DO {pack}
   PackedCity[K] := UnpackedCity[K];
```

or

```
pack (UnpackedCity,1,PackedCity);
```

Again, the 1 indicates the starting subscript in the unpacked array, which may be larger than the packed array. The subscript must be chosen to allow the entire packed array to be filled with values.

8.2 Fundamentals of Two-Dimensional Arrays

A two-dimensional array is an array whose components are themselves arrays. Before considering the general case, we look at arrays of character strings.

Arrays of Character Strings

Consider the problem of sorting a list of names. If we could structure the names as an array, we could use one of the sort algorithms from Chapter 7 to rearrange them. If 35 to 40 names are likely, an array capable of holding 50 names should be sufficient.

Suppose that we have such an array, Name. The effect of sorting this array is shown in Fig. 8.4. As you can see, the basic data entities in this

■ Figure 8.4
An array of strings (before and after sorting).

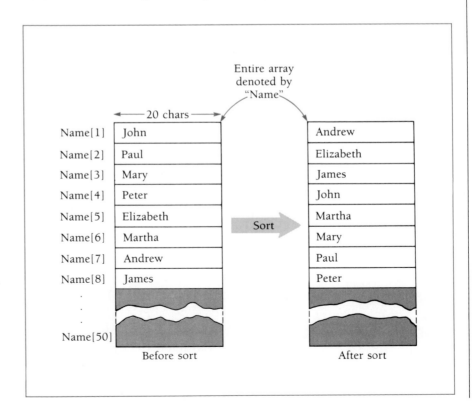

problem are names. At this level we do not need to worry about whether these names are fundamental within Pascal, that is, whether they consist of even simpler components.

If we use the bubble sort to rearrange the names in Name, we need no other arrays and can encode the main program immediately:

```
LoadArray (Name,Howmany);
Sort (Name,Howmany);
Display (Name,Howmany)
```

These procedures do the usual things: read a number of (Howmany) strings from the input stream into the array Name; reorder the strings in Name; and display the first Howmany strings found in the array Name.

Even the declaration of Name looks familiar:

```
CONST
  MaxNames = 50;
TYPE
  NameArray = ARRAY [1..MaxNames] OF CharString;
VAR
  Name: NameArray;
```

Declaration   Of course, this declaration is not complete; it presupposes a definition for the type CharString, the type pertaining to an individual name. If the longest name anticipated contains 15 letters, then to be on the safe side, each string variable will be allowed to hold 20 characters and can be declared as

```
CONST
  StringLength = 20;
TYPE
  CharString = PACKED ARRAY [1..StringLength] OF char;
```

When we combine these declarations, we have the complete declaration for Name, the key data object in our program:

```
CONST
  StringLength = 20;
  MaxNames = 50;
TYPE
  CharString = PACKED ARRAY [1..StringLength] OF char;
  NameArray = ARRAY [1..MaxNames] OF CharString;
VAR
  Name: NameArray;
  HowMany : 0..MaxNames;
```

Until now all the arrays you have encountered had simple variables as components. You now see more complex objects as array components, but their declaration and use are not very much different. The components of an array can be almost any data type, as long as they are all the same data type. Note that the NameArray type is not packed, although its components are.

   The complete main program is shown in Fig. 8.5. The fact that the array Name contains character string components does not affect the way it is passed among the procedures. LoadArray and Sort, the procedures that alter its contents, declare the corresponding formal parameter as variable-type.

```
PROGRAM SortNames (input,output);

   { Sort array of names in alphabetical order}

CONST
   StringLength = 20;
   MaxLength = 50;

TYPE
   CharString = PACKED ARRAY [1..StringLength] OF char;
   NameArray = ARRAY [1..MaxLength] OF CharString;

VAR
   Name: NameArray; {up to 50 names}
   HowMany: integer; { how many names stored in Name}

PROCEDURE LoadArray (VAR Name: NameArray;
                     VAR HowMany: integer);

      {See Figure 8.8}

PROCEDURE Sort (VAR Name: NameArray; HowMany: integer);

      {See Figure 8.7}

PROCEDURE Display (Name: NameArray; HowMany: integer);

      {See Figure 8.6}

BEGIN {SortNames}
   LoadArray (Name,HowMany);
   Sort (Name,HowMany);
   Display (Name,HowMany)
END. {SortNames}
```

■ Figure 8.5
Program to sort an array of names.

```
PROCEDURE Display (Name: NameArray; HowMany: integer);
   VAR
      Next: integer;
   BEGIN
      writeln; writeln; {skip 2 lines}
      FOR Next := 1 TO HowMany DO
         writeln( Name[Next] )
   END; {Display procedure}
```

■ Figure 8.6
Program to sort an array of names.

Even when we look at the procedures themselves, we receive few surprises. The Display and Sort procedures work exclusively at the level of complete names; their "view" of the data is that shown in Fig. 8.4. The Display procedure in Fig. 8.6 merely traverses the occupied portion of the array, writing out each string as a single entity.

Accessing rows of
array

```
PROCEDURE Sort (VAR Name: NameArray; HowMany: integer);
   VAR
      Sorted: boolean; {false when values interchanged}
      Temp: CharString;
      Psn: integer;
   BEGIN {Sort}
      REPEAT

         Sorted := true; {assume sorted}
         FOR Psn := 1 TO HowMany-1 DO
            IF Name[Psn] > Name[Psn+1] THEN {reorder}
               BEGIN {swap}
                  Temp := Name[Psn];
                  Name[Psn] := Name[Psn+1];
                  Name[Psn] := Temp;
                  Sorted := false
               END; {swap}
         HowMany := HowMany - 1

      UNTIL Sorted
   END; {Sort}
```

■ Figure 8.7
Bubble sort procedure.

The bubble sort procedure in Fig. 8.7 has exactly the same logic as the bubble sort in Section 7.3. The difference here is that each array component is a complete string. Hence the local variable Temp used in the swap must be declared as a CharString type. Full use is made of the ability to compare and assign packed arrays. Although this procedure reduces the parameter Howmany after each pass, these changes are never conveyed to the main program, since this parameter is of value-type.

Two-level input process
The input process has two natural levels. At the higher level, names must be read from successive input lines into successive positions in the array of names. This level still deals exclusively with entire strings.

However, an entire string cannot actually be read at one time. A lower level must "see" the internal structure of a string to read successive characters comprising a name into successive positions of a string. It is therefore natural to declare two procedures: one (LoadArray) to sequence through the strings of the array Name and another (ReadString) to handle the details of reading a single string.

You should carefully study these procedures, shown in Fig. 8.8 on p. 346. The outer procedure concerns itself exclusively with the strings comprising the array Name. When it calls ReadString, it expects an entire string to be returned to the string variable Name[Number]. Here only one component of Name is transferred between these two procedures on any one call.

On the other hand, ReadString deals only with the characters comprising a single string. It neither knows nor cares that its parameter, Line, may refer to an array component in an outside context. Regardless of where it comes from, ReadString initializes some object of type CharString. Of course, since Line is a packed array itself, its individual characters are denoted by subscripted variables (e.g., Line[CharsRead] and Line[Psn]). Note that ReadString fills out the array Line with blanks after it completes the input line (by executing readln). The logic here is the same as that of Fig. 8.3(a).

Visualizing, Declaring, and Referencing Two-Dimensional Arrays

Let's look again at the data structure used to hold the list of names. Its ultimate components, the character variables, were grouped into sequences called strings; the strings, in turn, were grouped into an array of strings. The result is a three-tiered hierarchy of data, as pictured in Fig. 8.9. The figure shows the data type and overall "shape" of each level in the hierarchy.

Hierarchy of data
If the outermost structure is known by the identifier Name, each character variable is ultimately a component of Name and can be identified in terms of this outermost structure. Identifying an individual character is really quite logical. Since the third string within Name is called Name[3], the fifth character of *this* particular string is simply the string name followed by the bracketed subscript [5], that is, Name[3][5]. Although perfectly legitimate, this notation is a bit clumsy and is usually written instead as Name[3,5].

```
PROCEDURE LoadArray (VAR Name: NameArray;
                     VAR Number: integer);


   PROCEDURE ReadString (VAR Line: CharString);
      CONST
         Blank = ' ';
      VAR
         CharsRead, Psn: integer;

      BEGIN {ReadString}
         CharsRead := 0;

         WHILE (CharsRead < StringLength) AND NOT eoln DO
            BEGIN {read another character}
               CharsRead := CharsRead + 1;
               read (Line[CharsRead])
            END; {character input}

         readln; {flush line, even if it still has data}
         FOR Psn := CharsRead+1 TO StringLength DO
            Line[Psn] := Blank {pad with blanks}

      END; {ReadString}


   BEGIN {LoadArray}
      Number := 0;

      WHILE (Number < MaxNames) AND NOT eof DO
         BEGIN
            Number := Number + 1;
            ReadString (Name[Number])
         END

   END; {LoadArray}
```

■ Figure 8.8
Input of names.

Use of this notation is illustrated in Fig. 8.9, but with variable rather than constant subscripts. Note that the more refined or specific the object being named, the more components we must include in its identifier to specify it. Each level in the hierarchy requires one additional subscript.

Figure 8.10 presents another image of Name, this time with its detailed structure more fully exposed. This structure appears as a two-dimensional grid, with each small square representing one character variable. The location of a particular character variable is given by specifying its distance downward and to the right (that is, its "south" and "east" coordinates) in that order,

```
CONST
    StringLength = 20;
    MaxLength = 50;
TYPE
    CharString = PACKED ARRAY [1..StringLength] OF char;
    NameArray = ARRAY [1..MaxLength] OF CharString;
VAR
    Name: NameArray; {up to 50 names}
```

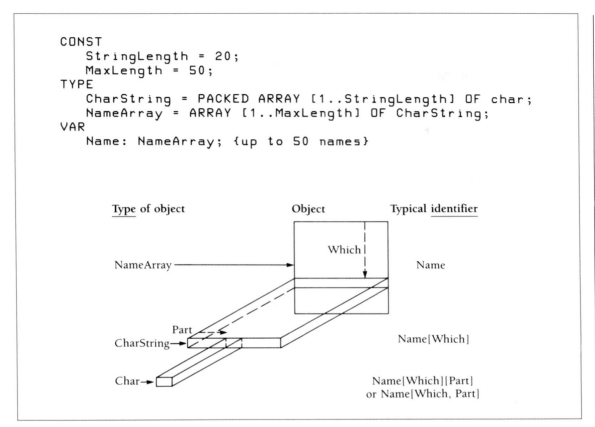

■ Figure 8.9
Hierarchy of data types and identifiers.

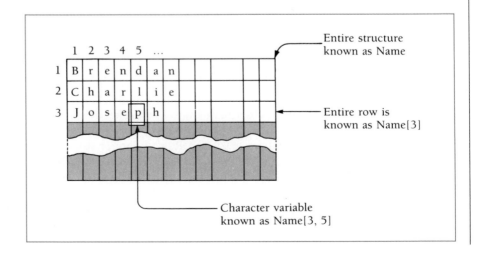

■ Figure 8.10
Name as a two-
dimensional array.

with the upper left corner being the reference point. We see the variable Name[3,5] located in the third row and at the fifth position of that row. Similarly, Name[2,3] = 'a', Name[3,2] = 'o', and 'd' is stored at Name[1,5].

This view of Name in two dimensions requires two subscripts, or coordinates, to identify any particular location. Such structures are called **two-dimensional arrays.**

two-dimensional
arrays

Some applications use two-dimensional arrays without any need for identifying particular rows as units. In these cases, we do not need to declare the rows (in our case CharStrings) as an explicit type; their structural specification may appear instead of their type identifier to describe the components of Name. Thus either of the following declarations would produce the same two-dimensional array shown in Fig. 8.10.

Alternative
declarations

```
TYPE
   CharString = PACKED array [1..20] OF char;
VAR
   Name: ARRAY [1..50] OF CharString;
```

or, alternatively,

```
VAR Name: ARRAY [1..50] OF PACKED ARRAY [1..20] OF char;
```

The fact that CharString is *packed* has no bearing on the naming conventions for the individual characters. (The only impact of packing is on the use of entire rows of Name as entities.) Suppose that CharString had been declared as an array but *not* a packed array. Then, Name would still have been a two-dimensional array with a structure like that shown in Fig. 8.10. The cell three rows down and 5 positions to the right would still be denoted by Name[3,5].

When intermediate levels are neither explicitly identified nor packed, we can condense the declaration of two-dimensional arrays even more. The three variations below are equivalent in terms of the structure they produce.

1.   TYPE Row = ARRAY [1 . . 20] OF char;
     VAR Name: ARRAY [1 . . 50] OF Row;
2.   VAR Name: ARRAY [1 . . 50] OF ARRAY [1 . . 20] OF char;
3.   VAR Name: ARRAY [1 . . 50, 1 . . 20] OF char;

Alternative (3) shows (within the brackets) the permissible range for each of the two subscripts required in a reference to an individual character.

Although both alternatives (2) and (3) suppress explicit mention of an intermediate level (the Row), there is still an underlying hierarchy of data types, and they still permit reference to an entire row, such as Name[3]. Of course, a row cannot be passed as a parameter to a subprogram unless it has been declared as an explicit type, as in alternative (1). Since these rows are not packed, their use is limited. They cannot be compared or displayed as single entities, for example. Also because its rows are not packed, Name as declared here does *not* have the same data type as it had in previous examples.

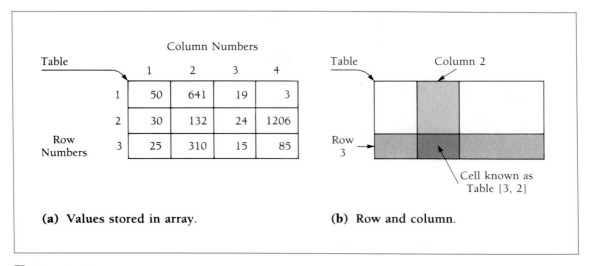

(a) Values stored in array.   **(b) Row and column.**

■ Figure 8.11
Another two-
dimensional array.

row

column

Consider the array shown in Fig. 8.11(a). This array contains 12 integers, arranged in three rows and four columns. The notions of row and column are quite important and, surprisingly, often confused in practice. A **row** is a horizontal slice of the array, and a **column** is a vertical slice. Each row cuts across all the columns and each column across all the rows. Thus each of the three rows in Fig. 8.11 has four elements, and each of the four columns has three elements. That array could be declared as

```
VAR Table: ARRAY [1..3, 1..4] OF integer;
```

In both the declaration and in all references to array components involving both subscripts, the first subscript identifies the row and the second the column. You should consider this order—row, column—inviolable. Figure 8.11(b) shows the location of an individual integer at the intersection of the particular row and particular column specified in the reference.

Sequential Processing of Two-Dimensional Arrays

In many applications dealing with two dimensional arrays, we often must traverse an individual row, an individual column, or the entire array. There are some standard techniques for this sort of processing.

Row traversal

Keeping in mind the row and column concepts it is easy to describe the traversal of two-dimensional arrays. For example, to set a boolean flag UnderTen if any value in the second row is less than 10, you could write

```
UnderTen := false;
FOR Col := 1 TO 4 DO
   IF Table[2,Col] < 10 THEN
      UnderTen := true;
```

Note how the row subscript is held fixed at 2, while the column subscript is sequenced through its four values. Even in two dimensions, traversal of an array usually involves FOR statements.

Column traversal

Similarly, to add the values in column 3, the column subscript is held fixed at 3, while the row subscript cycles through its values:

```
Sum := 0;
FOR Row := 1 TO 3 DO
  Sum := Sum + Table[Row,3];
```

Traversing entire array

When all the elements of a two-dimensional array are to be processed, you have the choice of organizing your task row-by-row or column-by-column. Thus, to search Table for the largest value, you could traverse one row at a time:

```
{for some particular value of Row and some
value of Max}
FOR Col := 1 TO 4 DO
  IF Table[Row,Col] > Max THEN
    Max := Table[Row,Col];
```

But you can do this for *each* of three rows by embedding this code in a loop that varies the row subscript:

```
Max := Table[1,1];
FOR Row := 1 TO 3 DO
  FOR Col := 1 TO 4 DO
    IF Table[Row,Col] > Max THEN
      Max := Table[Row,Col];
```

Column-by-column inspection would be similar, except that the FOR statements would be reversed. Although the order of traversal does not matter when you are finding the largest value, some problems dictate the order.

Row-by-row versus column-by-column

Similar alternatives are available for input and output of two-dimensional arrays as well. However, you must remember that the values come from the input stream in a particular order and that output must be produced line-by-line. Flexibility comes from accessing the array either by rows or by columns. Consider, for example, the output generated by the two code fragments shown in Fig. 8.12. Both use exactly the same array of values (reproduced from Fig. 8.11a). However, because of differences in the way they traverse the array, each output process delivers the values to the output device in a different order.

Subscripts of other ordinal types

The array subscripts may be of any ordinal type (making the FOR statement especially useful). Suppose that you own a small chain of three stores that carry a rather diversified line of stock: shovels, hats, trucks, and statues. You might record your inventory in the two-dimensional array of Fig. 8.13, which contains a total of 12 integers in three (horizontal) rows and

Table	Col. 1	Col. 2	Col. 3	Col. 4
Row1	50	641	19	3
Row2	30	132	24	1206
Row3	25	310	15	85

```
           output code                          generated output
FOR Row := 1 TO 3 DO
  BEGIN
    FOR Col := 1 TO 4 DO               50    641    19       3
      write (Table[Row,Col]:5);        30    132    24    1206
    writeln                            25    310    15      85
  END;
```

(a) Row by row.

```
FOR Col := 1 TO 4 DO
  BEGIN                                 50      30      25
    FOR Row := 1 TO 3 DO               641     132     310
      write (Table[Row,Col]:5);         19      24      15
    writeln                              3    1206      85
  END;
```

(b) Column by column.

■ Figure 8.12
Comparing row-by-row and column-by-column output.

Store Branch	Stock Items			
	Shovels	Hats	Trucks	Statues
Main Street	50	641	19	3
Park Avenue	30	132	24	1206
Suburban	25	310	15	85

■ Figure 8.13
Recording inventory for each of three stores.

four (vertical) columns. You could declare the array Stock as

```
TYPE
  Branch = (MainSt, ParkAve, Suburban);
  Item = (Shovels, Hats, Trucks, Statues);
  Goods = ARRAY [Branch,Item] OF integer;
VAR
  Stock: Goods;
```

You could obtain the total number of hats by summing the column Hats (assuming that Store is of type Branch and HatTotal is of type integer):

```
HatTotal := 0;
FOR Store := MainSt TO Suburban DO
  HatTotal := HatTotal + Stock[Store,Hats];
```

Once again, the row subscript Store varies over its range, while the column subscript remains fixed at Hats.

8.3 Maintaining Stock Prices

Consider the problem of maintaining the market prices of stock during one trading period. Whenever a sale occurs, an identification number and the amount per share at which that stock just sold are entered as input to the program. The identification number pertains to both the stock and the company. If the stock trades more than once, several sets of input will be processed for that stock.

The output should be a report generated at the end of the trading period, giving the high, low, and closing prices for each stock traded. The identification number must also accompany these three amounts. In addition, the report should give the average closing price for all the stocks involved.

Designing a Data Structure and an Algorithm

Simplified problem: one stock

A good starting point is to figure out how to handle a single stock. Since the four quantities to be printed for this company are numeric, they can all be stored in the same real-type array. Because only four quantities are involved, they might be kept in four simple variables, *if* there actually were only one stock of interest. However, anticipating a later extension to several stocks, we should collect these quantities into the same structure; hence the array. Although the identification number is an integer, we lose nothing by keeping it in a real variable and converting back to integer for output purposes. The structure to hold the information for a single stock can be defined as

```
TYPE
  StockInfo = (StockID,High,Low,Close);
  StockReport = ARRAY [StockInfo] OF real;
```

Processing is simple when there is only one stock to consider. The first transaction values read are used to initialize an array of type StockReport. The identification number goes into the first location and the amount into each of the other three. Whenever a subsequent transaction is read (presumably with the same identification number), the new selling price *may* replace either the high or the low and, being the most recent transaction, *certainly* will become the new closing amount. The output is just a display of these four values (with the identification number converted to an integer).

Declaration for all stocks

The next step is to consider several companies, each represented by an array and subject to the processing described above. Since all the StockReport arrays are similar, they themselves can be arranged into an array:

```
CONST
   MaxStocks = 10; {only 10 for now}
TYPE
   StockInfo = (StockID,High,Low,Close);
   StockReport = ARRAY [StockInfo] OF real; {one stock}
   StockArray = ARRAY [1..MaxStocks] OF StockReport;
VAR
   Stock: StockArray;
   HowMany: integer;
```

Each row of the array Stock pertains to a different company, and the variable HowMany indicates the number of stocks currently represented, that is, the frontier, or number of occupied rows in Stock. A snapshot of Stock is shown in Fig. 8.14.

■ **Figure 8.14**
Typical content of stock array.

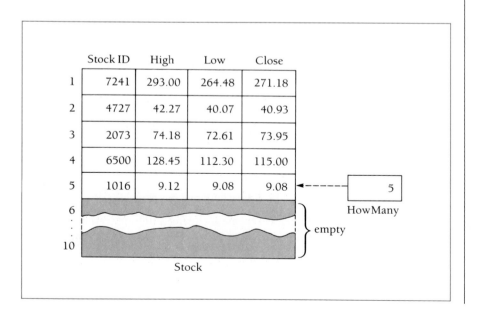

Processing the transactions for all stocks is an extension of processing one. The main difference is that the identification number must be used to find the appropriate row of values. In other words a search is made down the first column of Stock for a number matching the one just read. If none is found, a new row of Stock is initialized as described before, and the frontier HowMany is advanced. If a match is found, the selected row of Stock is updated exactly as before. In summary, the algorithm is

Algorithm

1. while transactions remain do:
1.1   read I.D. and selling price;
1.2   search array for information about this stock;
1.3   if search successful then
        update prices for that stock;
1.4   else {1st trade}
        establish and initialize new row;
2. report results for period; i.e.,
2.1   for each stock, report high, low and close; and
2.2   report average closing price for all companies;
3. stop.

Implementing the Solution

Main program

Assuming the use of end-of-file to terminate input and subprograms to carry out these actions, we can code this process as shown in Fig. 8.15. The Search function returns the row number (SelectedRow) where the company ID was found. This row number is needed by the Update procedure. But if the search failed, the row number is reported as 0, causing selection of the Enter procedure instead of the Update alternative.

From the main program the entire array Stock is passed among the procedures. The choice of which parameters must be variable-type is clear: Update and Enter both modify the data in Stock, and Enter advances the value of HowMany; all other parameters are value-type. Note that Search and Report need the value of HowMany to control their traversal of the array, whereas Enter needs it to know where to initialize the new row.

Search for Stock

The search function in Fig. 8.16 on p. 356 merely implements the search algorithm presented in Fig. 7.10(b) within the first column of the two-dimensional array. The comparison

```
IF Stock[Row,StockID] = Company THEN . . .
```

is made repeatedly using different values for Row but holding the column subscript fixed at StockID. Note again how 0 is returned if the company number is not found.

Update old Stock

The Update procedure in Fig. 8.17 on p. 357 uses the row number obtained by Search to select the row to be modified. Within this row, the update occurs as before. The High or Low value might be modified if the

```
PROGRAM StockMarket (input,output);

CONST
   MaxStocks = 10; {much larger in practice}
TYPE
   StockInfo = (StockID,High,Low,Closing);
   StockReport = ARRAY [StockInfo] OF real; {one stock}
   StockArray = ARRAY [1..MaxStocks] OF StockReport;
VAR
   Stock: StockArray; {major data structure}
   HowMany: integer; {rows occupied in Stock}
   Company: integer; {ID number of company}
   Price: real; {selling price of company stock}
   SelectedRow: integer; {result of Search}

FUNCTION Search (Stock:StockArray; Company: real;
                 HowMany: integer): integer;
         {See Figure 8.16}

PROCEDURE Update (VAR Stock: StockArray;
                  Identity: integer; Price: real);
            {See Figure 8.17}

PROCEDURE Enter (VAR Stock: StockArray;
                 Company, Price: real;
                 VAR HowMany: integer);
            {See Figure 8.18}

PROCEDURE Report (Stock: StockArray; HowMany: integer);
            {See Figure 8.19}

BEGIN {StockMarket}
   HowMany := 0; {array empty}
   WHILE NOT eof DO
      BEGIN
         readln (Company, Price);
         SelectedRow := Search (Stock, Company, HowMany);
         IF SelectedRow = 0 THEN {1st entry for Company}
            Enter (Stock,Company,Price,HowMany)
         ELSE
            Update (Stock,SelectedRow,Price)
      END;
   Report (Stock, HowMany)
END. {StockMarket}
```

■ Figure 8.15
Main program to report stock selling prices.

```
FUNCTION Search (Stock: StockArray; Company: real;
                 HowMany: integer): integer;

   {Search first HowMany rows of Stock for
    occurrence of Company; return 0 if not found}

   VAR
      Row: integer; {to traverse array}
      Found: boolean;
   BEGIN {Search}
      Found := false;
      Row := 0;

      WHILE (Row < HowMany) AND NOT Found DO
      BEGIN
         Row := Row + 1;
         IF Stock[Row,StockID] = Company THEN
            Found := true
      END;

      IF Found THEN
         Search := Row {where found}
      ELSE
         Search := 0 {to signal failure}

   END; {Search}
```

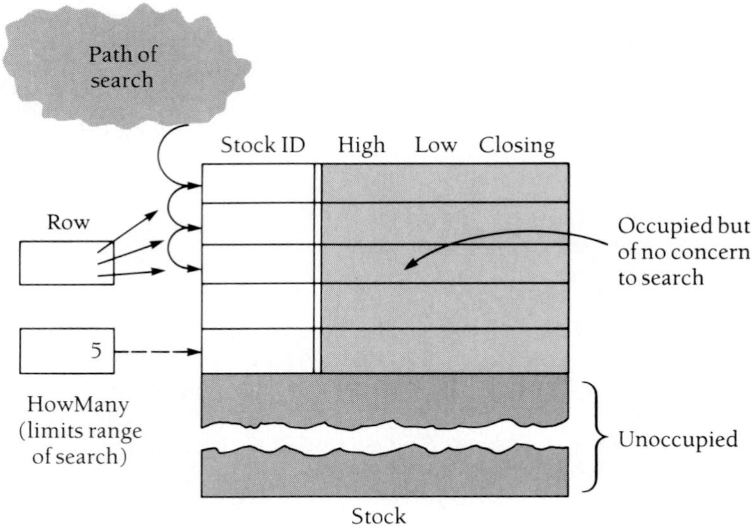

■ Figure 8.16
Search of two-dimensional array.

Enter new Stock

new Price is either higher or lower, respectively, and in all cases Price becomes the new Closing value.

After making sure that the array still has an available row, the Enter procedure in Fig. 8.18 on p. 358 advances the variable HowMany to denote the next empty row. (When this new value is returned to the main program through the variable parameter, it will represent the last occupied row.) In the Enter procedure, we use HowMany as the row subscript in every succeeding reference to Stock because the four components of this new row are given values.

Output report

The Report procedure in Fig. 8.19 on p. 359 traverses the array row-by-row, displaying each row on a separate output line. Before writing an identification number, this value is converted to an integer, so that the decimal point will not appear. As the procedure progresses, the closing price is added to a sum for the final display of the closing average.

Possible sort

A natural extension of the maintenance of stock prices would be to sort the array before displaying the report. With two-dimensional arrays, we have to choose the basis for sorting. For example, we could sort Stock by identification number or by any of the three prices, depending on the application. Whichever column of the array we choose, we could use any of the standard sort algorithms (such as selection or bubble). Although the comparisons would be based only on a specific entry in each row, any movement or rearrangement would involve entire rows, since all the data in each row must remain associated.

```
PROCEDURE Update (VAR Stock: StockArray;
                  Identity: integer; Price: real);

   BEGIN {Update}
      IF Price > Stock[Identity,High] THEN {new high}
         Stock[Identity,High] := Price;
      IF Price < Stock[Identity,Low] THEN {new low}
         Stock[Identity,Low] := Price;
      Stock[Identity,Closing] := Price
   END; {Update}
```

■ Figure 8.17
Updating an active stock at Row = Identity.

```
PROCEDURE Enter (VAR Stock: StockArray;
                    Company, Price: real;
                    VAR HowMany: integer);

    {to initialize new row of array Stock}

    BEGIN {Enter}
      IF HowMany >= MaxStocks THEN {no more space}
          writeln ('Sorry, array is full')
      ELSE {space available}
          BEGIN

              HowMany := HowMany + 1; {advance frontier}
              Stock[HowMany,StockID] := Company;
              Stock[HowMany,High] := Price;
              Stock[HowMany,Low] := Price;
              Stock[HowMany,Closing] := Price

          END
    END; {Enter}
```

■ Figure 8.18
Initializing new stock using first empty row.

8.4 Other Uses for Two-Dimensional Arrays

The two-dimensional array is one of the most common data structures and has wide applications in scientific computing. In this section we indicate just a few of these applications.

Output Applications

Just as one-dimensional arrays may be used as buffers in which to construct an output line before its actual display, two-dimensional arrays may be used to construct the details of two-dimensional displays. In a sense this was done in the stock-market example; the final report was basically a reproduction of the data array on the output device. However, this idea can be carried much further to include the preparation of purely pictorial output.

Bar chart   A simple example is the presentation of bar charts where the bars are vertical rather than horizontal. The difficulty in generating them directly is

```
PROCEDURE Report (Stock: StockArray; HowMany: integer);

   VAR
      Row: integer;
      Col: StockInfo;
      TotalClose: real;

   BEGIN {Report}
      TotalClose := 0;
      writeln ('Company':11,'High':9,'Low':9,'Closing':12);
      writeln;

      FOR Row := 1 TO HowMany DO
         BEGIN {row output}
            {show first entry without decimal point}
            write (trunc(Stock[Row,StockID]):10);

            FOR Col := High TO Closing DO {other cols}
               write (Stock[Row,Col]:10:2);

            writeln;
            TotalClose := TotalClose + Stock[Row,Closing]
         END {row output}

      writeln;
      writeln;
      IF HowMany > 0 THEN
         writeln ('Avg. closing price ',
            (TotalClose/HowMany):8:2)
      ELSE
         writeln ('No information available')
   END; {Report}
```

■ Figure 8.19
Output array of stocks row by row.

that the display characters must be sent to the output device row by row with no backtracking to fill in missing details. Each row transmitted may or may not contain small segments of the vertical bars. Although these segments can be calculated, it is much easier to first construct the vertical bars in a two-dimensional array by filling in appropriate columns. This allows the algorithm to move around to arbitrary places on a grid representing the output image. When all the columns are in place, the array is displayed row by row.

Let's briefly examine the production of a bar chart showing the relative proportion of even and odd integers read from the input stream. We will produce a simple bar chart containing only *vertical* bars and no labels or boundary characters. Assume that the variables Even and NotEven have already been computed to indicate the height of their respective bars in the histogram. (The identifier Odd cannot be used because the predeclared function odd would probably be used to separate the odd from the even integers.) A background grid (and hence an array) of 10 rows and 10 columns will be used for the bar chart. A bar of height 1 will represent 10 percent, and a height of 10 represents 100 percent.

The following algorithm produces a chart with bars that are each two columns in width.

1. initialize A to all blanks;
2. construct "even" bar in columns 3 and 4;
3. construct the "odd" bar in columns 7 and 8;
4. display all of A row by row.

The first step—initializing the entire array to blanks—is necessary to guarantee the presence of a "harmless," invisible character in all unused positions. The final step is the transmission of this "picture" to the output device, one row at a time. Figure 8.20 shows the corresponding code.

Use of giant letters

There are other intriguing possibilities for displaying output. For example, you might have available to you a library of giant letters that are simply two-dimensional arrays already initialized to particular patterns, resembling letters of the alphabet. You could copy a number of these patterns into sections of a large two-dimensional array in order to generate giant-letter messages.

Graphics

The patterns need not be simply letters. They can be circles, squares, or line segments of various types. Some systems allow a user to construct pictorial images from these basic elements and to perform certain operations on entire pictures (such as grow, shrink, duplicate, or rotate). When pictures containing small variations are transmitted to the screen in rapid succession, the visual impression is that of motion. This is one form of *computer graphics*.

Further Uses for Two-Dimensional Arrays

We cannot possibly cover all the applications for two-dimensional arrays in this book. However, two of them are so common that we want to at least mention them.

Consider an array having rows and columns that represent cities and entries that are the distances from any one city (row) to adjacent cities (columns). Such "distance matrices" can be inspected to find whether any route exists from city A to some distant city B by discovering a chain of consecutive adjacent cities. By systematically maneuvering the array, we can discover how many (possibly nonoverlapping) routes exist and which is the shortest or longest. Many other kinds of objects and relationships can be

Path or transportation problems

```
{Even and NotEven indicate the height of each vertical
 bar; each is an integer between 0 and 10, where
 Even + NotEven = 10; A is a 10 x 10 array of char in
 which the output image is prepared}

{Initialize A to all blanks}
FOR Row := 1 TO 10 DO
   FOR Col := 1 TO 10 DO
      A[Row,Col] := ' ';

{Construct 'even' bar in columns 3 and 4}
FOR Col := 3 TO 4 DO
   FOR Row := (11-Even) TO 10 DO
      A[Row,Col] := '*';

{Construct 'odd' bar in columns 7 and 8}
FOR Col := 7 TO 8 DO
   FOR Row := (11-NotEven) TO 10 DO
      A[Row,Col] := '*';

{Display histogram row by row}
FOR Row := 1 TO 10 DO
   BEGIN
      FOR Col := 1 TO 10 DO
         write (A[Row,Col]);
      writeln
   END;
```

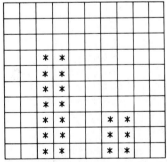
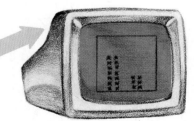

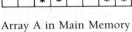
Array A in Main Memory

■ Figure 8.20
Construction of a bar chart inside a two-dimensional array.

represented and analyzed in this way. Many algorithms exist for inspecting two-dimensional arrays to solve such transportation problems.

Numeric applications   Another major application of two-dimensional arrays is in the solution of systems of equations. Most solution procedures involve writing down all the equations in some standard way, so that related terms in each equation are aligned. The coefficients are then manipulated to produce a solution. On a computer, the coefficients are usually stored in an array; each row corresponds to a different equation, and each column represents a different term. Again, a wealth of information about how to solve such problems is available.

8.5 Multidimensional Arrays

There is no reason why a number of identical two-dimensional arrays cannot be arranged into an array of their own. Such a structure would be a three-dimensional array because we would need to use three separate components to select an individual variable: one to identify the two-dimensional array being considered and two more to select its row and column.

In fact, we may declare any number of dimensions for arrays. We must reference each element in these arrays with as many subscripts as were **multidimensional** specified in the array declaration. **Multidimensional arrays** are obvious **arrays** extensions of one- and two-dimensional arrays and behave similarly in all respects.

Declaration   If we want to track daily stock prices over a five-day market week, we could set up five two-dimensional arrays or, better still, use one three dimensional array:

```
CONST
  MaxStocks = 200;
TYPE
  StockInfo = (StockID,High,Low,Closing);
  WeekDays = (Mon,Tue,Wed,Thu,Fri);
  StockReport = ARRAY [StockInfo] OF real;
  DailyStocks = ARRAY [1..MaxStocks] OF
                        StockReport;
  WeeklyStocks = ARRAY [WeekDays] OF DailyStocks;
VAR
  Market: WeeklyStocks;
```

Interpretation and   Such a declaration gives us in effect five copies of the old two-dimensional **access** array Stock, as shown in Fig. 8.21. This particular array, Market, contains 4000 real variables. The first dimension references the week days; the second, the stock in question; and the third, the prices. The high for stock number 66 on Tuesday would be referred to as Market[Tue,66,High]. We can vary any of these three subscripts to select a different location. The closing prices

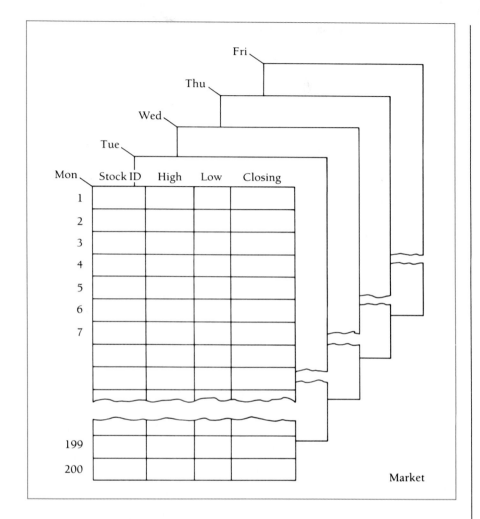

Figure 8.21
A three-dimensional array.

for stock 66 throughout the week could be displayed as

```
FOR Day := Mon TO Fri DO
   write (Market[Day,66,Closing]:10:2);
```

The hierarchy of structures with its associated hierarchy of names is one level deeper than before. For example:

Identifier	Refers to	Number of locations
Market	Entire structure	4000
Market[Wed]	One day's report	800
Market[Wed,125]	One stock for one day	4
Market[Wed,125,Low]	A single selling price	1

For some problems, multidimensional arrays emerge naturally. However, there is a trade-off when you use more dimensions. On the negative side, identifiers become more cumbersome, and more subscripts must be used in order to specify any location. On the positive side, more ways to handle natural cross-sections and subsets of locations become available; access to the data becomes more flexible.

8.6 Review of Rules

A. Any structured data type may be declared as PACKED. This often reduces the space consumed by the data and always produces a type different from, and therefore incompatible with, its nonpacked counterpart.

B. The most important packed structure is a packed array of characters having integer subscripts that begin at 1 and prescribe at least two components. Such a structure is known as a *character string*. Strings of different lengths belong to different data types, and strings of the same length have the same type.

C. Strings may be treated as units (that is, as if they were elementary objects) in three special contexts: in output, in comparison (among strings of equal length), and as string-type variables capable of being assigned an entire string constant as a value. (Of course, they also can be assigned and passed as parameters like unpacked arrays.)

D. There are two transfer procedures for copying an entire packed array to or from a continuous section of an unpacked array, beginning at position First in the unpacked array:

```
pack(UnpackedArray, First, PackedArray);

unpack(PackedArray, UnpackedArray, First).
```

E. The individual components of a packed structure can be accessed in exactly the same way as their unpacked counterparts. However, a *component* of a PACKED structure *cannot* be passed as a variable-type parameter, except to Pascal's predeclared read, readln, and new procedures.

F. It is possible to declare arrays of arrays (that is, two-dimensional arrays). The following declarations are equivalent.

```
VERSION 1
  TYPE RowType = ARRAY [Range2] OF Whatever;
  VAR Ary : ARRAY [Range1] OF RowType;

VERSION 2
  VAR Ary: ARRAY [Range1] OF ARRAY OF [Range2] OF Whatever;
```

VERSION 3
VAR Ary: ARRAY [Range1,Range2] OF Whatever;

Regardless of which form of declaration is used, the entire structure is referred to as Ary, a single row as Ary[RowID], and an individual value (of type Whatever) as Ary[RowID,ColumnID], where RowID is a member of Range1 and ColumnID is a member of Range2. However, only version 1 provides an explicit identifier for the row type and is therefore recommended in an application where an entire row is referenced (say, as a parameter).

G. The syntax diagram for any array declaration is

array type

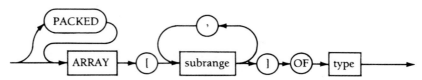

Since any number of subscript ranges may be prescribed and since the object may itself be an array type, it is possible to define any number of dimensions. This means that individual objects would be referenced using that number of subscripts.

KEY TERMS

column	row
multidimensional arrays	string-type variable
pack	two-dimensional arrays
PACKED ARRAY	unpack

EXERCISES

8.1 Implement a procedure to perform a selection sort using an array having components that are packed arrays of characters. Use this procedure in a program that reads up to 50 names, sorts them, and displays them in order.

8.2 Extend the information system of Exercise 7.15 that maintained two lists of taxicab ID numbers. Instead of only two lists, the system should now maintain up to five separate lists.

(a) Instead of using five one-dimensional arrays, use a single 20 × 5 two-dimensional integer array, with the columns representing the lists. The array number (from 1 to 5) specified in the commands will be used as a column index.

(b) Instead of using the initial positions in each column to hold ID numbers, define a 20 × 5 array of boolean values and associate each ID number permanently with a particular row. If ID number 316 corresponds to row r and cab 316 belongs to the list represented by column c, the value of position [r, c] is true. If this cab is not in that particular list, position [r, c] is false. (A one-dimensional array might be needed to keep track of the association between ID numbers and rows.)

8.3   Extend the information system of Exercises 7.16 and 8.2 by including the following commands.

```
b  ArrayJ  ArrayK
e  ArrayJ  ArrayK
```

where b requests the numbers belonging to both lists, and e requests the numbers belonging to either list (or both), as explained in Exercise 7.16. The particular pair of arrays must now be specified as operands of the commands.

(a) Use the two-dimensional integer array from Exercise 8.2(a) and perform merges to carry out the commands.

(b) Use the two-dimensional boolean array from Exercise 8.2(b). Consider each column a boolean vector and form the item-by-item product (AND) vector or the sum (OR) vector, respectively, of the two vectors specified by the command.

8.4   Instead of keeping track of taxicab ID numbers, as you did in Exercises 8.2 and 8.3, keep track of names of some friends. Use a two-dimensional array of names (that is, of packed arrays of char), similar to part (a) of those two exercises. Wherever one of the original commands specified an ID number, a name is now required instead.

8.5   A two-dimensional array of numbers is sometimes called a "matrix." If two matrixes have identical dimensions, their corresponding components can be added or subtracted to form a new matrix containing these sums or differences, respectively. The new matrix has the same dimensions as the two original matrixes and is known as their sum or difference, as appropriate. Write two procedures to produce matrix sums and differences, respectively. Use these procedures in a program that can manipulate two matrixes of 3 rows and 4 columns. The program begins by filling both matrixes with 0's. It then implements the following commands.

```
n K n1 n2...n12      {to supply new values for matrix K}
+ K  J               {to add matrix J to matrix K}
− K  J               {to subtract matrix J from matrix K}
d K                  {to display matrix K}
```

In every case the first array (K) is either modified or displayed. The n command fills array K row by row with 12 numbers. The values of K and J must be 1 or 2. The d command displays the matrix in two dimensions, using three rows and four columns.

8.6   Extend Exercise 8.5 to maintain two identical two-dimensional arrays, whose effective dimensions can be specified at run time, but are not to exceed 10 rows and 10 columns. These logical arrays will be stored in the upper left corner of actual 10 × 10 arrays. The first command must be

```
s  row#  column#
```

to set (s) the number of rows and columns that will be used. Every succeeding n command must specify enough values to fill all row# × column# components of the array. Again, these values are stored row by row.

8.7 Extend Exercises 8.5 and 8.6 to maintain up to five 2-dimensional arrays, using a single 5 × 10 × 10, 3-dimensional array for the data. Initialize the entire array to 0. The command format now changes to

s row# column#	{first command as before}
n arrayK n1 n2 . . . nN	{to supply values for array K}
+ arrayI arrayJ arrayK	{to form sum: I becomes J + K}
− arrayI arrayJ arrayK	{difference: I becomes J − K}
d arrayK	{to display array K in 2-D}

The command n is used to initialize any specified array by supplying row# × column# values to be stored row by row. The + and − commands now specify any two arrays (J and K) as operands and any third array (I) to hold the result. Arrays I, J, and K do not need to be different. Arrays are displayed only in response to the display (d) command.

8.8 Two matrixes, A and B, are said to be the transpose of one another if A is n × m, B is m × n, and $A[i, j] = B[j, i]$ for every position i and j. In other words, row i of A contains exactly the same values as column j of B, and vice versa.
  (a) Write a procedure to display—without actually constructing—the transpose of an n × m numeric matrix, where n and m are a known size (say, 3 × 4).
  (b) Write a procedure to actually construct the transpose of an n × m matrix in a second array. Let both the original and its transpose reside in the upper left-hand corner of physical 10 × 10 arrays. Test the procedure by displaying both its input matrix and its resulting matrix, using the same display procedure. The dimensions, n and m, must be supplied as parameters to these procedures and initially to the program.

8.9 In linear algebra, if A is a k × j matrix and B is a j × n matrix, then the product P is a k × n matrix, where each element $P[r, c]$ is given by:

$$P[r, c] = \sum_{m=1}^{j} A[r, m] \times B[m, c].$$

Write a Pascal program to perform matrix multiplication.

8.10 Design a tic-tac-toe game to be played by two players. When the game starts, and after each move, display the standard three-by-three grid, including the two vertical and two horizontal lines. Each player indicates his or her move by responding to prompts for the row number and the column number by indicating where to place the next mark. The system should handle the alternation between X's and O's, test the validity of each player's request, display the marks as requested, and determine when someone has won or a draw has occurred. *Hint:* The image to be displayed (such as the grid) can be stored as an appropriate pattern in a two-dimensional array.

8.11 (a) Implement a simplified giant-letter program. Predefine three giant letters (say A, B and C) by storing appropriate patterns in two-dimensional arrays. When the user specifies a letter as a command, the corresponding giant letter should be displayed on the screen, using the same display procedure each time.
  (b) Store these three giant letters as parts of a three-dimensional array, indexed by A, B, and C.

(c) Allow the user to specify two or three letters in a row, such as BAA, and print the corresponding giant letters side by side. This will require a new display procedure that uses the array described in part (b).

8.12 In Exercises 5.2 and 5.4, rows of tables were generated in response to input from the terminal. However, during interactive development, the input and output were intermixed on the screen. To allow the table to be viewed as an intact table, either the input had to come from a file or the output had to be directed to a file for later viewing. This is no longer the case. The output can now be stockpiled in main memory inside a two-dimensional array and viewed whenever the user wishes (by issuing a new display command). Rewrite either of these programs, so that it becomes entirely interactive.

8.13 Implement a simple word processing program that accepts text as input and aligns the text along both the left- and right-hand margins. The program stores incoming text in a two-dimensional array, using only as many columns as you specify in an initial command. This number of columns determines the width of the eventual output. As words are being entered, only entire words may be placed in a line. If a word would extend beyond the right-hand margin, the entire word must be placed on the following line. When all the words comprising a line have been entered, they should be repositioned within the line, so that they have about the same number of spaces between them and the last word ends at the right-hand margin—except for the final line. The text is output in response to another special command. Use an array with 20 rows (lines) and 80 (max) columns.

8.14 When a figure or image is scanned by a digitizing device, the result may be a set of points on a two-dimensional grid, corresponding to the borders of the object being scanned. Consider a two-dimensional array (20 × 30) that already contains such an outline. The figure may be represented by 1's in an integer array or by trues in a boolean array. For simplicity, assume that the figure is a sequence of one or more horizontal or vertical line segments, connected end to end. Thus, a "curve" would actually be a collection of very short line segments with tiny jagged edges. If the figure meets itself at all, it must form a closed contour. These assumptions imply that for any point on the grid, at most two adjacent positions will contain other points.

(a) Write procedures to enter a set of points from the terminal and display the figure traced out by these points considered in succession. Each point is specified by a pair of coordinates. If the figure is a line rather than a closed contour, the first pair of numbers entered will specify one of the end points. In any case, this first point will be the starting point for analysis of the figure.

(b) Since the figure occupies only a small fraction of the two-dimensional array, it may be encoded for more compact storage in a one-dimensional array. One way to do this is indicated for the neighborhood of an arbitrary point:

The positions surrounding any point can be specified by an integer from 1 to 4. Using two integers to designate the first point, you can describe each succeeding point on the line by appending one more integer to indicate the direction of travel. This sequence of integers provides a point-by-point description of how to trace the original figure on the grid. The end of the line or the return to the starting point in a closed contour can be indicated by appending 0 as the final point. For example, the sequence

2 3 2 2 3 3 2 2 2 1 1 4 0

represents the following pattern.

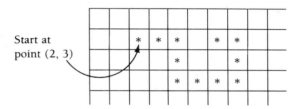

This sequence of integers can be stored in a one-dimensional array. Write a procedure to encode two-dimensional figures this way.

(c) Write a procedure to accept a sequence of integers that represents the encoded form of a figure and to reconstruct the original figure in a two-dimensional array.

(d) The encoding of a figure is not unique. Write a program to accept two encodings and determine whether they denote the same figure. *Hint:* use the procedure from part (c).

8.15 Use the procedures from Exercise 8.14(a) as part of a program to enter a "maze" as a set of points in a two-dimensional array. Include the code to find a path through this maze, as described in Exercise 1.15.

8.16 A dating service uses a two-dimensional array, with the rows representing women and the columns representing men. Assume that there are the same number of each. For now, to preserve anonymity, each person is designated by a row or column number, rather than by name. Men are to be matched with women according to compatibility measures. These measures have already been computed and are entered as the values of the array. For example, $A[i, j]$ indicates the compatibility between woman i and man j. A short and simple technique is to pair the most compatible couple, eliminate them from further consideration, and pair the most compatible of the remaining people, and so on, until all have been paired. This requires successive searches for the maximum compatibility value in successively smaller subarrays of the original. Implement this procedure by effectively eliminating a row and a column from the original array whenever a match is found.

8.17 With the compatibility data from Exercise 8.16, you can give each person an "amiability rating," which is determined by his or her total compatibility with every person of the opposite sex under consideration.

(a) Find the most amiable man and the most amiable woman. (*Note:* these two may not be compatible with each other.)

(b) Display the IDs of the women in order of decreasing amiability.

(c) Display the IDs of the men in decreasing order of amiability.

8.18 A system of linear equations, $Ax = b$, can be solved by a technique known as Gaussian elimination. If A is an N × N matrix and b is a vector of length N, then A and b can be stored in an N × (N + 1) array. The fundamental algorithm for Gaussian elimination is

```
1.    for c := 1 to N − 1 do:
1.1      for r := c + 1 to N do:
1.1.1       m := A[r,c] / A[c,c];
1.1.2       for k := c to N + 1 do:
1.1.2.1        A[r,k] := A[r,k] − m * A[c,k]
2.    stop.
```

where r is the row index, c the column index, A[c, c] is assumed to be nonzero, and k is a "moving" column index.

Write a Pascal program to perform Gaussian elimination. The output of the resulting array A should reveal that every element below the main diagonal is zero.

8.19 The Gaussian elimination technique described in Exercise 8.18 can be enhanced by using "partial pivoting." This enhancement helps avoid some nasty arithmetic problems, the solution of which are beyond the scope of this book. Simply stated, partial pivoting involves finding the row Pos that contains the largest absolute value in column c and then interchanging rows c and Pos. In pseudocode form this is

```
1.    Pos := c;
2.    for r := c + 1 to N do:
2.1      if |A[r,c]| > |A[Pos,c]| then
             Pos := r;
3.    interchange row c and row Pos;
```

which should be incorporated in the pseudocode of Exercise 8.18 between steps 1 and 1.1. Write a Pascal program to implement Gaussian elimination with partial pivoting.

8.20 Upon completion of Gaussian elimination, you are in a position to find the values for x that satisfy $Ax = b$. Since the matrix A is in upper triangular form, you can immediately find the value of x[N] as A[N, N + 1]/A[N, N]. You can find the other values of x by backward substitution, or

$$x[r] = (A[r,N+1] - \sum_{c=r+1}^{N} A[r,c] * x[c]) / A[r,r]$$

Note that if A[r, r] = 0 for any $1 <= r <= N$, then the system is singular (that is, has an infinite number of solutions or no solution). Write a Pascal program to solve a nonsingular system of linear equations using Gaussian elimination with partial pivoting and backward substitution.

9

Records and Sets

In many applications we deal with different types of data that are logically related, say, to the same customer, inventory item, or experimental event. Customer data, for example, may consist of a name (PACKED ARRAY of char), an account number (integer), and a balance owing (real). Collecting such related data into one structure to represent their association and identify them as a group is often desirable. Since the data are not all of identical type, they cannot be collected into an array. Fortunately, another structured data *record* type, known as a **record**, is capable of gathering components of different types into one common structure having its own type and identifier. Because of the common need to associate dissimilar values, records play a prominent role in practical programs. In this chapter we introduce records and present some of their uses. Many more applications are included in the chapters that follow.

Another structured data type, the SET, permits the representation and manipulation of sets as found in mathematics. A set in Pascal may contain as members only ordinal values belonging to the same data type, but such values can be inserted, removed, and tested for membership with ease. Since entire sets can be manipulated with primitive operations, sets provide a convenient way to associate similar values for certain kinds of processing. Sets are also explained in this chapter.

9.1 Simple Records

Suppose that we are interested in individual stocks in an investment portfolio. Each stock might have an abbreviated name (a string type), a stock identification number (an integer), *and* three (real) amounts: the high, low, and

371

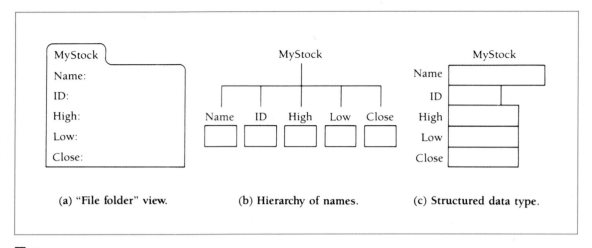

(a) "File folder" view.   (b) Hierarchy of names.   (c) Structured data type.

■ Figure 9.1
Images of a particular record.

closing prices. These five items can be made part of a single record MyStock.
Figure 9.1 shows three different ways of visualizing this record's structure.
In all three, specific values may be stored in five slots or locations. These

fields   locations are called **fields,** and each has its own unique identifier. The
identifier MyStock refers to the entire collection.

Figure 9.1(b) shows that a record implies a hierarchy of names and that
the actual data values are associated with the bottom level of the hierarchy.
Figure 9.1(c), though meant to suggest that the aggregate contains different
data types, is not meant to imply anything about the physical storage of the
data.

Record Fundamentals

Figure 9.2 shows how to declare this record in Pascal. Here StockType is the
record type, just as StringType identifies an array type. We declare an actual
record, MyStock, in the variable declaration part, as usual.

The individual fields are prescribed between the reserved words RECORD
and its matching END. The END is used to indicate exactly where the field
Record definition   definitions terminate. Each field is prescribed by (1) its identifier; and (2) its
type. In fact, we declare the fields within a record just as we declare the
variables in the VAR part. For example, we can declare consecutive fields
having the same type by writing a list of field identifiers having a common
type that is specified at the end of the list. Any number of fields can be
declared, and they can be of any legitimate data type.

■ Figure 9.2
Declaration of the
record MyStock.

```
TYPE
  StringType = PACKED ARRAY [1..10] OF char;
  StockType =
    RECORD
      Name : StringType;
      Id : integer;
      High,
      Low,
      Close : real
    END
VAR
  MyStock : StockType;
```

■ Figure 9.2
Declaration of the
record MyStock.

Record field references

Figure 9.3 shows how individual fields are referenced within a program. The record identifier must be included to distinguish between various records of the same type. The record identifier forms the first part of the name and the field identifier forms the second; the record and field identifiers are separated by a period.

The notation can be compared to that for referencing an individual array component, where the array name is followed by the position index, enclosed in square brackets. The differences are that record components are selected by a field name instead of by an index and that the syntax requires a period instead of brackets to separate the record name from the field name.

Use of record fields

Of course, the fields are merely objects that may be used like any other objects of their particular type. For example, MyStock.High is just a simple real variable; its name is more complex because of its membership in a record.

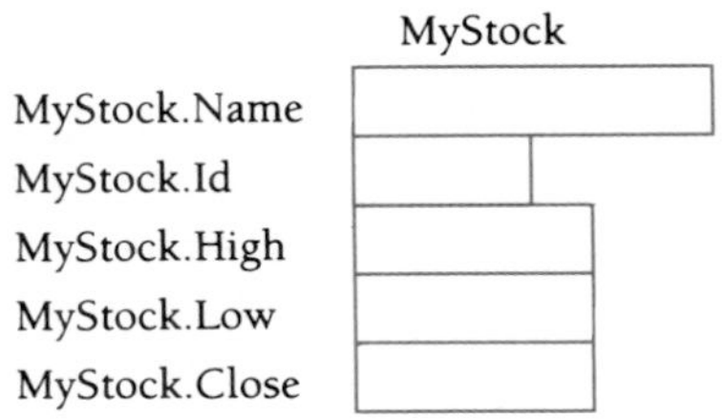

■ Figure 9.3
Referring to
individual fields
within the record
MyStock.

MyStock

MyStock.Name
MyStock.Id
MyStock.High
MyStock.Low
MyStock.Close

Nevertheless, it behaves like any other real variable. It may have a value read into it:

```
read (MyStock.High);
```

It may be assigned or compared to another numeric value:

```
IF CurrentPrice > MyStock.High THEN {revise}
   MyStock.High := CurrentPrice;
```

Or it may be used in an arithmetic expression:

```
MidPrice := (MyStock.High + MyStock.Low) / 2;
```

The first field, MyStock.Name, on the other hand, is a packed array of characters and as such must be manipulated in ways appropriate to this data type, such as

```
MyStock.Name := 'AlGoldMine';
```

Fields as parameters   The individual fields may be passed as parameters to subprograms having formal parameters that are of the appropriate type. For example, the function Midrange in Fig. 9.4 finds the midpoint between *any* two real numbers, regardless of their source. They could have represented the low and high ends of the range of prices paid for MyStock, as in

```
Avg := MidRange( MyStock.Low, MyStock.High );
```

An entire record can also be passed as a parameter, provided the subprogram has defined a formal parameter with the corresponding record type.

Entire records as parameters   The procedure ShowStock in Fig. 9.4 accepts a record of type StockType and displays the name, the identification number, the average of the high and low prices, and the closing price. Note that the formal parameter identifier Stock is used to identify the entire record within this procedure, but the field identifiers remain unchanged from the original declaration of StockType at the outer program level. Hence the complete field references within the subprogram are Stock.Name, Stock.Id, Stock.High, and so on. The average is calculated by the function Midrange. Note how the field values from Stock are passed as ordinary real numbers to this function.

Figure 9.4 also shows a typical call to ShowStock, as well as the output produced for a particular set of field values. Since the ShowStock procedure displays only the field values, its record arrives through a value-type parameter. As usual, a variable-type parameter is required whenever a subprogram might alter *any* portion of an entire record passed as a parameter.

Record assignment   Finally, we can copy an entire record into another record of identical type, using only a single assignment statement. Thus, if we have three records of StockType, as in

```
VAR MyStock, YourStock, ExtraCopy: StockType;
```

```
FUNCTION MidRange (Value1,Value2: real): real;
  BEGIN
    MidRange := (Value1 + Value2) / 2
  END;

PROCEDURE ShowStock (Stock: StockType);
  BEGIN
    writeln (Stock.Name);
    writeln ('i.d.#',Stock.Id:8);
    writeln ('Mid Price: ',
      MidRange(Stock.Low,Stock.High):10:2);
    writeln ('Closing Price: ',Stock.Close:6:2)
  END;

BEGIN {main program}
    .
    .
    .
  ShowStock (MyStock); {assuming MyStock contains values}
    .
    .
    .
```

These record values . . .   yield . . .   This display

MyStock

| A1GoldMine |
| 2727 |
| 51.75 |
| 23.25 |
| 24.63 |

```
A1GoldMine
i.d.#     2727
Mid Price:       37.50
Closing Price:   24.63
```

■ Figure 9.4
Use of records and
fields as parameters.

then we can interchange all five fields of MyStock and YourStock by executing the statements:

```
ExtraCopy := MyStock;
MyStock  := YourStock;
YourStock := ExtraCopy;
```

As with unpacked arrays, an entire record may be referenced in only two situations: (1) assignment from one record to another of identical type; and

Record Definition Style

Records are defined throughout the text as follows:

1. The record identifier and the "=" appear at the same level of indentation as other types.
2. The reserved word RECORD appears on the next line, indented one level from the record identifier.
3. All field names and field types appear on separate lines and are indented one level from RECORD.
4. The END appears at the same level as the corresponding RECORD.

EXAMPLE

```
TYPE
  SampleRec =
    RECORD
      Field1: integer;
      Field2: real;
      Field3: char
    END;
```

(2) as a parameter in a subprogram reference. The latter is one of the major reasons that records are used: to allow an arbitrary collection of objects to be passed to subprograms as a single package by means of a single identifier.

In other situations, only individual fields may be referenced or manipulated. The relational operators, for example, cannot be applied to entire records; one would have to test whether MyStock and YourStock were equal by separately comparing all five pairs of corresponding fields.

The WITH Statement

The specification of field names can cause statements that reference parts of a record to become fairly long. Consider displaying all the fields of the record MyStock on a single output line. The writeln statement could look like

```
writeln (MyStock.Name,MyStock.Id:8,
         MyStock.High:10:2,
         MyStock.Low:10:2,MyStock.Close:10:2);
```

Even though all the fields in this statement were chosen from the same record, the record identifier was mentioned five times.

Pascal provides a way of specifying the record identifier (such as MyStock) only once, without having to repeat it in every field reference within the

WITH statement statement. This construct, called the **WITH statement,** is written

> WITH ⟨record identifier⟩ DO
> ⟨statement⟩;

and means "with the record identifier indicated here, manipulate its fields according to the following executable statement." The statement following it need not include the record name; any field identifiers contained in it are assumed to pertain to the record selected by the WITH statement.

Our display example can therefore be rewritten as

```
WITH MyStock DO
  writeln(Name,Id:8,High:10:2,Low:10:2,Close:10:2);
```

Not only does this form reduce the amount of writing, it also clarifies the following statement. In a sense it allows you to factor out the record identifier, so that neither this identifier nor the intervening periods needs to appear in the field references of the following statement.

As usual, the statement governed by WITH may be a compound statement. Thus, to display the fields of MyStock on three separate lines, we could use

```
WITH MyStock DO
  BEGIN
    writeln (Name);
    writeln (Id:8);
    writeln (High:10:2,Low:10:2,Close:10:2)
  END; {influence of WITH}
```

The statement governed by WITH may still contain other variable references besides the fields of the selected record. These other references are unaffected by WITH. An explicit record identifier always overrides any record identifier implied by a surrounding WITH statement.

WITH can govern multiple records If we want to manipulate more than one record type in a segment of code, we can include a list of record identifiers in the preceding WITH. However, this form is generally not recommended. Associating a field name with the correct record requires knowledge of the record declarations and the technicalities of the WITH statement. Any isolated field name that belongs to more than one record in the list is associated with the rightmost applicable record. However, the possibility of confusion suggests using WITH in moderation, usually to identify just a single record over a very limited region of the code.

Distance between Points

Consider the problem of finding the straight-line distance between two points. Each point is specified by a pair of coordinates in a plane, usually written (x,y). The coordinates could be grouped into a single record, so that the points can be represented by a single identifier.

If we let records P1 and P2 represent the two points and use subprograms to handle the details, the main program is trivial:

```
ReadCoord (P1);
ReadCoord (P2);
ShowDistance(P1,P2);
```

```
PROGRAM PointDistance (input,output);

TYPE
   Point =
      RECORD
         Xpart: real;
         Ypart: real
      END;
VAR
   P1, P2: Point;

PROCEDURE ReadCoord (VAR Pt: Point);

   {Read one pair of numbers to initialize one point}

   BEGIN
      write('Enter x and y coordinates for one point:');
      WITH Pt DO
         readln (Xpart,Ypart)
   END; {ReadCoord}

PROCEDURE ShowDistance (P1,P2: Point);

   VAR
      Distance : real;

   BEGIN
      Distance := sqrt(sqr(P1.Xpart - P2.Xpart)
                       + sqr(P1.Ypart - P2.Ypart));
      writeln ('Distance is ',Distance:10:2)
   END; {Distance }

BEGIN {PointDistance}

   ReadCoord (P1);
   ReadCoord (P2);
   ShowDistance (P1,P2)

END. {PointDistance}
```

The important feature of this program is that it deals entirely at the level of "points"; we do not need to consider their internal representations. At this stage of program design, the programmer is spared from further details. The complete program is shown in Fig. 9.5. Note that the declarations first specify the structure of a record and then create two instances of it. (It does not matter that the record components both have the same type in this example; they do not have to differ.)

The input to the program consists of two lines, each containing two real numbers representing the (x,y) coordinates of a point. The procedure ReadCoord reads one pair of values into the two fields of a record. A complete record is then passed to the main program through its variable formal parameter. Since this procedure deals exclusively with a single record, the WITH statement simplifies and clarifies the code.

The result is calculated and displayed by the procedure ShowDistance. Since this procedure deals with two records having the same data type and identical field names, using the WITH statement here would be pointless and confusing. ShowDistance calculates its result using the formula

$$s = \sqrt{(x_2 - x_1)^2 + (y_2 - y_1)^2}$$

where the two points have coordinates (x_1, y_1) and (x_2, y_2).

9.2 Arrays of Records

Declaration Many applications involving records deal with several records of the same type. A program concerned with stock activity is a typical example. An individual record of type StockType might be provided for each of several Stocks being analyzed. The records pertaining to all of these stocks can be assembled into an array. The declaration of such an array is no different from before, except that its components happen to be records.

```
TYPE
    StringType = PACKED ARRAY [1 . . 10] OF char;
    StockType =
      RECORD
        Name: StringType;
        Id: integer;
        High, Low, Close: real
      END;
    AllStocks = ARRAY [1 . . 10] OF StockType;

VAR
    Stock: AllStocks;
```

Reference Membership in an array does not change the nature of any individual record. It merely adds some complexity to the record identifiers. Instead of a simple name, each record, being part of an array, now has an array subscript as part of its identifier. The third record in the array is called Stock[3], and its fields are referenced by Stock[3].Name, Stock[3].Id, Stock[3].High, and so on. We can display these fields by writing

```
WITH Stock[3] DO
  writeln(Name,Id:8,High:10:2,Low:10:2,Close:10:2);
```

Thus the only change is in the name of the entire record.

Hierarchy of data and procedures

The addition of one more level to the structure of the data is often accompanied by one more level in the hierarchy of subprograms. Consider the use of a procedure, Report, to display all of the current stock information. This procedure (shown in Fig. 9.6) accepts from the calling program the entire array of records plus the number of records to be displayed.

The calling program deals with only the whole array and not with its interior structure. A typical call would be

```
Report (Stock,HowMany);
```

The Report procedure is responsible for sequencing through the array but not for dealing with the interior of any record. It hands entire records (one at a time) to another procedure, WriteStock. This latter procedure extracts the individual fields and passes them to writeln for the actual output. Thus the main procedure supplies the entire array to the display process, Report selects a record from the array, WriteStock isolates fields from the record, and writeln processes the fields. In summary:

Procedure	Action
Main program	Initiates output of entire array
Report	Selects records from array
WriteStock	Selects fields from record
writeln	Displays field

Each procedure deals either with a limited object or with a complex object in a limited way. Thus none of the procedures is burdened with the complexities of specifying full field references, and all are extremely simple.

In contrast to the procedure approach, the main program could have used writeln itself (with no help from subprograms) as follows:

```
FOR Current := 1 TO HowMany DO
  WITH Stock[Current] DO
    BEGIN
      writeln ('Name of stock: ',Name);
      writeln ('Identification: ',Id);
      writeln (High:10:2,Low:10:2,Close:10:2);
      writeln
    END;
```

```
PROCEDURE Report (Stock: AllStocks; HowMany: integer);

    VAR
        Current: integer;

    PROCEDURE WriteStock (Issue: StockType);

        BEGIN {WriteStock}
            WITH Issue DO
                BEGIN
                    writeln ('Name of stock: ',Name);
                    writeln ('Identification: ',Id);
                    writeln (High:10:2,Low:10:2,Close:10:2)
                END
        END; {WriteStock}

    BEGIN {Report}
        FOR Current := 1 TO HowMany DO
            BEGIN
                WriteStock(Stock[Current]);
                writeln
            END
    END; {Report}

BEGIN {main program}
    .

    .
    Report(Stock,HowMany);
    .
    .
    .
```

■ Figure 9.6
Hierarchy of procedures to display hierarchical data.

Although this code is not difficult to understand, it would tend to clutter the main program with unnecessary detail.

Maintaining Information on Stocks

Let's reconsider the problem of maintaining stock information, presented originally in section 8.3. The major difference here is that the company name is to be included along with the numeric data pertaining to each stock. Consequently, we must use a record (rather than an array) to group the data for each company.

The basic problem is as before: to interactively read pairs of numbers (a stock identification number and a selling price) and to revise the current information (high, low, and close) for that stock. If a search of currently active stocks reveals that this one has just begun to trade, a new record is initialized to represent this new stock. In this version of the problem, the initialization includes prompting the user for the company name to be included in the record. The final report displays the data for each active stock (using the code from Fig. 9.6).

Except for the declarations, the stock-market program in Fig. 9.7 is almost identical to the one in Fig. 8.15. At this highest level of logic, the organization of company data into records, as opposed to arrays, has not made any substantial difference.

Searching an array of records

The position function in Fig. 9.8 on p. 384, which determines the position in the array occupied by the desired record, uses the same logic as the Search function from Fig. 8.16. In this code however, because the array component Stock[Psn] identifies a record, we refer to the company identification number stored in that record as Stock[Psn].Id. This reference may be thought of as a template that covers an entire record, enabling us to "see" the Id portion but masking out all the other fields. The action of Position is to move this template from one record to the next (by varying Psn) until we see the desired company number through the "window" or until we have inspected all records.

Update procedure

The Update procedure of Fig. 9.9, also on p. 384, is given one entire record and the most recent selling price for that company's stock. The procedure revises the closing price and, if applicable, either the high or low price. This procedure does not know or care that the record is part of an array, it is capable of altering this array component, passed as a variable parameter. Since it deals with a single record, the entire interior of this procedure is under the influence of a WITH statement. Note how the code introduced by WITH refers both to fields of the record and to the real-valued parameter Price with no confusion. Compare this procedure with the array version in Fig. 8.17.

Enter procedure

Finally, the Enter procedure in Fig. 9.10 (p. 385) behaves much like its counterpart in Fig. 8.18, except that we initialize a record, requiring reference to record fields. Note that WITH can refer to a record that is part of an array. Its effect even extends to parameters, so that the call to ObtainName causes a character string to be placed in Stock[HowMany].Name.

The other difference here is in obtaining the company name. We use the auxiliary procedure ObtainName for this purpose; it reads characters from the terminal and supplies additional blanks in the usual way for an array of 10 characters. Although the array for the name is part of a record in the Enter procedure, ObtainName treats it as a simple packed array.

```
PROGRAM Market (input,output);
CONST
   MaxStocks = 10; {much larger in practice}
TYPE
   LineType = PACKED ARRAY [1..10] OF char;
   StockType =
      RECORD
         Name : StringType;
         Id : integer;
         High, Low, Close : real
      END;
   AllStocks = ARRAY [1..MaxStocks] OF StockType;
VAR
   Stock: AllStocks;   {major data structure}
   HowMany: integer; {psns occupied in Stock}
   Company: integer; {ID number; input item}
   Price: real;{of stock; input item}
   SelectedPsn: integer;   {result of Search}

FUNCTION Position (Stock: AllStocks;
                      Company,HowMany: integer): integer;

PROCEDURE Update (VAR ThisStock: StockType; Price: real);

PROCEDURE Enter (VAR Stock: AllStocks;
                  Company: integer; Price: real;
                  VAR HowMany: integer);

PROCEDURE Report (Stock: AllStocks; HowMany: integer);

BEGIN {StockMarket}
   HowMany := 0;        {array empty}
   WHILE NOT eof DO
      BEGIN
         readln (Company, Price);
         SelectedPsn := Position(Stock,Company,HowMany);
         IF .SelectedPsn = 0 THEN {1st sale for stock}
            Enter (Stock,Company,Price,HowMany)
         ELSE
            Update (Stock[SelectedPsn],Price)
      END;
   Report (Stock, HowMany)
END. {StockMarket}
```

■ Figure 9.7
Main program to report stock selling prices.

```
FUNCTION Position (Stock: AllStocks;
                   Company,HowMany: integer): integer;

   {Determine position in Stock array where Company
    i.d. is located. Return 0 if i.d. not found.}

   VAR
      Psn: integer;    {to traverse array}
      Found: boolean;

   BEGIN {Position}
      Found := false;
      Psn := 0;
      WHILE (Psn < HowMany) AND (NOT Found) DO
         BEGIN
            Psn := Psn + 1;
            IF Stock[Psn].Id = Company THEN
               Found := true
         END;

      IF Found THEN
         Position := Psn {where found}
      ELSE
         Position := 0 {to signal failure}
   END; {Position}
```

■ Figure 9.8
Function to search array of records for company i.d.

```
PROCEDURE Update (VAR ThisStock: StockType; Price: real);

   BEGIN
      WITH ThisStock DO
         BEGIN

            IF Price > High THEN       {new high}
               High := Price;
            IF Price < Low THEN        {new low}
               Low := Price;
            Close := Price

         END    {manipulation of ThisStock}
   END; {Update}
```

■ Figure 9.9
Updating an already active stock record.

```
PROCEDURE Enter (VAR Stock: AllStocks;
                      Company: integer; Price: real;
                      VAR HowMany: integer);

   PROCEDURE ObtainName (VAR Name: StringType);

      VAR
         Psn, K: integer;
      BEGIN {ObtainName}
         writeln ('New stock; enter company name');
         Psn := 0;
         WHILE NOT eoln AND (Psn < 10) DO
            BEGIN     {input name}
               Psn := Psn + 1;
               read (Name[Psn])
            END;
         readln;
         FOR K := Psn+1 TO 10 DO    {pad with blanks}
            Name[K] := ' '
      END; {ObtainName}

   BEGIN {Enter}
      IF HowMany >= MaxStocks THEN {no more space}
         writeln ('Sorry, array is full')
      ELSE
         BEGIN {space available}
            HowMany := HowMany + 1;
            WITH Stock[Howmany] DO
               BEGIN {initialize record}

                  ObtainName(Name);
                  Id := Company;
                  High := Price;
                  Low := Price;
                  Closing := Price

               END {influence of WITH}
            END {Initialization}

   END; {Enter}
```

■ Figure 9.10
Initializing new stock using first empty row.

9.3 Records Containing Structured Data

You have already encountered records containing an array-type field to hold a character string. The fields of a record can be any legitimate type, including arrays of any description and even record structures.

Records Containing Array-Type Fields

One common reason for placing an array inside a record is to combine the array and its effective length in a single structure having a single identifier. This allows all the information pertaining to the array to be passed among subprograms through a single parameter.

Referring to arrays that are fields

Consider the record Student, which we declared in Fig. 9.11(a) and diagrammed in Fig. 9.11(b). This record has a field Score; its complete reference is Student.Score. Because this reference also identifies an array, the second component in that array is identified by including the subscript in square brackets after the array name, or Student.Score[2]. All three scores could be displayed by the code:

```
FOR K := 1 TO 3 DO
   write (Student.Score[K]);
```

The record identifier can be isolated in a WITH statement by either

```
FOR K := 1 TO 3 DO          or     WITH Student DO
   WITH Student DO                     FOR K := 1 TO 3 DO
      write (Score[K]);                   write (Score[K]);
```

Note that we have introduced no new rules. We used the usual rules governing either array or record referencing at each level, depending on the type of object that must be accessed at that level. Keeping the different types straight is the difficult part.

Arrays of records with array fields

These names become even more exciting when dealing with an array of such records (such as the array Class, declared in Fig. 9.11a). In this structure, each record has the same form as Student, but now the record identifier itself is an array component. The 17th student record is known as Class[17], his or her identification number is Class[17].StudentId, and the first recorded score is Class[17].Score[1]. This overall structure is shown in Fig. 9.11(c).

Hierarchy of input data and procedures

In Fig. 9.12 on p. 388, we present a hierarchy of procedures that could be used to initialize the entire array of records, assuming that each line of input consists of a student number followed by three (integer) scores. As before, we keep the various levels separate. InitialClass merely traverses the Class array, calling InitialStudent to provide values for each record. InitialClass is not involved with the interior of the records. InitialStudent, in turn, calls

```
CONST
  ClassSize = 40;
TYPE
  ScoreType = ARRAY [1..3] OF integer;
  StudentInfo =
    RECORD
      StudentId: integer;
      Score: ScoreType;
      Avg: real
    END;
  ClassType = ARRAY [1..ClassSize] OF StudentInfo;

VAR
  Student: StudentInfo;
  Class: ClassType;
```

(a) Actual declarations.

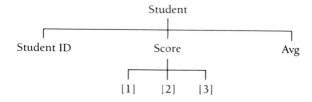

(b) Structure of the single record Student.

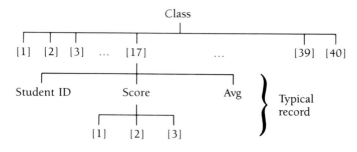

(c) Structure of the array of records Class.

■ Figure 9.11
Declaring an array of records with array-type fields.

ReadScores to provide values for the array portion of the record. InitialStudent need not know that the record is part of an array, and it need deal only with the major components of the record. It makes no difference to ReadScores that the array of scores may be part of a record.

By going down just one additional level in the hierarchy of data, we have each procedure perform a limited task and can use fairly simple names, appropriate to the level of data object the procedure deals with. Establishing

```
PROCEDURE ReadScores (VAR Score: ScoreType);

   VAR
      K: integer;
   BEGIN
      FOR K := 1 TO 3 DO
         read (Score[K]);
      readln
   END; {ReadScores}


PROCEDURE InitialStudent (VAR Student: StudentInfo);

   BEGIN
      WITH Student DO
         BEGIN
            read (StudentId);
            ReadScores (Score);
            Avg := (Score[1]+Score[2]+Score[3]) / 3
         END
   END; {InitialStudent}


PROCEDURE InitialClass (VAR Class: ClassType;
                        VAR HowMany: integer);
   BEGIN
      HowMany := 0;
      WHILE NOT eof AND (HowMany < ClassSize) DO
         BEGIN
            HowMany := HowMany + 1;
            InitialStudent (Class[HowMany])
         END
   END; {InitialClass}
```

■ Figure 9.12
Hierarchy of input procedures.

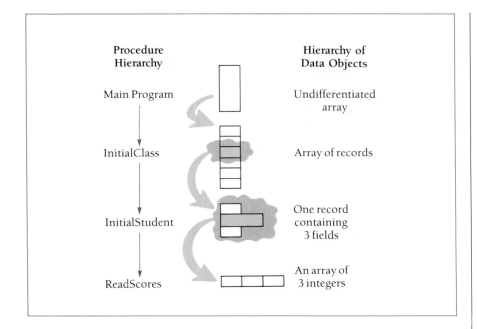

■ Figure 9.13
Corresponding
procedure and data
hierarchies.

a hierarchy of procedures to parallel the hierarchy of data types greatly simplifies the identification of the components of complex record structures. We illustrate this correspondence in Fig. 9.13.

Records Containing Record-Type Fields

The fields of a record may be of any legitimate type, including a previously defined record type. These constructions arise quite naturally in many problems.

Defining records with record fields

Suppose that a student record is to contain the student's name, as well as his or her identification number and scores. The name would probably consist of at least two character strings, one for the first name and another for the last name. This would permit the last name to appear first in an alphabetical list but to appear after the first name in another application, such as a mailing. The actual data associated with each student would then consist of the six items shown in Fig. 9.14(a). We could establish these six items as six separate fields in a single record type, but collecting the three scores into a single array-type field makes them more convenient to manipulate and pass as a group to subprograms.

Treating the two components of the name as a unit may also be useful. One application, such as posting scores identified only by student number, may involve all the numeric data but not the name. Another application, such

| Fred | Klein | 30616 | 92 | 41 | 56 |

(a) The data pertaining to one student.

```
TYPE
  ScoreType = ARRAY [1..3] OF integer;

  StudentInfo =
    RECORD              {like Fig. 9.11 without Avg}
      Id: Integer;
      Score: ScoreType
    END;
  StringType = PACKED ARRAY [1..20] OF char;

  NameType =
    RECORD
      First,
      Last: StringType
    END;
  StudentType =
    RECORD
      Name: NameType;
      Info: StudentInfo
    END;
VAR Student: StudentType;
```

(b) Definitions and variable declaration.

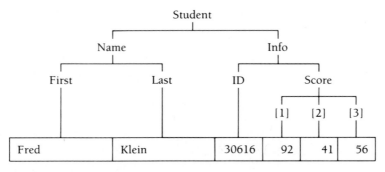

(c) Combined structure.

■ **Figure 9.14**
Declaring a record with record-type fields.

as generating class lists, may use only the name and not the other information. The two strings representing the name can be grouped into one record type and the remaining (numeric) information grouped into another. This approach permits us to identify and process either set of items as a unit and leads to the first two record definitions in Fig. 9.14(b).

For those applications using both the name and scores, all the information about a student should be collected into a single unit. This is done in the third record definition in Fig. 9.14(b), which establishes an overall student record with two fields that are the previously defined record types.

Structure

Figure 9.14(c) shows the combined structure of the overall student record. We have simply taken the original six data objects and grouped them in a hierarchy to facilitate their processing.

References

Referring to components of this record requires knowledge of the hierarchy but involves no new concepts. Take the student name, for example. The entire name is Student.Name. This object is itself a record of type NameType, whose fields are specified by including the field identifier and another period. The separate parts of the name are

Student.Name.Last   and   Student.Name.First

Similarly, the identification number is stored in the variable Student.Info.Id, and the second score recorded for the student is Student.Info.Score[2]. We construct the complete field reference by choosing a name from each level of the hierarchy and separate consecutive levels with a period. A field name, then, corresponds to a path from the top of the hierarchy to a specific location at the bottom.

More about the WITH statement

The WITH statement is still applicable, with more options than ever before. Since two different levels represent records, either can be isolated in the WITH statement. The following code fragments show four equivalent ways of displaying the first and last names.

```
writeln (Student.Name.First, Student.Name.Last);

WITH Student DO
  writeln (Name.First, Name.Last);

WITH Student.Name DO
  writeln (First, Last);

WITH Student DO
  WITH Name DO
    writeln (First, Last);
```

The last code fragment shows that the nesting of WITH statements can parallel the nesting of data objects. This nested form is useful when various subrecords of the outer record must be manipulated. However, if used to excess, it can cause confusion.

Records and the Scope of Identifiers

Recall from Section 4.5 that the term *scope* refers to the extent of a program over which any particular declaration of an identifier applies. Since only one declaration can apply at a time, the same identifier can be used in different program modules with different meanings in each.

Effect of record identifier

Similarly, whenever a record is defined, its field names pertain only to that type of record. We may declare the same identifier inside different record types and as a stand-alone identifier. There is never any confusion about which declaration applies when the identifier appears in a reference. An identifier used in conjunction with some record identifier refers to a component of that record. An identifier used by itself (assuming that it has a valid, independent declaration) does not refer to a field of any record.

The record identifier therefore gives a new meaning to the field identifier, which supersedes any other meaning the field identifier may have. In other words, the record identifier imposes a new context or region in which the interpretation given by the record declaration applies.

Effect of WITH

The WITH statement expands this region to cover one or more subsequent statements, instead of just an individual field reference. Thus every identifier within the influence of WITH that could possibly refer to a field of the indicated record does indeed do so. The interpretation imposed by the WITH statement overrides any other meaning that identifier may have outside this context. Until now the scope boundaries always coincided with some collection of program modules, but in the context of records they can also be prescribed by complete field references and by WITH statements.

To see the effect of these additional scope rules, let's consider the declarations in Fig. 9.15(a). Since X is undefined outside record R, X cannot be used as a stand-alone variable. The identifier Y, on the other hand, is declared both as a simple variable and as a field of record Q. When used by itself, Y refers to a boolean variable, but when used with record identifier Q, it refers to a real variable inside the record (Fig. 9.15b). Similarly, the identifier Z can be legally declared as a field name having different meanings in the different record types R and Q (Fig. 9.15c).

Effect of nested WITH

When WITH statements are nested, their regions of influence are also nested. If an identifier is used in both regions and identifies a field in both record types, the inner region applies. This parallels exactly our experience with nested subprograms.

When a WITH statement contains a list of records, such as

```
WITH A,B,C DO
```

this is equivalent to the nesting:

```
WITH A DO
  WITH B DO
    WITH C DO
```

```
TYPE
  FirstType =
    RECORD
      X: real;
      Z: char
    END;

  OtherType =
    RECORD
      Y: real;
      W: integer;
      Z: real
    END;

VAR
  R : FirstType;
  Q : OtherType;
  Y : boolean;
```

(a) Declarations.

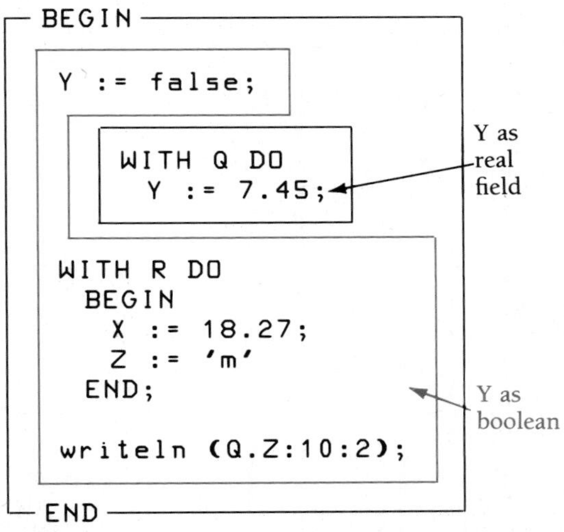

```
┌─ BEGIN ─────────────────────────┐
│                                 │
│   Y := false;                   │        Y as
│   ┌─────────────────────────┐   │        real
│   │   WITH Q DO              │   │        field
│   │     Y := 7.45;◄──────────┼───┼──────
│   └─────────────────────────┘   │
│                                 │
│   WITH R DO                     │
│     BEGIN                       │
│       X := 18.27;               │
│       Z := 'm'                  │
│     END;                        │        Y as
│                                 │◄────── boolean
│   writeln (Q.Z:10:2);           │
│                                 │
└─ END ───────────────────────────┘
```

(b) Program showing scope for two
different declarations of Y.

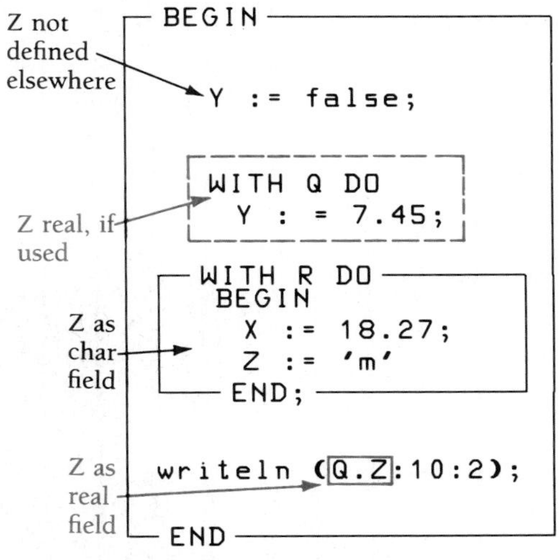

Z not
defined
elsewhere

Z real, if
used

Z as
char
field

Z as
real
field

```
┌─ BEGIN ─────────────────────────┐
│                                 │
│   ──►Y := false;                │
│                                 │
│   ┌ ─ ─ ─ ─ ─ ─ ─ ─ ─ ─ ─ ┐     │
│   │  WITH Q DO              │    │
│   │    Y : = 7.45;◄─────────┼────┼
│   └ ─ ─ ─ ─ ─ ─ ─ ─ ─ ─ ─ ┘     │
│   ┌─ WITH R DO ──────────────┐  │
│   │    BEGIN                  │  │
│   │      X := 18.27;◄─────────┼──┼
│   │      Z := 'm'             │  │
│   │    END;                   │  │
│   └───────────────────────────┘ │
│                                 │
│   writeln (⌐Q.Z:10:2);◄─────────┼──
│                                 │
└─ END ───────────────────────────┘
```

(c) Program showing scope for two
different declarations of Z.

■ Figure 9.15
Scope rules pertaining to records.

Therefore, if a field identifier pertains to more than one record in such a list, the identifier is associated with the latest mentioned record to which it could refer. Although the scope rules sort out the interpretation of identifiers at every point in the program, you should generally avoid multiple declarations of the same identifier in order to eliminate possible confusion.

Records in the Context of Text Processing

Representing varying length strings as records

As you learned in Chapter 7, a character string of arbitrary length can be represented by two components. Its characters are stored in an (unpacked) array, and its effective length—the number of currently significant characters—is stored in an integer variable. If we combine the length variable and the character array into a record, the entire string can be identified by a single name and passed as a single entity. Fig. 9.16 shows two of these strings when they contain data.

Input

Representing a varying length string as a record does not change the logic of string processing; it only simplifies some of the notation. For example, Fig. 9.17 shows a ReadLine procedure that reads characters from the terminal into a string. The values shown in Fig. 9.16 might have come from executing

```
ReadLine (A);
ReadLine (B);
```

This procedure works exactly like its counterpart in Fig. 7.32. However, the record-oriented version needs only one parameter and expresses all of its operations in terms of record fields. In fact, its entire executable section is

■ Figure 9.16
Records to represent varying length character strings.

```
TYPE
  LineType =
    RECORD
      Length: integer;
      Info: ARRAY [1..10] OF char
    END;

VAR
  A, B: LineType;
```

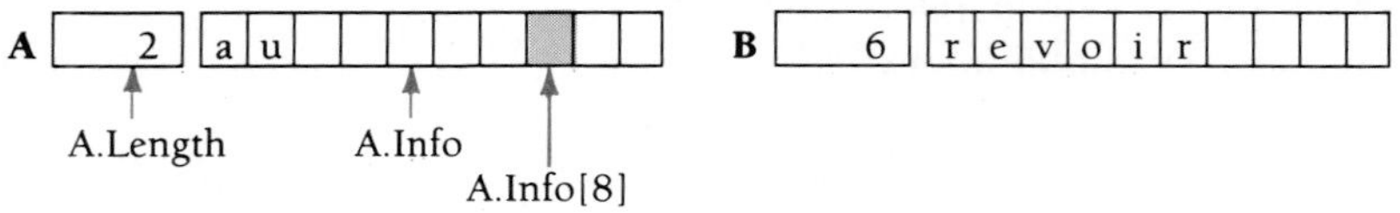

A [2 | a | u | | | | | | |]   B [6 | r | e | v | o | i | r | | |]

A.Length   A.Info

A.Info[8]

```
PROCEDURE ReadLine (VAR NewLine : LineType);

    {Obtain new line of text from terminal
     and install it together with its length
     in the record, NewLine}

    BEGIN
        WITH NewLine DO
            BEGIN

                Length := 0;
                WHILE NOT eoln AND (Length < MaxChars) DO
                    BEGIN
                        Length := Length + 1;
                        read( Info[Length] )
                    END;
                readln

            END {influence of WITH}
    END; {ReadLine}
```

■ Figure 9.17
Initializing a string stored in a record.

within the scope of a WITH statement. Note the read statement in Fig. 9.17: Each execution places a value in a character variable having the full name

```
NewLine.Info[NewLine.Length]
```

In Fig. 9.18 on p. 396, we show a procedure to append new input text to the end of an existing line. This procedure calls ReadLine to transfer the text from the terminal into another record, NewText, and then copies the characters from this record to the end of Line. The text is not read directly into Line, in case there is more input than would fit.

9.4 Record Variants

record variants

Some applications involve a variety of similar (but nonidentical) kinds of records that require similar (but nonidentical) kinds of processing. We can gather these different record structures, called **record variants,** into a single data type. This allows their common parts to be processed by the same code.

```
PROCEDURE Append (VAR Line : LineType);

   {read and append new text to end of Line}

   VAR
      NewText : LineType;
      Psn : integer;

   BEGIN
      ReadLine (NewText);
      IF NewText.Length + Line.Length > LineLimit THEN
         writeln('combined line too long')
      ELSE
         BEGIN {actual append}

            FOR Psn := 1 TO NewText.Length DO
               Line.Info[Line.Length + Psn] :=
                  NewText.Info[Psn];
            Line.Length := Line.Length + NewText.Length

         END
   END; {Append}
```

■ Figure 9.18
Appending NewText to existing line.

Furthermore, when dealing with entire records, all the variants can be treated in an identical way. For example, any variant can be passed to a subprogram through the same formal parameter, regardless of their differences.

To see how this is done, consider a small bank that offers three services to its customers: checking accounts (which everyone dealing with the bank must maintain), savings accounts, and personal loans. Any customer, then, may have (1) a checking account only; (2) a checking account and a savings account; (3) a checking account and a personal loan; or (4) all three services.

These four categories of service define the four customer types recognized by the bank and the four varieties of record needed in the processing program. Each customer record will contain identifying information and the current balance in each pertinent account. Certain fields will appear in every record, regardless of account type. These fields are called the **fixed part** of the record, and in our example include the account number, the name, and the checking account balance. A customer may or may not have a savings balance, loan balance, or both. The corresponding fields, which differ from one customer

fixed part

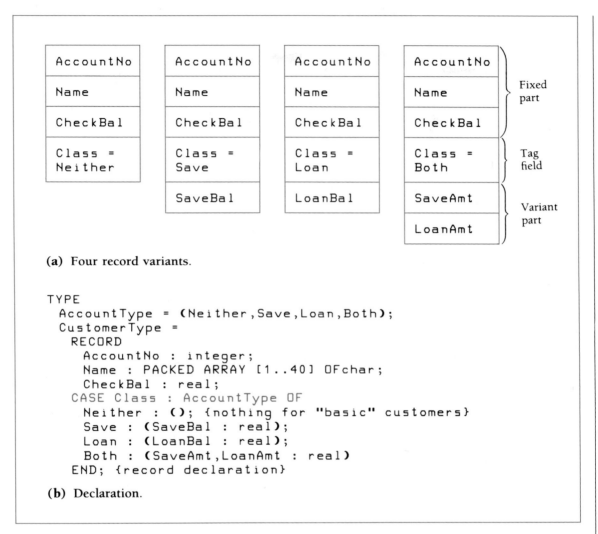

(a) Four record variants.

```
TYPE
  AccountType = (Neither,Save,Loan,Both);
  CustomerType =
    RECORD
      AccountNo : integer;
      Name : PACKED ARRAY [1..40] OF char;
      CheckBal : real;
    CASE Class : AccountType OF
      Neither : (); {nothing for "basic" customers}
      Save : (SaveBal : real);
      Loan : (LoanBal : real);
      Both : (SaveAmt,LoanAmt : real)
    END; {record declaration}
```

(b) Declaration.

■ Figure 9.19
Visualizing and declaring record variants.

variant part
tag field

Definition of record variants

class to the next, constitute the **variant part** of each record. After adding one more field, called the **tag field,** to indicate which customer class the record represents, we have the four record variants shown in Fig. 9.19(a).

Figure 9.19(b) shows a declaration that defines all four variants as a single record type. The fixed part must be declared before the variant part, and the fields in the fixed part are declared as usual. The four sets of variant fields are introduced by a construct resembling the CASE statement, and each is prefixed by an identifying *case constant (list)* and a colon. The fields comprising each variant are enclosed by parentheses, but otherwise are defined like ordinary record fields. The parentheses are needed to show just how many fields each variant contains; parentheses are required even when the variant contains no fields. Each variant must have unique field identifiers. Thus SaveBal is used in one variant and SaveAmt in another, even though they both refer to similar quantities.

The value of the tag field indicates which particular variant follows. The tag field—Class, in our example—is declared inside the CASE part. Its type must be described by an ordinal type identifier (that has already been declared). In addition all possible values of this ordinal type must be listed among the case list constants. This limits the ordinal type to one having very few values (that is, not simply integer).

This use of the reserved word CASE is not the same as that of the executable CASE statement. Among other differences, using CASE in a declaration does not give rise to an additional END; since the variant part must always be the final part of a record, a single END terminates the entire record declaration.

Controlling access to variant fields by value of tag field

The declaration of Customer actually produces a record with up to six fields, four of them being the same in all cases and the remainder depending on the value of the tag field for interpretation. In fact the tag field value dictates which set of variant fields may be accessed. When the value of Class is Save, for example, the definitions in the variant part labeled by Save are said to be *active*. This permits access to Customer.SaveBal, while disallowing use of any other variant fields. If the value of Class changes to Loan at run time, use of Customer.SaveBal becomes an error, and reference to Customer.LoanBal becomes valid.

Before using any fields in the variant part of a record, the program can check the tag field to determine which variant is currently active. Selecting the appropriate processing code is usually done with a CASE statement that parallels the CASE structure inside the record declaration. A procedure to list all the pertinent balances for all customers might contain the following code.

```
PROCEDURE Display (Customer: CustomerType);

  BEGIN {Display}
    WITH Customer DO
      BEGIN
        write (Account:10, Name:40, CheckBal:9:2);
        CASE Class OF
          Neither: writeln; {no more data}
          Save : writeln (SaveBal:10:2);
          Loan : writeln (LoanBal:20:2);
          Both : writeln (SaveAmt:10:2,
                          LoanAmt:10:2)
        END {case}
      END {with}
  END; {Display}
```

Note how any of the four variants can be passed through the same formal parameter. This permits their fixed fields to be accessed in the same way, that is, as Customer.Name.

As long as the same customer is being processed, normal usage will leave the tag field unchanged and deal only with the one variant of the record type. However, a few cases may require that the same record be accessed first from one point of view and then later from another. As long as the tag field is reset before the second mode of access, referencing the *same data* through two different variants is permitted. This works because the variants *are physically overlaid,* which means they share the same physical storage (as suggested in Fig. 9.19a).

Overlays

However, tampering with the tag field is a dangerous practice. The field types and sizes of one variant do not necessarily match the field types and sizes of the others.

discriminated type union

A record with variant parts specified by a tag field is sometimes called a **discriminated type union.** The word *union* reminds us that the record type is actually a union of different record structures that are physically super-imposed on the same storage. The word *discriminated* refers to the tag field, which identifies the active variant and thereby prescribes the interpretation.

free type union

The tag field is not strictly necessary. When it is omitted, the resulting record is known as a **free type union.** The program is assumed to always "know" which mode of access to the data is appropriate. Declaration of such an *untagged* record with variants is shown in Fig. 9.20. Note that the CASE

```
TYPE
     AccountType = (Neither,Save,Loan,Both);
     CustomerType =

     RECORD
         AccountNo : integer;
         Name : PACKED ARRAY [1..40] OF char;
         CheckBal : real;

     CASE AccountType OF
         Neither : (); {nothing for "basic" customers}
         Save : (SaveBal : real);
         Loan : (LoanBal : real);
         Both : (SaveAmt,LoanAmt : real)

     END; {record declaration}
```

■ Figure 9.20
Declaring record variants with no tag field.

line still specifies a type identifier (but not a field identifier) and that the variants are each introduced by a case constant of that type. The only difference is the absence of an explicit tag field. Each assignment to a variant field of an untagged record causes the corresponding variant to become active. In this case alternate use of different variants becomes even easier—and more susceptible to error.

9.5 Sets

Sets constitute a structured data type in Pascal. You have already encountered sets (in Section 6.5) as a way of grouping a number of similar objects together. For example, the following set contains all the characters that possibly could be involved in representing an integer.

['+', '−', '0' . . '9']

Recall that the members of any set must always belong to the *same ordinal data type;* they can never be real values or anything more complex than the ordinal types. The preceding set contains 12 characters as its members. Sets of integer, boolean, or user-defined type may also be defined. The ordinal type from which a set's members are drawn is known as the **base type** for that set.

base type

Although subrange notation may be used to specify sequences of values that belong to a set, the members of the set have no particular internal ordering; no member comes before any other or occupies a particular position within the set. The only relation that can exist between an individual item and a set is membership (or lack of membership). The sets [3,3] and [3] each contain only the integer 3 and are therefore equivalent; 3 is a member or it isn't. There is no concept of multiple occurrences in a set.

Testing membership

We can test set membership by the boolean-valued operator IN, as follows:

```
IF TestObject IN ['+','-','0'..'9'] THEN...
```

The TestObject must be an individual value from the base type of the set (char in this example).

We can also depict a set as a bounded region that encompasses precisely its own members within its boundary. The IN operator tests whether a particular value lies inside or outside the boundary. A value may happen to belong to more than one set at the same time. For example, the integer 6 belongs to both of the sets [2,4,6,8] and [3 . . 7]. These sets, illustrated in Fig. 9.21, have overlapping regions so that common values appear inside both.

empty set

A special set, called the **empty set,** is denoted by square brackets enclosing nothing, or [ ]. Although it contains no values, the empty set is a true set and plays an important role in the realm of sets, analogous to the role of 0 in the realm of numbers.

Figure 9.21
Two sets of single digit integers having some common members.

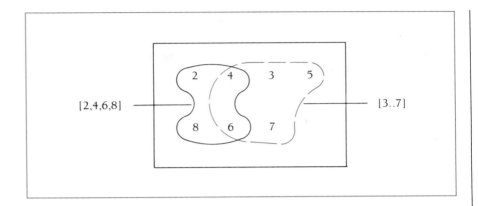

$[2,4,6,8]$ $[3..7]$

Set Variables

Until now you have encountered only set constants, that is, sets having members that are explicitly specified constants from some underlying ordinal data type. The term *set constant* reminds us that its contents never change. However, sets need not be so static and rigid. Just as sets in mathematics may acquire new members or lose old ones, so their counterparts in Pascal may be manipulated, tested, and combined to form new sets.

A simple extension of the set concept is the inclusion of *variables* inside the square brackets. In fact, more complex ordinal-valued expressions are also allowed. The square brackets are **set constructors,** and generate a set from whatever values are listed inside them (provided these values are all the same ordinal type). Thus when $x = 2$ and $y = 3$, the set $[x,y,x+y]$ would be equivalent to the set $[2,3,5]$. If x were 4 and y were 0, $[x,y,x+y]$ would be the same as $[0,4]$.

set constructors

Set variables

We may also declare set variables, as shown in Fig. 9.22. This declaration associates the set identifiers Friends and Neighbors with the base type Acquaintances.

Sets have the same type if their base types are the same. Like other variables, a set may be assigned a value, and its value may be changed at run time. The assigned value must be a set of the same type or at least a set with current members that all belong to the base type of the target set. The empty set is compatible with every set type and can thus be assigned as the value of any set variable.

Assignment to sets

The assignment statements shown in Fig. 9.22 supply values for the sets Friends and Neighbors. Being *set-type* variables, the values they receive must also be sets. Even if only a single object is assigned to a set, this object must be enclosed by square brackets. Thus the first statement below would be wrong and the second correct:

```
Friends := Joe;      {incorrect—incompatible types!}
Friends := [Joe];    {set variables must get set values}
```

```
TYPE
  Acquaintances = (fred,joe,ralph,tom,sam);
  PeopleSet = SET OF Acquaintances;

VAR
  Friends, Neighbors : PeopleSet;

BEGIN
    .
    .
    .
  Neighbors := [tom,joe];
  Friends := [fred,tom,sam];
```

(a) Code.

All values in
base type
Acquaintances — — — — — — — Current set
of Friends

Current set
of Neighbors

(b) Set diagram.

Set variables may also appear on the right-hand side of the assignment operator. We could make the set of Friends equal to the set of Neighbors by writing

```
Friends := Neighbors;
```

Sets as parameters　　　Just as they may be copied by assignment, sets may be passed as parameters. The function in Fig. 9.23 searches an array for *any* of a number of values. The possible target values are handed through a single set-type parameter. The function returns the position of the first item in the array that also belongs to the set (or 0 if no member of the set occurs in the array). Defining an explicit set type in the TYPE definition part of the surrounding program provides a type identifier for use in the parameter declaration. As with assignment, all members of the actual set parameter must belong to the base type of the formal set parameter. Note also the two typical calls of the function.

```
CONST
   SizeOfArray = 40;

TYPE
   SetType = SET OF 1..99;
   AryType = ARRAY [1..SizeOfArray] OF integer;
      .
      .
VAR
   Choices : SetType;
   Ary : AryType;
      .
      .

FUNCTION FindAny (Ary : AryType;
                  TargetSet : SetType):integer;

   {find position of first array value that
   also belongs to the TargetSet; 0 if none}

   VAR
      Index : integer;
      Found : boolean;

   BEGIN
      Index := 1;
      Found := false;

      WHILE (Index <= SizeOfArray) AND (NOT Found) DO
         IF Ary[Index] IN TargetSet THEN
            Found := true
         ELSE
            Index := Index + 1;

      IF Found THEN
         FindAny := Index
      ELSE
         FindAny := 0    {failure signal}
   END; {FindAny}

BEGIN {main program}
      .
      .
   Choices := [24,62,88];
   Where := FindAny(Ary,Choices);          Typical
                                           calls
   Place := FindAny(Ary,[15,75]);
      .
      .
```

■ Figure 9.23
A search for any of several values.

Unlike arrays and records, however, a set is not a collection of memory locations containing separate values. A set-type variable behaves more like a single memory location with "flexible sides," capable of expanding or contracting to accommodate whatever objects are members at the moment. Sets also differ from arrays and records in that we have no way to directly access individual set members; all we can do is test whether a candidate value is IN the set.

The underlying base type of a set may not contain more than some maximum number of values. This maximum number depends on the particular Pascal implementation and is sometimes not very large. Most implementations will allow at least as many values as the number of characters (typically 128), thus permitting the declaration:

```
VAR CharSet : SET OF char;
```

Restrictions on size of base type

However, some versions of Pascal do not permit this. In the interests of portability, it is better to specify a subrange to restrict the number of characters permitted, such as

```
VAR CharSet : SET OF 'a'..'z' ;
```

The set of integers is decidedly too large. Thus variables that hold sets of integers must always be defined over some suitably small subrange, as in

```
VAR IntSet : SET OF 0..99;
```

This sort of declaration appeared in Fig. 9.23. On certain implementations even this subrange might be too large for sets.

Operations on Sets

Binary set operators

To actually manipulate sets, we can use the three binary operators shown below; each generates a third set from two original sets.

Name	Algebraic Notation	Pascal Notation	Resulting Set
Union	∪	+	All items from either or both original sets
Intersection	∩	*	Only the items common to both original sets
Difference	−	−	Items from the first set that do not belong to the second set

For example, assuming that Friends and Neighbors have the values assigned in Fig. 9.22,

Friends + Neighbors	yields the result	[tom,joe,sam,fred]
Friends * Neighbors	yields the result	[tom]
Friends − Neighbors	yields the result	[fred,sam]

■ Figure 9.24
Set operations.

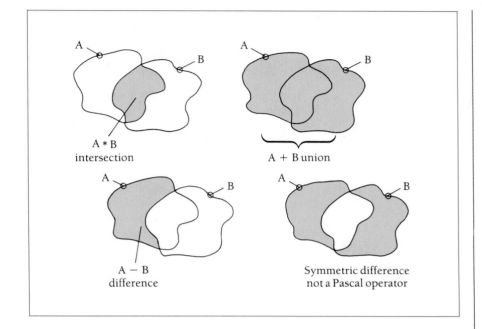

A * B
intersection

A + B union

A − B
difference

Symmetric difference
not a Pascal operator

**Union, intersection,
and difference**

These set operations are depicted in Fig. 9.24. Their results correspond to the region covered by either set (+), both sets simultaneously (∗), or only the first (−) of the two original sets. The order of operands is important in set difference, where only members of the first operand set will show up in the resulting set—provided they do not also occur in the second operand set. For example, the set of Neighbors who are not Friends would be written as Neighbors − Friends and would yield [joe] as a value.

Symmetric difference

Expressions involving set operators may be built up much like arithmetic expressions. For example, the set operation known as symmetric difference produces the set containing members from one or the other, but not both, of the original sets. Although it is not a predefined operation in Pascal, symmetric difference can be expressed by using the available operators. Suppose that A and B are the original sets. Their symmetric difference is equal to their union, excluding any items in their intersection:

$$(A + B) − (A * B)$$

An alternative formulation is to combine the portion of A not belonging to B with the portion of B not belonging to A:

$$(A − B) + (B − A)$$

If you think that the value of this expression should be 0, remember that the expression involves sets, not numbers. Although these Pascal operators may resemble the arithmetic operators, their action is entirely different in the context of sets.

Modifying an existing set

A common use of set-valued expressions is to modify the current membership of an existing set. If you have a fight with Fred, the following statement will remove him from your set of Friends.

```
Friends := Friends - [fred]
```

If Ralph moves into your neighborhood, he can be added to the set of Neighbors by the statement:

```
Neighbors := Neighbors + [ralph]
```

Expanding a set

The latter form may be used iteratively to expand a set one new member at a time, starting from the empty set [ ]. Figure 9.25 contains a program that interactively maintains a list of identification numbers of people who are scheduled for some unspecified duty. Assuming that the numbers do not cover too great a range and have no associated information, they can be maintained as a set. When a person is scheduled, his or her number is added to the set; when the duty is completed, the number is removed. Individual inquiry can be made at any time. Incidentally, adding an item that is already in the set will have no effect, since the item already has full membership. Likewise, attempting to remove an item that does not belong to the set has no net effect.

Displaying a set

Provided the number of values is small and their type is ordinal, sets provide an extremely simple means of maintaining and searching lists of values. However, it is not so easy to display all the members of a set. The only way is to individually test every possible value from the base type for membership. For example, to display all the ID numbers currently contained in the set OnDuty in Fig. 9.25, we would execute

```
FOR IDNumber := 1 to 99 DO
    {test each possible member}
    IF IDNumber IN OnDuty THEN
        writeln(IDNumber);
```

Interactive input of an entire set is not possible. Its elements are usually read, enclosed by square brackets, and added to the set one element at a time, as we did with identification numbers in Fig. 9.25.

Comparison of Sets

Two sets may be directly compared using the standard relational operators. As usual, the outcome is either true or false, allowing the outcome of set comparison to govern flow of control. However, since sets are not simple objects, we must explain the meaning of these comparisons.

Set equality and inequality

Two sets are equal if they contain exactly the same members and unequal if they differ in at least one member. Of course, the order and notation for

```
PROGRAM DutyRoster (input,output);

    {interactively maintain set of i.d. numbers
    of people currently assigned to duty}

    TYPE
        ValidNumber = 1..99;
        Personnel = SET OF ValidNumber;

    VAR
        OnDuty : Personnel;
        IDNumber : ValidNumber;
        Command : char;

    BEGIN
        writeln('Enter command (a,d,i), followed by i.d.');
        Writeln('Enter q to quit');
        writeln;

        OnDuty := [];
        REPEAT

            read(Command);
            IF Command <> 'q' THEN
                read(IDNumber);
            readln; {clear line}

            IF Command IN ['a','d','i'] THEN
                CASE Command OF

                    'a' : OnDuty := OnDuty + [IDNumber];
                    'd' : OnDuty := OnDuty - [IDNumber];
                    'i' : IF IDNumber IN OnDuty THEN
                               writeln('currently assigned')
                           ELSE
                               writeln('not on duty')

                END {Case}
        UNTIL Command = 'q'

    END. {DutyRoster program}
```

■ **Figure 9.25**
Modifying a set.

specifying the members makes no difference. Thus, the following comparisons are all true.

$$[1,2,3] = [3,2,1]$$
$$[1,2,1+2] = [1 . . 3]$$
$$[1 . . 4] <> [1 . . 3]$$
$$([1 . . 4] - [4]) = [1 . . 3]$$
$$([1,3] + [2,3]) = ([1 . . 5] * [1 . . 3])$$
$$([7] - [7]) = []$$
$$['a' . . 'z'] <> ['A' . . 'Z']$$

Containment relations

The relation A $<=$ B tests whether every member of set A is also a member of set B; that is, whether A could be represented by a region lying entirely inside the boundary of B. Set B may have additional members that are not in A (Fig. 9.26b), or A and B may be equal (Fig. 9.26a). But if A has a member not in B, then A $<=$ B is false. If A $<=$ B is true, then A is said to be a *subset* of B.

The relation A $<$ B is true if all members of A are also in B *and* if B contains at least one member that is not part of A. Thus if A $<$ B is true, then A $=$ B is false. A is said to be a *proper subset* of B in this case. The six

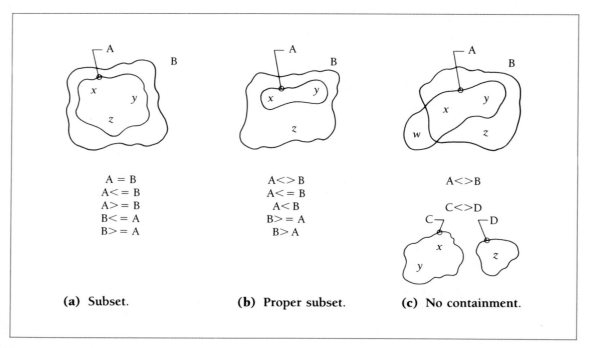

(a) **Subset.**   (b) **Proper subset.**   (c) **No containment.**

■ Figure 9.26
Comparing sets.

relations are as follows:

Pascal Relation	Mathematical Notation
=	=
<>	≠
<=	⊆
<	⊂
>=	⊇
>	⊃

Direct comparison of two entire sets is a powerful operation. If the values were stored in arrays instead of sets, these comparisons would require element-by-element matching of the two arrays, which is a much more involved process to code.

To see how these relations might be used, imagine a fleet of taxicabs, each identified by a two-digit integer. Just as we maintained one duty roster for a group of employees in Fig. 9.25, we can maintain several sets pertaining to the group of cabs. The sets might represent vehicles scheduled for repairs or repainting. The following Pascal expressions answer the questions indicated.

Repair <= Repaint	Do all cabs needing repair also need repainting
(Repaint − Repair) <> [ ]	Do any cabs needing repainting not need repair?

Now, let's consider a loop that might terminate for any of a variety of conditions. We will call these the "fatal" conditions. In addition, various other "harmless" conditions that do not cause termination might be detected in the loop. More than one condition might arise during any iteration of the loop, and all detected conditions should be distinguishable after termination.

We can use a generalization of a flag to control this loop. A boolean flag can distinguish only the "abnormal" condition from the "normal" state. A more versatile simple variable can directly record only one state at a time: the most recently detected condition. However, we can use a set to collect and retain all the conditions arising during execution of the loop. Also, if there is more than one fatal condition, the test for any fatal condition(s) can be made by testing whether the sets of detected and fatal conditions overlap. This strategy is outlined in Fig. 9.27. Following the loop, we could ask

```
IF Detected <= Fatal THEN...
```

to find out whether all the detected conditions were fatal. A warning message could be issued if any harmless conditions occurred; that is,

```
IF (Harmless * Detected) <> [] THEN...
```

or

```
IF (Detected - Fatal) <> [] THEN...
```

```
TYPE
   Conditions = (normal,hidata,lowdata,range,retry,warn);
   ConditionSet = SET OF Conditions;

VAR
   Fatal,Harmless,Detected : ConditionSet;
     .
     .
     .

BEGIN
     Fatal := [hidata,lowdata,range];
     Harmless := [retry,warn];
       .
       .
       .
     Detected := []; {initially no conditions detected}

     WHILE (Detected * Fatal) = [] DO
        BEGIN
          .
          .
          .
          Detected := Detected + [hidata];
          .
          .
          Detected := Detected + [retry];
          .
          .
          .
        END; {loop interior}
```

■ Figure 9.27
Use of sets as multipurpose flags.

9.6 Review of Rules

Records

    A. A RECORD is a structured data type whose constituent parts, called fields, do not all need to be of the same type. In its simplest form, a record type is declared as

⟨record type⟩ =
  RECORD
    ⟨field identifier1⟩: ⟨field type1⟩;
    ⟨field identifier2⟩: ⟨field type2⟩;
              .
              .
              .
    ⟨field identifierN⟩: ⟨field typeN⟩
  END

The simplified syntax diagram for a RECORD is

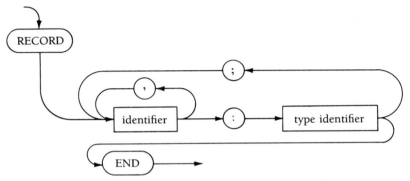

B. If ⟨record variable⟩ is an identifier of record type, each of its fields is
    referenced as

    ⟨record variable⟩.⟨field identifier⟩

    This refers to the particular object comprising the field and can be used
    in any context where a variable of that field type is permitted (say, as a
    parameter, in an expression, or as the target of an assignment statement).

C. Entire records can be used in only two contexts:

    1. when assigning the value(s) of one record to another of the same
        type; and
    2. when passing the whole record as a parameter.

D. You may declare an array having record-type components. In this case,
    each record identifier is an array component indexed in the standard
    way, causing a field reference to have the form:

    ⟨array identifier⟩[⟨index⟩].⟨field identifier⟩

E. The fields of a record may be array or record type. If a field is an array
    type, an individual component of the array would be referenced as

    ⟨record variable⟩.⟨field identifier⟩[⟨index⟩]

If the field is a record type, an individual field would be

⟨outer record⟩.⟨inner record⟩.⟨inner field⟩

This kind of nesting of data may continue to several levels, with similar rules applying at each level.

F.   The WITH statement, written

WITH ⟨record variable⟩ DO
⟨statement⟩

allows the ⟨statement⟩ part to contain field references without explicitly mentioning the record identifier. Its syntax diagram is

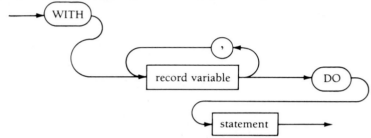

G.   WITH statements may be nested to correspond to the hierarchy of records with record-type fields. As shown by its syntax diagram, WITH may contain a list of record variables, such as

WITH R1, R2, R3 DO
⟨statement⟩

which is equivalent to

WITH R1 DO
  WITH R2 DO
    WITH R3 DO
      ⟨statement⟩

Each WITH statement prescribes a region over which its record field names are potentially defined. If some identifier in overlapping regions is a field name for two or more of these records, it will refer to the innermost applicable record.

H.   A single record type having variant realizations may be declared as follows:

TYPE
  ⟨record type identifier⟩ =
    RECORD
      ⟨field1⟩ : ⟨type1⟩;
        .
        .
        .
      ⟨fieldN⟩ : ⟨typeN⟩;

CASE ⟨Tag identifier⟩ : ⟨Tag type⟩ OF
　⟨constant1⟩ : (⟨variant1 field declarations⟩);
　⟨constant2⟩ : (⟨variant2 field declarations⟩);
.
.
.
　⟨constantM⟩ : (⟨variantM field declarations⟩)
END;

The field identifiers in all variant parts must be unique. Every value from the tag type must appear among the constants that introduce the variant parts. When space for a record with a variant part is allocated, the amount of space used is equal to the length of the longest field list; other field lists are overlaid on this space. When a tag-field identifier is present in the record definition, only the field list corresponding to the current value of the tag field is "active"; all other field lists are undefined. When the tag-field identifier is absent, the list currently being accessed is considered to be the active one.

Sets

I. A set of objects from the same ordinal type may be generated by listing the objects between square brackets. The values in the list may be constants, variable values, or values of appropriate expressions. The ordinal type from which the set members are drawn is called the base type.

J. A set-type variable may be declared as follows:

TYPE
　SetType = SET OF ⟨ordinal base type⟩;
VAR
　SetVariable : SetType;

Two sets have the same type if their base types are the same. The maximum size of a set is determined by the implementation. Set variables may be assigned set values either through the assignment statement or through the parameter mechanism.

K. The syntax diagram for a set value is

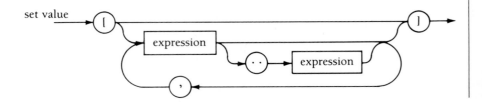

L.   If A and B are two sets of the same type, new sets may be generated from them by three binary set operators:

A * B   The set of values belonging to *both* A and B.
A + B   The set of values belonging to *either* A or B or *both*.
A − B   The set of values belonging to A but *not* to B.

M.   Two sets of the same type, A and B, may be compared using the relational operators. The = and <> operators test for identical and nonidentical membership, respectively. The other four test whether and how one set is contained in the other.

KEY TERMS

base type
discriminated type union
empty set
fields
fixed part
free type union
overlay

record
record variants
set constructors
tag field
variant part
WITH statement

REVIEW PROBLEM:
TEXT ANALYSIS

Strategy

When analyzing text, we often find it useful to determine the number of times each word is used. This problem involves development of a program to keep track of word usage in a small sample of text. In particular, we will produce a list of words from the text in order of frequency of occurrence, with the most frequently used word first.

To isolate the input from the analysis, we will first read all the text and then scan it word by word. The purpose of the scan is to build a dictionary containing each word used in the text together with a frequency count of how often that word is used. When the scan is finished, the dictionary is displayed in descending order of frequency. This discussion suggests an algorithm with three major steps:

1.   read all the text;
2.   build the dictionary including frequency information;
3.   display the words in decreasing order of frequency.

Algorithm

The heart of the problem is building the dictionary. As the text is scanned, each word must be isolated and searched for in the dictionary. If the word already appears, its frequency count is incremented. Otherwise, a new entry with a frequency of 1 is added. The dictionary therefore begins with nothing in it and is built one entry at a time. Since the dictionary is so dynamic during the construction phase, it may not be wise to maintain it in word order. Since the frequencies are continually being updated, it is also impractical to maintain the dictionary entries in order of frequency. Consequently, a sort will be required before generating the report. This provides the details for the expanded algorithm:

1. read all the text;
2. while text remains do:
2.1   locate next word of text;
2.2   search dictionary for that word;
2.3   update dictionary (if found, increment frequency;
            if not, append new word with count of 1)
3. sort dictionary in order of decreasing frequency;
4. display dictionary;

Data structures

This algorithm is encoded as the main program in Fig. 9.28. Note the declarations, especially in the TYPE section. Once a word is formed, its interior characters are never required. The words will be stored as packed arrays of type CharString to facilitate final output as well as comparison during the search and sort. A record type (WordType) allows frequency counts to be associated with words. The dictionary consists of an array of these records together with the number of words it currently contains. This array of entries and the word count are combined into a single record structure (type DictType) to allow all information concerning the dictionary to be passed as one parameter. The dictionary structure is shown in Fig. 9.29.

Because the input text will remain in memory, a very large array of characters is needed to hold it (type TextAry). Finally, since we will pass sets of characters as parameters, we need a set of characters (CharSet) as a data type.

Use of sets to test for legal characters

The set-type variable Content plays a role in the main program that is not indicated by the algorithm. While the ReadText procedure is reading characters in the usual way, it also collects all the characters encountered into the set Content. Before beginning the analysis, this set is checked to make sure that only legal characters are included. This is done by testing whether Content is contained in the set of all legal characters, which is formed by the union of alphabetic characters and other permissible nonalphabetic characters. Thus we have the statement

```
IF Content <= (Letters + OtherChars) THEN . . .
```

If Content contains only permissible characters, dictionary construction will proceed as planned. But if any character in Content is neither in Letters nor in OtherChars, the dictionary construction will be bypassed, and the sort and display will produce nothing.

The main program begins by initializing the set-type variables, Letters and OtherChars. Since their membership never changes, these identifiers are used like symbolic constants. However, because set constants cannot be defined in the CONST section (at least not in standard Pascal), sets must be given their values in the executable part.

```pascal
PROGRAM WordCounter (input,output);
CONST
   Terminator = '#';
   MaxText = 1000;
   MaxWords = 200;
TYPE
   CharString = PACKED ARRAY [1..20] OF char;
   WordType =
      RECORD
         Word : CharString;
         Freq : integer
      END; {record}
   DictType =
      RECORD
         Entry : ARRAY [1..MaxWords] OF WordType;
         WordNum : integer
      END;
   TextAry = ARRAY [1..MaxText] OF char;
   CharSet = SET OF char;
VAR
   Dictionary : DictType;      {dictionary}
   Stream : TextAry;           {input stream}
   TextPsn : integer;          {position in Stream}
   NewWord : CharString;       {object of search}
   WordPsn : integer;          {outcome of search}
   Content,                    {set of chars read}
   OtherChars,                 {allowed between words}
   Letters : CharSet;          {allowed within words}
{PROCEDURE and FUNCTION declarations appear here}

BEGIN {main program}
   Letters := ['a'..'z' , 'A'..'Z'];
   OtherChars := [' ',',','.','?',';',':','-','!'];
   Dictionary.WordNum := 0; {empty dictionary}
   ReadText(Stream,Content);
   TextPsn := 1;
   IF Content <= (Letters + OtherChars) THEN {valid}
      WHILE (Stream[TextPsn] <> Terminator) DO
         BEGIN
            NextWord (Stream,TextPsn,NewWord);
            WordPsn := Search (Dictionary,NewWord);
            Update (Dictionary,NewWord,WordPsn);
         END;
   Sort(Dictionary);
   Display(Dictionary)
END. {WordCounter}
```

■ Figure 9.28
Main program for dictionary construction.

Figure 9.29
Dictionary structure.

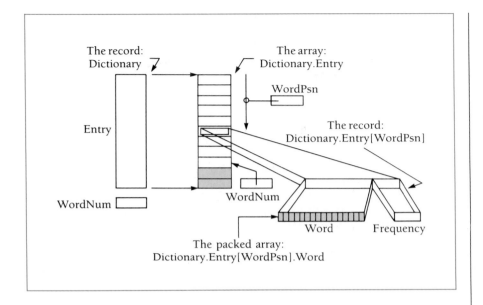

The record:
Dictionary

The array:
Dictionary.Entry

WordPsn

Entry

The record:
Dictionary.Entry[WordPsn]

WordNum

WordNum

Word   Frequency

The packed array:
Dictionary.Entry[WordPsn].Word

Subprogram actions

Our main program relies heavily on subprograms. ReadText provides the input stream and the set of characters it contains (Content). The variable, TextPsn, indicates the location of the next word in the input Stream. The NextWord procedure supplies this word as a packed array and advances TextPsn to the beginning of the following word. Search attempts to find the position of this new word in the dictionary. Update either increments the frequency count at dictionary location WordPsn, or it appends a new entry after advancing the dictionary size WordNum. The Sort and Display procedures perform their conventional roles.

Input processing

Figure 9.30 contains the subprograms that deal with the input text. We have already mentioned how the main program tests the input to determine whether it contains only legal characters. The ReadText procedure generates the set (Content) of input characters by starting with the empty set and adding each newly read character by means of set union. Of course, adding a character that is already a member has no net effect. The Content set is returned to the main program through a variable set-type parameter.

The ReadText procedure transfers all the input into the array Stream. Input line structure is ignored; whenever an end of line component is encountered, a blank is placed in Stream. When end-of-file is reached, Readtext appends a special Terminator character to the end of the legitimate text. Because it will be used as a sentinel by the text scanning code, Terminator is chosen so that it is not a legitimate input character. Since this sentinel is available to halt the scan, there is no need for ReadText to supply the number of characters read, which is the usual practice. Note that ReadText reserves space in the Stream array for inclusion of the Terminator.

```
PROCEDURE ReadText(VAR Stream:TextAry;
                   VAR Content:SetType);
    CONST Blank = ' ';
    VAR Num: integer;
    {GLOBAL...MaxText,Terminator}
    BEGIN
        Content := []; {initially no chars input}
        Num := 0;
        WHILE (NOT eof) AND (Num < MaxText) DO
            BEGIN
                Num := Num + 1;
                read( Stream[Num] );
                Content := Content + [ Stream[Num] ]
            END;
        Num := Num + 1;
        Stream[Num] := Terminator {install sentinel}
    END; {ReadText}

FUNCTION Scan (Stream : TextAry; Where : integer;
               AllowedChars : CharSet) : integer;
    BEGIN
        WHILE ( Stream[Where] IN AllowedChars ) DO
            Where := Where + 1;
        Scan := Where        {first char not Allowed}
    END; {Scan}

PROCEDURE NextWord (Stream: TextAry; VAR Start: integer;
                    VAR NewWord : CharString);

    CONST
        Blanks20 := '                    ';
    VAR
        Stop,StreamPsn,NewPsn : integer;
    {GLOBAL...Letters,OtherChars}
    BEGIN
        {find end of current word in stream}
        Stop := Scan(Stream,Start,Letters);
        NewWord := Blanks20;
        {copy word from Stream into NewWord}
        NewPsn := 1;
        FOR StreamPsn := Start TO Stop-1 DO
            BEGIN {copy}
                NewWord[NewPsn] := Stream[StreamPsn];
                NewPsn := NewPsn + 1
            END; {copy}
        {advance Start to beginning of next word}
        Start := Scan(Stream,Stop,OtherChars)
    END; {NextWord procedure}
```

■ Figure 9.30
Subprograms to process the text Stream.

418

```
FUNCTION Search (Dict:DictType;
                 Target:CharString):integer;

    {return position of Target string in Dictionary
    or 0 if the Target string is not found}

    VAR
        Found : boolean;
        Psn : integer;

    BEGIN
        Psn := 1;
        Found := false;
        WHILE (NOT Found) AND (Psn <= Dict.WordNum) DO
            IF Dict.Entry[Psn].Word = Target THEN
                Found := true
            ELSE
                Psn := Psn + 1;
            IF Found THEN
                Search := Psn
            ELSE
                Search := 0      {failure signal}
    END; {Search}


PROCEDURE Update (VAR Dict: DictType;
                  NewWord: CharString;
                  WordPsn: integer);

    {either update frequency of existing word,
     or add new word to dictionary}

    BEGIN
        IF WordPsn <> 0 THEN {word already present}
            WITH Dict.Entry[WordPsn] DO
                Freq := Freq + 1
        ELSE    {append new word...}
            BEGIN
                Dict.WordNum := Dict.WordNum + 1;
                Dict.Entry[Dict.WordNum].Word := NewWord;
                Dict.Entry[Dict.WordNum].Freq := 1
            END
    END; {Update}
```

■ **Figure 9.31**
Procedures to build and maintain the dictionary.

Text scanning

Just as a word is a sequence of alphabetic characters, the gaps between words are sequences of certain nonalphabetic characters. Stream therefore consists of alternate sequences of letters (words) and other characters (gaps). We call these two different sets of characters Letters and OtherChars, respectively. (As we have seen, their union is the set of all legitimate characters.)

Finding next word

A word extends from its starting position up to (but not including) the next character that is not a Letter. The following gap begins at this position, immediately after the word. This gap extends up to (but not including) the next character that is not one of OtherChars. The position in Stream immediately following the gap will then be the start of the next word (or the Terminator). Thus the scan alternates between traversing words and traversing gaps; its mode reverses whenever it encounters a character that belongs to the other type of sequence.

Except for the sets of characters constituting the two kinds of sequences, the processes of finding words and finding gaps are identical. Hence, the Scan function carries out this process of locating the next character that is not a member of some specified set. The particular set is supplied through a value-type parameter known as AllowedChars inside the function. Between calling Scan to traverse the current word and to traverse the gap before the next word, the NextWord procedure merely copies the characters of the current word into a packed array for use elsewhere.

Use of records

Figure 9.31 on the preceding page contains the subprograms for searching and updating the dictionary, and Fig. 9.32 contains the procedures to sort and display the dictionary. Their logic is straightforward and operates just like earlier versions in other applications. The feature of interest here is their need to access records and record fields. The dictionary itself is a record containing an array of entries and an integer indicating the number of active entries. Similarly, each entry is a record containing a word and its frequency count. Consequently, some of the accessed items have rather elaborate references. These record references are highlighted in these subprograms.

EXERCISES

9.1 A small liquor business keeps the following kinds of stock on hand at each of three locations.

75 brands of wine:
    30 brands of white
    35 brands of red
    10 brands of champagne

25 brands of whiskey:
    9 brands of Scotch
    10 brands of rye
    5 brands of bourbon
    2 brands of Irish

6 brands of gin
4 brands of vodka
5 brands of brandy

Define a Pascal record that could be used to help the owners keep track of the number of bottles on hand in each category at each store.

```
PROCEDURE Display ( Dict : DictType );

    VAR
        Psn : integer;
    BEGIN
        FOR Psn := 1 TO Dict.WordNum DO
            WITH Dict.Entry[Psn] DO
                writeln( Freq:3, Word:22)
    END; {Display}


PROCEDURE Sort ( VAR Dict : DictType );

    {bubble sort by decreasing frequency}

    VAR
        Pair : integer;        {index}
        Sorted : boolean;
        Temp : WordType;       {entire record}
        N : integer;{working copy of WordNum}

    BEGIN
        N := Dict.WordNum;
        WITH Dict DO        {whole procedure affects Dict}
            REPEAT

                Sorted := true; {assume sorted}
                FOR Pair := 1 TO N-1 DO
                    IF Entry[Pair].Freq < Entry[Pair+1].Freq THEN
                        BEGIN {swap}
                            Temp := Entry[Pair];
                            Entry[Pair] := Entry[Pair+1];
                            Entry[Pair+1] := Temp;
                            Sorted := false
                        END; {swap}
                    N := N - 1 {reduce effective length}

            UNTIL Sorted
    END; {Sort}
```

■ Figure 9.32
Procedures to sort and display the dictionary.

9.2   Consider the following:

```
TYPE
  A = RECORD
    Region: PACKED ARRAY [1..5] OF char;
    OfficeNo: integer;
    BadgeNO: integer;
    Industry: PACKED ARRAY [1..10] OF char
    END;
  B = RECORD
    Quota: real;
    Sales: real;
    Commission: real
    END;
  Sales = RECORD
    YearToDate: B;
    ThisMonth: B
    END;
  SaleStaff = RECORD
    Person: A;
    SalesRecord: Sales
    END;
VAR
  SalesForce: ARRAY [1..100] OF SaleStaff;
```

(a) How many storage locations are associated with the variable SalesForce?

(b) Write the Pascal code to display all the information available on the 37th member of the sales force.

(c) Write the Pascal code to display the information available on all members of the sales force for the current month.

9.3   The standing of any team in a certain league is calculated from the record consisting of

■ team name (up to 10 characters);
■ number of games played, P (integer);
■ number of games won, W (integer);
■ number of games tied, T (integer);
■ number of games lost, L (integer);
■ points for, F (integer);
■ points against, A (integer); and
■ percentage, Pct (real).

You obtain the percentage by using the formula

$$Pct = \frac{(W + 0.5 * T) * 100}{P}$$

There are eight teams in the league (hence four games each week) and each week the scores of each game are reported to the league office. As league manager you have to automate the process of updating the league standings. To simplify matters, you may assume that the process begins at the start of the season. Your program should include a procedure Update, which will examine each game result and update the records for each team. When all the games for a week have been passed through the Update procedure, another procedure, Sort, should then sort the teams into descending order by percentage. In the case of a tie in percentage, the higher standing should be given to the team with the largest difference in points for and against. Your program should handle several weeks' scores, printing out the team standings at the end of every set of games. The standings report should have a heading such as

```
Team  P  W  T  L  F  A  Pct.
```

9.4   Here we reconsider and extend the review problem from Section 9.7. For a particular fragment of text, you can represent each word by a record of the form:

```
Word = RECORD
   Length: integer;
   Content: ARRAY [1 . . 20] OF char;
   Freq: integer
END;
```

Content is the actual word, Length is the number of characters in the word, and Freq is the number of times the word Content appears in the text. For the purposes of this exercise, a word is any sequence of alphabetic characters terminated by one or more spaces, periods, commas, semicolons, colons, or question marks. Further, words are not allowed to continue from one line to another. A line of input is not to exceed 80 characters in length; you may assume that the text contains no more than 200 unique words and that no word exceeds 20 characters in length. The objective of the program is to read input text one line at a time, decompose the line into unique words, count the frequency of each word, and ultimately display the words in collating sequence (alphabetical) order.

You are to utilize the following procedures, in addition to those required for sorting. GetALine will read a single line of input and pass it back to the calling program. GetAWord will be given the input line, pick off the next word from the line, and pass it back to the calling program after removing this word from the line. Also, design your program so that it is insensitive to the case of the letters. In other words, code your program so that words like "THE," "the," and "The" are all considered to be the same.

9.5   Consider a system to maintain grades for a class of students. Each student is identified by ID number and a name of up to 20 characters. Each student record should contain these identifying items and an array for recording up to six grades. Each grade reflects the performance on a particular test. As the year progresses, more tests are taken, and more grades are recorded. For each test taken so far, assume that every student will have a grade entered.

(a) Write a procedure to enter up to 30 student names and ID numbers in an array of records. Assume that these records are entered in alphabetical order of names (last, then first).

(b) Enable the user to enter the grade of every student for one particular test. Include commands to find the grade entered for a particular student, given the name, and to replace any particular grade by an updated one.

(c) For any particular test, find and display the name of the student with the highest grade.

9.6   Consider a system for maintaining customer records for a small branch bank. Each customer record will contain a (20-character) name, an ID number, the balance at the start of the month, the number of withdrawals, the number of deposits, and the current balance.

(a) Have your program do the following: initialize an array of customer records as it might appear at the beginning of a month; and enter the accounts in increasing order of account number. Display all customer data in order of account number, on request.

(b) Expand your program to handle interactive updates. Allow a particular customer to make a deposit or withdrawal and be able to locate his or her account record either by account number or name. Allow a teller to view an individual customer record.

(c) Add the capability to display all customer data in alphabetical order of name.

9.7   If the master customer records in Exercise 9.6 are kept at the main branch, immediate update may not be feasible. In this case the updates may be stockpiled in a local array and periodically incorporated into the master records. For this problem, keep track of the name in the master records, but assume that all updates and inquiries are based on the account numbers.

(a) One approach is to maintain a second array of customer records (each without any value in the name field and with an initial balance of 0) for recording individual transactions. This array starts out empty. When any deposit or withdrawal occurs, the customer record in this auxiliary array is updated. If no record yet exists for this customer, a new one is created when the first transaction occurs. When a display of customer data is requested, the following happens before the display occurs.

> The auxiliary array of recent transaction records is sorted by increasing account number; these customer records are merged with the master records, updating the master record fields in the process; then the transaction records are all discarded, leaving the auxiliary array empty again.

Do not worry if a withdrawal causes the current balance to become negative. (This is a modern bank.)

(b) An alternative way to handle the task is to store only the account number, transaction type, and transaction amount in a new record of the auxiliary array for each transaction that occurs. When a display is requested or the auxiliary array becomes full, the transactions are sorted by account number, merged into the master records, and discarded. However, since there may be several transactions for the same account, they will be moved to consecutive positions in the auxiliary array by the sort, and the entire sequence of such records will be used to update a single master record.

(c) To make the system more realistic, extend and modify the approach in part (a) in the following manner. Do not have new transaction records start with a balance of 0. The master file is consulted to determine the current balance when an auxiliary record is created. After that, the auxiliary record contains up-to-date information. When a withdrawal is requested, require the current balance to cover this amount before the withdrawal actually takes place. Inquiries are also allowed. The auxiliary array is searched first, but if the customer record is not found there, the master array is then searched to answer the query.

9.8   Use record variants to represent the crucial dimensions of the following geometric shapes.

Shape	Dimensions
Circle	Radius
Rectangle	Length, width
Trapezoid	Top, bottom, height

Provide a tag field to designate the shape depicted by each record. Write a procedure to read the values for any of these shapes. Provide a procedure to accept a shape-type record as a parameter and calculate and display the area of the object.

9.9   Using an array of record variants, implement a system to maintain the payroll of a small company. Each employee is to be represented by a record that includes a name, ID number, and status indicator. The status shows whether the employee is hourly or salaried. The record for a salaried employee shows his or her annual rate (equivalent to 250 working days). Hourly employee records show an hourly rate, number of hours worked, and number of hours overtime. After initializing the array (in order of ID number), provide individual hours by entering

h   IDNumber   hours

or

o   IDNumber   hours

for regular (h) or overtime (o) hours, respectively. At the end of the pay period, issue a command indicating the number of working days since the last payday, display the pay amount for every employee, and reset the hours worked to 0.

9.10 (a) Write the declarations and assignment statements to define Lower, Consonant, Vowel, SomeSet, and OtherSet as sets of lowercase alphabetic characters, so that Lower contains all these characters and Consonant and Vowel contain the characters their names imply. Initialize Consonant in terms of Lower and Vowel.

      (b) Assume that SomeSet and OtherSet have values and write boolean expressions to answer the following questions.
           (i)   Is 'm' a member of SomeSet?
           (ii)   Is 'm' a member of both SomeSet and OtherSet?
                  (Express this in two different ways.)
           (iii) Are SomeSet and OtherSet different in any way?
           (iv)   Is every member of SomeSet a consonant?
           (v)   Does OtherSet contain all the vowels?

      (c) Write set-valued expressions to determine
           (i)   the vowels that belong to OtherSet;
           (ii)   the members of SomeSet that are not vowels; and
           (iii) the characters that are either vowels or members of OtherSet, but not both.

9.11 (a) Implement Exercise 8.2 (and 7.15) using five sets to represent the five lists of taxicab IDs.

      (b) Implement Exercise 8.3 using sets.

9.12 Consider a two-dimensional array that represents a region of physical space. Certain entries in the array (1's as opposed to 0's) depict objects located at the corresponding coordinates. The straight-line (Euclidean) distance between two objects is given by the familiar Pythagorean right-triangle theorem. After entering the coordinates of several objects in a 20×30 space, construct a distance matrix (two-dimensional array) in which the Jth row and Jth column each represent the Jth object, and the $[i, j]$ entry represents the distance between object i and object j. (The entries at positions $[i, j]$ and $[j, i]$ will be the same.) Have your program display the coordinates of the objects and the distance matrix.

(a) Cluster the objects into two groups by first choosing the two objects at the greatest distance from each other as the starting members of the two groups. Next, select the object that does not yet belong to either group and having the least distance to one of objects selected, and place this object in that group it is nearest. In case of a tie, place it in the "first" group. Keep making selections and assignments to the nearest group until all objects have been placed in some group. Use sets to keep track of the two groups and, if convenient, of all the selected and unselected objects. Display the result by showing the original space (two-dimensional array) with members of the two groups encoded by different values.

(b) Cluster the objects without knowing the number of groups in advance. Initially every object constitutes an individual set. The general strategy is to repeatedly coalesce sufficiently close sets of objects into larger and larger sets. However, the program is to merge only sets that are closer than some user-supplied threshold. The distance between two sets is defined as the minimum distance between any member of one set and any member of the other. Beginning with the nearest pair of objects belonging to different sets, if their distance is below the threshold, merge their two containing sets into one. Then take the next smallest distance, and if close enough, merge these two sets into one. Repeat this process until all remaining distances are as large as the threshold (or all points have been merged into one set). Use an array of sets to depict the groupings. Show the result as a space (two-dimensional array), with members of different groups denoted by different values.

9.13 Implement an interactive text-scanning system that is given a subject string of characters and an arbitrary set of individual characters, and answers some simple questions about the subject string in terms of that character set. The input begins with up to 100 characters, terminated by #. Then a number of commands (including q to quit) may be entered to direct the scan of this string. These commands have the following format.

    FROM MODE CharacterSet Ⓡ

There are no spaces between the FROM, MODE, and Character set fields; blank may appear only as a member of the character set. The fields have the following meanings.

FROM is an integer that refers to the position in the string where the scan should begin.

FROM	may be	0	to designate the CURRENT position
	or	n	to designate position n (1 = start)
MODE	may be	+	to seek only characters IN set
	or	−	to seek only chars NOT in set

For example, the command

    1+abcd

asks for the first instance of a, b, c, or d, anywhere between the first and last positions in the string. The command

```
0-abc
```

asks for the next character that is not an a, b, or c, starting from wherever the last command ended. The result, if successful, is to display both the position number and the character that ended the scan. The user is informed if the scan failed.

10

File Processing Fundamentals

file   Each distinct source of input data and each possible destination for output data is known as a **file.** To the operating system and to an individual program, however, the term *file* means slightly different things. For the *system* and its users a file is a collection of related data that may be stored on a secondary memory device or transmitted together from the same input/output device. A system file is a data aggregate that has a unique name and must be either allocated long-term storage space or associated with an input–output device. System files are independent of any program and may exist for a long time— much longer than the execution of a single program. Files therefore provide a place for programs to save values from one execution to the next or to convey values to other programs.

What concerns us more is the lower-level perspective of a single Pascal program. For the *program* a file is a structured data type. Unlike other data structures that are confined to main memory, a file has almost unlimited storage capacity. Files are the data structures through which a program may transfer data to and from the outside world. Any time a program interacts with either secondary memory or an input–output device, it is interacting with a file. Files provide the *only* avenues of access beyond a program's boundaries. In this chapter we will explore how a program may use files and how files allow one program to communicate with another.

10.1 File Fundamentals

You are already familiar with two very special files: Input, which is permanently associated with the standard input device, and Output, which designates the screen or printer. Whenever your programs execute read or write procedures,

429

data are transferred between program variables and one of these two special files. The same procedures are used to move data to or from other files, having other names and residing on various devices—provided that you have made the proper declarations and taken the other necessary preparatory steps.

Defining Files

file identifiers

The names Input and Output are examples of **file identifiers.** Since these two special files are *predeclared* in Pascal, you can use them immediately, without most of the preliminaries required before accessing other files. However, you have to declare the names of other files in the VAR section of the program.

file components

Like arrays, records, and sets, files in Pascal are a way of structuring data. Each file is a collection of simpler objects, called **file components.**† These basic units of data may be moved to or from the file by the read and write procedures. Even if a file component turns out to have some internal structure, nothing smaller than an entire file component can be transferred between a file and a program variable.

Components all the same type

Pascal requires that all components of a particular file be exactly the same data type. Permissible types range from basic ones, such as char or integer, to more complex ones, such as some designated array or record type. You specify the component type when declaring the file identifier. For example, to declare that Numbers designates a file with integer components, you could write

```
VAR Numbers : FILE OF integer;
```

File declaration

As with other Pascal types, an explicit file type may also be declared. The following code defines both Test1 and Test2 to be files having real components.

```
TYPE
  RealFile = FILE OF real;
VAR
  Test1,Test2 : RealFile;
```

The components can be structured types of almost any complexity; for example,

```
TYPE
  SampleData = ARRAY [1..6] OF real;
  SampleFile = FILE OF SampleData;
VAR
  Sample : SampleFile;
```

The only restriction is that the components cannot themselves be file types or structures with file-type components. Read or write operations on the file Sample would transmit entire arrays of six real values. It would be impossible

---

† Actually, *file component* is a term peculiar to Pascal; outside the Pascal context the term *record* is more common, but this may be confused with the Pascal data structure known as a record.

to access an individual real value on the file, since nothing less than an entire component may be transferred.

internal files

Pascal files do not necessarily correspond to actual system files. File-type data structures that have no reality outside the program are called **internal files.** Data transferred to these files cease to exist after program execution.

Need for files

On the other hand, we often need to save data from one execution of a program to the next. In applications such as text editing, inquiry systems, or maintaining stock prices or student scores, it is important that the data survive the program. We simply cannot reenter the data manually each time we execute some processing program. Nor can we run the program continuously, in order to maintain access to its data. The only feasible solution is to keep the data on files until needed again.

external files

Thus most files used by a program refer to some system-level file (that is, to an actual storage or input–output device). These are called **external files.** All external file identifiers must appear in the PROGRAM heading. For example, we routinely place input and output in the program heading:

PROGRAM Typical (input,output,Sample);

The similarity between this list of file names and the parameter list of a procedure heading emphasizes that external files are, in a sense, the parameters of a program, or its points of interaction with anything outside the program. If the file identifier does not appear in the heading, it is considered internal, by default, somewhat like a local variable.

Except for the appearance of the identifier in the heading, external and internal files are the same in terms of the program's actions; the same operations apply to both. Since external files are far more common and provide greater capability, we will discuss external files only.

Linking program-level and system-level files

Like formal parameters, the file identifiers in the heading are local to the program and do not need to correspond to the file names used in the operating system. Each computer system has its own conventions for naming, maintaining, and manipulating files. Because a system may be responsible for thousands of files, its file names and rules of access may be fairly complex. On some systems the association between a system file and a file identifier within the program requires a system-level command from the user. Unfortunately, the conventions vary widely among systems and the details depend on the particular system, so we can say little about them here. Whatever the details, we will assume throughout this chapter that the program and the system use the same identifiers. We will leave to you the burden of finding out how to bind the file identifiers in the program with the file names used by your system.

Using Files

Sequential processing

Standard Pascal permits only sequential processing of files. The components do not have unique names or any other features that would enable a program to access an arbitrary component. They may be accessed only in the order in which they are stored on secondary memory or presented through an input–output device. Furthermore, sequential processing must start with the very first component. (Some versions of Pascal—such as Turbo—do permit direct access to individual file components, but this feature is not standard.)

This description of a file as a linear arrangement of identical components may sound somewhat like an array, which is also a linearly organized collection of like components. However, it is worth noting some crucial differences:

1. An array is an occupant of main memory and then only for the duration of the defining program's execution, whereas an external file may be a long-term resident of secondary memory, quite independent of any processing program.
2. Any component of an array may be directly accessed by means of its index, whereas the components of a standard Pascal file must be accessed in sequential order, starting with the first component.
3. An array has a predefined, fixed size, whereas a file may be expanded almost indefinitely, with the addition of components to one end.
4. Values in an array may be alternately inspected or replaced, whereas a Pascal file may operate in only one mode, the **inspection mode** or the **generation mode,** at a time; when the file is being inspected (read), writing is forbidden, and when the file is being generated (written), no reading is allowed; these two modes of operation cannot be intermixed.

inspection mode
generation mode

We can illustrate these last three points by using the familiar file, input. The program cannot jump ahead to read input without traversing all the intervening input. Data must be read in the same order as they are keyed. Since no upper limit exists on how much data can be provided, the user can type until he or she gets tired. Also, it is an error to attempt to write on the input file. All Pascal files permit only one mode of access at any one time. (This particular one happens to be the inspection mode permanently, since the keyboard is incapable of displaying output.)

For files other than input and output, the mode of operation or direction of data transfer must be specified before any data can actually be moved. Depending on the direction in which the data will flow, this is done by executing one of the two procedures:

Setting the mode during execution

reset(⟨file identifier⟩);   {retrieve data from the file}

rewrite(⟨file identifier⟩);   {generate data on the file}

Both of these procedures position the file at the first component in preparation for sequential reading or writing, respectively. Incidentally, you should *not* use these procedures with the predeclared files input and output; their direction of transmission is determined by their respective devices.

reset

Since these procedures are executable, the file may be repositioned at the beginning more than once during the program. **Reset** allows the entire file to be scanned more than once or to be read after components have been written onto it. However, executing reset or rewrite for the same file more than once is usually undesirable and often incorrect. Performing rewrite on an existing file must be done with special care. Since **rewrite** prepares the file for writing starting with its first component, all former components of the file may be lost. (The actual result of this operation depends on your computer's operating system.)

Since generation mode implies starting at the beginning of the file, standard Pascal does not allow reading a file up to the end and then appending new components at that point. Appending new components must be done by copying the existing file onto a new file and continuing to write the new components on the new file while it is still in generation mode.

We finally come to the actual transmission of data, for which we use the procedures read and write. You can use read only with a file that is in inspection mode. Read transfers a component from the file to a program variable. You can use write only with a file that is in generation mode to transfer a component from the program to the file.

You can also use the familiar eof function to test for the end of a file. In order to direct their actions to other files, read, write, and eof allow the file identifier to be specified as their first parameter. Until now, this has not been necessary because input or output is always assumed in the absence of an explicit file identifier. However, even these file names may be optionally included in the statements that manipulate them. Thus the following statement pairs are equivalent.

```
read (X);              read (input,X);
WHILE NOT eof DO       WHILE NOT eof (input) DO
write (Y);             write (output,Y);
```

The file identifier is simply included as the first parameter when desired or necessary. Of course, the name is required when dealing with any user-declared file.

In summary, Pascal specifies a user-declared file and its manipulation in four different places. (Only 1 and 4 apply to the predeclared files input and output.)

1. External file identifiers appear in the heading.
2. The file identifier is declared in the VAR section, where its component type is also specified.
3. Generation or inspection of the file is specified by executing rewrite or reset, respectively.
4. Actual transfer of file components and testing of status is accomplished with read, write, or eof, as required.

Figure 10.1 shows a simple program that writes a series of real numbers onto a disk file called Info. We numbered the statements pertaining to this file according to the four kinds of statements in the preceding list.

This program reads nothing from the terminal, and so the standard file identifier Input does not need to appear in the program heading. Note how

(margin notes:)
rewrite
Rewrite may erase existing data

Read

Write

Eof

File generation

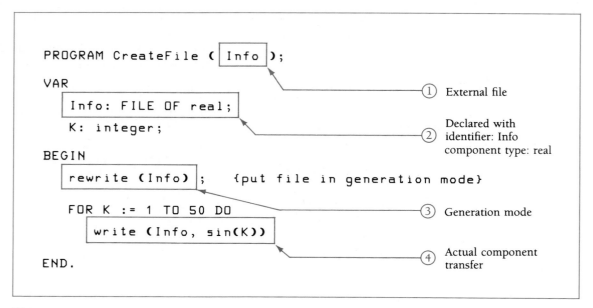

■ **Figure 10.1**
Writing to a file in Pascal.

we specified Info as the first parameter of the write statement:

```
write(Info,sin(K))
```

Although K is an integer variable, sin(K) is a real-valued expression and the declaration of Info as a FILE OF real requires that only real values be transmitted to the file. Not only must rewrite (Info) be executed before any write statement that places (real) components on Info, but it must also be executed before entering the loop. If you mistakenly place it inside the loop, the output file would be repeatedly erased and repositioned to the beginning. The file would wind up with only a single component: the last one written.

After the program terminates, Info will remain on the disk, available for future use. Although we happen to know that 50 real values were placed on Info, we do not need to remember this fact because the eof function can be used by another program to detect the end of the file during subsequent reading.

File copy   Figure 10.2 shows a program that might later copy this file of reals from Info to a new file named Master. Since two external files are involved, their identifiers, Info and Master, must appear in the program heading. Because they are nonstandard, both files must be declared and placed in the proper mode before actual transfer of the data. Since the data are being retrieved from Info and since Master is being created, the required statements are

```
reset (Info);        {inspection mode}
rewrite (Master);    {generation mode}
```

```
PROGRAM FileCopy (output,Info,Master);
   {copy real values from file Info to file Master}
TYPE
   RealFile: FILE OF real;
VAR
   Master,              {destination file}
   Info: RealFile;      {source file}
   Component: real;      {file component type}
   Count: integer;      {no. of values copied}

BEGIN {FileCopy}
   reset (Info);        {inspection mode}
   rewrite (Master);    {generation mode}
   Count := 0;

   WHILE NOT eof(Info) DO
      BEGIN {copying from Info}
         read (Info,Component);
         write (Master,Component);
         Count := Count + 1
      END; {copy}
   writeln (output,Count:3,' components copied')

END. {FileCopy}
```

(a) Copying the contents of a disk file.

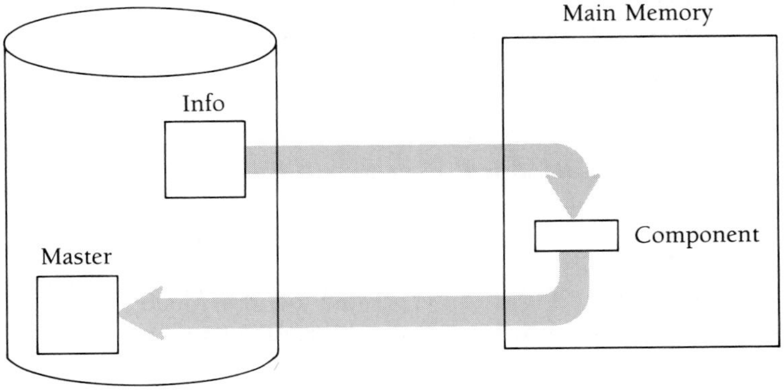

(b) Route of the data.

■ Figure 10.2
Making a copy of a disk file.

Select mode of access outside processing loop

Both reset and rewrite must lie outside any loop, so that their actions occur only once. For example, if you had mistakenly placed reset inside the loop in Fig. 10.2(a), the first component would be read every time, end-of-file would never be detected, and the loop would never terminate.

The actual data transfer is managed by the read and write statements inside the loop. The read statement obtains the next component from Info, and the write statement directs the value just read to the new disk file Master. Reading does not affect the data on Info, and they continue to be available. Observe that the loop governing the data transfer is terminated by reaching the end of the source file Info, which must be explicitly mentioned as part of eof, or

```
WHILE NOT eof(Info) DO
```

Type compatibility

Just as sequences of input statements in earlier programs had to agree with the type of data supplied from the terminal, so must they agree with data arriving from other sources. Although all components of any file must have the same type, you must know and specify the type of component that will be arriving.

In our example, the source file Info contains real components, meaning that:

1. Info must be declared with real components.
2. Read statements pertaining to Info must place the incoming components into real variables.

File identifiers are local

Using the same file identifier (Info) that was used when the file was created implies nothing about the nature of the file. The file identifier is local to the program and does not need to be the same as the identifier used by the system or by any other program referring to the same file. Thus Info (or whatever name you wish to use) must be declared with the same component type as the existing system-level file.

empty file

An **empty** input **file** should always be considered as a possibility. Note that if the file Info exists but contains no data, the program in Fig. 10.2(a) will execute and produce a Master file containing no data—a faithful copy of Info. An **undefined** (nonexistent) **file** is not the same as a file containing no data. Any attempt to retrieve data from an undefined file always results in a run-time error. The program in Fig. 10.2(a) is based on the assumption that Info already exists and thus that some other action (such as execution of the program in Fig. 10.1) generated the first version of the file.

undefined file

Although the program in Fig. 10.2(a) merely copied components intact, a similar program could have easily inspected or transformed each component as it visited main memory on its way from one file to another. In fact, the structure of Fig. 10.2(a) should be considered the normal way of sequentially processing a file. In particular, it begins by issuing reset and rewrite and then uses a loop to read, modify, and write components, one by one. Since only one component at a time resides in memory, the size of the files imposes no restriction on the memory requirements of the program.

Cannot place updates back on source file

Output must go to a file different from the original. The requirement that reading and writing cannot be intermixed on a file prevents the modified components from being immediately written back to the same file from which they came. (The solution is definitely *not* to reset and rewrite continually within the loop; this keeps returning the file to its first component and prevents the loop from stopping. A better solution is shown in Section 10.3.)

Files must be VAR parameters

File identifiers may be passed as parameters to subprograms, but *files must always be passed through variable parameters,* even if the subprogram will not alter the file in any way.

10.2 Text Files

Nontext files

A file that consists of characters can be read by people, whereas a file with another component type may generate gibberish if an attempt were made to display it. For example, if you asked the operating system to display directly the Info file in Section 10.1, you probably would not be able to read it. The reason is that the file's real components are represented in the internal coding of the machine as true reals, rather than as sequences of numeric characters.

text file

On the other hand, a **text file** is a file whose components are individual characters. For this reason, a text file can be directly displayed or printed in readable form. Until this chapter, we have dealt exclusively with text files, namely, input and output. These two are text files because they are associated with character-oriented devices designed for human communication.

Not all files are intended for use by people. Info, for example, might have been used only to store some real data that other programs would later read and utilize. Since these values were reals to begin with and will be used as reals later, there is no reason to store them as numeric character sequences— unless they will also be transmitted through a character-oriented device, such as a terminal. Why bother converting from numeric to character form and then back again, when the original numeric encoding can be stored just as well?

On the other hand, some files are intended for direct human use. Human readability might require that they be text files. You can certainly define your own; input and output are not the only possibilities.

text

Text file declaration

Text files are so common that Pascal provides a predeclared type, **text**, which is equivalent to FILE OF char. Thus we can declare text files in either of the following ways.

```
VAR   HisFile : text;
      HerFile : FILE OF char;
```

However, the declaration

```
VAR YourFile : FILE OF PACKED ARRAY [1..20] OF
               char;
```

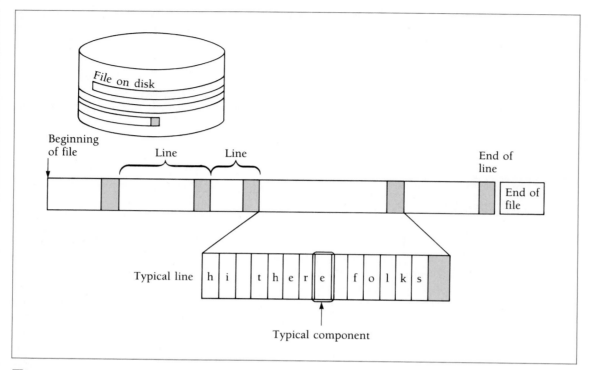

■ Figure 10.3
A text file as a
sequence of lines.

is valid but does *not* produce a text file. Even though all the data are ultimately recorded in character form, the file components are arrays and not individual characters.

Division into lines   Text files have special properties with which you are already familiar, but which are not shared by more general kinds of files. *Text files are subdivided into "lines,"* each of which is terminated by an end-of-line component. In fact, a text file is required to have end-of-line as its last component, giving text files the line-oriented nature of most input–output devices. For other kinds of files, the concept of lines is meaningless. Text files therefore have two levels of organization: (1) the file is a sequence of variable-length lines; and (2) each line is a sequence of char components. We illustrate this notion in Fig. 10.3.

Use of eoln, readln,   Three additional predeclared subprograms are available to deal with the
and writeln   line structure of text files. You are already familiar with these special subprograms: eoln, readln, and writeln. End-of-line components in the file can be sensed using the function eoln or bypassed by executing readln. Executing the writeln procedure generates an end-of-line component in an output file (which may cause the associated device to position itself at the beginning of a new display line). These actions are typical of all text files, even those stored on disk. Of course, you cannot use these subprograms with files of other types.

Automatic char/
numeric conversion

Another special feature of text files is *automatic conversion between certain simple data types to or from the required character form*. Although input and output are text files containing only character data, we have been routinely transmitting integers, real numbers, and other types of data between main memory and these files. In other words, the data types in main memory do not always *seem* to correspond to the type of the file component. Regardless of how they appear, the physical components of a text file are always individual characters.

In fact, read and write are procedures that (1) utilize more primitive subprograms to actually transmit each individual character; and (2) do the necessary conversion between the type of object in memory and the char type of the file component. For example, in order to display an integer value, the write procedure must extract the individual digits from the number, convert their encodings from numeric to character form, and transmit the numeric characters one at a time. Again, this conversion between numbers and characters is provided only when transmitting data to or from text files.

Text versus nontext

Because things are not always as they seem, beginning programmers often fall into traps. A common error is to use the editor to create a file, enter "integers" into it, and then try to access this same file from a Pascal program as a *file of integers*, which cannot be done. Even though the file may look like a collection of integers, it is actually a collection of characters or, in other words, a text file.

■ **Figure 10.4**
Important
characteristics of
different file types.

We can now characterize the differences between text files and other kinds of files and between text files that are predeclared (input and output) and those declared by the user. Figure 10.4 summarizes these differences.

PROPERTY	KIND OF FILE		
	Text		Nontext
	Predeclared (Input/Output)	User-Declared	
Definition			
Identifier in program heading	Whenever ident. used	Usually	Usually
Identifier declared in VAR section	Never	Always	Always
Access			
Need to specify mode (reset/rewrite) before use	Never	Always	Always
May use eof, read, write	Yes	Yes	Yes
May use eoln, readln, writeln	Yes	Yes	Never
Features			
All components are characters	Yes	Yes	No
Automatic conversion between char and numeric	Yes	Yes	No
Identical components, sequential access, one mode at a time	Yes	Yes	Yes

Text file copy preserves line structure

Figure 10.5 shows another file copy program. This time the files are both text files, and the line structure of the original is faithfully reproduced in the duplicate. The input structure is identical to that used with input of variable-length strings from the terminal; only the file names have changed in this example. The heart of the loop copies one character at a time to the output file, and every detection of end-of-line in the original file causes writeln to generate an end-of-line in the new version. Incidentally, if this program were converted to a procedure, use of input or output as parameters could cause a problem because of the implementation-dependent result of executing reset and rewrite on these files.

Any text file can look just like the terminal to a program trying to read its contents. The need for correspondence between input statements and the arriving data still applies. Consequently, all the input considerations from Chapter 5 are pertinent to any text file. The difference here is that the data already exist. There is no chance to prompt a user for the proper data, nor is there any chance to try again after reading an erroneous input value.

One last procedure provided for text files in generation mode is

■ **Figure 10.5**

Copying a text file.

Page (⟨TextFile⟩);

```
PROGRAM TextFileCopy (output,Source,Destin);
   VAR
      Destin,            {destination file}
      Source: text;      {source file}
      C: char;           {text file component}
   BEGIN
      reset (Source);    {prepare to read}
      rewrite (Destin);  {prepare to write}

      WHILE NOT eof(Source) DO
         BEGIN

            WHILE NOT eoln(Source) DO
               BEGIN
                  read (Source,C); {get next char}
                  write (Destin,C) {copy to new file}
               END; {inner loop}

            readln(Source);        {bypass end of line}
            writeln (Destin)       {append end of line}

         END; {outer loop}
      writeln('copy complete')
   END. {TextFileCopy}
```

which always generates an end-of-line component. When dealing with the standard output file, it also generally causes subsequent output to begin on a new page (or a fresh screen). However, its effect on other text files depends on the system.

10.3 Files Having Records as Components

Need for files of records
Many applications require that several items of data pertaining to the same subject, such as customer, inventory item, and so on, be maintained on files. The usual practice is to group the data about each object or person into a record and to keep these records together on a file representing all the objects or people. This file would then have records as its components.

Files of Records Having Fixed Structure

Consider the problem, originally discussed in Section 9.3, of maintaining the scores for a class of students. At that time, the student records were arranged in an array. Long-term storage provided by external files is more suitable for such information, so that it remains available from one use to the next.

Declaration
Two such files are declared in the following code. The record declaration (repeated from Fig. 9.11) represents each student by an identification number, three scores, and an average.

```
TYPE
  ScoreType = ARRAY [1..3] OF integer;
  StudentInfo =
    RECORD
      StudentID : Integer;
      SCORE : ScoreType;
      Avg : real
    END;
  ClassType = FILE OF StudentInfo;
VAR
  ClassFile,
  TempFile : ClassType;      {files of students}
  Student  : StudentInfo;    {single student}
```

File update
Suppose that we have an old class list (in a system file) that contains the student scores as of the second test for the term. A third test has just been graded, and we want to update the records to include this new information. The students may be processed independently, which means that the class list may be processed sequentially. We have a classic *file update* situation.

Class lists, as well as many other files, are kept in some specific order to simplify operations involving the whole file. If we assume that both the student records and the new scores are arranged by increasing identification

```
PROGRAM ClassUpdate (Input,Output,ClassFile);
TYPE
   ScoreType = ARRAY [1..3] OF integer;
   StudentInfo =
      RECORD
         StudentID : integer;
         Score : ScoreType;
         Avg : real
      END;
   ClassType = FILE OF StudentInfo;
VAR
   TempFile,                        {INTERNAL file!}
   ClassFile : ClassType;           {file of students}
   Student   : StudentInfo;         {single student}
   NewScore,                        {WHICH score is new}
   This      : integer;             {index of current grade}
BEGIN
   reset(ClassFile);   {prepare to read}
   rewrite(TempFile);  {prepare to write}
   writeln ('Which mark is being added to file?');
   readln(NewScore);    {presumably 1, 2, or 3}
   WHILE NOT eof(ClassFile) DO
      BEGIN {file inspection}
         read(ClassFile,Student);
         WITH Student DO
            BEGIN {processing Student}
               write('score for student# ?', StudentID);
               readln( Score[NewScore] );
               FOR This := 1 TO NewScore DO
                  Avg := Avg + Score[This];
               Avg := Avg / NewScore
            END; {processing Student}
         write(TempFile,Student) {save updated record}
      END; {inspection}
   reset(TempFile);       {reverse file modes before}
   rewrite(ClassFile);  {copying records back}
   WHILE NOT eof(TempFile) DO
      BEGIN {file copy}
         read(TempFile,Student);
         write(ClassFile,Student)
      END {copy}
END. {ClassUpdate}
```

(a) Program to update file.

■ Figure 10.6
Updating a file of records.

number, a merge-type process, involving tandem traversal of the file and the new scores, will do the job. The logic is that described in Section 7.4.

Assume that the class list is on a file and that the new scores will be entered from the terminal. The algorithm is

Repeat for each student in the class:
1. read the old student record;
2. read the new score for that student;
3. add the new score to the record and revise the average;
4. save the revised student record.

The only problem (in standard Pascal anyway) is that we cannot immediately store the revised record on the same file from which the old records are being read. As mentioned previously, a file cannot be in both the inspection and generation modes at the same time.

A solution is to transfer the new records to a different file as they are being revised. When all the records have been processed, the new file is copied back to the original and then discarded.

This approach is implemented by the program in Fig. 10.6. TempFile holds the updated records until ClassFile has been completely read. TempFile

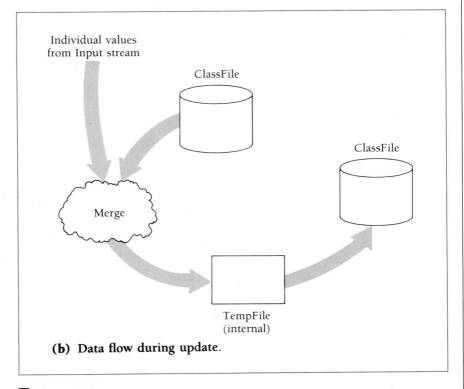

Individual values
from Input stream

ClassFile

ClassFile

Merge

TempFile
(internal)

(b) Data flow during update.

■ Figure 10.6
(Continued)

can be an *internal* file, since it contains nothing before program execution and is not needed afterward. The omission of the identifier from the program heading makes it internal.

During the first phase of processing, when the records are being updated, ClassFile is in inspection mode and TempFile is in generation mode. But during the copy phase TempFile becomes the record source and ClassFile the destination, requiring their modes to be reversed before the copy begins.

Every read or write statement dealing with these record files transmits exactly one file component, an entire record. The correct way to write the record is

```
Write (TempFile,Student);
```

We cannot transmit anything less than a complete component. Even though the following code would work with a text file, it is completely unacceptable here.

```
WITH Student DO  {actually...don't do}
   write(TempFile,StudentID,Score[1],Score[2],
      Score[3],Avg);
```

Although we mention all the fields of the Student record, this write statement attempts to output five simple numeric fields as five separate objects.

Similarly, when any of these files is being read, its components must be read as complete records and should be placed in record variables that are structurally the same as the file components; that is, the number and types of the fields of the record in memory should match the arrangement of data in a typical component.

Files of Records with Variant Parts

Record variants permit mixture of record types on file

The requirement that all file components be exactly the same type appears to forbid natural associations of data that could be stored on the same file. However, because of records with variant parts, no such problem arises. Differing records are simply treated as variants of the parent type that comprises the file components. Let's return to the student record problem. In our file of student scores, almost all of its records might pertain to individual students, but one or two might pertain to the class as a whole.

"Label" record introduces file

Suppose that only the first record is a "label" for the file, identifying the class by name and giving the number of student records in the file. All following records contain information on individual students. The declarations provide a single record type to serve as the file component type. However, this particular type includes two variants that allow two kinds of records to actually appear on the file: one to be used as the file label, the other to hold the data for an individual student.

Untagged variants

Since only the first record on the file will be a label, it is not necessary to explicitly tag each record or for the program to do any verification. Hence the free type union (untagged variety) of record variant is declared. The fields of the first record are immediately interpreted as label information. All subsequent records are processed as student data.

Tagged variants   Now suppose that, in addition to the label record, the student file contains a mixture of record types, so that you cannot know what kind of record you are dealing with until it has been read. For this situation you should use a discriminated type union (tagged) form of variant record declaration. Encoding the variant type in a tag field allows the program to select the appropriate processing by consulting this field.

In Fig. 10.7 on p. 446, we show the declarations and code for handling intermixed, tagged records from the file. We again assume that records come in two varieties: those that are textual and those that pertain to student scores. The textual variety of record might appear throughout the file because it is used to store extra data about particular students, such as personal history or academic comments.

Since the textual information may vary considerably from one student to another, we use variable-length strings to store it. In particular, text is stored in a record consisting of a character array and a length field. This record type, in turn, is a field of one of the record variants appearing on the file.

An important reason for utilizing variant records on files is to avoid using too much space for subjects with little information, while providing sufficiently large records for subjects with larger amounts of data.

10.4 Using the File Buffer Variable

get and put
procedures

Read and write are not the only means of transmitting data between files and main memory. Another pair of procedures, the **get procedure** and the **put procedure,** are the fundamental input–output routines used by read and write to carry out their detailed operations.

file buffer variable
(window)

Get and put transfer file components without explicitly reading to or writing from program variables. Pascal automatically provides a **file buffer variable** for every file identifier your program uses. Get and put move data between the file and this buffer variable. Put transfers data from the buffer into the file, and get transfers data from the file into the buffer. Both procedures transmit one component at a time, which, in the case of text files, means that precisely one character is moved by each call.

The buffer variable acts like a "window" through which the program can access one component of the file. As the file is being processed, this window is moved sequentially through the file and always identifies the current component. The file buffer variable is denoted as

⟨file identifier⟩ˆ   or   ⟨file identifier⟩ ↑

We will use the caret (˄) notation.

```
PROGRAM MixedFile (Input,Output,ClassFile2);
TYPE
   ScoreType = ARRAY [1..3] OF integer;
   VariableString =
      RECORD
         Length : integer;
         Content : ARRAY [1..40] OF char
      END; {record}
   KindOfRecord = (Individual,Textual);
   FileComponent =
      RECORD
      CASE Tag : KindOfRecord OF
         Textual    : (Info : VariableString);
         Individual : (StudentID : integer;
                       Score : ScoreType;
                       Avg : real)
      END; {record}
   FileType = FILE OF FileComponent;
VAR
   ClassFile : FileType;
   NextRecord : FileComponent;

BEGIN {MixedFile}
   reset(ClassFile);  {prepare to read}
   read(ClassFile,NextRecord); {the file label}
   {Process NextRecord.Info.Content}

   WHILE NOT eof(ClassFile) DO
      BEGIN
         read(ClassFile,NextRecord);
         WITH NextRecord DO
            CASE Tag OF {must check Tag}
               Individual: BEGIN

                        processing of fields...
                        StudentID, Score,Avg

                     END; {individual}
               Textual  : BEGIN

                        processing of fields...
                        Info.Length & Info.Content

                     END {textual record}
            END {case}
      END {loop}
END. {MixedFile}
```

■ Figure 10.7
A file containing intermixed tagged records.

Window acts like a variable

An assignment statement can move values between the file buffer variable and other program variables of the same type. Since a file buffer variable is provided automatically for every file identifier used in the program, it must not be declared separately.

The put procedure has the general form:

put (⟨file identifier⟩);

Action of put

The action of put is defined only when the file is in generation mode. The execution of put appends the data from the buffer variable onto the file, moves the file pointer (the window) beyond this latest component, and leaves the contents of the file buffer variable undefined. This means that the program cannot depend on the contents of the file buffer variable being the same after the execution of put as they were before.

Put and write

The effect of put is shown in Fig. 10.8. Note that when the data are stored in the buffer variable, nothing happens to the file. The buffer contents are written onto the file only after execution of put. For example, if DataOut is a *variable* and FileOut is a *file* of the same type, the following code fragments are equivalent.

```
rewrite (FileOut);                  rewrite (FileOut);
    .                                   .
    .                                   .
    .                                   .
write (FileOut,DataOut);            FileOut^ := DataOut;
                                    put (FileOut);
```

Clearly, if the data to be transferred already reside in a program variable, it is easier to use write.

The get procedure obtains the next component from the file and has the general form:

get (⟨file identifier⟩);

Action of get

The action of get is defined only when the file is in inspection mode and eof is false (that is, some unread component remains on the file). If the last component is already in the buffer variable, execution of get causes the value of eof to become true and the file buffer variable to become undefined. Attempting to inspect the file buffer variable after eof has become true is an error, as is attempting another get.

Although end-of-line may be represented in a different way, it behaves like an ordinary file component that looks like a blank, except to readln, reset, and eoln. The value of eoln is true when this special component is in the buffer.

Reset puts first component in buffer

As mentioned before, a reset operation must occur before any input can be obtained. *When reset is executed, the first file component is transferred to the file buffer.* The program therefore has the first file component available to it immediately after reset and before executing any get operation. Consequently, if the program executes the get procedure immediately after a reset, the first file component will be overwritten. You may think of reset as putting a file

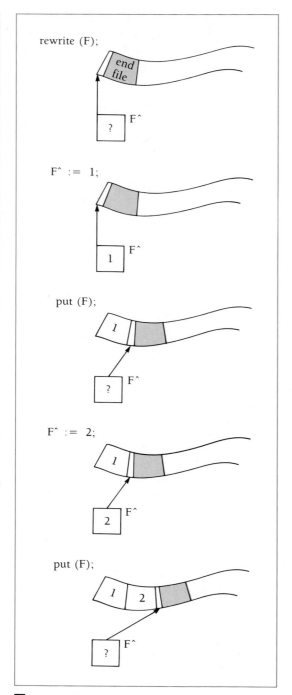

■ Figure 10.8
Action of the put procedure.

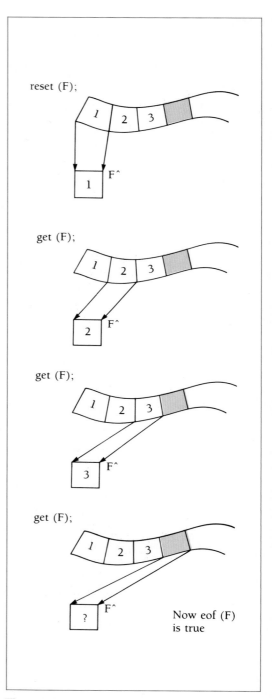

■ Figure 10.9
Action of the get procedure.

in inspection mode, initializing the file window to the beginning, and then doing the equivalent of a get operation. The action of the get procedure is shown in Fig. 10.9.

Get and read   The following code fragments have an equivalent effect.

```
read (FileIn,Data)        Data := FileIn^;
                          get( FileIn )
```

The behavior of reset and of get result in the following form for reading an entire file. It is shown below the equivalent familiar form using read.

Overall input process

```
reset (FileIn);
WHILE NOT eof(FileIn) DO
  BEGIN
    read (FileIn,DataIn);
    .
    . ┌─────────────────┐
    . │ process one     │
    . │ component       │
      └─────────────────┘
  END
```

```
reset (FileIn);
WHILE NOT eof(FileIn) DO
  BEGIN
    DataIn := FileIn^;
    .
    . ┌─────────────────┐
    . │ process one     │
    . │ component       │
      └─────────────────┘
    get (FileIn)
  END
```

In Chapter 7 we discussed the problem of merging two sorted arrays into one. The same problem carries over into file handling. To demonstrate, we will merge two files of names and addresses, a situation that often comes up in the direct-mail business. We assume that each file is sorted by name and that the components of each file are described as follows:

```
TYPE
  ShortString = PACKED ARRAY [1..2] OF char;
  LongString = PACKED ARRAY [1..20] OF char;
  CustomerData =
    RECORD
      Name: LongString;
      Initials: Shortstring;
      Street,
      City: LongString;
      Zip: PACKED ARRAY [1..5] OF char
    END;
  CustomerFile = FILE OF CustomerData;
```

```
PROGRAM Merger (File1,File2,MergedFile);
    {TYPE DECLARATIONS FROM TEXT APPEAR HERE}
VAR
    File1,   {two source files assumed...}
    File2,   {to be in order by Name}
    MergedFile : CustomerFile;

PROCEDURE FileAppend (VAR Source,Destin: CustomerFile);
    {copy remainder of Source onto end of Destin}
    BEGIN {FileAppend}
        WHILE NOT eof(Source) DO
            BEGIN
                Destin^ := Source^;
                put(Destin);
                get(Source)
            END
    END; {FileAppend}

BEGIN {Merger}
    reset(File1);
    reset(File2);
    rewrite(MergedFile);
    WHILE NOT eof(File1) AND NOT eof(File2) DO
        BEGIN {selection}
            IF File1^.Name < File2^.Name THEN
                BEGIN {choose File1}
                    MergedFile^ := File1^; {select component}
                    get (File1)        {advance window}
                END
            ELSE
                BEGIN {choose File2}
                    MergedFile^ := File2^; {select component}
                    get (File2)        {advance window}
                END;
            put (MergedFile)            {move component to new file}
        END; {selection}

    {At this point, one of the source files is used up}
    {Append whichever file still contains data}
    FileAppend (File1,MergedFile);
    FileAppend (File2,MergedFile);
END. {File Merge program}
```

■ Figure 10.10
Program to merge files (duplicates preserved).

Ordered file merge   The logic in merging two ordered files is the same as that for merging two ordered arrays. As long as both source files still contain unselected data, the current components from the two files are compared. The component with the smaller Name field value is chosen and copied to the new file. Then the window is advanced in the file from which that component was chosen. When one of the source files has been exhausted, the remaining data on the other are appended to the new file. Since no processing other than inspection is required, we can handle all data movement and comparison through the file buffer variables. The program for merging ordered files is shown in Fig. 10.10.

Using data in the
buffer   Note that we can refer to data in a buffer variable, just as if we had declared it as a normal variable of type Customer. For example, File1^.Name refers to the Name field of the component currently in the buffer of File1. Since both source files have been reset, there are always components in their respective file buffer variables (at least until the end of the file is encountered). Whichever component is chosen by a comparison must be moved from its buffer before the get procedure advances to the next component of that file.

File append   After one source file has been used up, we must copy the remaining records from the other source file to the end of MergedFile. Since the code to do this is identical regardless of which file still contains unprocessed data, we can implement the copy by using FileAppend, a procedure based on the assumption that the reset and rewrite operations have already been performed on the two files. This means that Source^ will already contain a component from the Source file when the procedure begins. Observe the order in which data are moved between the two file buffers and the files. Again, note that all file names must be passed as variable parameters.

If the same name appears on both File1 and File2, it will appear twice on MergedFile. It is possible to modify the program so that duplicate records are avoided.

10.5   Review of Rules

A.   If a file identifier appears in the program heading, it is for an external file, which means that it is associated with a system file and allows communication with an input–output device or a long-term storage device. Otherwise, the file is internal and is merely a run-time data structure.

B.   Files are declared in the variable declaration section as either

VAR ⟨file identifier⟩: FILE OF ⟨component type⟩

or

VAR ⟨file identifier⟩: ⟨filetype⟩

where ⟨filetype⟩ is either *text* or a previously defined type, such as

TYPE ⟨filetype⟩ = FILE OF ⟨component type⟩

C. A file is placed in inspection mode (prepared for reading) by

reset (⟨file identifier⟩);

or placed in generation mode (prepared for writing) by

rewrite (⟨file identifier⟩);

A file may be in only one mode at a time; data may flow in only one direction. Also, standard Pascal allows only sequential access, beginning with the first component. Whenever a new access mode is entered (by reset or rewrite), the file is repositioned to the beginning. Executing rewrite effectively erases any previous contents of the file.

D. File components may be transmitted by the procedures read, write, get, or put. In inspection mode, the procedures read or get may be applied to any kind of file, and the function eof can be called to detect the end of a file. With text files in inspection mode you may also use the readln procedure for data transfer and test for end-of-line with the eoln function. In generation mode the procedures write and put may be applied to any kind of file, and the procedure writeln can be used with text files only. All these subprograms specify the file name as the first parameter. If the file name is omitted, a predefined text file (input or output) is assumed.

E. When applied to files of type text, read and write provide automatic conversion between the internal encodings of certain standard types and the character representation used on all text files.

F. The file buffer variable is denoted by

⟨file identifier⟩ˆ   or   ⟨file identifier⟩ ↑

and is used by the get and put procedures to move components to or from the file. It is supplied with every file identifier in the program and may be used like a normal variable. Note that it is initialized to the first component of a file when reset is executed.

G. The relationships between read and get and write and put are summarized by the following equivalent sequences.

```
reset (F);              reset (F);
read (F,Data);          Data := F^;
                        get (F);


rewrite (F);            rewrite (F);
write (F,Data);         F^ := Data;
                        put (F);
```

H. The predefined files input and output must not be declared or used as arguments to reset or rewrite in standard Pascal.

I. File identifiers may be passed as parameters but always as variable parameters.

KEY TERMS

empty file
external file
file
file buffer variable
file component
file identifier
generation mode
get procedure

inspection mode
internal file
put procedure
reset
rewrite
text
text file
undefined file

EXERCISES

10.1 (a) Write two separate programs to exchange a message through a text file. The first program transfers the message from the terminal to the file. The second program reads the file and displays the message on the screen.

(b) Add to the second program the capability of replacing one message by another. When the second program begins, it displays the most recent version of the message stored on the file. After asking the user whether a different message is desired, the program may write a newly entered message on the same file before quitting, overwriting the message that was previously stored there.

(c) Try to implement part (b) without using the first program to store the original message on the file. On some systems, an empty system-level file may have to be generated before running this program.

10.2 An important use for files is to store the results of one program for later use by another. The "other" program may be simply a subsequent execution of the first. For example, the text prepared by a text editor may be modified later by the same editor. To explicitly move the data back and forth between main memory and the file, you may need two new commands:

l   {to load the data from the file}
k   {to keep the data on the file}

When you enter the quit command, the system should ask whether you want to keep the text before the program terminates. When a program starts up, it may automatically execute load to initialize its data structure.

(a) Incorporate these "load" and "keep" options in the program to maintain a single list of student grades, using the information in Exercise 7.12. The grades may be stored on either (i) a text file; or (ii) a file of integers.

(b) Include the load and keep commands in the program to maintain two lists of taxicabs in Exercise 7.15. Here, you may store both lists on the same text file, but must make provision for recognizing which cabs belong to each list.

10.3   To save the effort of reentering large amounts of data each time a program is executed, the data may be kept on a file for easy retrieval whenever it is needed. Several previous exercises have required considerable amounts of data to be entered before processing could begin. Implement data entry as a separate program that stores the data on a file and revise the original program to obtain its data from such a file. You may do this for any of the following exercises.
(a) The text to be analyzed in Exercises 7.11, 8.13, or 9.4.
(b) The maze to be searched in Exercise 8.15.
(c) The compatibility array used in Exercises 8.16 and 8.17.
(d) The matrix of coefficients used in Exercises 8.18–20.
(e) The spatial positions of objects to be clustered in Exercise 9.12; store either the two-dimensional array or the raw coordinates.

10.4   This exercise requires three programs that pass their results from one to the other through files. The first program simply transfers up to 50 names (of no more than 20 characters each) from the terminal to a file. The second program reads these names from the file, sorts them, and produces another file of alphabetically ordered names. The third program displays the names from either (but usually the ordered) file on the screen.
(a) Write the second program using the selection sort. The selection sort can generate its output file during the sorting process, eliminating the need for a second array.
(b) Write the second program using the insertion sort. (See Exercise 7.9.) The insertion sort can produce an ordered array during the input process, eliminating the need for a second array.
Instead of using text files, let the file components be packed arrays of characters; this will save some effort in the input processes.

10.5   Write a program to accumulate text on a file. There are four interactive commands:

Command	Meaning
a	Append the following text (up to but not including the sentinel, #) to the file.
d	Display all the text on the file.
e	Erase the file.
q	Quit.

Only one external (text) file may be used, but an internal file might prove useful. The primary objective here is to implement the append operation.

10.6   In Exercises 5.1 and 5.2, output lines were generated in response to interactive input. Although the output lines were supposed to produce a table, the table was difficult to view when input and output were intermixed on the screen. This problem was solved in Exercise 8.12 by storing the output lines in an array until the user wanted to view the entire collection of lines constituting the table.
(a) Instead of using an array, store this output on an INTERNAL file for later display.
(b) Add the option of storing this internal file on an external file before terminating the program, in case the user wants to view the report at a later time.

10.7   Sometimes, data are specially encoded for storage on a file. When such data are retrieved for later use, they must be decoded back to their original, usable form. One motive is security. Data may be encrypted during their residence on the file to prevent theft or unauthorized inspection. Another reason may be to consume less file space; this type of encoding is called data compression.

(a) The encoder/decoder ring of Exercise 7.18 provides a simple encryption scheme. Write one program to encode some uppercase alphabetic data using the method in Exercise 7.18(a) and save the secret message on a file. Write another program to read this coded message and display the original. To facilitate the decoding, you can write the letter with which 'A' is encoded as the first character on the file to be used by the message recovery program in generating its decoding array.

(b) In Exercise 8.14, a line or closed contour (originally, entries in a two-dimensional array) was encoded as a sequence of integers indicating how to trace the original shape. Write a program to convert such a two-dimensional array containing one of these shapes into a sequence of integers and store this encoding on a file. Write another program capable of reading the encoding from a file and recovering the original shape for display on the screen.

(c) A common form of data compression, called text compression, compacts text for more efficient storage. One technique replaces extremely common words or character sequences by some shorter, easily recognized pattern during residence on the file. Write one program to perform text entry and compression and another program to restore and display the original text from the version stored on the file. Use the following simple encoding scheme.

Original Sequence	Encoded Version
the	#1
und	#2
ing	#3
2 or more blanks	@n, where n = number of blanks

Thus the word "underling" would be encoded as #2erl#3, a saving of two characters. Assume that the text itself does not contain any instances of the special characters (# and @).

10.8 Sensitive computer data are frequently stored in encrypted form; that is, some coding scheme is used so that the meaning of the data is not immediately intelligible to someone who accidentally (or maliciously) gains access to the file. Of course, there must be some way of decoding the data so that they are meaningful to the people authorized to read the data. A trivial coding scheme that can be applied to character data in a text file (assuming use of the ASCII code) is to replace every character in the raw data with a two-digit numeral. In the ASCII code all printable characters occupy consecutive locations in the collating sequence, and their positions can be determined by the ord function. Unfortunately, some of the characters will yield three-digit integers when supplied as arguments to ord. For example, ord('z') is 122. To reduce these values to the required two-digit range, you can take ord(c) − ord('ᵇ'). The reason is that the smallest "printing" character in the ASCII sequence is the blank. Since ord('ᵇ') is 32, reducing each ordinal value by ord('ᵇ') produces numbers that do not exceed two digits. Also, if ord(c) − ord('ᵇ') is a number between 0 and 9, make sure that two characters are generated. This technique will double the number of characters in the coded version of the text. You cannot replace each character with a two-digit integer; you must replace the characters with two numeric characters and not numbers. Specifically, the character string 'Joe' will be encoded as '427969'. Write a Pascal program that will read a text file RawFile and produce its encoded version CodedFile, using the technique described. Then write the program to read CodedFile and recover the original raw data.

10.9 The patterns comprising giant letters are natural candidates for storage on files. (See Exercise 8.11.)

(a) Using a 10 × 10 array to construct the pattern, write a program to repeatedly enter a giant letter and store its shape on a file. The file components should be records having two fields: One is a 10 × 10 array containing a giant letter pattern; the other is a char-type field indicating which letter is encoded in the array. A second program enables the user to request output of particular giant letters. When a letter is requested, the display program searches the letter file, reading in records until the one containing the desired letter appears. Try this with the letters A, B, and C.

(b) To avoid a file search each time a letter is requested, you can store each giant letter on a separate file. The user's request will then cause a specific file to be read and displayed. Use an array of files(!) to simplify the code and index this array by associated letters. Then when the user specifies a letter, the appropriate file can be accessed immediately.

10.10 Maintain the student records of Exercise 9.5 on a file of records. The records are entered and stored in alphabetical order by a "class initialization" program.

(a) Write an inquiry program to display either the entire class file or an individual student record, based on a search of the file by either name or ID number. You must include some information on the file to indicate how many tests have already been given. This information can be retrieved by inspecting the first record.

(b) Write an update program that enters the grades for a new test and modifies the existing file accordingly.

10.11 Modify the program of Exercise 9.7(c) for maintaining information about bank customers. The master records now reside on a file and never in an array. Inquiries may be directed to the file, but updates are stockpiled in an array until the array is full or a complete report is requested. Using the array of update items as one source and the master file as the other, do a two-way merge to create a revised master file and store it on the original file, replacing the original values.

10.12 Rewrite the program of Exercise 9.9 to maintain the variant payroll records on a file. Write separate programs for each of the following tasks.

(a) Generate and initialize the original employee file.

(b) Do a weekly update of the number of hours worked by hourly employees.

(c) Generate a payroll report based on the data in the employee file. Reset the hours worked to 0 using this program but only in response to an explicit command.

10.13 Generate three ordered files of integers and write a program to perform a **three-way** merge of these files. By simultaneously traversing all three source files, a single ordered file containing all the original data should be produced.

(a) Write the program at the read/write level.

(b) Write the program at the get/put level.

11

Recursion and Special Topics in Control

A recent version of the compact edition of the Oxford English Dictionary says that the word **recursion** is "rare or obsolete" and then goes on to define it as "a backward movement, return." The term may very well be obsolete in everyday English, but it is commonly used in computer science to describe subprograms that can call themselves. In fact, *recursive subprograms* are powerful tools for solving certain problems. We introduce this technique in this chapter. In addition, we will discuss other topics concerning subprograms and control. Postponed until now because they are either advanced or specialized or nonstandard, these topics include passing subprogram names and generalized arrays as parameters.

11.1 Recursion

We have all heard concepts defined in terms of the same concept. For example, one "definition" of microcomputer is: the product produced by a microcomputer manufacturer. Although amusing, this description is a useless working definition, presuming as it does that you already know what "microcomputer" means. This is an example of a circular definition.

On the other hand, we can define something in terms of a *more primitive version of the same thing*. We could describe the height of a child as last year's height plus the past year's growth. Although the term "height" is used in the definition of height, the two references pertain to different years, and the larger height is defined in terms of the smaller. Assuming that we can obtain the amount of growth for each year, we can apply this definition repeatedly to define the current height in terms of any previous height. This approach helps us more than a purely circular definition, but we run into trouble when we try to apply it before the first year.

This definition needs two things. First, to stop the application of the definition when it has been extended back to the year of birth, we must add the restriction that it applies only when the year in question is greater than or equal to 1. Second, we must provide an alternative, primitive definition for the meaning of height at birth. For example, define the starting height (year 0) as length at time of birth, a definition that does not use the term "height."

recursive definition

This is a recursive definition of height. A **recursive definition** uses the term being defined in its own definition but with two provisions:

1. The version of the term appearing in the definition should be simpler than the version being defined.
2. There must be an alternative definition of the term, involving only other (primitive) elements.

This second feature is necessary to break the cycle and ultimately resolve the definition without using the term being defined.

Of course, human beings rarely need such precision for understanding. We usually known when to stop "looping" on the term being defined. In programs, however, precision is required.

Introduction to Recursion in Pascal

A subprogram defined (directly or indirectly) in terms of itself is recursive. *Pascal permits only subprograms to be recursive.* Thus it is possible to declare a procedure containing a reference to itself. At execution time this procedure might call itself, at which time it starts executing again from scratch. During

activation

this second **activation**—the process of executing the subprogram—it may call itself for a third time, and so on. Obviously, just as you must avoid circular definitions in English, you must design recursive subprograms with great care to prevent an infinite succession of calls. However, this recursive programming technique greatly simplifies certain problems. The early examples in this section are not among those problems, but they do provide a gentle introduction to recursive programming.

Define unsigned integer

Consider defining an unsigned integer. After a digit has been defined as one of the symbols 0, 1, 2, . . . , 9, you might describe an unsigned integer as a digit, possibly followed by another digit, possibly followed by another digit, and so on. Attempting to define an unsigned integer solely in terms of a simpler concept (digit) leads to the unfortunate use of "etc." A recursive definition for an unsigned integer is much neater and more precise: (1) a digit; or (2) a digit followed by an unsigned integer. In any concrete application of this definition, the integer involved in (2) is simpler (by having fewer digits) than the integer being defined, and alternative (1) provides a way out of the cycle.

Many Pascal syntax diagrams are recursive. For example, the following syntax diagram is comparable to the above definition of unsigned integer.

The recursion here arises from the path that includes the "unsigned integer" box.

Recursive verification

Let's attempt to verify that "123" is an unsigned integer according to our recursive definition. Since 123 is not a digit, we must determine whether it conforms to part (2) of our definition. The first character "1" is a digit, and "23" may be an unsigned integer. Now we are faced with the problem of testing whether "23" is actually an unsigned integer, which means reapplying the definition to this shorter string of symbols.

Since "23" is not a digit, we apply part (2) of our definition and discover that "2" is a digit, followed by a possible unsigned integer, "3." Once more we apply the definition to the still simpler candidate, "3." This time we find that "3" is a digit, and hence an unsigned integer according to part (1) of our definition.

Having broken the cycle, we now reverse direction and answer the questions posed by each attempt to apply the definition. We know that "3" is an unsigned integer. We therefore know that "23" is a digit followed by an unsigned integer and is therefore itself an unsigned integer. Continuing to work backwards, we confirm that "123" is a digit followed by an unsigned integer and conclude that "123" is an unsigned integer. This approach may seem tedious, but it does work.

Each successive application of our definition was to a successively shorter candidate. The repetitive application of part (2) is guaranteed to stop because you will either encounter a character that is not a digit or work down to a single digit that can be tested using only part (1) of our definition.

Recursive algorithm

In a programming context, the candidate would be a character string, and we would want to verify that all its characters are numeric. We can use our recursive definition to write an algorithm:

To test whether a string represents an unsigned integer . . .

if first character is not numeric then answer is *no*
else {still have a candidate}
   if only one character in string then {1} answer is *yes*
   else {2}
   if *remainder of string is unsigned integer* then answer is *yes* else answer is *no*

In order to test whether the remainder of the string is an unsigned integer, we apply this same algorithm to that fragment of the original string. This is the point at which recursion occurs. Testing whether a string is numeric may require testing whether a (shorter) string is numeric. You can easily see how successive applications of this algorithm correspond to the application of our original definition.

Recursive subprogram

The next step is to write a corresponding subprogram. If it is a boolean-valued function PureInteger, and the record containing the string is Subject, the original function call might look like

```
IF PureInteger (Subject, 1) THEN. . .
```

Using 1 as the second parameter tests the entire substring, starting with the first character. In general, if the second parameter has the value K, the subprogram will test the substring beginning at position K.

The corresponding function declaration is shown in Fig. 11.1, which is a direct encoding of the algorithm. Its key feature is its reference to itself, or

```
PureInteger := PureInteger( Subject, Start + 1);
```

The reference on the left provides the function result to its calling program. This result pertains to the substring beginning at position Start. At this point in the code, however, the character at position Start is known to be a digit, so that the outcome depends on whether the substring beginning one character beyond position Start is an unsigned integer. The reference to PureInteger on the right invokes the function to test this following substring.

Like the English and algorithmic examples of recursion, this function contains alternative branches that avoid self-reference, permitting it to terminate and return normally, and it calls itself only when it needs to know about a simpler string.

Each activation like a new subprogram

Consider how it works at execution time, when asked to test whether '123' is an unsigned integer. Whether the call originates from outside or from within the function, each activation starts from scratch, as though the function were being invoked for the first time. Figure 11.2 illustrates the three activations of PureInteger required to analyze '123'. Parameters are passed and control is returned in the usual way. When a second, third, or nth activation of a subprogram ends, control returns to the appropriate part of the first, second, or $(n - 1)$th activation, respectively.

Local identifiers

When a subprogram calls itself, it is as though some totally different subprogram were being referenced, as far as the current activation is concerned. All local identifiers (notably local variables and value-type parameters) are "shielded" from other parts of the program. Although all activations use the same identifiers, each instance in each activation refers to a different item in much the same way that a local variable is distinguished from variables of the same name elsewhere in the program.

Printing character strings in reverse

Recursive subprograms are not limited to testing whether some subject conforms to a recursive definition. A recursive approach is often used to produce more comprehensive effects. Consider the problem of displaying the characters of a string in reverse order. Although this is easy to do by simply scanning backwards through the string, this problem also has two straight-forward recursive solutions.

```
TYPE
   StringType =
      RECORD
         Length : integer;
         Data   : PACKED ARRAY [1..10] OF char
      END;
VAR
   Subject : StringType;



FUNCTION PureInteger (Subject : StringType;
                      Start : integer) : boolean;

   {Verify whether the Subject.Data characters, in
   positions Start to Length, are all numeric}

   BEGIN
      WITH Subject DO

         IF NOT (Data[Start] IN ['0'..'9']) THEN
            PureInteger := false
         ELSE {possible candidate}

            IF Length = Start THEN {one numeric char}
               PureInteger := true
            ELSE {check remainder}

               PureInteger := PureInteger (Subject,Start+1)

   END; {PureInteger function}
```

recursive call

```
BEGIN {main program}
      .
      .
```

original call

```
      .
   IF PureInteger (Subject,1)
      .
      .
      .
```

■ Figure 11.1
Test for an unsigned integer.

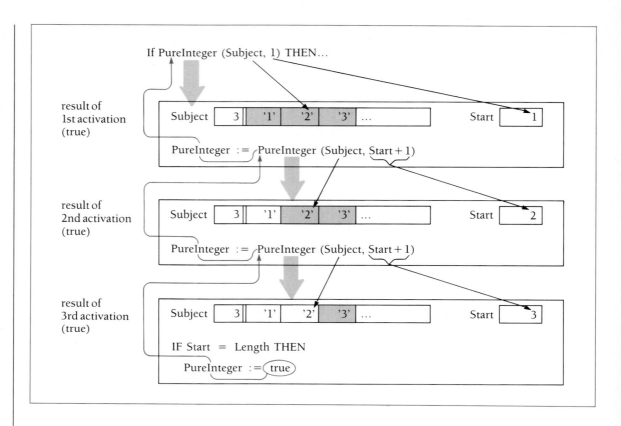

If PureInteger (Subject, 1) THEN…

result of
1st activation
(true)

Subject   3   '1' '2' '3' …   Start   1

PureInteger := PureInteger (Subject, Start + 1)

result of
2nd activation
(true)

Subject   3   '1' '2' '3' …   Start   2

PureInteger := PureInteger (Subject, Start + 1)

result of
3rd activation
(true)

Subject   3   '1' '2' '3' …   Start   3

IF Start = Length THEN

PureInteger := (true)

■ Figure 11.2
Activations of a
recursive function.

To achieve a recursive frame of mind, we do not consider the string as a whole. Rather, we consider how to process some individual character. We can choose the final character for our focus, since it will appear first in the reverse order. After displaying the final character, we can disregard it. We then deal with all the preceding characters of the string. However, we must display these characters in reverse order. This is the original problem applied to a shorter string. We thus have a recursive approach. We can apply our original strategy to reversing this substring and, if necessary, to reversing the initial substring of this substring, and so on. Each time we do this, the initial substring becomes shorter by one character. Eventually the recursion stops when we reach a character that has no preceding substring. We can now write our first algorithm.

Algorithm 1: To *reverse* the characters of a string . . .

1. display the final character;
2. if this character is not the first, then
   reverse the characters that precede it.

The corresponding recursive procedure is shown in Fig. 11.3(a). The string is represented as usual by a record containing a char array and its

Figure 11.3
Recursive procedure
to reverse a string.

```
TYPE
  CharString =
    RECORD
      Data : ARRAY [1..20] OF char;
      Length : integer
    END;
    .
    .
    .

PROCEDURE Reverse1 (Subject : CharString;
                    Final : integer);
  BEGIN
    write( Subject.Data[Final] );
    IF Final > 1 THEN
      Reverse1( Subject, Final-1 )
  END; {Reverse1}
```

(a) Recursive procedure code.

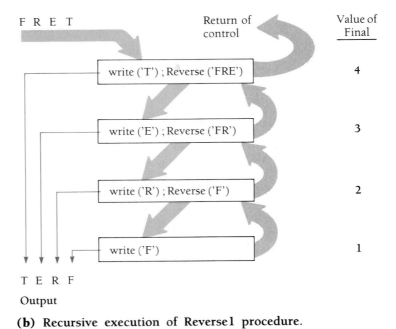

(b) Recursive execution of Reverse1 procedure.

actual length. This record remains unchanged as it is passed from one activation of the procedure to another. However, the other parameter indicates how many characters of the string are to be reversed. Its value gives the position of the final character in the substring to be considered by the current activation. Since this parameter's value is decreased by 1 each time the procedure is called, some activation will receive an actual value of 1 for the substring length. At this point the recursion will stop.

Figure 11.3(b) shows a sketch of this procedure applied to a particular character string. Although each activation of the procedure returns to the activation that called it, nothing happens during the sequence of returns. All the output occurred "on the way down."

Another approach to reversing character strings
In contrast, a second recursive algorithm results if we focus on a different character for special treatment, or the first instead of the last. Since the first character will appear at the end of the reverse order, all characters following it in the string should be processed before the first character is displayed. Again, the processing consists of displaying these following characters in reverse order, and recursion emerges.

Algorithm 2: To *reverse* the characters of a string . . .

1. if the substring has more than one character,
     reverse the characters following the first;
2. display the first character of the substring.

The procedure to implement this algorithm appears in Fig. 11.4, along with an outline of its application. In this implementation the second parameter also represents a substring length, but here the substring occurs at the end of the original string. In this case, no output occurs during the succession of procedure calls; instead, the results are produced "on the way back" from the deepest level of recursion. Compare this approach to the one shown in Fig. 11.3.

Numeric Examples of Recursion

Many numeric problems and formulas have a recursive form and therefore give rise to a recursive solution procedure. Consider, for example, the problem of finding the prime factors of a given positive integer. (We will consider only positive integers in what follows.) Recall that a *prime number* is an integer that is exactly divisible by only itself and 1. In a sense, the primes are the basic building blocks of integers. Every positive integer is the product of a *unique* combination of prime numbers. For some positive number, our problem is to discover all its prime factors.

The integer 60, for example, can be expressed as the following product of primes: $2 * 2 * 3 * 5$. No matter how we might factor 60, we will eventually discover the same prime numbers. This is what we mean by a unique set of prime factors. We could represent 60 as $5 * 12$, observe that 5 is already

■ Figure 11.4
Another recursive
procedure to reverse
a string.

```
TYPE
  CharString =
    RECORD
      Data : ARRAY [1..20] OF char;
      Length : integer
    END;
    .
    .
    .

PROCEDURE Reverse2 (Subject  :  CharString;
                    First : integer);
  BEGIN
    IF First < Subject.Length THEN
        Reverse2( Subject, First+1 );
    write( Subject.Data[First] )
  END; {Reverse1}
```

(a) Recursive procedure code

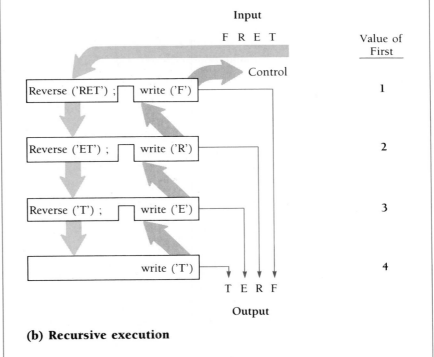

(b) Recursive execution

prime, and factor the nonprime 12 into 2 * 2 * 3. Alternatively, we could rewrite 60 as 6 * 10, factor 6 into 2 * 3, and factor 10 into 5 * 2. Using any approach, we will always come up with 2, 2, 3, and 5 as the factors of 60.

One systematic approach is to try finding the smallest prime factor first. Since 1 divides every integer, we can ignore it. We therefore start with 2 and test successively larger values for exact divisibility into the original number, N. Testing continues until some number is found that divides N exactly. If the divisor is smaller than N, the divisor is a prime factor of N. (If this number were not prime, some even smaller number would have divided N.) But if N's first divisor is equal to N, then N itself is prime, and further factorization is impossible.

Finding prime factors

Suppose that N is not prime and that its first prime factor, A, has been discovered. If we divide N by A, the result will be the product of all the remaining prime factors of N. Thus, in order to completely factor N, we must first find its smallest factor, A, and then completely factor (N DIV A). The recursive solution should now be apparent.

To *factor* a positive integer, N, where N > 1 . . .

   1. find and display A, the smallest factor of N;
   2. if A < N then *factor* (N DIV A).

Applying this algorithm to the problem of factoring 60, we would first discover the divisor 2 and then look for factors of 60 DIV 2 = 30. Since the first divisor of 30 is also 2, we would next seek the factors of 30 DIV 2 = 15. Since the first divisor of 15 is 3, we would next seek the factors of 15 DIV 3 = 5. A final application would show that 5 is prime. Note that the factors discovered are again 2, 2, 3, and 5 (in that order).

Finding greatest common divisor

Now consider the problem of finding the greatest common divisor (GCD) of a pair of positive integers M and N, written GCD(M,N). The GCD is the largest integer that exactly divides both M and N. The GCD, like all positive integers, is a product of prime numbers. Since the entire GCD exactly divides both M and N, so do all of its prime factors. Its prime factors are therefore prime factors of M and N as well. In fact, GCD(M,N) is the product of all prime factors that are common to both M and N. For example, let

    M = 3234 = 2 * 3 * 7 * 7 * 11

and

    N = 2205 = 3 * 3 * 7 * 7 * 5.

Since their common factors are 3, 7, and 7, their GCD is the product of these factors, namely, 147.

Finding the GCD of two numbers involves a process somewhat like finding the prime factors of a single number. Suppose that D is the smallest integer (other than 1) that exactly divides both M and N. Thus D will certainly be one factor of GCD(M,N). If D is less than both M and N, there may be other common factors whose product will be the GCD of M DIV D and

■ **Figure 11.5**
Calculating the
greatest common
divisor.

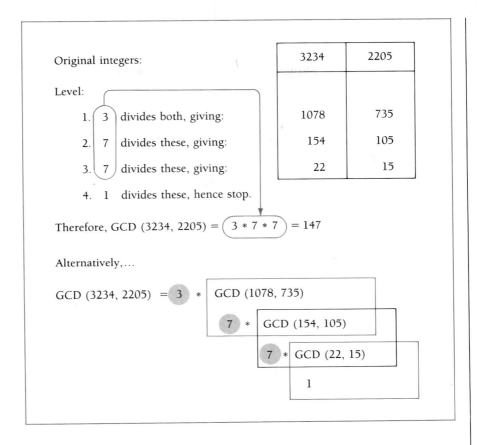

Original integers:

	3234	2205

Level:

1. 3 divides both, giving: 1078   735

2. 7 divides these, giving: 154   105

3. 7 divides these, giving: 22   15

4. 1 divides these, hence stop.

Therefore, GCD (3234, 2205) = (3 * 7 * 7) = 147

Alternatively, ...

GCD (3234, 2205) = 3 * | GCD (1078, 735)
                        7 * | GCD (154, 105)
                           7 *| GCD (22, 15)
                                1

N DIV D. We can summarize this approach by the formula

```
GCD(M, N) = D * GCD(M DIV D, N DIV D)
```

For example, consider finding the GCD of 3234 and 2205, as shown in Fig. 11.5. The smallest common divisor is 3. Therefore 3 will be a factor of the GCD. To find the other common factors, we seek the GCD of 3234 DIV 3 = 1078 and 2205 DIV 3 = 735. But to find GCD(1078, 735), we must first find the largest common divisor of these two numbers, which is 7. Thus 7 is another factor of the original GCD, and so on. When M and N have no common divisor other than 1, the quest for more common divisors is futile, and the process should terminate. A recursive procedure to find the GCD of two integers is shown in Fig. 11.6.

**Beware of global
identifiers**

It is no accident that all the identifiers in Fig. 11.6 are either value-type parameters or local variables. Global variables and variable-type parameters can be particularly troublesome in recursive subprograms because they can cause subtle interactions among different activations of the same subprogram.

```
FUNCTION FirstFactor ( M, N : integer) : integer;
   {If such a divisor exists, return the first integer
   greater than 1 which exactly divides both M and N;
   otherwise, return 1 (which always divides both) }
   VAR
      Divisor : integer;
      Successful : boolean;
   BEGIN
      Successful := false;
      Divisor := 2;
      WHILE (NOT Successful)AND
            (Divisor <= M ) AND (Divisor <= N ) DO
         IF ( M MOD Divisor = 0 ) AND
            ( N MOD Divisor = 0 ) THEN {exact divisor}
            Successful := true
         ELSE
            Divisor := Divisor + 1;

      IF Successful THEN
         FirstFactor := Divisor
      ELSE
         FirstFactor := 1
   END; {FirstFactor}

FUNCTION GCD ( M, N : integer) : integer;
   {Recursive function to determine Greatest Common
    Divisor of M and N. Each activation of GCD
    calls FirstFactor to determine the first integer
    (greater than 1 if possible) that exactly divides
    both M and N; this common divisor will be one
    factor of the GCD. Assume positive integers only}

   VAR
      Factor : integer;
   BEGIN

      Factor := FirstFactor(M, N);
      IF Factor > 1 THEN
         GCD := Factor * GCD(M DIV Factor, N DIV Factor);
      ELSE
         GCD := 1

   END; {GCD Function}
```

■ Figure 11.6
Recursive procedure for greatest common divisor.

Suppose, for example, that in the GCD function in Fig. 11.6 we had neglected to declare Factor as a local variable. If we had declared Factor as an integer variable in the main program, its use in the function would refer to a "legal" global variable. However, this erroneous version of the function would always return the value 1. Consider evaluating GCD(6, 12), which has a correct value of 6. The first activation of GCD would correctly identify 2 as the first common divisor of 6 and 12. The second activation would identify 3 as the first common divisor of 3 and 6 and replace the value of the global variable Factor by 3. The third activation would then identify 1 as the first common divisor of 1 and 2 and replace the value of Factor by yet another 1. Since each activation of the function accesses the same memory location to retrieve the factor it contributes to the GCD, each level would multiply by 1 the GCD obtained from lower levels. Hence the result will always be 1. By correctly declaring Factor as a local variable, we give each activation its private version of Factor, enabling each level to correctly remember the divisor it computed.

The Binary Search

binary search

One way to search an ordered array is to jump through it in giant steps until you have determined the region where the desired item must reside, if in fact it is present. A technique known as the **binary search** provides an even faster way to focus on the target area in an ordered array.

Binary search algorithm

Assume that you have an array with elements in ascending order and want to search it for a specific item. The basic idea is simple: When you are looking for a specific item in a sorted array, the most useful place to begin is in the *middle*. If the middle item is not the one you are seeking, at least you know which half of the array to search. If the middle element was too large, you would look in the first half of the array. Otherwise, you would concentrate on the second half of the array. Whatever the outcome, this single comparison eliminates half the array from further consideration. We can write this general strategy as

find middle element of array;
if middle element is desired element then
   the search terminates in success
otherwise
   if middle element > desired element then
     search first half of array;
   otherwise
     search second half of array;

A good way to search the remaining half of the array is to use the binary search. In other words, you apply *exactly* the same algorithm to one half of the array with which you began. If the desired item is not at the midpoint of this portion of the array, then the binary search algorithm chooses one half of this portion for inspection and disregards the other half. Since each successive application of the algorithm subdivides the remaining portion of the array in half, the range of the search is narrowed very quickly. To illustrate, Fig. 11.7 shows the application of this algorithm to an array of length 9.

How to stop
We also need some way to quit when the desired item is not present. An item is recognized as missing when successive calls to search have narrowed the possible range to less than one position, that is, when the lowest subscript of the range to be searched becomes greater than the highest subscript of the range. Thus we get the algorithm of Fig. 11.8(a).

In the corresponding function we need to supply the name of the array to be searched and the value sought. Since each call deals with a different segment of the array, we must also provide the first and last positions of the segment involved as parameters. Each recursive call of Search adjusts one or the other of these position numbers to reduce the difference between them. Since the function has no need to modify any of these values in the calling program, they can be passed as value-type parameters. The resulting code appears in Fig. 11.8(b).

■ Figure 11.7
Successive steps in binary search for value 18.

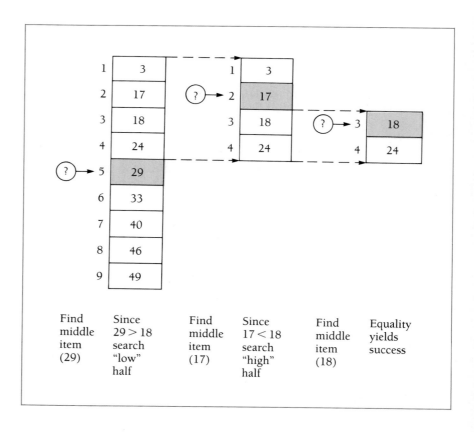

1. if LowBound > HighBound then
      report failure;
2. otherwise:
2.1   find the middle element;
2.2   if middle element is desired value then
          report success;
2.3   otherwise:
2.3.1   if middle element > desired element then
              search first half of array;
2.3.2   otherwise
              search second half of array;
3. stop.

(a) Binary search algorithm.

```
FUNCTION Search (A: ArrayType;
                 Low,Hi,Target: integer): integer;
   {Search from A[Low] to A[Hi] for the location
    of the Target value}

   VAR
      Mid : integer;
   BEGIN
      IF Low > Hi THEN {nothing left to search}
         Search := 0          {failure indicator}
      ELSE
         BEGIN {look for value}

            Mid := (Low + Hi) DIV 2;
            IF A[Mid] = Target THEN       {success}
               Search := Mid
            ELSE {look in half of the array}

               IF A[Mid] > Target THEN {'lower' half}
                  Search := Search(A,Low,Mid-1,Target)
               ELSE {'upper' half}
                  Search := Search(A,Mid+1,Hi,Target)

         END {look}
   END; {Search}
```

(b) Function to implement the binary search.

■ Figure 11.8
Algorithm and code for binary search.

■ Figure 11.9
Execution of
recursive search
function.

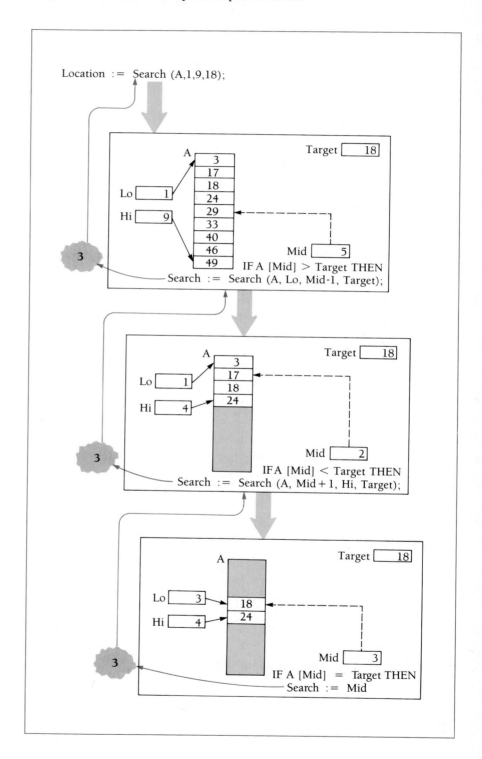

Note the two different uses of the function name Search. In four places it is the target of an assignment statement for returning a value to its calling program. In two other places the identifier is used as a function call (to itself). Figure 11.9 shows the flow of control through three activations of Search, while it looks for the value 18 in the array from Fig. 11.7.

Binary search, like finding the greatest common divisor, can be implemented without recursion, but the code would be more involved. However, some problems are much more difficult (if not impossible) to solve without using recursive subprograms. The QuickSort algorithm discussed in the next section is one such problem. You will encounter others in Chapter 12.

Quicksort

Quicksort

Another approach to sorting an array, known as **Quicksort,** begins by selecting an arbitrary value from the array, usually the first. Using this *partitioning value* as the basis, all the remaining values are then partitioned into two sets, with one set containing all values smaller than the partitioning value and the other set containing all values larger. (Assume no duplicates.)

Partitioning the data

In an ordered array, all the values in the "smaller" set will appear before the partitioning value, and all the values from the "larger" set will appear after it. The partitioning operation achieves some degree of ordering; at least it places the partitioning value at the correct position with respect to all the other elements of the array. By sorting the smaller elements and the larger elements separately, we can find an ordering for the entire array. This idea is illustrated in Fig. 11.10(a).

Sorting the partitioned data

In practice, these sets of elements from the original array are kept in two other arrays (or disjoint portions of the same array). Each of these arrays is then ordered by the method just described. Its elements are further partitioned into two subarrays whose values are, respectively, smaller or larger than its first element. If necessary, the resulting subarrays can themselves be partitioned further. At each application, the partitions become smaller. Eventually, the partitions will contain only single values. At that point, the relative ordering among the partitions constitute an ordering of the original array.

Thus Quicksort consists of a partitioning operation applied recursively to successively smaller subarrays of the original array. Figure 11.10(b) presents a high-level algorithm, and Fig. 11.10(c) shows a complete application of Quicksort.

One possible Quicksort procedure is shown in Fig. 11.11. The primary objects of interest are arrays of integers. However, each array is combined with its effective length in a record. Thus the parameters are actually records. The array received by the sort procedure is first partitioned into Smaller and Larger arrays. If either of these contains more than one item, it is sorted by a recursive call to QuickSort. The original parameter array is then erased and reconstructed by appending first Smaller (now sorted), then the partitioning value, and finally Larger (now sorted). Thus the Original array is returned

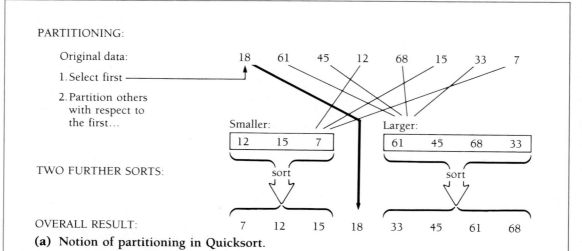

PARTITIONING:

Original data:

1. Select first

2. Partition others
   with respect to
   the first...

TWO FURTHER SORTS:

OVERALL RESULT:

(a) Notion of partitioning in Quicksort.

1. select first element of array;

2. partition other array elements with respect to it into two
   subarrays: Smaller and Larger;

3. if Smaller contains > 1 item then SORT(Smaller);

4. if Larger contains > 1 item then SORT(Larger);

5. combine Smaller, First element, and Larger in that order
   into a single array as the result.

(b) General Quicksort algorithm.

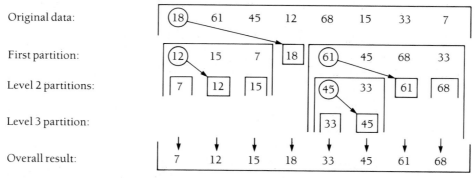

Original data:

First partition:

Level 2 partitions:

Level 3 partition:

Overall result:

(c) Complete operation of Quicksort.

■ Figure 11.10
Sorting an array with Quicksort.

```
TYPE
   IntegerArray = ARRAY [1..20] OF integer;
   Structure =
      RECORD
         Data : IntegerArray;
         Number : integer
      END;

PROCEDURE AppendItem (VAR Target : Structure;
                          Item : integer);
   {append single integer to Target.Data
   and increment Taget.Number}
PROCEDURE AppendArray (VAR Target : Structure;
                           Source : Structure);
   {append entire Source.Data array to Target.Data
   array, and update Target.Number accordingly}

PROCEDURE QuickSort (VAR Original : Structure);
   VAR
      Psn,
      PartitionValue : integer;
      Smaller,
      Larger : Structure;
   BEGIN
      Smaller.Number := 0;
      Larger.Number := 0;
      PartitionValue := Original.Data[1];
      FOR Psn := 2 TO Original.Number DO {partition}
         IF Original.Data[Psn] < PartitionValue THEN
            AppendItem (Smaller, Original.Data[Psn])
         ELSE
            AppendItem( Larger, Original.Data[Psn] );

      IF Smaller.Number > 1 THEN
         QuickSort (Smaller);
      IF Larger.Number > 1 THEN
         QuickSort (Larger);

      Original.Number := 0; {erase before rebuilding}
      AppendArray (Original, Smaller);
      AppendItem (Original, PartitionValue);
      AppendArray (Original, Larger)
   END; {QuickSort}
```

■ Figure 11.11
Recursive procedure for Quicksort.

with its values now arranged in order. Since this array will be altered by the procedure, it must arrive through a variable-type parameter.

The presence of two append procedures simplifies the code. Their details are not shown, but their actions should be familiar. They correctly update the length of the augmented array. If the source array contains no values, AppendArray has no effect.

Each activation of our QuickSort procedure allocates two additional arrays. More sophisticated implementations of QuickSort avoid this extra space at the cost of more complex parameters and code.

11.2 Mutual Recursion

mutual recursion

In the preceding section we examined subprograms that call themselves directly. One subprogram may also call another, which then calls the first. Of course this new activation of the first may again call the second, which may call the first once more, and so on. This process is called **mutual recursion.** Subprograms that call themselves indirectly are called *mutually recursive subprograms.*

You may have already noticed that mutual recursion can occur among Pascal syntax diagrams. We show a specific example in the highly simplified syntax diagrams in Fig. 11.12(a), which define "block" as a structure that may contain subprogram declarations. However, a subprogram declaration includes a "block." Following the cross-references between these syntax diagrams corresponds to defining nested subprogram declarations. Eventually, you must stop the recursion by declaring a subprogram that contains no other subprogram declarations.

Consider the outline of two mutually recursive procedures in Fig. 11.12(b). These procedures can call one another at execution time, as indicated. To break the cycle, one (or both) must follow a path of execution that does not invoke its partner.

Usual declaration will not work

Although mutually recursive subprograms may be defined in Pascal, they cannot be declared exactly as shown in Fig. 11.12(b). There is no problem with SubB calling SubA because the procedure SubA has been defined before the reference. However, the call from SubA to SubB does present problems, because nothing is known about SubB when the compiler first encounters this reference inside SubA. Pascal does not allow references to objects for which definitions have not yet appeared.

The FORWARD Directive

Solution: detach heading of second subprogram

Nevertheless, a mechanism has been provided for declaring mutually recursive subprograms. Suppose that we decide to declare SubA ahead of SubB, as we did in Fig. 11.12. In order to analyze the reference to SubB occurring in

■ Figure 11.12
Mutual recursion.

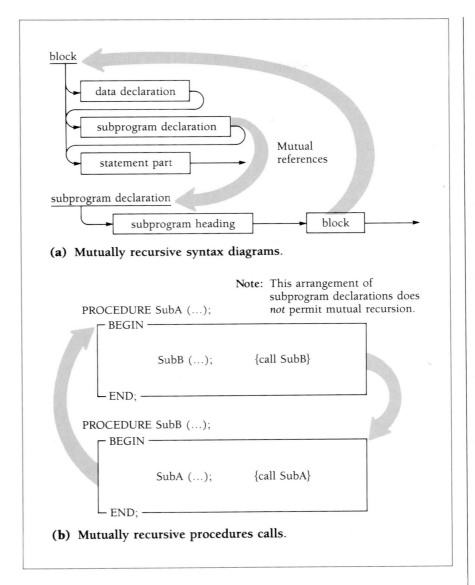

(a) Mutually recursive syntax diagrams.

Note: This arrangement of
subprogram declarations does
not permit mutual recursion.

(b) Mutually recursive procedures calls.

SubA, the compiler needs to know only how SubB is to be called. This
information is contained in the *heading* of SubB. The basic idea is to separate
the heading of SubB from its block and place this heading before the
declaration of SubA. However, we have to tell the compiler what is going on.

directive   We can use a **directive** in a program to inform the compiler of this (and
FORWARD directive   other) special situations. The **FORWARD directive** is the one to use here.
This directive allows the subprogram heading to be separated from the rest
of the subprogram declaration. It appears after each *detached heading* and
informs the compiler that the corresponding block of the subprogram will

■ Figure 11.13
Using the FORWARD
directive.

```
PROCEDURE SubB (...); FORWARD;
     {block will come later}
PROCEDURE SubA (...);
  BEGIN

    ·
    · SubB (...);
    ·

  END; {SubA}
PROCEDURE SubB;
  {note absence of parameter list}
  BEGIN

    ·
    · SubA (...);
    ·

  END; {SubB}
```

appear later in the program. For example, to use the directive in conjunction with the procedure SubB of Fig. 11.12, write

```
PROCEDURE SubB (...); FORWARD;
```

Introduce block when it appears

But we still need a way to recognize which subprogram is being declared when the block of code finally does come along. We therefore introduce the code defining the subprogram by either PROCEDURE or FUNCTION and the subprogram identifier. The *formal parameter list must not be repeated*.

The net result is shown in Fig. 11.13, where the mutually recursive procedures from Fig. 11.12(b) are correctly declared. Note especially the declaration of SubB, which consists of two parts:

1. The full header, followed by FORWARD; and eventually
2. The block, introduced only by PROCEDURE and the subprogram identifier.

Documentation idea

For documentation purposes, it is helpful to include the parameter list as a *comment*. For example, if the FORWARD declaration were

```
PROCEDURE P (A: real; VAR B: integer); FORWARD;
```

then at the point where the block is required, the first line would read

```
PROCEDURE P {A: real; VAR B: integer};
```

This approach allows the reader of the program to ascertain the subprogram's parameters without having to search back through the code for the FORWARD declaration.

11.3 Special Parameter Types

Consider a program that will compute a table of $X - Y$ coordinates for the function

$$y = ax^2 + bx + c$$

Assume that the function Quad has been written to evaluate a quadratic equation of this form for any specific real value of X. A procedure called Coord could call Quad repeatedly to compute the Y coordinates for several X values. The main program would supply Coord with an array of reals in which the procedure would store the Y values corresponding to a range of X values. The X values could be specified by three parameters: the first, the last, and a step value between the first and last. A version of Coord is shown in Fig. 11.14.

Subprogram Identifiers as Parameters

Passing function name as a parameter to procedure

Now suppose that we want to use Coord to evaluate another function with a different name. Coord can be generalized to handle a wider variety of cases if one of its actual parameters indicates the name of the function to be evaluated. To do this, we must add a formal parameter to Coord that indicates

■ Figure 11.14
Function limited to finding the values of one other specific function (Quad).

```
PROCEDURE Coord (VAR Y: Points; {array of real}
                     First,Last,Step: real);
VAR
    Psn : integer;
    X : real;
BEGIN
    Psn := 1; {array index}
    X := First;
    WHILE (X <= Last) AND (Psn <= ArraySize) DO
        BEGIN
            Y[Psn] := Quad(X);
            X := X + Step;
            Psn := Psn + 1
        END {loop}
END; {Coord}
```

how to access the function; this formal parameter resembles the heading of the function itself. The following revised heading allows Coord to evaluate any real-valued function having one real-valued argument.

Heading

```
PROCEDURE Coord (FUNCTION F (X : real): real;
                 VAR Y : Points;
                 First,Last,Step : real);
```

In this form, Coord has five parameters: a function, an array, and three reals. Hence, it must be called with five arguments. The first actual parameter will be a function identifier *only*; no argument list for this function should accompany the function identifier. Thus in Fig. 11.15 the function name Quad is the first argument in the call to Coord, or

Call

```
Coord (Quad,Y,0,10,0.5);
```

Figure 11.15 shows the new, more flexible version of the Coord program with the changes highlighted. Incidentally, the X mentioned in the formal parameter list of F has no meaning inside Coord; its appearance in the heading merely indicates the need for F to be called with one real parameter.

Although we can now call Coord to evaluate *any* real-valued function requiring one real argument, we cannot use it to handle other kinds of functions. The function passed to Coord must conform to the calling conventions described in Coord's formal parameter.

Rules

Procedure names can also be passed as parameters using this mechanism. For example the procedure

```
PROCEDURE This( PROCEDURE That(VAR A,B : real) );
```

could be called by the statement

```
This (What);
```

where What can represent any procedure having two variable-type real-valued parameters, such as

```
PROCEDURE What (VAR  X,Y : real)
```

The only restriction is that predeclared subprograms cannot be passed as parameters. Any subprograms passed as parameters may themselves have any number or type of formal parameters.

Conformant Array Parameters

One of standard Pascal's most serious drawbacks is that subprograms cannot deal with arrays of arbitrary length; array parameters must have fixed bounds. In some applications the same sort of processing needs to be performed on generally similar but nonidentical arrays. This means that you have to write separate subprograms to handle each array type, even though the processing steps are the same for each type. The resulting duplication in code and effort is unfortunate.

```
PROGRAM XYAgain (input,output);
CONST
   ArraySize = 200;
TYPE
   Points = ARRAY [1..ArraySize] OF real;
VAR
   Y : Points;
   First,Last,Step : real;
   Index,Number : integer;

FUNCTION Quad (X : real) : real;
   BEGIN
      Quad := 2.32*X*X + 6.14*X + 0.88
   END; {Quad}
```

> Coord can accept any real-valued function of one real argument

```
PROCEDURE Coord (FUNCTION F (X : real) : real;
                 VAR Y: Points; First,Last,Step : real);
   VAR
      Psn : integer;
      X : real;
   BEGIN
      Psn := 1; {array index}
      X := First;
      WHILE (X <= Last) AND (Psn <= ArraySize) DO
         BEGIN
            Y[Psn] := F (X);
            X := X + Step;
            Psn := Psn + 1
         END {loop}
   END; {Coord}
```

> Generalized function reference

```
BEGIN {XYAgain}
   readln (First,Last,Step);
   Number := Trunc((Last - First) / Step) + 1;
   IF Number > ArraySize THEN
      Number := ArraySize;

   Coord ( Quad ,Y,First,Last,Step); {generate array Y}

   FOR Index := 1 TO Number DO        {display array Y}
      writeln (Index,Y[Index])
END. {XYAgain}
```

> Specific function identifier

■ Figure 11.15
Computing the values of a general function.

conformant array
parameter

Although not necessarily implemented by your compiler, a second Pascal "standard" (known as level 1) does recognize the need for more flexibility in the rules for passing arrays. In particular, a formal parameter type, called a **conformant array parameter,** allows the actual array argument to be of any size and to be indexed over any range. The subscript type and component type must be fixed. However, until the moment of its execution, the called subprogram needs to know only these types and does not need to know the allowable range values for referencing a conformant array. The particular array size and subscript range will be provided each time the subprogram is called at run time.

bounds identifiers

The formal parameter declaration for a conformant array includes **bounds identifiers.** Each time the subprogram is called, these identifiers may refer to different values, which are the physical subscript limits of the array being passed. The subprogram can reference these bounds identifiers to determine the permissible subscripts range. However, their values may not be modified by the subprogram.

In general, the simplest form of the conformant array parameter specification for a one-dimensional array is

⟨identifier⟩: ARRAY [⟨lower⟩ . . ⟨upper⟩: ⟨ordinal type⟩] OF ⟨type⟩

While the array elements may be of any type, the bounds identifiers must be ordinals. The formal parameter may be of value-type or of variable-type and may be packed or unpacked.

An example should clarify their use:

```
PROCEDURE Init
  (VAR  A: ARRAY [Low..High: integer] OF integer);
VAR
  Psn: integer;
BEGIN
  FOR Psn := Low TO High DO
    A[Psn] := 0
END;
```

This procedure initializes each component of an array to 0. Its single parameter is a one-dimensional array, A, of integers with bounds that can be *any subrange of the integers.* We specify the index type and the array component type in the formal parameter definition. The lower and upper bounds during any particular execution of the subprogram are stored in Low and High, respectively. While regular formal parameters require a specific type identifier, we see here a generalized description of what the actual array might be.

Suppose that the calling program contains two integer arrays, as in

```
VAR
  Mini: ARRAY [1..5] OF integer;
  Maxi: ARRAY [-100..200] OF integer;
```

Each of these arrays could be passed to Init by

```
Init (Mini);
Init (Maxi);
```

When the first call is executed, Low will be given the value 1, High will take on the value 5, and the loop will execute 5 times. On the second call, Low will be -100, High will be 200, and the loop will execute 301 times. The execution of Init depends on the bounds of the actual array on which it is called to operate.

Returning to the program in Fig. 11.15, the Coord procedure produces a number of Y-values, depending on the range of X-values and step size given by the main program. We can now make Coord more general by supplying a conformant array parameter. This allows different real-valued arrays of different sizes to be passed. Presumably, we would chose an actual array of adequate size to hold the number of Y-values to be computed. The revised program is shown in Fig. 11.16 on p. 484. The call to Coord remains the same as before:

```
Coord(Quad,Y,First,Last,Step);
```

Only the array identifier is mentioned in the call. The bounds in this case are 1 and 200; these values are obtained from the declaration of Y in the main program.

Each conformant array specification in the subprogram heading establishes a distinct type for its formal parameter. Thus

PROCEDURE Zing (A : ARRAY [L1 . . H1: integer] OF boolean;
                              B : ARRAY [L2 . . H2: integer] OF boolean);

Distinct array types   makes A and B distinct types. Within the procedure Zing, A and B are *not* assignment compatible, even if the actual parameters are of identical types. If assignment compatibility is desired, the formal parameters must be specified with one descriptor, as in

PROCEDURE Zing (A,B : ARRAY [L . . H: integer] OF boolean);

In this case, both actual parameters *must* be the same type, whereas in the previous case they *may* be the same type.

11.4 The GOTO Statement

GOTO statement   One more Pascal control statement that—because of its potential for misuse—we have not yet discussed is the **GOTO statement.** Its general form is

GOTO ⟨label⟩;

When this statement is executed, it will cause control to transfer to the statement prefixed by ⟨label⟩.

```
PROGRAM XYFinal (input,output);
CONST
    ArraySize = 200;
TYPE
    Points = ARRAY [1..ArraySize] OF real;
VAR
    Y : Points;
    First,Last,Step : real;
    Index,Number : integer;

FUNCTION Quad (X : real) : real;
    BEGIN
        Quad := 2.32*X*X + 6.14*X + 0.88
    END; {Quad}

PROCEDURE Coord (FUNCTION F (X : real) : real;
                 VAR Y : ARRAY [Lo..Hi : integer] OF real;
                 First,Last,Step : real);
    VAR
        Psn : integer;
        X : real;
    BEGIN
        Psn := Lo; {array index}
        X := Start;
        WHILE (X <= Last) AND (Psn <= Hi) DO
            BEGIN
                Y[Psn] := F (X);
                X := X + Step;
                Psn := Psn + 1
            END {loop}
    END; {Coord}

BEGIN {XYFinal}
    readln (First,Last,Step);
    Number := Trunc((Last - First) / Step) + 1;
    IF Number > ArraySize THEN
        Number := ArraySize;

    Coord (Quad, Y ,First,Last,Step);      {generate array Y}
    FOR Index := 1 TO Number DO{display array Y}
        writeln (Index,Y[Index])
END. {XYFinal}
```

Coord can now accept any array of reals having an integer-valued index range

Specific values of index range

Mention only the array identifier as actual parameter

■ Figure 11.16
Conformant array parameters.

label

label declaration part

A **label** is any string of digits in the range 0 through 9999, inclusive, which has been declared in the **label declaration part**. This part appears before the constant definition part and has the form:

LABEL ⟨list of labels⟩;

The label itself may prefix almost any statement, as in

⟨label⟩ : ⟨statement⟩;

Note that the label is separated from the statement by a colon.

There are some restrictions on the destination to which GOTO can transfer control. Briefly, you cannot branch into the interior of a control structure (such as subprogram, IF, loop, or compound statement) from the outside. You can, however, branch from the inside to the outside. Also, the GOTO statement must be within the scope of the label.

Used only for fast
exit from loops

GOTO should be used only to make immediate exits from loops, as illustrated in Fig. 11.17. Here some condition is detected that should cause

```
PROGRAM Whatever (input,output);
LABEL 99;      {other labels could be included in list}
CONST ...
VAR ...
BEGIN {program action}
   .
   .
   WHILE true DO
     ┌─BEGIN──────────────────────────────────────────┐
     │    .                                            │
     │    .                                            │
     │    IF FatalCondition1 THEN     {exit at once}   │
     │       GOTO 99;                                  │
     │    .                                            │
     │                                                 │
     │    IF FatalCondition2 THEN     {exit at once}   │
     │       GOTO 99;                                  │
     │    .                                            │
     └─END; {loop}────────────────────────────────────┘
  99 : CASE Status OF ...    {label first statement after loop}
     .                       {target of GOTO statements}
     .
END. {program}
```

■ Figure 11.17
Using GOTO to exit from loop.

the loop to terminate without executing any more code inside it. Normally, bypassing the remainder of the loop would require setting flags and testing conditions, but here a GOTO causes an immediate exit.

In Fig. 11.17, we defined the label 99 at the beginning of the program and attached it to the *first* statement *following* the loop, that is, the point to which control is directed whenever either GOTO is executed. Since all the possible reasons for leaving the loop do so by means of GOTO, the WHILE condition is permanently "true," in order to keep the loop executing until some GOTO is activated.

Problems with use   Indiscriminate use of GOTO to branch throughout a program often leads to tortuous or "spaghetti" control structure. Such programs are so difficult to read, debug, and modify that the use of GOTO is almost completely forbidden in modern programming practice. *We do not advocate the use of GOTO.* About the only situation in which GOTO may even be considered is when making an emergency exit from a loop.

11.5 Review of Rules

A. A recursive subprogram can call itself. Each successive call causes a new activation equivalent to starting with a new, unused copy of the subprogram code; the local variables and value-type parameters refer to different things in each activation.

B. Mutually recursive subprograms call themselves indirectly. Thus A and B are mutually recursive if A calls B and B in turn calls A. In these cases, one of the subprograms must be given the FORWARD directive. The subprogram, whose block is defined last, has its heading detached and placed first. This heading is immediately followed by the reserved word FORWARD:

⟨subprogram heading⟩; FORWARD;

This declaration states that the actual subprogram block will appear at a later point in the program code. When the block appears, it must *not* be preceded by a full subprogram heading; instead, only the subprogram keyword, followed by its identifier, is supplied:

PROCEDURE ⟨identifier⟩;

or

FUNCTION ⟨identifier⟩;

C. Subprogram identifiers may be passed to other subprograms as arguments. If a parameter is to represent a subprogram, it is declared in the parameter list in a form identical to the ordinary subprogram heading.

D. Level 1 Pascal allows conformant array parameters, that is, arrays that have index ranges of some predetermined, ordinal type but no predetermined values for these bounds. In their simplest form, these conformant array parameters have bounds identifiers included in the formal parameter declaration:

⟨identifier⟩ : ARRAY [⟨low⟩ . . ⟨high⟩: ⟨ordinal type⟩] OF ⟨type⟩

When the parameter is described in this form, the corresponding argument may be any array with the same component type, having upper and lower subscript bounds that belong to the ordinal type. At the time of call, ⟨low⟩ and ⟨high⟩ will take on the values of the actual lower and upper bounds of the argument array. The subprogram may *not* modify the bounds identifiers.

E. A label is a number containing from one to four digits listed in the label declaration part, which appears as the first line of a (sub)program block:

LABEL ⟨label1⟩,⟨label2⟩, . . . , ⟨labeln⟩;

Execution may be directed to another (labeled) executable statement by means of the statement:

GOTO ⟨label⟩;

The statement to which control is transferred must be identified by a preceding label, as follows:

⟨label⟩ : ⟨statement⟩

KEY TERMS

activation
binary search
bounds identifiers
conformant array parameter
directive
FORWARD directive
GOTO statement

label
label declaration part
mutual recursion
Quicksort
recursion
recursive definition

EXERCISES

11.1 You are familiar with the Fibonacci sequence from Exercises 6.5 and 7.5. Write a recursive function, called Fib, to calculate the nth Fibonacci number. Its only parameter is the desired value of n, and it returns the value of the nth member of the sequence. Thus the value of Fib(4) would be 2. Test this function with an interactive program that allows a user to specify various values for n. In order to watch the progress of the recursive execution during the test phase, you should have Fib display the value it received for n and the value it calculated. Since the members of this sequence become very large very quickly, do not supply large values for n. (Determine the maximum value of n for your system.)

11.2 The Towers of Hanoi is a classic recursive problem. The problem begins with a row of three vertical pegs (designated A, B, and C) and a set of k rings of different sizes. The holes in the centers of the rings allow them to be placed over the pegs. All the rings start out around peg A. The rings are ordered so that the largest ring is on the bottom and the smallest on the top. The objective is to move all the rings from peg A to peg B. This would be simple, except for two constraints:

- you may move only one ring at a time; and
- a larger ring can never be placed on top of a smaller one.

You can solve the original problem of moving k rings by using a series of similar but simpler problems, each involving movement of only $k - 1$ rings, subject to the same constraints, of course. In particular, to move k rings from peg A to peg B,

- move $k - 1$ rings from peg A to peg C;
- move the one remaining (largest) ring from A to B; and
- move $k - 1$ rings from peg C to peg B.

Write a recursive procedure to solve the Towers of Hanoi problem for any value of k (keep k fairly small) given to the main program by the user. Identify the rings by the integers $1, 2, \ldots, k$, with 1 being the smallest and k being the largest. Each activation of the procedure should display the ring number, source peg, and destination peg for any individual ring(s) it moves.

11.3 Write and test a recursive procedure to generate and display all permutations (various linear orderings) of the first n integers. For example, the permutations of the first four integers are

1234	1243	1324	1342	1423	1432
2134	2143	2314	2341	2413	2431
3124	3142	3214	3241	3412	3421
4123	4132	4213	4231	4312	4321

Since n objects can be arranged in $n!$ ways, avoid using large values for n. Note how the numbers in the preceding example were generated. The sequences in the first line begin with 1, followed by all permutations of 2, 3, and 4. The sequences in the second line begin with 2, followed by all permutations of the remaining numbers, 1, 3, and 4. At this level, anyway, successive values are held fixed in the first position, while the remaining values are arranged through all their permutations. If you concentrate on the next level, the same holds true. For example, consider the last line, where 4 appears at the start of each sequence. You can forget about 4 and concentrate only on the permutations of 1, 2, and 3, namely, 123 132 213 231 312 321. Here the first two sequences have 1 fixed, while 2 and 3 are shown in their two permutations. The next two orderings fix 2 as first element followed by the permutations of 1 and 3, and so on. These observations provide the strategy for the recursive procedure:

Supply two arrays as parameters. The first array contains the numbers that will appear in the same fixed positions in every arrangement to be generated at this level. The second array contains the remaining numbers to be cycled through all their possible permutations. If the second array contains only one value, the position of every number is determined, and the current permutation can be written out immediately by the current activation of the procedure. However, if the second array contains more than one value, say k values, this procedure calls itself k times, each time with a different one of the numbers it was supposed to permute now assigned to a fixed position and with the remaining numbers to be permuted by a new activation at a lower level.

With the procedure designed in this way, the first call to find all permutations of four numbers would have no elements in the first array parameter and all four in the second.

11.4 Consider the problem of scanning an arithmetic (and/or logical) expression to determine whether the parentheses are correctly matched. In a correctly formed expression, every left parenthesis must have a matching right parenthesis, and every right paren must be preceded by its matching left paren. This matching left paren is the nearest preceding left paren that has not already been matched by some other right paren; this rule ensures proper nesting.

Write a main program to read a line of text, assumed to be an expression, and test for correct parenthesis matching. During a left to right scan, the appearance of a left paren causes the program to call the procedure Match, which continues scanning to locate the corresponding right paren. If Match is successful, the higher level scan continues from the point following this right paren, all intervening text having being validated by Match. If Match reports a problem, or if the main program's scan encounters a right paren (which is therefore not preceded by any matching left paren), an error has been detected. If the scan reaches the end of the string without an error, the parentheses are considered to be correct.

The Match procedure should be defined with four parameters:

- the character string being analyzed;
- the position where the left paren was found;
- the position where its matching right paren is located by Match; and
- a success/error indicator, presumably boolean.

Match conducts a scan starting just after the position indicated by its second parameter. When Match encounters a right paren, it returns the location and a success indication to its caller. If Match first encounters a left paren, it calls itself recursively to discover the corresponding right paren for this interior left paren. The recursion will continue to whatever number of levels the nesting occurs. When the recursive call of Match concludes, the calling level of Match continues its scan immediately after the matching right paren, just as the main program does. Test Match using several expressions, some of which are invalid.

11.5 Suppose that you have a maze with pathways represented by 1's at various positions throughout a two-dimensional array. Most other positions correspond to solid walls and contain 0's. However, the entrances and exits are denoted by 2's. One way to find a path to an exit is to "search" for a consecutive sequence of 1's until you reach a different value or an intersection (a fork in the road). If you find a 2, the search was successful. If you find a 0 (a dead end) or circle back to some previously visited spot, this particular search path should be abandoned. Whenever you reach an impasse, you should return to the previously visited intersection and try some other corridor from there. Whenever you reach an intersection for the first time, you should place a special indicator there (say, by altering the value to a 3), so that you can recognize the place in case you circle back to it later.

Use these ideas to write a recursive path-searching procedure, Link. Link conducts a search down one path of the maze until it either reaches a definite conclusion to its quest or else arrives at an intersection. After leaving its mark at the intersection, it then calls itself recursively to try an outgoing path. As long as these attempts fail to reach an exit and alternative outgoing paths remain, Link keeps calling itself to explore these other paths. If an attempt succeeds, a path through this intersection leads to an exit. But if all attempts fail, Link must return to its caller with a report of failure. Test this procedure by supplying a maze in a 20 × 20 array. The path traversal can be followed visually if the Link procedure changes every 1 it encounters to some other value, such as 4, and displays the entire array at every decision point. The sequence of 3's and 4's will provide a map of the territory explored. The coordinates of the starting point in the maze must be supplied as input. Assume that all corridors in the maze are either vertical or horizontal and that any two parallel corridors have the distance of at least one "wall" between them.

11.6 Suppose that the "maze" in Exercise 11.5 has several exits. Write a procedure to discover the shortest of several possible ways out. (The objective is no longer to find just any path from a source to an exit.) The actual shortest path need not be identified—only its length must be found. "Length" refers to the number of array locations that must be traversed to travel from the starting point to an exit, including the exit itself. Thus each successful activation of Link contributes the length of one corridor (to an exit or the next intersection) to the total length of the current path.

11.7 Stage a contest between the binary search and the estimated entry search, using several inquiries into an ordered array of 60 values. Pattern the contest after the one in Exercise 7.14.

11.8 Exercise 6.12 contains the formula for approximating the value of a definite integral using the trapezoidal rule. Application of this rule requires repeated evaluation of the particular function whose integral is being computed. Consequently, the program to evaluate integrals was restricted to finding integrals of only one particular function. To generalize the program, rewrite the integration program as a subprogram and give it the particular function identifier as a parameter. As long as the particular function conforms to the parameter type, the same subprogram can apply the trapezoidal rule to it. Assume that the particular function will be real-valued and has a single real-valued parameter, such as $f(x)$. Demonstrate the result with a main program that contains at least three other functions for which integrals are being evaluated.

11.9 Try your hand at conformant array parameters, but only if your version of Pascal supports this feature. Write a function that can assess the similarity between two boolean-valued arrays of the same length. However, the array length may differ from one call to the next. All array positions are assumed to contain values. The similarity measure is the number of corresponding positions in which the two arrays have identical values, divided by the number of values per array. Two identical arrays will have similarity of 1, and disagreement in every position produces a similarity of 0. Thus the function is real-valued, and its result ranges between 0 and 1, regardless of the array lengths. Write the function with two conformant array parameters. The test program should contain at least two types of boolean arrays with different lengths. The user should be able to specify either a short or a long sequence of 0's and 1's, to be encoded as boolean values in a short- or long-type array, respectively.

12

Pointers and Lists

Suppose that you had to design a data structure to represent a hierarchy, such as a family tree, a company's organizational chart, or a procedure nesting tree. None of the mechanisms discussed so far is really suitable. Arrays and files directly represent only linear relationships, and sets have no internal structure at all. Hierarchies of records can be defined, but they produce cumbersome references and remain completely inflexible. Their structures must be declared in advance and cannot be developed or altered during execution.

Need for complex connections among data objects

Some problems require a representation of relationships much more complex than a hierarchy. For instance, planning a Christmas shopping spree may involve making lists of recipients, gift ideas, and stores where these items may be found. Entries in these lists can be associated by drawing lines between them. The resulting weblike structure may associate some gift with several stores or several recipients. Any person or store may be connected to a number of different gifts. The lists may have lines and arrows all over the place, but this presents no problem for a person whose eye can easily follow the lines through the diagram.

Need for dynamic connections among data objects

Not only is this diagram complex, but at execution time it is subject to dramatic change. Names and gifts are crossed out as purchases are made, and new gift ideas are added as new products are encountered. The original associations are continually being adjusted.

A program that maintains or makes decisions based on such complicated data organizations needs some mechanism to (1) explicitly depict arbitrary relationships among objects; and (2) allow growth and rearrangement of these relationships at run time. Pointer variables in Pascal permit run-time connections among distinct data objects, much like drawing lines on a piece of paper. An associated mechanism allocates main memory as needed and releases unneeded storage for reuse by other data objects. This permits data structures to shrink, grow, and change within the capacity of main memory. In this chapter we present and discuss these capabilities and some fundamental techniques for using them.

12.1 The Basics of Pointers

Ideally, we would like to allocate memory locations as needed and establish arbitrary links among these locations at run time for keeping track of dynamic relationships among data objects. We will consider dynamic allocation in the next section, but, for now, let's consider how one data object can refer to another.

Until now we have always referred to memory locations through identifiers. Although an identifier can be mentioned in the *code,* producing a reference to its associated memory location, it cannot be used as *data.* Identifiers are relevant only at compile time; they allow the compiler to build predetermined references into the code. Identifiers refer to a static world of objects with which the program is stuck throughout its execution.

Cannot use identifiers as run-time links

One data object can refer indirectly to another by containing an encoded indicator from which the program can infer the related object. A CASE statement, for example, might use this indicator to select the code containing the correct reference. Another way is to store array indexes, so that array components may refer to other positions within the array or within a particular companion array.

Although such links can exist as data, they are indirect and inflexible. Links depicted in these ways only imply the designated object; a program is required to interpret and resolve them. More important, every potential link must be anticipated in advance by the programmer. For example, an encoded indicator can guide a CASE statement in choosing from only a *predetermined* set of alternative objects. Until now, the programs that we have introduced could not generate new data objects and then establish interconnections among them. However, pointers provide the means to *directly* reference *arbitrary* objects.

Declaring and Making References with Pointers

To get some notion of pointers, imagine an apartment where everyone is identified by unit number: "I hear that the woman in 421 is dating the man from 117." These numbers can be used as "data" by the residents. A note on the door of 117 can redirect inquiries to unit 421. More than one unit can refer to 421, and a note on the door of 421 can point to yet another location: "Enter through 420."

pointer

Pointer is a direct reference

pointer variable

domain type

Declaration

Actual pointer value unknowable

This example is close to the notion of a pointer in Pascal. A **pointer** is an address of some other location that can itself be stored as data. Unlike the unit numbers above, a pointer is not an ordinary numeric quantity. Its value can never be displayed or arithmetically manipulated. Even the notion of larger or smaller does not apply to pointer values. A pointer is simply a reference to another data object.

A pointer is clearly a new type of data object. It must be stored in its own type of variable, called, naturally enough, a **pointer variable.** A pointer can be visualized as an arrow, with the arrow head pointing at the designated object and the tail of the arrow anchored inside a pointer variable. Just as we have different types of data objects, we also have different types of pointers. A particular pointer in Pascal cannot reference just any sort of object; it may reference only objects from an associated data type, known as its **domain type.** The domain type can be any predefined type or any user-defined type *declared in the same type definition part.* Thus every data type can have an associated pointer type, and when a pointer variable has been declared, its contents can point only to members of its domain type. This preserves the separation of types at every level of Pascal.

The general form for defining pointer types is

> TYPE
>   ⟨pointer-type⟩ = ^⟨domain-type⟩

or

> ⟨pointer-type⟩ = ↑⟨domain-type⟩

As before, we will use the caret (^) rather than the arrow.

We can now declare a pointer variable in the variable declaration part. For example, we can write

```
TYPE
  IntegerPointer  = ^integer;
  RealPointer     = ^real;
VAR
  P,Q : IntegerPointer;
  R   : RealPointer;
```

These declarations establish P and Q as variables capable of referencing integer-type storage locations. Similarly R is a variable to be used for referencing real-type locations. Although these statements prescribe the pointer variables, they do *nothing* to generate the pointer values themselves. As with any other variable in a program, the contents of P, Q, and R are undefined when the program begins to execute; they do not yet point to any storage locations.

Pascal never allows the actual pointer value to be revealed; we have no way to print or even "deduce" what the pointer value really is. We can know only *where* its value is stored, but that is enough to let us use it. All references through pointers entail naming or otherwise referencing the variable where the pointer is stored. The designated object has no name of its own; it will always be accessed as "the object pointed to by the pointer stored in some particular pointer variable." Figure 12.1 illustrates these ideas.

References through pointers

Assuming that P and Q already contain pointers to some integer variables (you will soon see how the pointers are established), the integer variable that P points to may now be referred to as P^. It may be given the value 12 by executing

```
    P^  := 12;
```

The following statement stores the value of P^ plus 1 in the location that Q points to.

```
    Q^  := P^ + 1;
```

In these examples the operations involve only integer values and integer

■ Figure 12.1
Using pointers.

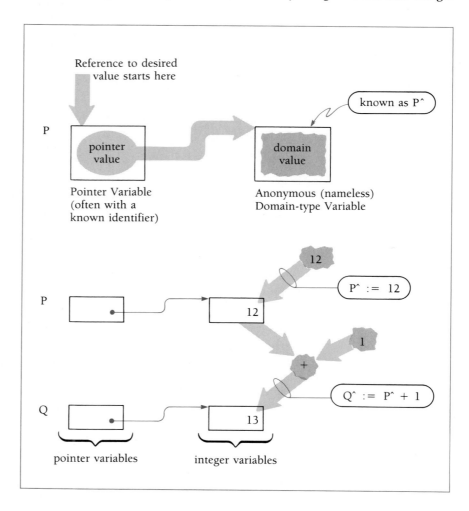

variables. These variables merely have pointer references rather than conventional identifiers. We can use P^ and Q^ to designate ordinary integer variables in any context in which an integer variable name would be valid.

Pointers cannot be manipulated but can be compared

The operations permitted on the pointers themselves are extremely limited. Since pointers do not even have magnitude, arithmetic operations cannot alter their values, and relational operators cannot determine which is larger or smaller. Pointer variables cannot be manipulated by the program; they are merely references to other values. About all you can do is compare two pointers (of the same type) for identical values, using the "=" or "⟨⟩" relational operators. Equality implies that both pointers point to the same data object (or to no data object). For example,

IF P = Q THEN . . . {both designate same object}

The contents of a pointer variable can be modified in only three ways:

Putting values in pointers

1. by assigning the NIL value to it;
2. by a call to the procedure, new; or
3. by giving it the value of another pointer, through either an assignment statement or the parameter mechanism.

A pointer can also be returned as the value of a function.

NIL

The special symbol **NIL** represents the only pointer value that can be explicitly written; for example,

    P := NIL;

NIL can be used like a "constant" of type pointer. When assigned to a pointer variable, NIL explicitly indicates that the variable currently points to no other data object. Since it is an error to attempt a copy or comparison using an undefined (pointer) variable, P cannot be accessed unless it has *some* value. Assignment of NIL does provide a genuine value and elevates the variable out of its original "undefined" state, even though it may not be referencing anything at the moment.

Assuming that P is either NIL or points to something else, we can find out if it does currently point to anything by writing

IF P <> NIL THEN . . . {P points to something}

An unusual feature of NIL is that it may be used with *any type* of pointer. In many respects it resembles the empty set, which is a true set that has no contents and is compatible with every set type.

Assigning the value NIL and copying from one pointer variable into another does not get us very far. We as yet have no way to generate new pointer values to new data objects. The only way to establish a new reference is through a call to the procedure "new." There is no way to generate a pointer reference to an already declared and allocated object having its own identifier. An object is referenced either by its own identifier or through a pointer—but never in both ways.

Dynamic Allocation in Pascal

new procedure

In conjunction with pointers, Pascal provides a predefined procedure, the **new procedure,** to generate a new element from some domain type and establish a pointer to this new element. Its general form is:

new (⟨pointer-variable⟩);

dynamic storage allocation

In particular this call (1) allocates a block of storage as required by the domain type for this pointer type; and (2) causes the pointer variable to take on the address of the new storage. The allocation of the new piece of storage is done at run time and is sometimes referred to as **dynamic storage allocation.** The new block of storage is anonymous; that is, no formal identifier is associated with it, and its content is undefined. However, we can now construct a reference to it, using the pointer variable's identifier, as explained before:

⟨pointer-variable⟩ˆ

New produces long-term storage allocation

Another unusual feature of dynamic storage allocation is that storage allocated by the procedure new remains allocated throughout the execution of the program, even if the allocation occurs in a subprogram. Other locally declared storage is lost when a subprogram terminates, including local variables that contain pointers. But the objects generated by the procedure new continue to exist until they are removed by a call to the procedure dispose.

Consider the program:

```
    PROGRAM Dynamic (input,output);
    TYPE
1     Pointer = ^integer;
    VAR
2     Ptr : Pointer;
    BEGIN
3     new (Ptr);
4     Ptr^ := 1999;
5     writeln (Ptr^)
    END.
```

Allocation mechanism

When this program begins to execute, precisely one storage location will be allocated for its use: the pointer variable P. Because P's content is undefined, we cannot use P as a memory reference before the execution of the procedure call in line 3. The memory initially available to the program will be nothing more than

Ptr [   ]

The call in line 3 will cause the allocation of a memory location suitable for holding integer values, and the address of this location will be stored in the variable P. Then, after completion of the call, the program's available

memory will be

Ptr

The new storage location's content is undefined, and no permanent identifier is associated with it. However, it is referred to in line 4 as P^, where the assignment statement places a value in it, giving the following memory picture.

Ptr  1999

Line 5 shows that this kind of reference can be used in any context in which an ordinary integer variable name could appear.

The code in Fig. 12.2 shows that a pointer can point to objects with structured types and that an object may be referenced by more than one pointer at a time. As before, when the program begins to execute, we find space for only P and Q, both of which are undefined. Line 4 allocates more memory, capable of holding 10 characters in a packed array, with its address in P.

Line 5 copies the address of this newly allocated storage into Q, giving us two references to the same storage location.

■ Figure 12.2
Pointing to an array
with two pointers.

```
     TYPE
1      String = PACKED ARRAY [1..10] OF char;
2      Pointer = ^String;
     VAR
3      P,Q : Pointer;
     BEGIN
4      new (P);     {space for string; address in P}
5      Q := P;      {copy string's address into Q}
6      P := NIL;    {remove address from P}
7      Q^ := 'Notre Dame'; {refer to string thru Q}
           .
           .
           .
```

At this point we can refer to the new storage as either P^ or Q^ because both contain its address. Since neither P nor Q "knows about" the other, the program must keep track of which pointers refer to which objects, but more about this later.

Referencing components

Since the designated object is an array, we can reference any of its individual character variables. We may reference the whole array as P^ or Q^ and access its components in the usual way: by placing a subscript in square brackets immediately after the array reference. Thus we may indicate the Kth component of the array by either P^[K] or Q^[K]. We could display the array character by character as follows:

```
FOR Psn := 1 TO 10 DO
  write( P^[Psn] );
writeln;
```

Returning to Fig. 12.2, line 6 disconnects P from the character string storage area by setting P to NIL. We can still keep track of the array, since its address remains in Q.

Reference through P^ would now be an error, because P does not point to anything. Finally, line 7 actually stores a value in the new space, referring to it through its address in Q.

Now consider what would happen if we add one more line to the code, after line 7:

```
Q := NIL;
```

This assignment will overwrite the address in Q, leaving no way to retrieve the value previously stored in the packed array. The array will remain in memory somewhere, but the program will never be able to access it again. As far as the program is concerned, the array is lost forever.

dispose procedure

Sometimes we really are finished with a dynamically allocated item. Rather than simply losing track of it and allowing it to clutter main memory, we should release the space it occupies, so that the space may be reused for other purposes. Pascal provides another predeclared procedure, the **dispose procedure,** which permits us to dispose of a dynamically allocated item when it is no longer required.† This procedure has the following general form.

dispose (⟨pointer-variable⟩);

How dispose works

It undoes the work of new by releasing the storage whose address is contained in the ⟨pointer-variable⟩ and leaving the pointer undefined. To call dispose with a pointer that does not contain a valid address is an error.

In the context of our previous pointer example, consider executing the sequence:

```
new (P);
P^ := 'Tom & Joe ';
dispose (P);
```

After executing the first two statements, we will have in memory:

However, when the third statement executes, our recently allocated packed array vanishes, the content of P is left undefined, and all we have in memory is

P ▓▓▓▓▓

If, instead, we had written

```
new (P);
Q := P;
dispose (P);
```

then, not only would the storage be freed and P be left undefined, but Q would also be undefined. The values of P and Q will not even be NIL, and neither can be used again until a new value has been assigned. When an object is deallocated (disposed), the program should set all of its referencing pointers to NIL. Failure to do so can cause problems later when any of these pointers is accessed.

Memory management

Without dynamic allocation, the program is constrained to refer to only those memory locations that have been preallocated in the variable declaration

---

† Some implementations do not bother to actually free the physical space for possible reuse. However, we choose to show physical disposition in the examples. In any event, the space disposed of is no longer available to the program.

part of the program. At one extreme, we tend to waste memory space by declaring more variables than the program will ever need; at the other, we may cause the program to terminate prematurely by failing to allocate sufficient space. New and dispose allow programs to allocate just as much space as they require (within the bounds of the particular computer) and to reuse formerly allocated space as required.

New and dispose with record variants

New and dispose can also be used to allocate and release storage for records with variant parts. These procedures have an alternate form that allows them to allocate only enough storage for one particular variant. Suppose the variant record declaration is

```
TYPE
  Form = (Short,Long);
  VariantRecd =
    RECORD
      IDNumber : integer;
    CASE Tag : Form OF
      Short    : (TotalAmt : real);
      Long     : (Gross,Expenses,NetAmt : real)
    END; {record}
    Pointer = ^VariantRecd;
VAR
  NextRecd : Pointer;
```

To generate a record variant of the short form, we would write

```
new( NextRecd, Short );
```

and the counterpart to release its storage is

```
dispose( NextRecd, Short );
```

A similar pair of calls with Long as the second parameter could manage the storage for the long form of the record. The first parameter, of course, is still a pointer to the record type. The second parameter must be a case constant specifying the particular variant. A variant generated with this special form of new can be released only by the corresponding special form of dispose. (If the record type has variant parts within its variant parts, we can specify additional case constants as additional parameters of new and dispose. These must specify consecutive levels of nested variants, beginning with the outermost; however, innermost levels need not be specified.)

Using Pointers with Records and Arrays

You saw in Fig. 12.2 that an array could be allocated by the procedure new and accessed through a pointer. Similarly, records may be generated by new and accessed through pointers. In practice, records are probably the most common objects to which pointers refer.

Consider the declaration:

```
TYPE
  TestRecord =
    RECORD
      Field1 : ARRAY [1..20] OF char;
      Field2 : integer;
      Field3 : real
    END;
  RecordPtr   = ^TestRecord;
VAR
  P : RecordPtr;
```

These lines of code establish P as a pointer to records of type TestRecord. When we call new(P), one such record will be allocated with its address stored in P. The record itself will be known as P^.

Although the newly allocated record has no identifier associated with it, its component fields inherit their types and identifiers from the record-type definition in the usual way. Since the entire record may be referenced as P^, the individual fields are identified by P^.Field1, P^.Field2, and P^.Field3. Similarly, the individual characters of Field1 are accessed as P^.Field1[K], where K is an appropriate integer.

Pointers as components of structured types
Pointer variables themselves may be components of structured types. Figure 12.3 shows an extension of the previous declaration, in which we declare an entire array of pointer variables. Here we see several records accessed through pointers stored in the array.

```
TYPE
  RecordType =
    RECORD
      Name   : ARRAY [1..20] OF char;
      IDNum  : integer;
      Amount : real
    END;
  PointerType = ^RecordType;
  ArrayType   = ARRAY [1..10] OF PointerType;

VAR
  Customer : ArrayType;       {pointers to customer recds}
  NewCust  : PointerType;     {to newly generated recd}
  Number   : integer;         {number of customers}
```

(a) Declarations for an array of pointers.

■ Figure 12.3
Records referenced by an array of pointers.   *(Continued)*

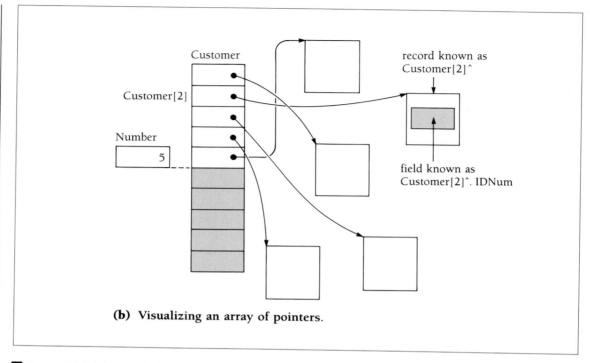

(b) Visualizing an array of pointers.

■ Figure 12.3 (*Continued*)

Generating several pointer references

Figure 12.4 presents a program fragment to generate this data configuration. An input loop generates and initializes new records, as long as the input continues and space remains in the array for an additional pointer. After the main program advances the array frontier, it allocates a record using the procedure new. The actual record is then passed as a parameter to an initializing procedure, which supplies values for its fields. After the call to Initial, the value of NewCust—a pointer to the newly initialized record—is stored in the next free position of the array. This causes Customer[Number] to reference the new record as well. With a pointer to the new record safely stored in the array, NewCust can be reused by new to reference yet another newly generated record.

Note that it makes no difference to the Initial procedure whether its record-type parameter is specified on the outside by an identifier or by a pointer reference (as it is here). Whatever the case, it sees only an ordinary record, which it fills with data in the usual way.

The array components are pointer variables, so we could have used an array component directly in the procedure new. This would have resulted in

```
TYPE
    RecordType =
        RECORD
            Name   : ARRAY [1..20] OF char;
            IDNum  : integer;
            Amount : real
        END;
    PointerType = ^ RecordType;
    ArrayType   = ARRAY [1..10] OF PointerType;
VAR
    Customer : ArrayType;         {pointers to customer recds}
    NewCust  : PointerType;        {to newly generated recd}
    Number   : integer;           {number of customers}
    .
    .
    .
PROCEDURE Initial (VAR Client : RecordType)
    VAR
        CharPsn: integer;
    BEGIN
        WITH Client DO
            BEGIN
                write('enter name:');
                CharPsn := 0;
                WHILE NOT eoln AND (CharPsn < 20) DO
                    BEGIN
                        CharPsn := CharPsn + 1;
                        read( Name[CharPsn] )
                    END;
                readln;
                write('enter i.d. and amount:');
                readln( IDNum, Amount )
            END {WITH}
    END; {Initial procedure}

BEGIN {main program}
    Number := 0;
    WHILE (Number < 10) AND NOT eof DO
        BEGIN
            Number := Number + 1;
            new(NewCust)
            Initial(NewCust^);         ← Passing actual record
            Customer[Number] := NewCust ← Assigning pointers
        END;
```

■ Figure 12.4
Initializing records and an array of record pointers.

```
PROGRAM...

    {TYPE and VAR declarations same as Figure 12.3(a)}

PROCEDURE Initialize ( NewClient : PointerType );

    VAR
       CharPsn: integer;
    BEGIN
       WITH NewClient^ DO
          BEGIN
             write('enter name:');
             CharPsn := 0;
             WHILE NOT eoln AND (CharPsn < 20) DO
                BEGIN
                   CharPsn := CharPsn + 1;
                   read( Name[CharPsn] )
                END;
             readln;
             write('enter i.d. and amount:');
             readln( IDNum, Amount )
          END {WITH}
    END; {Initialize procedure}

BEGIN {main program}
   Number := 0;
   WHILE (Number < 10) AND NOT eof DO
      BEGIN
         Number := Number + 1;
         new( Customer[Number] );
         Initialize( Customer[Number] );
      END;
      .
      .
      .
END.
```

Passing record pointer

■ Figure 12.5
Passing the record pointer instead of the record.

the following main program loop:

```
Number := 0;
WHILE NOT eof AND (Number < 10) DO
  BEGIN
    Number := Number + 1;
    new( Customer[Number] );
    Initial( Customer[Number]^ )
  END;
```

Note the call to Initial. The main program now references the new record through the pointer stored in the array.

Pointer as a parameter

Another possibility would have been to rewrite Initialize so that it accepted a *pointer* rather than the record itself as a parameter. This convention is shown in Fig. 12.5. In this case, the parameter does not need to be variable type; the pointer itself is not altered by the procedure, even though the object it points to is. Inside the procedure, we must designate the record by a pointer reference.

Yet another possibility would have been to generate and initialize the record without using a procedure. The objects at each level would be identified as

Object	Identifier
Entire array of pointers	Customer
The pointer at location Psn	Customer[Psn]
The record referenced from the pointer at location Psn	Customer[Psn]^
This record's Name field	Customer[Psn]^.Name
First char of that Name field	Customer[Psn]^.Name[1]

However you implement the initialization, the final result looks like Fig. 12.3(b). The pointers appear in their order of creation, but you could arrange them in any order, say, according to alphabetical ordering among the record Name fields. The records can then be accessed in some logical ordering, determined by the ordering among the pointers. You can represent multiple logical orderings by multiple arrays of pointers, with each array referencing the same records but in different respective orders.

12.2 Linear List Structures

Just as a pointer may be the value of an array item, so it may be a field within a record. Consider for a moment a collection of records, the logical ordering of which is depicted by a sequence of pointers in an array, as in Fig. 12.3. Now imagine that each of these pointers (except the first) is removed from the array and stored inside another record. Specifically, the pointer to the Kth record is placed in record $K - 1$, so that each record (except the last) points to its successor in the original logical ordering. The pointer to the first record can be anchored in any object outside the set of records, so that the array becomes irrelevant. The result is a self-contained linear sequence of records, where each record points to the next one in the ordering. By following the sequence of pointers, a program can encounter all the records in the proper order. This important structure is the linear list.

Introduction to Linear Lists

When a pointer field is part of a dynamically allocated record, each record can point to some other record. This permits records to be interconnected in a way that resembles drawing lines on paper among related objects.

linear list

A **linear list** is a data structure consisting of objects connected in a sequence, with each object pointing to the next, such as

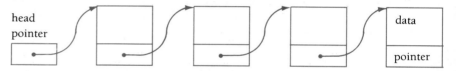

Records are the only objects that make sense in a list because the data to be linked should include other types besides pointers, and only a record can hold a combination of dissimilar types. Since our focus is on the connections among records, we will often assume that a record consists of only two general parts: (1) data and (2) a pointer to another record. These structures are often

nodes

called **nodes.**

head pointer

In order to locate a list, the pointer to its first node must be anchored somewhere outside the list itself. This initial pointer is often called the *head* of the list or **head pointer.** The *predecessor* of any interior node is the node pointing to it, and its *successor* is the mode to which it points.

Lists are versatile and dynamic

A linear list is a versatile structure with many applications. A group of related records can be associated by placing them on the same list. The membership may change during execution, and there is no predetermined limit on the number of constituent nodes. The ordering of nodes may be significant or it may be arbitrary; the entire list of objects can be passed among subprograms simply by passing the head pointer.

and require sequential processing

A linear list is a sequential structure that must be accessed through the head pointer, and its nodes must be accessed in the order in which they appear on the list.

Order of nodes independent of physical position

One of the greatest advantages of list structures is the ease with which they can be modified. Changing the membership does not require any movement of existing nodes. A node may be deleted by simply updating the pointer in its predecessor to bypass the deleted node and point directly to its successor. A new node may be spliced into the list at any spot by rerouting a pointer or two.

In Fig. 12.6, we illustrate how to modify linear lists. Moving from the top to the bottom of this figure, you see the node marked X being inserted into an existing list between nodes marked A and B. The pointer in node X is directed toward node B, and the pointer in A is redirected toward X. With these two simple changes, the insertion is complete. Deletion of node X from the list, shown in the progression from the bottom toward the top of Fig. 12.6, requires only that the pointer in node A be redirected to the node following X in the list, namely, node B.

■ Figure 12.6
Modifying linear lists.

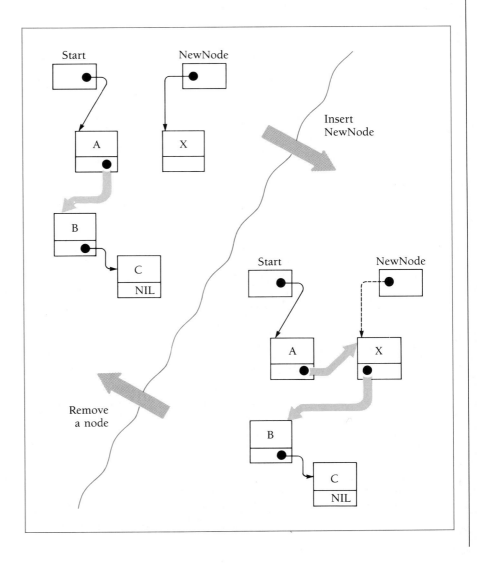

Creating an Unordered Linear List

If we are going to create a list, its nodes must be records that contain at least one data field and one pointer field for referencing another node. Furthermore all records on a list must be of the same type, that is, the domain type of the pointers. The declaration below provides what we need: the record type; the pointer type; and two pointer variables, one for the head of the list (Start) and another for referencing newly generated nodes (NewNode).

```
TYPE
  NodePtr = ^Node;
  Node =
    RECORD
      Data : integer;
      NextNode  : NodePtr
    END;
VAR
  Start,              {references head of list}
  NewNode : NodePtr;
```

The arrangement of type declarations shown in the preceding code fragment is the only option permitted. The pointer type *must* be declared before the record type that is its domain.

Suppose that we have already generated a list containing two records:

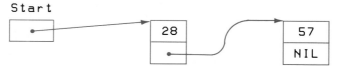

We can generate a new record and initialize its data field by executing

```
new (NewNode);
readln (NewNode^.Data);
```

The situation at this point is shown in Fig. 12.7(a).

Placing new node at head of list

Since the list is not ordered, the easiest place to insert the new node is at the beginning. This requires changes to two pointer values:

1. The new node must point to its eventual successor, currently the first node on the list; and
2. The head pointer must point to the new node, making it the first node on the revised list.

These steps must be implemented in the order given, because updating the head pointer first, when nothing else was pointing to the list, would cause the entire list to be lost. Both steps require just a simple copy of pointer values, or

```
NewNode^.NextNode := Start;
Start := NewNode;
```

This sequence of assignment statements is so important that we illustrate the effect of each separately. Since Start already points to the first node of the list, its value is copied into the pointer field of the new node. This causes the new node to reference the remainder of the list, as shown in Fig. 12.7(b). By copying the value of NewNode into Start, Start will point to the new node, making it the first element on the list, as shown in Fig. 12.7(c).

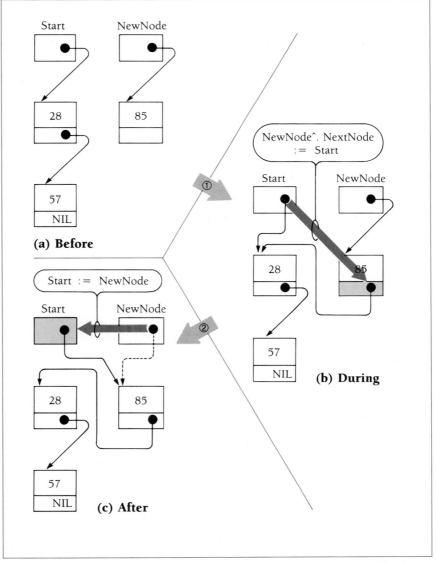

■ Figure 12.7
Pushing a node onto the head of a list.

```
PROCEDURE Push (VAR Start : NodePtr; NewNode : NodePtr);
  {Place record referenced by NewNode at front of list}
  BEGIN
   NewNode^.NextNode := Start;
   Start := NewNode
  END; {Push procedure}
```

(d) Push procedure.

■ Figure 12.7 *(Continued)*

These operations are encoded as a procedure in Fig. 12.7(d). To allow outside access to the updated list, the parameter, Start, must be variable-type. The procedure name is "Push," a term sometimes used to describe adding a new element to the head of a linear list.

Final node contains NIL pointer

The figure shows a value of NIL in the pointer field of the final list element. This NIL value is an important safeguard to prevent an attempt to access a nonexistent "next" record beyond the end of the list. A list with no nodes is often referred to as an **empty list.** Testing for an empty list amounts to asking

empty list

```
IF Start = NIL THEN...{empty list}
```

Suppose a pointer Current is pointing to some arbitrary node in the list. This node will be the final node if its pointer field is NIL; or, in Pascal,

```
IF Current^.NextNode = NIL THEN...{end of list}
```

Pushing first node onto an empty list

Here we are concerned with showing that the Push procedure works correctly when placing the first node on an empty list. The list starts with no members, which is indicated by a NIL value in Start. Push will place this NIL value in the pointer field of the first node placed on the list. As long as new nodes are always pushed onto the head of the list, this NIL pointer will remain at the end of the list, as required. Figure 12.8 shows how this works.

Building an entire list

Figure 12.9 on p. 512 shows the entire operation of reading integers and placing each successive integer on a list. The generation and initialization of new nodes is carried out by a procedure, as is the attachment of new nodes to the head of the list.

In the main program we need to declare only the two pointer variables Start and NewNode. These two starting points allow access—at least indirectly—to all the records containing the input values. Of course, pushing each new integer onto the head of the list produces a list in reverse order of integer arrival.

Figure 12.8
Pushing first node
onto empty list.

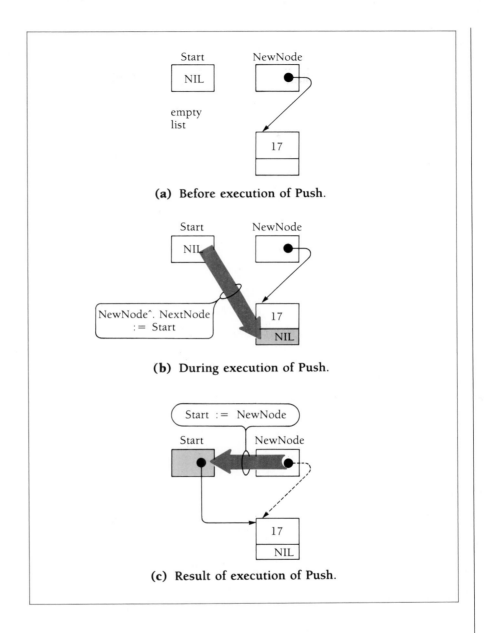

(a) **Before execution of Push.**

(b) **During execution of Push.**

(c) **Result of execution of Push.**

Consider what will happen when this program is executed with three
input values: 111, 222, and 333, in that order. The program begins by
initializing the head pointer to NIL. It calls the ProduceNode procedure to
allocate space for a new record and read the value 111 into its data field. A
pointer to the new record is returned through the variable-type parameter.

```
PROGRAM CreateList (input,output);
TYPE
   NodePtr = ^Node;
   Node =
      RECORD
         Data : integer;
         NextNode : NodePtr
      END;
VAR
   Start,                   {head of list}
   NewNode : NodePtr;

PROCEDURE ProduceNode (VAR NewNode : NodePtr);
   {Generate new node and initialize its two fields}
   BEGIN
      new( NewNode );
      WITH NewNode^ DO
         BEGIN
            readln( Data );
            NextNode := NIL
         END
   END; {ProduceNode}

PROCEDURE Push (VAR Start: NodePtr;
                    NewNode: NodePtr);
   {Put record referenced by NewNode at front of list}
   BEGIN
      NewNode^.NextNode := Start;
      Start := NewNode
   END; {Push procedure}

BEGIN
   Start := NIL;     {begin with empty list}
   writeln('enter integers, one per line');
   WHILE NOT eof DO
      BEGIN
         ProduceNode( NewNode );
         Push( Start, NewNode )
      END;
```

■ Figure 12.9
Program fragment to create unordered list of integers.

The data structure now appears as

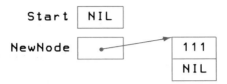

To which block does this new space belong? Although the space was requested inside a procedure, its allocation continues to exist until such time as the program disposes of it, and it will be accessible to any block that has access to its pointer.

The call to Push makes the new record the sole member of the list.

The presence of more input data allows the loop to execute a second time. The call to ProduceNode generates another record containing a data value, or

Another call to Push places the new node at the head of the list.

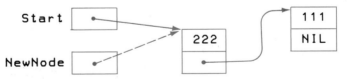

The final execution of the loop creates a third record and adds it to the head of the list, leaving

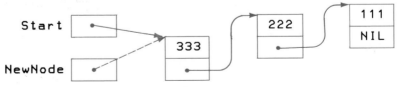

The end of data causes the loop to stop at this point.

Traversing linear lists

List traversal: a sequential process

Traversing a linear list means moving through it sequentially, node by node, which is the only way of processing a list. Processing the data portion of any node may be quite complex, but the general approach always follows the same pattern:

1. begin at the first node;
2. while nodes remain to be processed do:
2.1   process the "current" node;
2.2   advance to the "next" node;

This is standard sequential processing, except that pointers are involved in every step.

Maintaining current node pointer

The program needs some pointer variable through which it can access each node along the list. As the nodes are inspected, one after the other, this pointer must be updated to keep up with the current position in the list. It serves the same purpose as an index variable for stepping through an array. As a reminder of its role, we will use the identifier Current for this pointer variable.

Starting pointer

Finding the first node is no problem; its address is stored in some known head pointer, Start in our example. Current begins with this value, that is,

```
Current := Start;
```

Advancing pointer

Assuming that the list has been partially traversed, Current will point to the node under consideration. Moving to the next node (step 2.2) involves updating the value of Current. Its new value will be the address of the record that the current record is pointing to. In other words, the address contained in the pointer field of the current record is placed in Current, or

```
Current := Current^.NextNode;
```

Study this statement carefully. It represents the key operation in traversing a linear list. Its effect is shown in Fig. 12.10.

Deciding when to stop (step 2) depends on whether some "next" node remains to be inspected. If the list is empty, we are already finished. Assuming that Start was properly initialized to NIL, the list is empty if Current = NIL.

Stopping the traversal

Otherwise, there will be nodes to process. If we traverse the entire list, Current will eventually point to the final record. This record will be processed (step 2.1), and its pointer field will be copied into Current (step 2.2). Since this final pointer field is NIL, Current becomes NIL, and once again the loop terminates because Current = NIL. Thus, whether the list is empty or not, processing is governed by the statement:

WHILE Current <> NIL DO . . .

The code in Fig. 12.11(a) displays all the integer values stored in our list and reflects the programming ideas just discussed. If the value of Start is

Figure 12.10
Advancing current
node pointer through
a list.

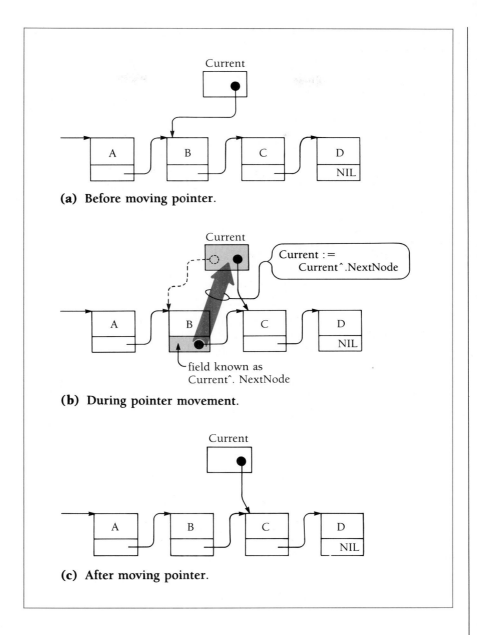

(a) Before moving pointer.

(b) During pointer movement.

(c) After moving pointer.

altered, nodes near the front of the list may be lost forever. In particular, Start itself should never be used to maintain the position during traversal; some other pointer variable (here Current) serves this function.

A generalized procedure to traverse a list is shown in Fig. 12.11(b). When the procedure is called with Start as an actual parameter, Start's value

```
TYPE
   {Declare NodePtr and Node types, as in Figure 12.9}
VAR
   Start,
   Current : NodePtr;
BEGIN
   .
   .
   {Assume Start points to first node on list (or NIL)}
   Current := Start;
   WHILE Current <> NIL DO
      BEGIN
         writeln (Current^.Data);        {display}
         Current := Current^.NextNode   {advance}
   END;
```

(a) Displaying contents of a linear list.

```
PROCEDURE Traverse (Current : NodePtr);
   BEGIN {Traverse}
      WHILE Current <> NIL DO
         BEGIN

            ┌──────────────────────────────────────────┐
            │ code to process Current^.Data goes here   │
            └──────────────────────────────────────────┘

            Current := Current^.NextNode {advance pointer}

         END {loop}
   END; {Traverse procedure}
```

(b) Skeleton procedure to traverse a linear list.

■ Figure 12.11
Linear list traversal.

becomes the initial value for the formal parameter Current. Hence, there is no explicit initialization of Current inside the procedure. Although the procedure contains the statement,

```
Current := Current^.NextNode;
```

use of a value-type parameter protects Start in the calling program from being altered.

Searching a list   A common reason to traverse a list is to locate some particular data value. We will use a function to find the node, if any, containing an integer, Target. The most useful form for the result is either the address of the node containing the Target value or NIL, if the Target is not found. Thus we want a pointer-valued function. The parameters to the function will be the head pointer and the value sought. This function has two stopping criteria: (1) when all nodes have been searched without success; or (2) when the desired value has been found. The code is shown in Fig. 12.12.

Beware of trying references through NIL pointer

The boolean flag to signal a successful search appears for a very good reason. You might be tempted to abbreviate the code by including the test for the Target value as one of the WHILE conditions. Your proposed search loop might look like the following.

{WARNING: this code might cause an error!}

```
WHILE (Current <> NIL) AND
      (Current^.Data <> Target) DO{not use}
```

```
FUNCTION TargetNode (Current: NodePtr;
                     Target: integer): NodePtr;

   {Find the first occurrence of Target
    in list starting at Current}

   VAR
      Found : boolean; {true when Target found}

   BEGIN
      Found := false;

      WHILE (Current <> NIL) AND NOT Found DO
         BEGIN {traverse}
            IF Current^.Data = Target THEN
               Found := true  {success}
            ELSE
               Current := Current^.NextNode {advance}
         END; {loop}

      TargetNode := Current
         {if Target not Found then Current = NIL,
          which is still the correct result}

   END; {TargetNode}
```

■ **Figure 12.12**
Finding where a target value occurs in a linear list.

Although this loop does not need a flag, it also might not work correctly. The problem occurs when the end of the list has been reached and the value of Current has become NIL. In that case Current^.Data is undefined, but there is no guarantee that this illegal reference will not be attempted. Even when one of the conditions is false, they might all be evaluated. Furthermore, conditions are not always evaluated from left to right. Therefore you should *never* use a pointer reference in a loop (or anywhere else) unless you are certain that the pointer actually points to some node. In Fig. 12.12 the reference appears inside a loop that is not entered unless the condition Current <> NIL is true.

Pointer-valued functions

Although pointer-valued functions are perfectly legal, their returned values must be stored in pointer variables by the calling program; they cannot be used directly to reference a data object [as in Illegal(X)^.Data]. The proper call is

```
DesiredNode := TargetNode( Start, Target );
IF DesiredNode <> NIL THEN
    {DesiredNode^.Data contains Target}
```

Removing Nodes from Linear Lists

Remove node from list before disposing

When its presence on a particular list is no longer appropriate, a node may be removed. The deleted node may be reused elsewhere, or it may be discarded by calling dispose. If a node is no longer needed, it must not be disposed while it is still a member of a list. This is like shooting a hole in the middle of the list, causing all the successors of the deleted node to be lost along with it. The node must first be removed from the chain of pointers forming the list, regardless of the purpose for the deletion.

Actual deletion step

Deletion from a list is illustrated in Fig. 12.6. The key operation involves redirecting a pointer around the node being removed, causing that node to be bypassed. In particular, if Current is the node to be deleted, its predecessor must be made to point to its successor. Of course, the Current node's NextNode field references its successor. If the predecessor is referenced by the pointer Predecessor, the following assignment accomplishes the bypass.

```
Predecessor^.NextNode := Current^.NextNode;
```

The details of deletion are shown in Fig. 12.13. Inserting a NIL value into the pointer field of the deleted node is not strictly necessary, especially if the node is about to be disposed. However, this simple precaution prevents the deleted node from continuing to reference the remainder of a list in which it does not belong.

Finding the predecessor of node to be deleted

Knowing which node to delete is not enough. We must have some way of accessing the deleted node's predecessor, and finding the predecessor is the hard part. We cannot travel backwards from the node to be deleted. The

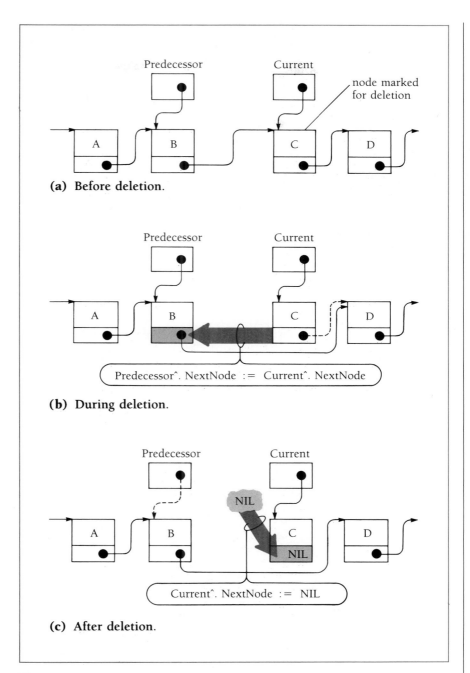

Figure 12.13
Deleting a node from a list.

```
PROCEDURE FindAndDelete (VAR Start, Result: NodePtr;
                              Target: integer);
   {Find Target value in list, remove it from list, and
    return its address in Result; return NIL if Target
    not found}

   VAR
      Current,
      Predecessor: NodePtr;
      Found: boolean;

   BEGIN {FindAndDelete}
      Found := false;
      Current := Start;
      Predecessor := NIL; {no predecessor to first node}

      WHILE NOT Found AND (Current <> NIL) DO
         BEGIN {search}
            Found := Current^.Data = Target;
            IF NOT Found THEN
               BEGIN {advance pointers}
                  Predecessor := Current;
                  Current := Current^.NextNode
               END
         END; {search}

      IF NOT Found THEN
         Result := NIL
      ELSE
         BEGIN {remove from list}
            IF Current = Start THEN {first node}
               Start := Start^.NextNode
            ELSE
               Predecessor^.NextNode := Current^.NextNode;
            Current^.NextNode := NIL;
            Result := Current
         END {remove}
   END; {FindAndDelete}
```

■ Figure 12.14
Finding and deleting a node from a list.

predecessor must be discovered during a list traversal; it can be determined as part of the algorithm that locates the actual node to be deleted.

Assume that deletion is based on finding a particular data value in the node. The search procedure can simply remember the predecessor of whatever node it is currently inspecting. As the Current pointer is advanced through the list, another pointer, designating its predecessor node, is advanced along with it. This is like moving two fingers through a list, where one always stays immediately behind the other. The statements to advance to the next position in the list are therefore

```
Predecessor := Current;
                             {Predecessor catches up}
Current := Current^.NextNode;
                             {Current moves ahead}
```

Deletion of first node is a special case

Deleting the *first* node on the list is treated as a special case. Because it has no predecessor, the head pointer, rather than an ordinary pointer field from a record, must be updated. Hence the head pointer must be passed as a variable-type parameter to a deletion procedure. Such a procedure is shown in Fig. 12.14.

If the first node is the only node on the list, its deletion leaves the list empty. However, in this case the node is also the last on the list, and its NextNode field will be NIL. This NIL value will be copied into Start, correctly indicating an empty list.

The procedure in Fig. 12.14 conducts a search for a specific data value, removes the first node containing that value from the list, and returns a pointer to the deleted node (which still exists, of course). A NIL value indicates that no node was removed from the list. The procedure imitates the search in Fig. 12.12, with the addition of initiating and advancing the Predecessor pointer, so that it follows the Current pointer through the list.

Insertion and the Insertion Sort

In contrast to pushing a new node onto the top of a list, we may want to *insert* a new node at a specific position in the list, presumably between two existing, consecutive nodes. The insertion can be made without moving any nodes, simply by rerouting pointers, as indicated previously in Fig. 12.6.

The insertion step

Figure 12.15 shows the details of splicing NewNode into a list, immediately *after* its predecessor node and before its successor node. Since it will eventually point to the new node, the Predecessor node must be known before an insertion is possible.

Finding predecessor of insertion point

You should always think of insertion as occurring *after* a particular predecessor node. Because the successor node's address is already stored in the field, Predecessor^.NextNode, this address need not be explicitly stored

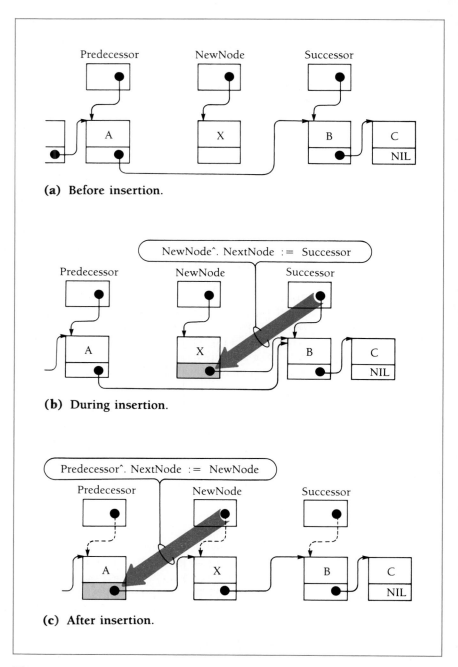

(a) Before insertion.

(b) During insertion.

(c) After insertion.

■ Figure 12.15
Inserting a new node in a list.

in a separate pointer variable. Nevertheless, an explicit Successor pointer is usually available, owing to the way the position for insertion is determined.

The most common reason for requiring insertion is to maintain some sort of order among list elements. Suppose that a list is ordered by increasing value of the data fields. A new item should be inserted after the last node having a smaller value and before the first node having a larger value (if one exists). This spot must be found by traversing the list. Because all the early items will have smaller values than the new node, we cannot know that we have reached the last node having a smaller value until we have *passed* it and discovered one with a larger value. At that moment the current node will be the Successor, and its predecessor will be the Predecessor of the node to be inserted.

The search for the insertion spot will be based on finding the first node, designated as (potential) Successor, for which

```
Successor^.Data > NewNode^.Data
```

If the Predecessor pointer has been following immediately behind the Successor during the traversal, we are ready to perform the insertion as soon as this condition becomes true. The use of strict inequality in the comparison causes the new node to be inserted after all other nodes that contain the same data value.

Figure 12.16 contains a procedure for making this search and insertion. The search portion of the code looks just like that in the deletion procedure of Fig. 12.14, except for the different stopping criterion. Note how the Predecessor and Successor pointers are advanced in tandem, so that they always point to consecutive nodes.

First node is a special case

Again, insertion at the beginning of a list is treated as a special case. Note that it does not matter whether the node is being added to the start of an existing list or is becoming the first node on a previously empty list. Because a new first node requires that we alter the head pointer, Start must be passed as a variable-type parameter.

If no larger value is found in the list, the new element will be *appended* to the end. In this case the loop will halt with Successor equal to NIL and Predecessor pointing to the final node. However, the final node should be the predecessor of the new element, and the new node's pointer field should be set to NIL. Thus the procedure handles this situation correctly, without requiring any special tests or processing.

insertion sort

Insertion of one item at a time into an ordered list is the basis for a familiar sorting method called the **insertion sort.** This technique is used to place new cards in a library card file. Although this kind of sorting can be done using arrays, the cost of moving elements to make room for new ones can become prohibitive as the number of values grows. A better approach is to maintain the values to be sorted in a linear list where the sorting involves only the changing of pointers.

```
PROCEDURE Insert (VAR Start: NodePtr; NewNode: NodePtr);

   {Find first value in list larger than NewNode's value
    and insert NewNode immediately before this node; if
    no larger value found, put NewNode at end of list}

   VAR
      Successor,
      Predecessor: NodePtr;
      Found: boolean;

   BEGIN {Insert}
      Found := false;
      Successor := Start;
      Predecessor := NIL; {no predecessor to first node}

      WHILE NOT Found AND (Successor <> NIL) DO
         BEGIN {search}
            Found := Successor^.Data > NewNode^.Data
            IF NOT Found THEN
               BEGIN {advance pointers}
                  Predecessor := Successor;
                  Successor := Successor^.NextNode
               END
         END; {search}

      IF Predecessor = NIL THEN
         BEGIN {Add to start of list}
            NewNode^.NextNode := Start;
            Start := NewNode
         END {first node}
      ELSE
         BEGIN {insert after Predecessor}
            NewNode^.NextNode := Successor;
            Predecessor^.NextNode := NewNode
         END
   END; {Insert}
```

■ Figure 12.16
Inserting a node onto an ordered list.

```
PROCEDURE Pop (VAR Start,TopNode : NodePtr);

   {Remove first node from list; return it as TopNode}

   BEGIN
      TopNode := Start;          {NIL if stack empty}
      IF Start <> NIL THEN       {delete first node}
         BEGIN
            Start := TopNode^.NextNode;
            TopNode^.NextNode := NIL
         END
   END; {Pop}
```

■ Figure 12.17
Popping the top node from a stack.

Push Down Stacks

push down stack

A **push down stack** is a linear list to which nodes may be added only at the start and from which nodes may be removed only from the start. In most applications only the topmost node may be inspected. Thus all the action takes place at the head of the list.

You are already familiar with the Push procedure (Fig. 12.7d) to add nodes to a stack. The name "push" is a standard term for placing an item on top of a stack. The counterpart operation is to remove or "pop" the top item

Pop procedure

from a stack. The **Pop procedure** is shown in Fig. 12.17. Note that Pop returns a pointer to the node that formerly occupied the first position on the list. If the list is empty, NIL is returned. A stack is initialized by setting the top-of-stack pointer to NIL, and whenever the stack is empty, its value is reset to NIL.

Items in a stack are always removed in reverse order of their arrival onto the stack; this order is referred to as *last-in–first-out (LIFO)* or *last-come–first-served (LCFS)*. A familiar example is that of processing the backlog of papers on your desk, when you begin with the most recently added item—the one on top.

Incidentally, a stack can be implemented inside an array, in which all additions and deletions occur at the frontier. The advantage of using a linear list is the absence of any restriction on the number of items the stack can hold.

Queues

queue

tail

Append at tail, remove from head

Head and tail pointers

A **queue** is simply a waiting line. Most of us are all too familiar with queues in everyday life. They operate on the principle that new arrivals join one end of the queue (the **tail**), and service is given to the person at the other end (the *head*).

A queue in a computer system is another special case of a linear list. It has a head and a tail; new nodes may be added only at the tail end of the queue, and only the node at the head of the queue may be removed. This leads to a mode of processing called *first-come–first-served (FCFS)* or *first-in–first-out (FIFO)*. Programs that must simulate waiting-line behavior usually do so with the queue data structure.

Besides a head pointer, a queue should also have a second special pointer to reference its final node. Although not strictly necessary, this tail pointer greatly expedites additions to the end of the queue. Both pointers can be combined into a single record, which represents the queue inside the program. Typical declarations are shown at the top of Fig. 12.18. With these definitions, a queue will have the following general structure.

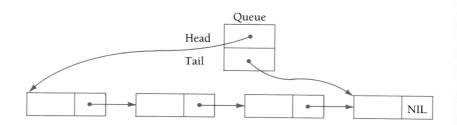

Initializing a queue

Removing a node

Adding a new node

You initialize a queue by setting its head and tail to NIL. You can test for an empty queue by checking either of the pointers for the NIL value. The queue has only one node when HEAD and Tail both refer to the same thing, as in

$$(Queue.Head = Queue.Tail) \text{ AND } (Queue.Head <> NIL)$$

Removing a node from the head of a queue is similar to a pop operation. Most of the time the head pointer is updated without any change to the tail pointer. However, Tail is involved when the node being removed is the last one on the queue, making the queue empty. In this case the value of Tail must be made NIL.

Adding a node to a queue is an append operation, but the availability of the Tail pointer makes it simple. The addition itself consists of two basic steps: (1) pointing to the new node from the end of the existing queue; and (2) adjusting the tail pointer to reflect the presence of the new node. The

```
TYPE
   NodePtr =^Node;
   Node =
      RECORD
         Data : integer;
         NextNode : NodePtr
      END;
   QType =
      RECORD
         Head,
         Tail : NodePtr
      END;
VAR
  Queue : QType;
  :

PROCEDURE AddToQ (VAR Queue: QType; NewNode: NodePtr);
   BEGIN
      WITH Queue DO {covers references to Head or Tail}
         BEGIN
            NewNode^.NextNode := NIL; {will end list}
            IF Head = NIL THEN{empty queue}
               Head := NewNode
            ELSE    {add new node to tail of queue}
               Tail^.NextNode := NewNode;
            Tail := NewNode
         END {WITH}
   END; {AddToQ}
PROCEDURE RemoveFromQ (VAR Queue: QType;
                       VAR TopNode: NodePtr);

   BEGIN
      WITH Queue DO {covers references to Head or Tail}
         BEGIN
            TopNode := Head;{NIL if queue empty}
            IF Head <> NIL THEN
               BEGIN {true removal}
                  Head := TopNode^.Next; {bypass first}
                  IF Head = NIL THEN {last node removed}
                     Tail := NIL;
                  TopNode^.NextNode := NIL {precaution}
               END {removal}
         END {WITH}
   END; {RemoveFromQ}
```

■ Figure 12.18
Procedures to manage a queue.

following code adds NewNode to an existing queue:

```
WITH Queue DO
  BEGIN
    Tail^.NextNode := NewNode;
    Tail := NewNode
  END;
```

Adding first node   Addition of a node involves the head of the queue only when the queue is empty to begin with. In this case, both the head and the tail pointers must be adjusted to signify the presence of the first node. Figure 12.18 shows complete procedures for adding a node to and removing a node from a queue.

Recursive Processing of List Structures

Recursion is natural with lists   We had no difficulty traversing a linear list by iteratively moving a pointer from node to node. However, list structures also lend themselves quite naturally to recursive processing. Being of uniform type, every node on a list looks like every other. Moreover, when any particular node has been reached, all previous nodes become history; the current node is the first node of the remaining list. Since each node requires similar processing and initiates a sublist, the subprogram can be written to process only this first node. By passing the remainder of the list to another activation of the same subprogram, the next activation will process this "next" node, which appears to it as the first. Of course, the "head pointer" to this remaining list happens to be stored in the current node. The code is therefore always processing the first node on a series of lists of ever-diminishing size and stops when the list finally shrinks to an empty list.

Search application   Consider searching a linear list. The iterative program in Fig. 12.12 has the following process at its core.

```
WHILE not at end of list AND item not found DO
  If Current node contains desired value then
    halt successful search
  else
    advance Current to next node
```

The recursive approach is only slightly different:

```
If not at end of list AND item not found then
  If current (first) node contains desired value then
    halt successful search
  else
    search remaining list for desired value
```

Figure 12.19 shows a recursive search function. As before, the search function inspects the node addressed by its pointer parameter. But if this

```
TYPE
   NodePtr = ^Node;
   Node =
      RECORD
         Data : integer;
         NextNode : NodePtr
      END;
VAR
   Start : NodePtr;
   Target : integer;
      .
      .
      .

FUNCTION Search(ThisNode: NodePtr;
                Target: integer): NodePtr;
   BEGIN
      IF ThisNode = NIL THEN     {end of list}
         Search := NIL           {failure}
      ELSE
         WITH ThisNode^ DO

            IF Data = Target THEN
               Search := ThisNode
            ELSE
               Search := Search( NextNode, Target )

      END; {Search}
```

■ **Figure 12.19**
Recursive search of a linear list.

node does not contain what we want, the function calls itself to search the sublist consisting of the previous list without its first node. The head pointer to this sublist is called ThisNode^.NextNode. Unlike the algorithm, the code tests for end-of-list first. Besides providing a NIL result, this strategy avoids referencing fields of an undefined record, in case the end has been reached.

Recursion provides another important advantage when processing list structures: A particular procedure activation does not lose control just because it makes a recursive call that temporarily moves the center of activity to some other node. Consider the nth activation of Search to inspect the nth record of the original linear list. Its call to Search may ultimately lead all the way to the end of the list, but control is guaranteed to return to the nth activation.

Consequently, the data in the *n*th node are still available for use. This is like being able to "peek ahead" in the list without sacrificing access to the current node.

12.3 A Glimpse of Nonlinear Structures

The problem posed in the chapter introduction was the run-time representation of hierarchies. We now have the tools to solve this problem. A record is not limited to just one pointer field; there can be as many pointer fields as required. A record could represent a parent in a family tree, with one pointer to each child. Of course, the children could themselves be parents, and each of their records could point to their respective children, and so on. The interconnections could be even more involved than a simple hierarchy.

Binary Trees in General

binary tree

Among the many possible structures that we could examine, we will consider only the **binary tree,** which is the simplest nontrivial hierarchical structure. Figure 12.20 contains some examples of binary trees. Regardless of their orientations, these examples all have the structure of trees: (1) they each have one special node, called the **root,** from which all the paths emanate; and (2) only one path exists from the root to any node of the structure.

root

Binary tree has two pointer fields per node

These trees are *binary* because at any node the path arriving from the root may branch into at most two outgoing paths. In terms of the records that represent the nodes, each record contains *two* pointer fields, allowing it to reference as many as *two* other nodes. Being "trees," each node can be *referenced by* at most *one* other node (that is, it can have at most one incoming pointer). In contrast, the two structures shown below are *not* binary trees.

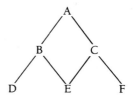

leaves

An abstract binary tree structure is shown in Fig. 12.21, along with a data structure to represent it. No node has more than two outgoing pointers, and all have one incoming pointer. The root is considered the starting point of the structure and is referenced by some outside pointer (like the first node on a linear list). The nodes at the "bottom" with no outgoing references are known as **leaves.**

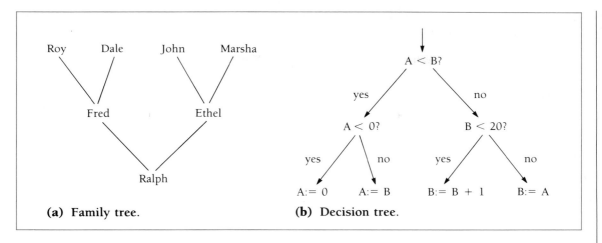

(a) Family tree.   **(b)** Decision tree.

■ Figure 12.20
Examples of binary
trees.

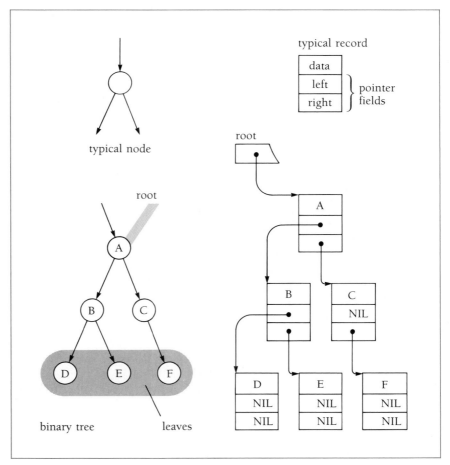

■ Figure 12.21
Binary tree structure.

Unique path to any node

Each unique path from the root to a leaf node is somewhat like an entire linear list. However, every node that has two outgoing pointers represents a choice. Traversing a path in a binary tree therefore involves a sequence of decisions about which direction to take.

If you cut any branch (or erase any line) in a binary tree, you could remove a separate piece from the original. This piece would also have a tree structure, and its root would be the node that was entered by the broken branch. Every node in a tree introduces the top of a smaller tree structure; thus every node is the root of a **subtree**, as shown in Fig. 12.22. The only access to the nodes in this subtree is through this root. Consequently, every pointer in the original tree references an entire subtree. This observation is the basis for all the recursive procedures that build and manipulate trees. By the way, even an individual node with no pointers (a leaf) still fits the definition of a tree, even though it looks more like a bud.

subtree

■ **Figure 12.22**
Subtree structure.

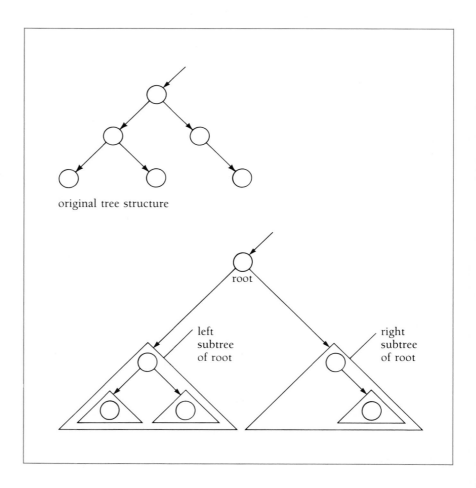

Left and right subtrees

Every node in a binary tree has three fields: a data field (which may be of considerable complexity in practice) and two pointer fields. These pointers refer to the *left subtree* and *right subtree*, respectively. Binary trees make a clear distinction between the left and right subtrees. Thus the following trees are *not* necessarily equivalent.

Now for some family terminology: If N1 is any node and N2 is the root of one of its subtrees, then N1 is called the *parent* of N2, and N2 is the *right offspring* or the *left offspring* of N1. Two nodes are *siblings* if they have the same parent. The *level* of a node is its distance from the root and may be found by assigning 0 to the root node and, to any other node, a level of one more than its parent.

Figure 12.23(a) contains a typical record declaration for a binary tree node and a procedure CreateNode to allocate and initialize one of these nodes (see p. 534).

Attaching a node to a tree

Suppose in an existing binary tree we are inspecting a node addressed by the pointer Current. Attaching a new node as the left subtree of Current^ involves creating a new node and storing its address in Current^.Left. To perform this attachment, we need only write

```
CreateNode (Current^.Left,NewData);
```

This operation is illustrated in Fig. 12.23(b). We can add a right subtree in a similar manner. The very first node would be produced by calling

```
CreateNode (Root,NewData);
```

where Root is some pointer variable outside the tree.

Since there are no unique final nodes or "next" nodes in a tree, knowing where to place new nodes requires some preliminary searching of the tree. We must therefore explore some common methods of moving through a tree before we can explain how to actually build one.

Binary Tree Traversal

Let's first consider the problem of traversing an entire tree to encounter all its nodes. Whenever a node is encountered, three things must happen: (1) the data in the node must be processed; (2) the left subtree must be processed; and (3) the right subtree must be processed. By convention, *the left subtree is (almost) always visited before the right subtree*. Thus there are three basic ways of ordering these steps. The approaches are characterized (and named)

Three approaches

preorder

inorder, postorder

by whether the data in the current node is processed before (**preorder**), between (**inorder**), or after (**postorder**) the two subtrees. The schematic

```
TYPE
  NameType = PACKED ARRAY [1..10] OF char;
  NodePtr = ^NodeType;
  NodeType =
    RECORD
      Data : NameType;
      Left,
      Right: NodePtr
    END;
    :
PROCEDURE CreateNode (VAR Ptr : NodePtr;
                          NewData : NameType);
  BEGIN
    new (Ptr);
    Ptr^.Data := NewData;
    Ptr^.Left := NIL;
    Ptr^.Right := NIL
  END; {CreateNode}
```

(a) Procedure to generate a binary tree node.

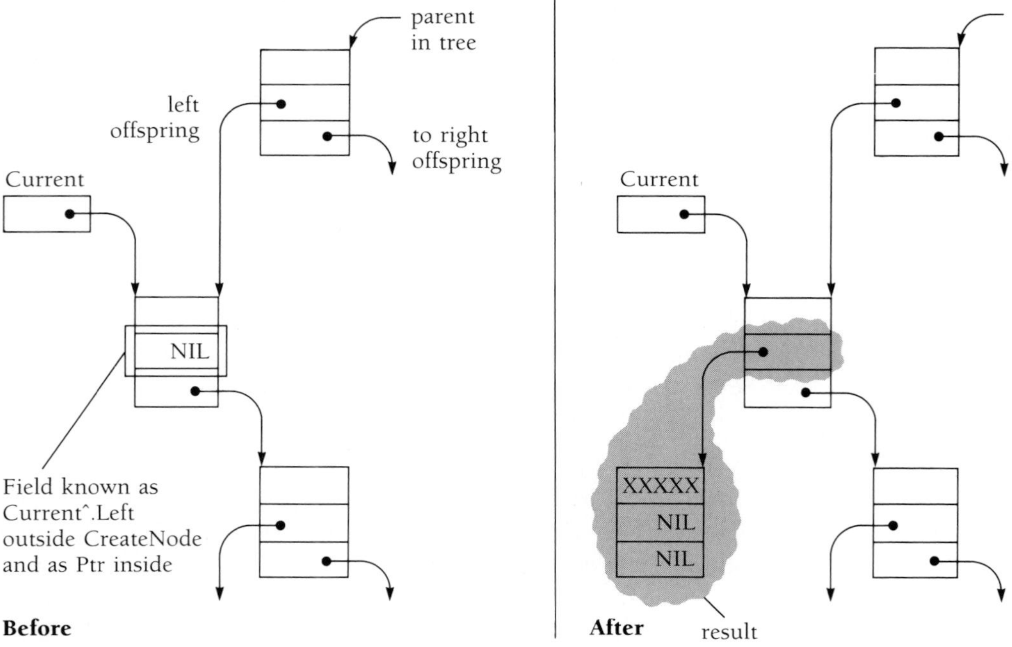

parent
in tree

left
offspring

to right
offspring

Current

NIL

Field known as
Current^.Left
outside CreateNode
and as Ptr inside

Before

Current

XXXXX
NIL
NIL

After   result

(b) Attaching a node to a binary tree.

■ Figure 12.23
Creating and attaching a binary tree node.

outlines for these three approaches are

Preorder	Inorder	Postorder
1. Current node	1. Left subtree	1. Left subtree
2. Left subtree	2. Current node	2. Right subtree
3. Right subtree	3. Right subtree	3. Current node

Preorder traversal

Tree traversal is usually done by a recursive procedure. We will develop the preorder traversal approach; the details of the other two will be apparent after you study preorder closely. Specifically, preorder traversal starts at the root and proceeds as follows:

1. Process data in the root.
2. Traverse the left subtree *in preorder*.
3. Traverse the right subtree *in preorder*.

Steps 2 and 3 lead us to the recursive solution in which each activation of the processing procedure deals only with the data field(s) in the root of a (sub)tree. The recursion stops when we reach a tree having neither right nor left subtree. In Fig. 12.24 we outline a procedure to traverse a binary tree in preorder.

■ **Figure 12.24** Outline of preorder traversal of nonempty binary tree.

```
TYPE
    NodePtr = ^NodeType;
    NodeType =
        RECORD
            Data: integer;
            Left,
            Right: NodePtr
        END;

PROCEDURE Preorder (Node: NodePtr);
    { Traverse nonempty binary tree in preorder}
    BEGIN

        { Process Node^.Data }

        IF Node^.Left <> NIL THEN
            Preorder (Node^.Left);

        IF Node^.Right <> NIL THEN
            Preorder (Node^.Right)

    END;
```

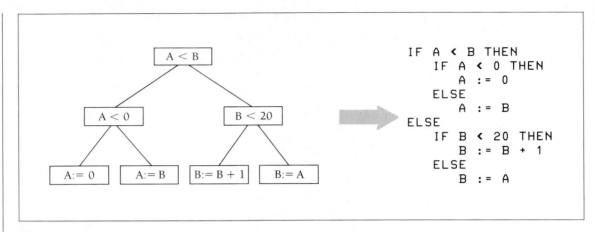

■ **Figure 12.25**
IF statements in a binary tree.

Preorder to generate nested IFs

The amount of processing to be done for each node depends on the application, as illustrated in the following example. Consider a decision tree of nested two-way conditions and conditionally executed statements, like the one in Fig. 12.20(b). Every interior node in the decision tree contains a conditional expression as its data field; the leaves contain the ultimate nondecision statements to be selected by a sequence of tests. Figure 12.25 shows the equivalent nested IF statements, and Fig. 12.26 shows a recursive procedure using preorder traversal to construct such nested IF statements for any given decision tree.

Before any line of output is printed, the appropriate number of blanks are generated to provide the proper level of indentation. The level of nesting must be passed as a parameter, so that each activation of the procedure can identify the level of the node it is inspecting. The entire process is begun by the call

        Display (Root, 0);

Binary Search Trees

binary search tree

Figure 12.27(a) shows a binary tree of names. This tree is a **binary search tree,** which means that the data fields of its nodes have a special relationship to each other. The relationship, depicted in Fig. 12.27(b), is:

> For any node in the tree, the value in its data field is larger than any data value in its left subtree and is smaller than any data value in its right subtree.

```
TYPE
    CharString = PACKED ARRAY [1..10] OF char;
    NodePtr = ^NodeType;
    NodeType =
        RECORD
            Data : CharString; {the action or condition}
            Action  : boolean; {whether action or condition}
            ThenPart,
            ElsePart : NodePtr
        END;
          .
          .
PROCEDURE Display (Node : NodePtr; Level : integer);
    {Generate nested IF statements implied by
     tree of conditions}
    CONST
        Blank = ' ';
    BEGIN
        WITH Node^ DO
            IF Action THEN {a statement governed by IF}
                BEGIN
                    write(Blank : (3*Level));
                    writeln(Data)
                END
            ELSE
                BEGIN {a condition of an IF statement}
                    write(Blank : (3*Level));
                    writeln('IF ',Data,' THEN');

                    IF ThenPart <> NIL THEN
                        Display(ThenPart,Level+1);

                    write(Blank : (3*Level));
                    writeln('ELSE');

                    IF ElsePart <> NIL THEN
                        Display(ElsePart,Level+1)
                END
    END;{Display procedure}
```

■ Figure 12.26
Procedure to generate nested IF statements from tree in Fig. 12.25.

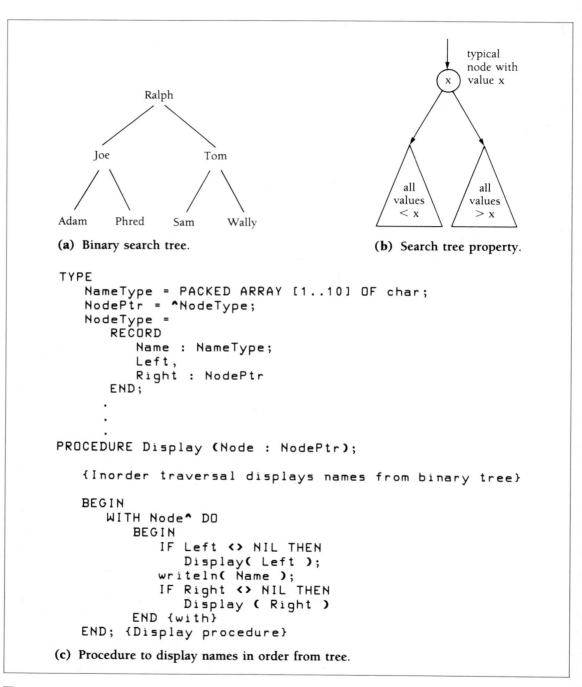

(a) Binary search tree.   **(b)** Search tree property.

```
TYPE
    NameType = PACKED ARRAY [1..10] OF char;
    NodePtr = ^NodeType;
    NodeType =
        RECORD
            Name : NameType;
            Left,
            Right : NodePtr
        END;
        .
        .
        .

PROCEDURE Display (Node : NodePtr);

    {Inorder traversal displays names from binary tree}

    BEGIN
        WITH Node^ DO
            BEGIN
                IF Left <> NIL THEN
                    Display( Left );
                writeln( Name );
                IF Right <> NIL THEN
                    Display ( Right )
            END {with}
    END; {Display procedure}
```

(c) Procedure to display names in order from tree.

■ Figure 12.27
Binary search tree property and traversal.

Since the value in any node lies strictly between the values in its respective subtrees, inorder processing will display the tree in ascending order. Figure 12.27(c) contains the corresponding recursive display procedure.

This property—or something like it—is needed in order to follow the path directly from the root to any particular value stored in the tree. Without some relationship among node values, a search algorithm would have no way to decide which direction to travel from any node. As the name *search tree* suggests, the path to any existing value can be traced directly, without any wrong turns.

Search tree property allows fast access

The Search strategy follows immediately from the node ordering property:

Starting at the root (of the current subtree) . . .
>   IF (current node = desired value) OR (at dead end) THEN
>   halt the search here
>   ELSE
>   IF desired value < current node THEN
>   *Search* Left Subtree
>   ELSE {desired value > current node}
>   *Search* Right Subtree

Recursive search strategy

After comparing the value in the current node with the value being sought, the decision about which subtree to pursue is clear, since all smaller values are in one subtree and all larger values are in the other. Each subtree is searched as though it were the original: Its root determines which of *its* subtrees to pursue. The search subprogram simply calls itself recursively to process the selected subtree. Of course, it can go no farther if it reaches a NIL pointer, the end of the path.

A search function is shown in Fig. 12.28 (see p. 541). Like other tree processing subprograms, this one is called with a pointer to the root (the tree is assumed to be nonempty). However, unlike other search functions, this one always returns a pointer to a node, regardless of whether the Target value was found. Rather than return a NIL pointer if the Target value is not found, this function returns a pointer to the node that was last inspected. A typical call sequence would look like:

    LastNode := TreeSearch(Root, Target);
    IF LastNode^.Name = Target THEN {search was successful . . .}

If the search was *not* successful, the search function reached a "dead end"; it was directed toward a subtree that did not exist. LastNode will then point to the node where the final decision was made, that is, the decision that would have led directly to the Target node, if Target had been present in the tree.

Adding a node

Carrying this one step further, if we want to add a node containing the Target value to the tree, we have just found the place where it should be attached. We now have the algorithm for adding a new node to the tree; its

code is

```
LastNode := TreeSearch( Root, Target );
WITH LastNode^ DO
    IF Name <> Target THEN          {search "failed"; add Target}
    IF Target < Name THEN                        {add to left}
        CreateNode(Left,Target)
    ELSE                                        {add to right}
        CreateNode(Right,Target)
```

We assume that the CreateNode procedure (see Fig. 12.23a) generates a new record, initializes its fields, and stores its address in either LastNode^.Left or LastNode^.Right. Nodes are never inserted in the interior of the tree; the newly added node will always be a leaf. This code does not permit adding a value that already exists in the tree.

Building an entire tree

If we know how to attach a single node to an existing binary tree, we can add any number of nodes by repeating this process any number of times. This method can be used to build an entire binary search tree. When we have a root, we have a binary tree. Only the very first value requires any special handling, since it will be stored in the root. Figure 12.29 contains a program for generating an entire binary search tree from names entered at the terminal.

To see the effect of executing this program, consider what happens when the following list of names is entered.

| Oliver | Paul | Daniel | Inez | George | Naomi |
| Carol | Brian | Roberta | | | |

We begin by establishing "Oliver" as the root of the tree, since this name appears first. For all subsequent additions we will return to the root as the starting point in the decision-making process. To add "Paul" we compare it with "Oliver" (at the root), discover "Paul" is greater, and take the right branch. However, there is no right subtree, so one is created and added.

"Daniel" is less than "Oliver," so we add a left subtree to accommodate the new name.

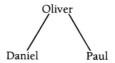

To add "Inez" we visit the root again and follow the left subtree (because "Inez" is less than "Oliver") and then compare "Inez" with "Daniel." This

```
TYPE
   NameType = PACKED ARRAY [1..10] OF char;
   NodePtr = ^NodeType;
   NodeType =
      RECORD
         Name : NameType;
         Left,
         Right : NodePtr
      END;
         .
         .
         .


FUNCTION TreeSearch (Node: NodePtr;
                     Target: NameType): NodePtr;

   {Return pointer to node closest to Target; Node NOT NIL}

   BEGIN
      WITH Node^ DO
         BEGIN

            TreeSearch := Node; {for now}
            IF (Target < Name) AND (Left <> NIL) THEN
               TreeSearch := TreeSearch( Left );
            IF (Target > Name) AND (Right <> NIL) THEN
               TreeSearch := TreeSearch( Right )

         END {with}
   END; {TreeSearch}
```

■ Figure 12.28
Searching a binary search tree.

comparison yields a right branch but also finds that there is no right subtree. Adding the new right subtree gives

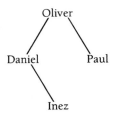

```
PROGRAM BuildTree (input,output);
TYPE
   NameType = PACKED ARRAY [1..10] OF char;
   NodePtr = ^NodeType;
   NodeType =
       RECORD
          Name : NameType;
          Left,
          Right : NodePtr
       END;
VAR
   Root : NodePtr;
   NewName : NameType;
FUNCTION TreeSearch (Node: NodePtr;
                     Target: NameType): NodePtr;
                {See Figure 12.28 for details}
PROCEDURE ReadName (VAR NewName : NameType);
   {read next name from terminal into NewName}
PROCEDURE CreateNode (VAR NewNode: NodePtr;
                      NewName: NameType);
   {Generate and initialize new node}
   BEGIN
      new(NewNode);
      WITH NewNode ^ DO
         BEGIN
            Name := NewName;
            Left := NIL;
            Right := NIL
         END {with}
   END; {CreateNode}
BEGIN {main program}
   ReadName(NewName);
   CreateNode(Root,NewName); {install name in new root}
   WHILE NOT eof DO
      BEGIN
         ReadName(NewName);
         LastNode := TreeSearch(Root,NewName);
         IF LastNode^.Name <> NewName THEN {add to tree}
            WITH LastNode ^ DO
               IF NewName < Name THEN
                  CreateNode(Left,NewName)
               ELSE
                  CreateNode(Right,NewName)
      END; {input loop}
      .
      .
END. {BuildTree}
```

■ Figure 12.29
Constructing a binary search tree.

When adding "George," comparison with "Oliver" takes us left; with "Daniel," we go right and then left again at "Inez," which yields

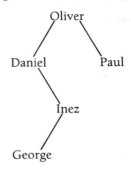

Continuing this process produces the following binary tree.

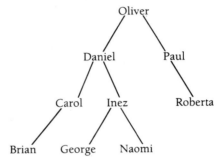

12.4 Review of Rules

A. Pointer types and variables are declared as follows:

```
TYPE
    PointerType = ^DomainType;
VAR
    PointerVar : PointerType;
```

At run time the pointer variable may be given as its value the address of any object from the associated domain type (and from no other domain type). The domain type may be any predeclared type or any other type declared within the same block. If the domain type is a record containing a PointerType field, the pointer type must be declared first.

B. A new unit of storage for the domain type is generated by a call to the procedure new, as follows:

```
new( PointerVar );
```

This call places the address of the new storage in the pointer variable. Even if control leaves the defining block, the new storage (though not necessarily the pointer) remains allocated until its release by a call to the dispose procedure:

dispose(PointerVar);

After executing a call to dispose, the value of the pointer variable parameter is undefined and it must not be used until it has been given some other value.

C. The object to which a pointer variable points is referenced by

PointerVar^

This referenced variable may be used in any context appropriate to its domain type. However, an object cannot have both a pointer reference and its own declared identifier.

D. Pointer variables may be components of structured types. When a pointer points to a structured type, the components of that type are accessed in the usual way, after the object itself has been referenced through the pointer; for example,

RecordPointer^.FieldName

or

ArrayPointer^[Subscript]

E. The only operations permitted on the pointer variables are comparison for equality (= or <>) and assignment among pointer variables of the same type. Pointer values may be passed as parameters and may be returned as function values (in which case they must be stored before use). The NIL pointer value, belonging to every pointer type, depicts a pointer that is not in use.

KEY TERMS

binary search tree	NIL
binary tree	node
dispose procedure	pointer
domain type	pointer variable
dynamic storage allocation	pop
empty list	postorder
head pointer	preorder
inorder	push down stack
insertion sort	queue
leaves	root
linear list	subtree
new procedure	tail

EXERCISES

12.1 Write a program to enter up to 30 names (of no more than 20 characters each) and store each name in a dynamically allocated record. Collect the pointers to these new records in an array. Then sort the names by rearranging the order of pointers in the array. Display the ordered names to confirm that the sort was successful.

12.2 Using the insertion sort to create an ordered list of names, generate two ordered lists of names.

(a) By traversing the two lists in tandem, determine which names appear in both lists.

(b) Merge the two lists into one, destroying the original lists and eliminating any duplicate names in the process; that is, no name should appear more than once in the final list. Display this list to check your result.

12.3 Linear lists provide a convenient way to represent a polynomial in one variable, say x. Each list element corresponds to one term of the polynomial and contains the coefficient and the power to which x is raised in that term. For example, the polynomial: $12x^3 - 6x^2 + 4$ would appear as

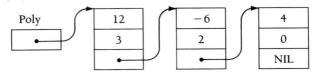

(a) Write a program that allows the user to interactively enter a polynomial one term at a time, store the nonzero polynomial terms in list form, and display the complete polynomial as a sequence of coefficients with a sequence of corresponding powers of x underneath. All powers of x should be included in the output, even if they do not appear in the linked list. Of course, those that do not appear in the list will have a coefficient of 0. For example, the polynomial $12x^3 - 6x^2 + 4$ would appear as

```
Coefficients:  12   -6    0    4
Power of x:     3    2    1    0
```

(b) Allow up to four polynomials to be entered and stored as an array of (up to four) lists. By issuing commands of the form

```
+ J K     or     - J K
```

replace the Jth polynomial by the sum or difference of the Jth and Kth polynomials, respectively, where J and K are integers between 1 and 4. By typing d J, the user will obtain a display of the current Jth polynomial.

12.4 A two-way linked list has nodes containing two pointer fields. The pointers in the first field connect the nodes into a normal left-to-right linear list. The pointers in the second field also define a linear list, but one in which the nodes are encountered in exactly the reverse direction. In other words, one pointer indicates the successor (as you have always done), and the other indicates the predecessor.

(a) Write a procedure to construct an ordered two-way linked list of names while entering names in alphabetical order. Maintain external pointers to both ends of this list. Write another procedure that can display the names in both alphabetical and reverse alphabetical order. Note how the two lists are superimposed on the same nodes and that the head of one list is the tail of the other.

(b) Repeat part (a), but this time enter the names in random order and perform an insertion sort as the names are being entered. Explain how insertion becomes simpler when you use a two-way list.

12.5 (a) Write a program that allows messages to be entered from a terminal and later displayed on the screen (in response to an explicit request). The messages may be of any length. However, the text is to be stored in dynamically allocated blocks, capable of holding at most 80 characters each. Whenever a message extends beyond its current storage block, a new block is allocated and connected from the present block by a pointer. Thus the message may require a linked list of one or more blocks. (This practice is commonly used to avoid allocating storage much in excess of that actually required.)

(b) Devise a way of storing these blocks of text on a file at the end of program execution (if so directed by another command) and a way of recovering the text from that file into a similar linked list at the beginning of the next run. Note that pointers cannot be stored on files. Thus you should save only the text and anything else you might need to identify the block. You will need some conventions about the storage, so that the list can be rebuilt when the text reenters memory.

12.6 Write a program to test for properly nested parentheses in an expression, as you did in Exercise 11.4. This time, however, use a stack to replace the recursion. A stack is simply a linked list in which all additions and deletions occur at the head. The strategy is to first scan the input string from left to right. Then, whenever a left paren is encountered, simply place it on (the head of) the stack; when a right paren appears, its matching left paren should be at the head of the stack, and if the stack is not empty, simply remove the left paren from the stack and continue the scan. However, if the stack is empty when a right paren is found, you have detected an error. Finally, at the end of the scan, the stack should be empty; if not, there were too many left parens. Use this approach to analyze several expressions, some of which are invalid.

12.7 Write an interactive system to maintain records for a small number of employees. Each employee record contains only a name (of up to 20 characters) and the number of hours worked during the current pay period. The important point is that the records will be stored on a linked list.

(a) Allow the user to enter an arbitrary number of names in arbitrary order. Each name will be stored as a separate node of a list. Provide a procedure which, in response to a reset (r) command, sets the hours-worked field in every node to 0. In response to a display (d) command, display the employee records in alphabetical order.

(b) Write procedures to search the list for a specific employee record in response to each of the following commands:

f name	Find and display employee record.
a hours name	Add specified number of hours to record.
c hours name	Correction, to indicate new hours.
t name	Terminate employee; remove name from list.

All four commands supply the name to guide the search. The correction command makes the new value of hours equal to the number specified in the command. The procedures should handle the case of a name that is not present.

(c) Implement the command maximum (m) to display the record for the employee with the most hours.

12.8 Enter several names and associated ID numbers as data. Place the two data items for each person in a record that also contains two pointer fields. As the data are being entered, insert these newly generated records into a list in alphabetical order. Use only the first pointer field for this list. Once the list of names is complete, link these same nodes together in numeric order, using only the second pointer field in each record to represent this list. Again, employ an insertion sort to produce this ordering, but this time there are two important differences. The values are encountered by traversing the alphabetical list of names, rather than being read from the terminal. Also, no new nodes need to be generated; the nodes are already initialized and available to be spliced into this second list. The final result is two logically independent lists, superimposed on the same physical nodes. Verify that both lists exist by displaying the node values in both alphabetic and numeric order.

Appendix A

Reserved Words

The following words are reserved in standard Pascal. They may be used in a program only in the context in which Pascal defines them. You cannot redefine a reserved word for any other use. Some implementations of Pascal have other reserved words in addition to these.

AND	END	NIL	SET
ARRAY	FILE	NOT	THEN
BEGIN	FOR	OF	TO
CASE	FUNCTION	OR	TYPE
CONST	GOTO	PACKED	UNTIL
DIV	IF	PROCEDURE	VAR
DO	IN	PROGRAM	WHILE
DOWNTO	LABEL	RECORD	WITH
ELSE	MOD	REPEAT	

Appendix B

Standard Identifiers

The following words have predefined meanings in Pascal. You may redefine them in any program but doing so eliminates their standard meanings. We recommend that novice programmers do not modify these identifiers.

Constants

false   true   maxint

Types

real   integer   char   boolean   text

Program Parameters

input   output

Functions

abs	arctan	chr	cos	eof	eoln
exp	ln	odd	ord	pred	round
sin	sqr	sqrt	succ	trunc	

Procedures

get	new	pack	page	put	read
readln	reset	rewrite	unpack	write	writeln

Appendix C

Character Sets

The ordering of the printable characters for the ASCII (American Standard Code for Information Interchange) and EBCDIC (Extended Binary Coded Decimal Interchange Code) codes are given in the following tables. The ordinal number for each character is given in decimal form. The blank character is denoted by "ƀ." Missing numbers or blanks in the tables indicate nonprinting control characters.

ASCII Character Set

Left digit(s)	Right digit → 0	1	2	3	4	5	6	7	8	9
3			ƀ	!	"	#	$	%	&	'
4	(	)	*	+	,	−	.	/	0	1
5	2	3	4	5	6	7	8	9	:	;
6	<	=	>	?	@	A	B	C	D	E
7	F	G	H	I	J	K	L	M	N	O
8	P	Q	R	S	T	U	V	W	X	Y
9	Z	[	\	]	^	−	`	a	b	c
10	d	e	f	g	h	i	j	k	l	m
11	n	o	p	q	r	s	t	u	v	w
12	x	y	z	{			}				

EBCDIC Character Set

Left digit(s) \ Right digit	0	1	2	3	4	5	6	7	8	9
6					♭					
7					¢	.	<	(	+	|
8	&									
9	!	$	*	)	;	¬	−	/		
10								,	%	—
11	>	?								
12			:	#	@	'	=	"		a
13	b	c	d	e	f	g	h	i		
14						j	k	l	m	n
15	o	p	q	r						
16			s	t	u	v	w	x	y	z
17										
18										
19				A	B	C	D	E	F	G
20	H	I								J
21	K	L	M	N	O	P	Q	R		
22							S	T	U	V
23	W	X	Y	Z						
24	0	1	2	3	4	5	6	7	8	9

Index

W